T0293747

ADDITIONAL PRAISE

"Alexander brings five decades of experience in the field of finance to create a how-to book for finance leaders guiding their companies through the complex inner workings of information asymmetries in the global macroeconomy."

—Dennis Edwards Ph.D., Professor of Economics,
Past Chair of Finance and Economics Department,
Coastal Carolina University

"Jack Alexander has unraveled the complex and sometimes mysterious ways of the finance world in a comprehensive yet clear, concise, and readable format. He illustrates how these topics work in the real world, and deals with the challenges presented by the new economy and business landscape. This is clearly a 'must read' and a reference book for any person who wants a seat at the proverbial table."

—Warren Davis, Vice President, Human Resources,
WTI Inc.

FINANCIAL MANAGEMENT

FINANCIAL MANAGEMENT

PARTNER IN DRIVING PERFORMANCE AND VALUE

Jack Alexander

WILEY

Copyright © 2024 by Jack Alexander. All rights reserved.

Published by John Wiley & Sons, Inc., Hoboken, New Jersey.
Published simultaneously in Canada.

No part of this publication may be reproduced, stored in a retrieval system, or transmitted in any form or by any means, electronic, mechanical, photocopying, recording, scanning, or otherwise, except as permitted under Section 107 or 108 of the 1976 United States Copyright Act, without either the prior written permission of the Publisher, or authorization through payment of the appropriate per-copy fee to the Copyright Clearance Center, Inc., 222 Rosewood Drive, Danvers, MA 01923, (978) 750-8400, fax (978) 750-4470, or on the web at www.copyright.com. Requests to the Publisher for permission should be addressed to the Permissions Department, John Wiley & Sons, Inc., 111 River Street, Hoboken, NJ 07030, (201) 748-6011, fax (201) 748-6008, or online at http://www.wiley.com/go/permission.

Trademarks: Wiley and the Wiley logo are trademarks or registered trademarks of John Wiley & Sons, Inc. and/or its affiliates in the United States and other countries and may not be used without written permission. All other trademarks are the property of their respective owners. John Wiley & Sons, Inc. is not associated with any product or vendor mentioned in this book.

Limit of Liability/Disclaimer of Warranty: While the publisher and author have used their best efforts in preparing this book, they make no representations or warranties with respect to the accuracy or completeness of the contents of this book and specifically disclaim any implied warranties of merchantability or fitness for a particular purpose. No warranty may be created or extended by sales representatives or written sales materials. The advice and strategies contained herein may not be suitable for your situation. You should consult with a professional where appropriate. Further, readers should be aware that websites listed in this work may have changed or disappeared between when this work was written and when it is read. Neither the publisher nor authors shall be liable for any loss of profit or any other commercial damages, including but not limited to special, incidental, consequential, or other damages.

For general information on our other products and services or for technical support, please contact our Customer Care Department within the United States at (800) 762-2974, outside the United States at (317) 572-3993 or fax (317) 572-4002.

Wiley also publishes its books in a variety of electronic formats. Some content that appears in print may not be available in electronic formats. For more information about Wiley products, visit our web site at www.wiley.com.

Library of Congress Cataloging-in-Publication Data is Available:

ISBN 9781394228362 (Cloth)
ISBN 9781394228492 (ePDF)
ISBN 9781394228379 (ePUB)

Cover Design: Wiley
Cover Image: © yuanyuan yan/Getty Images
Author photo: Courtesy of the author

SKY10062235_121123

To my family:
My wife Suzanne, for five decades of love, support, and friendship.
My parents Marian and Jack, who are at peace with the Father.
My sons Rob and Tom, and their wives Courtney and Felicity.
My sisters Karen and Carol, and their families.
And especially to my granddaughters Emmy and Lienna, who bring
indescribable joy and happiness to our lives!

Contents

Preface

WHY THIS BOOK?

In the late 1970s, as I was starting my career, I came across an article that identified the traits a chief executive officer was looking for in a chief financial officer (CFO). Since I had already set my sights on becoming a CFO, I jotted down the key takeaways from the article, something that I developed a habit of doing over my career and continue to this time. Unfortunately, I did not note the article, publication, or CEO to give them credit here or to recognize the soundness of the points articulated in the article. Figure P.1 is a copy of my notes that I have retained to this day:

FIGURE P.1 **Top Gun CFOs.**

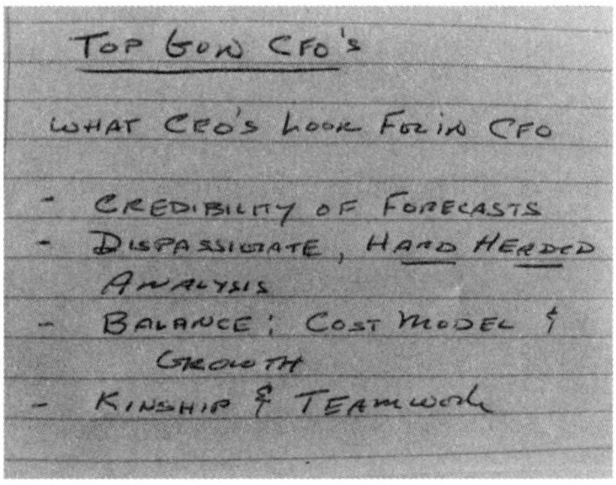
TOP GUN CFO's

WHAT CEO's LOOK FOR IN CFO

- CREDIBILITY OF FORECASTS
- DISPASSIONATE, HARD HEADED ANALYSIS
- BALANCE: COST MODEL & GROWTH
- KINSHIP & TEAMWORK

My initial reaction to the article was a realization that the CEOs did not include many of the traditional functions in accounting and finance, including control and external reporting (my role in public accounting at the time of the article), transaction processing, tax, treasury, and many others. Over time I recognized that CEOs and boards take these functions for granted. . .unless there are weaknesses or issues! Finance executives must execute well on the blocking and tackling *and* provide the service and advice appreciated by CEOs.

Each of the recommendations has proven to be true in my experience and form the foundation of being a "Partner in Driving Performance and Value." Of course, this assumes that financial controls and reporting are also well executed. CFOs and finance teams must be able to develop, evaluate, and assist in achieving planned and forecast results. The succinct phrase "dispassionate, hard-headed analysis" made a deep and lasting impression. Financial leadership must be impartial and objective. Finance teams must be prepared to identify and expose both problems and opportunities, often in a hard-headed way. CFOs and their teams must strike a balance between focusing on the cost model and directly and indirectly contributing to growth. *Kinship* refers to developing a trusted advisor and partner relationship with the CEO and other operating executives. And of course, finance must be viewed as a member of the team, supporting and executing to achieve the organization's objectives.

This article led me to focus on activities that contribute to the firm's success as a "Partner in Driving Performance and Value." Throughout my 45-year career, I have found that these value-added finance activities that contribute to performance improvements and value creation are the most important roles the finance team plays. I became a student of financial analysis early in my career and can directly attribute attaining my goal of becoming a CFO in large measure to a strong focus and emphasis on FP&A, decision support, and other value-added activities throughout my career.

I define *value added finance activities* very broadly, as evidenced by the scope of this book. These draw on several academic areas, including managerial accounting, financial accounting, finance, operations and process management as well as new disciplines in analytics, data visualization, and artificial intelligence. Today, the finance team is called on to lead the development of plans and projections, evaluate trends and variances, evaluate complex investment decisions, value and increase the value of the enterprise and acquisition candidates, among many others.

The title of this work is *Financial Management: Partner in Driving Performance and Value*. The term *financial management* recognizes that many "value-add activities" occur in other areas outside the typical FP&A function. This book will emphasize that finance should be a partner with other executives in achieving organizational goals. Finally, finance can and should play a key role in driving overall performance of the organization and maximizing shareholder value.

Even with the broad scope and increasing importance of financial management, there are very few resources available to senior financial managers, analysts, and FP&A departments. The objective of this book is an effort to address that void by providing a comprehensive and practical guide to FP&A and other key finance contributions.

USING THIS BOOK

The book can be utilized in one of three ways. First, a cover-to-cover read for those deeply involved (or aspiring to participate) in all facets of financial leadership. Second, many readers may peruse the entire book and then focus on specific areas of current interest. Finally, my hope is that the book will be retained for use as a future reference.

This book is organized into seven parts:

Fundamentals and Key Partner Capabilities

Financial Leadership in the 21st Century

Enterprise Performance Management

Business Projections and Plans

Planning and Analysis for Critical Business and Value Drivers

Valuation and Capital Investment Decisions

Summary and Supplemental Information

Part I: Fundamentals and Key Partner Capabilities

Part I includes a review of fundamentals of finance and key analytical tools. It also covers important FP&A capabilities, including developing models, building analytical capability, and presenting and communicating financial information.

Part II: Financial Leadership in the 21st Century

In Part II, several areas in which finance can provide leadership across the organization, including value creation, strategic planning, supporting growth, human capital management, and technology utilization, are presented. The management challenge, including finance, has intensified in recent years, especially owing to the impact of the Covid-19 pandemic and aftermath. This section includes frameworks to deal with the level of uncertainty and pace of change we are experiencing in business, including monitoring external forces, scenario management, and enterprise adaptability.

Part III: Enterprise Performance Management

Part III includes an introduction to enterprise performance management and best practices in developing key performance indicators and dashboards. It also provides guidance on institutionalizing performance management, that is, integrating it with other management processes. Additional topics include the measurement of innovation, agility, and human capital as well as applying performance measurement to external forces, including benchmarking and competitive analysis.

Part IV: Business Projections and Plans

Part IV covers best practices in developing projections and plans. Topics include budgets, operating plans, rolling forecasts, business outlooks, and long-term projections. Special attention is given to techniques to deal with the uncertainty and rapid change that exists in the 21st century.

Part V: Planning and Analysis for Critical Business and Value Drivers

This section covers techniques for planning, analyzing, and improving on key performance drivers: revenue growth and margins, operating effectiveness, capital management, and the cost of capital.

Part VI: Valuation and Capital Investment Decisions

Part VI addresses business valuation, value drivers, and analysis of mergers and acquisitions. In addition, the evaluation of capital investments is covered, from basic concepts through advanced topics, including dealing with risk and uncertainty.

Part VII: Summary and Supplemental Information

Part VII summarizes key points from throughout the book and provides suggestions on improving our ability to contribute as a "Partner in Driving Performance and Value."

WEBSITE

A number of illustrative analyses, performance dashboards, and models used in the book are available on the website. These items are identified in the book with a 💿. The dashboards, spreadsheets, and analysis are intended as working examples and starting points for the reader's use. An important theme of this book is to underscore the importance of selecting the appropriate measures and dashboards. It is very important to carefully select the measures that are most appropriate for each circumstance. Accordingly, most of the dashboards and models will have to be tailored to fit the specific needs of the user.

The spreadsheets contain the data used in the examples provided in the book. In all cases, the input fields are highlighted in blue. The reader can save these files under a different name and use them to begin developing dashboards and analysis for their specific needs. Using the models on the website requires Microsoft Excel software and an intermediate skill level in the use of that software. Additional information on the use of the website can be found in Appendix A: What's on the Website.

GLOSSARY

A glossary of commonly used financial, value, and performance management terms is included at the back of the book.

—Jack Alexander

1

Partner in Driving Performance and Value

"Try not to become a person of success but rather a person of value."
—Albert Einstein

Financial management, financial planning and analysis (FP&A), and other financial business partners (FBPs) play important roles in the overall success of any enterprise. In this chapter, we will introduce the critical value-add activities that contribute to becoming a "Partner in Driving Performance and Value," and we will preview the contents of the remainder of this book.

WHAT IS A FINANCIAL BUSINESS PARTNER?

I define an *FBP* as those individuals or teams that support the business in achieving goals for performance, and ultimately, value creation. In this text, I have chosen the label FBP rather than FP&A. FP&A is somewhat limiting and the role of FP&A varies from organization to organization. Much of what we define as a FBP occurs outside FP&A, for example, merger and acquisition (M&A) support, Capital Investment evaluation, financing, and so on.

Finance wears many hats in most organizations. These include varied responsibilities such as transaction processing, statutory compliance, financial control, and financial reporting. While these areas represent important functions and activities, they are not considered value-add activities by most nonfinancial senior executives (until they break!). This book will focus on the value-add finance roles we describe as the FBP. However, finance cannot function at this level unless the core elements of reporting and financial control are effective. If vendors and employees are not paid, or if financial reports are not timely and reliable, then finance must address these to shore up the foundation, enabling contributions at the higher FBP level. This can be conceptualized as a pyramid as illustrated in Figure 1.1, similar to Maslow's hierarchy of human needs.

FIGURE 1.1 **Business partner pyramid.**

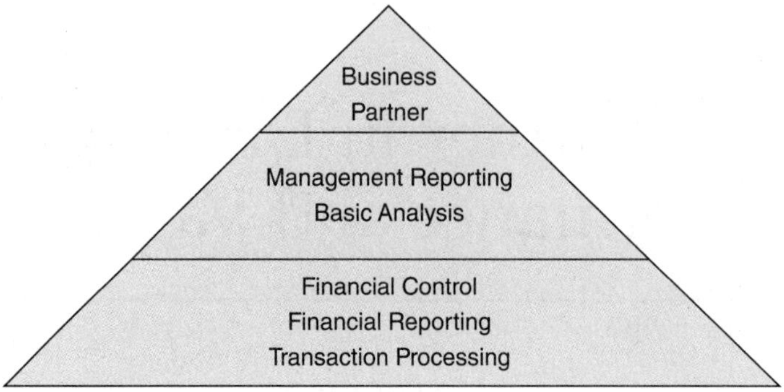

Under the leadership of the CFO, business partner roles may exist across the finance organization as shown in Figure 1.2. Shaded areas represent those areas considered value-add within finance, with the potential to drive performance improvements and create shareholder value.

FIGURE 1.2 **Chief Financial Officer responsibilities.**

Chief Financial Officer					
FP&A	**Control**	**Treasury**	**Investor Relations**	**Tax**	**Other**
Monthly Reporting	Monthly Reporting	Capital Structure	Investor Communication	Tax Planning	M&A support
Performance Analysis	Financial Reporting	Cost of Capital	Investor Presentations	Tax Compliance	Real Estate
Financial Plans and Projections	Compliance	Cash Planning & Optimization			Information Technology
Decision Support	Internal Control	Investment Evaluation			Strategic Planning
Scenario Management	Financial Data	Cash Management			Value Creation
		Other			

FINANCIAL ANALYSIS AND ENTERPRISE PERFORMANCE MANAGEMENT (EPM)

A major area that adds value across the organization is financial analysis and enterprise performance management. Figure 1.3 presents the instrument panel in the cockpit of the space shuttle, which represents a great illustration of key objectives of EPM. At a glance, the pilot can get a highly visual report on the shuttle's altitude, on its attitude, and on every major system in the aircraft. The radar in an airplane allows the pilot to spot and identify potential external threats long before visual contact. At first, the panel appears very complex, but you can bet the pilot knows where every needle and dial should be and the importance of any changes! Pilots compare this information with the feel of the plane, visual observation, experience, and intuition to make adjustments in real time, as indicated, to operate the craft to safely execute the flight plan or mission.

FIGURE 1.3 **Space shuttle cockpit instrument panel.**

Photo used with permission of NASA.

In a nutshell, one of the fundamental roles of finance is the development and delivery of information to run a business and achieve an organization's goals, just as the instrument panel assists the pilots of an aircraft to execute their mission.

Key Features from Cockpit Instrument Panel

1. Real-Time and Predictive Insights.
2. High Visual Impact.
3. Focus on the Important Measures.
4. Provides Insight into External Factors and Environment.
5. Combine with Observation, Experience, and Intuition.

Our definition and application of the FBP is very broad and inclusive. It includes all activities that assess, plan, improve, and monitor critical business activities and initiatives. EPM is a critical aspect of the management processes of the enterprise. Performance management is closely aligned with, and overlaps FP&A in many respects. Key characteristics of effective EPM include:

- Achieving an organization's goals and objectives, including strategic and operational initiatives, forecasts, and planned results.
- Projecting and modeling future financial performance.
- Monitoring performance on key value and business drivers.
- Increasing visibility into critical areas of business performance, allowing managers to assign and enforce accountability for performance.
- Providing an effective framework, allowing managers and employees to understand how their activities relate to operating and financial performance, and ultimately, the value of the company.
- Providing early detection of unfavorable events and trends, such as manufacturing problems, supply chain disruptions, competitive threats, and product performance issues.
- Delivering critical information to managers and executives in effective displays or presentation formats that aid in identifying trends, problems, opportunities, and so on.
- Integrating into other management practices in the overall system of management processes that we will call the performance management framework (PMF).
- Identifying, monitoring, and mitigating risks.
- Providing information to managers to run the business.
- Supporting growth.
- Identifying and managing risks and uncertainty.
- Scenario analysis and planning.
- Monitoring progress on critical projects and programs.

FP&A and EPM must be integrated into other management processes as shown in Figure 1.4. Analysts and others involved in EPM must play an active role in the management of the organization. They are not reporters or historians; they should help shape the outcome of the enterprises' efforts.

Understanding How Decisions Are Made

Since a substantial part of finance's value-add contribution involves developing and providing information and analysis to managers, partners should

FIGURE 1.4 **EPM integration with other management processes.**

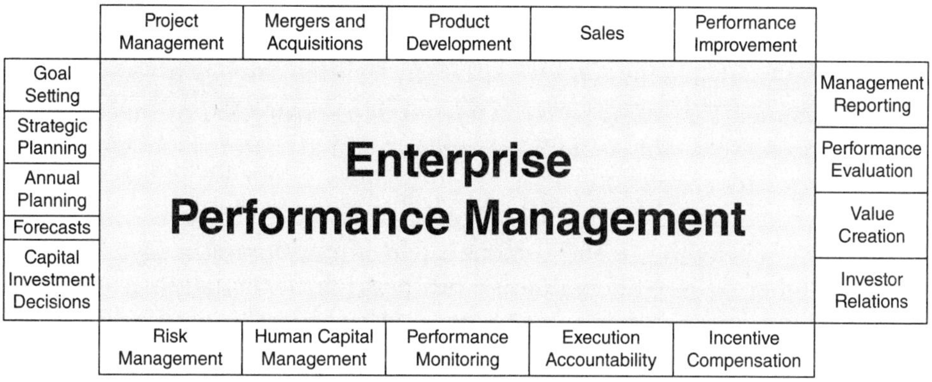

	Project Management	Mergers and Acquisitions	Product Development	Sales	Performance Improvement	
Goal Setting						Management Reporting
Strategic Planning			**Enterprise Performance Management**			Performance Evaluation
Annual Planning						Value Creation
Forecasts						
Capital Investment Decisions						Investor Relations
	Risk Management	Human Capital Management	Performance Monitoring	Execution Accountability	Incentive Compensation	

develop an understanding of how the human mind receives and processes information as part of evaluating options and making decisions. The analyst bears a responsibility to develop and present findings in an objective manner that reduces bias and the tendency to reach less than optimum decisions.

A primary theme throughout this book is the need to present and communicate business information effectively. This subject is the focus of Chapter 5, "Presenting and Communicating Financial Information."

Preview of the Book

The book has been written to address key areas of financial management from a practical point of view. While theory and technical aspects are included throughout the book, I have tried to incorporate real business applications from my 45-year career in business accounting and finance. Some readers will explore the entire text, while others may dive into a specific topic of particular interest at the time. Where appropriate, I have included cross-references to other parts of the book that cover related material to assist the reader.

Most of the illustrations are Excel-based since nearly all analysts have access to Excel, and it facilitates illustrating key concepts.

The book contains seven parts:

Part I: Fundamentals and Key Partner Capabilities

Part II: Financial Leadership in the 21st Century

Part III: Enterprise Performance Management (EPM)

Part IV: Business Projections and Plans

Part V: Planning and Analysis for Critical Business and Value Drivers

Part VI: Valuation and Capital Investment Decisions

Part VII: Summary

Part I: Fundamentals and Key Partner Capabilities   Part I builds a foundation for effective planning, analysis, and performance management. It includes a comprehensive review of financial statement analysis and presents analytical tools that can enhance the effectiveness of FP&A. For many finance professionals, Chapter 2 is primarily a review so a quick perusal of this material may be appropriate. This material serves as a foundation for many concepts presented in later chapters.

In order to complement technical subject areas in the book, we cover best practices in developing financial models and in developing analytical capability and other skills to add value as a business partner. Finally, we address a significant weakness in many finance organizations: presenting and communicating business information.

Part I contains these chapters:

2: The Fundamentals of Finance and Financial Statement Analysis

3: Skills, Knowledge, and Attributes for Financial Business Partners

4: Developing Predictive and Analytical Models

5: Presenting and Communicating Financial Information

Part II: Financial Leadership in the 21st Century   In Part II, we present several areas in which finance can provide leadership across the organization, including value creation, strategic planning, supporting growth, human capital management, and technology utilization. This part also includes frameworks to deal with the level of uncertainty and pace of change we are experiencing in business, including monitoring external forces, scenario management, and enterprise adaptability.

Part II contains these chapters:

6: Essential Ingredients for Value Creation: Growth and ROIC

7: Managing Human Capital and Building a High-Performance Finance Team

8: Strategic Analysis and Planning

9: The Role of Finance in Supporting Growth

10: The External View: Markets, Competitors, and Economic and Geopolitical Forces

11: Course Corrections: Business Transformations and Restructurings

12: Leveraging and Promoting Technology Investments

13: Scenario Analysis, Planning, and Management

14: Adaptability: Innovation Agility and Resilience

Part III: Enterprise Performance Management (EPM)   In Part III, we focus on subject matters traditionally associated with performance management. After introducing keys to effective EPM, we present the best practices in selecting key performance indicators (KPI) and creating dashboards. In order to fully achieve the benefits of EPM, it needs to be integrated with other key management processes. We introduce a challenge to business leaders to focus on *what's important*, not just what is easy to measure. Since performance management should also look outside the enterprise, benchmarking and competitive analysis are also presented in this section.

Part III contains these chapters:

15: Enterprise Performance Management and Execution

16: Dashboards and Key Performance Indicators

17: Institutionalizing Performance Management

18: Benchmarking Performance

Part IV: Business Projections and Plans   In Part IV, we cover best practices and techniques for planning, projecting, and forecasting future performance. In addition to traditional budgeting and operational planning, the implementation of rolling forecasts or business outlooks are also presented. Finally, we cover the unique challenges in projecting performance over an extended time horizon.

Part IV contains these chapters:

19: Business Projections and Plans—Introduction and Best Practices

20: Budgets, Operating Plans, and Forecasts

21: Long-Term Projections

Part V: Planning and Analysis for Critical Business and Value Drivers   This part presents best practices and illustrations for planning, measurement, analysis, and improvement of key business and value drivers.

Part V contains these chapters:

22: Revenue and Gross Margins

23: Operating Effectiveness—Costs and Expenses

24: Capital Management and Cash Flow—Working Capital

25: Capital Management and Cash Flow—Long-Term Capital Assets

26: Risk and the Cost of Capital

27: Capital Structure and Financial Leverage

Part VI: Valuation and Capital Investment Decisions   Part VI presents analysis and evaluation of critical business decisions, including capital investment decisions, techniques for valuing a business and analyzing value drivers. This part concludes with techniques to value a business, and the planning, analysis, and evaluation of mergers and acquisitions (M&A).

Part VI contains these chapters:

28: Capital Investment Decisions—Introduction and Key Concepts

29: Capital Investment Decisions—Advanced Topics

30: Business Valuation and Value Drivers

31: Analysis of Mergers and Acquisitions

Part VII: Summary and Supplemental Information

32: Summary and Where To from Here?

Supplemental information is also provided, including a glossary, an index, an appendix listing all models and illustrations, and information on the website available to purchasers of this book.

SUMMARY

Financial management and business partners have the potential to add tremendous value to the enterprise beyond simply closing the books and paying the bills. Combining elements of classic FP&A with EPM can unleash significant analytical horsepower that can assist the organization in executing its mission and achieving its objectives.

Before embarking on an initiative to improve the performance of FBPs, practitioners should develop a context based on the company's strategy and objectives, performance, and critical initiatives. This will ensure that the focus of our efforts is directed to critical areas in the organization. Material found in Chapter 3, "Skills, Knowledge, and Attributes for Financial Business Partners" and Chapter 7, "Managing Human Capital and Building a High-Performance Finance Team" will be helpful to this cause.

Part One

Fundamentals and Key Partner Capabilities

2

The Fundamentals of Finance and Financial Statement Analysis

The traditional and most fundamental aspect of financial management and analysis is the ability to understand and evaluate financial statements and financial performance. This chapter will present a brief introduction (or refresher) to financial statements and financial ratios. Many finance professionals will use these financial ratios as overall measures of a company's performance or as overall measures of performance on a particular driver of value.

BASICS OF ACCOUNTING AND FINANCIAL STATEMENTS

The three primary financial statements are the Income Statement, the Balance Sheet, and the Statement of Cash Flows. We need all three statements to properly understand and evaluate financial performance. However, the financial statements provide only limited insight into a company's performance and must be combined with key financial ratios, and ultimately, an understanding of the company's market, competitive position, and strategy before evaluating a company's current performance and value. A significant limitation of financial statements is that they present historical results, that is, the past. Other measures and mechanisms must be utilized to see what is happening in the present and to predict and manage future outcomes.

Financial statements are based on generally accepted accounting principles (GAAP). A key objective of financial statements prepared under GAAP is to match revenues and expenses. Two significant conventions arise from this objective: the accrual method of accounting and depreciation. These two conventions are significant in our intended use of financial statements for economic evaluation and business valuation purposes since they result in differences between accounting income and cash flow.

Accrual Accounting

Financial statements record income when earned and expenses when incurred. For example, the accrual basis of accounting will record sales when the terms of the contract are fulfilled, usually prior to collection of cash. Similarly, expenses are recorded when service is performed rather than when paid.

Depreciation   GAAP requires that expenditures for such things as property, plant, and equipment with useful lives longer than a year be recorded as assets and depreciated over the expected useful life of the asset. As a result, when a firm spends cash to purchase equipment, it records it as an asset on the Balance Sheet and depreciates (expenses) the cost of that asset each year on the Income Statement.

Income Statement (aka Profit and Loss)   The Income Statement, or what is frequently referred to as the Profit and Loss (P&L) statement, is a summary of all income and expense transactions completed during the period (year, quarter, etc.). Typical captions and math logic for a basic Income Statement include these examples:

Sales	+$1,000
Cost of Goods Sold	−500
Gross Margin	= 500
Operating Expenses	− 200
Operating Income	= 300
Income Tax Expense	− 100
Net Income	= 200

Many different measures, terms, and acronyms are used in practice to describe various elements of the P&L. Table 2.1 illustrates how some of these common measures are determined as well as how they relate to one another.
Following are definitions of key terms used in Table 2.1.

Net Income: Residual of income over expense, sometimes referred to as profit after tax (PAT).

TABLE 2.1 **Comparison of common P&L measures.**

	Abbreviation	**P&L**	**EBIT**	**EBIAT**	**EBITDA**	**EP/EVA**
Sales		$100,000	$100,000	$100,000	$100,000	$100,000
Cost of Sales	COGS	50,000	50,000	50,000	50,000	50,000
Gross Margin	GM	50,000	50,000	50,000	50,000	50,000
% of Sales		50.0%	50.0%	50.0%	50.0%	50.0%
R&D		5,000	5,000	5,000	5,000	5,000
SG&A	SG&A	15,000	15,000	15,000	15,000	15,000
Depreciation & Amortization (D&A)		10,000	10,000	10,000	–	10,000
Operating Profit	OP	20,000	20,000	20,000	30,000	20,000
% of Sales		20.0%	20.0%	20.0%	30.0%	20.0%
Interest Expense		3,000				
Profit before Tax	PBT	17,000				
Income Tax	35.0%	5,950		7,000		7,000
Net Income	PAT	11,050				
%		11.1%				
Earnings before Interest and Taxes	EBIT		20,000			
Earnings before Interest after Taxes	EBIAT			13,000		13,000
Earnings before Interest, Taxes, D&A	EBITDA				30,000	
Capital Charge						10,000
Economic Profit/Economic Value Added	EP/EVA					3,000

EBIT: Earnings before interest and taxes. This measure reflects the income generated by operating activities (generally equals or approximates operating income) before subtracting financing costs (interest) and income tax expense.

EBIAT: Earnings before interest after taxes, aka NOPAT (net operating profit after taxes) aka OPAT (operating profit after tax). This measure estimates the "after tax" operating earnings. It excludes financing costs, but does reflect income tax expense. It is useful in comparing and evaluating the operational performance of firms, excluding the impact of financing costs.

EBITDA: Earnings before interest, taxes, depreciation, and amortization. EBITDA adjusts EBIT (operating income) by adding back noncash charges for depreciation and amortization. This measure is used in valuation and financing decisions since it approximates cash generated by the operation. It does not include capital requirements such as working capital and expenditures for property and equipment.

Economic Profit (EP): Economic profit measures subtract a capital charge from the earnings to arrive at an economic profit. The capital charge is computed based on the level of capital employed in the business. EP is a comprehensive measure since it reflects both profits and the level of capital employed to generate those profits.

Many companies also use "adjusted" or "pro-forma" income measures:

- "adjusted EBITDA"
- "adjusted EPS" versus "GAAP EPS"

These adjustments are intended to eliminate nonrecurring items and other expenses that management feels should not be included in the results. Care should be exercised due to the lack of standards and inconsistency in reporting "adjusted" results.

Balance Sheet   The Balance Sheet is a critical financial report and frequently does not get the attention it deserves in evaluating the performance of an entity. It is a summary of the company's assets, liabilities, and owner's equity, and importantly, it represents a snapshot of all open transactions as of the reporting date. For example, the inventory balance represents all materials delivered to the company, work in process, and finished goods not yet shipped to customers. Accounts payable represents open invoices due vendors that have not been paid as of the Balance Sheet date. As a result, the Balance Sheet can be a good indicator of the efficiency of an operation. For example, a firm with a very efficient manufacturing process will have lower inventory levels than a similar firm with less effective practices.

The Balance Sheet is constructed as shown in Table 2.2.

TABLE 2.2 **Assets = Liabilities + Shareholders' Equity.**

Assets		Liabilities and Equity	
Cash	150	Accounts Payable	100
Receivables	200	Accrued Liabilities	100
Inventories	200	Debt	200
Fixed Assets, net	50	Total Liabilities	400
		Stockholders Equity	200
Total Assets	600	Total Liabilities and Equity	600

Another way to look at the Balance Sheet is to reorder the traditional format (Table 2.2) to identify the net operating assets and the sources of capital provided to the organization. This presentation, as illustrated in Table 2.3, is more useful in understanding the dynamics of the Balance Sheet. The net operating assets are those assets that are required to operate and support the business. The net operating assets must be funded (i.e., provided to the firm) by investors, either bondholders or shareholders.

TABLE 2.3 **Net operating assets/Invested capital illustration.**

Net Assets		Sources of Capital	
Cash	150		
Receivables	200		
Inventories	200		
Fixed Assets, net	50		
		Debt	200
Total Assets	600		
Less Operating Liabilities		Shareholders' Equity	200
Accounts Payable	−100		
Accrued Liabilities	−100		
Net Assets	400	Total "Invested Capital"	400

Statement of Cash Flows (SCF)   The Statement of Cash Flows (SCF) summarizes the cash generated and utilized by the enterprise during a specific period (year, quarter, etc.). Since cash flow will be a focus of our economic valuation and is an important performance measure, we will pay particular interest to cash flow drivers and measures. The Statement of Cash Flows starts with the net income generated by the company over the period, as reported on the Income Statement.

Since net income is based on various accounting conventions, such as the matching principle, the SCF identifies various adjustments to net income to arrive at cash flow. In addition, we also need to factor in various cash flow items that are not reflected in net income, such as working capital requirements, dividends, and purchases of equipment. A simplified format for a Statement of Cash Flows is shown in Table 2.4.

TABLE 2.4 **Statement of Cash Flows: Indirect method.**

Cash Flow Statement	$m
Net Income	200.0
Depreciation and Amortization	10.0
(Increase) Decrease in Working Capital	(25.0)
Purchases of Property and Equipment	(25.0)
Operating Cash Flow	160.0
Dividends	–
Debt Repayments	(60.0)
Cash Flow	100.0

Since the Statement of Cash Flow starts with net income and then is adjusted by multiple different factors to arrive at the final cash flow amount, many nonfinancial folks (okay, some finance folks, too) find this cumbersome and not intuitive. Rest assured that the "cash flow" amount reported here in this so-called "indirect method" will be the same result of all checks written and deposits recorded in the enterprise's checking account. In fact, those interested in projecting and managing cash flow closely will utilize the "direct method" shown in Table 2.5. It is easily understood and is consistent with the way most of us think about our own personal cash flow.

TABLE 2.5 **Statement of Cash Flows: Direct method.**

	Cash Flow Direct Method
Inflows:	
Payments from Customers	950.0
Interest Income	
Other Receipts	
Total Cash Inflows	950.0
Outflows:	
Payroll and Taxes	200
Payments to Vendors	250
Taxes	100
Repayment of Debt	60
Operating Expenses	195
Capital Expenditures	25
Dividend	
Other	20
Total Cash Outflows	850
Net Cash Flow	100.0

Note that net cash flow is the same under the two methods.

The Income Statement, Balance Sheet, and Statement of Cash Flows are interrelated. Understanding these relationships is critical to evaluating business performance and valuation and is presented in Figure 2.1. For example, net income (or PAT) flows from the Income Statement to increase shareholders' equity in the Balance Sheet. Net income for the period is also the starting point for the Statement of Cash Flows. Other elements on the Statement of Cash Flows are the result of year-to-year changes in various Balance Sheet accounts, including capital expenditures, changes in working capital, and reductions or increase in borrowings. Finally, financial ratios look at the relationship of various line items both within each financial statement and across all financial statements (e.g., return on assets).

FIGURE 2.1 **Financial statement interrelationships.**

Income Statement	Year 2	Year 1	Change
Sales	1000	900	100
Gross Margin	500	425	75
Operating Expenses	200	190	10
Operating Profit	300	235	65
Net Income	200	157	43

Cash Flow	Year 2
Net Income	200
+Depreciation	10
–Capital Expenditures	–25
(Inc) Decrease in Operating Capital	–25
Operating Cash Flow	160
Financing	–60
Cash Flow	100

Balance Sheet		
Cash	150	50
Receivables	200	150
Inventories	200	150
PP&E: Cost	100	75
PP&E: Accumulated Depreciation	–50	–40
Total Assets	600	385
Accounts Payable	100	75
Accrued Liabilities	100	50
Debt	200	260
Equity	200	0
Liabilities and Equity	600	385

Balance Sheet Change column:

	Change
Cash	100
Receivables	50
Inventories	50
PP&E: Cost	25
PP&E: Accumulated Depreciation	–10
Total Assets	215
Accounts Payable	25
Accrued Liabilities	50
Debt	–60
Equity	200
Liabilities and Equity	215

Ratio Analysis	
Profitability	20%
Days Sales Outstanding	73.0
Asset Turnover	1.67
Return on Assets — Net Income / Assets	33%
Return on Equity — Net Income / Equity	100%

17

Behind the Numbers... I was fortunate to start my career in public accounting, auditing transactions and financial records. This included documenting and reviewing business processes such as the revenue process and supply chain management. My first position in industry was as a Financial Accounting Manager, responsible for transaction processing (invoicing, payroll, payables), maintenance of the general ledger (summary of all financial transactions and balances), and financial and management reporting. These combined experiences afforded me a thorough understanding of business processes and how transactions were recorded and reflected in the financial statements. Throughout my career, I have worked with analysts and other financial staff who did not have the benefit of being grounded in these fundamentals. To provide a foundation for others, I developed the analysis in Table 2.6 to illustrate how transactions are recorded in the financial statements. This analysis further supports the interrelationship of financial statements illustrated earlier and provides a basis for understanding the relationships of business processes and transactions to the financial statements. The analysis starts with the Balance Sheet from Year 1 and then records all transactions in Year 2, resulting in an Income Statement, Balance Sheet, and Statement of Cash Flows for Year 2.

Transaction Description:

Sales on Account
    This entry records sales on account, increasing both sales and accounts receivable. At the same time, the cost of those inventory items shipped would be recorded as a Cost of Sales and deducted from inventory.

Record Collection of Accounts Receivable
    This transaction results in an increase to cash and a reduction of outstanding receivables.

Purchase Inventory
    Inventory purchased from vendors on credit increases inventory and accounts payable.

Pay Vendors
    The payment of invoices for inventory purchases reduces cash and accounts payable.

Purchase Property, Plant, and Equipment
    The purchase of PP&E increases PP&E balance and is a reduction to cash.

TABLE 2.6 **Behind the numbers.**

Year 2 Transactions (columns: Sales on Account through Pay Debt)

Balance Sheet	Balance Year 1	Sales on Account	Record Collections	Purchase Inventory	Pay Vendors	Purchase PPE	Accrue Expenses	Pay Expenses	Pay Payroll	Record Depreciation	Pay Taxes	Other	Pay Debt	Balance Year 2	Inc (Dec)
Assets															
Current Assets															
Cash	50		950		(250)	(25)		(195)	(200)		(100)	(20)	(60)	150	100
Accounts Receivable	150	1,000	(950)											200	50
Inventory	150	(500)		275			125		150					200	50
Total Current Assets	350	500	–	275	(250)	(25)	125	(195)	(50)	–	(100)	(20)	(60)	550	200
Property Plant & Equipment															
Cost	75					25								100	25
Accumulated Depreciation	(40)									(10)				(50)	(10)
Net PP&E	35					25				(10)				50	15
Total Assets	385	500	–	275	(250)	–	125	(195)	(50)	(10)	(100)	(20)	(60)	600	215
Liabilities	Year 1													Year 2	
Current Liabilities															
Accounts Payable	75			275	(250)									100	25
Accrued Liabilities	50						245	(195)						100	50
Tot Current Liabilities	125			275	(250)		245	(195)						200	75
Long-term Debt	260												(60)	200	(60)
Owners' Equity															
Common Stock	10													10	–
Retained Earnings	(10)	500					(120)		(50)	(10)	(100)	(20)		190	200
Tot Owners' Equity	–	500					(120)		(50)	(10)	(100)	(20)		200	200
Tot Liabilities & Equity	385	500	–	275	(250)	–	125	(195)	(50)	(10)	(100)	(20)	(60)	600	215

Income Statement

Income Statement	Year 2	Sales on Account	Accrue Expenses	Pay Payroll	Record Depreciation	Pay Taxes	Other
Net Sales	1,000	1000					
Cost of Goods Sold & Expenses	690	500	120	50			20
Depreciation	10				10		
Operating Profit	300	500	(120)	(50)	(10)		(20)
Interest Paid	–						
Taxable Income	300	500	(120)	(50)	(10)		(20)
Taxes	100					100	
Net Income	200	500	(120)	(50)	(10)	(100)	(20)

Cash Flow (Indirect Method)

Net Income	200
+ Depreciation	10
– Capital Expenditures	(25)
(Inc Dec in Operating Capital)	(25)
Operating Cash Flow	160
Financing	(60)
Cash Flow	100

19

Accrue Expenses

This entry records expenses incurred but not paid. Some of the invoices relate to the manufacturing of inventory ($125) and the balance represents operating expenses.

Pay Expenses

This transaction pays invoices previously recorded, reducing accrued liabilities and cash.

Pay Payroll

Payroll for the period is split between manufacturing (increasing inventory balance) and operating expenses.

Record Depreciation

This entry records depreciation for the year, resulting in an increase in accumulated depreciation.

Pay Taxes

This entry records taxes paid for the year. In practice, this may be accrued and then paid in two separate entries.

Pay Debt

The company made a debt payment resulting in a decrease in debt and cash.

FINANCIAL RATIOS AND INDICATORS

The basic financial statements are simply raw financial results and are of limited value. Financial ratios can be very useful tools in measuring and evaluating business performance as presented in the basic financial statements. Ratios can be used as tools in understanding profitability, asset utilization, liquidity, and key business trends, and in evaluating overall management performance and effectiveness.

Usefulness   Using financial ratios can provide a great deal of insight into a company's performance, particularly when combined with an understanding of the company and its industry. In addition to providing measures of performance, ratios can be used to monitor key trends over time and in comparing a company's performance to that of peers or "best practice" companies.

Variations   There are a number of different financial terms and ratios, and variations of each of these, in use. This leads to potential confusion when similar sounding measures are computed differently or used interchangeably. It is important to clearly define the specific ratio or financial measure used.

TABLE 2.7 **LSA Technology Company.**

Historical and Estimated Financials				
	2020	2021	2022	2023
P&L				
Net Sales	79,383	84,000	91,000	100,000
Cost of Goods Sold	36,000	38,000	41,000	45,000
Gross Margin	43,383	46,000	50,000	55,000
SG&A	25,403	26,880	29,120	32,000
R&D	6,351	6,720	7,280	8,000
Operating Income	11,630	12,400	13,600	15,000
Interest (Income) Expense	600	600	600	600
Other (Income) Expense	5	7	6	5
Income Before Income Taxes	11,025	11,793	12,994	14,395
Federal Income Taxes	3,748	4,010	4,418	4,894
Net Income	7,276	7,783	8,576	9,501
Balance Sheet				
Cash	25	2,404	4,400	7,944
Receivables	15,877	16,800	18,545	20,000
Inventories	14,400	15,200	16,400	18,000
Other	200	800	975	900
Current Assets	30,502	35,204	40,320	46,844
Net Fixed Assets	15,877	16,800	18,750	20,000
Net Goodwill and Intangibles	14,000	13,000	12,000	11,000
Other Noncurrent Assets	200	210	428	205
Total Assets	60,578	65,214	71,498	78,049
Accounts Payable	3,600	3,800	4,100	4,500
Notes Payable, Bank	–	–	–	–
Accrued Expenses & Taxes	4,000	4,500	4,750	5,000
Current Liabilities	7,600	8,300	8,850	9,500
Long-Term Debt	10,000	10,000	10,000	10,000
Other	3,083	2,536	3,194	3,794
Stockholders Equity	39,895	44,378	49,454	54,755
Total Liabilities and Equity	60,578	65,214	71,498	78,049

Other Information:					
Stock Price		9.22	9.78	10.00	10.59
Shares Outstanding (in millions)		16.7	16.8	16.9	17.0
Market Value of Equity		153,974	164,304	169,000	180,030
Interest Rate	6%				
Income Tax Rate	34%				
Dividends		3,000	3,300	3,500	4,200
Capital Expenditures		3,000	4,200	4,800	5,000
D&A		2,800	3,277	2,850	3,750
Employees		411	450	460	490

Other Information:

Comparable Companies are trading in the following ranges (trailing 12 months):

	LOW	HIGH
Sales	1.3	2.0
Earnings (P/E)	16.0	20.0
EBITDA	8.0	10.0
PEG	1.3	2.0
Cost of Capital (WACC)		12%

Key Financial Ratios To illustrate key financial ratios, we will use the information in Table 2.7 for LSA Technology Company (LSA). Unless otherwise indicated, the ratios will be computed using the estimated results for 2023.

Operating Measures Operating measures will include ratios that provide insight into the operating performance of the company. These measures will typically utilize the information presented in the Income Statement.

Sales (or Revenue) Growth Sales growth is an important determiner of financial performance. Based only on information in the Income Statement, we are limited to measuring the sales growth rate over the periods reported. Two key sales growth measures are year-over-year growth and compound annual growth rate (CAGR):

> **Year over Year Growth** LSA Technology Company's sales are expected to grow from \$91,000 in 2022 to \$100,000 in 2023. This represents a growth of 9.9% in 2023:
>
> $$= (\$100,000/\$91,000) - 1 = 9.9\%$$
>
> **Compound Annual Growth Rate** This measure looks at the growth rate over time (n years). The CAGR from 2023 to 2020 is computed as follows:
>
> $$= [(\text{Sales } 2023/\text{Sales } 2020)^{1/n}] - 1$$
> $$= [(\$100,000/\$79,383)^{1/3}] - 1$$
> $$= 8\%$$

Revenue growth contributed by acquisitions has significantly different economic characteristics than that contributed by the existing business. As a result, total revenue growth is frequently split between "acquired" and "organic" growth.

Chapter 22 will provide an in-depth review of revenue drivers, measures, and analysis.

Gross Margin % of Sales

How Is It Computed? Gross margin % of sales is simply the gross margin as a percentage of total revenues.

$$\text{Gross Margin } \% = \text{Gross Margin}/\text{Sales}$$
$$= \$55,000/\$100,000$$
$$= 55\%$$

What Does It Measure and Reflect? Gross margin % is an important financial indicator. Gross margins will vary widely across industries, ranging from razor-thin margins of 10% to 15% (e.g., grocery retailers) to very high margins approaching 70% to 80% (technology and software companies).

The gross margin % will be impacted by a number of factors, and therefore, will require substantial analysis. The factors affecting gross margin include:

- Industry.
- Competition and pricing.
- Product mix.
- Composition of fixed and variable costs.
- Product costs.
- Production variances.
- Material and labor costs.
- Overall effectiveness of Supply Chain Process.

Chapter 22 will provide an in-depth review of gross margin drivers, measures, and analysis.

R&D % Sales

How Is It Computed?

$$= R\&D/Sales$$
$$= \$8,000/\$100,000$$
$$= 8\%$$

What Does It Measure and Reflect? This ratio reflects the level of investment in research and development (R&D) compared to the current period total sales. This ratio will vary significantly from industry to industry and from high-growth to low-growth companies. Some industries, for example, retail, may have little or no R&D, whereas other firms, such as pharmaceuticals or technology companies, will likely have high R&D spending. Firms in high-growth markets or those investing heavily for future growth will have very high levels of R&D % to Sales, occasionally exceeding 20% of sales. Chapter 23 will provide an in-depth review of product development drivers, measures, and analysis.

Selling, General, and Administrative (SG&A) % Sales

How Is It Computed?

$$= SG\&A/Sales$$
$$= \$32,000/\$100,000$$
$$= 32\%$$

What Does It Measure and Reflect? Since this measure compares the level of SG&A spending to sales, it provides a view of spending levels for selling and distributing the firm's products, and in supporting the administrative aspects of the business. The measure will reflect the method of distribution, process efficiency, and administrative overhead. In addition, SG&A will often include costs associated with initiating or introducing new products.

Chapter 23 will provide an in-depth review of operating process and expense drivers, measures, and analysis.

Operating Income (EBIT) % Sales

How Is It Computed?

$$= \text{Operating Income}/\text{Sales}$$
$$= \$15,000/\$100,000$$
$$= 15\%$$

What Does It Measure and Reflect? This is a broad measure of operating performance. It will reflect operating effectiveness, relative pricing strength, and level of investments for future growth.

Return on Sales (Profitability)

How Is It Computed?

$$= \text{Net Income}/\text{Sales}$$
$$= \$9,501/\$100,000$$
$$= 9.5\%$$

What Does It Measure and Reflect? This is an overall measure of performance. In addition to the factors described under operating income % of sales, this measure will reflect taxes, and other income and expense items.

Asset Utilization Measures   Asset utilization is a very important element in total financial performance. It is a significant driver of cash flow and return to investors. Chapter 24 will provide an in-depth review of working capital drivers, measures, and analysis.

Days Sales Outstanding (DSO)

How Is It Computed?

$$= (\text{Receivables} \times 365)/\text{Sales}$$
$$= (\$20,000 \times 365)/\$100,000$$
$$= 73\,\text{days}$$

What Does It Measure and Reflect? DSO is a measure of the length of time it takes to collect receivables from customers. It will be impacted by the industry in which the firm participates, the creditworthiness of customers, and even the countries in which the firm does business. In addition, DSO is affected by the efficiency and effectiveness of the revenue process (billing and collection), by product quality, and even by the pattern of shipments within the quarter or the year.

Inventory Turns

How Is It Computed?

$$= \text{Cost of Goods Sold (COGS)}/\text{Inventory}$$
$$= \$45,000/\$18,000$$
$$= 2.5 \text{ times (turns)}$$

What Does It Measure and Reflect? Inventory turns measure how much inventory a firm holds compared to sales levels. Factors that will affect this measure include: effectiveness of supply chain management and production processes, product quality, degree of vertical integration, and predictability of sales.

Days Sales in Inventory (DSI)

How Is It Computed?

$$= 365/\text{Inventory Turns}$$
$$= 365/2.5$$
$$= 146 \text{ days}$$

What Does It Measure and Reflect? This measure is impacted by the same factors as inventory turns. The advantage to this measure is that it is easier for people to relate to the number of days of sales in inventory. It is easier to conceptualize the appropriateness (or potential improvement opportunity) of carrying 146 days' worth of sales in inventory than to conceptualize 2.5 inventory turns.

Operating Cash Cycle

How Is It Computed?

$$= \text{DSO} + \text{DSI}$$
$$= 73 + 146$$
$$= 219 \text{ days}$$

What Does It Measure and Reflect? Operating cash cycle measures the overall efficiency and the length of time it takes the business to convert inventory into cash. It is calculated by combining the number of days of inventory on hand with the length of time it takes the firm to collect invoices from customers. The factors impacting this measure are the aggregate of those affecting DSO and inventory turns/DSI.

Operating Capital Turnover and Operating Capital % Sales

How Is It Computed?

$$= \frac{\text{Operating Capital}}{\text{Sales}}$$

$$= \frac{\$29,400}{\$100,000}$$

$= 29.4\%$ or 3.4 turns per year

Operating capital computation

Receivables	20,000
Inventory	18,000
Other Current Assets	900
Accounts Payable	(4,500)
Accrued Expenses	(5,000)
Operating Capital	29,400

What Does It Measure and Reflect? These measures reflect the net cash that is required to support the operating requirements of the business. The factors impacting this measure are the aggregate of those affecting DSO and inventory turns as well as the timing of payments to vendors, employees, and suppliers.

Capital Asset Intensity (Fixed Asset Turnover)

How Is It Computed?

$$= \frac{\text{Sales}}{\text{Net Fixed Assets}}$$

$$= \frac{\$100,000}{\$20,000}$$

$= 5$ turns per year

What Does It Measure and Reflect? This measure reflects the level of investment in property, plant, and equipment relative to sales. Some businesses are very "capital intensive," that is, they require a substantial investment in capital, while others have modest requirements. For example, electric utility and transportation industries typically require high capital investments. On the other end of the spectrum, software development companies usually require minimal levels of capital.

Asset Turnover

How Is It Computed?

$$= \frac{\text{Sales}}{\text{Total Assets}}$$
$$= \frac{\$100,000}{\$78,049}$$
$$= 1.28 \text{ turns per year}$$

What Does It Measure and Reflect? This measure reflects the level of investment in all assets (including working capital, property, plant, and equipment, and intangible assets) relative to sales. It reflects each of the individual asset utilization factors discussed previously.

Capital Structure/Liquidity Measures Capital structure measures are indicators of the firm's source of capital (debt vs. equity), creditworthiness, ability to service existing debt, and ability to raise additional financing if needed. Liquidity measures examine the ability of the firm to convert assets to cash to satisfy short-term obligations.

Our definition of *debt* includes all interest-bearing obligations. The following measures will include notes payable, long-term debt, and current maturities of long-term debt (long-term debt due within one year).

For LSA Technology Inc.:

Notes Payable	$ –
Current Maturities of Long-term Debt	$ –
Long-Term Debt	$10,000
Total Debt	$10,000

Current Ratio

How Is It Computed?

$$\text{Current Ratio} = \frac{\text{Current Assets}}{\text{Current Liabilities}}$$
$$= \frac{\$46,844}{9,500}$$
$$= 4.93$$

What Does It Measure and Reflect? This measure of liquidity computes the ratio of current assets (that will convert to cash within one year) to current liabilities (that require cash payments within one year). As such, it compares the level of assets available to satisfy short-term obligations.

Quick Ratio

How Is It Computed?

$$\text{Current Ratio} = \frac{\text{Current Assets} - \text{Inventory}}{\text{Current Liabilities}}$$

$$= \frac{\$46,844 - 18,000}{9,500}$$

$$= 3.04$$

What Does It Measure and Reflect? The quick ratio is a more conservative measure of liquidity than the current ratio since it removes inventory from other assets that are more readily converted into cash.

Debt to Equity

How Is It Computed?

$$\text{D/E} = \frac{\text{Debt}}{\text{Equity}}$$

What Does It Measure and Reflect? Debt to equity measures the proportion of total book capital supplied by bondholders (debt) versus shareholders (equity).

Debt to Total Capital

How Is It Computed?

$$\text{D/TC} = \frac{\text{Debt}}{\text{Total Capital}\,(\text{Debt} + \text{Equity})}$$

$$= \frac{\$10,000}{(\$10,000 + \$54,249)}$$

$$= 15.3\%$$

What Does It Measure and Reflect? This measure computes the percentage of total "book" value (as recorded on the books and financial statements) of capital supplied by bondholders. A low debt-to-total-capital percentage indicates that most of the capital to run the firm has been supplied by stockholders. A high percentage, say 70%, would indicate that most of the capital has been supplied by bondholders. The capital structure for the latter example would be considered highly leveraged. This measure is also computed using market value of debt and equity.

Times Interest Earned (Interest Coverage)

How Is It Computed?

$$\text{TIE} = \frac{\text{EBIT (Operating Income)}}{\text{Interest Expense}}$$

$$= \frac{\$15,000}{\$600}$$

$$= 25 \times$$

What Does It Measure and Reflect? This measure computes the number of times the firm earns the interest expense on current borrowings. A high number reflects "slack," indicating an ability to cover interest expense even if income were to be reduced significantly. Alternatively, it indicates a capacity to borrow more funds if necessary. Conversely, a low number reflects an inability to easily service existing debt levels and borrow additional funds.

Overall Measures of Performance

Return on Assets (ROA)

How Is It Computed?

$$= \frac{\text{Net Income}}{\text{Assets}}$$
$$= \frac{\$9,501}{\$78,049}$$
$$= 12.2\%$$

What Does It Measure and Reflect? This measure computes the level of income generated on the assets employed by the firm. It is an important overall measure of effectiveness since it considers the level of income relative to the level of assets employed in the business.

Return on Equity (ROE)

How Is It Computed?

$$= \frac{\text{Net Income}}{\text{Equity}}$$
$$= \frac{\$9,501}{\$54,755}$$
$$= 17.4\%$$

What Does It Measure and Reflect? This measure computes the income earned on the book value of the company's equity.

Note that ROE is greater than ROA. This is because part of the capital of the firm is furnished by bondholders and this "financial leverage" enhances the return to stockholders (ROE).

ROE Tree   A very useful analytical tool that can be used to understand the drivers of ROE is to break the measure down into components. This methodology, often called the Dupont Model or return tree, is illustrated here:

$$\text{ROE} = \text{Profitability} \times \text{Asset Turnover} \times \text{Financial Leverage}$$
$$= \frac{\text{Net Income}}{\text{Sales}} \times \frac{\text{Sales}}{\text{Assets}} \times \frac{\text{Assets}}{\text{Equity}}$$

For LSA Technology Company:

$$17.4\% = 9.5\% \times 1.28 \times 1.43$$

Using this formula, we can compare the performance of one company to another by examining the components of ROE. It is also useful to examine ROE performance over time and to determine how a change in each of the components would affect ROE. For example, if we improve profitability to 10.5%, ROE will improve to 19%. The individual components (profitability, asset turnover, and financial leverage) can be further broken down into a tree to highlight the contribution of individual measures, for example, DSO or SG&A % of Sales. An expanded ROE Tree is illustrated in Figure 2.2.

Return on Invested Capital (ROIC)

How Is It Computed?

$$= \frac{\text{EBIAT (Earnings before Interest and after Tax)}}{\text{Invested Capital}}$$

$$= \frac{\text{EBIT} * (1 - \text{tax rate})}{\text{Debt} + \text{Equity}}$$

$$= \frac{\$15,000 * (1 - 0.34)}{\$10,000 + 54,755}$$

$$= \frac{\$9,900}{\$64,755}$$

$$= 15.3\%$$

What Does It Measure and Reflect? ROIC measures the income available to all suppliers of capital (debt and equity) compared to the total capital provided from all sources (debt and equity). Another way of looking at ROIC is that this measure indicates the amount of income a company earns for each dollar invested in the company, including both debt and equity investment. ROIC is a terrific measure of overall performance and will be discussed further in Chapter 6, "Essential Ingredients for Value Creation: Growth and ROIC."

Return on Invested Capital-Market (ROICM)   A variation to ROIC is to use the market value of capital rather than the historical book value.

How Is It Computed?

$$= \frac{\text{EBIAT (Earnings before Interest after Tax)}}{\text{Invested Capital}}$$

$$= \frac{\text{EBIT} * (1 - \text{Tax Rate})}{\text{Debt} + \text{Equity}}$$

$$= \frac{\$15,000 * (1 - 0.34)}{\$10,000 + 180,030}$$

$$= \$9.900 / \$190,030$$

$$= 5.2\%$$

FIGURE 2.2 **ROE analysis for LSA Technology Company.**

Return on Equity Analysis

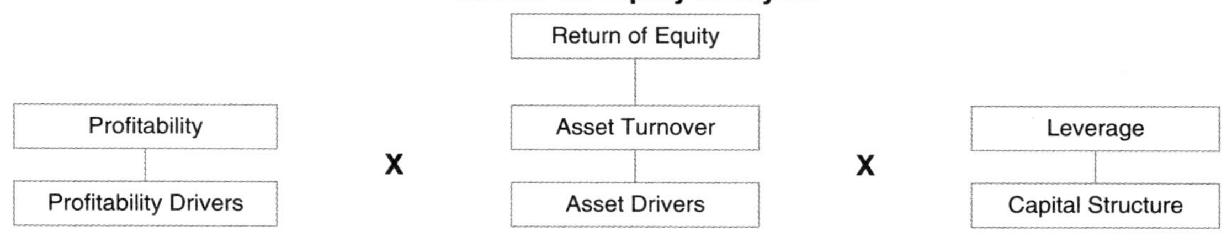

```
                    ┌──────────────────┐
                    │ Return of Equity │
                    └──────────────────┘
                             │
        ┌────────────────────┼────────────────────┐
 ┌───────────────┐    ┌───────────────┐     ┌──────────┐
 │ Profitability │  X │ Asset Turnover│  X  │ Leverage │
 └───────────────┘    └───────────────┘     └──────────┘
        │                     │                   │
┌──────────────────┐   ┌──────────────┐    ┌───────────────────┐
│Profitability     │   │ Asset Drivers│    │ Capital Structure │
│Drivers           │   └──────────────┘    └───────────────────┘
└──────────────────┘
```

ROE (Net Income/Equity) 17.4% = $\dfrac{9{,}501}{54{,}755}$

Profitability 9.5%	$	%
Sales	100,000	100.0%
Cos	45,000	45.0%
Gross Margin	55,000	55.0%
R&D	8,000	8.0%
Marketing	12,000	12.0%
Selling	12,000	12.0%
G&A	8,000	8.0%
Total Expenses	40,000	40.0%
Operating Income	15,000	15.0%
Other Income Expense	605	0.6%
Income Taxes	4,894	4.9%
Net Income	9,501	9.5%

X

Asset Turnover 1.28 X	Balance	% of Sales
Cash	7,944	8%
Receivables	20,000	20%
Inventory	18,000	18%
Other	900	1%
Total Current Assets	46,844	47%
Property & Equipment	20,000	20%
Goodwill & Intangibles	11,000	11%
Other	205	0%
Total Assets	78,049	78%
Asset Turnover(Sales/Asset)	1.28	
DSO:	73.0	
DSI:	146.0	

X

Leverage 1.43 X	
Liabilities	
Accounts Payable	4,500
Accrued Expenses	5,000
Long-Term Debt	10,000
Other	3,794
Total Liabilities	23,294
Shareholders Equity	54,755
Liabilities & Equity	78,049
Leverage	1.43
(Assets/Shareholders Equity)	

What Does It Measure and Reflect? ROICM measures the income available to all suppliers of capital (debt and equity) compared to the total capital provided from all sources (debt and equity) at current market values. While ROIC is a good measure of management effectiveness, ROICM relates current income levels to the market value of a company. A very low ROICM may indicate that the company's market value is very high compared to current performance. This may be due to very high expectations for future growth or a potential overvaluation of the company's stock.

Cash Generation and Requirements   In addition to measures such as EBITDA, others have been developed to measure and evaluate cash flow.

Cash Effectiveness (CE%)   Some managers and analysts measure the operating cash flow relative to the income generated as a measure of cash effectiveness and quality of earnings.

How Is It Computed?

The cash effectiveness for LSA Technology Company for 2023 is estimated to be 66% (see Table 2.8).

TABLE 2.8 **Cash effectiveness for LSA Technology Company.**

	$	%
Operating Profit after Tax	9,900	100%
Depreciation & Amortization	3,750	38%
Capital Expenditures	(5,000)	−51%
(Increase) Decrease in Operating Capital	(2,130)	−22%
Operating Cash Flow	6,520	66%

What Does It Measure and Reflect? The cash effectiveness ratio can be a good indicator of the relationship between reported income and cash flow. A significant decrease may signal that receivables collections are slowing or inventories are growing faster than income. Conversely, an increase in the percentage may indicate that the company is doing a better job in managing receivables, inventories, and capital investments. However, this measure is highly dependent on the rate of growth and the maturity of a business. A fast-growing company may have very low or even negative cash effectiveness percentage since asset levels must grow to support future sales growth. A company that is shrinking may find it easy to post CE% greater than 100% since capital investment levels will often decline faster than sales.

Self-Financing or Internal Growth Rate (IGR)   Managers must understand if the company is generating enough cash flow from operations to meet requirements to support future growth. A company that is self-financing will generate enough cash from operations to satisfy working capital and other requirements to support growth. Many companies test this requirement with future cash flow projections. Others use rules of thumb, for example, in order to support future growth levels of 15% our company needs a ROIC of 20%.

Ross et al. have developed a formula to estimate the self-financing growth rate given a firm's ROA and cash retention policy.[1]

How Is It Computed?

$$IGR = \frac{ROA \times r}{1 - (ROA \times r)}$$

where r is the percentage of net income retained in the business (i.e., not paid out as dividends to shareholders):

$$r = 1 - \left(\frac{Dividends}{Net\ Income}\right)$$

$$= 1 - \left(\frac{\$4,200}{\$9,501}\right)$$

$$= .5579$$

$$IGR = \frac{12.2\% \times .5579}{1 - (12.2\% \times .5579)}$$

$$= 7.3\%$$

What Does It Measure and Reflect? The IGR provides a high-level estimate of the rate at which the firm can grow without requiring outside financing. If this company grows at a rate faster than 7%, it will need to raise additional funds. If growth is under 7%, then the firm is generating enough cash to fund the growth. If the firm desires to increase the internal growth rate, it can retain a greater percentage of earnings or increase ROA.

Limitations and Pitfalls of Financial Ratios

Since the measures are based on financial statements that are prepared after the close of the period, these ratios are referred to as "lagging" measures of performance. We will discuss leading/predictive indicators a bit later.

Some managers place too much emphasis in blindly comparing ratios from one company to another. In order to effectively compare ratios across companies, it is important to understand the strategy, markets, and structure of each company. For example, a company that is vertically integrated will likely post significantly different financial results than one that is not. A company with a strong value-added product in a growing market will likely have very different characteristics than a company participating in a competitive, slower-growth market.

Financial ratios should be used as part of a broader diagnostic evaluation. These ratios will provide a great basis to identify trends, will complement other aspects of an overall assessment, and will be a great source of questions. Think of them in the same way a medical doctor uses key quantitative data about our health. Even in routine examinations, doctors will monitor key factors such as weight. But a patient's weight provides limited insight

[1] Ross, S.A., Westerfield, R.W., and Jordan, B.D., *Fundamentals of Corporate Finance*, Fifth Edition, McGraw Hill Companies, 2000, p. 102.

until combined with other insights, observations, and comparisons. How does the weight compare with others of the same age, height, and frame? Has the patient gained or lost weight since the last exam? If the patient has lost weight, why? This obviously could be good if intended as part of a fitness program or bad if a result of a health problem. Only through observation, discussion with the patient, and perhaps, additional testing can the doctor reach conclusions. So it is with many elements of financial performance.

Another potential limitation is that there is a great variety of similar ratios employed in business. An example is "return on capital." There are a number of potential definitions for both the income measure and the capital measure in such a ratio. It is important to understand exactly what is being measured by a formula before reaching any conclusions.

Similarly, it is important to understand the period to which the measure relates. Many measures could apply to monthly, quarterly, or annual periods. Further, an annual measure could be based on a balance at the end of the period or an average of the quarterly balances.

Putting It All Together

These individual ratios and measures take on greater meaning when combined as part of an analytical summary as shown below in Table 2.9.

TABLE 2.9 **LSA Technology Company: Performance assessment summary.**

	LSA Technology Company Analysis: Historical and Estimated Performance								
	2020	2021	2022	2023	2020	2021	2022	2023	CAGR
P&L									
Net Sales	$79,383	$84,000	$91,000	$100,000	100.0%	100.0%	100.0%	100.0%	8.0%
Cost of Goods Sold	36,000	38,000	41,000	45,000	45.3%	45.2%	45.1%	45.0%	7.7%
Gross Margin	43,383	46,000	50,000	55,000	54.7%	54.8%	54.9%	55.0%	8.2%
SG&A	26,000	27,500	29,500	32,000	32.8%	32.7%	32.4%	32.0%	7.2%
R&D	6,351	6,720	7,280	8,000	8.0%	8.0%	8.0%	8.0%	8.0%
Operating Income	11,032	11,780	13,220	15,000	13.9%	14.0%	14.5%	15.0%	10.8%
Interest (Income) Expense	600	600	600	600	0.8%	0.7%	0.7%	0.6%	0.0%
Other (Income) Expense	5	7	6	5	0.0%	0.0%	0.0%	0.0%	0.0%
Income Before Income Taxes	10,427	11,173	12,614	14,395	13.1%	13.3%	13.9%	14.4%	11.3%
Federal Income Taxes	3,748	4,010	4,418	4,894	4.7%	4.8%	4.9%	4.9%	9.3%
Net Income	6,679	7,163	8,196	9,501	8.4%	8.5%	9.0%	9.5%	12.5%
EPS	0.40	0.43	0.48	0.56					
EBIAT	7,281	7,775	8,725	9,900					
Balance Sheet									
Cash	25	2,404	4,400	7,944	0.0%	2.9%	4.8%	7.9%	
Receivables	15,877	17,500	17,800	20,000	20.0%	20.8%	19.6%	20.0%	
Inventories	15,500	16,250	17,000	18,000	19.5%	19.3%	18.7%	18.0%	
Other	200	800	975	900	0.3%	1.0%	1.1%	0.9%	
Current Assets	31,602	36,954	40,175	46,844	39.8%	44.0%	44.1%	46.8%	
Net Fixed Assets	15,877	16,800	18,750	20,000	20.0%	20.0%	20.6%	20.0%	
Net Goodwill and Intangibles	14,000	13,000	12,000	11,000	17.6%	15.5%	13.2%	11.0%	
Other Non current Assets	200	210	428	205	0.3%	0.3%	0.5%	0.2%	
Total Assets	61,678	66,964	71,353	78,049	77.7%	79.7%	78.4%	78.0%	

TABLE 2.9 (*Continued*)

		2020	2021	2022	2023	2020	2021	2022	2023	CAGR
				LSA Technology Company						
				Analysis: Historical and Estimated Performance						
Accounts Payable		3,600	3,800	4,100	4,500	4.5%	4.5%	4.5%	4.5%	
Notes Payable, Bank		-	-	-	-	0.0%	0.0%	0.0%	0.0%	
Accrued Expenses & Taxes		4,000	4,500	4,750	5,000	5.0%	5.4%	5.2%	5.0%	
Current Liabilities		7,600	8,300	8,850	9,500	9.6%	9.9%	9.7%	9.5%	
Long-Term Debt		10,000	10,000	10,000	10,000	12.6%	11.9%	11.0%	10.0%	
Other		3,083	2,536	3,194	3,794	3.9%	3.0%	3.5%	3.8%	
Stockholders' Equity		39,895	44,378	49,454	54,755	50.3%	52.8%	54.3%	54.8%	
Total Liabilities and Equity		60,578	65,214	71,498	78,049	76.3%	77.6%	78.6%	78.0%	
Operating Capital		23,977	26,250	26,925	29,400					
Invested Capital		49,895	54,378	59,454	64,755					
Market Value of Equity		153,974	164,304	169,000	180,030					
Cash Flow										
Net Income		6,679	7,163	8,196	9,501	8%	9%	9%	10%	
D&A		2,800	3,277	2,850	3,750	4%	4%	3%	4%	
Capital Expenditures		−3,000	−4,200	−4,800	−5,000	−4%	−5%	−5%	−5%	
(Inc) Decrease in OC			−2,273	−675	−2,475	0%	−3%	−1%	−2%	
FCF		6,479	3,967	5,571	5,776	8%	5%	6%	6%	
Employees		411	450	460	490					
Year/Year Revenue Growth		6.5%	5.8%	8.3%	9.9%					
Returns/Ratios:										
DSO		73.0	76.0	71.4	73.0					
Inv Turns		2.3	2.3	2.4	2.5					
DSI		157.2	156.1	151.3	146.0					
FA T/o		5.0	5.0	4.9	5.0					
Asset Turnover		1.3	1.3	1.3	1.3					
ROA		10.8%	10.7%	11.5%	12.2%					
ROIC		14.6%	14.3%	14.7%	15.3%					
ROE		16.7%	16.1%	16.6%	17.4%					
Economic Profit		7,281	7,775	8,725	9,900					
Interest Earned		18.4	19.6	22.0	25.0					
Debt to Total Capital (book)		20.0%	18.4%	16.8%	15.4%					
Debt to Total Capital (market)		8.1%	7.7%	7.7%	5.3%					
Leverage (Assets/Equity)		1.55	1.51	1.44	1.43					
Current Ratio		4.2	4.5	4.5	4.9					
ROE Analysis										
Profitability		8.4%	8.5%	9.0%	9.5%					
Asset Turnover	×	1.29	1.25	1.28	1.28					
Leverage	×	1.55	1.51	1.44	1.43					
ROE	=	16.7%	16.1%	16.6%	17.4%					
WACC					12%					

Creating a set of graphs capturing selected performance measures will generally be more useful to analyzing and communicating this information as shown in Figure 2.3.

A quick reference guide to key financial measures and ratios is provided in Table 2.10.

FIGURE 2.3 **Key performance trends for LSA Technology Company.**

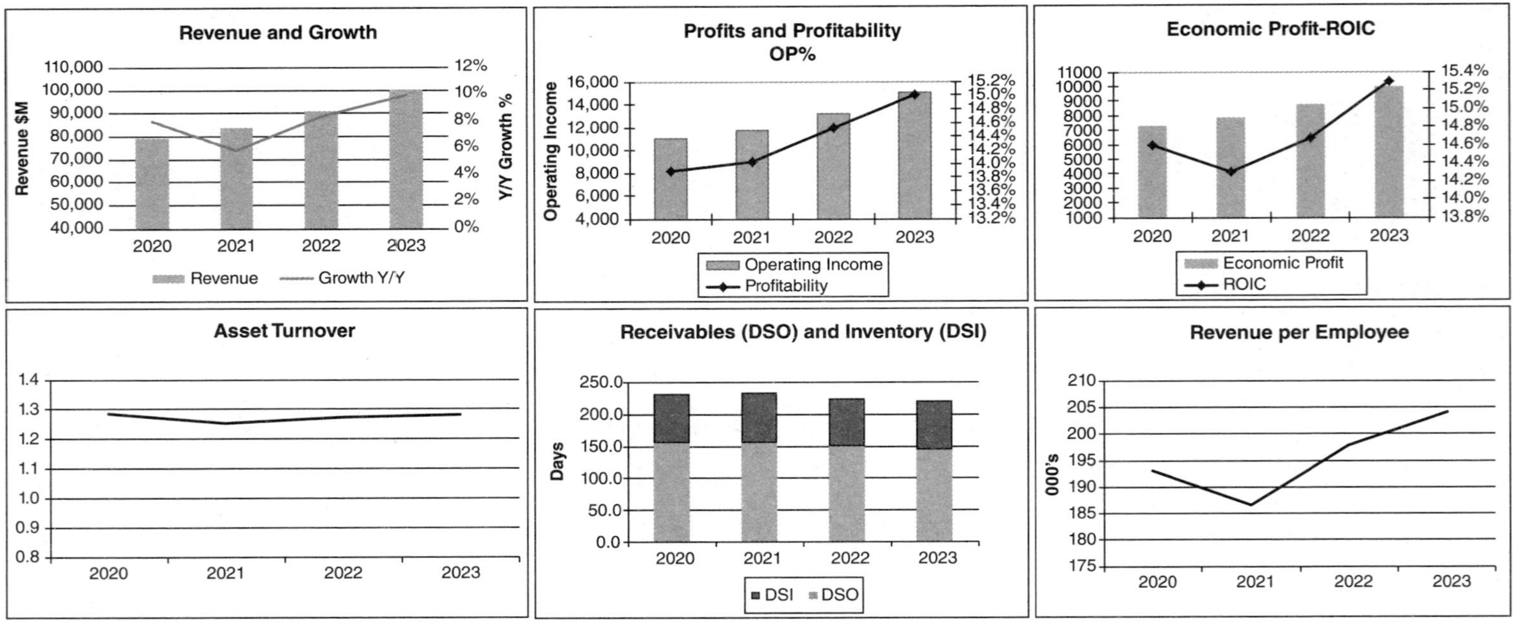

Revenue and Growth

Profits and Profitability OP%

Economic Profit-ROIC

Asset Turnover

Receivables (DSO) and Inventory (DSI)

Revenue per Employee

TABLE 2.10 **Key financial terms and measures: Quick Reference Guide.**

Measure/"AKA"	Description	Computed as. . .	Application
Value Creation and Overall Effectiveness			
ROE	Return on equity	Net income/Shareholders equity	Measures return to shareholders capital (equity)
ROIC	Return on invested capital	EBIAT/Invested capital	Measures return to all providers of capital (equity and debt)
EP	Economic profit	EBIAT − (Cost of capital × Invested capital)	Measures return to all sources of capital (equity and debt)
TRS	Total return to shareholders	Stock price appreciation + Reinvested dividends	Measure of management performance (and compensation)
Operating Measures			
COGS	Cost of goods sold	Total product cost including labor, material, overhead, and variances	
Gross Margin %	Gross margin as a % of sales	Gross margin/sales	Key operating measure
SG&A %	SG&A expenses as a % of sales	SG&A/Sales	Key operating measure
Operating Income/Profit		Sales − COGS − operating expenses	Key operating measure
EBIT	Earnings before interest and taxes		Key operating measure
Operating Margin %/ "Profitability"	Operating Income as a % of sales	Operating Income/Sales	Key operating measure
EBITDA	Earnings before interest, taxes, depreciation and amortization	EBIT + D&A	Adds back noncash expense items ("D&A")
EBIAT/OPAT	Earnings before interest after tax/Operating profit after tax	EBIT(1 − t)	Earnings available to all providers of capital
CAGR	Compound annual growth rate	$CAGR = [(LY/FY)^{1/n}] − 1$	Measure growth in a key variable over time (e.g., sales)
Asset Management			
DSO	Days Sales Outstanding	(Accounts Receivable x 365)/Sales	Measures time to collect from customers
Inventory Turns	Inventory turnover	Cost of goods sold/Inventory	Supply chain effectiveness
DSI/DIOH	Days sales of inventory/Days Inventory on hand	365/Inventory turns	A more intuitive measure of inventory levels/cycle time
Operating Capital Turnover	Operating capital levels relative to sales	Sales/Operating capital	Measure operating capital relative to sales
Operating Capital % Sales	Operating capital levels relative to sales	Operating Capital/Sales	Measure operating capital relative to sales
Operating Capital Cycle		DSO + DSI	Measure key operating capital elements relative to sales
Asset Turnover	Asset levels relative to sales	Sales/Total assets	Asset requirements and effectiveness
Capital Structure			
TIE/C	Time Interest Earned/Covered	EBIT/Interest Expense	Measures the ability to service debt
Debt to total Capital	% of capital contributed by lenders	Debt/(Debt + Equity)	Measures financial risk and capital structure
Valuation			
WACC/Cost of Capital	Weighted average cost of capital	WACC = (ke*we) + (Kd*wd)	Expected returns of equity and debt investors
Invested Capital	Total capital contributed by investors	Book equity + interest bearing debt	Historical investment from all investors
Enterprise value (EV)	Market value of debt and equity		Total value of the firm
Market Value/Market Cap	Market value of equity	Shares outstanding × Share price	Equity value of the firm

* Note: Definitions and uses of ratios often vary.

SUMMARY

Understanding and interpreting financial statements is a required competency for effective management and investing. Combining this competency with an understanding of the business, industry, and strategic objectives of a firm can significantly improve management effectiveness and decision-making. Historical and projected financial statements will serve as the basis for many decisions and are an important part of the foundation in building an effective performance management framework.

## 3

Skills, Knowledge, and Attributes for Financial Business Partners

As evidenced by opening the cover of this book, you have a desire to improve and develop your ability to contribute as a Financial Business Partner (FBP). This chapter will offer a number of ways the author has found helpful to improve our value as an FBP, and ultimately, as a financial executive. This chapter will provide suggestions on how individuals can assess their skills and competencies, learn and grow, and increase their value as a business partner. A broader view of building an overall finance organization will be covered in Chapter 7.

WHERE DO I STAND ON EXPERIENCE, SKILLS, AND ATTRIBUTES OF SUCCESSFUL FINANCE PARTNERS?

Successful FBPs (those perceived as adding value and assuming roles of greater responsibility) tend to have certain personal traits, core skills, specific knowledge, and overall business acumen (Figure 3.1). Not all of these knowledge or experience areas are important to all FBP roles nor can an individual be expected to achieve proficiency in all. This summary, and the assessment following tool, is intentionally broad to provide a comprehensive view of those characteristics and experience of individuals who assume greater roles as senior FBPs.

FIGURE 3.1 **Business partner characteristics, skills, and knowledge.**

Effective Business Partners
Characteristics, Skills and Knowledge

Personal Traits and Characteristics
- People Oriented
- Listener
- Communicator
- Agile/Adaptable
- Intellectually Curious
- Analytical
- Zoomability: From details to big picture
- Continual Learner
- Execution Orientation
- Credible and Objective

Core Skills
- Working knowledge of GAAP, accounting processes and financial statements
- Communication Skills: Written, Presentation, Story Telling
- Modeling transactions and projections
- Data Analysis (statistics or "data science")
- Ability to utilize Technology and Software

Specific Knowledge/Experience
- Financial Statement Analysis
- Valuation
- Key Value Drivers
  - Revenue and Margins
  - Operating Effectiveness
  - Capital Effectiveness
- Capital Investment Decisions
- M&A
- Investor Reporting and Relations
- Strategic Analysis & Planning
- Developing Projections and Business Plans
- Competitive Analysis
- Enterprise Performance Management (EPM)
- Business Restructuring and Transformations
- Business Process Improvement
- Exposure to other Disciplines (e.g., operations)

Note: This is a comprehensive list of important experiences a senior financial business partner (CFO, Controller, FP&A Director) should attain. All FBPs should be cognizant of this broad list and seek to gain exposure to these as they progress through their careers.

Business Acumen and Knowledge
- General Awareness of Business, Markets and External Forces
- Company Strategy
- Company's Market and Competitive Environment

Personal Traits

Successful financial planning and analysis (FP&A) contributors, FBPs, and financial executives tend to have some common personal traits. If you are an accountant or finance professional considering a change to a business partner role, these traits may be helpful in assessing whether you are well suited to the role (and likely will also improve your contribution in your current role). Some of these traits may have played a role in our choice of education majors; for example, a detail, quantitatively oriented individual may be more likely to major in accounting or math than marketing or entrepreneurship. While some of these traits may be hard coded in our DNA, my experience suggests that many can be improved on, or compensated for, over time.

One particular trait I have found especially valuable in the finance professionals I have worked with over my 45-year career is an Execution Orientation. It is supported by the old saying "If you want something done, give it to a busy person." Throughout my career, there were always individuals who were my "go to" staff when I needed something important done, ASAP. They always found the time to get it done, along with their preexisting workload. Needless to say, they became valuable partners and received exposure to many important subject areas.

Core Skills

There are certain core skills that are fundamental to success as an FBP. First, a basic understanding of generally accepted accounting principles (GAAP) is important to be successful as an FP&A analyst and in other key finance roles. This includes an understanding of the three primary financial statements. Without this basic foundation, it is difficult to analyze performance and transactions, or develop projections of future performance. Chapter 2, "The Fundamentals of Finance and Financial Statement Analysis," was a primer/ review of basic accounting principles and financial statement analysis.

FBPs must be effective communicators, including oral, written, and presentation (both development and delivery) capabilities. We cannot provide service to our clients if we are unable to effectively communicate with them. A great analysis is essentially useless if it is not effectively communicated. Effective communicators are also good listeners. Much of the value-added analysis and recommendations we make will be the result of attentive listening in discussions with our colleagues.

The development of financial models is also a core skill of successful FBPs. Models are a critical part of most financial analysis, business decisions, and financial projections. The development of analytical and financial models will be covered in Chapter 4.

Data analysis is increasingly important to business and finance. Formerly known as business statistics, the discipline has evolved to data science as the volume of digital data generated and stored has exploded over the last 30 years. At its core, this involves the collection, processing, storage, and analysis of various data sets. The analysis includes using basic statistical tools, including mean, median, quartile, Pareto, and regression analysis, and is progressing to the use of predictive tools based on artificial intelligence (AI). This subject will be addressed further in Chapter 12, "Leveraging and Promoting Technology Investments" and will be illustrated throughout the book.

The use of technology in business and finance has exploded over the last several decades. The ability to acquire and store data, and the development of software platforms to capitalize on this ability have resulted in a requirement for FBPs to understand and be able to utilize technology and software applications.

Specific Knowledge and Experience

Figure 3.1 lists a broad set of knowledge and experience categories for FBPs and senior finance contributors. The list is intentionally broad to present the full range of experience that is typically expected of senior finance executives. All FBPs should be cognizant of this broad list and seek to gain exposure to these areas as they progress through their careers. Each of these topics will be covered in subsequent chapters of this book.

Business Acumen and Knowledge

The best analysts and other FBPs develop an understanding of the business. To become an effective business partner, we must step back from our quantitative and technical orientation to develop a context and understanding of the overall business. A few ideas to increase your business acumen and contribution:

- Invest some time with operating managers to understand their challenges and objectives.
- Obtain and read marketing and strategic plans.
- Review investor presentations, analyst reports, and market reports.
- Inquire about areas where you may be able to assist by identifying opportunities or illuminating challenges.
- Replace accounting jargon with business terms.
- Simplify the analysis rather than complicate it.
- Act as players, not just reporters.
- Propose actions and solutions rather than offer criticism or just identify problems.
- Follow general business news and overall market trends. Macro trends may have a significant impact on your business. Many issues and opportunities a company may face may have been encountered in other industries, for example, a once high-growth company reaching maturity.

Whether you are considering a move to a business partner role, want to increase your ability to contribute in a current role, or desire to map out a long-term development plan, a thoughtful and deliberate evaluation should be employed. A tool such as the illustration in Table 3.1 will facilitate a self-assessment of where you stand and identify specific areas that you may choose to improve on over time. With gaps and improvement opportunities identified, a development plan can be created. This assessment tool can incorporate findings from your formal performance review and client surveys that will be discussed in Chapter 7.

BECOMING A MORE EFFECTIVE BUSINESS PARTNER

Having assessed where you stand on common skills and experience, you can develop a plan to close any gaps based on your personal career goals. Without a plan, it is highly unlikely that we will make progress on our personal goals for growth and advancement. Even if you are fortunate to be employed by an organization with a strong focus on organizational and people development,

TABLE 3.1 **Business partner assessment tool.**

		Self Assessment		
Traits, Skills and Knowledge Categories	**Why?**	**Rating**	**Comment**	**Indicated Action**
FBP Traits, Skills and Knowledge and Experience				
Personal Traits				
People Oriented	Must interact with partners, clients, and others	√		
Listener	Seek and understand information	√+		
Communicator	Must communicate observations and recommendations	-	Not confident or effective	Communication workshop & practice
Agile/Adaptable	Ability to adapt to ever-changing requirements and environment	√		
Intellectually Curious	Why? Why? Why?	√		
Analytical	Ability to define objective and process data for results	√+		
Zoomability: From details to big picture (and reverse)	Must see the forest from the trees	√+		
Continual Learner	Ability to grow and stay current	√		Need to add learning to weekly routine
Execution Focus	Must overcome obstacles to consistently complete assignments			
Credibility and Objectivity	Must be perceived as credible and objective to be valued as a FBP	√+	Trusted as fair and objective	
Core Skills				
Working knowledge of GAAP, accounting processes, and financial statements	Without this foundation, the ability to contribute will be limited	√+	CPA with general accounting experience	
Communication Skills	Any analysis or idea is useless unless effectively communicated	-	Not confident or effective	Communication workshop & practice
-Informal		√		
- Written		√		
- Develop Presentations		√		
- Data Visualization		√		
- Deliver Presentations ("Storytelling")		-	No Experience	
Modelling Transactions & Projections	Models are an essential part of many FPB services and projects	√+		
Data Analysis	Knowledge of data science principles imperative	√		
- Ability to leverage Technology and Software	Understanding and use of technology is critical to effective FBP	√		
- The Basics: Including Excel® PowerPoint®		√+		
- Enterprise Software (ERP)		-	Need training on ERP System	Attend user training
- FP&A software for planning, analysis and presentation		√		
- Data management and analysis		-	Need to learn new software	
- Ability to learn new applications	Rapid advancement in technology require learning new applications			
- Emerging use of artificial intelligence		-		Follow developments

(Continued)

TABLE 3.1 (CONTINUED)

	FBP Traits, Skills and Knowledge and Experience			
Traits, Skills and Knowledge Categories	**Why?**	**Self Assessment**		
		Rating	**Comment**	**Indicated Action**
Specific FBP Knowledge & Experience				
Financial Statement Analysis	Analysis of comprehensive financial performance	√+		
Valuation	Growing shareholder value is the ultimate goal for businesses	-		
Key Value Drivers	Understanding and analysis of value drivers is a critical responsibility	-		
- Revenue and Margins		-		
- Operating Effectiveness		√+	Focus is SG&A	
- Capital Effectiveness		-		
Capital Investment Decisions	Must be able to prepare and review proposed Investment decisions	-	No practical experience	
M&A	Support in evaluation, valuation, integration of acquisition candidates	-	No practical experience	
Investor Reporting and Relations	Vital function to satisfy reporting requirements and attract capital	√+	Reporting expertise, not investor relations	
Strategic Analysis and Planning		-	No practical experience	
Developing Projections and Business Plans	One of the most important roles of finance	-	Limited to SG&A area	
- Operational Plans		-	Limited to SG&A area	
- Forecasts, Business Outlooks		-	Limited to SG&A area	
- Strategic Planning		-	Limited to SG&A area	
- Scenario Planning		-		
Competitor and Customer Analysis	Significant way for finance to add value to our business partners	-		
Enterprise Performance Management (EPM)	Ensure organization achieves stated objectives	√	Responsible for SG&A KPI's and dashboards	
Business Restructuring and Transformations	All businesses eventually face this inevitable process	-		
Business Process Mapping, Diagnostics, and Improvement	Financial results are the product of various business processes	√	Experience in public accounting	
Exposure to other Disciplines (e. g. operations)	Broadens and Increases understanding of business	-	No experience outside of accounting	
Business Acumen and Knowledge				
- General Awareness of Business, Markets, and Other Forces	FBP must develop a broad perspective to be effective	-	Need to work on this	
- Company Strategy	Understanding the Company's strategic issues and goals is essential	-	No real exposure to strategy process	
- Company's Market and Competitive Environment	The market and competitors will influence financial performance	-	No knowledge of market and competition	

each of us has a responsibility to self-manage and contribute to our own career development. As one senior executive advised me early in my career: "You are in charge of your own career development." The following topics address specific actions that the individual can employ to broaden and enhance their skill set and contribution to any organization. Many of the specific areas are addressed throughout this book.

Develop a Personal Development Plan

Based on the results of the assessment tool and development needs addressed in recent performance reviews, the FBP can create a development plan. Without a written plan, it is unlikely that we will achieve our objectives for improved contribution. Where appropriate, review the assessment and plan with your manager and clients to validate your findings. To begin, focus on high-leverage improvement opportunities that will have the greatest impact. The plan should include specific objectives, actions, and timelines. Progress on the plan should be reviewed each month. An example of a Business Partner Development Plan is presented in Table 3.2.

TABLE 3.2 **Business Partner Improvement Plan.**

Business Partner Development Plan				
Objective	**Why?**	**How?**	**When?**	**Notes**
This Year				
Improve presentation skills	Critical skill for finance managers	Attend an interactive workshop	Jun 30	
		Seek out additional opportunities to present	Ongoing	
Learn XYZ software package	Need to query and write reports	Training	May 25–26	Scheduled
Evaluate current reports		Prepare list; evaluate quality and client usage	Sep 30	
Identify and survey key "clients"	A BP must be a service provider	1. Survey SG&A clients	Apr 15	
		2. Meet with Department managers	May	
		3. Identify and plan actions	June	
Increase understanding of business	Need context to be effective BP	1. Volunteer to support strategic analysis	Feb 1	email
		2. Develop Competitor Analysis	Oct 15	
Expand or rotate beyond SG&A analysis	Need to expand experience	1. Volunteer in Revenue or Margin Analysis	Jul 31	Meet with team
Continuous Learning	Survival and growth	Listen to podcast 1 per week	Feb 28	
		Attend two conferences per year	Jan 31	Identify
Longer Term				
Transfer from SG&A group	Career development	Lateral move to product revenue analyst	Dec 31	Performance and development review

Evaluate Your Current Reports and Analysis

One of the best ways to evaluate your effectiveness as an FBP is to collect all reports, dashboards, and on-demand reports that are provided to managers, executives, directors, investors, and other important constituencies. These should include recurring reports (e.g., monthly or quarterly) as well as ad hoc requests for analysis. I recommend collecting paper copies of these reports and spreading them out on a conference table for full visual impact.

These reports can then be evaluated for professional appearance, relevancy, usefulness to clients, and so on. This review should also be performed for the finance team as a whole as will be illustrated in Chapter 7.

Shift Emphasis to Value-Add Activities

One of the greatest impediments to improving our effectiveness as finance professionals is that "we are too busy processing transactions, closing the books, preparing reports, and working on annual and quarterly filings." Few finance professionals have slack time to assume additional challenges.

The key is for finance professionals to continue pursuing process improvements across the nonvalue or lower value-add activities, so that more time is available for higher value activities including FP&A. This can be done at both the personal and organization level (which will be discussed in Chapter 7). Finance professionals can identify potential areas to recapture time:

- ❑ Track and analyze where we spend our time. What opportunities do we have to reduce or eliminate nonvalue or inefficient activities? How much time is spent in ineffective meetings? Gathering and cleansing data versus analysis?
- ❑ Identify opportunities to utilize software and data sources to eliminate manual efforts in data collection and processing.
- ❑ Prepare a list of our work products and review with our clients and finance leaders. Are all of these products valued? Eliminate reports and analysis that are not effective, are redundant, or are not utilized, and utilize the time to develop better analysis or service.

Survey Your Clients (or Partners)

One of the most effective ways to assess our contribution as business partners is to ask for feedback from those we serve, whether we think of them as partners or clients. This can be as simple as a discussion to ask how we are doing, how we could add more value, and obtaining an understanding of our client's challenges. A client survey form could also be utilized. While the ratings are informative, the greatest value tends to come in the form of comments, suggestions, and subsequent conversations. This can also be formalized and performed across the finance team as will be discussed in Chapter 7.

Client Survey

Financial Planning and Analysis

Your input is important to us!

FP&A is one of the most important functions of the finance organization, providing management and others with objective insight into the performance of the organization.

What best describes your level of responsibility?*

Executive	Manager	Lead
Director	Supervisor	

	L H
Quality of presentation	1 2 3 4 5
Quality of content provided in reports and analysis	1 2 3 4 5
How would you rate your level of understanding of finance and accounting	1 2 3 4 5
Timeliness of reports and responsiveness to requests	1 2 3 4 5
Overall, how do you rate the performance of FP&A	1 2 3 4 5

What reports do you use on a regular basis?

In which business areas would you like more insight and analysis?

What improvements are needed?

Are the reports and analysis concise and well-presented business summaries of the topic covered?

What are your biggest challenges and key objectives? How can we help?

Do you view me (or the FP&A team) as a resource you can utilize?

Other Comments and Suggestions:

*Note: In scale, 1 is lowest and 5 is highest score.

Formal Training

A large number of training programs exist that are geared to financial analysis, managerial accounting and reporting, and related topics. Unfortunately, many are very basic and do not extend very far beyond traditional financial statement and ratio analysis and other "academic" areas. These are fine for the junior analyst, but fail to address important business drivers, current trends, and advanced topics.

For advanced levels of training, seek programs that cover a range of topics, practical tools, and new developments in the science.

- Planning and forecasting.
- Enterprise Performance Management.
- Diagnostic tools, including Pareto and root cause analysis.
- Developing financial models.
- Capital investment decisions.
- Valuation and value drivers.
- Presenting and communicating business information.

Also choose a workshop or seminar leader offering practical experience in the application of these tools and experience that rounds out the technical aspects of financial management.

Utilize Reference Materials (the Objective of This Book)

Few professional books or textbooks fully explore FP&A and other important topics for FBPs. Some works on corporate or managerial finance include a chapter or two on analysis, but the emphasis is on "technical" or "academic" finance subjects. Many books and publications focus on the theoretical aspects of a topic without exploring the real-world issues that the business partner routinely encounters.

Recognizing the void in this area, I began creating my own reference materials and developing analytical tools. The objective of this book is to provide such a reference to others. Most of the analytical templates reviewed in this book are available to purchasers of this book. For more information, please refer to the Appendix, "Website Info."

Read and Collect Examples of Outstanding Analysis

As a student of financial analysis and performance management, I set up a file (actually a paper file, back in the day!) in which I placed a copy of any superior analysis or presentation that caught my eye. Some were terrific spreadsheets; others had unique or very effective methods of summarizing and presenting complex information. In many cases, the analysis was not directly applicable to anything I was likely to need. However, there were often kernels that high-lighted best practices in analyzing or presenting findings such as statistical summaries, dual axis graphs, and waterfall charts.

Many of these thought-provoking examples were plucked from magazine (later digital) articles, conference materials, consultant reports, marketing and promotional materials, and research analyst reports.

Maintain a Portfolio of Your Analytical Works

Just as artists maintain portfolios of their works, so should the financial analyst. This portfolio can be electronic or paper or both. It can serve as a source of ideas and will also limit "reinventing the wheel."

My portfolio filled an entire file cabinet of paper, and more recently, a sub-stantial part of my hard drive. I often find materials that I had long forgotten, but that are directly applicable to a current project. My ability to leverage this past work, of course, is very dependent on my ability to retrieve a paper, or better yet, the digital file. Good filing, indexing, and labeling are critical. The portfolio can also be useful in employment searches and for reference in performance reviews.

Go beyond "Crunching the Numbers"

Many finance professionals believe that the analysis is complete when the spreadsheet is complete. They simply pass on the spreadsheet without any true analysis or effort to effectively communicate the findings. As a financial executive, I often received "analysis" from professional staff that was simply a spreadsheet. They expected me to make observations and interpret the data, identify implications, and propose recommended actions. This limited their development and advancement, and likely left important observations and suggestions unidentified (and made more work for the reviewer). Finance executives should require analysts to present complete analysis.

Improve Communication and Presentation Skills

One of the greatest improvement opportunities for most finance professionals is to develop their communication and presentation skills. The analytical pro-cess is not complete until the results are presented and understood. Chapter 5 will provide some specific and concrete ways for us to improve the way we present and communicate financial and business information.

Develop a Reputation for Credibility and Objectivity

To be an effective business partner, it is important to be viewed as an objective player. Too often, we finance folks have a "rep" of always having a negative perspective and being critical of all programs and performance. Operating managers will "tune out" input from analysts they believe are always pessimistic or negative, or have a hidden agenda or motive. To counter this, we must strive to be balanced, and occasionally, point out the positives! Our analysis and presentations should always be objective and fact-based.

One effective technique for creating a balanced view is to present the "Highlights" and the "Improvement Opportunities." This balanced presentation will strengthen the weight of your findings and build credibility as an impartial reviewer of business performance and projects. Another technique is to present several scenarios and risks and upsides of projections to point out concerns without always appearing negative about future prospects.

Demonstrate Business and Emotional Maturity

Finance managers are engaged in analysis of highly sensitive business issues, problems, and opportunities. They will be interacting with senior executives and with a wide range of associates within the organization. Analysts need to build trust with associates to ensure access to information. In many cases, the analysis is a component of the evaluation of a project, business, team, or even an individual manager. In addition to the need for confidentiality of sensitive information, analysts must also be thoughtful and considerate in their interactions with other associates and managers.

Volunteer to Work on Important Analytical Projects and Presentations

Another way to develop and hone analytical and presentation skills is to volunteer or assist in important, high-level presentations. Due to their importance, many projects and presentations get a lot of attention, and therefore, a lot of professional assistance. Volunteer to work on these projects and you will be exposed to the "big picture," solid thought leaders (consultants, investment bankers, senior managers, and executives) and good presentations of business information. A few examples of reports and projects:

- ❑ Reports and presentations to investors, analysts, and shareholders.
- ❑ Reports to the board of directors.
- ❑ Customer proposals.
- ❑ Large capital decisions, including new products or acquisitions.
- ❑ Strategic assessments and plans.

Improving the Financial Literacy of Nonfinancial Managers

Throughout my career as an auditor, controller, CFO, lecturer, and advisor, it was apparent to me that most nonfinancial managers do not have a solid foundation in finance. Even worse, most finance folks do not attempt to compensate for, or address, this issue. It should not come as any surprise that many of our attempts to communicate fall on deaf ears. In addition, without a foundation of basic finance, it is difficult for nonfinance folks to understand the ways in which their functions impact financial results.

Several years ago, I conducted a survey across business managers from first-line managers to middle managers to the executive suite. Although I had anticipated low scores, I was astonished at the results (see Figure 3.2). Even at the executive suite, there is a limited understanding of financial terms and concepts.

FIGURE 3.2 **Financial acumen scores.**

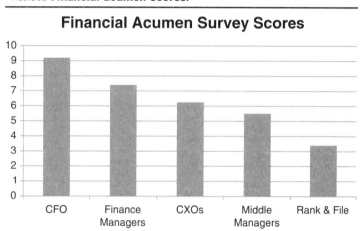

We can help our associates at all levels to develop a better understanding of finance and accounting. The specific ways we can help will vary depending on the organization, level of manager or associate, and background of team members. Here are a few suggestions:

- Avoid using accounting jargon and acronyms. Work at explaining issues and opportunities in business, not financial terms.

- Infomercials. Take the time during a presentation or meeting to provide an explanation or educate participants on the subject at hand. This can be a very effective way to reach senior managers, who are unlikely to sign up for a more formal training session. Another example of an opportunity for an infomercial is during a quarterly presentation to all associates.

- Lunch sessions. Best practice finance organizations have offered short sessions during lunch to cover important subjects.

- Formal programs. Business schools and other service providers offer training in finance to managers.
- In-house workshops. Offering an in-house workshop has the advantage of tailoring the material to the organization.
- Comprehensive financial training programs. Very progressive organizations realize the importance of associates understanding the key elements of financial performance and for the associates to understand how their individual function impacts key drivers of financial performance, value creation, and the organization's goals.

Whatever forum we choose, we must be aware that some associates may be knowledgeable in certain subjects, and therefore, may be offended by our attempts. Take care to couch the information appropriately and avoid any appearance of a condescending attitude.

Develop a Measured Tolerance to Risk Management Most finance professionals were educated and trained to be risk averse. Many nonfinance managers believe that finance opposes nearly all investment and business opportunities due to perceived risk. While part of our role is indeed to manage risks, FBPs must develop a balanced view of risks and rewards, and contribute to mitigating, managing, or reducing risks.

Continuous Learning There is no final destination for learning. The world is changing at a rapid pace across technology, business practices, and many other areas. A successful FBP will include ongoing learning into their professional objectives and weekly routines. Sources of learning include books, periodicals, conferences, podcasts, webinars, professional associations, and LinkedIn communities.

SUMMARY

Contributing as an FBP or senior financial manager requires a broad set of technical, business, and soft skills. Perhaps one of the most important traits is to become a "life-long learner," with a commitment to continued growth and development to contribute in an ever-changing world. FBPs should also review Chapter 7 and participate in the evaluation of the overall finance team's performance and the development of improvement plans.

4

Developing Predictive and Analytical Models

One of the greatest tools in the business partner's bag is the ability to create a "model" of future business results. Models are typically used to evaluate business decisions, analyze alternatives, or predict future business results. If you turned to this chapter hoping to find the latest and greatest spreadsheet tricks, you will be disappointed. Instead, in this chapter, we will define models, highlight typical applications, review best practices, discuss best ways to present the results of a model, and explain how to establish a portfolio of models.

WHAT IS A FINANCIAL MODEL?

A model is essentially a mathematical representation of a transaction, event, or business, and typically involves the use of assumptions and relationships of various factors to predict an outcome. Most models rely heavily on historical results and past experience to project future outcomes.

A financial model allows us to project and test the dynamics of a business, project, or program. Developing an effective model of a business or significant project requires a sophisticated understanding of the business or opportunity at hand. The analyst will almost always need input from other business disciplines such as sales and marketing, operations, and research and development.

Several challenges arise in developing effective models. The first challenge is to create a model that will fully satisfy its primary objective. Second, almost all models include or develop projections of future performance, and therefore, they incorporate assumptions about future performance, which introduces uncertainty and risk. Finally, the analyst must develop a method for creating output or presentation summaries to effectively communicate the results of the model to other managers, the ultimate clients of the model. We will discuss best practices to address these challenges in the remainder of this chapter. An illustration of a model to project revenues and product margins is included at the end of this chapter.

APPLICATIONS FOR FINANCIAL MODELS

Under our broad definition, models are used in a wide range of applications. We review a few of the most common applications of models, but the potential application of models is nearly unlimited.

Operating Plans and Budgets

Nearly all organizations develop operating plans and budgets. These plans include a set of projections about future performance based on a series of assumptions. While the emphasis will vary based on the nature of the organization, the operating plan should include projections of sales, margins, expenses, profits, balance sheet accounts, and cash flow. We will discuss operating plans and budgets in detail in Chapter 20.

Forecasts/Business Outlooks

Most organizations prepare forecasts, or "business outlooks," that are essentially updates to the annual operating plans and budgets. These are an increasingly important part of business projections owing to the dynamic times in which we live and operate. Assumptions made in the annual operating plan will often have to be revised throughout the year. We will discuss forecasts and business outlooks in detail in Chapter 20.

Revenue Projections

Revenue projections are typically the most important and difficult to predict variables in developing a forecast or plan for an enterprise. Projections must reflect assumptions in the company's market and overall business environment as well as pricing, cost, and product introduction and life cycle. The illustrative model at the end of this chapter presents a simple case to project revenues over a multi-year horizon. Additional models and analysis addressing revenue are included in Chapter 22.

Cash Flow and Liquidity Projections

Most treasurers and CFOs must pay very close attention to cash flow, capital requirements, and liquidity. Often, the traditional or indirect financial statement approach is not the best method for short-term, even weekly or daily projections. Cash flow models focus on specific drivers of short-term cash flow. We will explore these models in Chapter 24, "Capital Management and Cash Flow—Working Capital."

Strategic Plans and Long-Range Forecasts

A strategic plan should include a set of financial projections. These projections are a financial representation of the estimated results of executing the strategic plan. The projections are typically done at a higher level than annual plans or forecasts. Owing to the difficulty in projecting financial results over an extended period of time (typically three to seven years), a number of scenarios are often included in the plan. We will explore these models in Chapter 21, "Long-Term Projections."

Capital Investment Decisions

Capital investment decisions include any expenditure with a long-term horizon, such as purchases of capital equipment, new product development, acquisitions of businesses or companies. These decisions often require a series of projections of both investment outlays and future cash inflows. We will explore these models in Chapters 28 and 29, which both address capital investment decisions.

Compensation and Incentive Plans

As part of the process to design and test compensation systems, it is essential to model potential outcomes. These models illustrate incentives earned under different scenarios and help to prevent inclusion of "unintended consequences." You can rest assured that executives and managers will spend a great deal of time modeling potential payouts and scenarios for their personal compensation plans!

Valuing a Business

Most sound methodologies for developing an estimated value for a business require projecting future operating performance and cash flows. The best valuation models include key performance drivers, projected Income Statements, Balance Sheet, and cash flow projections. We will explore these models in Chapter 30, "Business Valuation and Value Drivers."

Mergers and Acquisitions

The ability to project the results and evaluate the investment characteristics of a merger or an acquisition is simply a combination and refinement of the business valuation model and the capital investment model. Additional metrics are included to focus on critical success factors and other unique aspects of these investment decisions. We will explore these models in Chapter 31, "Analysis of Mergers and Acquisitions."

Project and Proposal Estimates

Models are used to estimate the costs, benefits, and other attributes of projects, including development projects, plant and geographic expansions, and business transformation efforts. Models also are used to project and evaluate the business performance of business proposals.

BEST PRACTICES IN DEVELOPING MODELS

The best practices reviewed next can be applied to almost any predictive or analytical model. Models are illustrated and used throughout this book. We use a simple model to develop long-term revenue projections to illustrate these best practices.

Use the Four-Step Model Approach

For any analysis or model project, it is useful to view the activity in four major steps as illustrated in Figure 4.1. The traditional approach involved capturing

FIGURE 4.1 **Four-step model development process.**

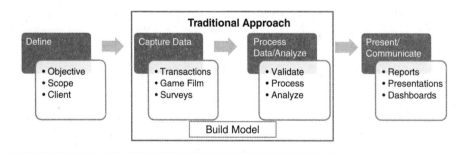

View Analytical Projects as a Four-Step Process

the data, setting up the spreadsheet, and then working the model. Large gains can be realized by taking a step back and defining the objective, scope and client for the model before we begin "coding" the spreadsheet model. In addition, we should begin with the end in mind, that is, how will the results of this model be presented and communicated? I have found it helpful to sketch out the graphs and tables that would be useful to effectively communicate the output of the model, often resulting in thoughts that are helpful in laying out the model. These summaries should identify key assumptions and important performance measures and analysis.

Define Objective

As a first step, analysts should step back and define the objective of a large modeling project. In many cases, the model is in response to a request from the CEO, CFO, or another operating executive. Taking a few minutes of time to define the objective and review with the internal client can save a great deal of time and rework later in the process. Defining the objective will also assist in designing the model and should address the following questions:

Who is the client or user of the model?

What answers (output) are we seeking?

What are the key variables that will impact the analysis?

What is the time horizon?

How frequently will the model be used, and by whom?

Who will partner with the financial analyst to provide business input and review assumptions?

And of course, when is the analysis needed? Answering this somewhat obvious question will define scope and complexity of the model.

Develop Architecture of Model

Many financial models are developed without well thought-out architecture. Pressed for time, the analyst sets up a spreadsheet or other tools without developing an overall framework for the model.

One of my hobbies is woodworking, including making furniture and creating wood models from scratch. I never embark on a project without at least sketching a rough drawing. A few attempts at doing so resulted in rework, wasted time and materials, or a finished project that was unsuitable for the intended purpose. Creating a drawing forces a consideration of size and dimensions as well as material requirements, and results in a product satisfying intended requirements. Similarly, I would not embark on the development of a financial model without a drawing or architecture. My favorite forum to conceptualize models is on a whiteboard, where revisions were easy to post and several colleagues could participate in the design.

Preferably, the analyst building on the stated objective of the model lays out the flow of the model, including required inputs, processing worksheets, and output summaries.

The architecture should include:

- Objective: What is the purpose of the model?
- Client: Who is the primary client/user of the report?
- Frequency: How often will the model be updated?
- Flow: In complex models, it is helpful to illustrate the flow of information in a model.
- Key assumptions: Identify, up front, the major assumptions and inputs required to use the model.
- Output and presentation: Based on the objective and identification of the client, develop the output summary.

Figure 4.2 is an example of the planning architecture for a cash flow projection model. This can be included as the first worksheet in an Excel model.

Documentation

One of the most common problems with financial models is that they tend to have little, if any, documentation. This presents a problem if another analyst attempts to use the model. In fact, for models that are used infrequently, even the developer of the model may waste a lot of time refreshing their memory (I am speaking from personal experience here!). Taking the additional time to properly document the model will save both the developer and other users substantial time in using and modifying the model in the future. The documentation should include key the inputs required and the steps required to update the model.

Identify Input Areas

For many models, it is very helpful to identify or even segregate input fields from processing or output fields. If input areas are not identified, the user must hunt and peck around the model looking for input fields. In large models, the input values may be several steps away from the final summary. A simple but effective technique is to simply shade all input areas in the model as a single color. This allows any user to quickly identify cells that can (and those that should not) be changed. Alternatively, some model developers prefer to have all key inputs and assumptions in one section of the model.

FIGURE 4.2 **Financial model architecture.**

Model Overview

Collections Forecast & Assumptions		Receivable Collections
Sales Forecast		Manufacturing Labor
Production Forecast		Material Purchases
		Capital Expenditures
		Other: Payroll

Cash Flow Projection → Cash Flow Presentation

Name of Model	Short-Term Cash Projections
Objective	Project cash flow
Primary Client	Treasurer
Secondary Clients	CFO
Frequency	Weekly
Estimated Hours to prepare	10

Key Assumptions/Input:	
Description	**Responsibility**
Sales Forecast	Shipping Department
Collections	Credit Department
Production Levels	Dir of Operations
Material Purchases	Materials Management
Payroll	Human Resources
Other Expenditures	Controller
Capital Expenditures	Controller

Output:
Key Assumptions
Cash Flow Projections
Exception/Alerts

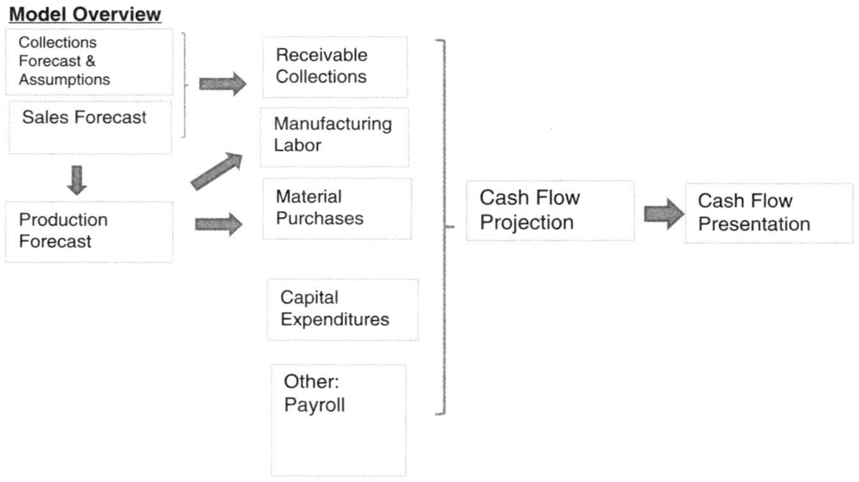

Identify Key Assumptions and Drivers

Models typically require making many estimates and assumptions. Not all inputs to a model have equal importance. Key assumptions and drivers in the model should be identified and highlighted. These critical inputs should be identified, documented, tested, reviewed, varied in sensitivity and scenario analysis, and included in output section of the model.

Incorporate Historical/Actual Results

In most cases, it is essential to incorporate actual results into the model. This serves two purposes. First, the historical information validates the model by replicating the actual results. Second, the historical information provides a baseline to compare and evaluate the projections used in the model.

For models that project annual results, three to four years of history should be included. For quarterly analysis, eight quarters generally provides sufficient historical perspective. Monthly or weekly analysis should generally include at least recent trends and the same periods from the previous year.

Protect Formulas

For models that will be used by several people, it is important to protect the cells with formulas to prevent inadvertent changes. For the record, I have often wished I had protected some of my own models from myself—from inadvertently keying over a formula.

Ownership and Buy-in

Most models should not be viewed as a finance exercise or product of finance. While it is okay for finance to be the developer/facilitator, the inputs and major assumptions must be understood and agreed to by the appropriate managers. Generally, it is preferable to obtain key inputs from the operating manager responsible for achieving the projected results. For example, the sales forecast should be provided by the senior sales and marketing executive, or their designee. If finance develops the major assumptions and inputs without buy-in of the cognizant manager, finance will own the projected results, which reduces the accountability of the responsible manager.

Robust and Flexible

The model must be flexible so that changes to key assumptions can easily be made and reflected throughout the model. For example, changing interest rates, currency rates, or sales projections in one input field should ripple throughout the model, resulting in revised outcomes. Too often, models are fragmented and require multiple manual entries to effect a single change.

In addition, contrary to the wildest dreams of the analyst, most models are not one and done. Typically, the client will want to change assumptions or run additional scenarios.

Keep It Simple

There is a tendency for model developers to create models that are unnecessarily complicated. Sometime this is to use the latest and greatest Excel® feature or to show off their expertise. Formulas in individual cells are often complicated, combining several functions. I recommend keeping it simple for two reasons. First, others (and you) will find it easier to review and revise when you use the model in the future. Second, simpler models are easier to review for understanding and testing reasonableness of outcomes. The analyst or reviewer can more easily follow the flow of calculations and understand the model results. Third, by replacing complex formulas with multi-steps, you can facilitate an increased understanding of the model and the results of the model.

Avoid "Black Box" Models: Show Your Work

Many models that I review are "Black Boxes." It may be clear what the inputs are and the answer is identified, but the model does not provide visibility into the processing dynamics (Figure 4.3). This is the equivalent of not "showing your work to receive partial credit" in school. Black Boxes are difficult to review, difficult to evaluate the answer, and provide little insight into the dynamics of the transaction or projection that is being modeled.

FIGURE 4.3 **The Black Box.**

Input ⇨   ⇨ "Answer"

A good illustration is the calculation of net present value (NPV) in Table 4.1. You can simply use the net present value (NPV) formula, but a more useful presentation provides the dynamics of the calculation. In the one-step computation, the NPV of future cash flows for Years 1–6 is $103,432. No additional insight is provided.

However, in the multi-step, insightful computation, we present the computations embedded in the present value computation. This allows us to see the contribution to NPV of each year's cash flow and highlights the important contribution of Year 6, presumably the terminal value. This method also allows us to reinforce the importance of the time value of money, that is, cash flow realized earlier is of greater value than cash flow realized in later periods. For more information on the time value of money, refer to Chapter 26.

TABLE 4.1 **Unpacking formulas to provide insight.**

Discount Rate	12%						
		Cash Flow by Year					
		1	2	3	4	5	6
		11,000	11,000	11,000	11,000	11,000	125,889
One-step							
Present Value	103,432						
Multi-step, Insightful							
Present Value Factor		0.893	0.797	0.712	0.636	0.567	0.507
Present Value of Cash Flow		9,821	8,769	7,830	6,991	6,242	63,779
Sum of PVFCF	103,432						

Revision Control

Certain models, for example, projections underlying a large capital investment or business acquisition, will likely be revised several times. Without some effective file naming, it can be frustrating to open a folder full of files that all sound the same. It is helpful to adopt a practice of labeling the models as illustrated below:

> Acquisition Analysis ABC Company Rev 0
> Acquisition Analysis ABC Company Rev 1 Refined Synergies
> Acquisition Analysis ABC Company Rev 2 Refined Revenue Projections

It is also useful to label different scenarios for clarity and additional use:

> Acquisition Analysis ABC Company Scenario 1 Base
> Acquisition Analysis ABC Company Scenario 2 Aggressive Revenue Case
> Acquisition Analysis ABC Company Scenario 3 Downside Revenue Case
> Acquisition Analysis ABC Company Scenario 4 Conservative Synergy

Review for Accuracy and Reasonableness

There is no quicker way to destroy personal and department credibility than to produce reports and analysis that contain errors. The analyst and finance team should implement measures to identify and correct any errors.

The following review techniques can reduce errors and improve the overall quality of the analysis:

Independent Review. It can be very difficult to effectively review an analysis that we have personally prepared. Where possible, the analysis should be reviewed by an analyst or a manager who was not directly involved in the process.

Review Key Inputs, Assumptions, and Flow of Analysis. The reviewer should perform a mini-audit of the model, to "tic and tie" key numbers to ensure they flow through the analysis, from detail worksheets to summaries.

Big Picture/Client Perspective. A great way to review for quality (and also prepare for presenting to client) is to review the analysis through the eyes of the client. Does it address the objective and issue at hand? Is the presentation clear? Are the results of the analysis/model sensible? In too many cases, the answer (output) is nonsensical because of some minor error in the model; this could easily be detected (and most assuredly will be discovered by the client!). It is helpful to estimate the result of a particular model and also to estimate the expected result of any changes. When presenting an analysis to one CEO I worked with, he frequently had developed an expected outcome of the analysis on the back of an envelope (and we discussed a high-level reconciliation of the two results if they differed!). I adopted this practice myself as a CFO and consultant. What additional questions does the analysis raise? What actions should be taken or recommended? This step also leads to growth and personal development of the analyst.

Sensitivity and Scenario Analysis

The model should also facilitate making changes to critical assumptions to create various scenarios and perform sensitivity analysis. The initial output of the model may be described as the "base" projection. Other versions of the model should be summarized and presented to the client since they add tremendous value in understanding the impact of assumptions and the overall dynamics of the situation or decision.

A sensitivity analysis will flex one or more sensitive assumptions. For example, what is the impact on total revenues if unit volumes are 10% lower than the base forecast? What is the result if unit volumes are 10% higher?

A scenario analysis will attempt to address "what-ifs." For example, what if a new competitor successfully introduces a product that competes directly with one of our key products. This scenario will likely result in reduced average sales prices *and* unit sales for this product. A model should easily accommodate estimating and presenting this and other scenarios. For additional examples of scenario analysis, refer to Chapter 13, "Scenario

Analysis, Planning, and Management," and Chapter 29, "Capital Investment Decisions—Advanced Topics."

Output and Presentation Summary

Nearly all analysis, spreadsheets, and models make poor presentation documents. Completing the analysis or model is just half of the job. Developing an effective way to summarize and present the results of the model is as important as the model itself.

For complex models, it is best to incorporate an output or presentation summary. By integrating the presentation summary into the model, it is updated any time the model is run or changed. I prefer a one-page summary highlighting key assumptions, a graphic presentation of results, and sensitivity and scenario analysis. This summary should be the primary presentation page or slide, with most spreadsheets and tables offered as supporting schedules. The model, or even one output from the model, represents a small part of the potential value of a model. The real value is in increasing the understanding of the dynamics of a particular investment, projection, or decision, and communicating this to the pertinent managers. An effective presentation summary also facilitates a quality review, which was discussed earlier in the chapter. We will cover this topic in greater detail in Chapter 5, "Presenting and Communicating Financial Information."

Establish a Portfolio of Models

In most organizations, the models are often stored by the individual who developed or uses the model. Many organizations have found it useful to develop an index of models and store them in a shared drive or cloud. This will serve to eliminate duplication of similar models. It will also encourage the sharing of best practices and techniques across the organization. The examples provided in Table 4.2 highlight the potential usefulness of this practice.

Use the Best Tool for the Job

The models illustrated in this book are developed using Excel® since this software is available to nearly all analysts and is widely used. This product has tremendous utility and is terrific for ad-hoc and relatively simple models. Microsoft continues to add new features to the product, further increasing functionality. However, Excel may not be the best software for all applications, especially complex models. For example, the development of an annual plan or rolling forecast for a large international enterprise would likely be better suited to one of the many planning software packages developed over the last quarter century.

TABLE 4.2 **Portfolio of financial models.**

Portfolio of Models and Analytical Tools

Subject Area	Title	Description	Developer	Last used
FS Analysis	Historical Performance Analysis	Ratio Analysis Financial Performance of Company Level	JFA	5/26/22
Revenue/Margins	Revenue and margin projections	Multi-year, product though Company summary	SVA	1/02/23
Valuation	DCF Sensitivity Analysis	Displays the sensitivity of share price to changes in assumptions	MTV	6/26/22
Projections	Expected Value/Probability	Probability weighted forecast	RJA	3/06/21
FS Analysis	ROE Analysis (Dupont)	Drill down analysis: components of Return on Equity	GO	10/14/22
Working Capital	Revenue Process/Receivable Analysis	Dashboard of Receivable levels, Measures and Drivers	KRV	5/26/18
Assessment	Activity Based Analysis	Allocate/Assign Costs based on activity and drivers	BVD	1/02/21
FS Analysis	Business Model: Comprehensive View	Presents Comprehensive Performance Analysis	TJA	6/26/22
Assessment	Benchmarking Financial Performance	Compares company performance to peers and admired	LSA	3/06/21
FS Analysis	Operating Leverage Analysis	Fixed and variable costs, breakeven, variable cont. margin	JFA	10/14/22
Assessment	FP&A Assessment	Assess FP&A performance and Identify improvement steps	SVA	9/17/17
Assessment	Report/Analysis Assessment	Review and Survey Users on Report Effectiveness	MTV	5/06/18
Assessment	FP&A Survey	Surveys clients of FP&A	RJA	5/26/18
Presentation	Dual Access Graphs	Presents 2 variables in single graph, e.g. Receivables/DSO	GO	1/02/21
Presentation	Reconciliation Graph	(aka waterfall chart)	KRV	6/26/22
Valuation	Valuation Summary	Value a project or Biz using Discounted Cash Flow	BVD	3/06/21
Assessment	Benchmarking Performance Graph	Compares company performance to peers and admired	TJA	10/14/22
Performance Measurement	KPI Development Worksheet	Develop KPI, objective, unintended consequences, etc.	JJC	5/26/18
Performance Measurement	Quarterly Corporate Dashboard	Displays key Corporate Trends	JFA	1/02/21
Performance Measurement	Weekly Dashboard	Tracks KPI weekly basis	JFA	6/26/22
Performance Measurement	Product Development Dashboard	Presents KPI for NPD function	SVA	3/06/21
Performance Measurement	Dashboard Specialty retailer	Overall Performance for specialty retailer	ERA	10/14/22
Performance Measurement	Dashboard Ski Resort	Overall Performance for Ski Resort	RJA	10/07/22
Performance Measurement	Dashboard Hospital	Overall Performance for Medical Center	GO	9/17/17
Performance Measurement	Assessing Environment for Innovation	Present KPI for Innovation	LAS	5/06/18
Performance Measurement	Agility Dashboard	Present KPI for Agility	BVD	5/26/18
Cost Driver Analysis	Cost of a New Hire	Computes the 5 year cost of a new hire	TJA	1/02/21
Performance Measurement	Human Capital Dashboard	Present KPI for Human Capital	JJC	6/26/22
Performance Measurement	Human Capital Portfolio Analysis	Visual Recap of Key Measures of Human Capital	JFA	3/06/21
Cost Driver Analysis	Headcount Trend	Visual Presentation of Headcount Levels and Trends	BVD	10/07/22
Projections	Rolling Forecast-Business Outlook	Projects future financial performance, with 12-month horizon	TJA	5/26/18

SUMMARY

Financial models are a critical part of the analysts' tool kit. Models are used to predict future results and to analyze actual performance. By employing best practices, the FP&A team can develop more effective models, save time, and present the results more effectively. Analysts should devote time at the beginning of a project to define the objective, identify their clients, determine key inputs and assumptions, design the architecture work flow of the model, and design how the results of the model will be presented. The model itself actually represents a small part of the potential value of a model. The real value is in increasing the understanding of the dynamics of a particular process or decision and communicating this to the pertinent managers.

APPENDIX: ILLUSTRATIVE MODEL

Our model to project revenues utilizes two separate spreadsheets, one for sales of existing products and another for sales of new products. The model was developed to reflect critical drivers and assumptions for this specific situation. Key variables and assumptions will vary for each specific company and situation. Other companies may need to modify the model to reflect other key drivers such as foreign currency rates, distribution channels, geographies, and other variables. It is also important to develop the model so that it is consistent with the "way the company runs the business." For example, in some organizations, product managers may be responsible for sales performance whereas others may place primary responsibility with the sales organization.

The model contains the following:

Architecture	Figure 4.4
Model documentation	Table 4.3
Revenue plan model—Existing products	Table 4.4
Revenue plan model—New products	Table 4.5
Model summary	Table 4.6

FIGURE 4.4 **Architecture.**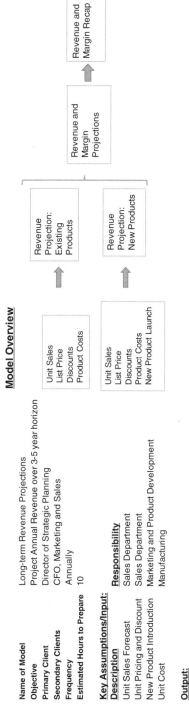

Financial Model Architecture Summary

Model Overview

Name of Model	Long-term Revenue Projections
Objective	Project Annual Revenue over 3-5 year horizon
Primary Client	Director of Strategic Planning
Secondary Clients	CFO, Marketing and Sales
Frequency	Annually
Estimated Hours to Prepare	10

Key Assumptions/Input:

Description	**Responsibility**
Unit Sales Forecast	Sales Department
Unit Pricing and Discount	Sales Department
New Product Introduction	Marketing and Product Development
Unit Cost	Manufacturing

Output:

Revenue and Product Margins by Year
Revenue Growth Rates
Sales by Products
Critical Success Factors

Revenue Projection: Existing Products

Unit Sales
List Price
Discounts
Product Costs

Revenue Projection: New Products

Unit Sales
List Price
Discounts
Product Costs
New Product Launch

Revenue and Margin Projections

Revenue and Margin Recap

TABLE 4.3 **Product revenue and margin documentation.**

Product Revenue and Margin Plan

Notes Page   **Model: Long-term revenue and margin projections**

Objective: This model will facilitate the development of long term projections of revenues. The working elements of the model are in two parts: (1) Existing Products (2) New Products Key variables and assumptions are entered on these two working spreadsheets to project revenues and margins for each product or product group. **Major assumptions:** -Pricing -List price and discounts -Unit volumes -Product costs -Introduction of new products Input fields are highlighted in grey **Summary Page** The summary page includes a table and a series of graphs to present the results of the projections. The tables and graphs are updated with any change to the underlying assumptions. Narrative comments must be manually updated to reflect changes in the model

TABLE 4.4 **Revenue plan model—existing products.**

Revenue Plan Model
Product Detail

Existing Products	2021	2022	2023	Future	2024	2025	2026	2027
Product 1200								
Unit Cost	400	416	433	4.0%	450	468	487	507
List Price	1000	1040	1080	4.0%	1123	1168	1215	1263
Average Discount	2.0%	2%	3%		4%	5%	5%	6%
Average Selling Price (ASP)	980	1019.2	1047.6		1078.272	1109.722	1154.11	1187.64
Unit Sales	245	270	300		320	275	260	240
Unit Sales Y/T Growth		10%	11%		7%	-14%	5%	8%
Revenue	240,100	275,184	314,280		345,047	305,173	300,069	285,034
Product Cost	98,000	112,320	129,900		144,102	128,792	126,637	121,572
Product Margin	142,100	162,864	184,380		200,945	176,382	173,432	163,462
%	59.2%	59.2%	58.7%		58.2%	57.8%	57.8%	57.3%
Product 1300								
Unit Cost		300	312	4.0%	324	337	351	365
List Price		799	820	4.0%	853	887	922	959
Average Discount		0%	1%		2%	2%	3%	5%
Average Selling Price (ASP)	0	799	811.8		840.01	873.61	894.72	911.32
Unit Sales		86	199		320	275	260	240
Unit Sales Y/Y Growth			131%		61%	-14%	-5%	-8%
Revenue	-	68,714	161,548		268,803	240,242	232,626	218,717
Product Cost	-	25,800	62,088		103,834	92,801	91,249	87,599
Product Margin	-	42,914	99,460		164,969	147,441	141,377	131,118
%		62.5%	61.6%		61.4%	61.4%	60.8%	59.9%

Revenue Plan Model
Product Detail

Existing Products	2021	2022	2023	Future	2024	2025	2026	2027
Product 960								
Unit Cost	700	732	650	4.0%	676	703	731	760
List Price	1200	1200	1100	4.0%	1144	1190	1237	1287
Average Discount	10.0%	12%	5%		8%	15%	17%	20%
Average Selling Price (ASP)	1080	1056	1045		1052.48	1011.30	1027.00	1029.48
Unit Sales	600	570	500		475	400	300	200
Unit Sales Y/Y Growth		-5%	-12%		-5%	-16%	-25%	-33%
Revenue	648,000	601,920	522,500		499,928	404,518	308,100	205,895
Product Cost	420,000	417,240	325,000		321,100	281,216	219,348	152,082
Product Margin	228,000	184,680	197,500		178,828	123,302	88,752	53,813
%	35.2%	30.7%	37.8%		35.8%	30.5%	28.8%	26.1%
Total Existing Products								
Revenue	888,100	945,818	998,328		1,113,778	949,934	840,795	709,646
Product Cost	518,000	555,360	516,988		569,036	502,809	437,235	361,252
Product Margin	370,100	390,458	481,340		544,742	447,125	403,561	348,393
%	41.7%	41.3%	48.2%		48.9%	47.1%	48.0%	49.1%
Year/Year Growth Rate		6%	6%		12%	-15%	-11%	-16%

TABLE 4.5 **Revenue plan model—new products.**

Revenue Plan Model
Product Detail

New Products	2021	2022	2023	Future	2024	2025	2026	2027
Product 2000								
Unit Cost			275	4.0%	286	297	309	322
List Price			600	4.0%	624	649	675	702
Average Discount			0%		2%	2%	3%	4%
Average Selling Price (ASP)	0	0	600		612	636	655	674
Unit Sales			75		140	225	325	425
Unit Sales Y/Y Growth					87%	61%	44%	31%
Revenue			45,000		85,613	143,096	212,768	286,381
Product Cost			20,625		40,040	66,924	100,535	136,727
Product Margin			24,375		45,573	76,172	112,233	149,654
%			54.2%		53.2%	53.2%	52.7%	52.3%
Product 3000								
Unit Cost			125	4.0%	130	135	141	146
List Price			300	4.0%	312	324	337	351
Average Discount			0%		2%	2%	3%	5%
Average Selling Price (ASP)			300		307	320	327	333
Unit Sales			0		100	200	300	450
Unit Sales Y/Y Growth						100%	50%	50%
Revenue			-		30,732	63,923	98,201	150,034
Product Cost			-		13,000	27,040	42,182	65,805
Product Margin			-		17,732	36,883	56,018	84,230
%					57.7%	57.7%	57.0%	56.1%

(continued)

Revenue Plan Model
Product Detail

New Products	2021	2022	2023	Future	2024	2025	2026	2027
Product 4000								
Unit Cost				4.0%	250	260	270	281
List Price				4.0%	600	624	649	675
Average Discount					8%	15%	17%	20%
Average Selling Price (ASP)			0		552	530	539	540
Unit Sales					40	125	250	300
Unit Sales Y/Y Growth						213%	100%	20%
Revenue			-		22,080	66,300	134,659	161,980
Product Cost			-		10,000	32,500	67,600	84,365
Product Margin			-		12,080	33,800	67,059	77,616
%					54.7%	51.0%	49.8%	47.9%
Total New Products								
Revenue	-	-	45,000		138,425	273,318	445,628	598,396
Product Cost	-	-	20,625		63,040	126,464	210,317	286,897
Product Margin	-	-	24,375		75,385	146,854	235,311	311,500
%			54.2%		54.5%	53.7%	52.8%	52.1%
Year/Year Revenue Growth					208%	97%	63%	34%

TABLE 4.6 **Model summary.**

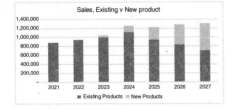

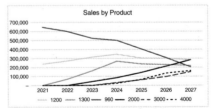

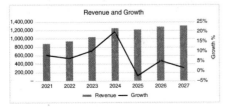

5

Presenting and Communicating Financial Information

"Tell me the facts and I'll learn. Tell me the truth and I'll believe. But tell me a story and it will live in my heart forever."
—Native American Proverb

All analytical projects are made up of several phases. First, the objective must be understood, the client identified, and the work flow planned. Second, the analytical work is completed, including research and "crunching the numbers." The third and most important phase is to present and communicate the findings of the analytical work. Rather than just present facts and figures, our presentations should tell a story to be impactful and memorable. The analysis should also call for some action and highlight alternative courses, and should recommend that a mechanism for monitoring progress be set in place. In this chapter, we will focus on the presentation and communication of the results of the analysis.

The greatest analysis will fail to achieve its objective if the results of the analysis are not presented or communicated effectively. In addition, financial managers should also recognize that, to a large extent, their career may be limited if they cannot effectively communicate. What do you call a strong finance professional with excellent communication and presentation skills? The CFO!

LAYING THE FOUNDATION FOR SUCCESS

There are a number of overall behaviors and practices that can enhance the effectiveness of communicating finance and business information. These include overcoming the accountant stereotype, knowing your audience, developing a messaging strategy, educating nonfinance managers, and choosing the best delivery method.

Overcoming the Accountant Stereotype

Accountants and financial types are often stereotyped as cold, dry, and impersonal. We are often seen as impediments to getting things done. We also often seem to be too busy to help operating managers; we are either closing the books, doing forecasts, filing tax returns, or whatever. Finance folks also typically do a poor job in communicating. It is not emphasized in our formal education, nor is it developed as a core competency in most finance organizations. Accounting tends to attract quantitative types, not orators. We speak in "accounting-ese," citing FASBs, journal entries, accruals, and other items that are foreign to operating managers. Many operating managers perceive finance as only focused on the numbers. Too often we are viewed as not understanding or even having an interest in the business.

Obviously, these stereotypes are not fair to all finance professionals or teams. One of the greatest ways to overcome these weaknesses, either real or just perceived, is to improve our delivery, communication, and presentation of business information to operating managers. Additional measures to improve capability for business partners were outlined in Chapter 3.

To become an effective business partner, we must step back from our quantitative and technical orientation to develop a context of the overall business. Invest some time with operating managers to understand their challenges and objectives. Obtain and read marketing and strategic plans. Review investor presentations, analyst reports, and market reports. Inquire about areas where you may be able to assist by identifying opportunities or illuminating challenges. Our accounting jargon should be replaced by business terms; we should simplify the analysis rather than complicate it; we should act as players, not just reporters; and we should propose actions and solutions rather than offer criticism or just identify problems.

Understanding How Decisions Are Made In order to effectively present business and analytical information, the analyst should develop an understanding of how the human mind receives and processes information as part of evaluating options and making decisions. The analyst bears a responsibility to present findings in an objective manner that reduces bias and the human tendency to reach less than optimum decisions. Michael Lewis, in his book *The Undoing Project*, does a great job of chronicling the lives and research of two Israeli psychologists, Daniel Kahneman and Amos Tversky. Together, they documented and exposed how the human mind works and errs when making decisions in uncertain situations, which of course, describes most business decisions.[1] Their observations strongly resonate with my personal experience. Analysts should consider the following in developing and presenting analysis:

Many Decisions Are Processed in the Subconscious Mind. While we may be focused on a particular issue in our conscious thinking, the wheels are turning in our subconscious. Without our recognition, our decision is often influenced by biases or past experiences that we would not want to be considered. Factual, comprehensive presentation and discussions of situations and decisions are essential to reduce this effect.

Executive Intuition Can Be Wrong. Most executives overvalue their intuitive senses and judgment. In part, we seem not to obtain or effectively process all the relevant information available to us. In addition, we are heavily influenced by our experience and models of the past. We tend to oversimplify situations and look for standard, easy solutions based on our past experience. We also tend to be highly influenced by recent events or trends (e.g., the strong stock market will continue to grow) in spite of much empirical evidence to the contrary. The same holds for views on the economy, competitive threats, or the impact of demographic changes. All experienced analysts are already familiar with the bravado about executive intuition and should recognize the importance of providing context and background information to any decision.

Management Bias. We all recognize that bias plays a role in any decision. Managers and executives almost certainly have pre-conceived views on most topics (and so may the analyst). Humans tend to look for facts that support their position and may ignore facts that are counter to their position (so called "confirmation bias"). Analysts must guard against their own biases, and anticipate and address pre-conceived conclusions of their clients.

Assumptions. Managers are likely to make a number of implicit assumptions about a particular issue. Managers also will likely overestimate the probability of many critical assumptions. The analyst can counter this by explicitly documenting and testing assumptions that underpin any projection or analysis. This subject will be covered in detail in Chapters 19–21 on business planning, and in Chapters 28—29 on capital investment decisions.

Presentation Matters. The way a particular issue is presented can have a significant effect on the interpretation and assessment by managers. In addition to the general subject covered in this chapter, analysts should

---

[1] Michael Lewis, *The Undoing Project* (New York: W.W. Norton, 2016).

be thoughtful about the way issues and decisions are framed and described. This is particularly true where downside risks are involved since humans are risk averse by nature.

Base Case. Managers often view the base case or status quo as a high probability scenario, even when the facts suggest otherwise. This may lead to deferring decisions or failing to act.

Tact, Diplomacy, and Emotional Intelligence   Analysts will find themselves working on analytical projects that are confidential or highly sensitive. They must accept this responsibility by safeguarding this information and by being discreet when communicating and presenting. In many cases the analysis is documenting or reporting negative performance that reflects on a team or executive, perhaps leading to the termination of a project, business, or even someone's career. Analysts should be sensitive to this aspect of their role.

Knowing Your Audience

Effective communicators tailor the message to their audience. Whenever I am engaged to make a formal presentation, I always strive to obtain a list of attendees or at least a profile of the group. What management disciplines and industries do they represent? How many years of experience do they have? If possible, understand what key issues they face. What language and cultural differences will I, as a presenter, encounter? How should each of these factors affect my presentation?

Another factor to consider is the level of understanding of financial concepts. In addition to contemplating this in developing and communicating presentations, consider improving the level of financial literacy of colleagues as was described in Chapter 3.

Here are a few audiences to consider. Obviously, the level of interest, understanding, and detail will vary significantly across these groups.

The CEO and Other Senior Executives   Senior executives are highly intelligent, are fast learners, and process information very quickly, or they wouldn't be senior executives. They are also very pressed for time. Most will not be interested in how you did the analysis, the Excel® formulas you employed, or how long it took to complete. Out of respect for their time and position (and your career advancement), you should bring your "A" game to any interaction with executives. Summarize the analysis, including a brief description of the objective, key findings presented in graphs and charts, and a summary with indicated actions. The detailed analysis should not be presented but can be included as an attachment, should there be a need or interest in "going into the weeds."

Watch the executive(s) for cues as to pace and reception. Make eye contact and look for signs of comprehension. If they start reading ahead, pick up the pace. Most conversations and presentations will be shorter than you expect. Be prepared to present the takeaways instead of working methodically through all of your materials.

The level of understanding of financial concepts across the executive suite varies significantly. For example, product development executives or technical scientists may have less exposure to finance and accounting than others, but no less cerebral capacity. Use common sense, and practical business explanations.

The CEO and other executives must focus on the big picture and the next move. Always present the full implications of the analysis and be prepared to offer suggested actions. For example, if you explain a variance for the most recent quarter, executives will undoubtedly want to know the impact, if any, on the future projections and possible mitigating actions.

Many interactions with executives are impromptu (and brief)! The CEO steps onto the elevator with the analyst and inquires about some trend, issue, or projection. In these cases, you do not have an opportunity to prepare. Develop a way of formulating concise explanations. . .the so-called elevator pitch. Do your best to respond with the major points in a succinct manner. As you progress through an analysis, start a working list of key takeaways. Interactions with the CEO may be both brief and infrequent, and serve as the basis of her assessment of you and your potential—make the most of it!

Board of Directors   My first experience presenting to a full board of directors came when I was named "acting" CFO while serving as vice president and controller of a large, publicly traded company. The board was very diverse: three CEOs of major corporations, two attorneys, two large company CFOs, and two university professors (one in finance and the other in nuclear physics). The audience was brilliant, and experienced, and most had deep business and finance experience. Information needed to be delivered in a concise manner and was absorbed at a rapid pace. Questions came fast, and due to the diversity of the group, they came from many different angles. It reinforced the need for deep preparation, including the need to anticipate likely questions.

Another learning experience occurred in that first board presentation: the need for the flexible presentation. The financial presentation was the last item on the agenda, and as in most meetings, the board meeting was running behind schedule. I was often asked to condense a 30-minute slot into 10 or even 5 minutes. Rather than attempt to rush through the full presentation, I decided to turn to the summary page at the end of the report. I knew that we had summarized all the key points there, so I stepped through these and took questions from the directors. This experience repeated itself throughout my career. I always included an "agenda/discussion topics" to preview and an "executive summary" to wrap up. Make sure that summaries are effective wrap-ups of the details of your presentation.

First Line Supervisors and Middle Managers   I am usually pleasantly surprised by the relative level of financial knowledge by many supervisors and managers, and even many associates within an organization. The wide adoption of 401(k) plans, increased levels of individual investing, and the availability of internet financial resources has substantially increased knowledge and interest in financial performance. However, most will not have a deep understanding of business accounting and finance. Always provide a link from financial outcomes to the processes and activities in which the employees are involved. Be especially careful to use general terms and commonsense explanations rather than accounting jargon. For example, say, "We need to reduce our customer payment cycle" versus "We need to reduce DSOs." Provide context for managers and supervisors if they are not generally exposed to this type of information. For publicly traded companies, the impact of a trend or variance can be linked to earnings per share (EPS) or even the share price.

Other Audiences   Senior finance managers may present to a wide set of audiences, even within a few days. Take the case of a CFO at the end of a quarter. He or she will likely present the results and business outlook to senior managers, the CEO, the board of directors, investment analysts, and associates in "town hall" meetings. In some cases, the same core presentation material can be used, but the presenter's "voice-over" accompanying the visuals and supplemental information is tailored to each group.

Developing a Messaging Strategy

If we were to talk to our marketing counterparts or a public relations firm about our communications and presentations, they would advise us to develop a "messaging strategy." This can be done for both our overall communications (e.g., focus on execution—hitting our goals) as well as each individual presentation (e.g., Why have margins declined from last year?).

For individual analytical projects, be sure to identify and state the objective. Examine the analytical worksheets and extract key observations. Step back and view the work as a senior business executive would review it. What is the best way to present these findings? What conclusions and recommendations should be made?

Develop talking points that focus on the key findings and observations as well as conclusions and recommendations. Make these concise and limited to the top three to five points. Do not dilute the message with minor details or distractions.

As with any message, repetition may be required. I recall becoming frustrated early in my career because we had repeatedly communicated a key finding or insight that didn't seem to stick and for which no apparent action was taken. We must be prepared to repeat and reinforce key observations; it may take time for managers to internalize the observations and even more time to address them. And it is often necessary to repeat key themes such as progress on critical initiatives and critical success factors (CSF) for achieving plans or other objectives.

Educating Nonfinance Managers

One of the barriers to effectively communicating finance information is that many managers do not have a solid understanding of basic accounting and finance functions and terms. If the foundation is weak, then many of our analyses and recommendations will not be fully understood. Chapter 3 presented options to help managers gain a better understanding of finance and accounting, ranging from formal training to lunch sessions to including infomercials in our analysis.

Choosing the Best Delivery Method

Just a few short years ago, most reports and presentations were developed on paper and sent or presented in person to the recipient. While this still occurs in many situations, technology and other changes have added additional delivery channels, ranging from email, on-line access, and query capabilities to dashboards to formal reports and presentations. In recent years, video calls and meetings have been utilized extensively in place of in-person sessions. Some reports are pushed by notification or alert; others are pulled (user initiated) as needed. Consideration must be given to client comfort with technology and whether clients will access information on their own initiative. We should never underestimate the potential importance of in-person communication to ensure that the information is understood. The automation of the delivery process often reduces the potential to add explanations and interpretive commentary.

DEVELOPING EFFECTIVE PRESENTATIONS AND REPORTS

Effective presentations start with a thoughtful outline of the presentation. The outline presented here is very effective in many situations, but it should be tailored to fit the requirements of each specific situation. Context and structure are very helpful to the audience (and the presenter!). In addition, the inclusion of an "Agenda" and "Summary" can facilitate schedule and time changes. Most business presentations are enhanced by visual aids such as handouts or PowerPoint® slides.

Agenda/Discussion Topics

The Agenda/Discussion Topics is essentially a preview of your presentation: here is what I'm going to tell you. This is a vital start to the pitch:

- ❑ It defines the objective of the presentation.
- ❑ It provides an overall context.
- ❑ It provides a flow of discussion topics and it previews the topics to be covered. This may help prevent premature questions on topics that will be covered later in the presentation.

Do not assume that the audience, whether a single manager or large group, understands the objective, scope, and context of the analysis. This overview can and should be brief, but developing a context and defining the objective of the exercise are very important.

Executive Summary—Preview

I often present the executive summary at the beginning of my presentations (as a preview) *and* at the end (to wrap up). I find it very effective to tell the group right up front the key findings and conclusions. The presentation then provides the basis of support for these findings. In other cases, especially where the findings are controversial or unexpected, I hold the executive summary until the end of the presentation.

Presentation Content

Distill all the analytical material to high-impact, visual summaries of your key findings. Do not include extraneous materials that are not relevant to the topic and key findings. Determine the best way to present your findings. Generally, this will involve graphs, tables, and other visual depictions to summarize the results of your detailed analysis. The order and flow of material is critical to an effective presentation. Avoid including detailed worksheets and tables in the presentation. These can be included in the appendix or as exhibits.

Briefly explain the methodology employed to complete the analysis. Did you review all transactions or just a sample? What was the scope? What period was covered? Be sure to credit others who assisted and provided input to the work. If the project involves projections, highlight the key assumptions utilized in the analysis. Do not describe the process in detail; no one cares!

The analytical tools used during the project are likely not the best tools to use in presenting the findings. Develop a few presentation slides that document and/or support key findings. Use highly visual tools to report findings. Graphs and charts with annotations are far superior to spreadsheets and tables. Eliminate any information that is not relevant or important to the objectives and findings of the analysis.

Identify Key Takeaways and Indicated Actions

In most cases, the objective of the analysis is not simply to *report* on a subject. The ultimate objective is to understand the implications of the findings and to develop and recommend one or more alternative courses of action. The value of the analysis is often exponentially increased if the analyst can recommend how to address the findings. Do not assume that the audience/reviewers would make the same observations or reach the same conclusions that you have reached. Since you have researched and studied the subject, your ability to understand the issue, implications, and to identify possible actions is likely to exceed that of managers hearing the information for the first time.

In some situations, it may be desirable that conclusions and actions be determined by the audience rather than presented as an outcome of the study. This can occur where you are trying to build consensus or have the team reach conclusions and develop indicated actions. In these situations, you should summarize findings and then facilitate a discussion and evaluation of solutions and alternatives.

Executive Summary and Recommended Actions

The executive summary, including recommended actions, is the most important part of your presentation. It is here that you will boil down and distill the results of your analytical work into key findings and recommended actions.

Often, there are alternative courses of action to address a problem. In this case, it is advised to list various alternatives and provide a financial evaluation of the various choices, in addition to your specific recommendation.

Exhibits

In our efforts to provide a very effective visual presentation of our findings, many supporting schedules and analyses are deemed not to be useful in the actual presentation. These can be included as an exhibit or in an appendix, should anyone wish to drill down.

Outline for Presentations and Reports

- ❑ Agenda/Discussion Topics.
- ❑ Executive Summary—Preview.
- ❑ Presentation Content.
- ❑ Executive Summary and Recommended Actions.
- ❑ Exhibits.

Delivering the Presentation

After following the guidelines outlined, the analyst needs to prepare to *present* the material and should consider using these best practices to improve delivery of the presentation. Preparation leads to confidence and successful presentations. In my first participation in a full board meeting (as acting CFO referred to earlier in the chapter), I was amazed by the CEO's ability to lead the meeting and articulate complex subject matter in a concise manner. After the meeting, I complemented him and asked for advice. He said that the key to effective communication is *preparation*.

❑ Flow. Review the flow of material to be presented to ensure that a story will be told and that the primary objective will be achieved.

❑ Talking Points. Develop talking points that tell a story. Script out your talking points for each slide. Do not read content on the slides since the audience will be viewing the material as you speak. Instead, use your "voice over" to complement and guide the audience's visual process. In developing talking points, strive for concise statements and labels that will "stick" in the audience's mind. Use of relevant quotations may be helpful, for example, "If we don't soon change our direction, we'll wind up where we are headed."

❑ Rehearse. Rehearse, but do not memorize your points. Time yourself as you rehearse to ensure that you can complete your presentation and address questions within the allotted time. If possible, visit the location of the meeting or presentation to familiarize yourself with the room and anticipate any problems that may arise.

❑ Complex Slides. Introduce complex slides with a quick description of the tables, charts, and other material on the slide. Then walk through the observations and takeaways. Tables and graphs should be accompanied by bullets highlighting key points.

❑ Flexibility. Be prepared for questions, changes in allotted time, and even appearances by "Mr. Murphy" of Murphy's Law: "when anything that can go wrong will go wrong." Time allotments may be reduced. Audio/visual devices may fail. Stay cool and develop a plan B. Always fall back on your primary objective and 3–5 primary talking points.

❑ Brevity. Be as brief and concise as possible. Respect people's time and remember that most people will stay more attentive if the pace is crisp. As Mark Twain and others have said: "If I had more time, I would have made this shorter."

❑ Eye Contact. Effective presenters make eye contact with the audience. This keeps the audience engaged. Also, effective eye contact allows you to determine the reception to your material, delivery, interest, and pace. Make adjustments as indicated.

❑ Anticipating Questions. Consider the questions members of the audience may ask and prepare responses. This is where "knowing your audience" is critical since questions will generally be based on the participants' role, responsibilities, and background.

❏ Avoidance of Jargon. Avoid technical terms and explanations; instead, where possible, use business terms rather than accounting terms.

❏ Stand Alone Value. The report or handouts are often passed on to others who were not present and are without the benefit of your "voice over." While it is not possible or desirable to include all your remarks, consider whether the printed material stands independent of verbal remarks. That is, could someone follow the main points of the presentation and follow observations and key takeaways? The use of bullet points to summarize key points and takeaways can be useful in achieving this objective.

❏ Objectivity. The analyst should remain objective in fact and in appearance. Avoid tendencies to be negative or critical. Provide balance by highlighting both "What's going well?" *and* "What needs improvement?"

❏ Confidentiality. If any of the information presented is confidential or is considered material, nonpublic information, a cautionary statement may be warranted at the beginning of the material.

DATA VISUALIZATION AND PRESENTATION: A PICTURE IS WORTH A THOUSAND WORDS

A well-designed graphic, visual, or dashboard is worth a thousand words. "Data visualization" has emerged as the label for this concept. Our objective should be to determine the data or information that is important and then develop the best method to present the information to facilitate understanding by the viewer, including highlighting trends, variances, and other insights. If not properly presented, these key insights may not be evident or easily discernable by the client. Consider the revenue process dashboard illustrated in Figure 5.1.

This dashboard presents the trend in receivables level and days sales outstanding (DSO), and also includes graphs representing the key drivers and leading indicators. The graphs facilitate understanding trends and relative magnitude that would not be easily determined by looking at a table containing the raw data. Effective use of charts and graphs can significantly improve the presentation product:

- They create visual interest in the material.
- Scale and relative size are evident in a manner that is difficult, if not impossible, to describe in words or present in tables.
- Trends are easily identified.
- They allow the viewer to see the salient aspects without having to work through the noise of a spreadsheet or table.
- Comprehension and retention rates skyrocket when you combine visual and hearing senses.

FIGURE 5.1 **Revenue process accounts receivable dashboard.** 🔢

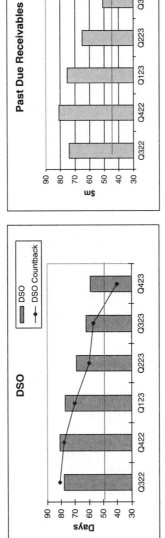
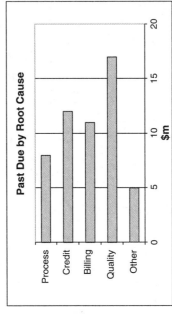
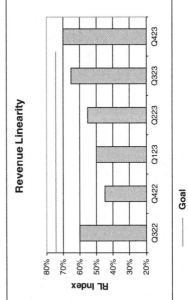

The graphs presented in this chapter are available on the book website. Refer to the "About the Accompanying Website" for additional information.

Use the Best Visual for the Job

Utilizing charts, graphs, and other visuals is essential to developing effective presentations. However, the inclusion of graphs does not necessarily increase the effectiveness of the presentation. Providing graphs of flawed analysis or extraneous information is not the objective. Equally important is to select the best graphic form for presenting the information or analysis.

The Pie Chart   The pie chart (Figure 5.2) is one of the most commonly used charts. In fact, it is sometimes overused or misused. It is best used to visually represent the relative size of component parts to a total population. It generally is not effective for comparing or presenting two sets of numbers. The number of slices in the pie should be limited to six or seven. If a large number of slices are included, the pie chart is difficult to interpret and the audience can get lost in matching slices to the legend description. It can also be hard to interpret the relative size of each slice compared to other slices.

FIGURE 5.2 **Cost pie chart.**

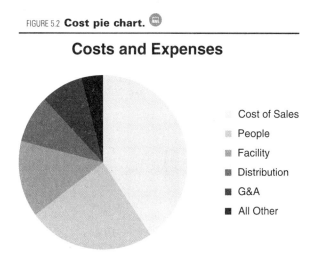

People
Facility
Distribution
G&A
All Other

The Histogram   An alternative to the pie chart is the histogram. The same data from the pie chart in Figure 5.2 is presented in the histogram in Figure 5.3. Data is clearly labeled and the relative size of each expense is evident. Presenting the segments in descending order also helps to focus attention on the largest, and likely most significant, items.

The histogram can also be used to effectively present comparative information as illustrated in Figure 5.4. Without any comment, the most significant expenses are evident and comparisons to prior years are also easily made. This is difficult to achieve by comparing two pie charts.

FIGURE 5.3 **Histogram of expenses.**

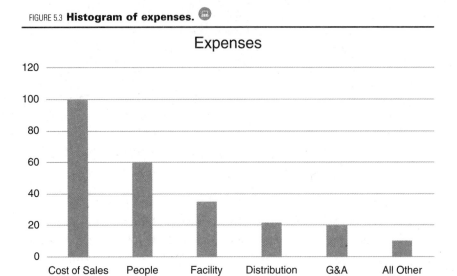

FIGURE 5.4 **Comparative histogram chart.**

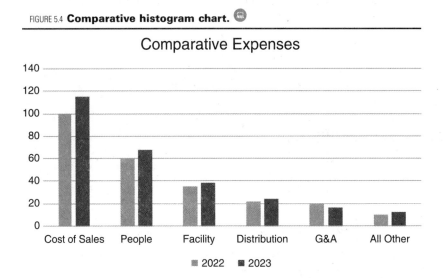

The Doughnut (or Ring) Chart   The doughnut, or ring, chart is a variant of the pie chart that has gained increasing popularity in recent years. This chart is illustrated in Figure 5.5. Some prefer this presentation since the proportions are easier to determine than the slices of the pie. The same cautions that apply to pie charts also hold for doughnuts. . .too many segments complicate the visual effect and processing of the information.

FIGURE 5.5 **Doughnut graph percentage completion.**

Development Project Percentage Completion

85%

The Line Graph   Line graphs are most suited to presenting trends over time. A classic application is the price of a stock over time. Line graphs can also be used to illustrate cumulative progress toward a goal, for example, annual sales, as shown in Figure 5.6. This example highlights a frequent situation where actual results trail planned results until the end of the period, in this case, annual sales.

FIGURE 5.6 **Line graph.**

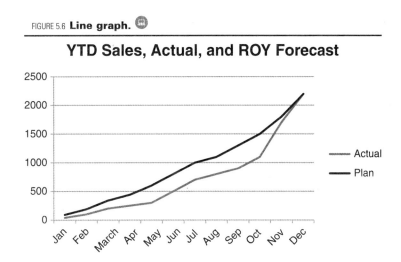

The Column Graph   The basic column graph is a great way to present comparative data sets, for example, actuals to budget. It is also useful for presenting trends. Subsets of data can be presented by stacking the columns. The stacked column illustration in Figure 5.7 presents the value and mix of revenue over time.

FIGURE 5.7 **Stacked column graph.**

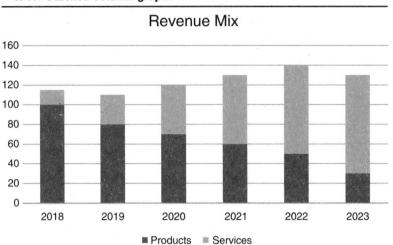

The basic column graph can be further enhanced by presenting a variance column that appears to "float." It is very effective in presenting variances in proportion to revenues and spending, for example, sources and uses of cash, and net cash flow as in Figure 5.8.

FIGURE 5.8 **Stacked columns with float.**

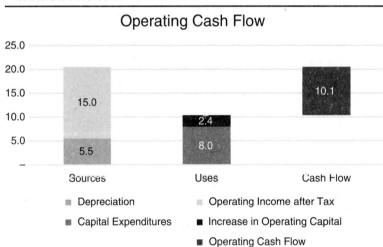

The Bar Chart   The bar chart is a variation of the column chart. In certain applications, the horizontal presentation fits better, especially when presenting distributions of entire data sets. In addition, by varying the mix of charts in a dashboard or presentation, we can create greater visual interest, variety, and attention. Figure 5.9 presents a summary of the performance evaluations for a company's associates.

FIGURE 5.9 **Bar chart.**

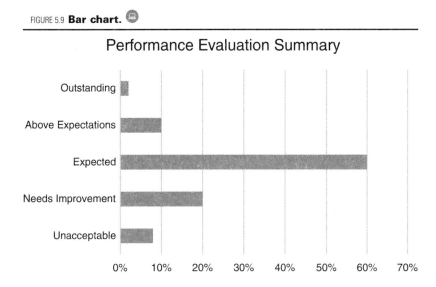

The Dual Axis Graph   The dual axis graph is a great way to present two related data sets. It is a very effective method of overlaying a relative measure (e.g., days sales outstanding) over an absolute number (e.g., accounts receivable balance). Figure 5.10 shows that although the absolute level of receivables is increasing and varies due to seasonal sales patterns, the DSO is declining (improving), indicating progress in managing the drivers of DSO.

FIGURE 5.10 **Dual axis graph.**

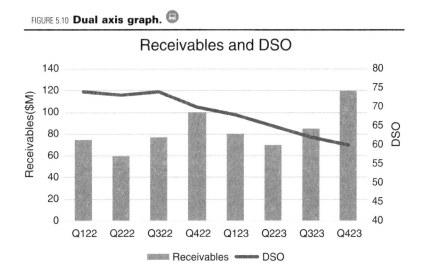

The Reconciliation Graph   The reconciliation graph, sometimes referred to as a waterfall graph, is a terrific way to compare, reconcile, or roll forward a specific financial measure. In Figure 5.11, it is used to compare next year's planned revenue to last year's actual result. The visual is extremely effective to present key changes, drivers, or other variables. The visual is more effective if you first start with the negative changes followed by the increments.

FIGURE 5.11 **Reconciliation (waterfall) graph.** 🔒

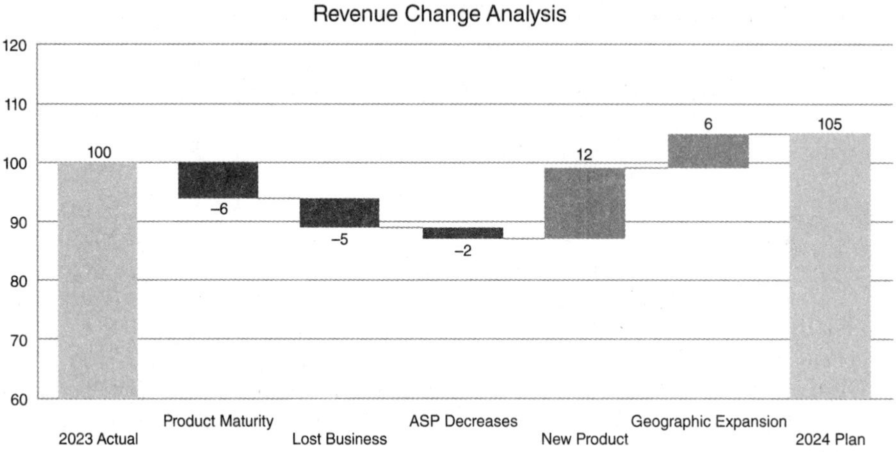

Revenue Change Analysis

The Sensitivity Chart   The sensitivity chart presents the sensitivity of an estimated result (base case) to changes in critical assumptions. In Table 5.1, the base case of a discounted cash flow (DCF) analysis indicated a value of $10.96 per share, assuming an 8% growth rate and 15% operating income. The table shows how the DCF value changes if you "flex," or change, the two critical assumptions.

TABLE 5.1 **Sensitivity chart.** 🔒

DCF Value Sensitivity Analysis

LSA Technology Company		Stock Price				
		Sales Growth Rate				
		4%	**6%**	**8%**	**10%**	**12%**
	20.0%	$12.11	$13.49	$15.04	$16.80	$18.77
Operating Income %	**17.5%**	10.52	11.68	13.00	14.49	16.17
	15.0%	8.92	9.88	10.96	12.18	13.56
	12.5%	7.33	8.08	8.92	9.87	10.95
	10.0%	5.74	6.27	6.88	7.57	8.34

The Speedometer Chart

A variation of the doughnut chart is the speedometer, or gauge, chart (Figure 5.12). It can add variety and visual interest to a dashboard to present progress or status of a project or to forecast performance.

FIGURE 5.12 **Speedometer chart.**

Cash Burn Rate

■ Green ░ Warning ■ Danger

To Scale or Not to Scale

The default setting on many graphic software tools, including Excel®, generally sets the axis at zero. This may hide or mask trends or variances, particularly if there is a mix of large numbers and small variances or other data points. The scale can be set at a different level so that trends and variables are more visible. However, caution must be exercised so that changes in the scale do not artificially magnify small changes or otherwise distort the presentation of the data.

An illustration of the choices in scaling are illustrated in Figure 5.13. The analyst should choose the scaling option that most appropriately presents the shortfall in revenue for Q1, a 6% shortfall. In most operations this would represent a significant variance and would have a large negative impact on earnings. With the axis set at zero, the variance appears relatively small. If the axis is set too high ($90 million), the variance may appear overstated. The graph with a moderate lower axis may be the most appropriate presentation.

Dashboards or Summary Charts   For certain purposes, it is useful to develop dashboards or summary charts that combine a number of graphs or charts into a single page presentation. They allow for a quick review of several key variables or metrics. They facilitate a quick, comprehensive way to see all parameters of a process or an activity. A few examples are presented here. Note the effectiveness of combining graphs and highlight comments in Figures 5.14 (Human capital management) and 5.15 (Valuation summary). Incorporating a variety of different chart types creates more visual interest and holds viewer attention for a longer period of time.

FIGURE 5.13 **Illustration of scale options.**

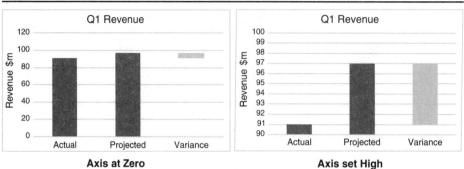

Axis at Zero   **Axis set High**

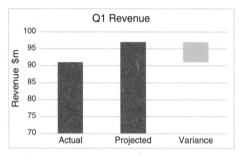

Axis Set Moderate

Dashboards are not ideal for every situation or client. For formal presentations, it may be preferable to present each graph separately. Some clients prefer individual views of the graphs versus a dashboard.

These dashboards are effective because they combine multiple views of performance. As mentioned, some executives prefer separate pages or slides to view performance. Formal presentations should generally break down the dashboards into separate slides.

Other Visuals   Images other than graphs and charts may also play an effective role in a presentation. They can be used to create visual interest and hold or extend the audience's attention. They can also add to or enhance the emotional attachment of the message. A photo of a team in a rowboat, a team in a meeting, a patriotic flag, or children living in poverty will evoke a response well beyond any spoken or written words.

FIGURE 5.14 **Human capital management assessment.** ⊞

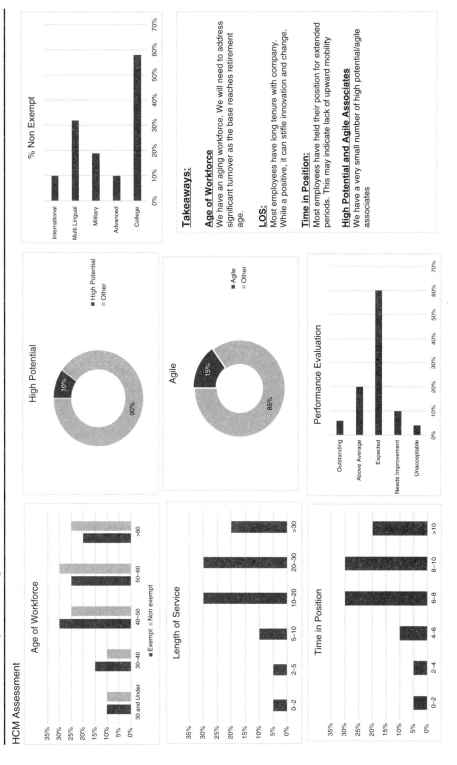

HCM Assessment

Takeaways:

Age of Workforce
We have an aging workforce. We will need to address significant turnover as the base reaches retirement age.

LOS:
Most employees have long tenure with company. While a positive, it can stifle innovation and change.

Time in Position:
Most employees have held their position for extended periods. This may indicate lack of upward mobility

High Potential and Agile Associates
We have a very small number of high potential/agile associates

FIGURE 5.15 **Valuation summary.**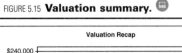

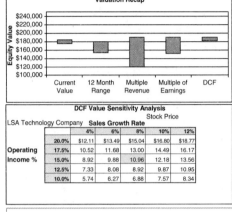

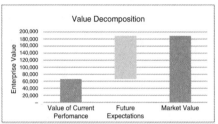

DCF Value Sensitivity Analysis

LSA Technology Company	Sales Growth Rate				
	4%	6%	8%	10%	12%
20.0%	$12.11	$13.49	$15.04	$16.80	$18.77
Operating **17.5%**	10.52	11.68	13.00	14.49	16.17
Income % **15.0%**	8.92	9.88	10.96	12.18	13.56
12.5%	7.33	8.08	8.92	9.87	10.95
10.0%	5.74	6.27	6.88	7.57	8.34

Key DCF Assumptions:

- Sales Growth: 8% CAGR
- Profitability: Gross Margins and Expenses are assumed to remain constant from 2023 performance
- Historical Cap Ex and Operating Capital %s

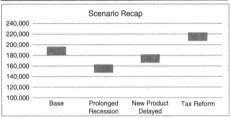

Summary

- Valuation is highly sensitive to Operating Income and Revenue Growth
- Current Performance only accounts for approximately 35% of total value
- Sales Growth is critical to valuation!

SUMMARY

Communicating and presenting the findings of our work is the most important aspect of the analysis. If not communicated effectively, the analysis is unlikely to achieve its objective. The quality of the presentation significantly impacts the credibility of both the analysis and the analyst.

Financial team members are often called on to present plans and to project analysis, financial results, and other analyses. We should work to improve our ability to develop and present business proposals, issues, and results. The actual analysis is typically not a good way to present the findings and recommendations. Analysts should utilize graphs, charts, and dashboards to communicate and present the results of their analysis. Choose the graph that best illustrates the point you are making. Improving the ability to crisply deliver the message will improve the reception of the analysis and the standing of the analyst.

Part Two

Financial Leadership in the 21st Century

6

Essential Ingredients for Value Creation: Growth and ROIC

The ultimate goal for business organizations is to create value for shareholders. Yet, many reports and analyses generated by finance do not reflect this important goal. For many decisions, the impact on shareholder value provides a terrific context and an important decision criterion. Two measures of performance that encapsulate all drivers of value creation are revenue growth and return on invested capital (ROIC).

VALUATION AND SHAREHOLDER VALUE

As the ultimate goal for business organizations is building sustainable shareholder value, it should be incorporated into essentially all reports, analyses and plans. Benefits of this focus include:

- Provides a context for business decisions.
- Highlights the importance of value creation, which is essential for the business to attract and retain capital.
- Allows business and strategic decisions to be evaluated in the context of long-term value creation.
- Facilitates the evaluation of alternative strategies and other decisions to be based on their potential to create long-term value.

In Chapter 30, we will cover valuation in great detail. A simple framework for analyzing value and linking to underlying performance is illustrated in Figure 6.1, Drivers of shareholder value. Long-term sustainable value is created by performance and expectations across six value drivers:

- Revenue growth.
- Relative pricing strength.
- Operating effectiveness.
- Capital management
- Cost of capital and capital structure.
- Intangibles.

These value drivers align with key drivers and assumptions in most valuation techniques, including discounted cash flow. Historical performance and future expectations can be analyzed and projected utilizing this framework. Each of these drivers can be linked to specific activities and measures that are relatable to managers and employees.

Figure 6.1 also illustrates that all of these drivers except revenue growth ultimately effect ROIC. Accordingly, we can look at growth and ROIC as two overall measures of valuation and value creation.

Growth is intuitively a significant driver of value. Consider the lofty valuations of high-growth companies, including Amazon, Microsoft, Tesla, Alphabet (Google), and Meta (Facebook). However, uncontrolled growth can lead to value destruction. Growth does not create sustainable value unless it is accompanied by an ultimate business model that delivers an ROIC higher than the firm's cost of capital. The level of income generated by a firm is only meaningful in the context of how much capital is invested to generate that income. ROIC is highly correlated with free cash flow and value creation. The value of a firm will be maximized if the mix of growth and ROIC is optimized.

VALUATION AND SHAREHOLDER VALUE

The most fundamental objective of company boards and executives is to create value for their shareholders. This objective must be reflected in all key management and investment decisions, and strategic and operational planning. A focus on revenue growth and ROIC will provide context and discipline for long-term value creation.

REVENUE GROWTH

Revenue growth is the most significant driver of shareholder value over the long term. All other drivers, such as operating effectiveness, can contribute

FIGURE 6.1 Drivers of shareholder value.

Focus on Drivers of Long-Term Value:
Then Link Value & Value Drivers to Business Processes & Activities

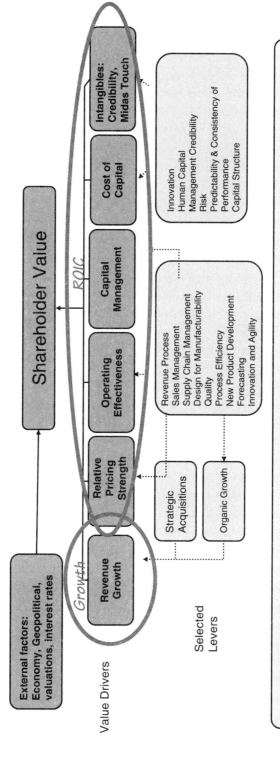

to value creation but usually reach a point of diminishing returns. Revenue growth can be disaggregated into organic and inorganic growth (mergers and acquisitions activity). Mergers and acquisition topics will be covered in Chapters 9 and 31; we will focus on organic growth drivers here. While the drivers are specific to each industry and company, the drivers illustrated in Figure 6.2 are fairly typical. They include contributions from new products and services, retaining and growing existing customers, acquiring new customers and new channels, and overall competitive and market forces.

For each driver, we can quantify the contribution to overall growth, link to key activities, and identify leading indicators that are predictive of ultimate growth.

For example, the revenue growth from retaining and growing existing customers can be linked to several key drivers and measures. We can measure (and project) the expected customer attrition rate. This rate is likely impacted by service levels such as product returns, on-time delivery performance, and customer satisfaction scores. The contribution of each revenue driver to overall revenue or growth can be quantified and modeled. This analysis, as well as other related analyses and performance measures, will be covered in detail in Chapter 22.

Key Performance Indicators (KPIs) can be identified and reported on a revenue growth dashboard as illustrated in Figure 6.3. The specific measures included on the dashboard should be situation specific, reflecting important drivers for that enterprise.

RETURN ON INVESTED CAPITAL (ROIC)

ROIC measures the return on capital invested in the business operations. It is computed as follows:

$$\text{ROIC} = \frac{\text{Operating Profit after Tax}}{\text{Invested Capital}\left(\text{Net operating assets}\right)}$$

The following ROIC analysis is based on the financial summary for Roberts Manufacturing Company in Table 6.1. ROIC is computed as:

OPAT = Operating Profit / Income $\times$ (1 – tax rate)

$20,126 \times (1 - 21\%) = 15,899$

Invested Capital = Debt + Equity*

$10,000 + 30,550 = \$40,550$

ROIC : $\$15,899 / \$40,550 = 39.2\%$

FIGURE 6.2 **Revenue growth drivers.**

Link Value & Value Drivers to Business Processes & Activities

Drill Down: Revenue Growth

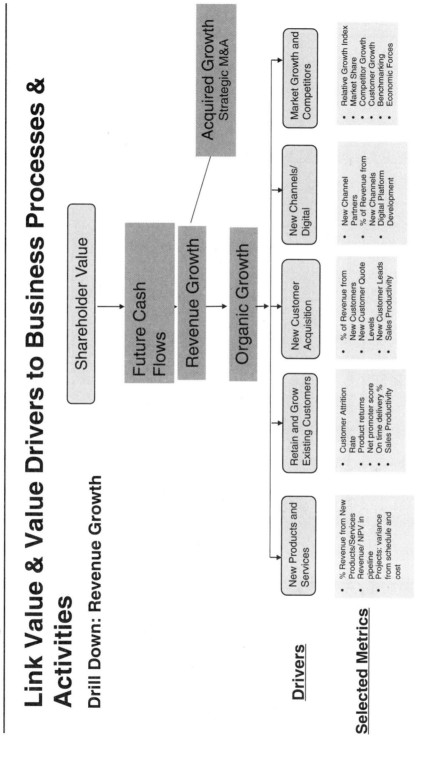

Drivers

Selected Metrics

Shareholder Value

Future Cash Flows

Revenue Growth

Organic Growth

Acquired Growth
Strategic M&A

New Products and Services
- % Revenue from New Products/Services
- Revenue/ NPV in pipeline
- Projects: variance from schedule and cost

Retain and Grow Existing Customers
- Customer Attrition Rate
- Product returns
- Net promoter score
- On time delivery %
- Sales Productivity

New Customer Acquisition
- % of Revenue from New Customers
- New Customer Quote Levels
- New Customer Leads
- Sales Productivity

New Channels/ Digital
- New Channel Partners
- % of Revenue from New Channels
- Digital Platform Development

Market Growth and Competitors
- Relative Growth Index
- Market Share
- Competitor Growth
- Customer Growth
- Benchmarking
- Economic Forces

FIGURE 6.3 **Revenue growth dashboard.**

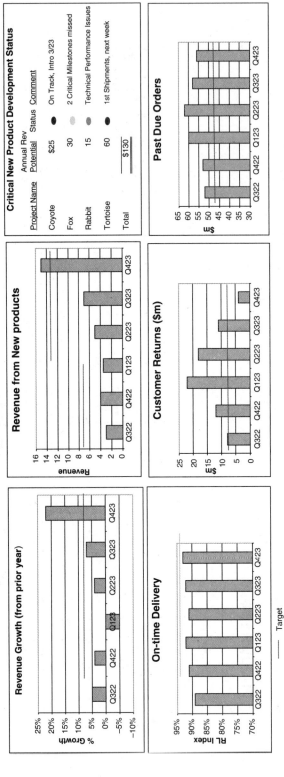

TABLE 6.1 **Roberts Manufacturing Company performance report.**

	2021	2022	2023
P&L			
Revenue	87,000	90,000	96,000
Gross Margin	24,709	28,134	30,926
SG&A	(9,000.0)	(10,000)	(12,000)
Adjustments	1,800	1,900	2,000
Adjusted EBITDA	17,509	20,034	20,926
D&A	(650.0)	(750.0)	(800.0)
Operating Income	16,859	19,284	20,126
Operating Income after Tax (OIAT)	13,319	15,234	15,900
Revenue Growth Y/Y	8.0%	3.4%	6.7%
Gross Margin	28.4%	31.3%	32.2%
SG&A	10.3%	11.1%	12.5%
Adjusted EBITDA Margin	20.1%	22.3%	21.8%
Operating Income after Tax Margin	15.3%	16.9%	16.6%
Invested Capital			
Receivables	19,333	21,429	24,000
Inventory	12,000	13,000	14,000
Property Plant & Equipment, net	3,200	3,950	5,150
Goodwill & Intangibles	1,000.0	1,000.0	1,000.0
Accumulated Amortization			
Other	2,610	2,700	2,880
Total Operating Assets	38,143	42,079	47,030
Accounts Payable	(1,305)	(1,350)	(1,440)
Deferred Liabilities	(1,088)	(1,125)	(1,200)
Accrued Liabilities	(2,610)	(3,600)	(3,840)
Invested Capital(Net Operating Assets)	33,141	36,004	40,550
Operating Cash Flow			
Operating Income After Tax	13,319	15,234	15,900
D&A	650.0	750.0	800.0
Capital Expenditures	(1,000)	(1,500)	(2,000)
Acquisitions			
(Inc) Dec in Operating Capital	(2,500)	(2,023)	(3,166)
Operating Cash Flow	10,469	12,462	11,533
Invested Capital Metrics			
Receivables DSO	81.1	86.9	91.3
Invested Capital Turnover	2.63	2.50	2.37
Profitability-OIAT/Revenue	15.3%	16.9%	16.6%
Return on Invested Capital (ROIC)	40.2%	42.3%	39.2%

Invested Capital is the net value of assets required to generate the operating income. Starting with the traditional Balance Sheet in Table 6.2, we can modify to compute invested capital by grouping operating assets and liabilities on the left side; note that the right side includes the sources of invested capital as illustrated in Table 6.3.

TABLE 6.2 **Traditional Balance Sheet.**

Assets = Liabilities + Shareholder Equity

Assets		Liabilities and Equity	
		Accounts Payable	1,440
Receivables	24,000	Accrued Liabilities	3,840
Inventories	14,000	Deferred Liabilities	1,200
Fixed Assets, net	5,150	Debt	10,000
Intangibles, net	1,000	Total liabilities	16,480
Other	2,880	Stockholders Equity	30,550
Total Assets	47,030	Total Liabilities and Equity	47,030

TABLE 6.3 **Converting traditional Balance Sheet to invested capital.**

Net Operating Assets/Invested Capital Illustration

Net Operating Assets (Invested Capital)		Sources of Capital	
Receivables	24,000		
Inventories	14,000		
Fixed Assets, net	5,150		
Intangibles Net	1,000	Debt	10,000
Other	2,880		
Total Assets	47,030		
Less Operating Liabilities		Shareholders Equity	30,550
Accounts Payable	(1,440)		
Accrued Liabilities	(3,840)		
Deferred Liabilities	(1,200)		
Net Assets	40,550	Total "Invested Capital"	40,550

ROIC Analysis

ROIC can then be further analyzed by examining the contribution from both profitability and investment turnover, as follows:

$$ROIC = Profitability \times Investment\ Turnover$$

$$= \frac{OPAT}{Revenue} \times \frac{Revenue}{Invested\ Capital}$$

$$= \frac{15,900}{96,000} \times \frac{96,000}{40,550}$$

$$39.2\% = 16.6\% \times 2.37$$

The analysis can be further disaggregated into an ROIC analysis tree in Table 6.4. This analysis allows us to identify the major contributors/drivers to ROIC and to perform "what-if" analysis to determine the effect on ROIC of changes in margins, spending, or asset levels.

TABLE 6.4 **ROIC analysis tree.**

Roberts Manufacturing Co.

	ROIC 39.2%	
Profitability 16.6%		Asset Turnover 2.37

OIAT	15,899.6	
Revenue	96,000	

Revenue	96,000	
Invested Capital	40,550	

Profitability	$	% Revenue
Sales	96,000	100.0%
Cost of Revenue	65,074	
Gross Margin	30,926	32.2%
Adjustments	2,000	
SG&A	(12,000)	−12.5%
Adjusted EBITDA	20,926	21.8%
D&A	(800)	−0.8%
Operating Income	20,126	21.0%
Operating Income after Tax (OIAT)	15,900	16.6%

Invested Capital	$	% Revenue	Measure	
Receivables (includes Service)	24,000	25.0%	91.3	DSO
Inventory	14,000			
PPE	5,150	5.4%		
Goodwill & Intangibles, net	1,000	1.0%		
Other	2,880	3.0%		
Total Operating Assets	47,030	49.0%		
Accounts Payable	(1,440)	−1.5%		
Deferred Liabilities	(1,200)	−1.3%		
Accrued Liabilities (1)	(3,840)	−4.0%		
Invested Capital (Net Operating Assets)	40,550	42.2%	2.4	T/O

This simple model enables sensitivity analysis on the key drivers. For example, in Table 6.5, we present a ROIC sensitivity analysis considering changes in both profitability and invested capital turnover.

TABLE 6.5 **ROIC sensitivity analysis.**

		ROIC Sensitivity Chart Invested Capital Turnover				
		1.6	2.0	2.37	2.8	3.2
	18.5%	29.6%	37.0%	43.8%	51.8%	59.2%
	17.5%	28.0%	35.0%	41.5%	49.0%	56.0%
OIAT%	**16.6%**	26.5%	33.1%	39.2%	46.5%	53.1%
	15.5%	24.8%	31.0%	36.7%	43.4%	49.6%
	14.5%	23.2%	29.0%	34.4%	40.6%	46.4%

This analysis is very useful but only considers financial measures. In Table 6.6, we can extend this analysis to link to business and operating processes, activities, and measures. This linkage is extremely important since most managers and employees will identify with process and activity measures much better than financial results and measures. For example, cost of revenues includes "people" costs, which are directly impacted by employee turnover, learning and development, productivity, and utilization. Accounts receivable and inventory balances and measures can be linked to payment terms, past due accounts, manufacturing cycle times, and supply chain measures.

We can also examine the drivers of accounts receivable and inventory levels, relating these results to key revenue and supply chain process measures such as past due accounts and manufacturing cycle times.

ROIC Dashboard. Figure 6.4 illustrates a dashboard for ROIC, providing insight into trends in profitability and investment turnover. This visual allows us to drill down under an essentially flat ROIC trend to see that improved profitability has been offset by declining investment turnover, represented by higher accounts receivable days sales outstanding (DSO) and higher days sales in inventory (DSI).

How does ROIC relate to other financial performance measures?

ROE. How does ROIC differ from ROE?

- ROE reflects financial leverage (debt) and non-operating income, assets, and liabilities.
- ROIC reflects only operating performance and does not include financial leverage.
- ROE is significantly impacted by financial leverage (e.g., leverage buyout transactions).
- ROIC allows performance comparisons across companies with different capital structures.

Figure 6.5 compares the ROIC to ROE computation. ROE is higher due to the reflection of financial leverage.

Economic Profit. Economic profit (EP), also referred to as economic value added™ (EVA), is consistent with ROIC. Economic profit reduces accounting profits for a carrying cost on the assets invested in the business. Where ROIC = OIAT/Net Investment, EP = OIAT – capital charge (assessed on net investment). For example, in 2023, EP is computed as:

OIAT		$15.9
Less Capital Charge:		
Invested Capital	40.6	
× Cost of Capital	12%	−4.9
Economic Profit		$11.0

TABLE 6.6 **ROIC performance tree.**

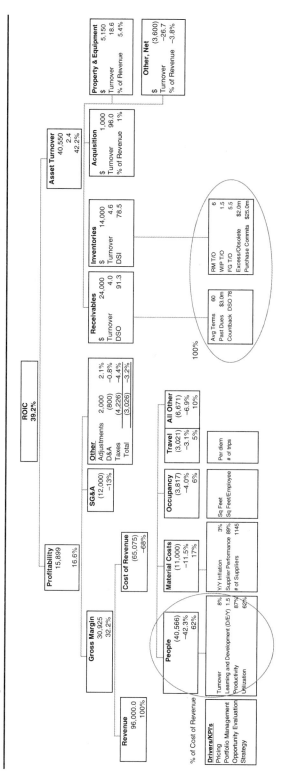

FIGURE 6.4 **ROIC dashboard.**

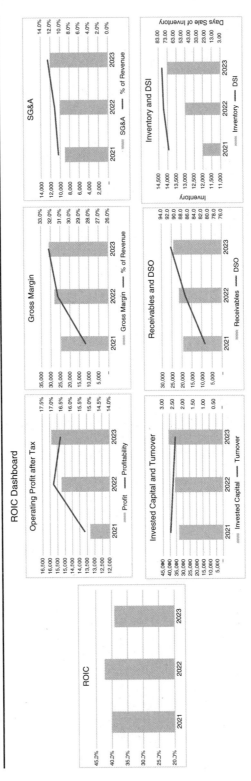

FIGURE 6.5 **ROIC versus ROE.**

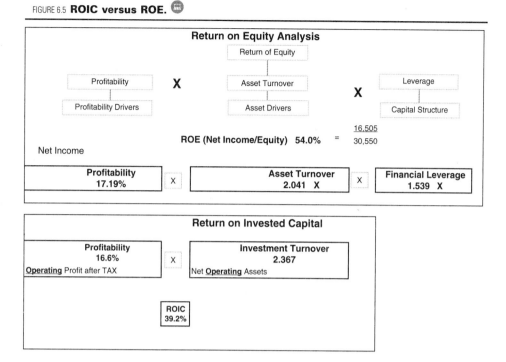

In this example, ROIC of 39.2% is greater than the cost of capital, consistent with a positive EP value of $11.0 million. EP has the advantage of incorporating the contribution of revenue growth and the net return over cost of capital. The objective is to increase the EP over time, leading to value creation. In the example in Table 6.7, even though ROIC has declined slightly, economic profit has increased because of revenue growth. My experience is that including both measures provides a comprehensive perspective of value.

The relationship between ROIC and EP is as follows and is illustrated in Table 6.8:

Where ROIC > cost of capital, EP is positive, leading to value creation in excess of cost of capital.

Where ROIC = cost of capital, EP = 0, leading to value created at a rate equal to cost of capital.

Where ROIC < cost of capital, EP is negative, leading to value dilution.

Cash Flow. Both ROIC and economic profit are highly correlated with cash flow generated by operating activities, often called operating or free cash flow. Free cash flow is the basis for valuing a company using discounted cash flow (DCF). Free cash flow computation accounts for operating income and changes in net investment as follows:

TABLE 6.7 **ROIC and economic profit.**

		2021	2022	2023
Roberts Manufacturing Company				
Revenue		87.0	90.0	96.0
Adj. EBITDA		17.5	20.0	20.9
D&A		−0.65	−0.75	−0.8
Operating Profit		16.9	19.3	20.1
Operating Profit after Tax (OPAT)	21%	13.3	15.2	15.9
% of Revenue		15.3%	16.9%	16.6%
Net Investment				
Accounts Receivable		19.3	21.4	24.0
Inventory		12.0	13.0	14.0
PP&E, net		3.2	4.0	5.2
Acquisition Assets		1.0	1.0	1.0
Other		2.6	2.7	2.9
Accounts Payable		−1.3	−1.4	−1.4
Accrued Liabilities		−2.6	−3.6	−3.8
Deferred Liabilities		−1.1	−1.1	−1.2
Net Investment		33.1	36.0	40.6
Net Investment Turnover		2.63	2.50	2.37
ROIC		**40.2%**	**42.3%**	**39.2%**
Economic Profit (aka EVA)				
OPAT		13.3	15.2	15.9
Less Capital Charge				
Net Investment		33.1	36.0	40.6
Cost of Capital	12%			
Capital Charge		−4.0	−4.3	−4.9
Economic Profit		**9.3**	**10.9**	**11.0**
Y/Y Growth			1.6	0.1

Operating Cash Flow after Tax

Add: Depreciation and Amortization

Less: Capital Expenditures

+ − Changes in Operating Capital

= Free Cash Flow

ROIC AND THE BUSINESS MODEL

Managers often describe the actual and targeted financial performance of their company as a "business model" or "financial model." The business model

TABLE 6.8 **ROIC and EP for Sheridan Express Co.** ⊕

Sheridan Express Co.		**Value Dilution**	**Break-even**	**Value Creation**
Revenue		100.0	100.0	100.0
EBITDA		8.0	9.0	15.0
D&A		−4	−3.4	−1.5
Operating Profit		4	5.6	13.5
Operating Profit after Tax (OPAT)	21%	3.2	4.4	10.7
% of Revenue		3.2%	4.4%	10.7%
Net Investment				
Accounts Receivable		40.0	32.0	25.0
Acquisition Assets		10.0	10.0	10.0
Other		3.0	3.0	2.0
Accounts Payable		−5.0	−4.0	−5.0
Accrued Liabilities		−4.0	−4.0	−4.0
Net Investment		44.0	37.0	28.0
Net Investment Turnover		2.3	2.7	3.6
ROIC		**7.2%**	**12.0%**	**38.1%**
Economic Profit (aka EVA)				
OPAT		3.2	4.4	10.7
Less Capital Charge				
Net Investment		44.0	37.0	28.0
Cost of Capital	12%			
Capital Charge		−5.3	−4.4	−3.4
Economic Profit		**−2.1**	**0.0**	**7.3**

represents the quantification of a company's strategy, market forces, and business practices. The business model framework provides a useful analysis for a number of business decisions ranging from product/service pricing to setting investment and expense levels. However, managers may lock into a single business model concept, limiting their ability to effectively compete or grow into other markets.

The common view of a business model represents a target profit & loss (P&L) model. The manager thinks of the business in terms of the P&L captions and the relationship of each line item as a percentage of sales as illustrated in Table 6.9 for LSA Technology Company.

Using this conceptual framework, managers will set prices, establish business plans, evaluate business proposals, set expense levels, and make other critical business decisions. For example, a company that is developing a product with a cost of $450 may set a target selling price of $1,000 to maintain the 55% margin, subject to competitive forces. In establishing the research and development (R&D) budget, the company may target spending at 8% of projected sales.

TABLE 6.9 **Business model illustration: Traditional view.** ⓐ

LSA Technology Company

	2023	% of Sales
Revenue	$ 100,000	100.0%
Cost of Sales	45,000	45.0%
Gross Margin	55,000	55.0%
SG&A	32,000	32.0%
R&D	8,000	8.0%
Total Expenses	40,000	40.0%
Operating Income	15,000	15.0%
Other (Income) Expense	605	0.6%
Profit before Tax	14,395	14.4%
Taxes	4,894	4.9%
Net Income	9,501	9.5%

The traditional P&L business model framework, while useful, provides an incomplete view of a company's economic performance since it does not reflect other critical aspects of business performance. Most importantly, it does not consider sales growth rates, capital requirements, cash flow, and returns. As discussed earlier in this chapter, the two critical determiners in building long-term, sustainable value are growth and return on invested capital (ROIC). Therefore, any comprehensive business model framework must incorporate at least these elements to be a useful decision support tool.

A broader, more comprehensive view of the business model is illustrated in Table 6.10. By including the additional measures reflecting growth and invested capital, we present a more complete picture of the company's performance. For example, managers or investors should not reach a conclusion on the reasonableness of R&D spending levels without considering the potential sales growth rates.

In addition, the profitability measures alone are incomplete for evaluating the performance of the organization. Only when we include the capital levels employed in a business, can we fully assess the financial performance of that business. The inclusion of a balance sheet and key metrics will allow us to determine and evaluate the ROIC. Many companies and entire industries generate significant returns despite relatively low profit margins as a result of low capital requirements or high asset turnover. The grocery industry is a prime example. This industry tends to operate with razor-thin margins, but requires lower invested capital by turning assets, primarily inventory, faster than other industries. Many mass merchandisers have a similar low-margin, high-turnover model.

TABLE 6.10 **Business model illustration: Comprehensive view.**

LSA Technology Company

		2023	% of Sales
Sales Growth Rate:	8.0%		
Profitability Model			
Sales		$ 100,000	100.0%
Cost of Sales		45,000	45.0%
Gross Margin		55,000	55.0%
SG&A		32,000	32.0%
R&D		8,000	8.0%
Total Expenses		40,000	40.0%
Operating Income		15,000	15.0%
Other (Income) Expense		605	0.6%
Profit before Tax		14,395	14.4%
Net Income		9,501	9.5%
Asset Utilization			
Days Sales Outstanding			73.0
Days Sales Inventory			146.0
Operating Capital Turnover			3.4
Fixed Asset Turnover			5.0
Intangible Turnover			9.1
Total Asset Turnover			1.3
Leverage			1.43
Debt to Total Capital			15.3%
Returns			
ROE			17.4%
ROIC			15.3%

Conversely, other industries such as equipment manufacturers, must post higher profitability to compensate for high capital requirements.

Review of Business Models   Table 6.11 provides a summary of various business models for some well-known companies. Take a moment to compare key performance measures across the companies, including growth, profitability, asset turnover, and financial leverage. The companies' performance on each of these variables can be related to the key ROIC and valuation measures. The differences in these business models arise from the following characteristics:

- Capital intensity. Certain industries, such as manufacturing and retail, have higher capital requirements due to physical locations.

TABLE 6.11 **Business model benchmark summary.**

$ms	Business Models, Returns and Valuation Metrics							
	3M	**Walmart**	**Microsoft**	**Apple**	**Accenture**	**ExxonMobil**	**Emerson**	**Merck**
Revenue and Growth								
Revenue	35,355	572,754	198,270	394,328	61,594	276,692	19,629	48,704
Rev. Growth (3 Year Hist CAGR)	2.6%	3.6%	16.4%	14.9%	12.5%	−0.3%	2.2%	11.6%
Profitability								
Gross Margin %	46.8%	25.1%	68.4%	43.3%	32.0%	23.5%	41.7%	72.0%
R&D %	5.6%	0.0%	12.4%	6.7%		0.4%		25.1%
SG&A %	20.4%	20.6%	14.0%	6.4%	16.8%	3.5%	21.6%	19.8%
Operating Margin	7,369	25,942	83,383	119,437	9,367	32,181	4,278	13,879
Operating Margin %	20.8%	4.5%	42.1%	30.3%	15.2%	11.6%	21.8%	28.5%
EBITDA	9284	36,600	97,843	130,541	11,455	52,788	5,317	17,079
%	26.3%	6.4%	49.3%	33.1%	18.6%	19.1%	27.1%	35.1%
Operating Profit after Tax	6,055	19,343	72,449	100,083	7,119	24,313	3,383	12,358
%	17.1%	3.4%	36.5%	25.4%	11.6%	8.8%	17.2%	25.4%
Asset Turnover and Returns								
DSO	48.1	5.3	81.5	26.1	69.8	42.7	55.9	69.2
DSI	96.8	48.1	71.6	9.0	0.0	32.2	69.9	159.5
PP&E, Net	9,429	112,624	87,546	42,117	4,677	216,552	3,361	19,279
% of Revenue	26.7%	19.7%	44.2%	10.7%	7.6%	78.3%	17.1%	39.6%
Goodwill & Intangibles, Net	18,774	29,014	78,822		13,133	18,022	21,386	44,187
% of Revenue	53.1%	5.1%	39.8%	0.0%	21.3%	6.5%	109.0%	90.7%
Net Asset (IC) Turnover	1.27	3.96	1.58	2.70	0.88	1.24	0.74	0.68
ROIC	21.7%	13.4%	57.8%	68.5%	10.2%	10.9%	12.7%	17.3%
Valuation								
Enterprise Value	86,430	387,000	387,000	2,430,000	178,200	481,900	65,000	273,000
Enterprise Value/Revenue	2.4	0.7	2.0	6.2	2.9	1.7	3.3	5.6
Enterprise Value/EBITDA	9.3	10.6	4.0	18.6	15.6	9.1	12.2	16.0

Source: Based on company reports and SEC filings.

- Product versus service or software. Service organizations generally have lower margins but also have lower investments in physical assets, including inventories and facilities. Software companies have higher margins, low inventory requirements, and high R&D requirements.

- Retail businesses. Retail businesses often have lower margins and significant inventory requirements. They do not carry significant receivables since cash or credit cards represent a significant portion of sales transaction.

- Acquisition activity. Significant acquisitions can result in higher growth rates and acquisition related investments carried as goodwill and intangibles.

- Process innovation. Companies that develop innovative business processes such as customer fulfillment or outsourcing may have lower inventory requirements, manufacturing investments, and accounts receivable. As realized during the supply chain crisis during and after the

Covid-19 pandemic, outsourcing can also increase risk and the impact of "black swan" events (an unforeseen but significant event), economic, health, and geopolitical events. This subject will be addressed in more detail in Chapter 13, "Scenario Analysis, Planning, and Management."

- Investment in development. Most product companies, and certainly most technology and pharmaceutical companies, will invest heavily in product development. A large part of these costs are reported as R&D expense when incurred.

While this summary is used to illustrate the business model concept, the format is also a terrific way of benchmarking performance across value drivers. We will build on this concept of benchmarking business models in Chapter 18, "Benchmarking Performance."

Varying Business Models within a Company   Most companies have two or more distinct business units under one corporate roof. When this situation exists, it is important that managers understand the differences in the various businesses and to resist the inclination to "force fit" the model from one business to another without due consideration. This is especially important when a company has one dominant business with smaller but different business units in the portfolio. Managers have a tendency to apply a single business model mindset, expecting similar ratios and performance across the businesses, which can result in dysfunctional decisions and missed opportunities.

This is a common problem when managers consider a related but different business opportunity. For example, there may be an opportunity to build a business based on the current product line, but requiring lower pricing, and therefore, lower costs. Managers may pass on this opportunity because of lower expected gross margins. However, it is possible that this product line may require lower levels of SG&A and inventory. This may result in returns approximating or even exceeding the levels achieved by the "high end business."

This phenomenon is striking at companies with diversified portfolios such as 3M, Textron, and United Technologies. These companies each contain business units with very different business characteristics. In 3M's case, the units range from office supplies to medical equipment to advanced materials. Each of these businesses will be shaped by different market and competitive forces. The businesses will have different growth rates, gross margins, operating expense levels, and asset requirements. An illustration of a diversified portfolio is presented in Table 6.12. This portfolio has five businesses, each with very different characteristics. These businesses record gross margins that range from 65% to as low as single digits. Some had very large levels of invested capital; other businesses required essentially no capital. Some of these businesses are growing and require capital to fund the growth; others were mature and were generating substantial cash flow. This diverse set of businesses could not have a "one-size-fits-all" business model. If the managers of this firm insisted on a single business model, the results would likely to be disastrous. For example, if managers evaluated each of these businesses on operating profitability alone, they could significantly misjudge the overall economic performance of each. To evaluate overall business performance, managers and investors need to consider expected growth rates and ROIC. Note in this example that the services business has the lowest operating margin, but due to low investment requirements, posts one of the highest ROIC.

TABLE 6.12 **Varying business models under the same roof.**

	Equipment		Components		
	Mature	**High Growth**	**Mature**	**High Growth**	**Services**
Estimated Sales Growth	5%	15–20%	5%	15–20%	3%
Gross Margin	65%	60%	45%	40%	15%
R&D	9%	12%	5%	3%	1%
SG&A	40%	35%	30%	18%	5%
Operating Margins	16%	13%	10%	19%	9%
Net Income	10%	8%	7%	12%	6%
DSO	60	60	50	45	75
DSI	120	90	70	50	0
Other Capital Requirements	L	M	M	H	L
Asset Turnover	3.0	4.0	5.0	4.0	8.0
ROIC	31%	34%	33%	49%	47%

Even in companies with a more homogeneous set of businesses, there is likely to be a significant variation in the performance characteristics of business segments. Businesses tend to have different product lines or end use markets with different business models. Geographic markets, ancillary products, and services also contribute differently to financial performance. Managers must understand and evaluate the individual business models and the contribution that each makes to total corporate performance. Table 6.13 presents different business models that may exist in what appears to be a homogeneous business.

TABLE 6.13 **Business models in a homogeneous company.** 🌐

| | Base Business | | | | | New | |
	End Use 1	End Use 2	End Use 3	Service	Parts	Market	Combined
Estimated Sales Growth	−2%	10–15%	20%	5%	6%	60%	12%
Gross Margin	60%	40%	54%	35%	30%	50%	53%
R&D	3%	8%	10%	0%	0%	15%	7%
SG&A	28%	20%	35%	7%	7%	20%	25%
Operating Margins	29%	12%	9%	28%	23%	15%	21%
Net Income	19%	8%	6%	18%	15%	10%	14%
DSO	60	60	100	45	45	90	70
DSI	90	115	200	100	160	150	118
Other Capital Requirements	L	M	H	L	L	H	M
Asset Turnover	5.0	4.0	2.5	5.0	5.0	2.7	3.5
ROIC	94%	31%	15%	91%	75%	26%	48%

Improving Return on Invested Capital

Operating and financial management can improve ROIC and contribute to revenue growth. The primary objective of this book is focused on improving critical performance and value drivers.

Improving ROIC

❏ Adopt ROIC as a key performance indicator ("what gets measured gets improved").

❏ Growth:
  • Organic revenue growth (Chapter 22).
  • Effective acquisition process (Chapter 31).

❏ Profitability:
  • Optimize pricing and gross margins (Chapter 22).
  • Improve productivity and overall operating effectiveness (Chapter 23).

❏ Investment Turnover:
  • Improve revenue process and accounts receivable management (Chapter 24).
  • Improve supply chain process and inventory management (Chapter 24).
  • Optimize capital investment decisions (Chapters 28–29).

❏ Reduce risk and the cost of capital (Chapter 26).

SUMMARY

The overarching objective of firms is to create long-term sustainable value for owners. It is important for financial managers to identify and review the key drivers of value creation: revenue growth, pricing power, operating and capital efficiency, and risk. These drivers can be aggregated into two overall measures of performance: growth and return on invested capital. These measures should be prominent in all business reviews, investment, and operating decisions and plans.

7

Managing Human Capital and Building a High-Performance Finance Team

Leaders of most organizations describe people as their "greatest asset." While executives may sincerely believe that associates are "resources" or "capital" or "assets," most organizations are far less disciplined in acquiring, managing, developing, evaluating human assets than they do other "capital" investments such as new products or programs, businesses, and equipment. How can we assess whether our human capital is appreciating (growing and developing) or depreciating? Have we deployed our human capital effectively? While it is often difficult to establish direct mathematical relationships between human capital management (HCM) and financial results, it is certainly worth the effort to develop conceptual relationships.

Financial leadership can play a role in elevating and improving key management processes to manage and develop human capital. We can also focus on developing a high-performance finance team. Regrettably, finance organizations often are perceived as less focused on human capital than managers in other functions. In this chapter, we will discuss the importance of HCM, critical processes, including HCM evaluation, and specific finance organization topics.

THE IMPORTANCE OF HUMAN CAPITAL MANAGEMENT (HCM)

There are two ways employees impact financial performance and value creation. First, *people costs*, defined broadly, are typically a major, if not the largest cost in any organization. Second, with very few exceptions, it is our people that execute the strategy, develop products, deal with customers and suppliers, and deliver or manufacture the company's services or products, and all other activities that are critical to an organization's success.

In addition to the belief that human capital is our "greatest asset," it typically is also the largest cost in most organizations. This fact is often not evident from examining most financial reports, budgets, and analyses. These tend to be prepared on a functional basis, rather than looking at total people costs (see natural expense analysis in Chapter 23). Most financial analysis of costs and expenses does not provide adequate visibility into total people costs, major drivers, performance and productivity, of our largest cost component. If an organization wants to be more productive, profitable, and successful, HCM must be more effective.

Consider the investment made in a new hire in Table 7.1. In this case, we are making an investment of over $937,500, when considering recruiting fees, internal staff time spent recruiting and evaluating candidates, annual salary, fringe benefits, annual bonus, and training and learning curve. This should get our attention on the importance of the recruitment and immersion processes as well as employee engagement and satisfaction.

This analysis is a cost-based analysis. Assuming the position is of importance, there is a huge opportunity cost if the hire is not successful or does not add full potential value to the company. For example, if the new hire is critical to the development and introduction of a new product, the potential value could be substantially greater than the "cost" view.

TABLE 7.1 **Investment in new hire.**

Investment in a New Hire			
Investment Description		**Notes**	**Investment**
Annual Salary	125,000	5 Year	625,000
Recruitment Fees	30%		37,500
Internal Recruiting Effort	20%	Interviews, Selection	25,000
Executive Search			125,000
Training and Learning Curve	50%	Assume 6 month	62,500
Estimated Annual Bonus	20%		25,000
Benefits	30%		37,500
Total Investment 5 Year			937,500

Human capital impacts all value drivers as shown in Figure 7.1. Satisfaction and engagement play a critical role in key performance drivers, including customer satisfcation, execution, productivity, and quality, just to name a few! We can all recall experiences as customers of an organization with a disaffected workforce. We can also contrast that with a highly engaged workforce. Any question that the customer experience is impacted by the level of engagement and satisfaction of associates?

FIGURE 7.1 **Human capital impacts all value drivers.**

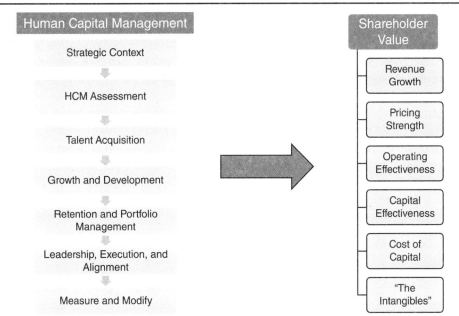

Many employees, at all levels, do not understand the organization's mission, strategic objectives, key priorities, and how their role fits into the broader picture. This contributes to both lower engagement and productivity since employees will likely not be focusing on the projects, processes, and activities that are vital to the company's success.

At the present time, there is an acceleration of major changes in the workforce, including the attitudes and engagement of employees toward their employers and work in general. Major demographic changes such as an aging (and retiring) workforce in developed countries, low birth rates, and suboptimal immigration policies have resulted in a shortage of qualified employees. Employee attitudes toward work in general have also been changing in recent decades. Many surveys report that satisfaction, engagement, and loyalty may be at all-time lows. The Covid-19 pandemic, related actions (e.g., lockdowns and work from home), and cumulative stress have greatly exacerbated this trend. Reported productivity has declined for the first time in recorded history.

Terms like *quiet quitting* and *career breaks* are now commonplace in business. The shortage of qualified employees has created an imbalance resulting in higher voluntary turnover, higher compensation levels, and reduced loyalty to current employers.

With full recognition of the importance of HC in the overall performance and success of the enterprise, we turn to an evaluation of our processes managing HC. How effective are our processes in acquiring, managing, developing, evaluating, and retaining human assets? Do our performance management, financial analyses, and HC analytics address this important topic adequately? Financial leadership can play an active role in elevating HCM, related analyses and metrics, partnering with HC leadership and promoting an effective HCM process across the entire company. Financial leadership must also ensure that we recognize the critical importance of HCM within our own organizations and invest in managing and developing financial talent.

HUMAN CAPITAL MANAGEMENT (HCM): KEY ELEMENTS

Due to the importance of HCM to the overall success of the enterprise, we briefly review key activities that contribute directly to an engaged, productive, and vital workforce.

Strategic Context

HCM must be an integral part of the strategic planning process and any evaluation of the company's talent and organization must be performed in the context of strategy and strategic objectives. For example:

- Can our existing team execute the plan?
- What additional resources and new competencies will be required to execute the plan?
- Identify and address demographic changes and impact on costs, experience, and turnover.

HCM Assessment

Many successful organizations have formal processes to review and evaluate the organization structure, demographics, workforce characteristics, and talent acquisition and development. This periodic assessment can represent the cornerstone of the overall HCM process. A comprehensive illustration of HCM assessment will be presented later in this chapter.

Talent Acquisition and Immersion

Recruiting new talent is critical to the success of the organization. An effective process will include:

- Assessment. HCM assessment to provide context and clarity on the need and definition of the position.
- Clear definitions. Define positions, responsibilities, and required skills and experience. This should also include soft or personal traits that are likely to be predictive of performance and cultural fit.
- Source of candidates. Ensuring that the search process targets appropriate candidate pools.
- Evaluate candidates. This should go beyond a strong interview and reference checking. HCM should analyze past experience and ensure a basis for predicting successful selections.
- Candidate management and communication. From a candidate's perspective, the hiring process is often characterized as a long, protracted activity with limited communication and feedback. This can result in losing specific candidates and in creating a poor reputation in the marketplace.
- Orientation. Programs to immerse or on-board the new associate will increase probability of a successful hire.

Growth and Development (G&D)

One of the most important functions within HCM is the identification of development needs and developing effective programs to meet those needs. In addition to developing the overall organization, employees consistently rate G&D as an important part of overall satisfaction. This should be a critical focus of the HCM assessment. Development is much broader than training, and should include effective feedback, rotational assignments, mentoring, and other steps. Financial leadership should set the tone for learning and development. This includes leading by example and instituting a formal development program.

Integrating Growth and Development into the Performance Evaluation Process. Identifying growth and development opportunities, discussing career goals and setting a development plan in motion are essential parts of performance evaluation and HCM assessment.

Measure Professional Development Days or Hours. Due to the pace of change in business, technology, and process, all associates should set a target or minimum number of professional development hours. Nearly all professional organizations require 40 hours per year to *maintain* accreditation or license status; a similar level may be an appropriate target for all managers and key employees. Professional development may include formal training, education, conference participation, webinars, reading, and other useful learning opportunities. Larger organizations should consider developing workshops tailored to the needs of the team. As a CPA, I was required to obtain 40 hours of professional development credits per year. This instilled a mindset of continual learning that I maintained throughout my career.

Rotational Assignments. Upward mobility for many employees is limited by their exposure to a narrow function or set of responsibilities. For example, a successful controller may not be promoted to CFO because they do not have investor relations, merger and acquisition, operational, treasury, or other specific experience sets. Rotating senior managers between these positions can be done, but is challenging as successful execution at these roles is critical. Rotational assignments are easier to accomplish earlier in careers, when the risk and disruption to the employee and organization are lower. One opportunity to overcome the challenge of rotating employee positions is to encourage participation in cross-functional teams, special projects, or assignments to provide exposure to other areas.

Mentoring Programs. Companies can develop formal or informal mentoring programs that provide an opportunity for employees with growth potential to have access to a manager for career and performance advice.

Portfolio Management

If we do view associates as assets, can we borrow techniques from financial portfolio management to evaluate and improve our talent portfolio? We can develop various views of the workforce across key elements, including demographics, performance, aptitude for growth, agility, experience, and diversity. This analysis almost always identifies issues and opportunities in our "portfolio of human resources."

Periodically, as part of the HC Portfolio management process or the annual organization and development review, we should look at the workforce across several variables, including:

- ❏ Turnover—General.
- ❏ Age.
- ❏ Length of service.
- ❏ Time in position.
- ❏ Education.
- ❏ Language proficiency.
- ❏ International experience.

❑ Performance.

❑ Aptitude for growth (high-potential associates).

❑ Agility.

❑ Experience.

❑ Diversity (broadly defined to include education, cultural, experience, etc.).

Engagement, Alignment, Evaluation, Accountability, and Retention

After effectively recruiting and on-boarding an associate, the organization must keep them engaged and ensure that their work is aligned with corporate objectives. We also must have effective methods for evaluating performance and holding associates accountable for responsibilities and achieving objectives.

The ability to retain employees is a result of multiple factors, including the external labor market, identification with the company mission and objectives, work-life balance, leadership, and growth opportunities. Employees are increasingly looking for employers with missions that contribute to objectives that they value, including health, social, environmental, and other causes. Younger generations reportedly value work-life balance more than prior generations. Finally, we need to ensure that the employee is satisfied and sees future opportunities for growth in the organization. Employee satisfaction, engagement, and retention (or alternatively turnover) can be measured and should be included on dashboards and other performance management summaries.

In spite of best efforts to acquire, on-board, develop, and encourage high performance, it is inevitable that some team members will not perform up to our expectations, or that their particular skill and experience sets are no longer required. In these cases, the firm should make every attempt to assist the employee in addressing shortcomings or finding another role that is better suited to the individual. These efforts should occur early, at the first signs of a performance issue. If the ultimate result is a decision to terminate the employee, every effort should be made to assist the employee in obtaining other employment and bridging financial hardships associated with the transition.

Other employees may choose to pursue opportunities outside the firm. Although we may prefer to retain these employees, this can be viewed as a healthy result of our efforts to acquire and develop a high-performing team.

Compensation and Incentives

The development of effective compensation and incentive plans is critical in attracting, retaining, and motivating associates. These plans must be fully integrated with broader performance management efforts in order to optimize effectiveness and ensure accountability for performance.

Leadership, Alignment, and Execution

One of the most important drivers of a high-performance team is the effectiveness of leadership, alignment, and execution. Financial leadership can focus on several activities to achieve these objectives.

Establish a Mission and Objectives   Creating a mission statement and specific objectives for quarterly and annual performance can be effective steps toward ensuring alignment of the leadership and the finance teams. The mission statement can outline major responsibilities, business standards, and service objectives.

Quarterly and annual objectives for the finance organization should be established and shared with the team. Objectives for individual departments and employees should be developed based on the overall goals for the finance team.

Communicate   CFOs and other financial leaders must communicate frequently with the organization. The CFO's calendar and various responsibilities present a substantial challenge to be visible and actively engaged with team members. Quarterly team meetings, skip-level meetings (meeting with small groups of employees in the trenches), and visibility and engagement on various projects and reviews all provide opportunities to motivate and communicate with employees.

Establish a Performance Management Process   After establishing goals and objectives, leadership must ensure that there is a process to review progress, identify challenges, course correct, or redirect based on changing circumstances.

Human Capital: Measure, Monitor, and Adjust

A number of measures, analyses, and other tools can be utilized to evaluate and improve human capital. Some of these may be part of a continuous reporting process; others may be utilized periodically, for example, as part of an annual or quarterly review. Others may be used on an ad-hoc or when-needed basis.

Human Resources (HR): Costs per Employee. How efficient is the HR department? What are the costs incurred in recruiting, providing benefits, and employee development and evaluating performance? How do these costs compare to other companies in our industry? To best practice companies?

Benefits per Employee. Employee benefits are a significant cost. Some of these costs, including healthcare premiums, have risen significantly in recent years. This measure is better than benefits as a percentage of payroll since payroll can be skewed by the inclusion of highly compensated managers and executives. Note that reducing the cost of employee benefits by reducing *benefits* may have implications on retaining and attracting talent.

Headcount Analysis. People-related costs are typically a significant percentage of total costs. Tracking headcount levels is essential to cost management. Significant changes to the cost model will result from additions or reductions to headcount. Tracking headcount by department over time can provide significant insight into changes in costs. Some companies include the full-time equivalent (FTE) of part-time, temporary, or contract employees in the analysis to provide a comprehensive view and to prevent "gaming" the measure by using resources that may fall outside the employee definition. In addition, tracking open employment requisitions, new hires, and terminations provides a leading indicator of future cost levels. An example of a headcount analysis is presented in Table 7.2.

Employee Engagement and Satisfactions Surveys. Employee surveys are typically done on a quarterly or annual basis. Occasionally, management may also want to take the pulse of the workforce after specific events, such as a change in leadership or workforce reductions. Quantitative results can be very useful, especially when combined with commentary. Survey questions, frequency, and methods should be designed by professionals. Management must be committed to providing feedback and action, where appropriate, to associates, or the surveys can do more harm than good.

Effectiveness of Training and Development Programs. Development programs, including training, can lead to growth and improved performance of the workforce. The programs must be thoughtfully chosen based on relevance and quality. It can be difficult to measure the effectiveness of training programs, especially in general topic areas. Where possible, develop specific objectives for the training, for example, to improve customer service on help lines. This objective could be supported by measuring call wait times, customer survey results, and other specific measures. By putting a stake in the ground, we can then measure improvements against that performance.

It is also useful to survey participants and their superiors and clients. Did the participants learn from the session? Did it meet the stated objectives? Did clients and superiors see improved performance after the session? For example, after the FP&A team attended a session on "Presenting and Communicating Business Information," did the clients of FP&A report an improvement?

TABLE 7.2 **Headcount trend analysis.**

	Headcount Analysis									
	2023	2024				2025				Increase (Decrease)
Department	Q4	Q1	Q2	Q3	Q4	Q118	Q218	Q318	Q418	Q424–Q425
Operations										
Manufacturing	125	123	126	135	126	127	125	140	132	6
Quality Control	7	7	7	7	7	7	7	7	7	0
Inspection	3	3	3	3	3	3	3	3	3	0
Procurement	8	8	8	8	8	8	8	8	8	0
Other	9	9	9	9	9	9	9	9	9	0
Total	152	150	153	162	153	154	152	167	159	6
R&D										
Hardware Engineering	15	15	15	15	15	15	15	15	15	0
Software Engineering	17	17	17	17	17	19	23	25	30	13
Other	2	2	2	2	2	2	2	2	2	0
Total	34	34	34	34	34	36	40	42	47	13
SG&A										
Management	7	7	7	7	7	7	7	7	7	0
Sales	15	15	15	15	15	15	15	15	15	0
Finance	11	11	12	12	14	14	14	14	14	0
Human Resources	4	4	4	4	4	4	4	4	4	0
Total	37	37	38	38	40	40	40	40	40	0
Company Total	223	221	225	234	227	230	232	249	246	19
Increase (Decrease)		–2	4	9	–7	3	2	17	–3	

Open Requisitions	Number	Annual Cost (000s)
Operations	3	$ 150
R&D	6	750
Finance	1	95
Human Resources	1	75
Total	11	$ 1,070

Average Training Hours per Employee. This measure provides a good indicator of the level of training and learning within the organization. Since training needs may vary across the organization, depending on the level and function of employees, this measure is often established and tracked separately for engineers, analysts, managers, technicians, and so on.

Retention, Engagement, and Satisfaction

Employee Satisfaction. Many companies survey employee satisfaction annually or on a rotating basis. These surveys test overall satisfaction as well as specific areas including compensation, perceived growth opportunities, communication, level of engagement, and management effectiveness. Another good way to get a pulse on employee satisfaction and underlying causes is for senior managers to meet with small groups of employees, without other managers and supervisors present. Some companies refer to these as skip-level meetings since several levels of managers may be skipped in the sessions. Employees are typically candid in these sessions, especially when the process gains credibility by providing anonymity of comments and action on issues they raise. The effectiveness of surveys and skip-level meetings is highly dependent on how employees perceive management's commitment to address the findings. If the findings are not communicated to employees or acted on, the process will lose employee participation and engagement.

Employee Turnover. Employee turnover can be very costly, as shown in Table 7.1 earlier in this chapter. There is significant time and cost incurred in recruiting, hiring, training, and terminating employees. Some level of turnover may be a positive indicator; if employees are leaving for great opportunities, the turnover can be a reflection of a strong company that is developing talent. A variation of this measure is to split this between involuntary and voluntary turnover. What are the root causes of each? Is the turnover due to employee dissatisfaction, compensation levels, poor hiring practices, culture, or lack of growth? It is also important to look at the characteristics of those departing. Are we losing high-potential and high-performing associates? What are the root causes?

Recruitment and Immersion

Time to Fill Open Positions. Since it is important to fill open positions in the shortest possible time, measuring the length to fill open positions is important. In keeping with our theme to balance measures, it will be important to view this measure in the context of the overall effectiveness of recruitment. We wouldn't want to encourage hiring the wrong individuals faster!

Percentage of Openings Filled Internally. Some companies have a stated policy of promoting internally. Others prefer a mix of internal promotions and hiring from the outside, leading to diversity in experience and background. This measure captures the actual mix of hiring and provides an indication of the effectiveness of the organization in developing talent for internal growth and promotion.

Percentage of Offers Accepted. Another way to assess the recruiting and hiring process is to track offers accepted as a percentage of offers extended. A low acceptance percentage may indicate a problem in assessing the potential fit of applicants or an unfavorable perception of the company developed by the candidates during the recruiting process. This measure will also reflect the conditions in the job market.

Successful Hire Rate Percentage. While it is important to fill open positions on a timely basis, it is obviously more important to fill the positions with capable people who will be compatible with the organization. This measure tracks the success rate in hiring new employees or managers. The percentage of new employees retained for certain periods, or achieving a performance rating above a certain level, is a good indication of the effectiveness of the recruiting and hiring process.

LINKING TO OVERALL PERFORMANCE AND CREATING AN HCM DASHBOARD

In order to ensure the relevance of our HCM measures, we should attempt to link these measures and underlying activities to overall performance and financial results as shown in Figure 7.2.

After identification of the most important aspects and critical initiatives, a dashboard can be developed for HCM as illustrated in Figure 7.3.

HCM ASSESSMENT PROCESS

Managing HC can be thought of as a business process, as illustrated in Figure 7.1. The process should begin with a review and assessment of the current environment, strategy, talent, and organization. Based on this review, a written plan should be developed to address key issues and opportunities.

Most high-performing organizations employ formal reviews of talent and organization that reflect the overall importance of managing the company's most important asset, human capital. The review typically covers the following subjects:

- Strategic Context.
- Situational Analysis (SWOT).
- Organization Chart.
- Talent Assessment Summary.
- Competency and Experience Analysis.
- Direct Reports and Key Associates:
  - Career Profiles.
  - Performance and Development Summary.
- Hi-Potential Summary.
- Succession Plan.
- Analytics Summary.
- FP&A Assessment.
- Summary and Action Plan.

The following illustrates this review for a finance organization.

FIGURE 7.2 **Human capital management and financial performance.**

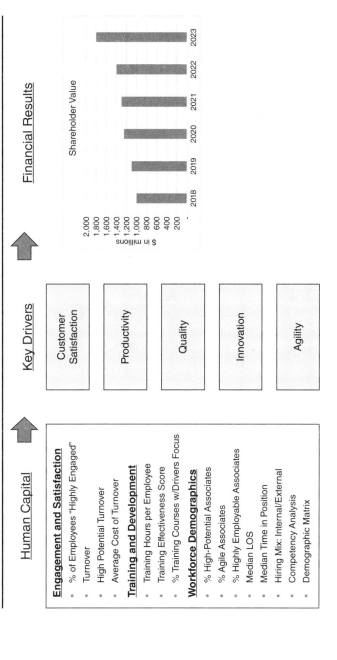

FIGURE 7.3 **HCM dashboard.**

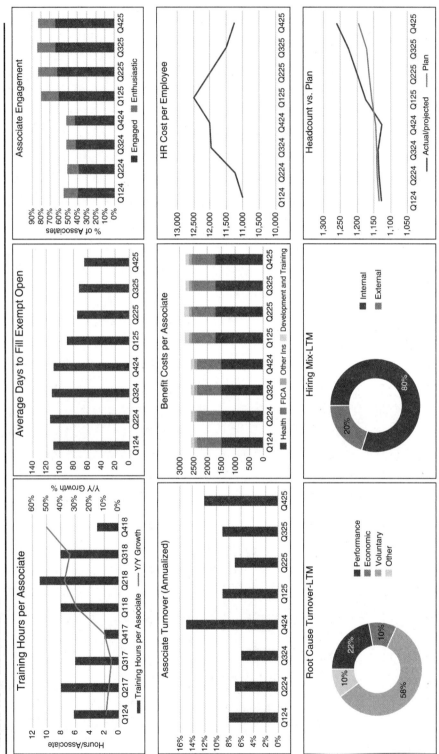

Strategic Context

Any serious analysis of operational or functional activities should start with a review of the company's strategy and strategic objectives. This ensures that the assessment of the finance team fully considers the priorities and initiatives that are vital to the organization's success. The strategic context can be developed by considering:

- Strategic issues.
- Mission, vision, and values.
- Strategic objectives.
- Execution plan.

These will be covered in detail in Chapter 8, "Strategic Analysis and Planning." A summary of these documents should serve as the introduction to our focus on talent and organization.

Organization

An organization chart provides an overview of how the team is structured and identifies senior members of the team. At face value, the chart may even identify inconsistencies with key objectives and priorities (Figure 7.4).

- What are the size of value-added functions relative to general accounting and transaction processing?
- Is there an optimum span of control (number of direct reports) at each level?

FIGURE 7.4 **Finance organization chart.**

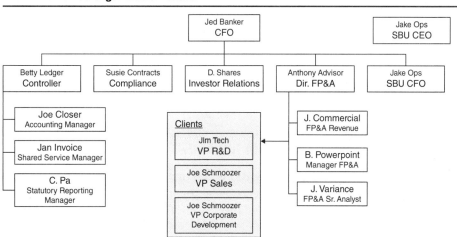

- Do critical functions, such as FP&A, report directly to the CFO?
- Are the reporting lines optimum for both financial control and service? Business unit financial leaders generally will have responsibilities both to the business unit leadership and corporate finance. This may be represented by a "dotted line" or dual "solid line" reporting relationships.
- Are certain functions centralized and others distributed or close to business leaders? For example, it likely makes sense to centralize transaction processing, but distribute FP&A members to support the business and operating teams.

Career Summary and Performance

For each key manager and team members with high-potential, a career (Table 7.3) and performance summary (Table 7.4) should be prepared to capture relevant information. This provides a concise summary of the experience, education, and performance of key associates.

The individual performance and career summary can then be used to prepare summaries of the finance team. We can then review the portfolio of our human assets in the same way we may look at a portfolio of businesses or investments. A talent assessment summary is a great way to start assessing the team. In Table 7.5, the talent in the FP&A department is summarized.

The talent recap allows the manager to look across all key staff for patterns, including length of service, time in position, and background and experience.

Another great assessment tool is to summarize performance of the team members using a bell curve. If performance evaluations tend to be "inflated" in an organization, it is useful to recast them in a performance summary curve as illustrated in Figure 7.5. This technique requires us to identify underperformers and star performers. Most of the team will fall into the middle, often referred to as the "vital" 70%.

Another tool to evaluate talent is the potential-performance grid shown in Figure 7.6. Team members are assessed for potential ability to grow in the organization. High-potential (Hi-Pots) employees are generally defined as "employees who have the potential to rise two or more levels in the organization or serve in a senior leadership role in the future." Identifying Hi-Pots is important; efforts should be made to retain and develop these employees to achieve their potential growth.

Experience, Competency, and Skills Inventory

High-performing finance organizations recognize that the development of key competencies and experience is critical to their success. Business acumen, communication and presentation skills, exposure to other disciplines,

TABLE 7.3 **Career profile.**

General Information					
Name:	Joe Ledger	**Date of Hire:**	7/25/2010	**Location:**	Somewhere, USA
Title	Controller	**Department:**	Finance	**Citizenship:**	USA
		Business Unit:	Corporate		

Education (Post High School)				
Dates	**Degree**	**Majors**	**School**	**Location:**
5/20/2019 to Present	MBA (8/12 courses completed)	Finance	Tullytown Tech	Tullytown PA
5/20/2005	BS Accounting	Accounting, Minor in Finance	Tullytown Tech	Tullytown PA

Training and Development (Last 24 Months)				
Dates	**Program Description**	**Days**	**Provider**	**Certification**
3/5/2023	Accounting Update	2.0	AICPA	
6/12/2022	Budgeting & Planning	1.5	Jack Alexander & Assoc	
Total		3.5		

Work Experience				
Dates	**Title**		**Company**	**Location**
6/2017 to Present	Controller		ABC Co	Somewhere USA
7/2010 to 6/2017	Assistant Controller		ABC Co	Somewhere USA
5/2005 to 7/2010	Staff and Senior Auditor		PWC	Phila, PA

Career Interests/Goals	
Short-term (0-2 Years):	Additional Responsibilities (Contracts, Billing)
Longer-term (3-5 Years):	CFO
Other:	

statistics, and data visualization are just as important as technical knowledge, including accounting principles and software expertise. Strong contributors will typically be strong in several of the following skills and experience:

❑ Business sense.
❑ Operating experience.
❑ Ability to learn and utilize technology solutions.
❑ Graphics.

TABLE 7.4 **Performance and development summary.**

Employee Name: Joe Ledger   **Date:** June 2023
Length of Service: 9 years, 1 month
Time in Current Position: 2 years

PERFORMANCE SUMMARY	Leadership Values	Rating
Joe is a hard working manager. He consistently exhibits strong leadership and is an advocate for continuous improvement in accounting and across the company. He has led the reduction of the closing cycle (5 days) and was a team leader on the ERP implementation this year.	Excellence	FS
	Teamwork	O/S
	Dedication	FS
	Leadership	FS
	Vision & Purpose	FS
Joe consistently delivers quality financial reports and coordinates with external auditors. No significant adjustments have been proposed in recent years. He does a good job of staying current on new accounting requirements.	Communication	MG
	Ethics & Integrity	EXC
	Bias for Action	O/S
	Innovation	FS
Joe needs to improve his evaluation and utilization of human resources. He has not developed a successor and has not acquired or developed enough high performers and high potential. He also needs to improve on his verbal and written communication skills and develop a better stand-up presentation capability.	Agility	FS
	Developing Talent	MG
	Customer Commitment	FS
	Performance	FS
	Rating Key	
	Outstanding	O/S
	Excellent	EXC
	Fully Satisfactory	FS
	Marginal	MG

Capabilities Summary	
Strengths	**Improvement Opportunities and Development Needs**
Financial Reporting	Personal Development
Internal control	Human Capital Management
Execution	Presentation and Communication Skills
Ethics and Integrity	

Development Actions and Timing	
Action	**Timing**
1. Complete HCM assessment and develop plan.	9/2023
2. Implement 1st Phase of Actions under HCM Plan	3/2024
3. Attend course on Presentation and Communication	8/2023
4. Increase personal training and development to 40 hours per year	12/2023

Signatures:

Manager   Date

Employee

Employee signature indicates that a joint discussion with the manager has taken place and does not necessarily signify employee's agreement with the manager's assessment and evaluation

❑ Oral communication and presentation.

❑ Written communication.

❑ Process mapping and improvement.

❑ Statistics.

❑ External reporting.

TABLE 7.5 **Talent recap.**

		Olin Industries			Department: FP&A	
Name Position	Anthony Advisor Director of FP&A	Bill Powerpoint Manager, FP&A	Jill Variance Senior Analyst	Tom Trend Analyst	Steve Detail Analyst	TBN Analyst
Primary Responsibility	Oversight	Executive Reporting	Variance Reporting	Budget	Ad-hoc	Rolling Forecast
Highest Degree	MBA	BS	BS	BS	BS	BS
Certifications		CPA		CMGI		
Years in Position	2	1	2	1	6	
Years with Company	5	1	2	1	8	
Total Experience	7	5	4	1	10	
Hours of Training (LY)	24	16	8	16	0	
Performance Rating	AA	OS	E	E	E	
Potential (High/ Moderate/Low)	M	H	L	M	L	H
Agile	Y	Y	N	N	N	Y
Flight Risk		Low	Moderate	High	Low	NA
Competencies:		Graphics Develop Presentations	Modeling ERP	Excel ERP	Excel	
Development Needs:	Presentation	Learn Business Modeling	Presentation Learn Business	Presentation Modeling Learn Business ERP Application	Presentation Modeling Learn Business	
Salary	$140,000	$84,000	$84,000	$70,200	$81,000	$62,000

If these skills and competencies are underrepresented in the team, consideration should be given to developing or acquiring those skill sets. Formal training is available, but analysts should also become active learners by reviewing top-quality analyses and presentations from consultants, research analysts, and presentations to the board and investors. Very successful finance organizations also strive for diversity in thinking and skills. For example, individuals with experience in quality initiatives and process improvement can make a

FIGURE 7.5 **Performance summary curve.**

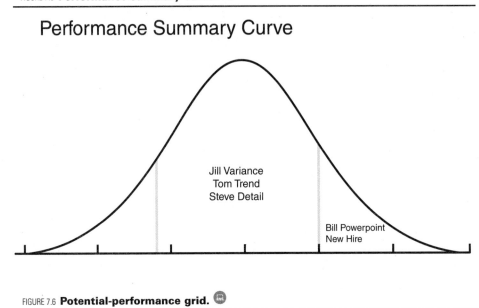

FIGURE 7.6 **Potential-performance grid.**

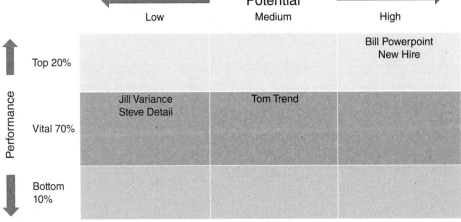

significant contribution to the overall FP&A effort. Table 7.6 is an example of a skills and experience inventory that highlights coverage and gaps.

Succession Planning

Succession planning is a critical component of any HCM assessment and plan. For each critical position, potential successors are identified. Each potential successor is then rated as ready now or potentially ready in the future. Key development opportunities should be identified to develop successors for each critical position (Table 7.7).

TABLE 7.6 **Experience, skill, and competency inventory.**

| | Skill and Competency Inventory | | | | | Olin Industries | | | | | | | |
Competency/Experience	CFO	Controller	Treasurer	FP&A Director	Senior Analyst	SEC Reporting	Analyst	Investor Relations Dir	Accounting Manager	Payroll	Payables	Credit Collection	Internal Audit
General													
General Management	X												
Operations Management	X	X											
Commercial and Sales				X									
Business Sense				X	X								
Strategic Planning	X							X					
Business Partner	X												
Supervisory and Management	X	X	X	X					X				
Treasury													
Cash Management	X		X										
Banking			X										
Investments			X										
Risk Management	X		X					X					
Capital Investment Decisions			X										
FP&A													
SEC(GAAP) Reporting		X				X			X				
Communication-Written		X				X		X					
Communication-Oral		X						X					
Presentation-Development		X					X	X					
Presentation-Delivery	X						X	X					
Graphics		X		X			X	X					
Statistics							X						
Business Application Software		X					X						
Process Mapping and Diagnostics				X	X				X				
Modelling				X	X		X		X				

(Continued)

TABLE 7.6 **(Continued)**

Olin Industries

Competency/Experience	Skill and Competency Inventory												
	CFO	Controller	Treasurer	FP&A Director	Senior Analyst	SEC Reporting	Analyst	Investor Relations Dir	Accounting Manager	Payroll	Payables	Credit Collection	Internal Audit
Transaction Processing													
Accounts Payable									X		X		
Payroll									X	X	X		
Credit and Collection									X			X	
General Ledger		X							X				
Other													
Public Accounting	X	X											X
Financial Control ("SOX")		X											X
Tax	X												
Cos: Accounting		X			X								
Cos: Management		X											X
M&A- Valuation, Due Diligence													
M&A- Integration													
International													
Contracts and Compliance													

TABLE 7.7 **Succession planning.**

Company: Olin Industries
Department: Finance

Succession Analysis

Readiness Code

RN	Ready Now
R1	Ready 1-3 Years
R2	Ready 4-6 Years

CFO

Incumbent	Jed Banker			**Hit by Truck Coverage:**	Betty Ledger
Yrs. In Position	5.5				

Successors:	**Position**	**Readiness**		**Development Needs**	**Actions**
Betty Ledger	Controller	R1		FP&A	Lateral Transfer Controller
Anthony Advisor	Dir FP&A	R1		Core Accounting	Lateral Transfer FP&A

Controller

Incumbent	Betty Ledger			**Hit by Truck Coverage:**	Joe Closer
Yrs. In Position	7				

Successors:	**Position**	**Readiness**		**Development Needs**	**Actions**
Joe Closer	Accounting Manager	R2		Various	See Development Plan

Dir of FP&A

Incumbent	Anthony Advisor			**Hit by Truck Coverage:**	Bill Powerpoint
Yrs. In Position	1.5				

Successors:	**Position**	**Readiness**		**Development Needs**	**Actions**
Bill Powerpoint	Manager, FP&A	R1		Learn Business	Focus on CEO, ETL Support

Manager, Compliance

Incumbent	Susie Contracts			**Hit by Truck Coverage:**	None
Yrs. In Position	1.25				

Successors:	**Position**	**Readiness**		**Development Needs**	**Actions**
None					Acquire Asst. Manager

Summary of Actions:
1. Lateral transfer, Controller and FP&A Director
2. B. PowerPoint to support CEO/ETL's
3. Develop or acquire Controller successor
4. Acquire/Develop Assistant Manager of Compliance

Conclusions
1. Limited bench strength
2. Immediate action required to develop succession tracks and HBT coverage

139

Human Capital by the Numbers

As with any analysis of performance, a graphic summary illustrated in Figure 7.7 can be used to highlight key trends and observations.

Developing an Improvement Plan

The results of the assessment can be overwhelming. Senior managers should review all assessment materials and identify the most important findings. The focus should be on high-leverage improvement opportunities that will have the greatest impact. The team should construct an implementation plan with specific objectives, responsibilities, and timeline. Progress on the plan should be reviewed each month. An example of an FP&A improvement plan is presented in Table 7.8.

FOCUS ON THE FINANCE TEAM

In addition to the general framework outlined in this chapter, there are a few additional areas that can improve the effectiveness of the finance team. These include developing a service mindset, client surveys and evaluating reports, and analytical products generated by finance.

Finance as a Service Organization

Leading finance teams have adopted the persona of a service organization. This simple shift in perspective can have a transformational change in how finance views its role and also in how it is perceived by operating managers and executives. While the term *business partner* has gained traction as a banner for working collaboratively and contributing broadly in the organization, I have found that a view as a service provider leads to better collaboration and contribution.

Finance teams can begin this journey by declaring this shift in focus and changing the relationship with our "internal clients." Services can be defined, ranging from transaction processing to trusted advisor, with an eye toward improving performance across the board.

Survey Your Clients (or Partners)

In addition to informal discussions, some organizations also survey customers or clients of finance. While the ratings are informative, the greatest value tends to come in the form of comments, suggestions, and subsequent conversations. Priority should be given to common themes. An example of a client survey was presented in Chapter 3, which can be adapted for use across the finance team.

FIGURE 7.7 **Human capital by the numbers.**

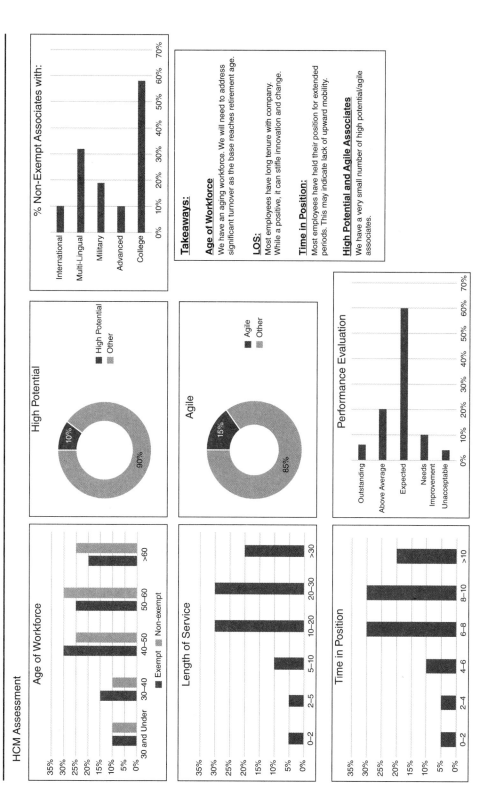

TABLE 7.8 **FP&A improvement plan.**

FP&A Assessment and Improvement
Timeline and Work Flow

Task	Who?	Status	Date Prior	Timeline (Week 1–30)
Assessment				
Skills and Competency Inventory	BR	Complete	6/15	X (wk 1)
Report Inventory	BR	Complete	6/22	X (wk 2)
Client Survey	BR	Complete	6/29	X (wk 3)
Summarize Findings	BR	Complete	7/6	X (wk 4)
Develop Plan	Team	In Process	7/13	X X (wk 4–5)
Low Hanging Fruit				
Eliminate Reports and Analysis	CD	In Process	7/22	X -- X (wk 6–8)
Talent Acquisition and Management				
Additional Position Senior Analyst	JD	Open	7/31	X Define (wk 8); X Hire (wk 10)
Group Training program	CD	Open	Var	X Contract (wk 10); X Session 1 (wk 16); X Session 2 (wk 20); X Evaluate (wk 24)
Communication Seminar	BR	Open	10/15	XX (wk 16); XX (wk 21–22)
Individual Development and Training Plan	BR	Open	11/5	
Develop Analysis				
List of new additions	JD	Complete	7/15	X (wk 4)
Develop Dashboard	CD	Open	Var	X Corporate (wk 5–6); X Product Development (wk 11); X Revenue Pipeline (wk 18)
Revise Capital Investment Decision Package	BR	Open	8/1	X X X (wk 8–10)
Implement Rolling Business Outlook	BR	Open	9/15	x x (wk 14–15); x x x x (wk 16–19)
Evaluation and Next Steps				
Evaluate Progress				X (wk 26)
Additional Actions				X (wk 27)
Conflicts				Closing (wk 1); CFO-Vacation (wk 6); Closing (wk 11); Closing (wk 21); IR (wk 24)

Evaluate Current Reports and Analyses Produced by the Finance Team

One of the best ways to evaluate your effectiveness as a finance team is to collect all reports, dashboards, and on-demand reports that are distributed to managers, executives, directors, investors, and other important constituencies. These should include recurring reports (e.g., monthly or quarterly) as well as ad-hoc requests for analyses. I recommend collecting paper copies of these reports and spreading them out on a conference table for full visual impact.

Evaluate these reports considering the following characteristics:

Graphic or visual presentation versus spreadsheet tables?

Relevancy: Do the reports cover key issues and progress toward goals, targets, and objectives?

What themes are we emphasizing? Are they appropriate?

Does our work support the attainment of strategic objectives and critical performance drivers of the organization?

Do the reports address business performance or just financial results?

Are the reports professional and consistent with the image the finance organization strives to present?

How much time was needed to produce?

The reports and analyses can be summarized as illustrated in Table 7.9. This process can be very illuminating! Typically, managers are surprised at the tremendous time invested in certain reports, including those with dubious utility. In some cases, reports can simply be eliminated. Others may be candidates for streamlining or developing a more efficient preparation process. This activity also identifies those reports that were introduced for a specific purpose at a point in time. . .that never get eliminated.

Next, interview key managers, executives, and other clients of your reports and analyses. In many cases, managers do not utilize or even look at substantial parts of reports. In one instance, not one recipient (of 22 senior managers and executives) in the organization found the monthly finance report useful. Few reviewed the report. A couple recipients referenced a single schedule for specific information. The report was old-school, almost entirely focused on the past and full of Excel® spreadsheets. We decided to eliminate the report entirely, saving over 12 days of preparation time! The report was replaced with more relevant weekly and monthly dashboards and more emphasis was placed on current performance and progress toward future performance targets and goals.

Ask the managers what information they need on a recurring basis to execute their responsibilities. Inquire of any specific problems or issues that FP&A can assist in resolving.

TABLE 7.9 **Report and analysis inventory and assessment.**

Olin Industry
FP&A
Reporting and Analysis Assessment

Illustrative

Page 1 of 8

Gather all Reports and Analysis Completed by the Finance Organization. List each report below:

Report Title	Frequency	Estimated Time	Preparer	Clients	Client Assessment	Value H/M/L	Business Focus	Visual	Professional Appearance	Indicated Actions
Monthly Package	Monthly	48 hours	Team	Sr Staff	Low Utilization, selected schedules valued - "Doesn't help me run the biz"...I use one schedule"	L	Accounting Oriented	None - all financials	Needs Improvement	Reduce to high value segments, add summary and narrative
Board Package	8x per year	30 hours	Sue B	Directors	Reference use, too historical	M	Accounting Oriented	Few	Tolerable,	Add graphs, exec summary
Margin Analysis	Monthly	2 hours	John H	Product Managers	Important info difficult to understand	M	Accounting Oriented		Needs Improvement	Revamp, add graphs and summary
Inventory Analysis	Monthly	4 hours	Jim B	Ops	No longer required	L	Accounting Oriented		Weak	Eliminate
Weekly Dashboard	Weekly	2 hours	John H	Sr Staff	"High Value" - single most useful thing coming out of finance	H	Biz Focus	Graphics	High	None Required
Forecast Summary	Monthly	3 hours	John H	CEO/CFO/Staff	Great recap of ST goals—effective communication of targets	H	Biz Focus	Graphics	High	None Required

Creating the Slack for Value-Added Activities

One of the greatest impediments to improving our effectiveness in finance as an organization is that "we are too busy processing transactions, closing the books, and working on annual and quarterly filings." Few if any organizations have excess resources; most have been purged of any excess years ago.

The key is for finance teams to continue pursuing process improvements across the nonvalue or lower value-added activities so that more time is available for higher value activities, including FP&A. In many organizations, there is still a huge opportunity to eliminate rework and redundant activities. Examples of areas where efficiency gains have been realized in many organizations include:

❑ The closing and reporting cycle.

❑ Transaction processing, including payables, travel expense, payroll, invoicing, and receivables management.

❑ Budgeting, planning, and forecasting, especially reducing detail work and multiple iterations.

❑ Eliminating reports and analyses that are not effective, are redundant, or are not utilized.

SUMMARY

The success of any organization is highly dependent on the human capital employed. HCM should be viewed as a critical management process to look holistically at all phases of optimizing the acquisition, utilization, development, and retention of employees. Companies should perform a comprehensive assessment of HC on an annual basis. KPIs, analyses, and dashboards should be utilized to monitor trends and performance. Finance teams can consider some additional measures, including developing a service mindset, surveying clients, and improving productivity.

8

Strategic Analysis
and Planning

Finance professionals can make a significant contribution to strategic planning. In some corporations, there is a strategic planning process in place, but finance may not be actively participating. Unfortunately, I hear many finance professionals complain that they "do not have a seat at the table."

In other firms, typically smaller and mid-size companies, the finance team may play a role in introducing a systematic strategic planning process. In either situation, finance business partners must understand strategic analysis and planning. In this chapter, we will discuss core principles of strategic planning, how we can "earn a seat at the strategy table," and the two ways we can assist in developing the firm's strategy, including strategic analysis and strategy development.

STRATEGIC PLANNING: CORE PRINCIPLES

Prior to rushing to join in strategic planning efforts, we should identify the objectives of strategic planning and invest time in learning the core principles of strategic planning. The objectives of strategic planning go far beyond the creation of the strategic plan document. A thorough process will provide an in-depth review of markets, competitors, and our competitive position in those markets. Recent historical performance trends should be reviewed to develop a context for evaluating performance and setting future direction. The organization will develop goals and objectives for the next three to five years. Possible alternative strategies should be identified and evaluated. Resource requirements, both financial and human, will be identified. The plan will provide a framework to evaluate potential future investments. The strategic plan will also include a summary execution roadmap that supports the projected financial results. The strategic planning process will also enable the effective communication of strategic priorities and alignment of resources.

The objectives of an effective strategic plan process:

- Thorough analysis and review of markets, competitors, and competitive position.
- Develop goals and objectives for 3–5 years.
  - Longer-term view of performance.
- Identify human and financial capital required to execute strategy.
- Encourage the identification and consideration of alternative strategies.
- Review and optimize asset allocation.
- Develop a framework to evaluate major investments and acquisitions in the future.
- Create alignment across the organization (direction, priorities, etc.).

It is important to emphasize that the greatest utility expected from the process is derived from the assessment, thinking, and discussion of the markets, competitive forces, and proposed strategy. While the strategic thinking and strategy will be documented in a formal plan, the research, analysis, discussion, and deliberations are typically of greater value than the plan document.

Strategic Planning Tools

A number of strategic planning tools and frameworks have been developed over the last century. Many of these have been incorporated into the framework that is described later in the chapter.

SWOT Analysis. The traditional SWOT (Strengths, Weaknesses, Opportunities, and Threats) is a terrific framework for situational analysis.

Porter's Five Forces Analysis. This framework looks at the attractiveness of markets based on five driving forces. I have found it a useful tool to evaluate overall industries and investment decisions, but of limited application in strategic planning for an individual company (unless facing resource allocation decisions across multiple industries or contemplating investments outside their primary industry).[1]

---

[1] This framework was introduced by Michael Porter in a 1979 *Harvard Business Review* article (Michael E. Porter, "How Competitive Forces Shape Strategy," *Harvard Business Review*, May 1979 (vol. 57, no. 2), pp. 137–145) and amplified in several subsequent books he authored on strategic and competitive advantage.

- Rivalry among existing competitors. How strong is the competition among players in the industry? Highly competitive industries are likely to result in lower returns.

- Relative bargaining power of suppliers. If the industry is reliant on a limited number of suppliers, it will limit returns of market participants. Consider the airline industry, where all firms must purchase aircraft from one of two dominant suppliers. This increases input costs and limits opportunity for differentiation among firms.

- Bargaining power of customers. If customers have higher relative bargaining strength over the firm, returns will be limited. For example, margins have declined for many consumer products companies due to the concentration of power in a few major retailers including Walmart and Amazon.

- Threat of substitutes. Is the product or service subject to potential substitutes? For example, a substitute for some business air travel, video-conferencing, has reduced demand for business travel.

- Threat of new entrants. How difficult is it for new competitors to enter the market? Are there barriers to entry such as time and costs, economies of scale, or intellectual property that reduce the ability of new competitors to enter the market?

PESTEL Framework. This framework looks at macro factors that impact markets, including political (geopolitical), economic, social, technology, environmental, and legal. This analysis can identify major tailwinds or headwinds facing the firm.

Portfolio Analysis. A number of frameworks have been used to assess the portfolio of products, services, and business units within the firm. The portfolio can be analyzed on various characteristics, including growth, profitability, strategic fit, and so on.

Strategic Planning Framework

Figure 8.1 presents an overview of an effective strategic planning framework. The strategic planning process encompasses four stages:

Strategic Analysis and Assessment. The first and most important is often the assessment and analysis of our market, competitive position, performance, trends, and major factors.

Strategy Development. Based on the strategic analysis, the team can develop a proposed strategy and objectives. This stage should also include the identification and consideration of alternative strategies. The strategic objectives must then be translated into specific action plans to achieve the strategic objectives.

FIGURE 8.1 **Strategic Planning Framework**

Execution Planning. The ultimate success of any strategy lies in the ability to effectively implement and execute it. Finance can play a large role in ensuring that the strategy is translated into actionable plans.

Monitor Performance and Establish Accountability. In order to ensure effective execution, the firm must develop the capability to monitor performance and execution on strategic objectives. This may include monitoring critical projects, important assumptions (e.g., economic), market trends, and competitive forces. The firm should be prepared to course-correct or change direction if warranted. An example of a table of contents for a strategic plan is included in the text box and each will be discussed later in this chapter.

- Executive Summary
- Historical Performance
- Strategic Analysis
  - Summary: Market, Customer, Competitor
  - Revenue Analysis
  - Competitor Summary
  - Competitor Analysis
  - Other Market Players
  - Benchmark Analysis
  - Portfolio Analysis
  - Talent and Organization Assessment
  - Growth Opportunities and Investments
  - Strategic Issues

- Strategy Development
  - Strategy and Strategic Objectives
  - Alternatives/Scenarios
  - Critical Assumptions, Upsides, and Risks
  - Financial Projections Summary
- Execution Planning
  - Execution Plan Summary
  - Historical and Projected Headcount Summary
- Executive Summary
- Appendix

STRATEGIC ANALYSIS

A substantial part of the value of strategic planning is strategic analysis, essentially an assessment of performance and an analysis of the current situation. I am a fan of one-page summaries and utilize this approach throughout the planning process. Others may prefer to divide the analysis into several slides or pages.

Executive Summary

Although the executive summary (Figure 8.2) of the plan is completed after developing the various components, it is helpful to summarize key observations and themes impacting the organization and strategy. The purpose of the executive summary is to preview/review the key factors presented in the strategic plan. Key topics that should be summarized in concise form:

- ❑ Historical perspective and performance trends.
- ❑ Key assumptions and uncertainties.
- ❑ Critical objectives.
- ❑ Brief statement of proposed strategy and projected results.

The same document can also be used as a summary at the end of the plan document.

FIGURE 8.2 **Strategic plan executive summary.**

Executive Summary

- After a long period of strong performance as market leader, the Company is facing major headwinds.

- The Company's flagship product platform is now technologically obsolete and a major investment is required to restore product leadership.

- The European marketplace represents a growth opportunity but will require significant investment in marketing, distribution, and manufacturing.

- Major macro headwinds include economic uncertainty and geopolitical risk.

- Existing Talent & Organization must improve to meet the rising challenges and execute the plan.

Historical Performance Recap

The purpose of the historical performance recap (Figure 8.3) is to present a summary of recent financial performance to provide context for the strategic discussion. This summary ensures that the discussions will not be detached from the recent performance trends.

The content for this summary should be tailored to that specific business and situation. Generally, revenue, growth rates, and profitability should be included. Asset levels and return on invested capital (ROIC) should also be presented, especially for capital-intensive businesses. For most companies, the summary may include the market value of the enterprise and stock price. A high-level revenue summary can also be presented. Finally, value-added commentary is helpful in underscoring key points.

Strategic Summary

This form (Figure 8.4) summarizes important strategic elements, including product or service definition; market and competitive factors; strength, weaknesses, opportunities, and threats (SWOT); and external factors. The form is generally prepared for each strategic business unit (SBU) and may be prepared for product lines within an SBU.

Product/Service Definition. Provide a succinct statement that describes the nature of your product or services.

Competitive Advantages. List significant competitive advantages from the perspective of customers/clients. Some considerations include:

❑ Are the advantages identified a true source of competitive advantage in the eyes of customers?

❑ Over which competitors are these advantages?

❑ Are they sustainable?

FIGURE 8.3 **Historical performance summary.**

Business Unit: Company

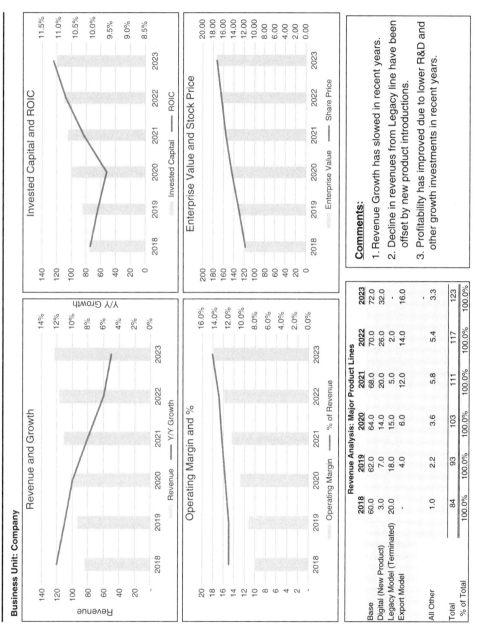

Revenue Analysis: Major Product Lines

	2018	2019	2020	2021	2022	2023
Base	60.0	62.0	64.0	68.0	70.0	72.0
Digital (New Product)	3.0	7.0	14.0	20.0	26.0	32.0
Legacy Model (Terminated)	20.0	18.0	15.0	5.0	2.0	-
Export Model	-	4.0	6.0	12.0	14.0	16.0
All Other	1.0	2.2	3.6	5.8	5.4	3.3
Total	84	93	103	111	117	123
% of Total	100.0%	100.0%	100.0%	100.0%	100.0%	100.0%

Comments:

1. Revenue Growth has slowed in recent years.
2. Decline in revenues from Legacy line have been offset by new product introductions.
3. Profitability has improved due to lower R&D and other growth investments in recent years.

153

FIGURE 8.4 **Strategic analysis summary.**

Strategic Analysis Summary
Strategic Business Unit (SBU):

Product/ Service Definition (Elevator Pitch):

Major network control and security devices

Customers (Description):

Major network providers and partners

Trends and Market Forces (PESTEL Forces):

- **Political:** Tax and regulatory environment unfavorable. Geopolitical uncertainty
- **Economic:** Recession likely
- **Social:** Significant workforce change
- **Technology:** Pace of change requires accelerated development cycles
- **Environmental:** Pressure to reduce energy consumption across all products
- **Legal:** Inadequate international intellectual property protection

Competitive Advantages (Strengths):

- Reputation
- Largest Installed Base
-
-
-

Opportunities:

- Expand underserved international market
-
-
-

Competitive Disadvantages (Weaknesses-Limitations):

- Technology outdated
- Product not suited for export
- Reliant on single supplier
-

Threats/Limitations:

- International Competitors
- Technological Obsolescence
-
-

Summary:

This SBU is under considerable competitive threats and pressure from market forces. Market share continues to decline due to technology obsolescence of our core product.

Significant investment required to maintain market presence and leadership.

Direct Market Analysis

Base Business Rank	Competitor	2021 Revenue	2021 Share	2022 Revenue	2022 Share	Y/Y Growth
1	Us	68.0	57.6%	70.0	53.4%	2.9%
2	TAEK	20.0	16.9%	22.0	16.8%	10.0%
3	Euronet	10.0	8.5%	11.0	8.4%	10.0%
4	NTD	5.0	4.2%	11.0	8.4%	120.0%
5						
6						
Others		15.0	12.7%	17.0	13.0%	13.3%
		118.0	100.0%	131.0	100.0%	11.0%

Competitive Disadvantages. List significant competitive disadvantages from the perspective of customers/clients.

- ❏ What are the implications of this weakness?
- ❏ Can these be addressed/overcome in this plan?
- ❏ Significant weaknesses should be addressed in "Strategic Objectives" and "Execution Planning" in the strategic plan.
- ❏ If these weaknesses cannot be addressed in the near term, the financial projections should reflect the expected impact.

Customers. Provide a description of the major customers (or customer types) you are serving.

Opportunities and Threats. Identify the major opportunities and threats for this SBU.

Trend and Market Forces. Consider forces and events that may impact the market. PESTEL factors include:

- ❏ Political: government policy, trade policy, labor laws, fiscal policy.
- ❏ Economic: economic growth or recession, interest rates, taxation, labor rates.
- ❏ Social: population growth, demographics, cultural trends.
- ❏ Technological: digitization, robotics, data analytics, artificial intelligence.
- ❏ Environmental: legislation, climate and weather, social pressure.
- ❏ Legal: health and safety, consumer rights, privacy laws.

Direct Market Analysis. Based on the definition of the market, we can estimate the market size, identify competitors, and estimate their revenue in this market (and include our revenue and share of the market). Many strategic planning experts advocate a broad definition of the market, avoiding narrowly defined markets where the company has a dominant market share. Figure 8.5 provides some guidelines in market definition and segmentation.

Revenue Analysis

Revenue is one of the most important drivers of performance and value. Many companies have a diverse set of revenue streams. They vary in terms of pricing, terms, risk, length, and nature (e.g., product vs. recurring service). These factors impact growth, profitability, risk, valuation, and other elements of

FIGURE 8.5 **Market definition and segmentation.**

Market Definition and Segmentation

- What market (Segments) are we addressing?
- What is the market size?
- Who are the major competitors?
- How much is our revenue in the market? Market share?
- Are we a $100m player in a $200m market or a $100m player in a $1.2 billion market?

Objectives:

- Useful to communicate and present to external parties (potential investors)
- Market segmentation can lead to useful strategic questions and opportunities
- Defining the market broadly provides more insight into opportunities and threats
  - Jack Welch, iconic CEO of GE, insisted that markets be defined so that GE had less than 10% market share

Direct Market Analysis

Base Business		2021		2022		Y/Y
Rank	Competitor	Revenue	Share	Revenue	Share	Growth
1	Us	68.0	57.6%	70.0	53.4%	2.9%
2	TAEK	20.0	16.9%	22.0	16.8%	10.0%
3	Euronet	10.0	8.5%	11.0	8.4%	10.0%
4	NTD	5.0	4.2%	11.0	8.4%	120.0%
5						
6						
Others		15.0	12.7%	17.0	13.0%	13.3%
		118.0	100.0%	131.0	100.0%	11.0%

> Defining markets and market segments is an imperfect exercise. The value is not in the precise definitions, but in the discussion and evaluation that occurs in the exercise.

performance. Figure 8.6 characterizes the major revenue stream by pricing, type, and geography. The measures included are situation-specific and will vary across organizations and change over time.

Competitor Summary

An essential element of strategic planning is to research and analyze the company's competitors. By researching and analyzing competitors and other market players, we introduce information and perspectives from outside the company. Figure 8.7 identifies key competitors and provides a summary of key attributes, including size, performance, ownership, and strategy. Sources of information include:

Public Companies: U.S. Securities and Exchange Commission forms 10k, proxy, and investor relations materials.

Private Companies: Since private companies are not required to disclose financial performance and other information to shareholders and other stakeholders, this information must be obtained from other sources or estimated. Provide your best estimate/understanding of their performance and strategy based on information available or based on your observations from their actions in the market.

FIGURE 8.6 **Revenue analysis.**

FIGURE 8.6 Revenue analysis.

Revenue Growth Analysis

Revenue from New Products

By Geographic Region

Revenue Type

Recurring vs. Non-Recurring Revenue

Revenue by SBU

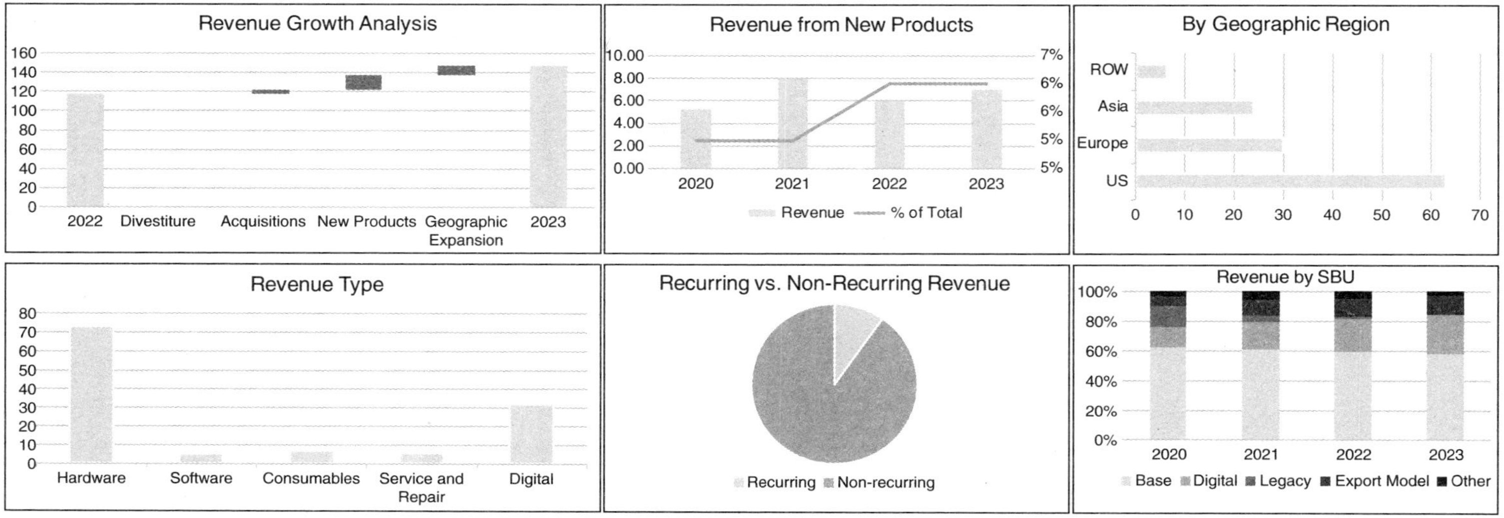

FIGURE 8.7 **Competitor summary.**

SBU: Base

Name	Us	TAEK	Euronet	NTD	Others (small local comapanies)
Revenue	$70.0m	$22.0m	$11.0m	$11.0m	$17.0
Profitability (EBITDA % Revenue)	12%	5%	9%	Low	Low
Ownership	ERA NetTech, Inc	Tai Electronics Corp	Private ownership	NTD Holdings	Generally privately held
Location	Annapolis MD	Taiwan	Zurich	Palo Alto, CA	
Total Revenue	$117.0m	$1b	$11.0	$250.0m	$17.0
Principal Service/ Business	Network Devices	Electronics	Network Devices	Broad offering of Network Equipment	Network Devices
Their Definition of Market	Network Control Devices	Electronics and Cloud	Network Control Devices	Network Devices	Network Control Devices
Their Strategy		Become market leader through significant investment in development	Leader in European NCD	Become market leader through advanced technologies	Local supplier to small network companies

Other Market Players

It can be useful to identify other market players beyond direct competitors (Figure 8.8). These players may have a significant influence on the market and our performance in the market, and also help us to shape an external perspective of the markets in which we participate. These may include:

❑ Potential/Indirect competitors in adjacent markets. Companies that do not currently compete with us at present may do so in the future. This is particularly true due to the formation of alliances and consolidation in many markets.

❑ Customers and clients. The growth and profitability of our customers and clients has significant implications for the company's performance.

❑ Partners and subcontractors. The performance of partners and subcontractors can also be insightful to our strategic analysis. They may also be competitors in the future.

❑ Financial investors. Financial investors (e.g., private equity firms) tend to focus on certain markets, technology, or service areas. They often develop strategies to accelerate growth or combine various portfolio companies to develop competitive advantages and ultimately create shareholder value. Certain industries become targets of private equity firms and this activity can have an impact on our market and should be considered in setting strategy.

FIGURE 8.8 **Other market players' summary.**

(Non-direct Competitors)
SBU: Base

Potential/Indirect Competitors	Customers/Client	Sub-Contractors / Channel Partners	Financial Investors/ (e.g. Private Equity)
Cloud Computing Hardware vendors	Cloud Computing Inc.	LSA Technology Co.	L&S Equity
	Enterprise Computing Company	Thomasso Electronics	Techgro Investment Co

Benchmark Analysis

A key part of the strategic analysis and assessment is to evaluate our company's performance against a relevant set of benchmark companies to provide a comparative analysis of our performance to competitors, partners, and selected "wildcard" (best practice) companies.

Benchmark Inclusions:

❑ SBU or company.

❑ Direct competitors.

❑ Customers, vendors, other market players.

❑ Best practice and most admired.

❑ Others of interest.

Generally, there are significant benefits to comparing a company's performance to other companies on key measures. This comparison typically leads to interesting observations, questions, and potential opportunities.

❑ External information is useful in providing context and "grounding" our view of our performance and competitive position.

❑ How does our performance compare to direct competitors? Revenue Growth? Profitability? Why?

❑ Does the performance of our customers raise concerns or highlight opportunities?

❑ Wildcard or most admired: What business practices, models, and process changes are in place to achieve that level of performance? Are any potentially relevant to us?

The financial performance benchmarking illustrated in Figure 8.9 can be enhanced by combining with an analysis of competitive position and market factors. Benchmarking will be described in more detail in Chapter 18, including the development of this analysis.

Portfolio Analysis

Important insights into a company's performance and future opportunities can result from looking at the "portfolio" of products or services within the company. Several similar frameworks have been introduced by strategy consultants over the years. The growth-profitability quadrant analysis illustrated in Figure 8.10 places SBUs in various quadrants based on their growth rate and profitability. The quadrants provide a basis for classifying the SBUs into stars (high growth and profitable), cash cows (low growth but profitable), questions or undetermined (high growth but not profitable), and underperformers (low growth and profitability). Generally, underperformers should be addressed in the plan. They may be candidates for a restructuring, liquidation, or sale depending on strategic importance. A company may find it useful to have SBUs across three quadrants to balance cash requirements and growth.

Most companies have several product groups, SBUs, and business lines. The company's portfolio may be diversified in terms of profitability, growth rates, and strategic fit. This can be represented in the sample grid in Figure 8.11. The visual, showing where each SBU fits on a growth-profitability matrix, is a terrific way to present the portfolio. The relative size of each business unit is also evident in the grid.

Several interesting observations typically arise. First is the diversity of the performance of each individual SBU. The largest SBU 4 has moderate growth and profitability, but all others are outliers. SBU 1 is high growth, but low profitability. Presumably, this SBU will attain profitability as it attains maturity and scale. SBU 2 has low growth, but high profitability, indicating perhaps a mature business contributing solid returns and cash flow. SBU 5 is both low growth and low profitability, and should be evaluated for restructuring or divestment. SBU 3 appears to be a star, attaining strong profitability while maintaining a high growth rate.

Talent and Organization

No strategic planning activity would be complete without considering the firm's most important asset: human capital. This asset will execute the

FIGURE 8.9 **Benchmark summary.**

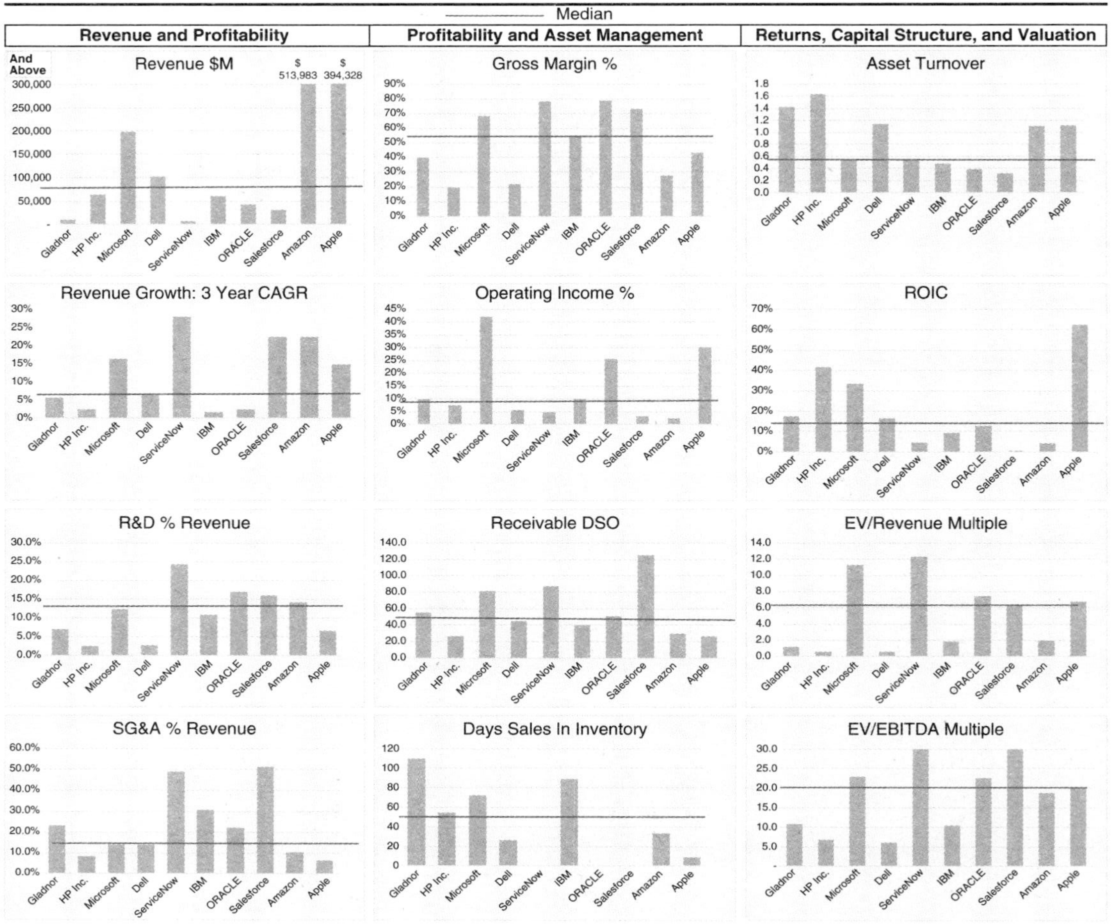

FIGURE 8.10 **Growth-profitability quadrant portfolio analysis.**

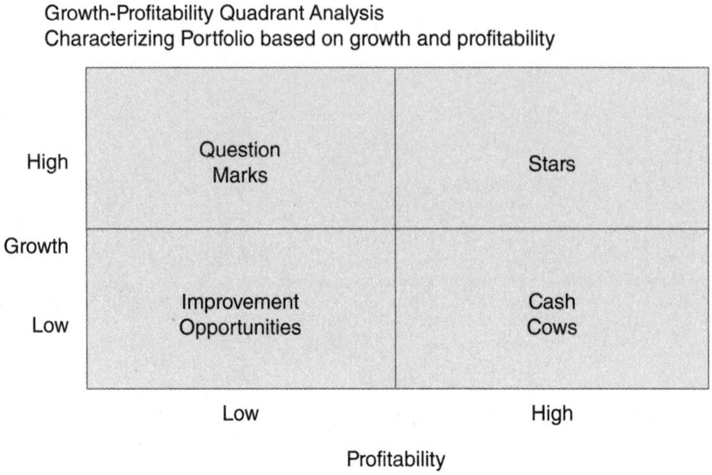

Growth-Profitability Quadrant Analysis
Characterizing Portfolio based on growth and profitability

	Low	High
High Growth	Question Marks	Stars
Low	Improvement Opportunities	Cash Cows

Profitability

FIGURE 8.11 **Portfolio analysis.**

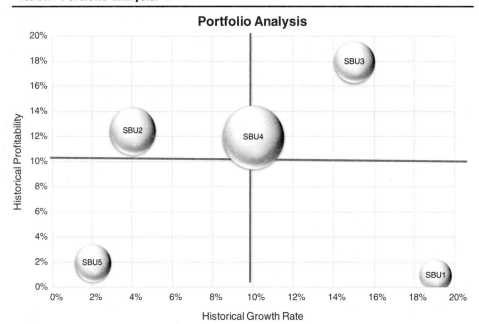

Portfolio Analysis

SBU	Growth	Profitability	Revenue	Future Investment	Strategic Importance
SBU1	19%	1%	9.4	High	High
SBU2	4%	13%	19.5	Low	Moderate
SBU3	15%	18%	14.8	Moderate	High
SBU4	10%	12%	34.5	Moderate	High (Core)
SBU5	2%	2%	12	Low	Low
Total			90.2		

strategic plan as well as drive the day-to-day operating activities. The objective of the Talent and Organization (T&O) section of the strategic plan is to evaluate the skills, experience, and depth of human capital in the context of the strategic analysis, objectives, and plan.

Talent and organization, which was the subject of Chapter 7, should be thoroughly evaluated in a separate process. The objective here is to ensure that T&O is evaluated in the context of the strategy to ensure that the resources required to execute the strategy are identified, developed, or acquired if not presently in place.

As part of the strategic assessment, HC can be viewed through three lenses:

❏ Organization chart (Figure 8.12) for reference.
❏ Talent and organization assessment (Figure 8.13).
❏ Talent and organization by the numbers (Figure 8.14).

A simple organization chart is a great place to start. The focus can be on the senior team that will set and drive strategy and performance. Is the leadership team in place? Are there gaps in terms of experience and competencies that could undermine execution? Have successors been identified?

FIGURE 8.12 **Organization chart.**

Talent and Organization Assessment
Organization Chart

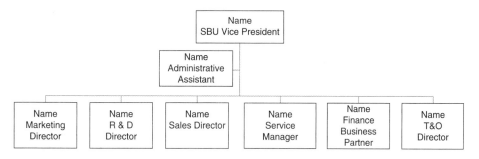

Talent and Organization Assessment   To assess the human capital environment, we can use Figure 8.13 as a guide. Key areas addressed are performance, potential, alignment of compensation, objective setting, succession, and engagement. Each organization should tailor for the specific situation at hand. Most of these are self-explanatory; we will highlight three important topics:

Talent on board to execute strategy? In order to ensure that the strategy will be successfully executed, the company should identify critical human resource requirements and determine whether additional resources are required.

Succession Planning. A succession plan will identify all key leadership and vital positions and identify potential successors. These individuals would be further evaluated to determine readiness to assume that position and then a specific development plan would be prepared to ensure future readiness.

High Potential Employee. Any individual who:

1. Is listed as a successor for a senior management or executive role.
2. Has the aptitude and potential to ultimately rise to a senior-level position within the organization.

Since these employees are likely to be key players in the future success of the firm, significant efforts should be made to retain and develop these individuals.

FIGURE 8.13 **Talent and organization assessment.**

Consideration	Assessment	Comments
Succession Plan in Place?	Informal and Incomplete	Limited number of Ready Now (RN) successors in place. Need to accelerate development and acquisition of high potential leaders
Organization Structure Aligned with Strategy?	Legacy Structure not optimum for future execution.	Functional structure not optimized for evolving business. Resources need to be allocated away from traditional functional departments to matrix and cross-functional teams
Compensation and Incentive Plans Consistent with Strategic Objectives?	Incentive plan weights revenue growth vs. profitability and other Strategic Objectives	Consider revising compensation structure, including incentive
Talent on Board to Execute Strategy?	Significant Gaps	Current team is not capable of competing in the future/ executing strategy
Estimated % of High Performing (HP) Employees	66% rated Above Average or higher	Current performance ratings inflated. Estimated HP closer to 15%; not adequate for future execution and growth requirements
Estimated % of High Potential Employees	18%	A substantial % of team are long-term employees and have reached Highest Potential Level of Contribution
Ability to Attract New Talent	Difficult	Very competitive environment. Compensation structure is inconsistent with competitive environment and shifting requirements for talent
Talent Development/Acquisition Plan in Place?	NO. Informal at best	Little emphasis in past on evaluation, L&D, acquisition of talent

Indicated Actions	
❏ T&O Assessment	September 2023
❏ Develop succession plan	October 2023
❏ Talent Development and Acquisition Plan	November 2022
❏ Implement Plan	October 2023–June 2024

Talent and Organization by the Numbers   Introduced in Chapter 7, a simple dashboard of key performance and demographics can provide insights to the broader workforce, and identify opportunities and challenges (Figure 8.14). Typical KPIs and other measures include age of workforce, turnover, diversity, time in position, performance distributions, length of service, and education. This quantitative analysis can surface important issues and opportunities across the workforce. For example, in using this dashboard with clients over the last decade, the vulnerabilities of an aging employee base and potential worker shortages were foreshadowed.

Growth Opportunities and Investments   During the strategic planning process, it is important to identify and evaluate existing and potential growth opportunities and investments over the plan horizon (e.g., 5 years), including required investments, probabilities, and risk (Figure 8.15). This allows us to validate the current status and revenue potential for existing programs, and also to identify and consider new potential programs. Key characteristics to include:

- Opportunity description.
- Indicate annual revenue potential over the next 3–5 years.
- Indicate probability of achieving revenue in the plan horizon.
- Indicate risk level of opportunity (high, moderate, low).
- Indicate whether the revenue and investments are included in the current operating plan. If not, consideration must be given to "affordability" of this investment.

Identify Strategic Issues   Another effective tool in strategic analysis is to create a list of strategic issues the organization faces (Figure 8.16). Some of the strategic issues will arise from the analysis that were described earlier in this chapter. Other issues may be identified by executives, the board of directors, or investors.

Based on the strategic analysis, the team can turn to the development of a strategy and execution planning.

STRATEGY DEVELOPMENT

After reviewing and discussing the strategic analysis, we can begin to formulate a strategy, including strategic objectives (Figure 8.17). The strategy should be a succinct statement that describes our intended direction and plan for the business. Strategic objectives should identify major programs and initiatives to implement the strategy. The strategy should also include identification and evaluation of alternative strategies.

FIGURE 8.14 **Talent and organization by the numbers.** 🌐 **HCM was covered in more detail in Chapter 7.**

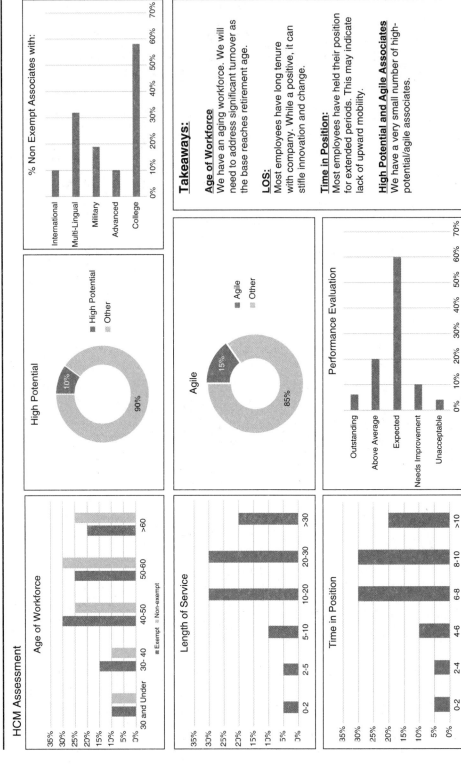

HCM Assessment

Age of Workforce
(Exempt / Non-exempt)
30 and Under, 30-40, 40-50, 50-60, >60

High Potential
High Potential 10%, Other 90%

% Non Exempt Associates with:
International, Multi-Lingual, Military, Advanced, College

Length of Service
0-2, 2-5, 5-10, 10-20, 20-30, >30

Agile
Agile 15%, Other 85%

Time in Position
0-2, 2-4, 4-6, 6-8, 8-10, >10

Performance Evaluation
Outstanding, Above Average, Expected, Needs Improvement, Unacceptable

Takeaways:

Age of Workforce
We have an aging workforce. We will need to address significant turnover as the base reaches retirement age.

LOS:
Most employees have long tenure with company. While a positive, it can stifle innovation and change.

Time in Position:
Most employees have held their position for extended periods. This may indicate lack of upward mobility.

High Potential and Agile Associates
We have a very small number of high-potential/agile associates.

FIGURE 8.15 **Growth opportunities and investments.**

SBU: Base

Description	Revenue Potential	Investment Required	Probability	Risk	Included in This Plan?	Included in current operating plan?
Develop Next Generation of NCD	$50m	$10m	60%	Moderate	Yes	
Expand International Market	$30m	$6m	50%	Moderate	Yes	
Acquire International Competitors	$30m	$50m	10%	Valuation and Execution Risk	No	

FIGURE 8.16 **Identifying strategic issues.**

Strategic Issues

- Our market leadership position is threatened by more technologically advanced products
- Our product offering is "hardware only" and does not present a total solution
- Absence of a clear executive succession plan
- We have serious gaps in Talent required to succeed
- Limited market position in Europe
- IT infrastructure is inadequate and will not support future expansion

Strategy Statement

A strategy statement is a brief declaration of the company's strategy. The statement should include the strategic goal (e.g., build market share) and a summary of how this will be accomplished. Examples:

- Build market share by accelerating investment in new products.
- Build market share by acquiring smaller market players.
- Expand market share by establishing a European distribution organization.
- Explore sale of nonstrategic SBU and redeploy proceeds in core business.
- Withdraw from market by selling or liquidating assets.

Strategic Objectives

The key strategic objectives that support the strategy should be identified. The objectives should also address important strategic issues identified earlier in the process (Figure 8.16). The strategic objectives should be integrated with the execution plan (key milestones) and the company's management by objectives (MBO) or objectives and key results (OKR) processes. All objectives should be supported by initiatives—the plans and activities that help to achieve the objective.

Strategic Objective Guidelines

- Clearly define strategic goal or objective.
- Selection consideration: What key programs and initiatives would we share with shareholders and employees in a brief and concise update?
- Convert the broad strategy into key initiatives.
- Identify specific, measurable, and time-based objectives.
- Generally, a company or SBU should identify six to eight strategic objectives.

FIGURE 8.17 **Strategy development.**

Strategy Development
SBU: Base

Business Unit Strategy:	Strategic Objectives
To regain market leadership by developing and introducing next generation of network control equipment and expanding to international markets	❏ Develop Next Gen NCE ❏ Expand International Market 　　❏ Sales and Service 　　❏ Manufacturing ❏ Develop redundancies in Supply Chain ❏ Develop T&O to enable market leadership

Possible Alternative Strategies:

Description	Reason Not Pursued
1. Acquire Company to Accelerate Technology	More effective to develop in-house
2. Sell to larger electronics firm	Less value created than primary strategy
3. Acquire European based firm to accelerate international expansions	More effective to expand

Consider Possible Alternative Strategies

Most strategy (and also operating) plans present a single scenario. That scenario was likely selected as the "optimal" among several alternative scenarios. For strategic plans, alternatives may include:

- Selling the business.
- Selling a segment or SBU.
- Accelerate implementation of strategy through acquisitions to obtain critical competencies and access to targeted market segments.
- Expand the service offering by acquiring related businesses or competencies.
- Narrow the focus to fewer market segments by divesting or exiting marginal or noncore businesses.
- Significant outsourcing, partnership, or joint venture opportunities.

In many cases, the primary scenario, or base case, may have been chosen without a comprehensive evaluation of other alternatives. A summary of strategic alternatives, illustrated in Figure 8.18, facilitates consideration of these alternate paths. For each scenario, we can project performance and value, consider advantages and challenges, and identify resource requirements and management actions.

FIGURE 8.18 **Summary of strategic alternatives.**

Strategic Alternatives
Recap

Alternative Strategies	Revenue 2026/ CAGR	Operating Income 2026 % Revenue	PV: Shareholder Value	Advantages	Risks and Challenges	Required Capital (Incremental)	Required Actions
1. Primary Strategy	$150m	15%	$225m	• Moderate risk • Maximizes Shareholder Value	• Headwinds • Execution Risk	$15m	• Accelerate Development • European Expansion
2. Acquisition of Technology Companies	$150m	10%	$180m	• Speed over in-house development	• Transaction Risk • Execution Risk	$30	• Identify Candidates • Assess M&A Readiness • Financing Flexibility
3. Sell to larger electronics firm			$150m	• High Equity Valuations • Strong M&A Environment • No Execution Risk	• Due diligence Process • Transaction Risk		• Due diligence readiness • Market Assessment
4. Acquire international competitors	$150m	10%	$190m			$0	• Assess Transaction Readiness • Engage Investment Banker

Critical Assumptions Risks and Upsides   Any plan, and especially strategic plans spanning three to five or more years, include a number of significant assumptions. Many times, these assumptions are implicit and have not been identified or evaluated. Critical assumptions should be identified and evaluated (Figure 8.19). This will facilitate a review and discussion about the appropriateness of each assumption and also highlights the presence of uncertainty in the plan. Once identified, these assumptions can be monitored over time. Key assumptions can then be modified to create upside or downside event scenarios. For each scenario, we can identify leading indicators, event trigger criteria, potential impact on plan, probability, expected value, and indicated management actions. For a more in-depth discussion on scenario planning, please refer to Chapter 13.

FIGURE 8.19 **Critical assumptions and risks.**

Critical Assumptions:
- Mild recession in 2023, followed by global economic expansion
- NextGen Product developed on time and favorable market reception
- Eurozone Expansion

Event Description	Leading Indicators	Event Trigger/ Criteria	Potential Impact Ann Rev. $m	Probability	Expected Value	Management Action
Upsides:						
No recession	Consumer Confidence Unemployment Rate	UR stays < 4%	+$5.0m	10%	.5m	(1) Monitor
Total Upsides			$+5.0m		.5m	
Downsides:						
Severe/Protracted Recession	Consumer Confidence Unemployment Rate	UR >4%	-$15.0m	30%	-4.5m	(1) Monitor (2) Develop Contingency Plan
New Product Delayed/ No performance gain	Project Milestones Performance Checkpoint	Delay	$-7.0	20%	-1.4m	(1) Monitor
Eurozone Expansion delayed/ lower share	Project Milestones	Delay	$-3.0	25%	$-.75m	(1) Monitor
Total Downsides			$-25.0m		$-6.65m	
Net U/D			$-20.0m		$-6.15m	

Projected Financial Performance

Projected financial performance is an important ingredient in developing and evaluating a strategic plan. An illustration of a summary of projected financial performance is presented in Figure 8.20. The content in the summary is consistent with the historical summary earlier in the chapter. This summary includes revenue and growth, profitability, invested capital to support the business,

FIGURE 8.20 **Projected financial performance.**

Business Unit: Company

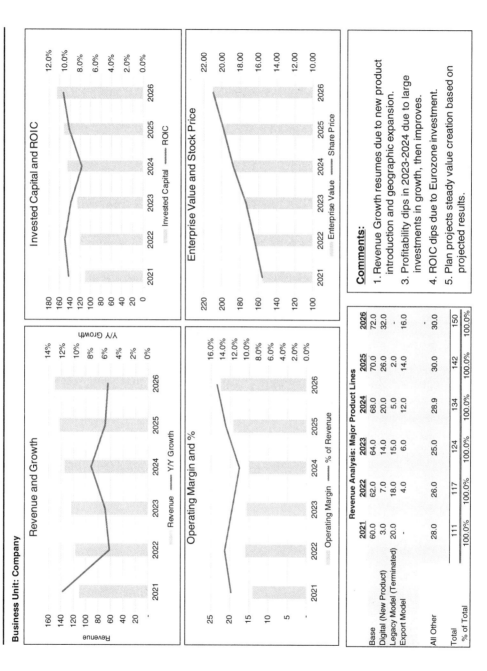

Revenue and Growth

— Revenue — Y/Y Growth

Operating Margin and %

— Operating Margin — % of Revenue

Invested Capital and ROIC

— Invested Capital — ROIC

Enterprise Value and Stock Price

— Enterprise Value — Share Price

Revenue Analysis: Major Product Lines

	2021	2022	2023	2024	2025	2026
Base	60.0	62.0	64.0	68.0	70.0	72.0
Digital (New Product)	3.0	7.0	14.0	20.0	26.0	32.0
Legacy Model (Terminated)	20.0	18.0	15.0	5.0	2.0	-
Export Model	-	4.0	6.0	12.0	14.0	16.0
All Other	28.0	26.0	25.0	28.9	30.0	30.0
Total	111	117	124	134	142	150
% of Total	100.0%	100.0%	100.0%	100.0%	100.0%	100.0%

Comments:

1. Revenue Growth resumes due to new product introduction and geographic expansion.
2. Profitability dips in 2023-2024 due to large investments in growth, then improves.
3. ROIC dips due to Eurozone investment.
4. Plan projects steady value creation based on projected results.

171

ROIC, and implied valuation based on the projections. The summary would be based on a comprehensive projection model including a multi-year P&L, Balance Sheet, and cash flow statements. Please refer to the "long-range planning" discussion in Chapter 21.

EXECUTION PLANNING

Even a great strategy that is not supported by an execution plan is unlikely to succeed. Developing a series of roadmaps supporting the plan is essential. Key product development projects must be planned and integrated with product launch, manufacturing plans, and revenue projections. Geographic expansion will involve support across many functions, including sales, marketing, legal, finance, and others. Other initiatives such as HCM and enterprise software implementation must also be planned and integrated with other areas of the plan. A summary of the execution plan is illustrated in Figure 8.21 and provides a high-level summary of each key initiative. This summary should be supported by detailed project plans for each initiative.

Due to the importance of human capital in executing the strategy, it may be helpful to provide a summary of the headcount plan, illustrated in Figure 8.22.

EARNING A SEAT AT THE STRATEGY TABLE

A common frustration for finance professionals is that they "do not have a seat at the table," that is, they are not invited to participate in strategic discussions. At one conference, I heard a speaker respond to a question on this issue by advising "You must *demand* a seat at the table." This approach is unlikely to have the desired result. A better way is to demonstrate that you can add value to the process by developing a business mindset, contributing to strategic analysis, and developing robust projections models to support strategic decisions.

Develop a Business Mindset

In order to be included in business and strategic discussions, finance professionals must be perceived as trusted advisors that have an interest and understanding of the company's business. We can demonstrate an interest and acumen in the business by investing time in reviewing market studies and analyst reports and by analyzing competitors and customers. Additional suggestions on developing a business mindset and becoming a "financial business partner" were included in Chapter 3.

FIGURE 8.21 **Strategic plan execution summary.**

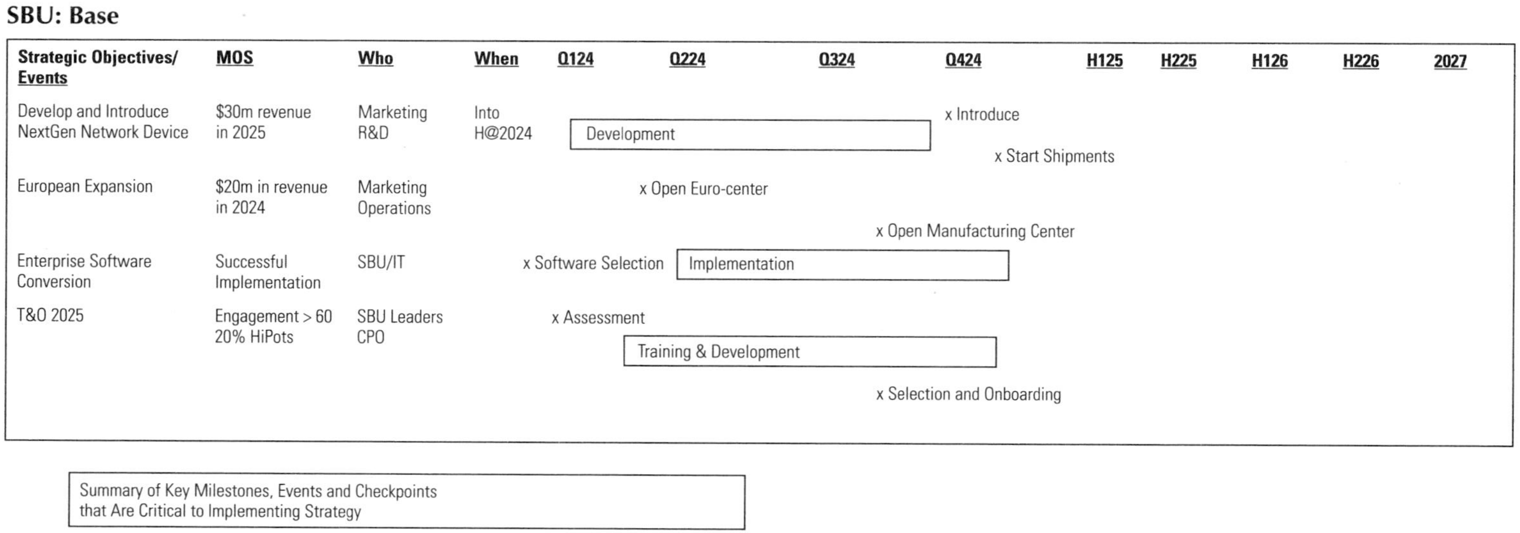

SBU: Base

Strategic Objectives/ Events	MOS	Who	When	Q124	Q224	Q324	Q424	H125	H225	H126	H226	2027
Develop and Introduce NextGen Network Device	$30m revenue in 2025	Marketing R&D	Into H@2024	Development			x Introduce	x Start Shipments				
European Expansion	$20m in revenue in 2024	Marketing Operations			x Open Euro-center		x Open Manufacturing Center					
Enterprise Software Conversion	Successful Implementation	SBU/IT		x Software Selection	Implementation							
T&O 2025	Engagement > 60 20% HiPots	SBU Leaders CPO		x Assessment	Training & Development		x Selection and Onboarding					

Summary of Key Milestones, Events and Checkpoints that Are Critical to Implementing Strategy

173

FIGURE 8.22 **Headcount analysis.**

Strategic Plan
Headcount Analysis

	History									Increase (Decrease)		Notes
	2021	2022	2023	2024	2025	2026	2027	2028	2029	2021-2024	2024-2029	
Leadership	2	2	3	4	4	4	4	4	4	2	0	
SBU Management	12	12	12	12	12	12	12	12	12	0	0	
R&D	14	15	16	17	18	18	19	20	21	3	4	
G&A	22	22	22	22	22	22	22	22	22	0	0	
Manufacturing	62	62	62	62	62	62	62	62	62	0	0	
Selling		7	12	18	19	19	20	21	22	18	4	
New SBU							8	12	22	0	22	
Admin	3	3	3	4	4	4	4	4	4	1	0	
All other	5	6	6	6	6	6	6	6	6	1	0	
Total Practice Area	120	129	136	145	147	147	157	163	175	25	30	
Y/Y Growth		7.5%	5.4%	6.6%	1.4%	0.0%	6.8%	3.8%	7.4%			
Revenue ($000)	20,000	22,000	23,500	25,000	26,000	26,000	27,500	28,750	31,000	5,000	6,000	
Y/Y Growth		10.0%	6.8%	6.4%	4.0%	0.0%	5.8%	4.5%	7.8%			
Revenue per Employee	166,667	170,543	172,794	172,414	176,871	176,871	175,159	176,380	177,143			

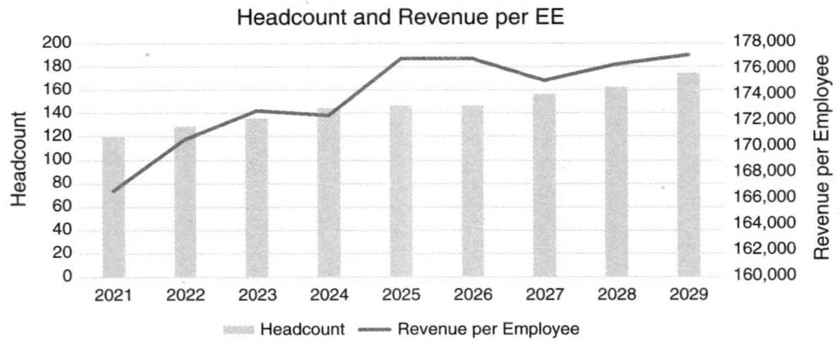

Summary:
Headcount Growth primarily driven by new SBU

Headcount and Revenue per EE

Legend: Headcount — Revenue per Employee

174

I have observed many finance professionals in strategic meetings over the years. Some FBPs have a tendency to focus only on the financial aspects, in particular, on the minor inconsistencies or even math errors. These can be addressed off-line, so that we can demonstrate that we understand the business and can contribute to the analysis and strategy development. We should focus more on the big picture and overall objectives and performance topics.

Prepare and Present Strategic Analysis

Even if not invited, we can contribute by preparing the content of strategic analysis and presenting to those involved in developing strategy. In addition to making a direct contribution to the strategic plan, this will undoubtedly demonstrate both an interest and ability to contribute to the process (which was illustrated in this chapter), include:

- Key analysis
- Historical performance analysis.
- Revenue analysis.
- Portfolio analysis.
- Talent and organization analysis.
- SWOT analysis.
- Benchmark performance of customers and competitors.
- Valuation analysis.

Develop Strategic Financial Projections and Analysis

Finance should develop projections models that facilitate strategic planning. The models should be comprehensive and identify and facilitate testing of critical assumptions. They should be robust so that we can process revised estimates and scenarios. Our skills in analyzing revenue projections can be used to provide a critical evaluation of revenue growth. Our projections models should include all major financial statements so that we can project resource requirements, cash flow, financing requirements, key ratios (e.g., ROIC), and implied value creation.

Incorporate Progress on Strategic Issues and Objectives in Performance Reporting

Finance can provide value by monitoring progress on the execution plan and underlying assumptions of the strategy plan. This will also result in participation of strategic matters on an ongoing basis.

SUMMARY

FP&A and other finance professionals have the potential to add value to strategic analysis, discussion, development, and execution. In fact, a great deal of the strategic analysis could be facilitated by finance. Finance must be involved with the development and evaluation of strategy to ensure that projected performance is consistent with the strategy.

## 9

The Role of Finance in Supporting Growth

Finance professionals are often viewed as impediments rather than contributors to growth. We often stand in the way with heavy process requirements and high-return hurdles. We have been trained to be risk averse and protect against the downside. While we should continue to be good stewards of the company's treasury and manage risks, we can actively contribute to efforts to grow revenue in support of value creation.

THE IMPORTANCE OF GROWTH

Revenue growth is the most important of the six drivers of long-term value creation, which is shown in Figure 9.1. While other drivers such as operating and capital effectiveness and cost of capital are important, there are practical limits and diminishing marginal returns for these drivers. Investors and owners place a premium on revenue growth and value those businesses at premiums over slower growth counterparts.

Revenue growth can also be projected and analyzed in terms of performance drivers. We can decompose expected or actual revenue growth into these drivers. While the drivers may vary from industry to industry, Figure 9.2 is a general representation for most companies. Drivers of organic revenue growth include:

- Introduction of new products and services.
- Retention and growth of existing customers.
- Acquisition of new customers.
- Develop new channels/markets.
- Generate market growth and competitive environment.

177

FIGURE 9.1 **Value drivers framework.**

Focus on Drivers of Long-Term Value:
Then Link Value & Value Drivers to Business Processes & Activities

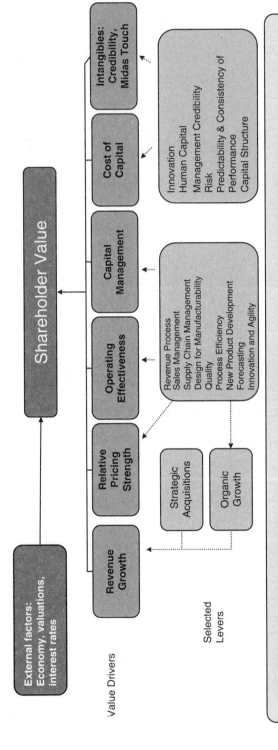

Value Drivers

External factors:
Economy; valuations, interest rates

Shareholder Value

| Revenue Growth | Relative Pricing Strength | Operating Effectiveness | Capital Management | Cost of Capital | Intangibles: Credibility, Midas Touch |

Selected Levers

Strategic Acquisitions

Organic Growth

Revenue Process
Sales Management
Supply Chain Management
Design for Manufacturability
Quality
Process Efficiency
New Product Development
Forecasting
Innovation and Agility

Innovation
Human Capital
Management Credibility
Risk
Predictability & Consistency of Performance
Capital Structure

Building long-term shareholder value is accomplished by highly motivated & competent employees satisfying customer needs & expectations

FIGURE 9.2 **Revenue growth drivers.**

Link Value & Value Drivers to Business Processes & Activities

Drill Down: Revenue Growth

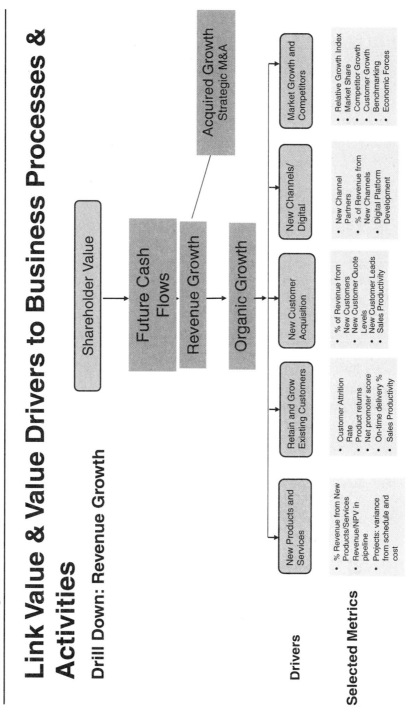

Drivers

Selected Metrics

Shareholder Value

Future Cash Flows

Revenue Growth

Acquired Growth
Strategic M&A

Organic Growth

New Products and Services
- % Revenue from New Products/Services
- Revenue/NPV in pipeline
- Projects: variance from schedule and cost

Retain and Grow Existing Customers
- Customer Attrition Rate
- Product returns
- Net promoter score
- On-time delivery %
- Sales Productivity

New Customer Acquisition
- % of Revenue from New Customers
- New Customer Quote Levels
- New Customer Leads
- Sales Productivity

New Channels/ Digital
- New Channel Partners
- % of Revenue from New Channels
- Digital Platform Development

Market Growth and Competitors
- Relative Growth Index
- Market Share
- Competitor Growth
- Customer Growth
- Benchmarking
- Economic Forces

We can analyze historical revenue growth using this framework, quantifying the contribution of each driver to overall growth. We can also drill down another layer to identify the processes and business activities (and performance measures) that impact that driver. For example, we can link the outcome for retaining and growing existing customers to key activities and measures, including quality, delivery performance, and overall customer satisfaction.

For revenue projections, we can estimate the expected contribution from each driver. This is a great way to validate and test the overall revenue growth rate. Each of these drivers can then be linked, conceptually if not mathematically, to levels of activity required to achieve that driver contribution to growth.

ANALYSIS OF REVENUE TRENDS AND GROWTH PROJECTIONS

It is imperative for finance to participate in the development and review of future revenue projections. In many organizations, finance directs more attention to costs and expenses than to revenues. Optimistic (low probability of occurring) revenue projections can actually limit growth by providing a false picture of the growth potential of the business, delaying necessary actions and investments that will ultimately lead to growth. A comprehensive approach to developing or evaluating revenue projections should include the following:

Review historical trends. Are the projections consistent with historical trends?

Extrapolate Historical Trends. What level of revenue is projected by simply extrapolating recent trends? What factors explain the difference from projected revenues?

Consider Product Life Cycles. All products and businesses progress through a product life cycle, eventually leading to a decline in revenue. Is this reflected in our projections?

Evaluate New Product Pipeline. What revenues can be expected from products currently under development? Are the projects on schedule?

Consider Order Funnels. Do levels of leads, requests for quotations (RFQs), quotes, and so on support the revenue projections?

Monitor Competitor and Customer Performance. Are projections consistent with those of competitors and customers? Why or why not?

Monitor Economic Conditions. What macro-economic assumptions are reflected in the projections? Recession versus economic growth? Inflation and interest rate environment? Do these assumptions consider regional and international variations?

Chapter 22 will be devoted entirely to analyzing and reporting revenue growth. The revenue growth dashboard from that chapter is also presented here in Figure 9.3 for consideration. The dashboard includes both historical (lagging) measures of revenue growth along with leading indicators, including delivery performance and status of new products.

FIGURE 9.3 **Revenue growth dashboard.** 🔲

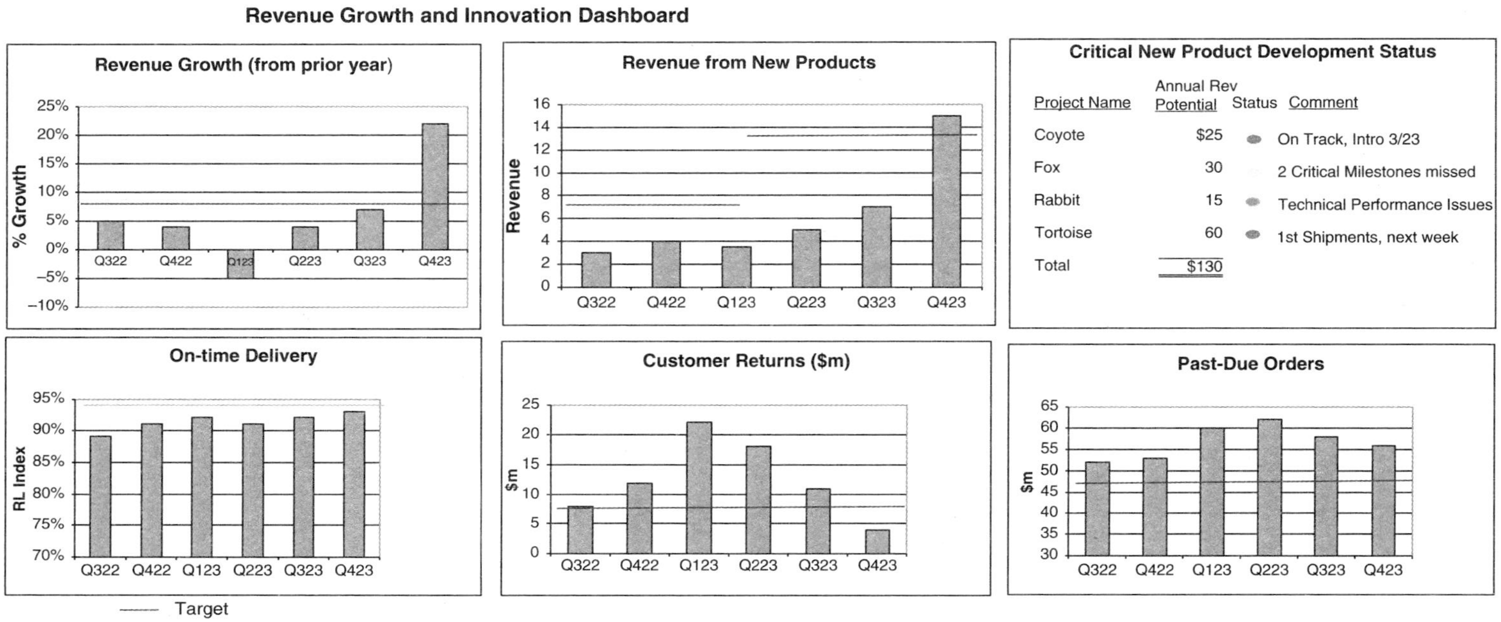

Revenue Growth and Innovation Dashboard

Critical New Product Development Status

Project Name	Annual Rev Potential	Status	Comment
Coyote	$25	●	On Track, Intro 3/23
Fox	30	●	2 Critical Milestones missed
Rabbit	15	●	Technical Performance Issues
Tortoise	60	●	1st Shipments, next week
Total	$130		

Finance should also review major components of revenues as illustrated in Figure 9.4. This analysis presents revenue by geography, type, recurring or not, and by major strategic business unit (SBU). Often, additional opportunities may be recognized by reflecting on the analysis. For example, is there an opportunity to increase relatively low software and service components of the business?

The KPIs and dashboards should be tailored to each individual organization and situation, but generally should reflect the key revenue drivers discussed in the beginning of this chapter: new product introductions, retention and growth of existing customers, acquisition of new customers, development of new channels and M&As. KPIs should be predictive in nature, allowing a present snapshot of current activity, ultimately resulting in revenue gains.

CONTRIBUTING TO STRATEGIC ANALYSIS AND PLANNING

An effective strategic planning process can identify and evaluate opportunities for growth. Finance can contribute by ensuring that a strategic plan process is in place and by directly participating in that process. Specifically, contributing to the following analyses:

- Historical revenue and trends.
- Evaluation of growth opportunities and investments.
- Portfolio analysis.
- Benchmark competitors and customers.
- Evaluation of critical assumptions.
- Develop and review projections.
- Encourage alternative strategies and scenarios.

Strategic analysis and planning was the focus of Chapter 8.

Competitor Summary

Purpose: An essential element of strategic planning is to analyze external information on competitors, customers, and suppliers. In addition, by researching and analyzing competitors and other market players, we introduce information and perspectives from outside the company. Figure 8.7 identifies key competitors and provides a summary of key attributes, including size, performance, ownership, and strategy. Sources of information include:

FIGURE 9.4 **Revenue analysis.**

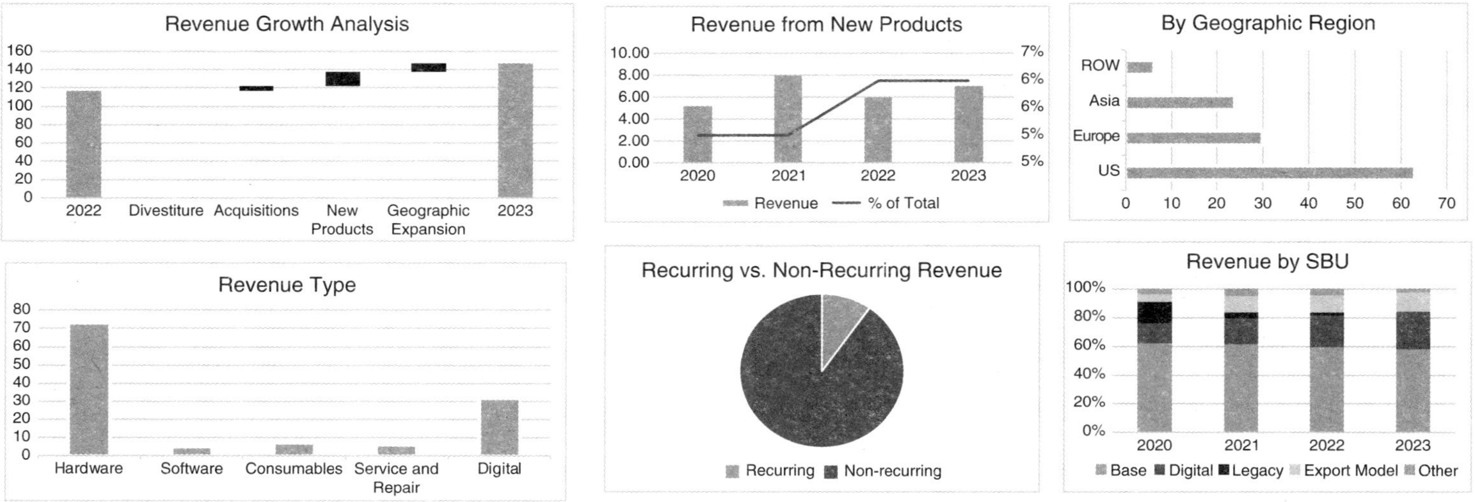

Public Companies: Securities and Exchange Commission (SEC) forms 10k, proxy, and investor relations materials available on the company's website. Consider preparing a comprehensive competitor analysis that will be illustrated in Chapter 10.

Private Companies: Since private companies are not required to disclose financial performance and other information to shareholders, this information must be obtained from other sources or estimated. Provide your best estimate/understanding of their performance and strategy based on information available or based on your observations from their actions in the market. In some cases, financial information may be found in competitive bid disclosures, government filings, debt registration, and other sources.

In some cases, there may be a large number of small competitors that are too numerous to list. In this case, the competitors can be described as group, for example: "We compete against single-shingle or small firms that focus on a particular state or region." These firms typically have an annual revenue of approximately $1.5 million.

A comprehensive analysis of competitors and customers will be covered in detail in Chapter 10, "The External View."

SUPPORTING GROWTH INITIATIVES AND PROCESSES

Finance professionals can support various growth initiatives and processes across the enterprise, including business development, proposals, and new product developments.

Business and Corporate Development (BD)

Many companies have an executive charged with identifying and exploring business opportunities outside the company's traditional customer set. These may include licensing agreements, joint ventures, minority investors, venture funds, and other opportunities to partner with other companies. Finance should view BD as a client or business partner, and provide support in analyzing and evaluating these opportunities.

Bid and Proposal

Many companies provide products, services, software, software as a service, and other services over an extended period of time. These long-term arrangements are covered by contracts generally awarded after an extended procurement process directed by the customer. Since the contracts are typically significant and can span several years, they can have a material effect on the future business performance. The length of these programs also increases performance and financial risk over time. Finance involvement should include:

- Develop a review and approval process commensurate with the size and risk of the opportunities.
- Develop projection models that provide reasonable estimates of the opportunity at hand (Table 9.1).
- Ensure that program margins and returns are consistent with targets established to support overall business objectives.
- Develop and review financial projections based on opportunity under consideration.
- Identify risks and ensure consistency with company's limits on risk tolerance (e.g., fixed price contact, limits on liabilities, etc.).
- Participate in negotiation of pricing, cost, liability, and other contract provisions. Ensure provisions are included to cover future cost increases (inflation).
- Report on profitability and returns of existing programs to hold managers accountable and to incorporate any changes to limit systemic variances into the review process (Table 9.2).

One of the most useful process tools is to review actual project performance compared to the estimates in the proposal as illustrated in Table 9.2. This can be done for both individual projects as well as in summary. This analysis provides useful feedback to estimators, delivery managers, and executives.

It can also be helpful to look at the performance across all projects. The graph in Figure 9.5 clearly indicates a downside bias since most projects come in under projected margins. The root causes of this failure to achieve target margins should be identified and corrected. Often, systemic process problems are identified, for example, consistently underestimating time requirements, invalid cost assumptions, poor management of scope creep, optimistic bias, and so on. Once identified, the team can address these deficiencies, improving the process and project margins.

Table 9.3 presents a listing of all significant programs compared to estimated performance and identifies the root cause of variances. In this example, certain patterns may be observed. Are many of the underperforming projects managed or proposed by the same individual or team? Do certain project types tend to overrun costs? What process changes are indicated by these findings?

TABLE 9.1 **Proposal estimate.**

Bel Air Consulting
Proposal Estimate

				Rates	Cost	Billing
Partner	RJA	**Project Summary:** FP&A: Improve forecast process, including adoption of Extended Business Outlook		Partner	400.00	800.00
Proposal Manager	MTV			Director	200.00	500.00
Engagement Manager	ED			Staff	100.00	250.00
Client	MNO, Inc			Fringe	25%	
				Overhead	15%	

Cost Estimate

	Phase 1	Phase 2	Phase 3	Phase 4	Total	% Total	Target Mix	
Estimated Labor								
Partner	15.0	12.0	12.0	20.0	59.0	5.4%	5%	
Director	25.0	75.0	50.0	50.0	200.0	18.2%	25%	
Staff	40.0	300.0	300.0	200.0	840.0	76.4%	70%	
Total	80.0	387.0	362.0	270.0	1099.0	100.0%	100%	
Labor Costs								
Partner	6,000	4,800	4,800	8,000	23,600	16.0%		
Director	5,000	15,000	10,000	10,000	40,000	27.1%		
Staff	4,000	30,000	30,000	20,000	84,000	56.9%		
Total	15,000	49,800	44,800	38,000	147,600	100.0%		
Labor	15,000	49,800	44,800	38,000	147,600	62.9%		
Fringe	3,750	12,450	11,200	9,500	36,900	15.7%		
Overhead	2,250	7,470	6,720	5,700	22,140	9.4%		
T&E	5,000	6,000	6,000	8,000	25,000	10.7%		
Outside Costs			3,000		3,000	1.3%		Software Licenses
Total Costs	26,000	75,720	71,720	61,200	234,640	100%		

Revenue Estimate

	Phase 1	Phase 2	Phase 3	Phase 4	Total	% Total		
Partner	12,000	9,600	9,600	16,000	47,200	13.2%		
Director	12,500	37,500	25,000	25,000	100,000	28.0%		
Staff	10,000	75,000	75,000	50,000	210,000	58.8%		
Total	34,500	122,100	109,600	91,000	357,200	100.0%		

Project Margin Summary

	Phase 1	Phase 2	Phase 3	Phase 4	Total			
Revenue @ Rates	34,500	122,100	109,600	91,000	357,200			
Discount					-			
Net Revenues	34,500	122,100	109,600	91,000	357,200			
Costs								
Labor and Fringes	18,750	62,250	56,000	47,500	184,500			
Overhead	2,250	7,470	6,720	5,700	22,140			
Other	5,000	6,000	9,000	8,000	28,000			
Total	26,000	75,720	71,720	61,200	234,640			
Project Margin	8,500	46,380	37,880	29,800	122,560		**Target**	
%	24.6%	38.0%	34.6%	32.7%	34.3%		**35.0%**	

TABLE 9.2 **Post-review B&P estimate.**

Bel Air Consulting
Proposal Estimate

						Rates	Cost	Billing
Partner	RJA	**Project Summary:** FP&A: Improve forecast process,				Partner	400.00	800.00
Proposal Manager	RCG	including adoption of Extended Business Outlook				Director	200.00	500.00
Engagement Manager	ED					Staff	100.00	250.00
Client	MNO, Inc					Fringe	25%	
						Overhead	15%	

Project Analysis

	Proposal	Actual	Variance	Comments
Estimated Labor				
Partner	59.0	60.0	−1.0	
Director	200.0	240.0	−40.0	More director time due to staff inexperience, scope change
Staff	840.0	865.0	−25.0	Less experienced staff utilized, resulting in additional time
Total	1,099.0	1,165.0	(66.0)	
Labor Costs				
Partner	23,600	24,000	(400)	See above
Director	40,000	48,000	(8,000)	
Staff	84,000	86,500	(2,500)	
Total	147,600	158,500	(10,900)	
Labor	147,600	158,500	(10,900)	
Fringe	36,900	39,625	(2,725)	
Overhead	22,140	23,775	(1,635)	
T&E	25,000	21,377	3,623	Less on-site contact required @ subsidiaries
Outside Costs	3,000	4,200	(1,200)	
Total Costs	234,640	247,477	(12,837)	
Revenue				
Partner	47,200	47,200	-	
Director	100,000	105,000	5,000	Customer agreed to scope change notice $5,000
Staff	210,000	210,000	-	
Total	357,200	362,200	5,000	
Project Margin Summary				
Revenue @ Rates	357,200	362,200	5,000	
Discount		-1000	(1,000)	Partial absorption scope change
Net Revenues	357,200	361,200	4,000	
Costs				
Labor and Fringes	184,500	198,125	(13,625)	Staff experience, scope creep
Overhead	22,140	23,775	(1,635)	
Other	28,000	25,577	2,423	
Total	234,640	247,477	(12,837)	
Project Margin	122,560	113,723	(8,837)	
%	34.3%	31.5%	−2.8%	

FIGURE 9.5 **Program margin variance.**

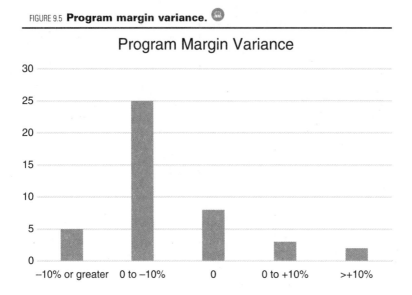

New Product Development (NPD)

The introduction of new products is always an important contributor to revenue growth. The investment in R&D and other efforts to develop new products are a substantial cost, often exceeding 10% of total revenues. Finance can add value to improve the effectiveness of NPD in several ways.

Disciplined evaluation and approval process. Although most R&D efforts are expensed when incurred, the costs of research and developing new products should be viewed as an investment and evaluated as such. The product development may include several years of development activity and cost followed by revenue and profit streams over an extended period of time.

The evaluation process should include an analysis of the economic characteristics of the investment. Evaluation techniques include internal rate of return (IRR), net present value (NPV), and payback. This will require projected costs of development, introduction, and manufacturing as well as projected future revenue and cash flows. All significant assumptions should be called out explicitly in the proposal. Since all product development and resultant revenues extend for several years, scenario planning should be added to the proposal review. The economic evaluation of investments will be covered in detail in Chapters 28 and 29. Scenario planning will be covered in Chapter 13.

A key value-added dimension of new product evaluation is to require a realistic project schedule as part of the approval process, including key checkpoints and feasibility checks. A project schedule will allow management to monitor progress and assess whether the project is on schedule both from a

TABLE 9.3 **Project margin summary.**

Project Description	Client	Delivery Manager	Proposal Manager	Revenue			Project Costs			Project Margins			Project Margin %			Notes
				Actual	Proposal	Variance	Actual	Proposal	Variance	Actual	Proposal	Variance	Actual	Proposal	Variance	
Forecasting	ABC Inc.	LSA	ERA	275,221	280,000	(4,779)	184,398	184,800	402	90,823	95,200	(4,377)	33.0%	34.0%	–1.0%	
BPM	NPO	RJA	TMT	127,500	125,000	2,500	86,700	82,500	(4,200)	40,800	42,500	(1,700)	32.0%	34.0%	–2.0%	Mid-year inflation adjustment not proposed
FP&A Transformation	AirPost	KRV	RCG	481,000	480,000	1,000	329,485	316,800	(12,685)	151,515	163,200	(11,685)	31.5%	34.0%	–2.5%	Mid-year inflation adjustment not proposed
Forecasting	MNO, Inc	EAD	RCG	361,200	357,200	4,000	247,477	234,640	(12,837)	113,723	122,560	(8,837)	31.5%	34.3%	–2.8%	Inexperienced staff, scope creep
O&D	Genfry	KAV	RCG	146,000	145,800	200	109,500	96,228	(13,272)	36,500	49,572	(13,072)	25.0%	34.0%	–9.0%	Underestimated complexity
Forecasting	Roberts Trucking	LSA	ERA	202,000	200,000	2,000	127,260	132,000	4,740	74,740	68,000	6,740	37.0%	34.0%	3.0%	Client contribution exceeded expectations
BPM	DJH	DAD	BJT	187,000	185,000	2,000	132,770	129,500	(3,270)	54,230	55,500	(1,270)	29.0%	30.0%	–1.0%	
FP&A Transformation	Zpharma	ROA	SVA	75,000	75,000	-	48,700	49,500	800	26,300	25,500	800	35.1%	34.0%	1.1%	
Forecasting	Tomasso	GRS	RCG	135,000	150,000	(15,000)	108,000	99,000	(9,000)	27,000	51,000	(24,000)	20.0%	34.0%	–14.0%	Client obstacles, project suspended
Management Reporting	ACS	MGA	JFA	162,500	162,500	-	107,250	107,250	-	55,250	55,250	-	34.0%	34.0%		

time and cost standpoint. If the success of a particular development hinges on achieving certain performance thresholds, these should be called out explicitly in the project proposal. If actual performance fails to achieve these thresholds, the project should be reevaluated.

Monitoring and tracking progress on cost and key project milestones, monitoring critical assumptions, and reviewing performance thresholds provide management with options to alter the development project, reevaluate revenue projections, or even terminate the project. By recognizing that a project will not meet expectations, management can cause the project to "fail fast," allowing the organization to redeploy human and financial resources to other projects.

Other Growth Opportunities

Other growth opportunities may include geographic expansion, offering products and services through other channels, and serving markets beyond those currently served. Finance can support the analysis and evaluation of each of these opportunities.

CONTRIBUTING TO A SUCCESSFUL MERGER AND ACQUISITION PROGRAM

Finance professionals can make a significant contribution to a company's merger and acquisition (M&A) efforts. Finance departments are often called on to participate in the valuation of prospective M&A targets. We can also participate in the development of a robust M&A process, including ensuring strategic fit, evaluation, valuation, due diligence, synergy and integration planning, and integration execution.

M&A Process

Many mergers and acquisitions fail to achieve objectives for growth and value creation. This often results in a write-off or write-down of acquisition assets arising from the transaction and a decrease in the market value of the firm. Yet many firms have successful M&A programs. In my experience, the success is generally attributable to an effective M&A process, as illustrated in Figure 9.6.

Strategy. The first component of a successful process is the development of a corporate strategy with well-defined strategic objectives. This strategy will allow the firm to envision the role that M&A may play in achieving these objectives. Strategic planning was covered in detail in Chapter 8.

FIGURE 9.6 **M&A process overview.**

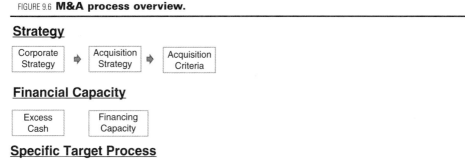

Strategy

Corporate Strategy ➡ Acquisition Strategy ➡ Acquisition Criteria

Financial Capacity

Excess Cash   Financing Capacity

Specific Target Process

Preliminary Evaluation ➡ Due Diligence ➡ Integration Planning ➡ Valuation Analysis ➡ Negotiation ➡ Transaction ➡ Post-Merger Integration ➡ Monitor

Financial Capacity. The firm should determine the level of financing flexibility available to support acquisitions. Financial resources are required for the purchase price, closing costs, and the cost to integrate and achieve synergies. The finance team should be proactive in identifying potential sources of capital, including excess cash, borrowing capacity, future cash generation, and potential equity issuance, which is illustrated in Figure 9.7. This analysis provides boundaries for one or more acquisitions. Financing conditions tend to change over time, with occasional periods where opportunities to raise capital are limited. This analysis should also consider interest rates and valuation levels.

Specific Target Process. The firm can then develop a strategy for M&A and develop specific acquisition criteria, as illustrated in Figure 9.8. This creates

FIGURE 9.7 **Financial capacity.**

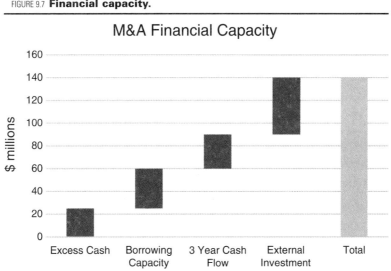

FIGURE 9.8 **Acquisition criteria.**

Objective: Supplement and accelerate organic growth
- Target range: $50.0-75.0m
- Targeting 30% of our Overall Growth

Acquisition Candidates:
- Should be consistent with stated strategy and strategic objectives
- Serve network or cloud markets
- Potential objectives:
  - Increase market share
  - Acquire competencies/technology/access
  - Enter faster growing market segments
  - Acquire Management Talent
  - Geographic Expansion
- Sustainable Growth Potential (≥ 15%)
- Well managed, (on track to be) profitable enterprises
  - EBITDA ≥ 15%

alignment and focus on the types of acquisitions the company would pursue in terms of size, valuation, market, and other attributes. Just as important, it records on paper the specific criteria, reducing the potential for opportunistic transactions that fall outside our strategy and criteria for size, profitability, and so on. Many of these "over-the-transom" opportunities are presented by investment bankers and sellers who can cause the company to drift away from strategic objectives.

Due Diligence. Historically, due diligence had been focused on confirming assets and unearthing potential surprises. In successful M&A programs, due diligence goes beyond this to validate earnings and cash flow projections that justify the valuation levels in the transaction. This includes confirming key value drivers and synergies.

Due Diligence
- Standalone value confirmation.
- Customer, pipeline, and revenue analysis.
- Competitive analysis.
- Business development and product pipeline.
- Confirm strategic fit.
- Management and human capital.
- Supply chain assessment.

Risk Management and Avoidance
- Validate financials and confirm asset valuation.
- Litigation and contingencies.

- Regulatory compliance.
- Technology and intellectual property.
- Information technology environment.
- Antitrust considerations.
- Environment exposure.
- Tax issues.
- Commitments and costs.
- Related-party transactions.

Synergies. Generally, the business case and financial justification for the acquisition includes an expectation of significant synergies. The intent is that the value of the combined entities would be greater than the sum of the parts (the two separate entities). Finance should work closely with other executives to validate the estimated synergies. Too often, synergies are estimated at a high level, without appropriate analysis. This tends to lead to more aggressive expectations of synergies and the absence of a specific plan to implement these potential synergies. The synergies are then unlikely to be realized. Examples of synergies include:

Revenue. The combined organization may increase revenues as a result of complementary distribution channels, customer access, new products, and other opportunities to leverage collective strengths.

Cost Savings. A combination of two companies generally enables cost reductions by eliminating redundant functions. For example, the combined firm will not need two CEOs, CFOs, and certain administrative functions such as a board of directors, accounting, and procurement. The combination may also result in combining sales and service functions resulting in elimination of redundant staff and facilities. One of the entities may have better business processes that can be applied to the other, including operational planning, performance management, supply chain management, and human capital management that ultimately result in improved performance. The combination can also achieve economies of scale by aggregating the two enterprises, for example, increasing the relative bargaining position with suppliers.

Integration Planning. I am always amused at the celebration of "closing" the acquisition transaction. While sellers and investment bankers may be done, the work is only beginning for those responsible for integrating the two firms and delivering the expected deal value. Finance can play a big role in developing integration roadmaps and action plans during the negotiation and due diligence phases as well as monitoring execution progress. Integration efforts often include the sales organization, R&D, financial systems and reporting, and human capital and benefits.

Resource Planning. Before embarking on acquisitions, the firm should assess the availability of key resources, including financial and human capital. The analysis of financial capacity for acquisitions was addressed earlier in the chapter. Of equal importance to the financial capacity is the organization's ability to execute across all stages of the acquisition process:

- Do we have talent with the experience and bandwidth to devote substantial time to this effort?
- Who will be included in the process to identify, evaluate, and value potential candidates?
- Do functional areas such as tax, treasury, accounting, HCM, and legal have the capability to perform due diligence, synergy, and integration planning, and ultimately, execution?
- Do we have business processes and enterprise technology systems to facilitate the combination of the firms?

M&A Valuation

M&A valuation includes two components. The first is the value of the target on a "standalone" basis. That is, what is the value of the projected performance of the company if it is not acquired. The second component is the value of expected synergies that will arise from the combination.

Standalone value will be addressed in detail in Chapter 30. The valuation analysis should include both discounted cash flow and comparable pricing analysis. In estimating value, a number of critical assumptions are required. Synergy value is the present value of cash flows arising from incremental revenues and lower costs. Finance can add substantial value by directly linking performance expectations and value. Valuations fluctuate greatly over time due to economic conditions, interest rates, stock market gyrations, and other factors. Special care should be taken during periods of "frothy" valuations; while the price may be supported based on market multiples, it may be difficult to earn a return on the capital invested to purchase the firm.

The economics of M&A will be covered in detail in Chapter 31.

SUMMARY

FP&A and other finance professionals have the potential to contribute to the growth of the organization in several ways. Key areas of contribution include analysis and evaluation of revenue trends and projections, strategic planning, evaluation of growth investments, new business proposals, and M&A. These areas are among the most important opportunities to partner with other business executives in driving performance and value.

10

The External View:
Markets, Competitors,
and Economic and
Geopolitical Forces

Traditionally, finance and FP&A have focused on the internal workings of the enterprise, including revenue, cost of revenue and expenses, headcount, manufacturing, receivables, inventory, and similar components of financial performance. However, the greatest drivers, threats, and opportunities typically arise outside the enterprise. These include competitive and market forces, government regulation, geopolitical trends and events, technological advances, economic factors such as inflation and monetary policy, and many others. Finance must monitor external forces and trends to understand the effect on the organization and monitor future potential impacts. We can also add value by providing analysis of competitors, suppliers, customers, and other relevant players. In Chapter 1, a space shuttle cockpit instrument panel was used to illustrate key principles of FP&A. One of the five key features was to "provide insight into external factors and environment."

Key Features from Cockpit Instrument Panel

1. Real-Time and Predictive Insights.
2. High Visual Impact.
3. Focus on the Important Measures.
4. ***Provides Insight into External Factors and Environment.***
5. Combine with Observation, Experience, and Intuition.

The military mantra used in combat, "Keep your head on a swivel and eyes wide open," seems appropriate for executives in the 21st century.

EXTERNAL FORCES

In Chapter 8, "Strategic Analysis and Planning," we introduced the PESTEL framework. The framework advocates an assessment and monitoring of six external forces: political (geopolitical), economic, social, technology, environmental, and legal. Finance must have a continuous eye on these factors to understand how they might impact the firm's operations and financial performance. In large corporations, finance will have the benefit of direct monitoring of and responding to these forces by separate functional managers such as General Counsel, Government Relations, Chief Technology Officer, and Chief Human Resources Officer. In smaller organizations, the finance team may have to monitor these areas directly.

Political (geopolitical). The political environment can have a significant effect on the general business environment and company operations. Within each specific country or jurisdictions that the business operates, the following should be monitored:

- Outcome of elections and political shifts.
- Tax policy.
- Monetary policy.
- Energy policy.
- Regulation.
- Trade.
- Government spending and debt.

Economic. Macro and micro trends generally have a significant effect on the performance of most industries. This force is so critical to business performance, we will dive deeper into this topic later in the chapter.

Social. In recent years, there have been many reports of significant changes in society that will impact business. The Covid-19 pandemic, plus government response and aftermath, have accelerated many changes, including work from home, and the relationship between employees and employers.

Also important are the significant demographic changes, for example, the aging population in developed countries such as the United States. The so-called postwar Baby Boomer generation is retiring from the workforce at a reported pace of 10,000 per day. This is a partial contributor to the shortfall of workers, increased spending on retirement and medical programs, and government spending. This particular factor should come as no surprise to anyone monitoring demographics, as it was a known trend since the "boom" occurred in the late 1940s to early 1960s. Lower birth rates in subsequent periods have resulted in a reduction in the pool of available workers.

Technology. Senior finance executives should be aware of advances in technology that may transform the way finance operates and also advances that may disrupt the market in which the company operates. Technology will be covered in more detail in Chapter 12.

Environmental. Environmental policy and regulation have increased dramatically over the last 60 years. Each year, government regulations address new potential risks of emissions, toxins in our water, and the food and products we use. More recently, the acceleration of "green," "climate change," and other movements have resulted in significant policy changes in Europe and the United States on the use of fossil fuels. Some of these policy changes have been draconian in that the restriction of coal, oil, and gas production has preceded the development of reliable, renewable alternative energy sources. This has contributed to inflation, energy shortages, and some believe, geopolitical conflicts (e.g., Russian invasion of Ukraine). CFOs should monitor proposed changes to environmental policy and the potential effect on the company and the broader economy.

Legal. Changes in regulatory and legal environments can also impact individual firms and the broader economy. Legislation, administrative policy, and court rulings can impact product regulation, mergers and acquisitions, immigration, patent protection, financial disclosures, and many others.

THE ECONOMIC ENVIRONMENT

Although most finance and operating executives intuitively recognize the relationship between broad economic events and business trends, many enterprises do not explicitly consider this in developing plans, projections, and capital investment decisions. In November 2019, I asked a polling question while presenting at a finance conference on the topic of scenario planning. Since most companies typically complete the operating plan for the next year in the fall, I asked what assumptions the recently completed plans were based on: expansion, moderate growth, recession, or no explicit assumption (Figure 10.1).

The vast majority of participants (senior financial and FP&A managers) responded that they did not make an explicit assumption about the economy in developing their operating plan. While this was not a complete surprise based on my experience as a CFO and consultant, I was stunned by the overall results. Some participants indicated that they were not in economically sensitive industries. In the three years following the conference, substantially all industries were significantly impacted by changes in economic forces. These include inflation, labor market conditions, interest rates, accelerating then reversing broad monetary policies (zero interest and quantitative easing), to name a few. Within three months of the conference, Covid-19 rocked the

FIGURE 10.1 **Economic assumptions in operating plans.**

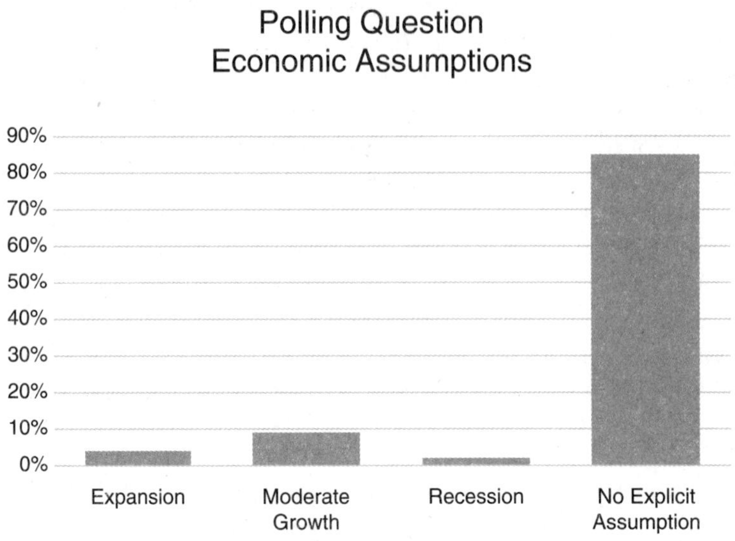

Polling Question
Economic Assumptions

world and accelerated or exposed a fragile economic environment. Any time spent in considering the economic environment and other potential scenarios and responses would have increased the level of preparedness. Scenario analysis, planning, and management will be presented in detail in Chapter 13.

General Economic Measures

There are several measures that economists, investors, and business leaders traditionally monitor. These include gross domestic product (GDP), unemployment, labor participation rates, consumer sentiment, and housing starts. These measures are general and each enterprise should also focus on measures that reflect key drivers for the industry and economies in which they participate. Other measures should be tracked given specific trends or events in the world, for example, energy and monetary policy discussed later. This set of measures include both lagging and leading indicators.

Lagging Indicators. Many economic measures are lagging, or backward looking. For example, gross domestic product (GDP) is reported on a quarterly basis with a lag of approximately 20 days. The general determination of a recession is "two consecutive quarters of declining GDP." So, by the time a recession is officially declared, the economy has experienced at least six months of contraction and may be on the road to recovery. It is useful to explain what has happened, but is of limited use as a future indicator of performance. Unemployment and labor participation rates are also backward views of conditions in the labor market.

Leading Indicators. While it can be insightful to look at historical trends, where possible, executives should focus on leading or predictive indicators of performance. Consumer sentiment may be predictive of future spending, a significant part of the U.S. economy. Housing permits or construction starts can signal a future change in spending and activity across a broad spectrum, including building materials, furniture, appliances, mortgage, and services related to household formation. Identifying and tracking leading indicators is generally more difficult than the lagging indicators provided by government institutions. Access to so-called "high-frequency" data such as daily retail sales, spending reflected in credit card and bank accounts, and real-time reporting of layoffs would be more insightful than lagging monthly or quarterly recaps.

In mid-2023, there was considerable disagreement among economists, business leaders, and journalists about the future direction of the economy. I recommend that finance teams monitor economic measures and projections in order to inform the development of business plans, projections, and scenario analysis. These measures can be summarized on a dashboard as illustrated in Figure 10.2. This dashboard should be available during business and plan reviews. I should disclose that the information is challenging to collect. Key indicators are reported separately across several government sites, as noted on the economic dashboards presented in Figures 10.2 to 10.5.

After a long period of relatively stable energy process, energy costs became very volatile in 2021. Analysts point to a number of factors, including aggressive measures to decrease use of fossil fuels, the invasion of Ukraine by Russia, and the impact of the reopening following the Covid-19 pandemic. The sharp increase in energy costs was a major contributor to high overall inflation in 2022, due to the combined effect of the costs of direct usage of energy and the indirect effect on all products due to energy usage in transportation of all goods and services. In addition, by-products of petroleum are also used in plastics and fertilizers, which were also driven higher. Given the volatility and impact of the energy markets, companies should track the cost of major energy components. Of interest, since this analysis was prepared in fall of 2022, energy costs have partially subsided but remain above 2020 levels. In particular, natural gas has fallen to approximately $2 within six months from a peak of $9. Among other factors, weather (a milder winter in the United States and Europe) is one of the principle drivers.

Another factor that is useful to understand and consider is the monetary policy undertaken by central banks (e.g., U.S. Federal Reserve Bank) in large economies. Central banks have a number of important functions in many countries. These include oversight and regulation, monitoring and moderating the economy, and mandates to achieve employment targets and control inflation. In many developed economies, these central banks engineered an artificially low level of interest rates (even negative rates in some cases) environment to cushion the impact of the great recession in 2008–2010. This was achieved by

FIGURE 10.2 **Economic dashboard: General economic indicators.**

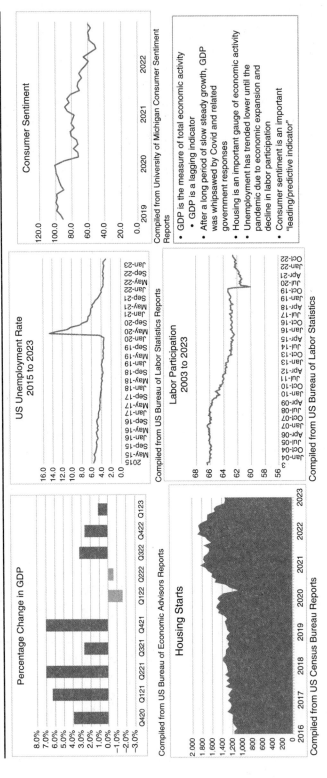

FIGURE 10.3 **Economic dashboard: Energy.**

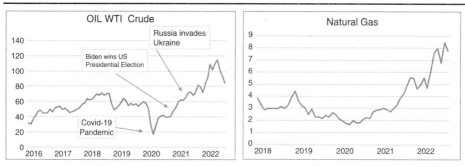

Compiled from US Energy Information Administration data

- Cost of energy impacts the cost of nearly all goods and services:
  - Transportation
  - Plastics
  - Fertilizer
- Drivers include:
  - Supply/Demand
  - Energy policies in Europe and US
  - Geopolitical Events (Russia/Ukraine)
  - Weather/Seasonality

reducing central bank lending rates and also by purchasing securities in the market to firm up bond prices, thereby further suppressing interest rates. This so-called "quantitative easing" essentially amounted to central banks printing money to purchase bonds to increase liquidity in the capital markets. The securities purchased by the central reserve was then carried on the central bank's Balance Sheet. As shown in Figure 10.4, the quantitative easing was never significantly reversed, and then was driven from $4 trillion to over $9 trillion as a result of government spending in response to the Covid-19 pandemic, lockdowns and resultant economic hardships, and additional stimulus well after the pandemic had subsided. This $5 trillion infusion into the economy (approximately 20% of total economic spending—GDP) was a significant contributor to the inflation reaching historical highs in 2021 and 2022.

In addition, artificially suppressing interest rates contributed to extremely high valuations across stocks and real estate since these asset values are inversely related to interest rates. In 2022, central banks began to reverse these policies by raising interest rates and "reducing their balance sheets" (quantitative tightening—selling securities they had purchased during quantitative easing). This is intended to reduce overall economic activity to reduce demand for goods and services, eventually reducing inflation. It has also resulted in dramatic reductions in valuation of most stocks and real estate, and more recently, the viability of marginal banks.

FIGURE 10.4 **Dashboard illustration: Monetary policy.**

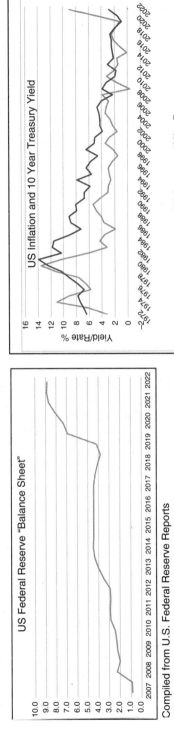

US Federal Reserve "Balance Sheet"

Compiled from U.S. Federal Reserve Reports

CPI

Compiled from U.S. Bureau of Labor Statistics Reports

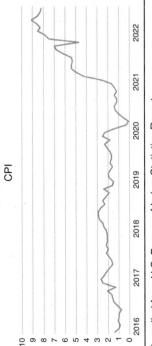

US Inflation and 10 Year Treasury Yield

—— Inflation —— 10 Year Treas

Compiled from data on www.macrotrends.net

- The US and other major economies experienced 40-year high levels of inflation in 2021-2022
- Yields on 10 year treasury generally were above inflation (as expected to cover inflation and provide a "real" return)
- Beginning in 2008 the US FR artificially lowered interest rates, resulting in yields less than or equal to inflation
- The US FDR also purchased trillions of Treasury (and other) securities, further driving down yields
- While the FDR has increased interest rates modestly, the rate of inflation currently exceeds treasury yields by 5%

FIGURE 10.5 **U.S. government deficit and debt trends.**

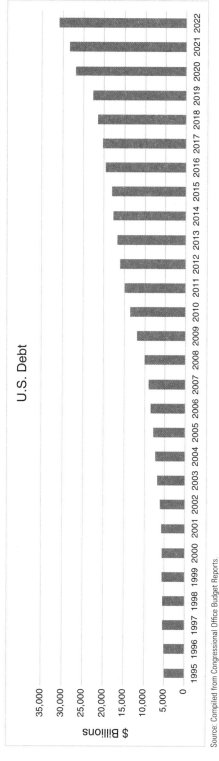

Surplus/Deficit by Year

$ Billions

500
0
−500
−1,000
−1,500
−2,000
−2,500
−3,000
−3,500

	1995	1996	1997	1998	1999	2000	2001	2002	2003	2004	2005	2006	2007	2008	2009	2010	2011	2012	2013	2014	2015	2016	2017	2018	2019	2020	2021	2022
Deficit	−164	−107	−22	69	125	236	128	−157	−377	−412	−318	−248	−160	−459	−1412	−1294	−1299	−1087	−679	−485	−438	−584	−665	−779	−984	−3131	−2775	−1375

U.S. Debt

$ Billions

35,000
30,000
25,000
20,000
15,000
10,000
5,000
0

1995 1996 1997 1998 1999 2000 2001 2002 2003 2004 2005 2006 2007 2008 2009 2010 2011 2012 2013 2014 2015 2016 2017 2018 2019 2020 2021 2022

Source: Compiled from Congressional Office Budget Reports.

Sovereign Debt

Over the last decade, I have become increasingly concerned about the deficit and debt level of the U.S. government, and more generally, governments in many developed countries. The pandemic, and related government actions, turbocharged government spending, resulting in record deficits and debt, further pushing government debt levels to alarming levels. Figure 10.5 recaps the U.S. deficit spending and debt levels.

The U.S. debt as a percentage of total GDP has grown from 62% in 2010 to over 100% and then reached 130% in 2021! The interest on this debt will soon surpass spending on all defense programs in the United States due to higher debt levels and interest rates returning to normal levels.

A financial leader should conclude from this discussion on external forces that there is a great deal of uncertainty and change, especially in geopolitical and economic forces. In addition, these forces suggest likely macro directional movements, including higher taxes, slower growth, and challenging labor markets in the future. The level of uncertainty and rate of change argue for the adoption of scenario analysis (which will be explored in Chapter 13) and increased organization agility (which will be explored in Chapter 14).

ANALYSIS OF MARKETS, COMPETITORS, AND CUSTOMERS

Another aspect of the external view is to monitor and evaluate the strategy, investments, and performance of other players in the markets in which the company participates. Finance professionals can add substantial value by contributing to the analysis of competitors, suppliers, customers, partners, and the overall market. We are uniquely qualified to obtain, evaluate, and present insights available in public financial and investor reports. This financial perspective can be integrated with traditional marketing competitive analysis focused on price, performance, service, and other factors.

Sources of Information

The digital age has resulted in a plethora of data that is readily available from multiple sources on the internet. In fact, the challenge has shifted from the availability of data to evaluating and selecting the most credible and relevant information to utilize.

Industry Reports

Most markets are covered by industry analysts or trade groups that follow market trends and key events. These reports also often provide rankings by revenue growth or other financial performance measures, and include news on product introductions and other important events.

Research Analyst Reports

Companies whose securities are traded on public exchanges (e.g., NYSE or NASDAQ in the United States or FTSE in the United Kingdom) are typically "covered" by research analysts from large investment and brokerage firms. These reports range from puff pieces to very thorough reports that go well beyond basic financial analysis to include performance drivers, problems and opportunities, and a perspective on valuation. These reports can (and should) be an independent assessment of performance, and often include a comparison to competitors or overall market trends.

Company Website

Publicly traded companies (and certain private companies) disclose considerable information on their websites, including press releases, financial statements, executive profiles, product information, corporate governance, and other information. Most of the relevant financial information can be found in the "Investor" section of the website.

Required Disclosures by Publicly Traded Companies

Securities laws mandate that publicly traded companies disclose substantial information to investors (and as a result, many others!). Much of this report is written by lawyers and accountants for other lawyers and accountants. As such, much of the meaning is lost on folks outside the legal and accounting profession. An FP&A professional who has experience in SEC (Securities and Exchange Commission) reporting can decode and interpret these reports.

Annual Report and Form 10k. While these reports may be helpful, they often are hundreds of pages in length. Areas of these reports that can be the most fertile sources for relevant information:

- ❑ Business description. This section can provide a useful perspective, including how the company defines its business and markets. This section includes a description of the company's business strategy and a description of their products, intellectual property, marketing and promotion, and competitors.
- ❑ Management's discussion and analysis (MD&A). The MD&A is one of the most important disclosures in the Form 10k. It is intended to be a review of the company's performance and financial condition "through the eyes of management." Topics that must be addressed in the MD&A include:
  - Business overview.
  - Results of operations.

- Review of current performance compared to prior years, addressing revenues, margins, expenses, and cash flow.
- Business combinations, acquisitions, and divestitures.
- Liquidity.

❏ Footnotes. While most footnotes are loaded with accounting jargon and will bore most people to tears (including the author), there are very important disclosures here, especially description of business, financial overview, accounting policies, acquisition activity, segment and geographical performance, and contingencies.

❏ Risk factors. Companies are required to disclose factors that may adversely impact financial results and the value of the company's shares.

Proxy Statement. The proxy statement includes information on management, directors, and compensation, and incentive levels and programs.

Quarterly Report/Form 10Q. Publicly traded companies are required to report a summary of quarterly financial results.

Press Release/Form 8-k. Publicly traded companies must disclose material events and provide updates on previous guidance on earnings.

Supplemental disclosures. Additional filings and disclosures are often required for special events or transactions, for example, acquisitions requiring shareholder approval or financing. These would include detailed information on the strategic case supporting the transaction as well as the basis for valuing the acquisition.

Company Presentations to Investors. Companies that meet or present to shareholders are required to share that same information with all investors under the SEC's Regulation FD (Full Disclosure). These presentations are generally posted to the company's website.

Earnings Conference Calls. Most companies hold quarterly conference calls where senior executives review the last quarter's performance and discuss the business outlook for the future.

Analysis and Presentation

Much of the information sources previously described would be too time-consuming to gather and too technical to be effectively utilized by executives and business unit managers. The analyst can consolidate and distill this information into useful analysis and reports. This information is useful in:

- Competitive intelligence for executives.
- A component of situational analysis for strategic and operational planning.
- A basis for evaluating strategic and operating plans by comparing competitor and customer trends to the assumptions incorporated into our plans and forecasts.

- Quarterly updates for executives.
- Alerts for special events.

Some best practice companies assign analysts to cover one or more competitors or customers. This also represents a terrific development opportunity for financial analysts due to the perspective and insight gained in this process.

A typical presentation for an analysis of a company would include summaries of financial performance, business and strategy, and segment information.

These summaries are illustrated for Microsoft Corporation (MSFT) in Figure 10.6 through 10.8.

The summary of financial performance would generally include revenue, margins, and return on invested capital (ROIC). The summary should be tailored to highlight key aspects of the specific company's performance. For example, Microsoft generates very high levels of cash flow from operations and retains approximately $100 billion in cash and equivalents. Cash and equivalents are the largest asset group on the company's Balance Sheet. While this has a significant (and dilutive) impact on returns, it does represents a large "war chest" to invest in development, make acquisitions, or return to shareholders. The report has been tailored to highlight this extraordinary feature.

Figure 10.7 presents a one-page summary of key business and strategic factors. Much of this content is disclosed in the company's annual report (Form 10-k). The summary includes a business description, growth and investment strategy, competitive and market environment information, and recent acquisitions.

Companies that operate with several business units are required to disclose summary information on performance of each segment. Figure 10.8 provides insight into major contributors to growth and profitability trends of major business segments.

Quarterly Update on Customer/Competitor

A one-page quarterly performance recap for a competitor or customer is presented in Figure 10.9. This recap can be used to highlight current performance and updates to the annual summary previously presented.

This recap is a very effective way to summarize and communicate the performance and recent events of a competitor, customer, or investment. The specific information presented would likely vary depending on the reason for monitoring the company. For example, investors may focus on revenue growth and operating income, while a supplier or subcontractor may be focused on signals about business performance and investments in the segment they do business.

FIGURE 10.6 **Microsoft research—Financials.**

Microsoft $in billions   FYE: 6/30   09/09/23   Analyst: Alexander

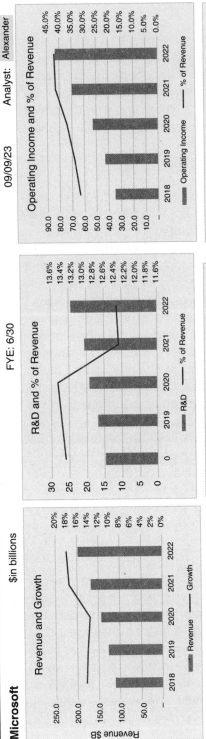

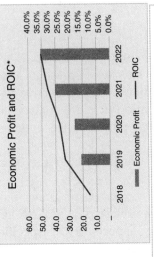

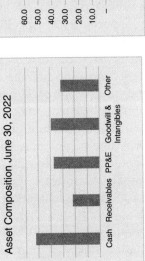

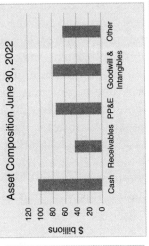

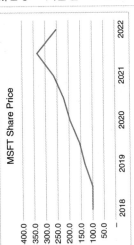

Summary:

MSFT consistently delivers mid-teen revenue growth and operating margins approaching 40% of revenues. Growth in recent years has included several large acquisitions.

Valuation Metrics:
EV/Revenue: 9.4x
EV/EBITDA: 19.4

* ROIC and Economic Profit include the Cash and equivalents (6/30/22 balance of $104.8b). Assuming that $20b is required to support operations, approximately $80b might be considered excess and available for acquisitions, share repurchases and returns, etc. Excluding the $80b from the ROIC would increase the 2022 returns to over 100%!

Source: Compiled from company SEC filings and press releases.

FIGURE 10.7 **Microsoft research — Business and strategy.**

Microsoft

Compiled from SEC reports including forms 10k and Proxy

Business Description. Microsoft is a technology company whose mission is to empower every person and every organization on the planet to achieve more. We strive to create local opportunity, growth, and impact in every country around the world. Our platforms and tools help drive small business productivity, large business competitiveness, and public-sector efficiency. We are creating the tools and platforms that deliver better, faster, and more effective solutions to support new startups, improve educational and health outcomes, and empower human ingenuity.

Founded in 1975, MSFT develops and supports software, services, devices, and solutions that deliver new value for customers and help people and businesses realize their full potential. We offer an array of services, including cloud-based solutions that provide customers with software, services, platforms, and content, and we provide solution support and consulting services. We also deliver relevant online advertising to a global audience. PART I Item 14 Our products include operating systems, cross-device productivity and collaboration applications, server applications, business solution applications, desktop and server management tools, software development tools, and video games. We also design and sell devices, including PCs, tablets, gaming and entertainment consoles, other intelligent devices, and related accessories.

Business Segments	Revenue	% of Total
Productivity and Biz Process	63.4	32%
Intelligent Cloud	75.3	38%
More Personal Computing	59.7	30%
Total	198.3	100%

Competitors

Vary by segment; highlights include:

Enterprise service competitors include companies such as Amazon, Google, IBM, Oracle, VMware, and open source offerings.

Office competitors include software and global application vendors, such as Apple, Cisco Systems, Meta, Google, IBM, Okta, Proofpoint, Slack, Symantec, Zoom, and numerous others.

Devices face competition from various computer, tablet, and hardware manufacturers.

Gaming faces competition from various online gaming ecosystems and game streaming services, including those operated by Amazon, Apple, Meta, Google, and Tencent.

Server Products. Includes competitors such as Hewlett-Packard, IBM, and Oracle.

Growth and Investment Strategy:

To lead the industry in several distinct areas of technology over the long term, which we expect will translate to sustained growth. We are investing significant resources in:

- Transforming the workplace to deliver new modern, modular business applications, drive deeper insights, and improve how people communicate, collaborate, learn, work, play, and interact with one another.
- Building and running cloud-based services in ways that unleash new experiences.
- Applying AI to drive insights and act on customers' behalf by understanding and interpreting their needs using natural methods of communication.
- Tackling security from all angles with our integrated, end-to-end solutions spanning security, compliance, identity, and management, across all clouds and platforms.
- Inventing new gaming experiences that bring people together.
- Using Windows to fuel our cloud business, grow our share of the PC market, and drive increased engagement with our services like Microsoft 365 Consumer, Teams, Edge, Bing, Xbox Game Pass, and more.

Competitive Advantages:
(Not identified by Company)

Risk Factors (Specific)
- Security of Information Technology
- Threat of new competitive products
- Government Regulatory and Litigation
- Acquisition Risk
- New Product Development Execution Risk

Market Environment
- Increased regulatory pressure on Tech companies
- Significant and rapid changes in technology
- Intense competition

Recent Acquisitions and Divestitures:

- March 2022, completed acquisition of Nuance Communications, Inc. for a total purchase price of $18.8 billion, consisting primarily of cash. Nuance is a cloud and artificial intelligence software provider.

- March 2021, completed our acquisition of ZeniMax Media Inc., the parent company of Bethesda Softworks LLC , for a total purchase price of $8.1 billion, consisting primarily of cash. Bethesda is one of the largest, privately held game software companies

- January 2022, entered into agreement to acquire Activision Blizzard, Inc. in an all-cash transaction valued at $68.7 billion.

Recent Events

FIGURE 10.8 **Microsoft research—Segment reporting.**

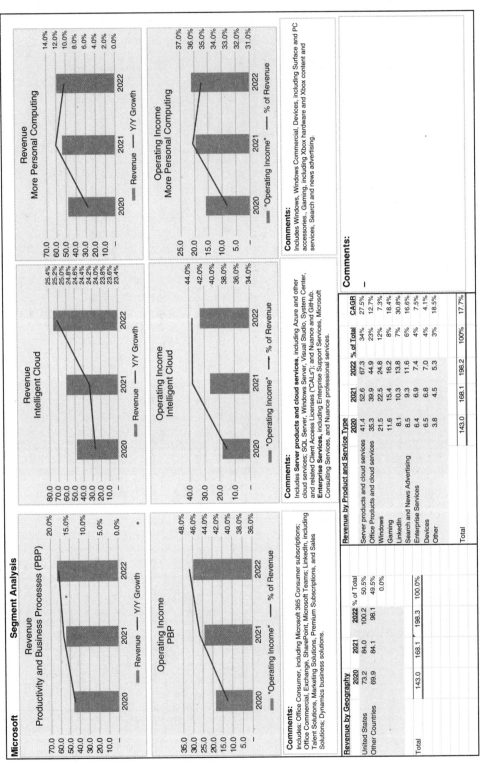

Microsoft   **Segment Analysis**

Revenue Productivity and Business Processes (PBP)
Revenue Intelligent Cloud
Revenue More Personal Computing
Operating Income PBP
Operating Income Intelligent Cloud
Operating Income More Personal Computing

Comments:
Includes: Office Consumer, including Microsoft 365 Consumer subscriptions; Office Commercial, Exchange, SharePoint, Microsoft Teams; LinkedIn, including Talent Solutions, Marketing Solutions, Premium Subscriptions, and Sales Solutions; Dynamics business solutions.

Comments:
Includes **Server products and cloud services**, including Azure and other cloud services; SQL Server, Windows Server, Visual Studio, System Center, and related Client Access Licenses ("CALs"); and Nuance and GitHub. **Enterprise Services**, including Enterprise Support Services, Microsoft Consulting Services, and Nuance professional services.

Comments:
Includes Windows, Windows Commercial, Devices, including Surface and PC accessories, Gaming, including Xbox hardware and Xbox content and services, Search and news advertising.

Revenue by Geography	2020	2021	2022	% of Total
United States	73.2	84.0	100.2	50.5%
Other Countries	69.9	84.1	98.1	49.5%
				0.0%
Total	143.0	168.1	198.3	100.0%

Revenue by Product and Service Type	2020	2021	2022	% of Total	CAGR
Server products and cloud services	41.4	52.6	67.3	34%	27.5%
Office Products and cloud services	35.3	39.9	44.9	23%	12.7%
Windows	21.5	22.5	24.8	12%	7.3%
Gaming	11.6	15.4	16.2	8%	18.4%
LinkedIn	8.1	10.3	13.8	7%	30.8%
Search and News Advertising	8.5	9.3	11.6	6%	16.6%
Enterprise Services	6.4	6.9	7.4	4%	7.5%
Devices	6.5	6.8	7.0	4%	4.1%
Other	3.8	4.5	5.3	3%	18.5%
Total	143.0	168.1	198.2	100%	17.7%

Comments:
—

FIGURE 10.9 **Quarterly performance recap: Microsoft Corporation.** 🖥

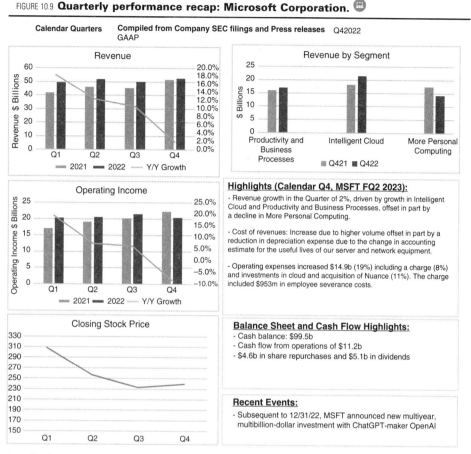

Calendar Quarters   Compiled from Company SEC filings and Press releases   Q42022
GAAP

Highlights (Calendar Q4, MSFT FQ2 2023):

- Revenue growth in the Quarter of 2%, driven by growth in Intelligent Cloud and Productivity and Business Processes, offset in part by a decline in More Personal Computing.

- Cost of revenues: Increase due to higher volume offset in part by a reduction in depreciation expense due to the change in accounting estimate for the useful lives of our server and network equipment.

- Operating expenses increased $14.9b (19%) including a charge (8%) and investments in cloud and acquisition of Nuance (11%). The charge included $953m in employee severance costs.

Balance Sheet and Cash Flow Highlights:
- Cash balance: $99.5b
- Cash flow from operations of $11.2b
- $4.6b in share repurchases and $5.1b in dividends

Recent Events:
- Subsequent to 12/31/22, MSFT announced new multiyear, multibillion-dollar investment with ChatGPT-maker OpenAI

Source: Compiled from company reports and SEC filings.

SUMMARY

Now, more than any time in relevant history, finance executives must closely monitor the environment in which they operate. The greatest threats and opportunities almost always arise outside the organization. The PESTEL (Political, Economic, Social, Technology, Environment, Legal) framework is a good overall approach, but a deeper dive is warranted in certain areas. Economic forces should be considered in developing projections and evaluating capital investments. Finance can also add substantial value by monitoring and analyzing competitors, customers, and the overall market in which the firm competes.

11

Course-Corrections: Business Transformation and Restructuring

All businesses are eventually forced to deal with the reality that the strategy, business model, or cost structure are not aligned with the reality they face in the markets. The business may fall short of growth and profitability targets. Staying the course is not a viable option. Financial management generally takes a leadership role in restructuring or transforming the business to be positioned for future success.

THE NEED FOR CHANGE. . .

All organizations will eventually have to consider making significant course-corrections. This occurs for a variety of reasons, including life cycle maturity, competitive pressures, disruptive forces, failed investments or strategy and economic cycles. Even high-growth technology companies with a long history of growth, including Amazon, Meta (Facebook), and Alphabet (Google), had to face this reality in recent years.

How Did We Get Here?

There are many paths that lead to a need for business transformation.

Competitive Threats. Nearly all enterprises face significant competition. This competition is often intensified by a new entrant to the market, or by an innovation in product, process, or distribution. This intensification will typically result in lower market share (volume) and price erosion with a significant impact on profitability.

Disruptive Forces and Black Swan Events. Many industries have been disrupted by significant changes in technology, and social, environment, or other forces. For example, brick-and-mortar retailers were slammed by on-line sellers early in the 21st century. The oil and gas industries were whipsawed by political and legislative shifts in recent years.

Black Swan events are significant downside events that cannot be reasonably foreseen. A recent example, Covid-19 has been labeled the "great accelerator," since it caused many trends already underway to accelerate beyond any pace imagined. Changes include work from home, remote learning, on-line retail, the Great Resignation, and many others. Entire industries have been reshaped, including technology tools, commercial real estate, and education.

Failed Acquisitions. Acquisitions are typically bold and significant investments for a company. They generally represent a high-risk investment, especially for companies without a solid acquisition process. Acquisitions that do not meet expectations result in the acquiring company missing earnings and growth targets and a probable write-down of goodwill and intangibles. Studies often report that 50% or more of acquisitions fail to meet the stated objectives for performance and value creation.

Organization Maturity. Nearly all products and companies follow a similar life cycle curve. The firm begins with little revenue to start, hopefully followed by a period of rapid growth. At some point in time, the growth rate is slowed due to saturation or competition in the market. Eventually the revenues reach a point where they decline, requiring a strategic reset. The S-curve life cycle model shown in Figure 11.1 illustrates this evolution.

FIGURE 11.1 **Product life cycle.**

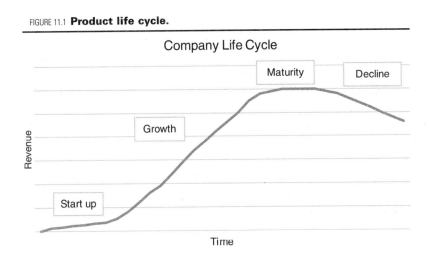

Making the Case

Many managers will delay on decisions to make strategic course-corrections. Some want to let more time elapse, hoping that current trends are temporary, or that more data points will provide additional insight (analysis paralysis). Others may be blinded by the prior successes of the executives and organization, and have confidence that they can avoid the inevitable. Many managers may only have experience in growth industries or companies and have not experienced the signposts or necessary actions to address the challenges.

Strategic changes, transformations, and cutting costs are not easy, and generally require time, insight, and resolve. Unfortunately, cost reductions almost always result in reductions in the workforce, directly impacting employees, their careers, and their families. Cost reductions involve tough decisions, including terminating projects and programs, forcing productivity improvements, and so on.

The strategic analysis included in Chapter 8 can be used to prepare a situational analysis and develop a call to action. Another helpful approach is to present the likely outcome of staying on the current course. This can be as simple as a scenario that extrapolates recent performance that can then be compared to the company's more optimistic projections for the future. This extrapolation, to which I apply Lao Tzu's "If we don't soon change our direction, we'll soon wind up where we are headed" can lead to interesting discussions about why the future will be different than the past. Consider the issues raised in the projected performance in Figure 11.2. What specific actions or events will lead to higher revenue growth? Higher profitability?

Analytical tools to inform course-corrections include those focused primarily on cost and process, and those focused on business and strategy. Many of these are not mutually exclusive and can be used in combination to provide a comprehensive view of alternatives.

ANALYTICAL TOOLS TO SUPPORT BUSINESS TRANSFORMATION–COST AND PROCESS

We have a number of different analytical tools to assist in the development of business transformations that focus on cost, business model, and process.

Periodic Pruning

As an avid gardener, I have long recognized the parallels between pruning plants and organizations. Most plants will not reach their full potential without thoughtful pruning. For example, tomato plants produce "suckers," shoots that will not produce fruit, but consume the plant's energy. They must be removed to maximize tomato production. Other plants produce branches

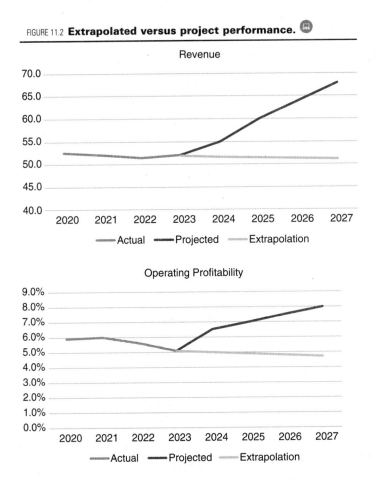

FIGURE 11.2 **Extrapolated versus project performance.**

that are weak or cross other branches leading to injury. Disease can often start in one section of the plant and spread to the remaining healthy sections over time. Other branches may be damaged by storm or pests. Removing these problem limbs generally results in a healthier and more productive plant. The same issues often occur with businesses. Over time, new departments or projects are formed that eventually outlive their usefulness. Some strategic business units (SBUs) do not meet expectations and will be a drag on the overall performance. Progressive companies address and may ultimately terminate employees who fail to perform at acceptable levels on a regular basis. The organization will be healthier if regularly pruning is employed.

Across-the-Board Cuts

Unfortunately, many organizations facing the need to reduce costs default to across-the-board cuts. After the total required cost reduction is determined, a top-down directive may require a 10% reduction across every unit or department in the organization. While this can be a useful starting point for consideration, it seldom results in optimum results. This approach does not consider:

- Strategic and business considerations.
- Some departments may be operating leaner than others.
- The need to support certain strategic or critical areas.
- Any differentiation as to relative contribution or importance, including specific talents and institutional knowledge.

However, this approach does start a conversation and an evaluation of costs and expenses across the organization. This can provide a sense of what pain would be caused by the reductions. However, a more thoughtful method will generally produce better results.

Address Leakers and Bleeders

Every business has certain projects, customers, business units, and products that drain resources. They may post outright losses or profits lower than the organization's goal. Others may require high investment levels that dilute returns. By identifying these drains on performance, we can develop a plan to fix or eliminate them, thereby raising the company's overall performance.

Zero-Based Cost Analysis (ZBCA)

One of the deficiencies in most operational planning processes is that the spend rate for next year is based on the spending in the current year. For example, the budget for next year may be set at 5% increase over the current year. In addition, costs are added to an organization for a specific reason or purpose with a limited duration. Often these programs become part of the "base" expense if they are not challenged.

In its simplest form, ZBCA is a fresh look challenging every position, cost, function, project, investment, and program in the organization. A critical evaluation of each expense is conducted, focusing on why the cost is incurred, what value is derived, and what would happen if the cost were eliminated. Some companies use a scoring or ranking convention, for example, mission critical, strategic investment, statutory requirement, or "up for grabs." Progressive organizations implement ongoing cost management programs as part of their operational planning process. ZBCA will be covered in more detail in Chapter 19 on business planning.

Activity-Based Cost Analysis (ABCA)

In many types of analysis, including product, customer, and business unit profitability, many general costs and expenses must be assigned or allocated.

The easiest and most common method is to allocate expenses on the basis of revenue dollars. This may be acceptable, if the amounts allocated are not significant, or if sales dollars are representative of the activities and drivers of that expense. For example, order processing, invoicing, and service activities may support all product lines within an enterprise. In preparing product line Profit and Loss statements (P&Ls), these costs are often allocated on the basis of sales dollars. However, in most situations, sales dollars are not reflective of the level of activity and time attributable to each product line. For example, the cost of processing and invoicing an order may be the same for a small-dollar repair order as it is for a $100,000 system. Service costs will be driven by the level of product failures and returns, not sales dollars. Inevitably, certain product lines will consume a disproportionate share of these activities. In order to better evaluate customer and segment profitability, it is important to *assign* costs properly. Table 11.1 presents an analysis of these activities and measures, and an allocation of total costs on the basis of sales dollars.

Note that the activity measures selected as representative of the drivers of time and cost for the department, namely, number of invoices generated and returns, vary significantly from the percentage of sales dollars for each product line.

Table 11.2 assigns the cost for order processing and billing (OPB) on the basis of the number of transactions (invoices) and assigns the customer service costs on the basis of product returns. The table also compares the costs

TABLE 11.1 **Order processing costs allocated by sale dollars.**

Activity-Based Cost Analysis

Order Processing and Customer Service

Order Processing and Billing (OPB)	1,200,100	
Customer Service	750,000	
Total	1,950,100	

	Sales	% Total	Allocation on Sales $	# Invoices	% Total	Average Transaction	Returns	% Total	Return Rate
Product Line 1	1,500,100	3%	56,519	862	11%	1,740	20	2%	2.3%
Product Line 2	2,105,000	4%	79,310	410	5%	5,134	61	6%	14.9%
Product Line 3	1,200,600	2%	45,235	600	8%	2,001	41	4%	6.8%
Product Line 4	8,001,000	15%	301,455	1600	20%	5,001	15	1%	0.9%
Product Line 5	4,200,500	8%	158,263	2300	29%	1,826	40	4%	1.7%
Product Line 6	12,400,500	24%	467,215	260	3%	47,694	12	1%	4.6%
Product Line 7	6,000,000	12%	226,063	525	7%	11,429	28	3%	5.3%
Product Line 8	14,750,000	28%	555,738	300	4%	49,167	1	0%	0.3%
Parts	1,600,486	3%	60,302	1000	13%	1,600	800	79%	80.0%
Total	51,758,186	100%	1,950,100	7,857	100%	6,588	1,018	100%	13.0%

TABLE 11.2 **Costs assigned based on activity.**

| | | OPB Cost | | Service | Comparison | | |
	% Invoices	Assignment	% Returns	Assignment	Total Assigned	Allocated Sales $	Change
Product Line 1	11.0%	131,664	2.0%	14,735	146,399	56,519	89,880
Product Line 2	5.2%	62,625	6.0%	44,941	107,566	79,310	28,255
Product Line 3	7.6%	91,646	4.0%	30,206	121,852	45,235	76,617
Product Line 4	20.4%	244,388	1.5%	11,051	255,440	301,455	(46,015)
Product Line 5	29.3%	351,308	3.9%	29,470	380,778	158,263	222,515
Product Line 6	3.3%	39,713	1.2%	8,841	48,554	467,215	(418,661)
Product Line 7	6.7%	80,190	2.8%	20,629	100,819	226,063	(125,244)
Product Line 8	3.8%	45,823	0.1%	737	46,560	555,738	(509,178)
Parts	12.7%	152,743	78.6%	589,391	742,134	60,302	681,832
Total	100.0%	1,200,100	100.0%	750,000	1,950,100	1,950,100	-

Costs assigned based on Activity Measures

allocated by sales dollars to the costs assigned by activity measures, highlighting a significantly different assignment of costs. The analysis also identifies some other notable concerns that should be pursued, for example, the large number of returns for parts. What are the root causes of returns and possible corrective actions? The company should also look at the profitability for parts to ensure that pricing covers the relatively high transaction costs.

This assignment of costs can then be used to address the drivers of cost and to prepare a better analysis of customer or SBU profitability.

Process Evaluation and Redesign

Substantially all costs are driven by one or more key business processes, including the revenue, supply chain, product development, employment, and administrative (e.g., business planning) processes. In addition to driving internal costs, these processes also affect other performance drivers such as customer satisfaction and innovation.

Process evaluation and improvement starts with documenting or mapping current processes. It will identify bottlenecks, defects, redundancies, and key performance indicators (KPIs). The objective of the review is to analyze overall process cycle time, reduce delays, improve quality, eliminate bottlenecks, and reduce costs. This type of analysis requires an understanding of business processes, process improvement, and diagnostic techniques. In many cases, these skills will not be resident within the traditional FP&A or finance departments. Many of these skills are developed in consulting firms or in quality or continuous improvement organizations within the enterprise.

Performance Improvement Tools and Disciplines

Root cause analysis.

Continuous improvement.

Six sigma.

Total quality management (TQM).

Benchmarking.

Lean manufacturing.

ANALYTICAL TOOLS TO SUPPORT BUSINESS TRANSFORMATION—BUSINESS AND STRATEGY

No business transformation should be undertaken without an analysis of the company's strategic situation and direction. In Chapter 8, several strategic planning tools were discussed. The following is a recap of those most relevant to business transformations.

Situational Analysis

An analysis of the current situation is a very important tool to identify and evaluate alternative actions. Key components include SWOT or SLOT (Strengths, Limitations, Opportunities, and Threats), competitive advantages and disadvantages, and forces impacting our business (e.g., PESTEL framework).

Business Portfolio Analysis

Every business is comprised of various strategic business units (SBUs), product families, and products. Typically, the company's overall performance is a blend of several businesses, including some that underperform. By analyzing the performance of the segments in the portfolio (Figure 11.3), we may identify opportunities for fixing, selling, or closing underperforming units.

We introduced the growth-profitability quadrant analysis (see Figure 8.10 in Chapter 8) as an important strategic analysis tool. This tool should also be utilized to identify potential actions as part of a business transformation. Generally, underperformers such as SBU 5, should be identified and addressed. They may be candidates for a restructuring or sale depending on strategic importance. SBU 5 is of low strategic value to the company, so it may be worth more to another company. The proceeds from the sale could be reinvested in a more strategic, complementary business, or returned to shareholders.

FIGURE 11.3 **Business portfolio analysis.**

SBU	Historical Growth	Historical Profitability	Revenue	Future Investment	Strategic Importance
SBU1	19%	1%	5.0	High	High
SBU2	4%	13%	11.0	Low	Moderate
SBU3	15%	18%	7.0	Moderate	High
SBU4	10%	12%	19.0	Moderate	High (Core)
SBU5	2%	-2%	10.0	Low	Low
Total			52.0		

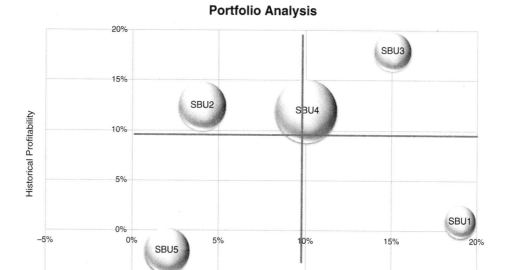

Portfolio Analysis

Product Portfolio Analysis

A review of the company's product portfolio can provide a more granular view of the business. This disaggregation will likely surface opportunities to evaluate and improve business performance. Table 11.3 presents an example of a detailed list of product sales, margins, and growth rates for SBU 3.

A few observations can be made from the raw data:

- The expected growth rates are declining. It appears that revenues are concentrated in a few products.
- Growth rates are low or even negative for several products.
- Accessories and service and repair have low margins, diluting the overall margins for the SBU.

While this analysis is interesting as presented, it can be greatly enhanced by sorting on key fields such as revenue dollars, margin percentage, and growth rates. Table 11.4 displays the analysis sorted by revenue dollars, Table 11.5 is sorted by margin percentage, and Table 11.6 is sorted by growth rate.

TABLE 11.3 **Product portfolio analysis.**

Product Portfolio Analysis

SBU 3

Product	Year Introduced	Unit Sales	ASP	Cost	Extended Revenue	Extended Cost	Margin	Margin %	3 Year Growth CAGR	Projected Growth Rate
3200	1998	200	1,900.00	1,100.00	380,000	220,000	160,000	42%	-9.0%	-10.0%
3205	2005	125	6,400.00	3,400.00	800,000	425,000	375,000	47%	4.0%	2.0%
3210	2006	42	8,900.00	5,000.00	373,800	210,000	163,800	44%	5.0%	3.0%
3215	2010	342	400.00	250.00	136,800	85,500	51,300	38%	2.0%	1.0%
3300	1999	895	25.00	17.00	22,375	15,215	7,160	32%	-2.0%	-5.0%
3350	2018	26	3,200.00	1,700.00	83,200	44,200	39,000	47%	5.0%	4.0%
3400	2019	48	2,200.00	1,200.00	105,600	57,600	48,000	45%	4.0%	3.0%
3410	2021	700	500.00	300.00	350,000	210,000	140,000	40%	7.0%	5.0%
3500	2022	520	1,000.00	600.00	520,000	312,000	208,000	40%	8.0%	8.0%
3500-2	2022	265	5,000.00	3,000.00	1,325,000	795,000	530,000	40%	7.0%	6.0%
3500-3	2022	450	6,800.00	3,975.00	3,060,000	1,788,750	1,271,250	42%	6.0%	6.0%
3600	2001	333	1,500.00	950.00	499,500	316,350	183,150	37%	-6.0%	-8.0%
3610	2009	605	2,200.00	1,500.00	1,331,000	907,500	423,500	32%	1.0%	0.0%
3615	2015	16	800.00	395.00	12,800	6,320	6,480	51%	4.0%	2.0%
3725	2018	2,895	105.00	60.00	303,975	173,700	130,275	43%	5.0%	4.0%
3750	2020	800	750.00	400.00	600,000	320,000	280,000	47%	6.0%	5.0%
3800	2023	200	95.00	50.00	19,000	10,000	9,000	47%	15.0%	12.0%
4000	2005	900	159.00	100.00	143,100	90,000	53,100	37%	15.0%	2.0%
4100	2010	200	75.00	42.00	15,000	8,400	6,600	44%	4.0%	3.0%
4250	2019	600	180.00	110.00	108,000	66,000	42,000	39%	2.0%	1.0%
4280	2021	500	75.00	40.00	37,500	20,000	17,500	47%	6.0%	3.0%
4400	2022	175	59.00	32.00	10,325	5,600	4,725	46%	5.0%	4.0%
4412	2022	146	200.00	110.00	29,200	16,060	13,140	45%	6.0%	0.0%
4550	2022	226	200.00	115.00	45,200	25,990	19,210	43%	8.0%	6.0%
5000	2001	326	200.00	120.00	65,200	39,120	26,080	40%	-3.0%	-5.0%
5100	2009	345	15.00	8.00	5,175	2,760	2,415	47%	-1.0%	-2.0%
5150	2015	320	215.00	170.00	68,800	54,400	14,400	21%	2.0%	1.0%
5500	2018	100	200.00	100.00	20,000	10,000	10,000	50%	3.0%	1.5%
5575	2020	125	225.00	100.00	28,125	12,500	15,625	56%	2.0%	1.0%
5800	1997	97	275.00	162.00	26,675	15,714	10,961	41%	-4.0%	-7.0%

5900	2001	10	1,050.00	650.00	10,500	6,500	4,000	38%	-1.0%	-2.0%
5906	2009	164	175.00	100.00	28,700	16,400	12,300	43%	0.0%	0.0%
5907	2015	157	119.00	65.00	18,683	10,205	8,478	45%	2.0%	1.0%
5920	2000	225	50.00	28.00	11,250	6,300	4,950	44%	-7.0%	-8.0%
6000	1998	117	150.00	80.00	17,550	9,360	8,190	47%	-8.0%	-10.0%
6100	2004	75	180.00	100.00	13,500	7,500	6,000	44%	2.0%	1.0%
6200	2008	119	150.00	85.00	17,850	10,115	7,735	43%	2.0%	1.0%
6300	2022	56	220.00	120.00	12,320	6,720	5,600	45%	2.0%	1.0%
Accessories	NA	5,000	15.00	10.00	75,000	50,000	25,000	33%	2.0%	1.0%
Service & Repair	NA	1,100	250.00	200.00	275,000	220,000	55,000	20%	2.0%	1.0%
Total					11,005,703	6,606,779	4,398,924	40.0%	4.0%	3.0%

TABLE 11.4 **Product portfolio analysis revenue sort.**

Product Portfolio Analysis

Sorted by Revenue

SBU 3

Product	Year Introduced	Unit Sales	ASP	Cost	Extended Revenue	Extended Cost	Margin	Margin %	3 Year Growth CAGR	Projected Growth Rate
3500-3	2022	450	6,800.00	3,975.00	3,060,000	1,788,750	1,271,250	42%	6.0%	6.0%
3510	2009	605	2,200.00	1,500.00	1,331,000	907,500	423,500	32%	1.0%	0.0%
3500-2	2022	265	5,000.00	3,000.00	1,325,000	795,000	530,000	40%	7.0%	6.0%
3205	2005	125	6,400.00	3,400.00	800,000	425,000	375,000	47%	4.0%	2.0%
3750	2020	800	750.00	400.00	600,000	320,000	280,000	47%	6.0%	5.0%
3500	2022	520	1,000.00	600.00	520,000	312,000	208,000	40%	8.0%	8.0%
3600	2001	333	1,500.00	950.00	499,500	316,350	183,150	37%	-6.0%	-8.0%
3200	1998	200	1,900.00	1,100.00	380,000	220,000	160,000	42%	-9.0%	-10.0%
3210	2006	42	8,900.00	5,000.00	373,800	210,000	163,800	44%	5.0%	3.0%
3410	2021	700	500.00	300.00	350,000	210,000	140,000	40%	7.0%	5.0%
3725	2018	2,895	105.00	60.00	303,975	173,700	130,275	43%	5.0%	4.0%
Service & Repair	NA	1,100	250.00	200.00	275,000	220,000	55,000	20%	2.0%	1.0%
4000	2005	900	159.00	100.00	143,100	90,000	53,100	37%	15.0%	2.0%
3215	2010	342	400.00	250.00	136,800	85,500	51,300	38%	2.0%	1.0%
4250	2019	600	180.00	110.00	108,000	66,000	42,000	39%	2.0%	1.0%
3400	2019	48	2,200.00	1,200.00	105,600	57,600	48,000	45%	4.0%	3.0%
3350	2018	26	3,200.00	1,700.00	83,200	44,200	39,000	47%	5.0%	4.0%
Accessories	NA	5,000	15.00	10.00	75,000	50,000	25,000	33%	2.0%	1.0%
5150	2015	320	215.00	170.00	68,800	54,400	14,400	21%	2.0%	1.0%
5000	2001	326	200.00	120.00	65,200	39,120	26,080	40%	-3.0%	-5.0%
4550	2022	226	200.00	115.00	45,200	25,990	19,210	43%	8.0%	6.0%
4290	2021	500	75.00	40.00	37,500	20,000	17,500	47%	6.0%	3.0%
4412	2022	146	200.00	110.00	29,200	16,060	13,140	45%	6.0%	0.0%
5936	2009	164	175.00	100.00	28,700	16,400	12,300	43%	0.0%	0.0%
5575	2020	125	225.00	100.00	28,125	12,500	15,625	56%	2.0%	1.0%
5800	1997	97	275.00	162.00	26,675	15,714	10,961	41%	-4.0%	-7.0%
3300	1999	895	25.00	17.00	22,375	15,215	7,160	32%	-2.0%	-5.0%
5500	2018	100	200.00	100.00	20,000	10,000	10,000	50%	3.0%	1.5%
3800	2023	200	95.00	50.00	19,000	10,000	9,000	47%	15.0%	12.0%
5907	2015	157	119.00	65.00	18,683	10,205	8,478	45%	2.0%	1.0%

Code	Year	Units						%	%	%
6200	2008	119	150.00	85.00	17,850	10,115	7,735	43%	2.0%	1.0%
6000	1998	117	150.00	80.00	17,550	9,360	8,190	47%	-8.0%	-10.0%
4100	2010	200	75.00	42.00	15,000	8,400	6,600	44%	4.0%	3.0%
6100	2004	75	180.00	100.00	13,500	7,500	6,000	44%	2.0%	1.0%
3615	2015	16	800.00	395.00	12,800	6,320	6,480	51%	4.0%	2.0%
6300	2022	56	220.00	120.00	12,320	6,720	5,600	45%	2.0%	1.0%
5920	2000	225	50.00	28.00	11,250	6,300	4,950	44%	-7.0%	-8.0%
5900	2001	10	1,050.00	650.00	10,500	6,500	4,000	38%	-1.0%	-2.0%
4400	2022	175	59.00	32.00	10,325	5,600	4,725	46%	5.0%	4.0%
5100	2009	345	15.00	8.00	5,175	2,760	2,415	47%	-1.0%	-2.0%
		19,545			11,005,703	6,606,779	4,398,924	40.0%		

# of Products							%	%	%
Top Quartile	10	4,040			9,239,300	5,504,600	3,734,700	40.4%	4.1%	3.3%
2nd Quartile	10	11,557			1,364,675	880,520	484,155	35.5%	4.1%	1.8%
3rd Quartile	10	2,610			2,75,458	152,084	123,374	44.8%	3.8%	1.4%
4th Quartile	10	1,338			126,270	69,575	56,695	44.9%	0.1%	-1.1%
Total	40	19,545			11,005,703	6,606,779	4,398,924	40.0%	4.0%	3.0%
Pareto	8	3,298			8,515,500	5,084,600	3,430,900	40.3%	3.9%
% of Total	20.0%	16.9%			77.4%	77.0%	78.0%		
Mean (Average)	489	1,155		664	275,143			
Median	276				55,200			

TABLE 11.5 **Product portfolio analysis margin percentage sort.**

Product Portfolio Analysis

Sorted by Margin %

SBU 3

Product	Year Introduced	Unit Sales	ASP	Cost	Extended Revenue	Extended Cost	Margin	Margin %	3 Year Growth CAGR	Projected Growth Rate
5575	2020	125	225.00	100.00	28,125	12,500	15,625	56%	2.0%	1.0%
3615	2015	16	800.00	395.00	12,800	6,320	6,480	51%	4.0%	2.0%
5500	2018	100	200.00	100.00	20,000	10,000	10,000	50%	3.0%	1.5%
3800	2023	200	95.00	50.00	19,000	10,000	9,000	47%	15.0%	12.0%
3205	2005	125	6,400.00	3,400.00	800,000	425,000	375,000	47%	4.0%	2.0%
3350	2018	26	3,200.00	1,700.00	83,200	44,200	39,000	47%	5.0%	4.0%
3750	2020	800	750.00	400.00	600,000	320,000	280,000	47%	6.0%	5.0%
4280	2021	500	75.00	40.00	37,500	20,000	17,500	47%	6.0%	3.0%
6000	1998	117	150.00	80.00	17,550	9,360	8,190	47%	-8.0%	-10.0%
5100	2009	345	15.00	8.00	5,175	2,760	2,415	47%	-1.0%	-2.0%
4400	2022	175	59.00	32.00	10,325	5,600	4,725	46%	5.0%	4.0%
3400	2019	48	2,200.00	1,200.00	105,600	57,600	48,000	45%	4.0%	3.0%
E300	2022	56	220.00	120.00	12,320	6,720	5,600	45%	2.0%	1.0%
5907	2015	157	119.00	65.00	18,683	10,205	8,478	45%	2.0%	1.0%
4412	2022	146	200.00	110.00	29,200	16,060	13,140	45%	6.0%	0.0%
6100	2004	75	180.00	100.00	13,500	7,500	6,000	44%	2.0%	1.0%
4100	2010	200	75.00	42.00	15,000	8,400	6,600	44%	4.0%	3.0%
5920	2000	225	50.00	28.00	11,250	6,300	4,950	44%	-7.0%	-8.0%
3210	2006	42	8,900.00	5,000.00	373,800	210,000	163,800	44%	5.0%	3.0%
6200	2008	119	150.00	85.00	17,850	10,115	7,735	43%	2.0%	1.0%
3725	2018	2,895	105.00	60.00	303,975	173,700	130,275	43%	5.0%	4.0%
5306	2009	164	175.00	100.00	28,700	16,400	12,300	43%	0.0%	0.0%
4550	2022	226	200.00	115.00	45,200	25,990	19,210	43%	8.0%	6.0%
3200	1998	200	1,900.00	1,100.00	380,000	220,000	160,000	42%	-9.0%	-10.0%
3500-3	2022	450	6,800.00	3,975.00	3,060,000	1,788,750	1,271,250	42%	6.0%	6.0%
5800	1997	97	275.00	162.00	26,675	15,714	10,961	41%	-4.0%	-7.0%
3500-2	2022	265	5,000.00	3,000.00	1,325,000	795,000	530,000	40%	7.0%	6.0%
3500	2022	520	1,000.00	600.00	520,000	312,000	208,000	40%	8.0%	8.0%
3410	2021	700	500.00	300.00	350,000	210,000	140,000	40%	7.0%	5.0%
5000	2001	326	200.00	120.00	65,200	39,120	26,080	40%	-3.0%	-5.0%

Product	Year	Qty	Price	Unit Cost	Revenue	Cost	Gross Profit	GP%		
4250	2019	600	180.00	110.00	108,000	66,000	42,000	39%	2.0%	1.0%
5900	2001	10	1,050.00	650.00	10,500	6,500	4,000	38%	-1.0%	-2.0%
3215	2010	342	400.00	250.00	136,800	85,500	51,300	38%	2.0%	1.0%
4000	2005	900	159.00	100.00	143,100	90,000	53,100	37%	15.0%	2.0%
3600	2001	333	1,500.00	950.00	499,500	316,350	183,150	37%	-6.0%	-8.0%
Accessories	NA	5,000	15.00	10.00	75,000	50,000	25,000	33%	2.0%	1.0%
3300	1999	895	25.00	17.00	22,375	15,215	7,160	32%	-2.0%	-5.0%
3610	2009	605	2,200.00	1,500.00	1,331,000	907,500	423,500	32%	1.0%	0.0%
5150	2015	320	215.00	170.00	68,800	54,400	14,400	21%	2.0%	1.0%
Service & Repair	NA	1,100	250.00	200.00	275,000	220,000	55,000	20%	2.0%	1.0%
		19,545			11,005,703	6,606,779	4,398,924	40.0%		

	# of Products	Qty	Revenue	Cost	Gross Profit	GP%		
Top Quartile	10	2,354	1,623,350	860,140	763,210	47.0%	4.8%	3.2%
2nd Quartile	10	1,243	607,528	338,500	269,028	44.3%	4.3%	2.5%
3rd Quartile	10	5,843	6,104,750	3,596,674	2,508,076	41.1%	5.3%	4.8%
4th Quartile	10	10,105	2,670,075	1,811,465	858,610	32.2%	0.7%	-1.2%
Total	40	19,545	11,005,703	6,606,779	4,398,924	40.0%	4.0%	3.0%
Pareto	8	1,892	1,600,625	848,020	752,605	47.0%	4.9%	
% of Total	20.0%	9.7%	14.5%	12.8%	17.1%			
Mean (Average)	489	1,155	275,143					
Median	1,507	664	160,913					

227

TABLE 11.6 **Product portfolio analysis projected growth rate sort.**

SBU 3

					Product Portfolio Analysis				Sorted by Projected Growth	
Product	Year Introduced	Unit Sales	ASP	Cost	Extended Revenue	Extended Cost	Margin	Margin %	3 Year Growth CAGR	Projected Growth Rate
3800	2023	200	95.00	50.00	19,000	10,000	9,000	47%	15.0%	12.0%
3500	2022	520	1,000.00	600.00	520,000	312,000	208,000	40%	8.0%	8.0%
4550	2022	226	200.00	115.00	45,200	25,990	19,210	43%	8.0%	6.0%
3500-3	2022	450	6,800.00	3,975.00	3,060,000	1,788,750	1,271,250	42%	6.0%	6.0%
3500-2	2022	265	5,000.00	3,000.00	1,325,000	795,000	530,000	40%	7.0%	6.0%
3750	2020	800	750.00	400.00	600,000	320,000	280,000	47%	6.0%	5.0%
3410	2021	700	500.00	300.00	350,000	210,000	140,000	40%	7.0%	5.0%
3350	2018	26	3,200.00	1,700.00	83,200	44,200	39,000	47%	5.0%	4.0%
4400	2022	175	59.00	32.00	10,325	5,600	4,725	46%	5.0%	4.0%
3725	2018	2,895	105.00	60.00	303,975	173,700	130,275	43%	5.0%	4.0%
4280	2021	500	75.00	40.00	37,500	20,000	17,500	47%	6.0%	3.0%
3400	2019	48	2,200.00	1,200.00	105,600	57,600	48,000	45%	4.0%	3.0%
4100	2010	200	75.00	42.00	15,000	8,400	6,600	44%	4.0%	3.0%
3210	2006	42	8,900.00	5,000.00	373,800	210,000	163,800	44%	5.0%	3.0%
3615	2015	16	800.00	395.00	12,800	6,320	6,480	51%	4.0%	2.0%
3205	2005	125	6,400.00	3,400.00	800,000	425,000	375,000	47%	4.0%	2.0%
4000	2005	900	159.00	100.00	143,100	90,000	53,100	37%	15.0%	2.0%
5500	2018	100	200.00	100.00	20,000	10,000	10,000	50%	3.0%	1.5%
5575	2020	125	225.00	100.00	28,125	12,500	15,625	56%	2.0%	1.0%
6300	2022	56	220.00	120.00	12,320	6,720	5,600	45%	2.0%	1.0%
5907	2015	157	119.00	65.00	18,683	10,205	8,478	45%	2.0%	1.0%
6100	2004	75	180.00	100.00	13,500	7,500	6,000	44%	2.0%	1.0%
6200	2008	119	150.00	85.00	17,850	10,115	7,735	43%	2.0%	1.0%
4250	2019	600	180.00	110.00	108,000	66,000	42,000	39%	2.0%	1.0%
3215	2010	342	400.00	250.00	136,800	85,500	51,300	38%	2.0%	1.0%
Accessories	NA	5,000	15.00	10.00	75,000	50,000	25,000	33%	2.0%	1.0%
5150	2015	320	215.00	170.00	68,800	54,400	14,400	21%	2.0%	1.0%
Service & Repair	NA	1,100	250.00	200.00	275,000	220,000	55,000	20%	2.0%	1.0%
4412	2022	146	200.00	110.00	29,200	16,060	13,140	45%	6.0%	0.0%
5506	2009	164	175.00	100.00	28,700	16,400	12,300	43%	0.0%	0.0%

3610	2009	605	2,200.00	1,500.00	1,331,000	907,500	423,500	32%	1.0%	0.0%
5100	2009	345	15.00	8.00	5,175	2,760	2,415	47%	-1.0%	-2.0%
5900	2001	10	1,050.00	650.00	10,500	6,500	4,000	38%	-1.0%	-2.0%
5000	2001	326	200.00	120.00	65,200	39,120	26,080	40%	-3.0%	-5.0%
3300	1999	895	25.00	17.00	22,375	15,215	7,160	32%	-2.0%	-5.0%
5800	1997	97	275.00	162.00	26,675	15,714	10,961	41%	-4.0%	-7.0%
5920	2000	225	50.00	28.00	11,250	6,300	4,950	44%	-7.0%	-8.0%
3600	2001	333	1,500.00	950.00	499,500	316,350	183,150	37%	-6.0%	-8.0%
6000	1998	117	150.00	80.00	17,550	9,360	8,190	47%	-8.0%	-10.0%
3200	1998	200	1,900.00	1,100.00	380,000	220,000	160,000	42%	-9.0%	-10.0%
		19,545			11,005,703	6,606,779	4,398,924	40.0%		

# of Products								
Top Quartile	10	6,257		6,316,700	3,685,240	2,631,460	41.7%	6.4%	5.9%
2nd Quartile	10	2,112		1,548,245	846,540	701,705	45.3%	5.2%	2.3%
3rd Quartile	10	8,023		771,533	536,180	235,353	30.5%	2.1%	0.9%
4th Quartile	10	3,153		2,369,225	1,538,819	830,406	35.0%	-2.4%	-3.7%
Total	40	19,545		11,005,703	6,606,779	4,398,924	40.0%	4.0%	3.0%
Pareto	8	3,187		6,002,400	3,505,940	2,496,460	41.6%	6.5%	
% of Total	20.0%	16.3%		54.5%	53.1%	56.8%			
Mean (Average)	489	1,155	664	275,143					
Median	107			15,502					

We can then break the portfolio into quartiles, compute Pareto values, and add statistical features, including mean and median.

These analyses raise a number of interesting observations, including:

- Overall, weighted average growth rates are declining.
- The quartile analysis shows a dramatic concentration of revenue dollars in quartile one (not unusual).
- 75% of the portfolio is projected to grow less than 3% per year and one fourth of the products are projected to have declining revenue.
- Using the Pareto rule, we determine that 20% of the products contribute 78% of the SBU revenue.
- One-fourth of the portfolio has low margins.
- Service and repair and accessories have very low margins.

Subject to further evaluation based on business considerations, the following actions should be considered to improve performance:

- Accelerate the introduction of new products to increase growth rates.
- Consider raising prices on accessories. In addition to diluting margins, these items typically require disproportionate shipping and handling costs, and inventory levels.
- Service and repair pricing should be evaluated and adjusted.
- Products with low margins should be evaluated for price increases or discontinuation.
- Older products with declining volumes could be discontinued.

Business Model Analysis

In Chapter 6, the importance of business model was addressed. Examining the business model and potential improvements can be useful in developing high-level estimates of changes required to achieve targeted performance levels and in identifying potential actions as part of a transformation. In Table 11.7, we start with an estimate of the current performance. In the "What if" column, we can model various changes that would lead to our goals for operating profitability (15%) and return on invested capital (40%). In addition to highlighting the scope and magnitude of required changes, possible actions to achieve in the what-if performance can be identified on a preliminary basis.

TABLE 11.7 **Business model "what if?" exercise.**

	Current Performance	What if?	Indicated Change	Comments
Revenue	52,000	52,000	-	
Product COGS	31,148	29,120	(2,028)	New supplier, SCM redesign
Product Margin	20,852	22,880	2,028	
	40.1%	44.0%	3.9%	
Other COGS	3,640	2,080	(1,560)	Elim Warehouse, reduce warranty
Gross Margin	17,212	20,800	3,588	
	33.1%	40.0%	6.9%	
R&D	3,640	3,640	-	
% of Revenue	7.0%	7.0%	0.0%	
SG&A	10,920	9,360	(1,560)	Consolidate sales office
% of Revenue	21.0%	18.0%	−3.0%	
Operating Profit	2,652	7,800	5,148	
% of Revenue	5.1%	15.0%	9.9%	
Operating Profit after Tax	2,069	7,800	5,731	
Net Investment				
Accounts Receivable	8,667	8,000	(667)	Revenue process redesign
Inventory	10,383	9,000	(1,383)	SCM redesign
Accounts Payable	(6,240)	(6,240)	-	
Accrued Expenses	(5,720)	(5,720)	-	
Property, Plant, and Equipment	13,000	13,000	-	
Net Investment	20,089	18,040	(2,049)	
Accounts Receivable DSO	60.8	56.2	(4.7)	
			-	
Days of Inventory	121.7	112.8	(8.9)	
			-	
Return on Invested Capital	10.3%	43.2%	33%	

Customer Profitability or Value Contribution

Not all customers are created equally in terms of the profit or value contribution to the firm. By estimating the profitability or value contributed (e.g., ROIC) by each customer (or customer type) we may identify opportunities to reprice services or restructure customer relationships. In some cases, the analysis may suggest that a customer is diluting overall performance, and the company should consider renegotiating pricing and other terms or even terminating that customer.

Table 11.8 is an illustration of a customer profitability analysis. We identified the two largest customers, Onerous and Benevolent, and grouped all distributors in a single category. Finally, all others are included as a group due to relative significance and homogeneous characteristics. Where possible, costs and Balance Sheet requirements are specifically assigned; other amounts are allocated based on sales. This analysis indicates that our business with Onerous is generating a loss. The ROIC is unacceptable due to the loss and high asset requirements. Onerous is a challenging customer that:

- Requires discounts on all products.
- Drives higher warranty and service costs.

TABLE 11.8 **Customer profitability and returns.**

	Total	Onerous	Benevolent	Distributors	All Other	Total
Revenue	52,000	6,000	20,000	10,000	16,000	52,000
Product COGS	31,148	3,780	11,200	6,400	9,768	31,148
Product Margin	20,852	2,220	8,800	3,600	6,232	20,852
	40.1%	37.0%	44.0%	36.0%	39.0%	40.1%
Other COGS	3,640	500	1,100	930	1,110	3640
Gross Margin	17,212	1,720	7,700	2,670	5,122	17,212
	33.1%	28.7%	38.5%	26.7%	32.0%	33.1%
R&D	3,640	600	1,300	650	1,090	3,640
% of Revenue	7.0%	10.0%	6.5%	6.5%	6.8%	7.0%
SG&A	10,920	1,380	4,280	1,900	3,360	10,920
% of Revenue	21.0%	23.0%	21.4%	19.0%	21.0%	21.0%
Operating Profit	2,652	(260)	2,120	120	672	2,652
% of Revenue	5.1%	-4.3%	10.6%	1.2%	4.2%	5.1%
Operating Profit after Tax	2,069	(203)	1,654	94	524	2,069
Net Investment						
Accounts Receivable	8,667	1,350	2,857	1,887	2,573	8,667
Inventory	10,383	1,600	3,319	2,133	3,331	10,383
Accounts Payable	(6,240)	(720)	(2,400)	(1,200)	(1,920)	(6,240)
Accrued Expenses	(5,720)	(660)	(2,200)	(1,100)	(1,760)	(5,720)
Property, Plant, and Equipment	13,000	1,500	5,000	2,500	4,000	13,000
Net Investment	20,089	3,070	6,576	4,220	6,224	20,090
Accounts Receivable DSO	60.8	82.1	52.1	68.9	58.7	60.8
Days of Inventory	121.7	154.5	108.1	121.7	124.5	121.7
Return on Invested Capital	10.3%	-6.6%	25.1%	2.2%	8.4%	10.3%

- Requires that we hold inventory and frequently changes delivery schedules.
- Consumes a disproportionate share of sales, customer service, and sales engineering.
- Required modification to existing product, increasing R&D costs.

The company should confirm this analysis and then evaluate the current relationship with Onerous. Each of the issues previously identified should be reviewed and considered. Pricing concessions to Onerous should be limited, if possible. Onerous business practices, such as high service demands and inventory service levels, should be challenged. Onerous should be charged for special R&D projects or pricing adjustments should be implemented to recover these costs. Finally, if Onerous is not reasonable in addressing these requirements, the firm should consider "firing this customer" after thoughtful deliberation and analysis.

DEVELOPING FINANCIAL AND EXECUTION PLANS AND MONITORING PROGRESS

Developing a Transformation Plan

Based on the cost and strategic analysis, the firm can develop a transformation plan. True transformations typically involve a broad set of actions to result in dramatic changes to financial performance. Our illustration includes the following actions:

1. Reduce headcount in specific departments.
2. Evaluate and redesign product development process to reduce development time and improve project management.
3. Evaluate and redesign supply chain management to reduce the cost of purchased materials and improve manufacturing cycle time resulting in reduced inventory levels.
4. Sell nonstrategic and unprofitable SBU.
5. Purchase complementary business.
6. Rationalize product portfolio.
7. Consolidate warehouse activities and sublease redundant space.

The estimated results of the transformation initiatives should be reflected in a pro forma financial analysis. The broad objectives in the transformation plan must be translated into an execution plan with specific actions.

Developing Financial Projections

The financial effects of the transformation should be estimated and incorporated into a pro forma financial summary as illustrated in Table 11.9. The analysis should go beyond the profit and loss statement to include net investment and return on invested capital and even valuation. The transformation cannot be evaluated in a comprehensive manner unless ROIC and shareholder value are considered. Ultimately, the plan should be evaluated on the ultimate goal of the company: to maximize shareholder value.

The results of the proposed business transformation dramatically improve both profitability and ROIC. The analysis also includes estimates of enterprise value using price-earnings multiple and discounted cash flow estimate (valuation will be covered in detail in Chapter 30).

Developing an Execution Plan

The projected results of the business transformation, whether it is cost-focused or includes strategic actions, will not be achieved without a comprehensive execution plan. The plan should include the critical success factors of project planning, including responsibility, progress checks, timing, and accountability. A high-level summary of the plan is illustrated in Table 11.10. This summary should be supported by detailed execution plans for each area.

Monitoring Progress

In order to ensure successful implementation of the business transformation plan, two key accountability tools should be employed. First, dashboards and other reports should be developed that monitor progress on key initiatives and update projections of ultimate results. An illustrative dashboard is presented in Figure 11.4. Second, the executive team should hold frequent review sessions to monitor progress and hold managers accountable to their plan.

TABLE 11.9 **Pro forma financial analysis business transformation.** 🖥

Pro Forma Financial Estimates

	Current	Headcount Reduction	Redesign R&D	Redesign SCM	Sell SBU 5	Purchase Company	Rationalize Portfolio	Consolidate Warehouse	Proforma Estimate
Revenue	52,000		2,000		(10,000)	10,000	(800)		53,200
Product COGS	31,148	-	1,198	(1,500)	(6,300)	5,800	(700)	(1,500)	28,146
Product Margin	20,852	-	802	1,500	(3,700)	4,200	(100)	1,500	25,054
	40.1%		40.1%		37.0%	42.0%	12.5%		47.1%
Other COGS	3,640	(100)	140	-	(700)	700	(56)	-	3,624
Gross Margin	17,212	100	662	1,500	(3,000)	3,500	(44)	1,500	21,430
	33.1%		33.1%		30.0%	35.0%	5.5%		40.3%
R&D	3,640	(100)	(100)	-	(700)			-	2,740
% of Revenue	7.0%		−5.0%		7.0%	0.0%	0.0%		5.2%
SG&A	10,920	(1,500)		-	(2,100)	1,500	(168)	-	8,652
% of Revenue	21.0%		0.0%		21.0%	15.0%	21.0%		16.3%
Operating Profit	2,652	1,700	762	1,500	(200)	2,000	124	1,500	10,038
% of Revenue	5.1%		38.1%		2.0%	20.0%	−15.5%		18.9%
Operating Profit after Tax	2,069	1,326	594	1,170	(156)	1,560	97	1,170	7,830
% of Revenue	4.0%								14.7%
Net Investment									
Accounts Receivable	8,667		(400)		(1,667)	1,667			8,267
Inventory	10,383			(2,000)	(2,100)	1,657	(400)		7,540
Accounts Payable	(6,240)				1,200	(1,200)			(6,240)
Accrued Expenses	(5,720)	800			1,100	(1,100)			(4,920)
Property, Plant, and Equipment	13,000				(1,200)	1,200		(200)	12,800
Net Investment	20,089	800	(400)	(2,000)	(2,667)	2,224	(400)	(200)	17,446
Accounts Receivable DSO	60.8		−73.0		60.8	60.8	0.0		56.7
Days of Inventory	121.7			486.7	121.7	104.3	208.6		97.8
Investment Turnover	2.6								3.0
Return on Invested Capital	10.3%	165.8%	−148.6%	−58.5%	5.9%	70.1%	−24.2%	−585.0%	44.9%
Valuation									
Multiple of Earnings	31,028								117,445
Discounted Cash Flow	34,477								130,495
Assumptions									
Tax Rate	22%								
P/E Multiple	15								
Expected Growth Rate	4.0%								
Cost of Capital	10%								

TABLE 11.10 **Business transformation plan.**

Business Transformation — Timeline and Work Flow

Task	Status	Date	Responsibility	Aug '23	Sep '23	Oct '23	Nov '23	Dec '23	Jan '24	Feb '24	Mar '24	Apr '24	May '24	Jun '24	Jul '24	Aug '24	Sep '24	Oct '24	Nov '24	Dec '24	Jan '25	Feb '25	Mar '25	Apr '25	May '25	Jun '25	Jul '25	Aug '25	Sep '25	Oct '25	Nov '25	Dec '25
Assessment and Plan																															
Cost Analysis & Assessment	Complete	8/15	JH (Controller)	X																												
Strategic Review	Complete	8/22	JA (CFO)	X	X																											
Preliminary Plan	Complete	8/29	JA (CFO)			X																										
Finalize Plan	Complete	9/6	JA (CFO)			X																										
Board Approval	In Process	11/15	JK (CEO)				X																									
Communication Plan																															
Employees			WD(HCM)				X																									
Investors			DL(IR)				X																									
Headcount Reduction																															
Finalize	In Process	10/31	WD(HCM)				X	X																								
Develop Severance and Outplacement Services		11/30	WD(HCM)																													
Implement		12/15	WD(HCM)					X	X																							
Redesign Product Development Process																															
Define Objectives	Open	7/31	GM(CTO)							X Define																						
Hire Consultant	Open	Var	GM(CTO)									X Hire																				
Assessment and Recommendations	Open	10/15	GM(CTO)											X		X																
Implement	Open	11/5	GM(CTO)																XX													
Redesign Supply Chain Management Process																															
Define Objectives	Open	7/31	DS(COO)							X Define																						
Hire Consultant	Open	Var	DS(COO)									X Hire																				
Assessment and Recommendations	Open	10/15	DS(COO)												X						X											
Implement	Open	11/5	DS(COO)																			X	X									

Sell SBU

Task	Date	Owner
Transaction readiness review (e.g. due diligence)	In Process 1/15	TT(BD)
Hire Investment Banker	2/15	TT(BD)
Auction	4/15	TT(BD)
Due diligence and Negotiation	6/15	TT(BD)
Close	7/31	TT(BD)

Purchase Complementary Business

Task	Date	Owner
Develop Acquisition Criteria	5/31	TT(BD)
Hire Banker	6/30	TT(BD)
Identify and Evaluate Targets	10/31	TT(BD)
Close Transaction	11/30	TT(BD)
Integration	2/28	TT(BD)

Rationalize Product Portfolio

Task	Date	Owner
Identify low volume products	10/31	SBU VP
Evaluate: Discontinue, price increases	1/31	SBU VP
Customer notification	3/31	SBU VP
Implement	6/30	SBU VP

Other

Task	Date	Owner	Note
Consolidate Warehouse, sub-lease warehouse C	3/31	DS (COO)	x Consolidate / x Sub-lease

Conflicts

Task	Owner
Board Meetings	
Quarterly Earnings	
Investor Day	
Annual Operating Plan	
Monthly Transformation Review	JA (CFO)

237

FIGURE 11.4 **Business transformation dashboard.**

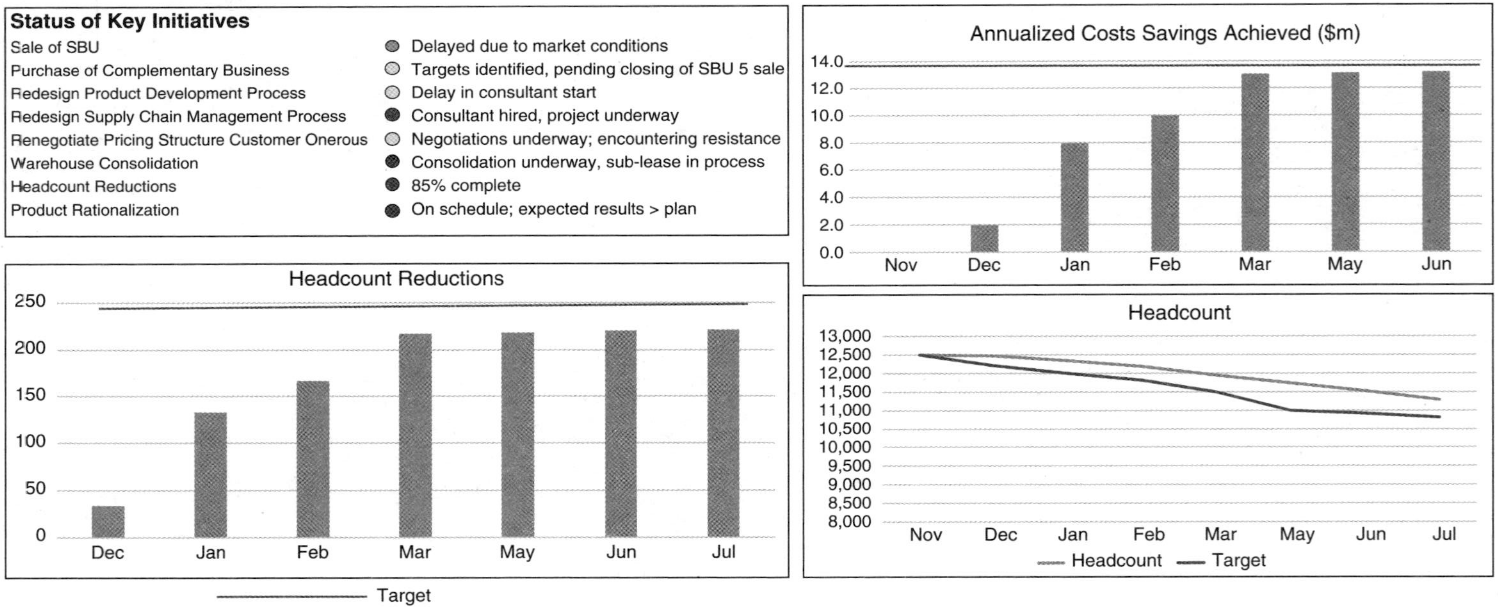

Status of Key Initiatives

Sale of SBU	⬤ Delayed due to market conditions
Purchase of Complementary Business	◓ Targets identified, pending closing of SBU 5 sale
Redesign Product Development Process	○ Delay in consultant start
Redesign Supply Chain Management Process	⬤ Consultant hired, project underway
Renegotiate Pricing Structure Customer Onerous	◐ Negotiations underway; encountering resistance
Warehouse Consolidation	⬤ Consolidation underway, sub-lease in process
Headcount Reductions	⬤ 85% complete
Product Rationalization	⬤ On schedule; expected results > plan

Annualized Costs Savings Achieved ($m)

Headcount

Headcount Reductions

SUMMARY

All businesses will eventually reach a point where they must course-correct. This occurs for a variety of reasons, including life cycle maturity, competitive pressures, disruptive forces, and economic cycles. Financial managers can highlight the need for action, analyze the current situation, contribute to the development of a transformation plan, and assist in monitoring the execution of the plan.

Course-corrections may necessarily involve both a focus on costs and strategic decisions. The transformation plan should be developed after assessing costs, process, market forces, competitive position, and likely outcome from "staying the course." Financial managers should estimate the effects of the transformation plan on the company's expected financial results on a comprehensive basis, including ROIC and shareholder value. The organization must develop and monitor an execution plan to ensure that the objectives of the transformation are achieved.

12

Leveraging and Promoting Technology Investments

The most daunting part of my expanded responsibilities when I was promoted to CFO in 1995 was assuming responsibility for the information technology function. Although I had been the financial lead on a major enterprise system (ERP) implementation at a major division a few years prior, I was overwhelmed by the complexity of issues, the rapid changes in technology and the need to ratchet up my knowledge of information technology (IT), broadly defined. Fortunately, we had a capable Chief Information Officer (CIO) with both a solid technology background, and importantly, a strong business orientation.

The purpose of this chapter is to provide a basic foundation in IT for finance managers and business partners. Of course, this subject is addressed in numerous conferences, books, articles, and webinars and those interested in digging below the surface should do so. Technology is impacting every aspect of our lives and businesses and disrupting entire industries with the promise of even greater impact with the rapid adoption of artificial intelligence (AI). Unfortunately, many organizations are well behind the technology adoption curve, limiting effectiveness and efficiency of finance and the overall enterprise.

Early in my tenure as financial executive, I was introduced to the People, Process, Technology (PPT) framework. Essentially, finance managers looking for improvements in processes and performance should consider these three interconnected elements. As such, technology evaluations or decisions should never be undertaken without understanding and addressing people and process dimensions. Technology alone should never be viewed as a silver bullet to fix process and performance issues.

IT OVERVIEW

In my experience, a wide range in the level of knowledge and understanding of IT occurs across financial management and business partners. The purpose of this section is to provide an overview of key technology areas, including IT applications and the IT strategy roadmap. Figure 12.1 provides an overview of IT software applications within a company from a finance perspective (many of my CIO friends would draw this very differently, but it will serve to frame our discussion here!).

FIGURE 12.1 **Information technology overview.**

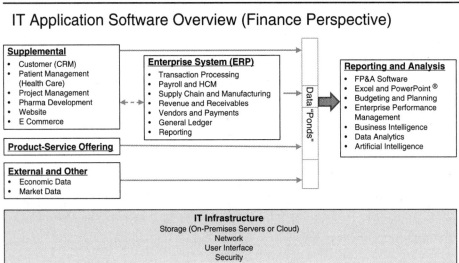

A list of representative application software and providers is shown in Table 12.1.

Enterprise System (ERP)

Nearly all companies have a software platform that serves to process core business transactions, generates business information, and provides a platform for managing the operations of the enterprise. These enterprise systems are referred to as ERP systems, short for enterprise resource planning. Ideally the key parts of this system are fully integrated, for example, so that transactions and data are shared across all applications. Applications in an ERP will likely include payroll and human capital management (HCM), supply chain and manufacturing, the revenue process (credit, billing, and receivables), vendors and payments, general ledger, and some level of reporting. As such, these applications are critically important to finance.

Large ERP vendors offer platforms that process general business transactions and are fully integrated. While many companies have adopted these solutions over the last several decades, many companies continue to operate on outdated legacy systems. The legacy systems may not be fully integrated and require the use of manual effort or supplemental software to connect the separate application packages. In some cases, these systems are no longer supported by vendors and may even fail to provide adequate internal controls and security. The ability to analyze business performance is often hampered in this environment as data is produced in different systems and stored separately, requiring substantial effort to gather, assimilate, and reconcile data from various sources.

An alternative to selecting a fully integrated ERP system from a single vendor, some companies choose a "best-in-breed" solution. Most ERPs have certain strong modules and certain other modules that are relatively weak. A best-in-breed approach selects the best modules (e.g., billing and receivables) from various different vendors, and then integrating those individual modules into an ERP. The advantage is utilizing the best available module for each process; the disadvantages are the need to integrate these individual packages, lack of standardization, and maintaining multi-vendor relationships.

Supplemental Systems

Nearly all companies utilize other software packages that are necessary for business execution within a certain industry or business model. Examples include point-of-sale applications in retail, patient care applications in healthcare, and development and regulatory approval process in the pharmaceutical industry. Ideally, these supplemental systems are then integrated with the enterprise platform.

Product and Service Offerings

An increasing number of enterprises have specialized software that represents a core piece of their product or service offering. A classic example is online retailers that have built shopping and fulfilment technology platforms. These platforms would then be integrated with the ERP solution.

External and Other Information

In Chapter 10 we explored the importance of financial managers and operating executives maintaining a view on forces that are external to the enterprise. These forces are not typically addressed by ERP systems, but are critical drivers of business performance and should be contemplated in the *information* technology environment. Examples include market, competitor, economic, weather, and demographic information. This external information is then integrated with other data by human effort or included in data repositories for use in analysis and developing financial projections.

Data Lakes (and Pools, Ponds and Puddles)

While technology providers and consultants refer to "data lakes" and data warehouses, where all critical data is collected, cleansed, stored, and available for analysis in a single repository, this is rarely the case in practice. While centralized data lakes are a great objective, critical data is often scattered across many systems, with inconsistent data structures, accuracy, and accessibility (pools and puddles). This limits the effectiveness and efficiency of performance management and financial analysis, and requires substantial effort to collect, combine, and process data. A long-term goal should be to create a comprehensive data repository to facilitate analytics and AI.

Reporting, Analysis, and Planning

One of the most important contributions of financial business partners (FBPs) is the reporting, analysis, and development of future projections of business performance. These activities often require assimilating data from a variety of sources and consolidating and refining the data, adding (hopefully) valuable observations and insights to develop business plans, dashboards, and performance reports. A wide array of products is available to analysts to perform these functions, including ERP reports, queries, Excel® and PowerPoint®, POWER BI®, and many other planning and reporting tools. In recent years, there has been proliferation of software tools to assist in FP&A and performance management, including Planful, Adaptive Planning, Apliqo Unified Performance Management, IBM Planning Analytics, to name just a few.

Although many criticize and have predicted its demise for years, Excel® remains a robust tool in the FBP's box. While it is often misused to perform large functions such as a comprehensive business plan, its flexibility, features, and cost-effectiveness are extraordinarily useful in ad-hoc financial analysis. Microsoft has also expanded the features to ensure its continued use and value.

IT Infrastructure

All of the application platforms and software previously described must be supported by a robust IT infrastructure, including processing equipment, storage, network and user interface, and security. Under the CIO's guidance, these functions represent a large portion of the IT budget and staffing. Finance involvement is typically limited to assisting in the financial analysis supporting these investments.

TABLE 12.1 **Representative application software and service providers.**

Representative Application Software and Service Providers			
CRM	**ERP**	**Data Analysis and AI**	**FP&A, PM and BI**
Sales Force	SAP	SAS Institute	Excel
NetSuite CRM	Oracle	AWS	PowerPoint
Pipeline	Net Suite (Oracle)	Microsoft Azure	Planful
	Workday	IBM	IBM Planning and Analytics
		Big Query	Tableau
		Vertex AI Prophet	Apliqo Unified Performance Management
		Google	Adaptive Planning
			Power BI
			Anaplan
			Cubewise

*This is a short list of representative product and service providers. Additional offerings are hitting the market at a rapid pace.

IT Strategy and Roadmap

The CIO should develop an overall strategy for IT in cooperation with the CFO and other senior executives. It is important that the CIO recognize the company's overall strategy, competitive position, and strategic objectives and develop the IT strategy in support of the company's strategic plan. The IT environment and developments should also be considered in the development of the IT strategy. As part of the IT strategy, an IT architecture roadmap should be developed. The roadmap is essentially an overview of key IT projects and timelines. Supported by detail project plans, it is a useful summary and communication tool (Figure 12.2).

In developing an IT strategy, the firm can utilize assessments, opportunity analysis, and benchmarks available through consulting firms and professional organizations. These tools can put a stake in the ground marking the current status relative to peers and best practice organizations, and provide a basis for setting the strategic course and developing the roadmap.

The strategy and roadmap should be updated at least annually and the roadmap will evolve as certain projects are completed and other initiatives are introduced. When I was promoted to CFO in 1995, our initial roadmap included evaluating and selecting standard ERP solutions across our 40 diverse operating divisions, setting up the company's initial website, establishing a local area network (LAN) and desktop roll-out, and preliminary evaluation of potential risks arising from Y2K!

ADVOCATING TECHNOLOGY

Financial leadership should be one of the voices supporting relevant investments in technology. With a broad perspective of the company's strategic issues and objectives, competitive landscape, potential sources of competitive

FIGURE 12.2 **IT strategy and roadmap process.**

Business Strategy

Information Technology
Assessment, Environment, and Developments

Information Technology Strategy

Information Technology Roadmap

Project	Jan	Feb	Mar	Apr	May	2024 Jun	Jul	Aug	Sep	Oct	Nov	Dec	2025 Q1
Security	Security Review		X Report			Implement Findings							
Cloud Conversion			X Hire Consultant	Evaluate Alternatives			X Decision	Implementation					
ERP	Kick Off	Convene Task Force	Define Requirements		Vendor Evaluation		X Vendor Selection		Implementation				
Artificial Intelligence		AI Opportunity Analysis and Data Assessment				X Proposal	Pilot Project						
Critical HCM Requirements	X Info Sec Manager			X ERP Application Staff (2)		X AI/Data Scientist Team							

advantage, and a leadership role in the allocation of capital, finance must play a leading role in IT. CFOs and other leaders need to develop and maintain a working understanding of technology applications, trends, and developments. Fortunately, in this information age, there are many opportunities to become IT literate, including articles published in IT magazines and websites, large consulting firm publications, webinars, and conferences. Many of these sources are now tailored to address issues and opportunities unique to CFOs and financial managers.

Finance can also lead by example by employing technology to improve efficiency and service in transaction processing, and access and delivery of business information to internal clients. I know from personal experience that it is challenging to promote technology best practices and investments when financial services such as transaction processing and performance management and reports are archaic!

Leveraging Technology Solutions in Financial Applications

Finance has a tremendous opportunity to leverage advanced technology across a broad set of applications, including enterprise computing, performance management and analysis, and in developing business projections.

Enterprise Computing. Finance and other disciplines have utilized technology solutions at most companies for over 80 years. Many of these were inflexible software packages installed on large mainframe computers. In my earliest position in industry, key users did not have direct access to the system. Journal entries had to be written out and keyed by a data entry operator onto punch cards for input to the system. Reports were inflexible, and any changes had to be proposed and submitted for development by IT professionals. We did not have an ability to query the system. The ERP systems available to serve these needs today offer much more flexibility, power, and user interface than the old systems. However, I find a surprising number of companies, especially small and mid-market enterprises, rely on outdated, outgrown, unsupported, and often fragile legacy systems. In many cases, these companies do not have the leadership or financial resources to implement new technology systems. Finance should articulate and advocate for adoption of the new "class" of enterprise systems. The example used in the following "Evaluating and Implementing Technology Solutions" is for an ERP system.

Performance Management and Analysis. The increase in digital transactions and other data, storage capacity, and the rapid development of computing power and software to manage and interpret the data have resulted in a huge potential opportunity to redefine performance management and analysis.

Projecting Business Performance. Historically, business projections were developed in the ERP platform's general ledger application and rudimentary supplemental tools (including paper spreadsheets). These generally were not robust tools to assist in the preparation of an operating plan, so forecast and finance teams turned to other tools, including Microsoft Excel®, to develop customized input templates, summaries, and review packages. Soon planning vendors began to market software that offered more capacity, features, and controls in the development of projections. More recently, AI and Machine Learning (ML) have been utilized in the development of revenue and profitability projections. AI/ML is discussed later in this chapter in the section "The Future of IT."

EVALUATING AND IMPLEMENTING TECHNOLOGY SOLUTIONS

Financial managers should play a key role in the evaluation, selection, and implementation of technology solutions. In this section, we illustrate the evaluation and implementation of an ERP system. Other technology projects have similar characteristics to this illustration.

Evaluating Technology Solutions

The evaluation and selection of technology solutions is crucial to the ultimate success of the project. A process chart for this activity is illustrated in Figure 12.3.

FIGURE 12.3 **Evaluating technology solutions.**

Technology Evaluation Process

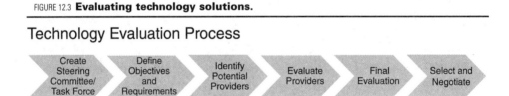

Create a Steering Committee and Task Force. In my experience, a steering committee and cross-functional task force should be created early in the process of considering technology solutions and evaluating potential vendors. These groups can be formed as soon as a decision is made to consider a new technology application or service. Failing to do so can result in not considering key issues, and may also result in lack of support and buy-in from those tasked with implementing the solution and the intended ultimate users.

The steering committee is typically comprised of senior-level executives with a broad perspective of business, operational, and financial matters. The steering committee will also be critical in marshalling support and resources for the implementation and usage of the technology.

The task force should be comprised of managers representing all functional areas impacted by the decision. For example, an ERP system should include managers from sales, marketing, operations, human capital management, finance, and IT. The members will have a detailed view of the requirements and suitability of potential solutions. This group will also be integrally involved in the implementation, and ultimately, usage of the solution. The task force will also include IT managers and potentially a project manager and consultant familiar with the specific technology options to supplement internal talent.

Define Objectives, Requirements, and Evaluation Criteria. An important role of the task force is to develop the overall objectives of the project, specific needs and requirements, and criteria that will be used in evaluating potential vendors. For example, there may be a specific requirement to provide robust project management and reporting or to easily integrate into other established technology systems employed at the firm. Certain industries will also develop specific and very different requirements based on their business (e.g., pharmaceuticals, manufacturing, service, and retail).

Identify Potential Providers. Knowledgeable IT professionals, application users, and consultants can usually develop a preliminary list of potential vendors. In many cases, IT, operations and financial professional associations, and IT research organizations frequently provide overviews of vendors in a particular space. Additionally, managers can consult with members of their professional network for experiences with technology solutions. Typically, this process will result in the identification of a small group of viable candidates. A request for proposal can be prepared and sent to a group of finalists.

Evaluate Providers. Once the search has been narrowed down to a small list of candidates, a more thorough evaluation should be performed. This process may include the following:

- Evaluate the solution against the criterion established by the task force.
- Evaluate vendors, who should demonstrate the technology to appropriate members of the task force and other users. These can be helpful in providing an overview of capabilities and features. However, demonstrations have significant limitations since they are generally based on vendor data sets and typically do not deal with specific nuances of the company's operation.
- Conduct site visits. I have found site visits or reference inquiries with existing users to be one of the most helpful ways to evaluate vendors. Existing users are typically very open about the positive and negative or limiting aspects of the solution and vendor relationship. Choosing a user engaged in a similar business will be most helpful. Attending the vendor's user group conferences is another excellent way to learn more about the solution's overall performance.

Conduct Final Evaluation. The field of potential candidates can be narrowed to a short list based on the preceding evaluation.

- Request a best and final offer (BAFO) from finalists. Vendors typically sharpen their pencils and develop a more responsive and complete competitive offering.

- A proof of concept (PoC) is essentially a test drive and is a useful way to evaluate final candidates. While demos are intended to show off features and functions, they do not identify limitations or thoroughly evaluate "fit for use" in your enterprise. A PoC essentially provides you with an opportunity to test how the system would perform in the company's environment with realistic data volume, complexity, and company-specific issues. This activity will reduce the possibility of discovering significant limitations after selection and during implementation.
- Prior to finalizing the decision to proceed and selection of vendors, an economic evaluation of the technology investment should be performed. A high-level estimate of costs and expected benefits should be developed early in the process and refined at this time. The merits of any investment will vary and it is important to be thorough in identifying costs and benefits. The illustration in Table 12.2 provides a list of implementation costs, ongoing costs, and savings of an ERP implementation.

TABLE 12.2 **Costs, savings, and benefits of an ERP system implementation.**

Implementation Costs	Ongoing Costs	Savings and Benefits
System Hardware	Annual license and support costs	Reduces staff support of legacy system
User Devices	Annual support and maintenance costs	Reduces manual effort due to limited functionality
Installation		Eliminates fees associated with older system
Site Preparation		
Upgrade Network	Additional staff	
Initial Software Licenses		
Consulting		
Training		**Soft and Intangible Benefits**
		Addresses control weaknesses in legacy system
		Results in digitization of all transactions and data
		Reduces financial closing cycle
		May facilitate better analysis and decision making
		Scalability: can support future growth
		Improved IT security

Many technology vendors advocate the use of a simple return on investment (ROI) metric, computed as follows:

$$ROI = \frac{Benefits - Investment}{Investment}$$

This ROI computation ignores the time value of money and generally overstates the ROI since the investments will be made in the near term and benefits will be realized over several years. Table 12.3 provides a better evaluation of the capital investment decision. Chapters 28 and 29 will present tools and best practices for evaluating capital investments. The investment analysis should also project the estimated impact on earnings per share and cash flow.

TABLE 12.3 **ERP investment analysis evaluation.** 🖥

		Project Investment Analysis					$000s (unless otherwise noted)		
ERP Investment									
Incremental Costs and Savings	**2024**	**2025**	**2026**	**2027**	**2028**	**2029**	**2030**	**2031**	
Initial Capital Investments *									
System Hardware	150,000								
User Devices	75,000								
Installation	15,000								
Site Preparation	25,000								
Upgrade Network	51,000								
Initial Software Licenses	425,000								
Consulting	200,000								
Training	25,000								
	966,000								
Additional Costs and Expenses									
Annual License Fees		50,000	50,000	50,000	50,000	50,000	50,000	50,000	
Annual Maintenance		75,000	75,000	75,000	75,000	75,000	75,000	75,000	
Additional Staffing		200,000	100,000	100,000					
Savings from termination of old system									
Annual Licensing Fees		—	−25,000	−125,000	−125,000	−125,000	−125,000	−125,000	
Reduce Staffing Supporting Legacy Problems			−100,000	−200,000	−200,000	−200,000	−200,000	−200,000	
Eliminate Outside Consultant Legacy System			−15,000	−75,000	−75,000	−75,000	−75,000	−75,000	
Reduce IT Facility Space									
Project Expenses									
Depreciation on Project Capital	50,000	193,200	193,200	193,200	193,200	193,200			
Incremental Operating Expenses	50,000	193,200	78,200	−81,800	−81,800	−81,800	−275,000	−275,000	
Incremental Operating Profit Impact	−50,000	−193,200	−78,200	81,800	81,800	81,800	275,000	275,000	
Tax 22%	11,000	42,504	17,204	−17,996	−17,996	−17,996	−60,500	−60,500	
Incremental Operating Profit after Tax	−39,000	−150,696	−60,996	63,804	63,804	63,804	214,500	214,500	

Operating Cash Flow:								
Depreciation		193,200	193,200	193,200	193,200	193,200		
(Inc) Dec in Accounts Receivable		−75,000	100,000				25,000	25,000
(Inc) Dec in Inventories		−100,000	75,000	50,000	25,000	25,000		
Capital Expenditures	−966,000							
Incremental Cash Flows	−1,005,000	−132,496	307,204	307,004	282,004	282,004	239,500	239,500
Cumulative Cash Flow	−1,005,000	−1,137,496	−830,292	−523,288	−241,284	40,720	280,220	519,720
Present Value Factor	0.909	0.826	0.751	0.683	0.621	0.564	0.513	0.467
Present Value of Cash Flows	−913,636	−109,501	230,807	209,688	175,102	159,184	122,901	111,729

Net Present Value (NPV)	**($13,726)**		
Internal Rate of Return (IRR)	9.6%	Discount Rate	10.0%
Payback	4.5 years	PH Growth Rate	0%

* Assume all expenditures are treated as capital

Proof   −13,726

This investment analysis, based on a number of key assumptions, shows a negative net present value (NPV) and an internal rate of return (IRR) lower than the discount rate. Technically, applying investment decision rules, this investment should not be approved (see Chapter 28). In addition to reviewing the underlying assumptions, decision-makers should consider the "soft" or intangible benefits of the project. The legacy system may be a weak internal control environment, which may pose a significant risk to the company's ability to report financial results. I have seen this as a real issue for several publicly traded companies and several private companies that are anticipating issuing shares to the public. The U.S. Securities and Exchange Commission (and other regulatory agencies) requires companies to certify on a quarterly basis that the systems of internal control are operating effectively. Of course, this same objective for internal controls should also exist in private organizations.

The new ERP system will result in the "digitization" of all transactions across an integrated system, facilitating access and analysis of important data. The system also will likely enable better analysis of operating and financial performance, leading to better decision-making, and ultimately, improved results. In certain situations, the new system will also address security weaknesses in the legacy environment and will likely be able to scale to support future growth.

Make Final Decision. Before making a final decision, it is useful to begin negotiations with the final two or three candidates. This ensures a competitive process. The final decision should be based on an informed view of the expected performance, costs, and benefits, including a realistic view of ongoing costs.

Implementing Technology Solutions

Planning and executing a successful implementation will determine the ultimate success of the project. As part of the evaluation process, before a final vendor selection and decision to proceed, the company should start developing an implementation plan, illustrated in Figure 12.4.

FIGURE 12.4 **Technology implementation plan.**

Technology Implementation Process

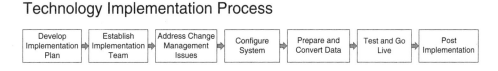

Develop Implementation Plan. The success of any project is highly dependent on the development of a quality implementation plan. The plan should detail the progression of key steps in the process, resource requirements, responsibilities, timeline, and critical path. Often these projects are so complex that a professional project planner is engaged to assist in developing the plan and monitoring progress. Periodic meetings of both the task force and steering committees should review progress and address any issues that arise.

Establish the Implementation Team. If a steering committee and task force were established as recommended in the evaluation phase discussed earlier in this chapter, the project is off to a good start. In my experience, it is imperative that those individuals tasked with implementation had a say in defining requirements and vendor selection. This increases buy-in and establishes responsibility for the success of this very significant project. The project team is typically expanded at this time, for example, the accounting representative will be joined by members of accounts payable, billing and receivables, general ledger, and other key staff. Similar involvement is required across all functions in the company.

Another important consideration is inclusion of consultants and other partners who will assist the project team. Unless the company has employees with experience in the new system and experience with ERP implementations, outside resources are a must. Most ERP vendors offer this service and also have a network of partners who specialize in specific software and industries.

Address Change Management. Implementation of large technology solutions, such as ERP systems, require significant change across the organization. Specific issues include:

- Implementation of a new system, which will change how nearly all employees perform their job. This warrants a plan to communicate, train, and address concerns. Some level of training may be required for all employees.

- The implementation usually results in an increased workload for most employees, as they assist in the implementation while continuing to perform regular duties. This often extends well into the post-implementation phase due to the learning curve and the need to continue to refine processes, key reports, and other required enhancements. Potential issues such as employee burnout, morale dips, and lower job satisfaction should be monitored and addressed by senior HCM professionals.

- Most systems require companies to change internal processes. For example, the billing process may be done on the new system, replacing a tailor-made legacy process with easily customizable features. The billing process will have to be revised to conform to the structure and processing of the new system.

- Most ERP implementations cause disruptions and introduce risks. For example, inventory levels at manufacturing and retail companies often rise during and immediately after conversion. This is due to new processes, automating actions that were manually controlled (e.g., reorder levels and lead times), absence of customized reports, and lack of familiarity with the new system. These risks can be minimized if considered up front and monitored during the conversion process. Other frequently encountered problems include disruption in customer deliveries, billings, paying bills, and so on. Key watch lists should be developed and monitored during and immediately after the implementation.

Configure System. Significant choices must be made to configure the system to a specific company. These choices will have significant effect on the system's performance, report structures, and many of these selections are not easily changed after implementation. A few examples:

- Chart of accounts.
- Cost centers.
- Business units or product lines.
- Product and service codes.
- Bills of material.
- Vendor and part codes.

Prepare and Convert Data. A very important and surprisingly challenging step is the collection, preparation, and conversion of data. Data from the legacy system may be resident in several distinct systems. The data may not be captured in a configuration consistent with the new systems. The data may also be corrupted and not suitable for use in the new system. A simple example is the conversion of data from the old general ledger (GL) to the new system. The new GL structure is likely different from the old, perhaps using a lower level of accounts that does not correspond to the old structure. Certain accounting entries may be recorded in other systems (e.g., consolidating and reporting software) in the past. The effort can be substantial in areas with large transaction or database volumes, including procurement and payables, customers and revenues, and manufacturing.

Test and Go Live. The functionality and accuracy of the new system should be tested before flipping the switch. A few important considerations include:

- Is the data in the new system accurate?
- Are core functions operating effectively (paying bills, processing orders)?
- Are critical reports and queries available to users?
- Is the system resourced properly to support all intended users and processing?
- Will accurate financial reports be produced within established timelines?
- Do the links with other critical systems function properly?
- Is the new system secure?

Some companies run the new and old systems in parallel to test functionality. This can be difficult. A variation is to perform a delayed parallel test, processing past data and transactions from the old system to test functionality of the new system. Vendors and partners have established robust protocols to effectively convert to and test the new system, reducing the chances for catastrophic outcome.

Post-Implementation. Significant issues will inevitably arise after implementation. The steering committee and task force should continue to meet and review the system's status and address any ongoing issues to ensure they are resolved.

THE FUTURE OF IT

One has only to look at the dramatic changes in technology and the way it has changed our lives over the last 50 years to begin to imagine the future changes that await us. Advanced imaging and AI have improved medical diagnostics; on-line retailers and streamers can recommend specific products or programs that we are likely to purchase; our homes employ smart technologies to control security, heating and cooling systems; law enforcement can predict crimes; machines can beat chess champions; chatbots address our questions on-line; just to name a few! Two critical areas already undergoing change that impact business and finance are cloud computing and artificial intelligence (AI).

Cloud versus On-Premises Computing

Cloud computing has seen significant growth over the last decade. In a traditional environment, storage (servers), software applications, support, and security are performed locally on the company's premises. In a cloud environment, these functions are performed by a provider, at the provider's location, and accessed remotely by the company's users. Considerations include:

- **Cost.** While cloud solutions appear expensive on the surface, a thorough analysis may challenge this after considering direct and indirect local support costs (staff, maintenance, facilities, etc.).

- **Service and Control.** On-premises often *appears* to offer more control and higher service levels. This assertion should also be challenged.

- **Scalability.** Cloud solutions, in general, provide more scalability. The provider has more flexibility to grow storage and transaction volumes.

- **Security.** The security of the company's information is paramount whether it employs a cloud-based or on-premises solution. While some perceive a higher risk with cloud solutions, this also should be challenged. Any evaluation should consider the cloud provider's security measures as compared to the security of the on-premises alternative.

- **Additional Risks.** Companies should also evaluate whether there are additional risks associated with cloud computing, for example, disruption of internet access to the cloud. Ownership of the data and how easy it is to transition to a new provider are also important considerations.

Artificial Intelligence (AI) and Machine Learning (ML)

Surprisingly, artificial intelligence (AI) has been a formal science since the 1950s. After envisioned by philosophers and mathematicians for centuries, the term *artificial intelligence* was coined at a summer research project at Dartmouth College in the summer of 1956.[1] J. McCarthy, a professor of mathematics at Dartmouth; A.L. Minksy, a computer and cognitive scientist; and representatives of IBM and Bell Telephone Company were among the participants of the six-week project (the longevity of the AI evolution is remarkable to the author since I was born in the summer of 1956, during the project, over six decades ago!). While AI progressed over the years, it was limited by the absence of both digitized data and computing power. In recent years, attention to and usage of AI has increased exponentially. The use of AI has been enabled by the tremendous increase in digital data and advances in technology that can acquire, store, and analyze large amounts of this digital data.

AI is essentially the ability of technology to perform tasks commonly associated with intelligent beings. Machine learning (ML) is the ability of digital technology to learn autonomously, without human assistance. Recently, considerable attention has been given to the potential use of artificial intelligence and related developments in finance with initial focus on the development of projections and forecasts.

Artificial Intelligence. The ability of a digital technology to perform tasks commonly associated with human (intelligent) beings.

Data Science. A broad term that includes developing insights from large amounts of data using statistical methods, algorithms, and processes. Data science integrates skills and techniques from computer science, mathematics, statistics, data visualization, and business analytics.

Data Scientist. A professional trained or experienced in the acquisition, cleansing, storage, retrieval, analysis, and interpretation of digital data.

Data Lake. A central repository that facilitates storage of data. The centralized data can then be processed to create or enable analytics, performance dashboards, statistical analysis, artificial intelligence, and machine learning.

Generative AI. Any type of artificial intelligence that can be used to create (generate) new text, audio images, video, or code.

Machine Learning (ML). ML refers to the ability of digital technology to learn autonomously from human control or guidance.

---

[1] Dartmouth website, https://home.dartmouth.edu/about/artificial-intelligence-ai-coined-dartmouth

AI and ML will continue to change the way we live and the way we operate in accounting, finance, business, and life in general. While it is uncertain exactly how AI and ML (and other new technology advances) will play out in the future, there are a number of issues, opportunities, and requirements that we should consider.

AI requires data. The most sophisticated AI applications will require access to quality data in central repositories. Data that is stored in multiple systems and formats will hamper the effectiveness of AI. Raw data must be processed to remove errors and inconsistencies, resulting in reliable data structured in a manner to facilitate analysis. In many companies, the use of AI today would be challenging due to "GIGO" (garbage in, garbage out) syndrome.

New competencies are required to be effective in the future. Finance managers and business partners must develop at least a minimal level of competence in data science. In addition, the finance and FP&A departments of the future will need to have data scientists on the team. Data science is essentially the application of statistical analysis to large data sets, identifying trends, patterns, and relationships that the human mind cannot easily determine. A core part of AI is the use of statistical tools at a scale that humans cannot perform. These include trend (time-series) analysis, regression analysis, decision trees, probability, Monte Carlo simulation, expected value, and predictive analytics. These techniques have been used in business for decades and are discussed throughout this book, but the technology now enables their application to large data sets.

AI and other advances in technology will change the way we work. Many news reports speculate on the likelihood of AI eliminating positions for humans. While this will certainly occur (as every advance in technology has in the past), it will also drive a transition away from clerical activities, including collecting the data and crunching the numbers to higher-value activities such as analysis, interpretation, communication, reviewing, and adjusting AI-generated materials, business consultation, and advice. FBPs should plan for this change and acquire or develop skills and competencies for this emerging workplace of the future.

Current AI Applications in Finance. One of the earliest uses of AI in finance is the development of projections, specifically revenue projections. Additional discussion on this subject will be included in Chapters 19 and 22 that cover developing projections and revenue and gross margins, respectively. Some pundits do not believe that AI can generate a full set of financial projections, including a P&L Statement, Balance Sheet, and Statement of Cash Flows. I disagree, since projecting costs and expenses may be relatively simpler to automate than revenue projections. Projecting the balance sheet and cash flow can be based on several decision rules and the relationship of various accounts in the financials (e.g., accounts receivable and revenue). Integrated financial statement models are illustrated in Part IV: Business Projections and Plans.

At present, the use of AI is in early stages in many companies and is often used to generate an "AI or machine version" of a projection. This version is then reviewed and compared to projections generated by traditional methods. The AI projection is typically adjusted (by humans) for errors or anomalies that are not presently considered by the machine, for example, the bankruptcy of a major customer, a geopolitical or economic shock, a one-time or nonrecurring activity, new product introductions, and so on. Finally, the development of projections in an uncertain and rapidly changing world is challenging even if AI and ML are utilized effectively. Undue confidence and reliance in the machine-generated projections may be unwarranted and even dangerous in this environment. Figure 12.5 recaps a typical process for utilizing AI in the development of revenue projections.

FIGURE 12.5 **AI process summary chart for revenue projections.**

Follow development in AI applications in finance. Finance managers must follow developments in the use of AI across business and especially within finance.

Acceptance of AI. Introduction of AI in business processes and decision-making should not be undertaken without recognition of the change management issues that will arise. Analysts and managers will be reluctant to move away from existing (even if imperfect) practices, say to forecast revenue. Widespread use of AI will require demystifying the "black box" output. Operating and financial executives will trust the output only if they have a reasonable understanding of the underlying data sets, algorithms, and decision rules. Reliable results over time will increase confidence in AI.

Indicated Actions

While the future evolution and utilization of AI is unknown, finance managers should:

- Increase the use of data science in financial analysis and developing projections. Where possible, "data scientists" (training and experience in the use of data management and statistical analysis) should be added to FP&A and IT organizations.

- Increase the use of technology, including key underlying business systems (ERP, CRM, etc.) to build and maintain relevant data, data science processing software, and software to share and present outputs.
- Adopt certain aspects of AI. Many of the key benefits of AI can be partially realized by introducing and adopting certain aspects, for example, time series and trend analysis for an extrapolated version of a projection.
- Monitor future developments in the application of AI/ML and modify approach accordingly.

SUMMARY

Technology is advancing at a rapid and even alarming pace. The advances have changed nearly every aspect of our lives, including the way we conduct and manage business. Financial managers must develop an understanding of the use of technology in their business; stay aware of new developments; and evaluate, promote, and facilitate the use of technology within the company.

## 13

Scenario Analysis, Planning, and Management

"It's tough to make predictions, especially about the future."
   "The future ain't what it used to be."

— **Yogi Berra**

Most plans and financial projections are based on a single course or scenario. Single-point projections and scenarios have a number of shortcomings. First, they ignore the presence of uncertainty: *The future will be different than we anticipate.* Second, they contain dozens of assumptions, many of which are critical and buried in the depths of our projection models. In times of uncertainty, scenario analysis and planning are critical tools. Scenario planning can be applied to all types of financial projections. Whether you are projecting financial earnings, estimating cash flow and liquidity, or evaluating product development or capital investment decisions, scenario analysis provides important context and encourages an awareness of uncertainty. It is not simply a financial planning tool; it can be an integrated approach that can assist enterprise-wide efforts in preparing for an uncertain future (Scenario Management).

SCENARIO ANALYSIS: DEFINITION, BENEFITS, AND APPLICATIONS

What Is Scenario Analysis and Planning?

Scenario analysis and planning are tools to assist in making decisions under uncertainty. In general, most operational plans and financial projections are based on a single course or scenario. This single scenario is based on many significant assumptions about the future that often are not explicitly identi-fied. Many of these assumptions involve levels of uncertainty that could have a significant effect on the projections. For example, what economic assumptions are our operating plans based on? Recession or growth? Inflation or stability? Interest rates? Labor market conditions?

While scenario analysis has rapidly gained attention during and after the Covid-19 pandemic (2020–2023), it has been utilized by well-managed companies for decades. My first exposure to scenario analysis was in my first role as a finance manager with a diversified technology and services company in the 1980s. The company required that business units identify significant risks and upsides to our operating plans, and then identify "trigger points" and anticipated responses to those events. That simple, one-page analysis prompted some important discussions about the likelihood of achieving the plan and dealing with known uncertainties.

We live and work in a time of unprecedented change and uncertainty. This was true before Covid-19, and the pandemic has accelerated and magnified both the rate of change and level of uncertainty in many areas of the business and the workplace.

Macro Uncertainties
- ❑ Tax policy
- ❑ Healthcare reform
- ❑ Immigration policy
- ❑ Economic policy and outlook (inflation and interest rates, growth or recession, etc.)
- ❑ Trade policy
- ❑ Government elections
- ❑ Other geopolitical events
- ❑ Cultural changes
- ❑ Pandemics
- ❑ Other unexpected events

Micro Uncertainties
- ❑ New product introductions
- ❑ Customer acquisition and retention
- ❑ Contract wins/losses
- ❑ Competitive actions/threats
- ❑ Regulation
- ❑ Technology
- ❑ Supply chain disruptions
- ❑ Many others. . .

Scenario analysis elevates planning and forecasting from an accounting exercise to a robust management activity. Dwight Eisenhower, a former U.S. General and President, often said, "In preparing for battle I have always found that plans are useless, but planning is indispensable." Essentially, the battle plan never survives the first contact with the enemy. The value in planning lies in the critical thinking, recognition of uncertainty, and identification of possible scenarios and alternative actions.

Scenario planning differs from sensitivity analysis in that it goes beyond flexing key variables (e.g., 10% revenue decline) to contemplating a complete story (e.g., a recession). Table 13.1 illustrates a sensitivity analysis that will be used in Chapter 30 and presents the sensitivity of growth and profitability assumptions on the value of a firm. While a very useful analysis, this illustration does not contemplate alternative *scenarios*.

TABLE 13.1 **Sensitivity analysis.**

		DCF Value Sensitivity Analysis				
					Stock Price	
LSA Technology Company			Sales Growth Rate			
		4%	**6%**	**8%**	**10%**	**12%**
	20.0%	$10.88	$11.93	$13.08	$14.36	$15.77
Operating	**17.5%**	9.43	10.30	11.27	12.35	13.53
Income %	**15.0%**	7.97	8.68	9.46	10.33	11.29
	12.5%	6.52	7.06	7.65	8.32	9.05
	10.0%	5.06	5.43	5.85	6.31	6.81

A scenario is a possible future narrative (a story). A *story* will typically impact a number of variables and drivers. For example, a recession scenario would likely impact a number of performance drivers, including unit sales volume, pricing, cost of materials, human capital turnover, and compensation levels. Scenario analysis will estimate the total impact of the story on a firm and encourage the development of a mitigating response.

Benefits of Scenario Analysis?

Utilizing scenario analysis has a number of important benefits:

- Promotes an awareness of uncertainty and provides a range of possible outcomes (scenarios).
- Counters "groupthink" by encouraging discussions about possible events and alternative outcomes.
- Encourages developing a deeper insight into critical drivers and assumptions, and developing a process to track leading indicators of these factors.
- Increases operational preparedness for a range of potential outcomes by identifying indicated responses to various scenarios.
- Leads to the recognition of the need for a robust and agile organization, which will be addressed in Chapter 14.

Scenario Analysis Applications

Scenario analysis can be utilized in any plan or projections about the future that involve uncertainty (all projections):

- Short-term earnings projections.
- Cash flow and liquidity projections.
- Annual planning and rolling forecasts.
- Strategic planning and long-term projections.
- Capital investment decisions:
  - New product development.
  - Mergers and acquisitions.
- Business continuity.
- Preparing for black swan events.[1]

STEPS IN SCENARIO ANALYSIS

Successful scenario analysis requires several key ingredients. These include developing a robust model, identifying potential scenarios and critical assumptions, leading indicators, and potential mitigating actions (Figure 13.1).

FIGURE 13.1 **Steps in scenario analysis.**

Steps in Scenario Analysis

1. Develop a Robust Projections Model	2. Identify Critical Assumptions and Uncertainties	3. Develop a Base Case and Identify Other Scenarios	4. Model Scenarios	5. Monitor Critical Assumptions	6. Take Indicated Actions
• Robust: assumptions easily changed to generate additional scenarios • Comprehensive: complete financial picture	• Explicit assumptions • Easily changed to generate key outcomes	• Base—most probable outcome • Plausible alternatives • Sequence of events • Estimate probabilities • Consider wide range of outcomes	• Estimated impact • Indicators • Trigger events • Indicated responses	• Focus on critical drivers and leading indicators • Integrate into performance management	• Eliminate improbable scenarios • Update remaining likely scenarios • Implement responsive actions

Develop a Robust Projections Model

Whether we are projecting the impact on revenues, earnings, or cash flow, scenario analysis requires a robust model to estimate the outcomes under different assumptions. Without a strong model, attempts at scenario analysis will be difficult at best. A financial model is a representation of a transaction, event, or business. Requirements include:

❑ The developers of effective models must have a thorough understanding of the underlying business dynamics impacting the projections. It is not simply a spreadsheet exercise.

❏ Assumptions must be explicitly identified so they can be evaluated and flexed.

❏ The model must be robust so that changes can be easily reflected to create different scenarios.

❏ The model should be comprehensive, generating the Income Statement, Balance Sheet, cash flow, and key performance measures, including ROIC and valuation, where appropriate.

❏ Outcomes on key measures (e.g., cash flow) must be autogenerated by the model to facilitate impact analysis and presentation.

Best practices in developing financial models was covered in more detail in Chapter 4, "Developing Predictive and Analytical Models."

Identify Critical Assumptions

Developing future projections requires the use of dozens of assumptions, including the economic conditions, outcome of major contract competitions, timing of new product introductions, M&A, and competitive forces. Critical assumptions must be identified and evaluated as part of setting the base case (based on most likely outcome on key assumptions). In my experience, critical assumptions are not routinely identified and evaluated in the process of developing projections.

Figure 13.2 presents a representative list of critical assumptions and uncertainties. This list should be tailored for each specific enterprise and would also vary over time.

FIGURE 13.2 **Major assumptions and drivers.**

Identify Critical Assumptions and Uncertainties

Revenue and Margins:
- ❏ Pricing
- ❏ Product life cycles
- ❏ New product intros
- ❏ Contract/programs
- ❏ Macroeconomic factors
- ❏ Market and competitive forces
- ❏ Currency

Significant Cost Drivers
- ❏ Human resources
- ❏ Commodities
- ❏ Significant inputs

Macro Economic Factors
- ❏ GDP (Growth or recession)
- ❏ Inflation
- ❏ Interest rates
- ❏ Geopolitical
- ❏ Public policy
- ❏ Demographics

Major Investments
- ❏ New products, programs
- ❏ Information technologies
- ❏ Major expansion
- ❏ Acquisitions

Human Capital Plan
- ❏ Headcount
- ❏ New hires, recruiting
- ❏ Incentives
- ❏ Inflation
- ❏ Healthcare and other benefits

Risks and Upsides
- ❏ New product/program delays
- ❏ Loss of contract
- ❏ Major expansion
- ❏ Acquisitions
- ❏ Black swan events

- ❏ For most organizations, 80% of attention should be focused on Revenue and Margins
- ❏ Every business has unique drivers, and scenarios should be tailored to specific circumstances

Simply by explicitly identifying and listing these critical assumptions, we enable managers and executives to review for reasonableness or change if appropriate. After identifying critical assumptions and drivers, they should be monitored as part of the ongoing performance management process.

Build a Base Case and Identify Other Possible Scenarios

During uncertain times, we need to identify and contemplate a variety of potential outcomes. In our example in Figure 13.3, the Donaldson Company identified a continued slow growth economy as our most probable outcome, representing our base case. The company also identified two other scenarios, a mild recession and a deep, protracted recession. For operating and strategic plans, it can also be helpful to identify other potential scenarios, such as a possible black swan event (recognizing the possibility of a low-probability, high-impact event occurring during the plan horizon, for example, Covid-19, geo-political events, etc.).

Possible scenarios should be identified and contemplated by all senior managers and should not represent a "finance exercise." Perspectives from finance, sales and marketing, operations, supply chain management, and human resources are all essential to identify all potential risks and upsides. To stimulate discussion, there are a few general conventions that may provoke possible scenarios:

- Extrapolate recent performance and trends. Plans and projections are often optimistic. Providing a scenario that simply extrapolates recent performance trends can be helpful in evaluating and testing management projections.
- Identify uncertainties. In military planning, consideration is given to "known unknowns," such as economic conditions, as well as "unknown unknowns," including geopolitical, health, and weather events.
- Consider predetermined outcomes. Managers should make sure they consider events or trends that are predetermined or scheduled. Examples include: demographic trends, economic and product life *cycles*, and known or scheduled events such as elections.

In addition to the economic uncertainty previously described, The Donaldson Company has also identified the uncertainty of the outcome of a large contract recompete. Reflecting both variables, the company has recognized

---

[1]The term *black swan events* was introduced by Nassim Taleb in his book *The Black Swan*. I highly recommend that all finance professionals read the second edition of this book (Nassim Talib, *The Black Swan*, 2nd edition [Random House, 2010]).

FIGURE 13.3 **Economic scenario illustration.**

Economic Scenarios
2024 Operating Plan

Donaldson Company

Current Situation	Scenarios	Trigger Event(s)	Revenue	Profit	Cash Flow	Probability	Indicated Actions
Slow/Negative Growth	**Base Case: Continued slow growth**	CCI remains above 60 and inflation on track to < 3%	125.0	15.0	10.0	50%	**Proceed with Operating Plan** • Conservative CapEx • Conservative Hiring
	Mild recession	CCI < 60 and inflation above 5%	118.0	11.8	7.0	40%	**Implement "Tap the Brakes"** • Limit hiring (essential only) • Terminate dubious projects
	Deep, protracted recession	CCI < 50 and inflation above 6%	110.0	8.8	4.0	10%	**Implement "Hard Brake"** • Hiring Freeze • Restructure/Force Reduction • Delay CapEx and R&D Investments

Expected Value | 120.7 | 13.1 | 8.2

Economic Dashboard: Key Indicators

	Leading	Lagging
Macro	Consumer Confidence Index (CCI) New housing starts 10 Year Treasury Rate Inflation Rate (CPI) Price of Oil	Gross Domestic Product Unemployment Rate
Micro	Order funnel Backlog	Revenue

six potential scenarios, illustrated in Figure 13.4. The company estimates the probability of winning the contract extension at 60%. The contract will be awarded after the customer reviews competitive bids, selects finalists, and negotiates best and final offers (BAFOs). This timeline of events can be monitored as early predictive outcomes of the contract that will commence in the next fiscal year.

FIGURE 13.4 **Identifying scenarios with multiple variables.**

Combining Variables to Create Scenarios

Example: A company identifies two major variables: the economy and a contract recompete

		Economic		
		Continued Slow Growth	Mild Recession	Deep, Protracted Recession
Contract Recompete	Contract Win	Slow Growth/Win	Mild Recession/Win	Deep Recession/Win
	Contract Loss	Slow Growth/Loss	Mild Recession/Loss	Deep Recession/Loss

Model Scenarios

After identifying scenarios and assumptions, we can create a script of how each scenario would likely play out. Using this script, we can then model various scenarios and identify leading indicators, critical decision points, and potential responses. Visuals such as event trees are helpful in understanding and communicating potential scenarios and related outcomes and mitigating actions. A summary of scenarios, illustrated in Figure 13.5, can be very useful for comparing and communicating potential outcomes. This summary includes several key items:

Leading indicators. Identify the leading indicators that will provide insight into the probability of a particular event occurring. Since we have two variables, economic and contract, key economic indicators and contract events are included.

Trigger event. A key part of effective scenario management is to identify "trigger points"; events or thresholds that will trigger the implementation of the responsive or contingency plan. These trigger points, set during the scenario planning process, reduce the tendency for managers to delay action, waiting for "one more update" (with more favorable trends). In our example, the company has determined that consumer sentiment and inflation are the two critical predictive indicators of economic impact on 2024 revenues.

Scenario probability. An estimate of the probability of each scenario is useful. While these estimates are typically subjective, it often reveals surprising insights, such as that the base case has a relatively low probability of occurring or that there is more downside risk than upside to the base projection. The probabilities can be estimated by a knowledgeable manager or by a group of managers. In some cases, the probabilities may be based on expert assessments, for example, probability of a recession. The probability can also be used to estimate an expected value (EV) or weighted average of outcomes. For example, for revenue:

Scenario	Revenue	Probability	EV
SCN-1	$125.0m	30%	$37.5
SCN-2	118.0	24%	28.3
SCN-3	100.0	6%	6.0
SCN-4	105.0	20%	21.0
SCN-5	98.0	16%	15.7
SCN-6	80.0	4.0%	3.2
Expected Value:			$111.7

This exercise should not be viewed as a precise statistical prediction, but rather as another insightful perspective on the uncertainty in the future projections and potential bias arising from optimism or management expectations.

Indicated actions. One of the most significant benefits occurs when leaders identify and evaluate potential actions indicated under each scenario. This allows business leaders to preview each scenario and determine the actions that would be necessary to respond to mitigate the resulting impact. In some cases, the same or similar actions are indicated under most or all scenarios. These actions are called "no-brainer" or "no regrets" by scenario planners as they have minor negative consequences and should be implemented under all scenarios. For example, given the uncertainty and potential impact on the Donaldson Company's performance and liquidity, it likely makes sense to implement cost avoidance or cost reductions immediately, as pending further information and clarity about the future will confirm the need for these actions.

Projected performance (unadjusted). The summary includes the impact of each scenario on financial performance. In this example, we presented the raw or unadjusted results, prior to implementing responsive actions. This view identifies the potential impact of the event or scenario if no mitigating action is taken to facilitate comparison across all scenarios. The effect of potential mitigating actions on financial performance should also be determined. The measures selected in the summary should be tailored to the specific facts and circumstances of the company and situation. In general, revenue, profitability, or earnings per share (EPS), and cash flow would be presented. In this

FIGURE 13.5 **Summary of scenarios.**

Scenario	SCN-1 Slow Growth Contract Win	SCN-2 *Mild Recession* Contract Win	SCN-3 Deep Recession Contract Win	SCN-4 Slow Growth Contract Loss	SCN-5 *Mild Recession* Contract Loss	SCN-6 Deep Recession Contract Loss
Leading Indicators Economy: - CCI - Housing Starts **Contract Events:** - Selected as Finalist - BAFO/Negotiation - Award						
Trigger Event Economy:	CCI > 60 Inflation < 3%	CCI < 60 Inflation > 5%	CCI < 50 Inflation > 7%	CCI > 60 Inflation <3%	CCI < 60 Inflation > 5%	CCI < 50 Inflation > 7%
Contract:	Contract Award	Contract Award	Contract Award	Eliminated from Process	Eliminated from Process	Eliminated from Process
Probability	30%	24%	6%	20%	16%	4%
Indicated Actions	• Cost Avoidance/Delay • Working Capital Improvement	**SCN-1 actions, plus:** • Level 1 Cost Reductions • Delay Capital Expenditures	**SCN-2 actions, plus:** • Level 2 Cost Reductions • Increase credit facility • Suspend share repurchase plan	• Level 2 Expense Reductions • Increase credit facility • Reduce contract specific costs	**SCN-4 actions, plus:** • Level 3 Expense Reductions • Delay Capital Expenditures • Suspend share repurchase plan • Increase Credit Facility	**SCN-5 actions, plus:** • Level 4 Expense Reductions (Restructuring) • Reduce Corporate Overhead • Suspend Dividend
Projections (Unadjusted) Revenue **Operating Profit** **Operating Cash Flow**	$125.0m 12.5m 4.0	$118.0m 8.3m 1.6	$100.0m 0.0 –4.0	$105.0m 8.5 0.8	$98.0m 4.3m –1.6	$80.0m –4.0m –7.2
Excess (Deficit) Liquidity	$10.0m	$7.6m	$2.0m	$6.8m	$4.4m	$–1.2m

example, we also included liquidity under each scenario since the company would face a liquidity crisis under several of the scenarios.

In this example, the Donaldson Company faces significant downside risks to the base case projections. Senior executives should be proactive in monitoring conditions and exploring and developing actions to mitigate the downside risks.

Monitor Assumptions and Leading Indicators

After identifying possible scenarios, we can track leading and predictive indicators that will determine which scenario is most likely to occur. How are events and data trends unfolding? Do they support our assumptions in the base case? Do the trends increase the probability of another scenario replacing the base case as most likely? A dashboard reflecting the leading indicators, as in Figure 13.6, should be integrated into our performance management and business review sessions. This will ensure that the key uncertainties and leading indicators are monitored on a periodic basis. As more information becomes available (e.g., consumer sentiment, unemployment rates), the scenario model can be updated to refine existing scenarios or generate additional possible outcomes.

Take Indicated Actions

Based on the trends evident in the economic dashboard and our predetermined trigger points, we can implement actions contemplated in the development of the scenarios. There is significant value in having a predetermined set of actions before arriving at the point of crisis. The predetermined actions can be implemented without delay, saving valuable time and resources.

UTILIZING SCENARIO PLANNING IN OTHER APPLICATIONS

In this chapter, scenario planning in projecting annual results in an uncertain environment was illustrated. Scenario planning can be utilized effectively in other areas where managers must make decisions involving uncertainty.

Strategic Planning and Strategic Alternatives	Chapter 8
Long-Term Projections	Chapter 21
Capital Investment Decisions	Chapters 28 and 29
Business Valuation	Chapter 30

FIGURE 13.6 **Dashboard of key assumptions.**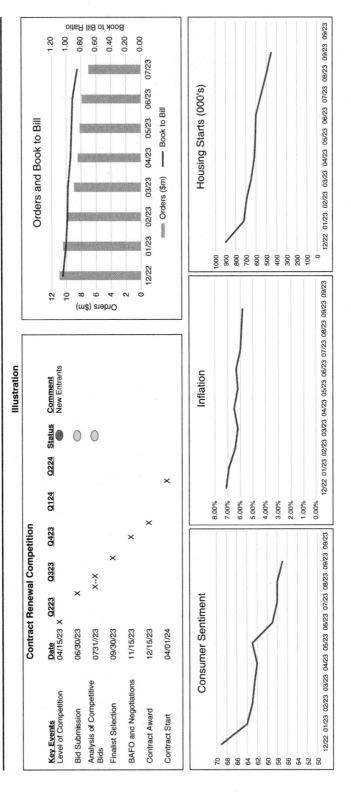

SUMMARY

As financial and operating managers, we are tasked with making decisions and operating in an uncertain future. Scenario analysis provides a structured way to identify a range of potential outcomes, estimate likely impact, and then identify and evaluate potential responsive actions. It reinforces the presence of uncertainty and increases our readiness to deal with a variety of potential outcomes. Scenario planning provides a disciplined approach to dealing with uncertainty and can be applied to any projections about an uncertain future. While scenario management is a useful framework for recognizing uncertainty and preparing for various possibilities, we can never imagine all potential events and outcomes. This realization should drive organizations to create robust and flexible organizations by promoting innovative and agile practices, which will be addressed in Chapter 14.

14

Adaptability: Innovation, Agility, and Resilience

In my 45-year career in business and finance, I cannot remember a period with greater uncertainty or with a higher pace of change. As I draft this chapter in mid-2023, we face a very uncertain future. The uncertainty includes geopolitical events and tensions, inflation, interest rates, regulation, energy, monetary policies, taxation, and pandemics, to name a few. The world is changing at a rapid pace. Much of this is driven by rapid developments in technology, enabling unprecedented computing power in our phones, work from home, a global economy, analytics, streaming, and most recently, artificial intelligence (AI).

Many companies, and specifically finance organizations, continue to operate with tools, processes, and a mindset that is not responsive to the *new* reality. While scenario management is a terrific step forward, future success and even survival ultimately requires an ability to adapt to a rapidly changing and unpredictable environment. Financial leadership can encourage and build adaptability into their organizations and the overall enterprise. Key requirements to quickly respond to changes include the ability to innovate, agility, and resiliency.

INNOVATION

Innovation has been hailed as a magic source of value. In fact, it has been the basis for value creation in a number of enterprises over the last 30 years. It is also a requirement for navigating during periods of rapid change and uncertainty. As an intangible, innovation is difficult to measure, but we know it when we see it!

While difficult to quantify, key conditions and enablers of innovation can indeed be measured. In particular, measurement of innovation requires identifying key performance indicators (KPIs) of critical business processes and activities that are targets for innovative practices, for example, radical improvements in "time to market." It is also possible to identify and assess certain conditions that tend to support and encourage innovations.

Types of Innovation

Innovation initiatives can be grouped into three broad categories: product, business model, and process. Product innovation is generally described as developing revolutionary new products or increasing the speed at which creative new products are introduced to the market—think of Apple's stream of new iPods, iPhones, watches, and other products (and now services). Business model innovation involves developing a new approach to delivering products and services that create significant competitive advantages in cost, customer service, or other important drivers. Examples include Uber's ride service and Netflix's mail-delivery, then their digital model of movie rentals, then streaming and content development.

Process innovation includes efforts to improve the quality and effectiveness of key business processes such as customer fulfillment or supply chain management. Walmart, for example, is notable as an innovator in supply chain, inventory, and vendor management. Other organizations, such as General Electric (in its heyday), Pepsico, and others create innovative *management* processes around strategy, planning, organization, and management development. Still others, like Amazon, innovate processes such as business intelligence and analytics, and cloud computing.

Some initiatives cut across two of these categories, and there is often a fine line between process and business model innovation. In addition, efforts to improve the new product development process reflect both process and product innovation. These distinctions can, indeed, be subtle, but the key point is that innovation is much broader than simply "rolling out new products" and can be directed to any business activity.

Will Innovation Efforts "Move the Needle"?

Before developing innovation programs and measures that can help move the needle, we first need to determine which dial we have in mind. What exactly are we trying to accomplish *through* innovation? In addition to enabling the adaptation and evolution required to survive for the long haul, common objectives include growth in revenue, boosts in profitability, and improvements in processes or product development effectiveness. Ultimately, most executives hope to accelerate progress on key strategic objectives, financial measures, and shareholder value.

Most consultants and academics, and most independent rankings of innovation focus on two or three measures of overall performance to evaluate innovation effectiveness. These measures, such as total return to shareholders (TRS) and revenue or profit growth, are good starting points, but they are by no means perfect or exclusive measures of innovation. Their principal deficiencies are that they are lagging indicators; historical measures don't help companies see where they are going. In addition, each of these measures is impacted by multiple factors besides innovation; TRS, for instance, is also subject to stock market variations, errors in valuation, cost reductions, and many other factors.

Developing an effective set of measures necessitates the identification of performance indicators that emphasize the direct contribution from innovation. This process, the development of a dashboard for innovation—can be facilitated by identifying key measures and activities that cascade from the objective of creating shareholder value.

Performance and Value Creation in Innovative Organizations

How have innovative companies performed on overall financial and value creation measures? Consider the dashboard of key financial and value indicators for Apple, which includes the following measures (see also Figure 14.1):

Revenue growth.

Operating margins.

Return on invested capital.

Asset turnover.

Growth in market value.

Apple's performance over an extended period of time is extraordinary. Revenues have nearly tripled while maintaining high profitability. Market value has quadrupled, reaching over $2 trillion. ROIC is strong, despite the dilutive effect of retaining substantial cash reserves. It is noteworthy that the growth rate has slowed in recent years. This is inevitable for two reasons. First, as the organization grows, it becomes more difficult to maintain a high percentage growth rate on a larger base. Increasing sales by $50 million on a $100 million base is a 50% growth rate; growing by $50 million on a $500 million base is "only" 10% growth, and $50 million growth on $5 billion is only 1% growth. Second, maintaining the innovation edge often seems to wane over time, and it is often more difficult to identify new product and new markets for extended periods of time. Some organizations, including Amazon,

FIGURE 14.1 **Historical performance recap: Apple.**

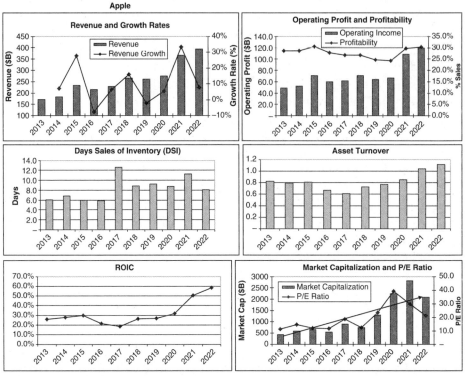

Source: Analysis based on company annual reports.

have continued to refresh growth by extending offerings to new markets and even leveraging technology competencies into new business opportunities (e.g., Amazon Web Services).

The power of innovation to drive differentiation within an industry is noteworthy as well. In my book *Financial Planning & Analysis and Performance Management*, I highlighted the early evolution in home video entertainment. The example is still powerful and continues to evolve to this day! Look at the contrast between the performance of the business model innovator Netflix (NFLX) and the traditional company Blockbuster (BBI) (see Figure 14.2) in the early 2000s. Netflix's innovative business model for DVD mail rental resulted in very rapid sales growth—at Blockbuster's expense. The Netflix business model also produced strong operating margins, even during high-growth periods, while Blockbuster's profits plummeted. Blockbuster's market capitalization and price-to-earnings (PE) multiple cratered as a result, whereas Netflix created substantial value. Netflix continued to innovate by pivoting away from the mail order DVD business to a digital platform, and then ultimately began developing their own programming content.

The Netflix story continues. . .after enjoying a leading and profitable position in developing and streaming content, competitors were inevitably

FIGURE 14.2 **Comparative performance Netflix and Blockbuster.**

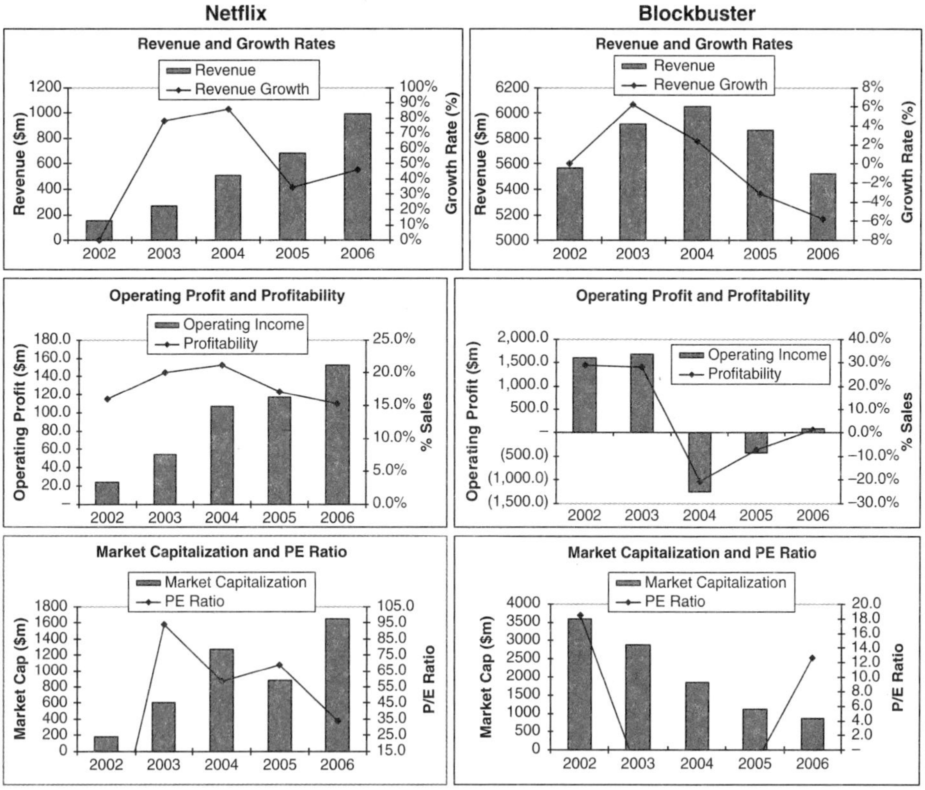

Source: Company filings with Securities and Exchange Commission.

attracted to the party. These competitors included other technology companies such as Amazon, Apple, and Google (YouTube TV) in addition to entertainment companies, including Disney, Paramount, and many others! This led to huge investments in developing content that have impacted cash flow and return on invested capital (ROIC). Netflix accounts for content development as an asset and amortizes these costs over time. As of year-end 2022, the company had $32.7 billion of "content assets," representing over 100% of current revenues. These capitalized costs were financed by operating cash flows and increased borrowings, and will be amortized against revenues in the future (Figure 14.3).

A similar transformation has been underway in retail. Amazon and other internet retailers have transformed the retail market, taking market share from traditional retailers at levels that threaten their very survival. Strong retailers, including Target and Walmart, have responded with their own digital platforms. Many others were not able to respond.

Innovator	Victims
Netflix	Blockbuster
Amazon	Walmart, Target, many others
Tesla	Traditional automobile manufacturers

FIGURE 14.3 **Netflix postscript.**

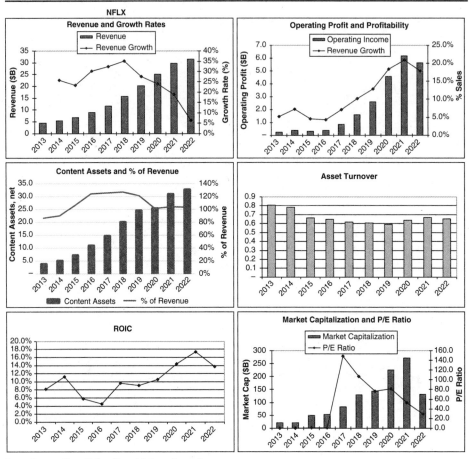

Source: Company filings with Securities and Exchange Commission.

Connecting the Dots: Innovation, Financial Performance, and Value

Innovation is most often discussed in the context of revenue growth. For this purpose, we focus on the five key drivers of organic growth: market size, market growth, and competition; new product introduction; new customer acquisition; new channels; and customer satisfaction/retention (Figure 14.4).

The importance of each of these drivers at this level will vary over time and from company to company. Organizations should select measures that address an improvement opportunity or a specific strategic objective. For example, if new product development is a priority, measures such as revenue from new products, project status, and other key metrics can be incorporated into a new product development dashboard (see Figure 14.5). Such a dashboard would be appropriate for Apple, but not relevant for Wal-Mart's focus on process innovation or Netflix's focus on business model innovation. If we were to create the revenue growth drill-down chart for Netflix, it would most

FIGURE 14.4 **Drilling down into sources of revenue growth.**

Link Value & Value Drivers to Business Processes & Activities

Drill Down: Revenue Growth

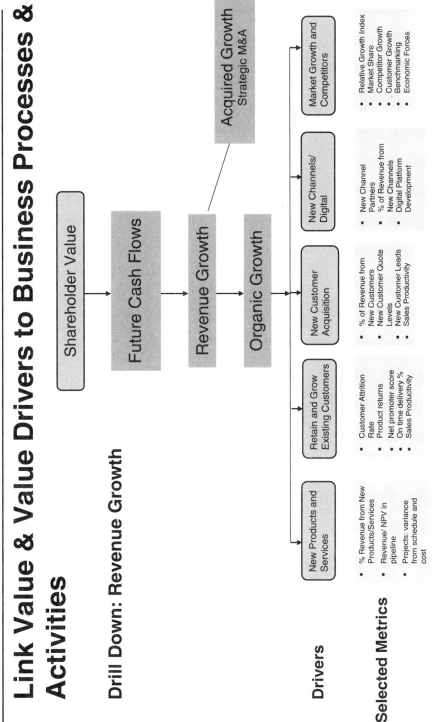

Drivers

Selected Metrics

281

FIGURE 14.5 **New product development dashboard.**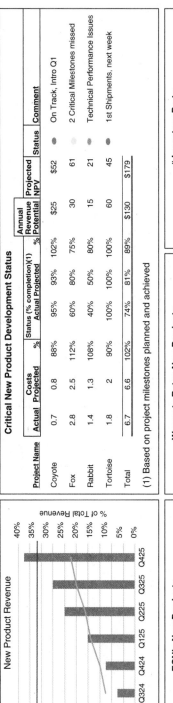

New Product Development Dashboard

Critical New Product Development Status

Project Name	Costs			Status (% completion)(1)			Annual Revenue Potential %	Projected NPV	Status	Comment
	Actual	Projected	%	Actual	Projected	%				
Coyote	0.7	0.8	88%	95%	93%	102%	$25	$52	●	On Track, Intro Q1
Fox	2.8	2.5	112%	60%	80%	75%	30	61	○	2 Critical Milestones missed
Rabbit	1.4	1.3	108%	40%	50%	80%	15	21	●	Technical Performance Issues
Tortoise	1.8	2	90%	100%	100%	100%	60	45	●	1st Shipments, next week
Total	6.7	6.6	102%	74%	81%	89%	$130	$179		

(1) Based on project milestones planned and achieved

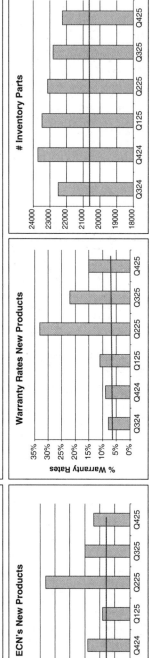

New Product Revenue

Warranty Rates New Products

Inventory Parts

ECN's New Products

— Goal

likely focus on customer acquisition, retention (or churn) activity, content development, and related measures.

Note that this new product development dashboard is balanced. In addition to containing vital information on new product status and development performance, it also presents information on the quality of the design process (engineering change notices from new products) and design for manufacturability (number of inventory parts).

Additional measures that provide insight into innovation effectiveness by specific value drivers are included in Table 14.1 and Figure 14.6. Managers should select measures from the list that best represent their situation-specific priorities and issues.

TABLE 14.1 **Key innovation measures.**

Overall	New Product	Business Model	Process
Revenue Growth-Organic	Relative Growth Index	Value Added per Employee	Asset Turnover
Total Return to Shareholders	Annual Revenue in Development Pipeline	Operating Leverage %	Customer Satisfaction (Warranty, OTD)
Profitability	Project Completion vs. Plan (Milestones and Cost)	ROIC (Asset Turnover × Profitability)	Cycle Time
Return on Invested Capital	% Sales from New Products	Customer Life Cycle Cost	Production Yields

In addition to developing key measures and dashboards, we can assess the conditions for innovation, utilize benchmarking and process evaluation tools, and project planning execution and tracking techniques. Do the culture, management systems, and practices of the company encourage or inhibit innovation?

Assessing the Environment for Innovation

Culture and Environment

- ❏ Tolerance for risk?
- ❏ View "failures" as an inevitable part of business and life?
- ❏ NIH (not invented here) syndrome?

People

- ❏ What happens to managers of "failed projects"?
- ❏ Are risk-takers and innovators rewarded?
- ❏ How many hours of training/development do our people get?
- ❏ Active membership in trade or professional organizations?

(*continued*)

(continued)

❑ Passionate Advocates or Bureaucrats?

❑ Diverse human capital: experience, education, age, culture, professional discipline?

Process

❑ Funding available for innovation, experimentation, skunk works, and pure research?

❑ How painful is it to advance new ideas in the company?

❑ Discipline in project planning, execution, and monitoring?

Leadership and Ownership

❑ Vision and strategy: communicated and understood?

❑ Investment and performance horizon: months, quarters, or years?

Focus: Internal or External

❑ Engage in partnerships and joint ventures?

❑ Performance benchmarking utilized?

❑ Hiring mix of internal and external candidates?

❑ Source of new product ideas?

MEASURING AND DRIVING BUSINESS AGILITY

Both the pace and magnitude of change have reached levels that threaten the success and even the very existence of many organizations. Leaders of all organizations must assess and improve their ability to see, recognize, respond to, and adapt to change. They must have the ability to move quickly to address threats and to capitalize on opportunities. Finally, in addition to measuring and assessing agility, it is essential for executives to provide tools for improving the organizations agility.

Business agility as the ability to anticipate, recognize, and effectively:

- Capitalize on opportunities.
- Mitigate risks and downside events.
- Prepare for and weather storms, including economic cycles and black swan events.

FIGURE 14.6 **Innovation dashboard.**

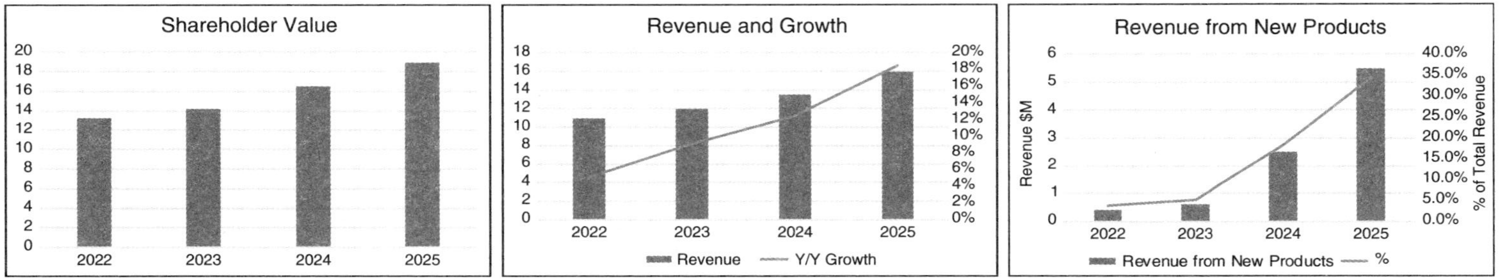

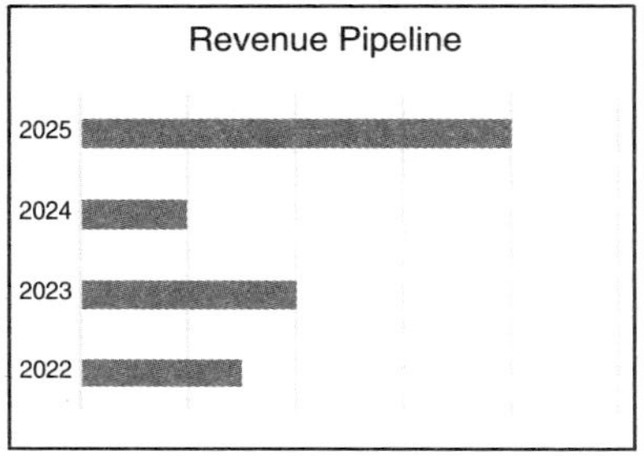

Critical New Product Development Status

Project Name	Costs Actual	Costs Projected	%	Status (% completion)[1] Actual	Status (% completion)[1] Projected	%	Annual Revenue Potential	Projected NPV	Status	Comment
Coyote	0.7	0.8	88%	95%	93%	102%	$25	$52	●	On Track, Intro Q1
Fox	2.8	2.5	112%	60%	80%	75%	30	61	●	2 Critical Milestones missed
Rabbit	1.4	1.3	108%	40%	50%	80%	15	21	●	Technical Performance Issues
Tortoise	1.8	2	90%	100%	100%	100%	60	45	●	1st Shipments, next week
Total	6.7	6.6	102%	74%	81%	89%	$130	$179		

(1) Based on project milestones planned and achieved

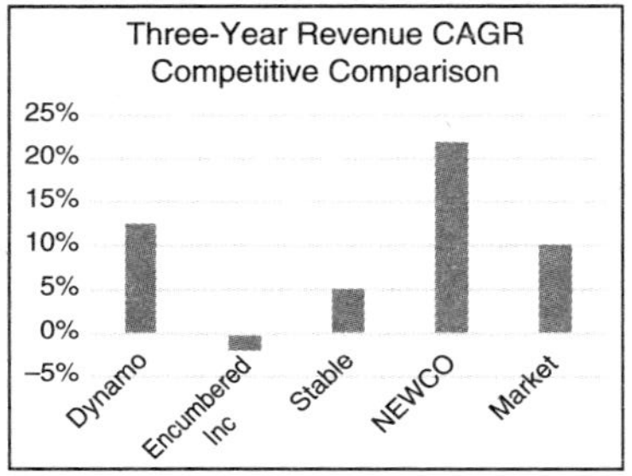

285

It is helpful to view agility as a three-part process as shown in Figure 14.7. First, do we have the *vision* to see a potential threat, opportunity, or event on the horizon? This is the most important component since if a threat or opportunity goes undetected, the organization cannot effectively respond. In addition, seeing the threat or opportunity at the earliest possible time extends the total time the enterprise has to respond to the event. Second, the organization must be able to *recognize* that an event or circumstance represents a threat or opportunity. Finally, the organization must have the ability to *respond*.

FIGURE 14.7 **Agility as a three-part process.**

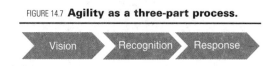

Can Your Organization Call an "Audible"?   One of the best examples of agility is found on the (American) football field. Prior to each play, the team "huddles-up" to call the next play. The plays were selected as part of a game-plan (operating plan) that was tailored to address the specific competitor, accounting for strengths and weaknesses of both teams. After calling a play in the huddle, the team lines up to execute the play. As the quarterback (team leader) comes to the line of scrimmage, he quickly surveys the opposing defensive personnel and formation to determine if the play he just called can be executed successfully. If he decides that the play will not work, he can call an "audible," changing the play called in the huddle to a different play that is more favorable to the defensive situation he has observed. He then has the ability to communicate this change to the team, by a single word or gesture, resulting in a different role or assignment for each player. This entire process takes only seconds.

Businesses and other organizations can learn a lot from this analogy. Many of us look across the "field" and see very different circumstances from what we had expected when we "called the play." Unfortunately, we do not have the ability to call an audible!

Let's examine the skills and preparation that enable the "audible" on the football field, using the Vision-Recognition-Response framework, and extend these to our business environment (Figure 14.8).

Vision   When the quarterback comes to line of scrimmage, he does so with tremendous "vision." While his eyes likely possess greater than average capabilities such as clarity and peripheral vision, he has been trained to survey the whole field. He scans key match-ups and assignments, and accounts for so-called "high-impact opponents." At first opportunity, he will review photographs taken to see the entire defensive alignment.

Businesses must also develop and improve their vision. FP&A and EPM play a large role in developing and improving the organization's vision.

FIGURE 14.8 **Improving agility.**

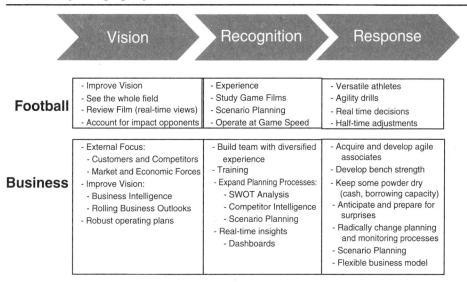

	Vision	Recognition	Response
Football	- Improve Vision - See the whole field - Review Film (real-time views) - Account for impact opponents	- Experience - Study Game Films - Scenario Planning - Operate at Game Speed	- Versatile athletes - Agility drills - Real time decisions - Half-time adjustments

Business	- External Focus:
	  - Customers and Competitors
	  - Market and Economic Forces
	- Improve Vision:
	  - Business Intelligence
	  - Rolling Business Outlooks
	- Robust operating plans
		- Build team with diversified
		  experience
		- Training
		- Expand Planning Processes:
		  - SWOT Analysis
		  - Competitor Intelligence
		  - Scenario Planning
		  - Real-time insights
		    - Dashboards
			- Acquire and develop agile
			  associates
			- Develop bench strength
			- Keep some powder dry
			  (cash, borrowing capacity)
			- Anticipate and prepare for
			  surprises
			- Radically change planning
			  and monitoring processes
			- Scenario Planning
			- Flexible business model

Play-callers (executives) must have a view of how their internal processes, players, and projects are performing to ensure they are ready to execute. Do we have the right players on the team? Does everyone understand the plan and their role? Unfortunately, many organizations do a poor job in communicating the game plan to all employees, significantly limiting the ability of the team to succeed.

As was discussed in Chapter 10, organizations also need to focus substantial attention to external forces. The vast majority of threats and opportunities arise outside the organization. Therefore, they must have the ability to see what is happening in the economy, their market, to their competitors, and regulatory and geopolitical events. Extending the techniques and horsepower of financial analysis and performance management to external factors can significantly improve the vision of the enterprise.

Capturing and presenting critical information in real time is essential to improving the organization's vision. The use of rolling forecasts and outlooks, which will be discussed in Chapter 20, facilitates the processing of new information and events, and understanding the impact on the company's performance.

Recognition   The best vision in the world would not help the quarterback if he did not have the ability to immediately recognize and evaluate what he was seeing on the field of play. This ability comes from both preparation and experience. The preparation includes long hours spent studying films of their opponent in prior games. Coaches and players review the tendencies of the other team in certain situations. The team develops different actions under various "what-if" scenarios.

Similarly in business, we must be able to interpret what we see and hear and understand the implications for our ability to execute our plans and achieve our objectives. A diversified and experienced executive team and board can increase the likelihood that events and patterns will be recognized and addressed. For example, an executive from another industry may recognize patterns from his past experience that are new to this industry. An experienced executive may recognize the early signals of a business or economic cycle. Identifying potential surprises and considering various scenarios will improve the ability of the organization to recognize and respond.

Response   After seeing and recognizing changing circumstances, the team must have the ability to respond. One of the key factors is having the right personnel. Since the team is not sure what it will encounter, a premium is placed on having highly versatile players who can play a variety of different roles as required. For example, using our football analogy a linebacker who can drop back in pass coverage or attack the line of scrimmage on a run play provides more flexibility than a specialist player. The players are coached and trained, and study the game plan. The hours of preparation allow the players to react at *game speed*. Teams work to develop both physical and mental agility. They practice and drill to ensure their ability to react quickly under many diverse situations.

Companies improve their ability to respond by acquiring and developing versatile (agile) associates that can be quickly re-deployed to address issues and opportunities the company faces. How deep is the bench? Do we prepare for changing circumstances by anticipating potential future events and developing responsive actions? By developing planning processes that identify and evaluate critical assumptions and possible scenarios, the organization will be better able to respond to any change in circumstances. Maintaining a flexible business model and keeping some financial powder (cash and borrowing capacity) dry will facilitate developing and executing responses.

The Agile (Versatile) Associate

Since our associates are vital contributors to our overall success, it also holds that they play a huge role in enabling the organization's agility and flexibility. Agile associates are constant learners and are highly adaptable; they can be reassigned based on changing conditions and priorities. Characteristics of agile-versatile associates include:

❑ Continual learner.
❑ Good communicator.

❑ Analytical.

❑ Project management skills.

❑ Team player.

❑ General business perspective.

❑ Able to jump across silos to contribute.

❑ A "go-to" person.

Not all roles need to be filled by agile associates. Companies should identify key roles and departments where agility is critical and set target levels for
those areas. Organizations can acquire or develop agile associates by employing the following practices:

❑ Hiring practices (identify and evaluate key competencies).

❑ Rotational assignments.

❑ Training and development.

❑ Promoting external activities and interests to broaden experience.

Anticipating and Responding to Business and Economic Cycles

Nearly all businesses are subject to business and economic cycles. Business
leaders must recognize that business downturns (and subsequent recoveries)
are inevitable and build an enterprise that can thrive on upturns and survive
on downturns:

❑ Develop business models that are successful across economic cycles.

❑ Utilize tools that provide a view forward, increasing the time to react.

In addition, all products, businesses, and markets are also impacted by
a finite life cycle. New products or businesses are developed, grow, reach a
peak at maturity, and then tend to decline. Successful companies are fully
aware of this cycle and monitor product life cycle stage. The impact can be
offset by developing and introducing new products as the older products
reach maturity.

Many businesses fail to recognize that they are approaching the peak and
heading toward slow or even negative growth. Signs that an organization is
approaching decline include:

❑ Growth rate slows.

❑ Revenue projections are missed.

❑ Product and gross margins decline.

Ignoring these signposts prevents the organization from revamping the business model to adjust for the road ahead or to accelerate the development of new businesses to refresh the growth curve. As a result, these organizations suffer from significant profit hits as revenues decline. In addition, pressure mounts to develop an acquisition program to replace the lost organic revenue growth. Failing to recognize the stage of maturity of the business can even lead to its ultimate demise.

FIGURE 14.9 **Economic and life cycles.**

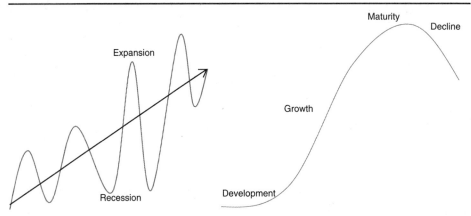

Economic Cycles Are Cyclical!   **Products and Businesses Have a Life Cycle**

What can finance do to better prepare the organization for the impact of business and life cycle changes?

- Provide context. Many executives and especially founders have great difficulty accepting that the company may be approaching a mature state. Preparing analysis that shows growth curves for products and the entire business can help. Overlaying competitor, customer, and other well-known life cycle curves can provide further support for the alert.

- Establish signposts or trigger events. Predetermining KPI levels or events that clearly indicate that a kink in the curve is imminent can help to prevent denial and facilitate earlier responses.

- Develop cyclical projection scenarios. As part of developing strategic plans, long-term forecasts, and even business outlooks, a business cycle or life cycle scenario should be prepared. This will introduce the possibility of a downturn into the thinking and allow the team to contemplate signposts and contingency efforts.

- Develop business models and practices accordingly. For companies that are in cyclical industries, they should develop a flexible business model. Shifting selected expenses from fixed to variable will afford more flexibility and reduce the impact of the shortfall on profits. For companies approaching maturity, investment levels and costs and expense levels can be adjusted for the road that lies ahead.

- Dampen irrational exuberance during peaks. Human beings tend to extrapolate the present conditions into the future (known as recency bias). Include a historical perspective in planning and analytical products to remind executives that it is not if, but when.

- Prepare for recovery during downturns. Companies that participate in cyclical industries should identify signal events and prepare plans to ramp up to capitalize on the recovery.

Agility Assessment and Metrics

KPIs that provide a perspective on the level of agility within an organization include:

Percentage of agile employees. It is not necessary that all associates are versatile. However, establishing a target level that will provide flexibility and developing practices to move toward that level is important. The organization should identify characteristics of an agile associate incorporating characteristics from the list above that are most relevant.

Associate length of service/time in position. Measuring the length of service and time in position can provide a view of versatility and agility. If a substantial number of associates have been locked in their present position for long periods, it may indicate a lack of mobility or agility or a need to increase rotational development assignments.

Breakeven sales level. This old-school measure is still very useful. It estimates the level of sales required to break even, based on contribution margins and fixed versus variable costs. It is an indication of preparedness, by highlighting the extent that revenue can decrease before incurring losses. Measuring the level over time will track progress in bracing for downturns; a decrease in breakeven sales is a positive result of converting fixed costs to variable. This analytical tool will be explored further in Chapter 23.

Reduce planning cycles. Companies should measure and reduce the length of time to generate the strategic and operating plan as well as business forecasts. A shorter time cycle usually indicates a more efficient process that can lead to a faster response to any changing circumstance. For example, reducing the length of time to develop an updated or alternative scenario business forecast would allow the company to quantify the potential impact and address surprises in a timely manner.

Manufacturing and procurement cycles. Shorter manufacturing and procurement cycles allow for greater flexibility in responding to change in demand.

Time to market, new product development. Companies that can introduce new products in a shorter time frame have a significant advantage in general, but especially in responding to competitive threats or market needs.

These measures can be utilized as part of a periodic assessment of agility. These measures can also be used to develop a business agility dashboard as is illustrated in Figure 14.10.

Increasing business agility:

❑ Establish measures that cover flexibility and agility.
❑ Shift business planning from detail financial budgets and forecasts to driver-based planning.
❑ Focus on scenario and contingency planning.
❑ Identify, evaluate, and monitor key assumptions.
❑ Identify and improve key aspects of flexibility and agility.
❑ Reduce planning and forecast cycles.
❑ Reduce time to market.
❑ Reduce manufacturing/procurement cycle time.

BUSINESS RESILIENCE

Disruptions, setbacks, problems, and other challenges are inevitable in life and business. Individuals and managers view and react to these challenges in different ways. Some hold an unrealistic expectation that nothing will go wrong and view challenges as catastrophic and are more likely to abandon ship. Others view challenges as inevitable and embrace them as learning experiences and opportunities in disguise. In early 2023, I hear senior executives often quipping that they are "wondering what the next crisis is going to be."

Executives and organizations that have overcome challenges in the past are more confident and better equipped to deal with future problems. This reality has been recognized for thousands of years. As Lucius Seneca, an ancient

FIGURE 14.10 **Agility dashboard.**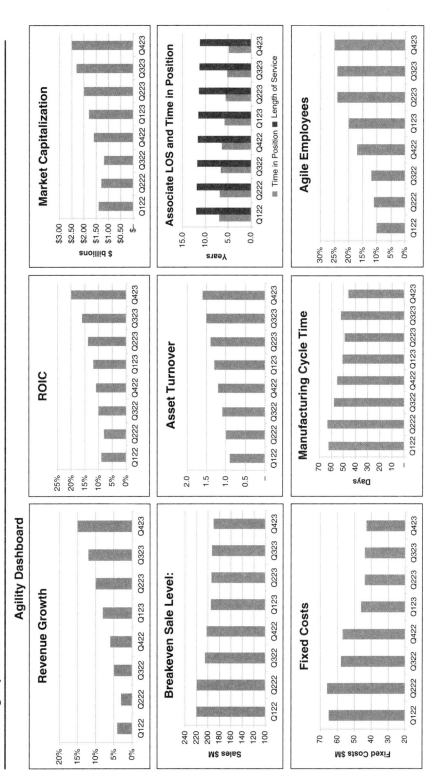

293

Roman philosopher, said, "A gem is not polished without friction nor a man perfected without trials." Another powerful statement attributed to many speakers and various proverbs is "Smooth seas do not make a skillful sailor."

Financial executives should encourage enterprise resilience by hiring and developing individuals who have overcome challenges, providing context and perspective, developing problem solving and contingency planning skills, promoting innovation and agility and leadership in the face of adversity.

SUMMARY

We live and conduct business during a challenging time, with significant uncertainty and rapid change. In order to be successful, enterprises must adjust to this environment by developing the ability to respond and adapt quickly to future events and changes. Key competencies to enable this adaptation are innovation, agility, and resilience.

Part Three

Enterprise Performance Management

15

Enterprise Performance Management and Execution

Enterprise performance management (EPM) is an essential aspect of leading and managing an enterprise. Contrary to the views of many authors and consultants, this is not a 21st-century epiphany, but an evolution and enhancement of practices that have roots in the earliest management principles. EPM (also referred to as business performance management) is far broader than developing glitzy dashboards! In this chapter, we will introduce key concepts of EPM, including developing a "context" for establishing performance measures.

In Chapter 16, we will cover the selection and development of KPIs and the development of dashboards.

In Chapter 17, we will outline key steps in implementing EPM and how to institutionalize and integrate performance management into other key management processes.

In Chapter 18, we will discuss using performance management to develop an outside-in view of performance, including competitive analysis and benchmarking.

WHAT IS ENTERPRISE PERFORMANCE MANAGEMENT?

Our definition and application of *EPM* is very broad and includes all activities that plan, assess, improve, and monitor critical business activities and initiatives across the *enterprise*. So how does financial planning and analysis (FP&A) relate to performance management? Under this broad definition of performance management, FP&A is actually an important dimension of EPM. The *F* in FP&A often limits the scope or perception of the function since we want to examine all aspects of performance. Many traditional FP&A activities are integral parts of performance management, including planning and forecasting, variance analysis, and financial reporting. FP&A may be an ideal function to expand into performance management since that function is already involved in many important aspects and has an overall context of important performance drivers.

EPM represents a key part of the overall management system as pictured in Figure 15.1.

FIGURE 15.1 **Overview of enterprise performance management process.**

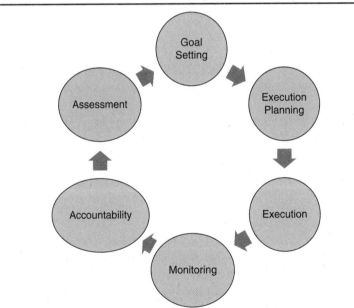

Performance management plays a role in each of these activities.

Assessment

Before setting goals and performance targets, there should be an assessment of the external environment and the current performance of the organization.

Market and competitive forces must be assessed and factored into the overall view of performance. Current levels of performance, including performance drivers and improvement opportunities, must be identified and understood.

The organization must also continually assess performance against established goals.

Goal Setting

Based on the assessment of the current environment and performance levels, goals can be established for the organization. The goals will eventually cascade down into objectives and targets for strategic and operating plans.

Benchmarking is a useful method of grounding performance expectations with the performance of competitors, customers, or best practices companies. Benchmarking will be explored in detail in Chapter 18.

Execution Planning

Execution planning is the process of determining how, in specific terms, the goals and performance targets will be achieved. We have all heard some variation of this statement: "Organizations don't plan to fail; they fail to plan."[1] In other words, an important aspect of achieving goals is to develop a plan to accomplish them.

Frequently, nonbusiness experiences provide great insight into business issues. One example from my personal experience relates to the Boston Marathon. Living and working near the marathon route for years, I marveled at the runners who participated and began to wonder how you train for such a feat. I had been a casual runner for decades, but never considered running long distances. A friend gave me a plan to train for a marathon from my humble three-mile-run base. Among other invaluable tips, the plan's author included programs to train an individual to run a marathon in 26 weeks, tailored to their current fitness and distance level. One of these programs, suited to a first-time marathon trainee (me), provided a program to get me from my three-mile runs to *finish* a marathon (26.2 miles). Other, more aggressive programs were intended to achieve a specific time goal, for example, to complete the course in four hours. The beauty of this program was that it provided a daily activity for each day over the next 26 weeks. The program is shown in Table 15.1.[2]

---

[1] Variants of this statement are often attributed to the Bible, Chinese proverbs, and Ben Franklin. . .all sources of great thoughts!

[2] This marathon training program is my recollection of the plan that I utilized and is here for illustrative purposes only. Please refer to plans currently available on most running and marathon sites if you are contemplating that challenge!

TABLE 15.1 **Marathon training program.**

Marathon Plan: To Finish							
Week	**Monday**	**Tuesday**	**Wednesday**	**Thursday**	**Friday**	**Saturday**	**Sunday**
	Run		Run		Run	Run	
1	3	Strength	3	Strength	3	3	Rest
2	3	Strength	3	Strength	3	4	Rest
3	3	Strength	3	Strength	3	3	Rest
4	3	Strength	3	Strength	3	6	Rest
5	3	Strength	3	Strength	3	3	Rest
6	3	Strength	3	Strength	3	8	Rest
7	3	Strength	3	Strength	3	4	Rest
8	3	Strength	3	Strength	3	10	Rest
9	3	Strength	3	Strength	3	5	Rest
10	3	Strength	3	Strength	3	12	Rest
11	3	Strength	3	Strength	3	6	Rest
12	3	Strength	3	Strength	3	14	Rest
13	3	Strength	3	Strength	3	7	Rest
14	3	Strength	3	Strength	3	16	Rest
15	3	Strength	3	Strength	3	8	Rest
16	3	Strength	3	Strength	3	18	Rest
17	3	Strength	3	Strength	3	9	Rest
18	3	Strength	3	Strength	3	20	Rest
19	3	Strength	3	Strength	3	10	Rest
20	3	Strength	3	Strength	3	22	Rest
21	3	Strength	3	Strength	3	11	Rest
22	3	Strength	3	Strength	3	24	Rest
23	3	Strength	3	Strength	3	12	Rest
24	3	Strength	3	Strength	3	26	Rest
25	3	Strength	3	Strength	3	10	Rest
26	3	Strength	3	Strength	3	Marathon	3

There are several takeaways from my use of this program:

- ❏ I knew what I should be doing, each and every day, to achieve the long-term goal.
- ❏ Each time I referred to this program (daily), I could connect my current activity (run) to the ultimate goal, completing the marathon.
- ❏ It reinforced accountability since I could see that missing a training session would jeopardize the attainment of the goal.
- ❏ I didn't reinvent the wheel, rather I used a program followed by thousands of aspiring marathoners.
- ❏ It worked!

In the business world, I often observe the success of teams that had well-developed execution plans. Conversely, the root cause of teams that failed to achieve objectives was often the absence of, or a poorly developed, execution plan. Even a simple plan, as illustrated in Table 15.2, will significantly increase the odds of successful execution.

TABLE 15.2 **Project plan: FP&A improvement.**

FP&A Assessment and Improvement
Timeline and Work-flow

	Resp	Status	Date	Week 1	2	3	4	5	6	7	8	9	10	11	12	13	14	15	16	17	18	19	20	21	22	23	24	25	26	27	Notes
Assessment																														
Skills and Competency Inventory	BR	Complete	6/15	X																											
Report Inventory	BR	Complete	6/22		X																										
Client Survey	BR	Complete	6/29			X																									
Summarize findings	BR	Complete	7/6				X																								
Develop Plan	Team	In Process	7/13				X	X																							
Low Hanging Fruit																														
Eliminate Reports and Analysis	CD	In Process	7/22						X	--	X																				
Talent Acquisition and Management																														
Additional Position Senior Analyst	JD	Open	7/31							X Define				X Hire																	
Group Training Program	CD	Open	Var																X Session 1					X Session 2			X Evaluate				
Communication Seminar	BR	Open	10/15											X Contract																	
Individual Development and Training Plan	BR	Open	11/5																XX					XX							
Develop Analysis																														
List of New Additions	JD	Complete	7/15				X																								
Develop Dashboard	CD	Open	Var					X Corporate					X Product Development																		
Revise Capital Investment Decision Package	BR	Open	8/1								X	X	X																		
Implement Rolling Business Outlook	BR	Open	9/15														x	x	x	x X Revenue Pipeline	x	x									
Evaluation and Next Steps																														
Evaluate Progress																											X		
Additional Actions																												X	
Conflicts				Closing						CFO-Vacation				Closing														Closing			IR

The existence of such a plan demonstrates that a considered, thoughtful approach to the project has been developed. The plan clearly identifies responsibilities, ensuring that each team member is aware of tasks and expected completion dates. Assigning responsibility and completion dates also facilitates accountability. The simple visual lays out the project flow, including sequencing and prerequisite tasks. The plan is a very effective way to communicate with the team and serves to provide assurance to senior executives that the program is supported by a solid plan.

Execution

The entire organization should be engaged in executing the goals, plans, and critical functions of the organization. This includes everything from developing new products and talent to delivering products and services. Getting things done and done on time is, in large part, a cultural dimension of the organization. The tone must be set from the top. Make your plan. Get it done. I know of one CEO of a large company who left no doubt with managers of this priority. At a cocktail party to celebrate the closing of an acquisition transaction he circulated to meet all the managers of the acquired company and told each "Make your plan!"

One caveat to this emphasis on execution is that it must be clear that legal and ethical boundaries are not to be breached as part of achieving goals and plans. Many examples of fraud are a direct result of high-performance targets and an unqualified mandate to "make your numbers."

The chances of successfully executing any task or activity increase substantially as the effectiveness of execution planning increases. Another critical element to successful execution is the expectation of monitoring and enforcing accountability.

Monitoring

Monitoring progress on key initiatives and projects, as well as monitoring the overall performance of the organization on key business processes, is an essential activity. Identifying problems, delays, exceptions, and changing assumptions on a timely basis will increase the probability of successful execution. EPM must also focus on events and trends external to the organization. The greatest threats and opportunities typically arise outside the organization (Chapter 10).

In order to be effective, the monitoring process must provide visibility into these key programs, processes, and performance drivers. Historically, progress and results in business were measured after the fact and reported on in financial reports. A far more effective method is to develop a series of reports or displays that present the key factors in a presentation format that has high visual impact, including graphs, charts, and tables. These user-friendly reports can be summarized in one or more dashboards that will allow managers and employees to quickly scan the series of charts, as a pilot would scan the instrument panel on an airplane. Running a business, or any organization, is similar to flying an airplane. Managers also need timely, visual reports on key aspects of their business. How well is the company performing on major systems? Where is the company headed? Are there threats on the horizon? In Chapter 16, we will explore performance monitoring by using key performance indicators (KPIs) and dashboards.

Accountability

Many organizations fail to achieve goals, or fail outright, because of lack of accountability. To hold people accountable, you first must state clear expectations in terms of responsibility, timing, scope of project or activity, and results. Managers with the responsibility for execution must participate in goal setting to achieve buy-in. It is also necessary to be able to measure performance against expectations. Performance targets must be well defined and *measurable*. There must be rewards for achieving objectives and consequences for failing to achieve. Accountability should be a primary objective of monthly or quarterly meetings on product development or business unit performance.

Organizations that are successful in holding associates accountable for performance integrate the goals, plans, and targets of the company into setting performance objectives and reviews for associates. Promotions, compensation increases, and incentive compensation must be consistent with the organization's overall EPM.

DEVELOPING OR ENHANCING EPM IN AN ORGANIZATION

Nearly all companies use performance measures. Many attempts to use or implement performance measures and to develop an overall framework for EPM fail to achieve the full potential value of such efforts. Many organizations jump to creating dashboards and selecting performance measures without creating a context that considers the company's strategy, financial performance, key initiatives, and other important considerations. Figure 15.2 highlights a four-step, systematic process for building an effective performance management framework leading to the maximization of shareholder value.

Creating the proper context and integration with other elements of the management system will also ensure that managers and employees will not view this project as just another "flavor of the month" initiative. This is not a short-term initiative, instead it will be integrated into the core of the company's management systems.

By utilizing a thoughtful and systematic way of developing an overall framework for performance management, the effort will ensure that it will be

FIGURE 15.2 **Implementing performance management framework.**

Establishing or Improving Enterprise Performance Management

Identify Objectives	Create Context	Build Framework	Institutionalize
❏ Integrate Financial and Operational Measures ❏ Accelerate Value Creation ❏ Alignment and Execution of Goals	❏ Strategy ❏ Key Initiatives ❏ Assess Performance ❏ Identify Threats and Opportunities ❏ Shareholder Value	❏ Select Key Performance Measures ❏ Build Dashboards and Reports ❏ Build Delivery Mechanisms	❏ Training ❏ Technology Platform ❏ Planning and Forecasting ❏ Performance Evaluation ❏ Compensation ❏ Evaluate/Refresh

directed toward areas of significance and importance. In addition, this approach will build credibility with executives and associates.

Define Specific Objectives

The organization should consider and agree on the specific objectives of EPM. While many of the objectives will be common across most organizations (e.g., value creation, improve visibility), others will vary from organization to organization based on specific circumstances.

What Should We Measure? Creating Context

Developing a context for EPM will ensure that the efforts will focus on areas that are important to the organization. Figure 15.3 illustrates the areas that should be considered as part of developing the context. This is a critical step toward building an effective performance management framework.

FIGURE 15.3 **Creating context for performance management.**

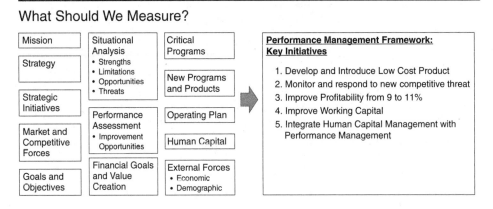

What Should We Measure?

Mission	Situational Analysis • Strengths • Limitations • Opportunities • Threats	Critical Programs	**Performance Management Framework: Key Initiatives**
Strategy		New Programs and Products	1. Develop and Introduce Low Cost Product 2. Monitor and respond to new competitive threat 3. Improve Profitability from 9 to 11% 4. Improve Working Capital 5. Integrate Human Capital Management with Performance Management
Strategic Initiatives	Performance Assessment • Improvement Opportunities	Operating Plan	
Market and Competitive Forces		Human Capital	
Goals and Objectives	Financial Goals and Value Creation	External Forces • Economic • Demographic	

Mission. What is the mission of the organization?

Strategy. What is the organization's strategy? What are the most important strategic objectives? What are the critical assumptions that should be monitored?

Market and Competitive Forces. Is the market growing or contracting? Are there specific forces that are shaping the market? Are new competitors entering the market? Is the market subject to disruptive technologies or business models? How can we identify and monitor emerging threats?

Strategic Initiatives. Effective managers have a short list of essential projects and programs that are critical to executing the strategic plan and achieving the long-term goals of the company. Examples of key strategic initiatives may be the introduction of a series of new products, the establishment of a distribution channel, or significant reduction to manufacturing costs for improving profitability and price competitiveness. These strategic initiatives should be documented and fully integrated into the development of a performance management system.

Situational Analysis. The SLOT (or SWOT) analysis can be helpful in developing a clear view of weaknesses, opportunities, and threats.

❑ Strengths: How can we leverage our existing advantages?

❑ Limitations/Weaknesses: Do we have a plan to address our major weaknesses and limitations?

❑ Opportunities: What are the largest opportunities? What are our plans to capitalize on these?

❑ Threats: What are the potential vulnerabilities? How can we develop plans to address them?

Assessing Performance. Before proceeding with the selection of performance measures, it is important to complement the strategic focus with an objective assessment of the company's performance. The assessment can begin with the performance evaluation introduced in Chapter 2. It should include a review of financial performance and recent trends as illustrated for LSA Technology Company in Table 2.8. While this analysis contains a great deal of useful information on the financial performance of the company, it will be more useful if key elements are summarized in graphical form as shown in Figure 2.3. The evaluation should also include benchmarking key elements of operating, financial, and value measures against a peer group and to best practice companies. The assessment of financial results should be linked to key drivers of performance, introduced later in this chapter.

Benchmarking Performance. Benchmarking the performance of your organization against a peer group and best practice companies can identify significant improvement opportunities. The selection of companies to be included in the benchmark group is very important. Many managers limit benchmarking to a "peer group" of similar companies or competitors. The potential for learning can be greatly expanded if the universe of companies in the benchmark is expanded to include best practice companies and most admired organizations.

Monitoring External Trends and Forces. All companies will be impacted by external forces and trends. These include economic, demographic, technological, and regulatory forces that should be reflected in the EPM. This subject was covered in detail in Chapter 10.

Performance Framework

Where possible, it is best to establish a framework for EPM that flows down from over-arching goals of the organization. Examples include value creation for most businesses or a specific goal for mission-oriented organizations, for example, eradicating polio or world hunger.

Value Creation

The most fundamental objective for most companies is to create value for shareholders. For these enterprises, we have successfully utilized a framework that links value creation and value drivers to key business processes and activities. The value performance framework (Figure 15.4) identifies six drivers of shareholder value:

- ❑ Revenue growth.
- ❑ Relative pricing strength.
- ❑ Operating effectiveness.
- ❑ Capital effectiveness.
- ❑ Cost of capital.
- ❑ The intangibles.

Factors such as interest rates, market conditions, and irrational investor behavior will, of course, affect the price of a company's stock. However, the preceding value drivers are those that management teams and directors can drive in order to build long-term sustainable shareholder value.

It is important to recognize that the significance of each driver will vary from firm to firm and will also vary over time for a particular firm. For example, a firm with increased competition in a low-growth market will likely place significant emphasis on operating and capital effectiveness. By contrast, a firm with a significant opportunity for revenue growth is likely to focus on that driver and place less emphasis on capital management or operating

FIGURE 15.4 **The value performance framework (VPF).**

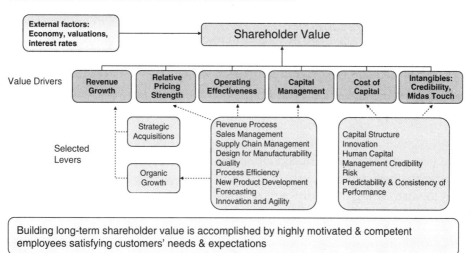

Focus on Drivers of Long-Term Value:

Then Link Value & Value Drivers to Business Processes & Activities

effectiveness. At some time in the future, however, this high-growth firm may have to deal with a slower growth rate and may have to shift emphasis to other drivers, such as operating efficiency and capital management.

To attain its full potential value, a firm must understand the potential contribution of each driver to shareholder value. It starts with the six value drivers that ultimately determine shareholder value. The contribution to value of each driver can be estimated using discounted cash flow (Chapter 30). Underneath these value drivers are some of the key activities and processes that determine the level of performance in each value driver. In addition, the framework identifies some of the key performance indicators that can be used to measure the effectiveness of these activities and processes. For example, revenue growth is a key driver of shareholder value. A subset of revenue growth is the level of "organic growth," excluding the contribution to growth from acquisitions. Organic sales growth will be driven by a number of factors, including customer satisfaction, which can be tracked by key metrics such as "on-time deliveries" (OTD) and the level of "past due orders."

At the foundation of the value performance framework is the employees. A firm cannot build sustainable value for shareholders without developing and retaining a competent and motivated workforce. This framework is very useful in helping employees and managers throughout the organization link their specific roles and objectives to the value of the company. A brief description of each of the value drivers within the framework follows. In Section V, each driver is explored in detail.

Revenue Growth   Revenue growth is the most significant driver of shareholder value over the long term. Other drivers are very important, but tend to reach a limit in terms of value creation. For example, a firm can improve management of working capital to a certain level, but will eventually reach a point of diminishing marginal contribution. However, a firm with a strong competitive advantage in an attractive market can enjoy revenue growth over an extended period of time. In due course, this driver also tends to slacken for nearly all firms as they approach the mature stage in the life cycle of a company.

Despite its importance, managers must not focus exclusively on revenue growth. To reach full potential value, some level of attention must be paid to each value driver. Additionally, it is important to note that not all growth leads to value creation. Revenue growth must be profitable and capable of generating positive cash flow and economic returns in a reasonable period of time in order to create value.

It is fairly straightforward and relatively easy to measure and track sales growth over time. Two common measures are the growth in sales over the prior year, and the growth over an extended period of time, usually measured as compound annual growth rate (CAGR). Predicting future revenue levels, however, is much more difficult and requires considerable thought and analysis. In fact, estimating future sales and sales growth is typically the most difficult element of any planning or forecasting process.

Under the VPF, we understand that value will be driven, to a significant extent, by the expectation of *future* revenue growth. Therefore, considerable emphasis will be placed on understanding the factors impacting future revenue levels. Key factors in evaluating potential revenue growth include: the market size and growth rate, the firm's competitive position in the market, pricing pressures, costs, product mix, new product introductions, product obsolescence, customer satisfaction, and impact of foreign currency exchange rates to name a few. The sales growth driver will be reviewed in greater detail in Chapter 22.

Growing the firm through acquisitions is a very different proposition than organic growth. This subject will be reviewed in detail in Chapter 31, "Analysis of Mergers and Acquisitions."

Relative Pricing Strength   The firm's ability to command a strong price for its products and services will have a significant impact on financial performance and building shareholder value. Clearly, if a firm has a strong competitive position, it should have greater pricing flexibility. This will allow the firm to set its pricing at a level that covers its costs and investments, and earns an acceptable return for shareholders. However, if the firm is in a relatively weak position in a highly competitive market, it could be subject to significant pricing pressure that will limit financial returns and drive cost containment and reduction. The subject of relative pricing strength will be explored more fully in Chapter 22.

Operating Effectiveness *Operating effectiveness* is a broad term that covers how effectively and efficiently the firm operates. It is an extremely important value driver and is often measured in terms of costs, expenses, and related ratios. Consider a firm that has operating margins of 15% of sales. This firm consumes 85% of its revenues in operational costs and expenses. If this firm can improve its productivity and reduce costs, a significant improvement in its financial performance, and ultimately its valuation, will occur.

A couple of obvious topside measures of operational effectiveness include gross margin and selling, general and administrative (SG&A) expenses expressed as a percentage of sales. These measures can be supported by a number of indicators of process efficiency. A less obvious, but no less important element of operational efficiency relates to the level of investments a company is making in future growth and the manner in which the firm manages these investments. Many firms have high levels of investment directed toward future growth. The disciplines around evaluating growth programs and eliminating dubious investments are important contributors to future financial performance and value creation. Eliminating investments in dubious projects at the earliest possible time allows managers to redirect the investment dollars to other projects or to improve margins.

An analogous issue for many companies is the frequency and diligence management uses to evaluate business units and/or products that routinely lose money. Thoughtful and disciplined managers can add significant shareholder value by addressing underperforming businesses or product lines. In addition to the ability to make the tough calls on these businesses, managers must have visibility into the true economic performance of the units and/or products. Chapter 23 will explore in further detail these and other business processes and key measures for operating effectiveness.

Capital Effectiveness An underutilized lever for improving cash flows and shareholder value is effective capital management. Capital effectiveness has two broad categories: operating capital requirements and investments in long-term assets, including property and equipment, and acquisitions of businesses. Failing to manage investments in operating capital and in property and equipment has a significant impact on cash flows and return on assets, and ultimately, on valuations.

Our definition of *operating capital* in the VPF includes accounts receivable and inventory, offset by accounts payable and accrued expenses. We will focus primarily on the business processes and conditions that drive the levels of receivables and inventories for a firm in Chapter 24.

For property, plant, and equipment (PP&E), we will look at the processes for reviewing and approving large expenditures, measuring utilization, and conducting post-implementation reviews. In addition, we will address the hidden potential value of assets that are quite frequently carried at low accounting values.

Long-term capital effectiveness will be explored in detail in Chapter 25.

Cost of Capital   The firm's cost of capital is a significant value driver because it is the rate used to discount future cash flows. Cost of capital is influenced by a number of factors, including the firm's capital structure, perceived risk of future performance, operating leverage, and stock price volatility. General economic factors, such as interest rates, also play a role in determining the cost of capital for a firm. Cost of capital, capital structure, and related topics will be discussed in Chapters 26 and 27.

The Intangibles   In addition to the more quantitative, hard factors previously discussed, there are any number of intangible factors that play a significant role in driving share value. These include: expectations of future performance, the reliability and consistency of financial performance, and the credibility of management. The intangibles were discussed in Chapters 7 (on human capital) and 14 (on innovation, agility, and resilience).

The key is to develop an effective performance management framework that supports the overall objective of the corporation to create value for shareholders. In Chapter 30, the VPF will be integrated with valuation techniques to maximize shareholder value. Projecting improved performance on spreadsheets is very easy. Achieving these improvements in actual results requires substantial planning, effort, and follow-through. Central to achieving these performance goals is the selection and development of effective performance measures.

Setting Targets   Realistic performance targets should be set for each measure that will lead to the achievement of strategic objectives and goals for value creation. This should be done by cascading the broad goals for value creation and performance down to the value drivers and individual process and activity measures. Setting targets must also consider the improvement opportunities identified in the process assessments.

Mission-Oriented Frameworks

While financial performance is critical to all organizations, mission-focused (aka not-for-profit) organizations are not created to build wealth. Instead, these organizations are founded to achieve (mostly) noble objectives such as curing cancer, eradicating polio, ending starvation, or educating youth. Accordingly, the focus of performance management in these organizations should be the attainment of specific objectives. However, financial management will still play a significant part in the overall success of the organization.

FIGURE 15.5 **Performance framework for mission-oriented organization.**

Mission-Oriented Framework

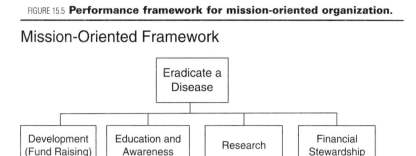

With a clear identification of the mission/goal, key activities required to support and achieve that goal can be identified as shown in Figure 15.5. Then specific objectives and measures can be established for each of these activities.

Measuring and Driving What's Important

Organizations must avoid the temptation to only measure activities and performance that is easy, where data is readily available. Chapter 14 discussed the application of performance management to important areas, including innovation, agility, and resilience. Human capital was addressed in Chapter 7. While these areas are far more difficult to measure, their importance mandates that they be included in any comprehensive EPM framework.

SUMMARY

Many companies use performance measures. Few have achieved the full potential benefits that a well-designed and well-implemented performance management framework can offer. The objective of EPM is to provide a systematic way of measuring progress on strategic initiatives and performance on key value drivers. A successful framework will increase visibility into critical areas of business performance and allow managers to assign and enforce accountability for performance. Managers and employees will also understand how their activities relate to operating and financial performance, and ultimately, the value of the company.

The single most important factor for achieving success with performance management is to create context for the measurement system. This is achieved by creating linkage among strategy, performance management, process and quality initiatives, financial performance, and shareholder value. It is also critical to integrate and link operating measures to financial measures and then to shareholder value measures. The time spent in establishing this linkage will improve understanding, and ultimately, the effectiveness of the framework.

We will explore the concepts introduced in this chapter throughout the rest of the book. In Chapters 22 through 27, we will drill down into each of the key value drivers, linking to critical business processes and identifying key performance measures. Chapter 16 will cover the selection of performance measures and the development of dashboards. Chapter 17 will explore the importance of "institutionalizing" EPM across the organization. Chapter 18 will present the use of EPM in developing an external view and benchmarking.

## 16

Dashboards and Key Performance Indicators

The use of performance measures and dashboards has exploded over the past 30 years. The effective use of key performance indicators (KPIs) and dashboards is illustrated throughout this book. This chapter will deal with some specific techniques in selecting and developing measures and dashboards.

OBJECTIVES OF DASHBOARDS AND KPIS

Organizations that *effectively* use performance measures and dashboards spend a great deal of time thoughtfully selecting appropriate measures and developing dashboards that are relevant to the organization's objectives and challenges.

Too often, organizations adopt measures or start using so-called canned dashboards without properly vetting what should be measured. Before jumping into KPIs and dashboards, it is very important to develop a context and framework as was explained in the previous chapter, an introduction to enterprise performance management (EPM).

As a potentially very useful part of EPM, we must start by focusing on the objective of EPM. We want to provide executives and managers with the information they need to run the business and achieve strategic goals. The cockpit of an aircraft provides us with a very useful visual to guide us in the selection of measures and the development of dashboards (Figure 16.1). I reflect on this image frequently during any EPM project.

FIGURE 16.1 **Shuttle cockpit instrument panel.**

Photo used with permission of NASA.

The instrument panel is essential in aviation. There are a number of important performance management principles that are illustrated by the cockpit.

Real-Time and Predictive Insights

The aircraft's pilot and crew are not asked to blindly fly the mission and then be handed a series of narratives and reports after the conclusion of the flight to tell them how it went. The crew is able to monitor the performance of the aircraft in real time.

The instrument panel provides *real-time insight* into the performance of every major system on the aircraft, everything from engine performance to fuel levels and consumption, hydraulics, and landing systems. The cockpit has a number of alerts (flashing lights or sound alarms) to call the pilot's attention to potential problems or threats.

High Visual Impact

This pilot does not have to interpret long-winded narrative or Excel spreadsheets to see how thing are going. With a quick scan of the instrument panel the pilot can see how every major system is performing and what's happening in the external environment. The pilot is not flying blind and then presented with a 50-page report of Excel spreadsheets after the plane has landed.

Initially this instrument panel is complex, but you can be assured that the commander knows where every dial and reading should be. This illustrates an important concept in EPM, now generally described as data visualization. Transforming important data into visual presentations that allow the user to quickly identify trends, scale, direction, and variances has great utility. The use of graphics and dashboards has greatly increased the effectiveness of reviewing business results.

Focus on the Important Measures

The instruments are measuring what's *important and relevant* to the mission. The pilot has confidence that a lot of thought, 100 years of aviation experience, and substantial tax dollars went into selecting the measures that are vital to a successful mission.

Providing Insight into External Factors and Environment

The instrument panel also provides insight about the aircraft's position and relationship with the *external environment*. There is external radar for potential threats, a navigation system, wind speed, altitude, and attitude. The pilot can identify storms and alter course. In many planes the pilot will be alerted that an adversary has the aircraft in their sights or on missile lock!

Combining with Observation, Experience, and Intuition

Finally, the pilot doesn't rely on the panel exclusively, but rather *combines it* with observation, intuition, and experience to complete the mission. One of the biggest mistakes we make is to presume that performance measures, dashboards, and other aspects of EPM eliminate or replace the need for executive judgment, decisions, and even intuition. Instead, these measures should be utilized to better inform decisions and where appropriate to challenge intuition to ensure that the best possible decision is made by the executive.

SELECTING APPROPRIATE PERFORMANCE MEASURES AND KPIS

A Nonbusiness Illustration

Let's assume that we have a goal to improve our health and fitness. We then decide that we want to measure our current state and future improvements by tracking our weight, cholesterol levels, and resting heart rate. We can measure our weight by jumping on the scale every hour, but we will not make progress until we identify and manage the key drivers, primarily food intake and our level of activity. The measures we have identified are really "results" or "outcomes" of our lifestyle (diet and exercise). To achieve different results, or outcomes, we must identify, manage, and measure food intake and activity, important drivers of health.

Fitness and nutrition journals (recording exercise and food intake, respectively) have been used successfully by athletic trainers, weight-loss programs, and nutritionists. They also underscore an important principle of EPM, that is, what gets measured gets attention.

Activity Measures	Result/Outcome Measures
Food Intake (Calories, Fat, Carbs)	Weight
Activity Levels	Cholesterol
Number of Steps	Resting Heart Rate
Minutes of Cardio Exercise	Blood Sugar Levels
Strength Sessions/Week	Lean Muscle Mass
Alcoholic Drinks/Day	Liver Study, Sugar Levels

By recognizing the likely cause-and-effect relationship among these measures, we can begin to track the results that our lifestyle changes have on the health indicators (weight, etc.). By capturing the activity levels and displaying the activity measures on a dashboard with related outcomes, we create a visual that typically tells a compelling story. Figure 16.2 is an illustrated dashboard for health and fitness. By tracking the measures, we create a discipline that makes us more likely to achieve our targets for increased activity and reduced food intake. By building a dashboard, we provide the linkage required to connect the dots and reinforce the cause-and-effect relationship.

Developing Appropriate Measures

After documenting the key strategic issues and initiatives, assessing performance and setting improvement goals in the context of valuation creation, as was described in Chapter 15, we can begin to select the measures that will be important for monitoring performance and progress across the company. What measures will track our progress in achieving strategic objectives and goals for value creation? What are the critical elements of our business that I want to see on a daily, weekly, monthly, or quarterly basis? What measures will serve as leading indicators to alert us to potential problems in time to make meaningful adjustments? Guidelines for selecting and developing performance measures include the following:

FIGURE 16.2 **Personal health and fitness dashboard.**

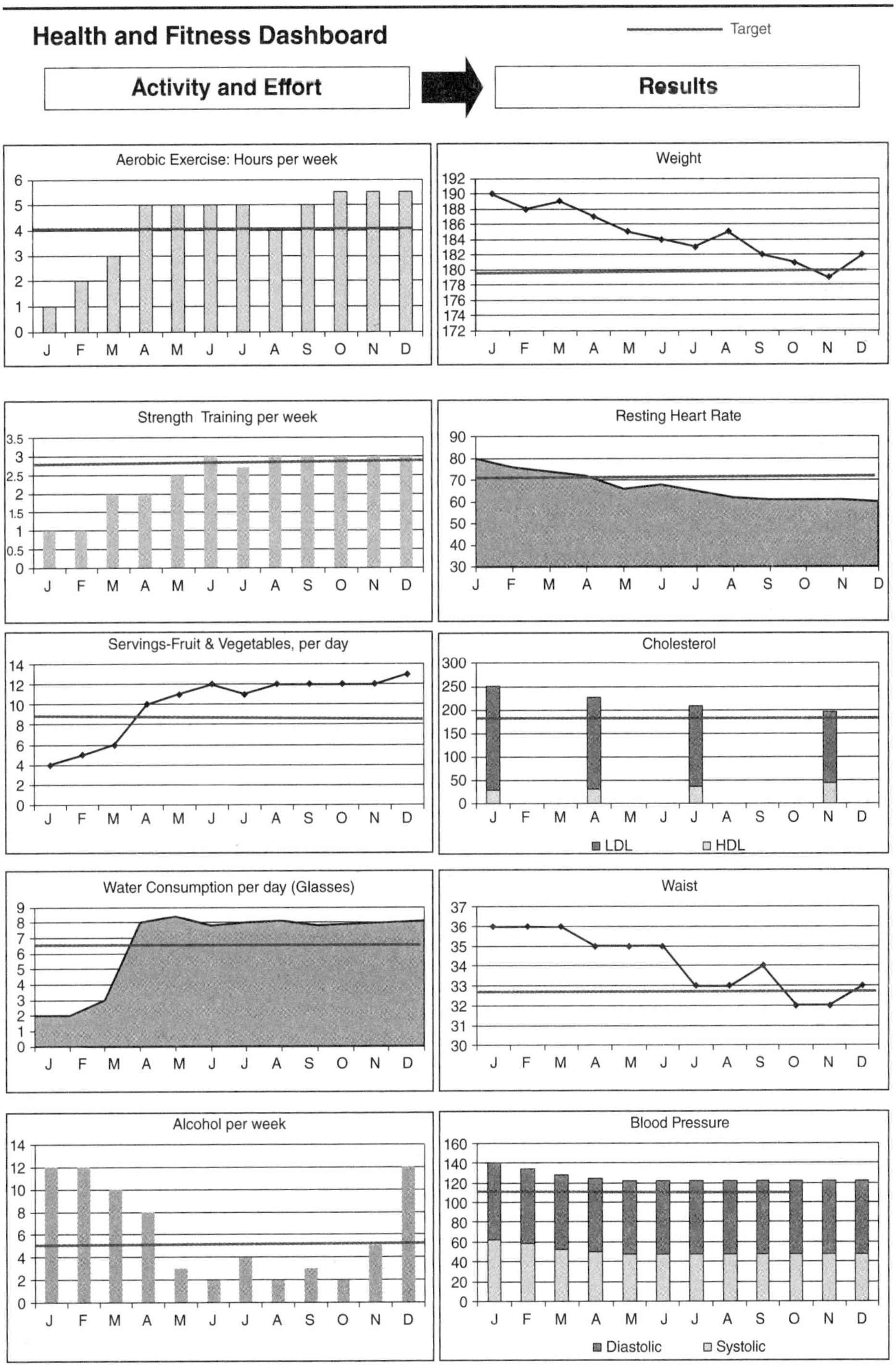

Relevancy. While it sounds obvious, many organizations track measures that are not relevant to important goals, objectives, or performance and value drivers.

Objectivity. To the extent possible, performance measures should be quantifiable and objective. Qualitative assessments are necessary in certain cases. However, care must be taken to promote objectivity and to complement qualitative assessments with quantitative measures.

Timeliness. Performance measures and dashboards must be available on a timely basis. This requires that systems and databases be maintained and updated on a current basis. This is generally not a problem for the primary business systems, but can be a problem in areas such as entering or updating sales leads or warranty experience, or where outdated or poorly integrated systems inhibit real-time access.

Balance. Performance measures should be balanced to reduce the risk of optimizing performance in one area at the expense of the long-term health and value of the organization. Said differently, the establishment of a seemingly benevolent measure may have unintended (and negative) consequences. For example, if inventory turns is selected as a key performance measure without a balancing measure such as on-time deliveries, it may result in reductions in inventory at the expense of customer satisfaction. By balancing the two measures, the company will promote the development of healthy process improvements that lead to improvement in both measures.

Emphasis on Leading Indicators of Performance. The systematic approach that is outlined in this chapter will provide confidence that the performance measures will be predictive of future operating and financial performance. More attention should be paid to measuring and improving the leading indicators of performance. For example, if a company sets a target of improving DSO from 75 to 55 days, it must develop targets and measure performance on leading indicators such as revenue patterns, quality, and collections.

Measurement **Definitions.** Specific definitions must be developed and documented for each measure. For example, what is the definition of *on-time delivery to customers*? Is it the date that the company committed to delivery or the date the customer originally requested? In one extreme case, we discovered that the date used to measure on-time delivery was changed to the most recent internal schedule update. Since this measure is an important part of customer satisfaction, we want to view this measure through the eyes of the customer, generally the availability when the customer placed the order or received order confirmation. Definition of performance measures is important and must be consistent with the objective of the measure. These definitions should be documented and approved by management.

Data Integrity. Implementing EPM without having the ability to generate performance measures and dashboards that present accurate data may be worse than not having measures at all. It is fairly typical for a company to encounter problems with data accuracy as it begins to use performance measures. In fact, this is a side benefit of the process, improving the accuracy of reported data. Each measure should be defined and approved by the appropriate managers. Data gathering and processing can be improved over time. Data integrity was discussed in a broader discussion of information technology in Chapter 12. It is a good idea to have performance measures reviewed by internal audit teams or the controller's staff to ensure the integrity of the measurement system.

Unintended Consequences. As we focus on certain measures of performance with the best of intentions, we must be alert to the potential of unintended consequences. This potential should be considered before adopting any specific measure and the broad set of collective measures selected to be used.

Less Is More. Since the organization will focus on the performance measures we select, it is important to limit the number of measures utilized. We should emphasize key priorities, drivers, programs, improvement opportunities, and other important stuff. If we measure too much, the message is diluted and the team is overwhelmed. Generally, six to twelve measures represent a reasonable number on which to focus attention for a team, department, or individual. Additional metrics may be used that are subordinate to these primary measures.

Several years ago, I met with an enthusiastic finance team that had begun the performance management journey. They had adopted a great practice of posting KPIs in the work area of the responsible team. The trouble was that I counted more than 40 measures for a team with a relatively straightforward mission and simple operating model. Most of the measures were not understood and were not associated with any specific projects or key business drivers. This organization lost an opportunity to select and emphasize a few very important measures and likely confused the members of the team.

The selection of measures and building performance dashboards can be improved by using a performance measurement worksheet, illustrated in Figure 16.3. This worksheet forces us to define the measures, identify the objective, address the critical success factors (CSF), anticipate unintended consequences, and place the measure in context.

FIGURE 16.3 **Performance management worksheet.**

Be Careful (Thoughtful) about What You Measure and Report!	
Performance Measure Worksheet	
Measure: Asset Turnover	**Next Higher Measure:** ROA, ROE, ROIC
Objective: Measure the effectiveness of asset management, a key driver of ROE and a good overall measure of operating effectiveness	**Key Subordinate Measures:** Inventory Turnover Days Sales Outstanding Fixed Asset Turnover
Definition/ Computation: Sales/Assets	**Processes Covered:** Supply Chain Management Revenue Process Management
☐ **Leading** ✓ **Lagging**	
	Owner: Controller
Unintended Consequences: May place too much emphasis on reducing assets at potential expense of revenues or efficiency	**Compensating Measures:** Customer Service Levels, Profitability Revenue Growth

CREATING PERFORMANCE DASHBOARDS

Having developed the objectives and a context for performance management as was described in Chapter 15, we then set off to build a reporting mechanism to provide insight into these critical activities. It is essential to provide managers and all employees with critical information about the health of the business and the effectiveness of the activities in which they participate. And if performance improvement is to be successful, information must be provided consistently and in a timely manner relative to the activity.

Managers have two key decisions to address in implementing dashboards across the organization. The first decision is to determine what dashboards should be developed. Beyond the corporate level dashboard, it will also be appropriate to have dashboards for various processes, divisions, functions, and departments. Many managers and employees also develop their own personal dashboards.

The second important consideration for developing any dashboard is to consider the optimum frequency for measuring performance and refreshing the dashboard contents. Some process and activity measures need to be monitored daily or continuously. Examples may include product yields from production processing in refinery or fabricating operations, order levels, or weather conditions. Other measures such as return on invested capital (ROIC) are typically measured at quarterly and annual intervals. Selecting the appropriate frequency for each measure is nearly as important as selecting the right measures.

Some organizations prefer the term *scorecards* over *dashboards*. While to some extent this is just a matter of semantics, words do matter. I prefer the concept of a dashboard or instrument panel because the inference is that we are visually monitoring a system in real time and have the ability to control at least some functionality within that system. A scorecard is often a document that records the results or outcome, as in recording the strokes on a hole of golf or runs scored in an inning of baseball.

Guiding Principles in Building Dashboards

Focus on what's important:

- Value Creation, Strategic Objectives, Key Drivers.
- Mix of Leading/Predictive and Lagging Measures.
- Balance across financial, strategic, customer, operational, and human capital.
- Limit to 6 to 12 measures.
- High Visual Impact.
- Integration with key management processes.
- Being careful (thoughtful) about what you measure.

Corporate or Division Summary. The corporate dashboard is the most critical dashboard (see Figure 16.4). Selecting the most important 8 to 12 measures that capture the key performance variables for the company is both important and difficult. Managers must ensure that all key value drivers are represented. All other dashboards should be developed to support the corporate-level summary.

Note that at first the dashboards can be visually overwhelming. However, after a few cycles, managers become familiar with where each dial and needle should be on the dashboard. Having a complete and highly visual dashboard covering the business provides great insight across all key value drivers and affords managers the opportunity to assess performance and progress on key strategic objectives.

This summary-level dashboard would be supported by a series of dashboards with additional and more detailed measures that focus on key processes and activities. This graphic affords managers the opportunity to examine performance and understand the interrelationships of key factors, for example, the relationship between forecast accuracy and operating capital.

While combining key measures in a single dashboard, some executives prefer, and certain circumstances warrant, breaking down the dashboard into individual views.

FIGURE 16.4 **Quarterly corporate dashboard.**

Quarterly Corporate Dashboard

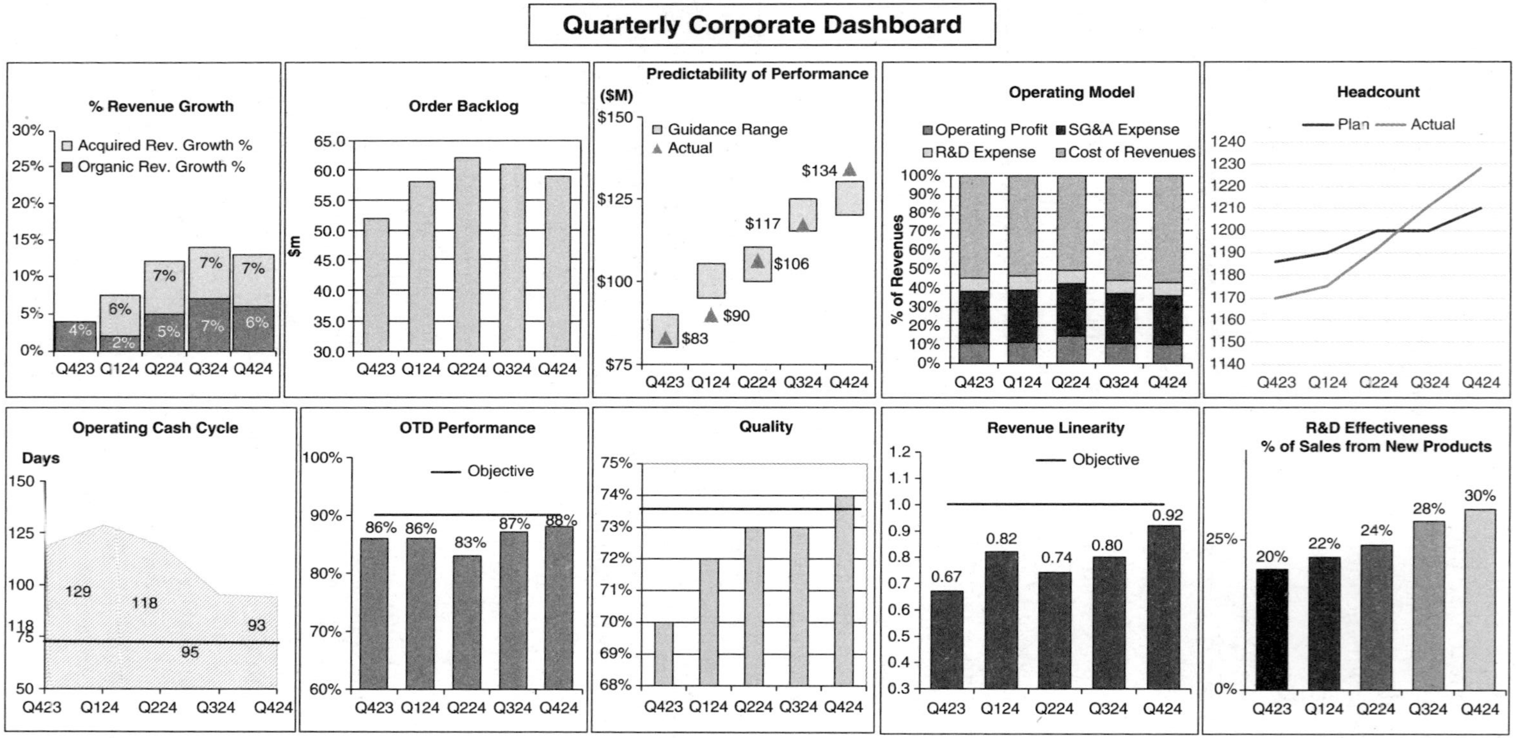

Daily and Weekly Dashboards. Many activities and events should be monitored more frequently than monthly or quarterly. In fact, a key part of achieving quarterly goals is to track progress on a weekly basis (see Figure 16.5). This not only tracks progress toward the goal, but in doing so, also allows the managers to course-correct or take additional actions if measured progress indicates that they are not on track to attain the performance target for the quarter.

Function or Department Dashboard. Dashboards should be developed for functional areas and departments such as information technology, finance, and human resources. These dashboards must support the corporate objectives and be consistent with the dashboards established for processes that the function leads or serves.

FIGURE 16.5 **Example of weekly dashboard.**

WEEKLY DASHBOARD

Q4'24 WEEK # 7 of 13   Percentage: 54%
($ in millions)

BOOKINGS	Week	Unit	QTD	Forecast	% Achieved	$ Required
	0.7	BU 1	12.0	25.0	48%	13.0
	-	BU 2	0.9	1.0	89%	0.1
	0.5	BU 3	4.0	6.0	67%	2.0
	0.4	BU 4	1.7	4.7	37%	2.9
	0.0	Other	0.1	-		(0.1)
	1.6	Totals	18.7	36.7	51%	18.0

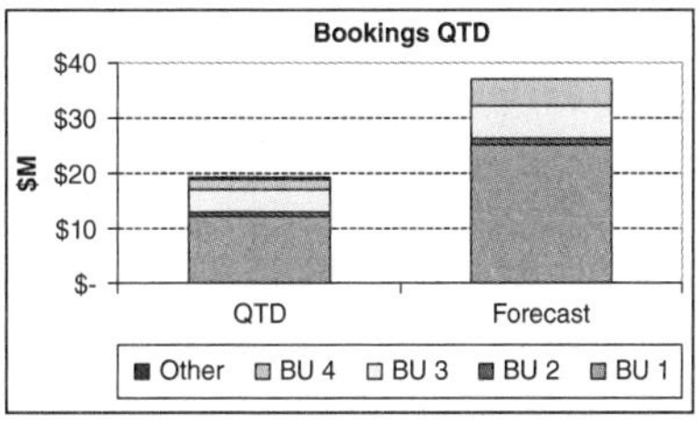

REVENUE	Week		QTD	Forecast	% Achieved	Backlog	Required Fill
	2.0	BU 1	13.0	28.0	46%	5.0	10.00
	0.4	BU 2	3.0	5.0	60%	1.0	1.00
	0.0	BU 3	3.0	6.0	50%	2.0	1.00
	2.6	BU 4	3.0	7.0	43%	1.0	3.00
	-	Other	-	-			
	5.0	Totals	22.0	46.0	48%	9.0	15.0

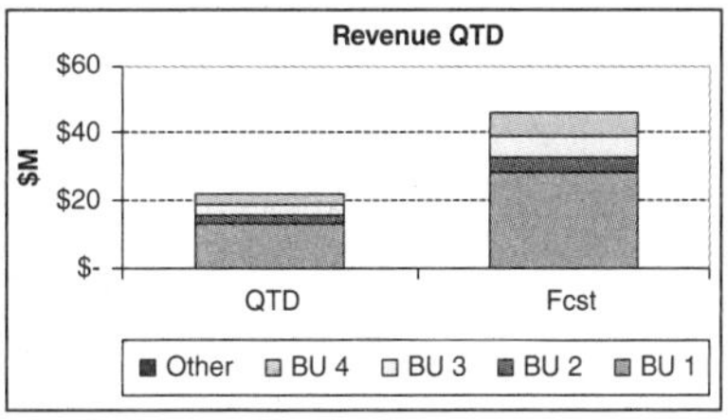

Receivable Collections (Cumulative)	Week	1	2	3	4	5
	Actual	1.0	5.0	19.0		
	Target	4.0	9.0	17.0	28.0	35.0

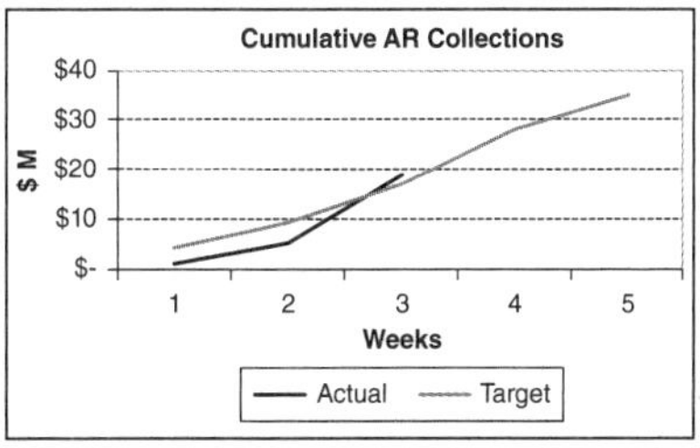

	Day	1	2	3	4	5
Process Yield		77%	80%	81%	68%	82%

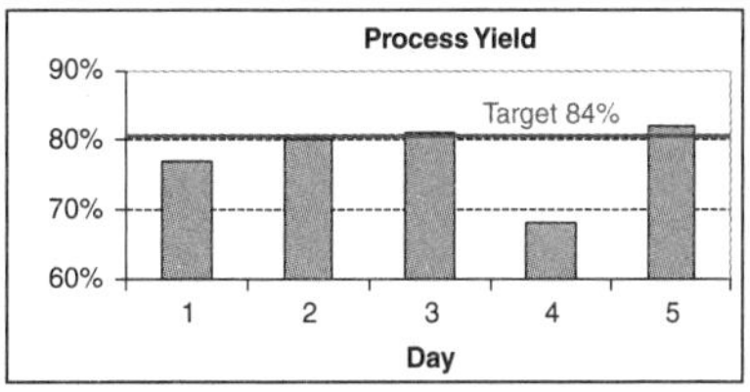

Process Dashboard. Since business and financial performance is largely the result of critical business processes, these are the most critical supporting dashboards (see Figure 16.6). Examples of key business processes include:

❑ Revenue process.
❑ Supply chain management.
❑ New product development.
❑ Mergers and acquisitions.

Dashboards for other processes are presented in Part V, "Planning and Analysis for Critical Business and Value Drivers."

Project Dashboards   A very useful application for dashboards is to set goals and track performance on key projects.

Performance Improvement Dashboards   Dashboards are terrific ways to evaluate and diagnose performance issues and to track progress on performance improvement initiatives, for example, improving the management of receivables in Figure 16.7. In fact, performance improvement initiatives are terrific ways to introduce KPIs and dashboards to an organization.

Individual Manager Dashboards   In some cases, an individual's dashboard may correspond to a process, functional, or corporate dashboard. For example, the CEO can look at the corporate dashboard as his or her personal dashboard. Similarly, a vice president of R&D may choose the new product development dashboard. Other individuals may develop dashboards that include performance measures that cover critical activities and objectives within their respective responsibilities. Care must be exercised to ensure that these individual dashboards are consistent with the objectives and measures of the company and to the function or process to which the individual contributes.

Exception-Based Reporting (EBR) and Alerts   A very effective tool that has gained wide acceptance is a notification or alert to an analyst or manager when a rogue transaction occurs, trends change, or exceptions or unusual events occur. As a result, the manager does not have to constantly monitor a process or activity, but will be alerted to some activity warranting attention. EBR leverages analyst's and manager's time by eliminating the need to review every transaction or event, and allowing them to focus on those that have certain characteristics or are outside of predetermined boundaries.

FIGURE 16.6 **New product development dashboard.** 🔲

New Product Development Dashboard

Critical New Product Development Status

Project Name	Costs			Status (% completion)(1)			Annual Revenue Potential	Projected NPV	Status	Comment
	Actual	Projected	%	Actual	Projected	%	%			
Coyote	0.7	0.8	88%	95%	93%	102%	$25	$52	●	On Track, Intro 3/24
Fox	2.8	2.5	112%	60%	80%	75%	30	61		2 Critical Milestones missed
Rabbit	1.4	1.3	108%	40%	50%	80%	15	21	●	Technical Performance Issues
Tortoise	1.8	2	90%	100%	100%	100%	60	45	●	1st Shipments, next week
Total	6.7	6.6	102%	74%	81%	89%	$130	$179		

(1) Based on project milestones planned and achieved

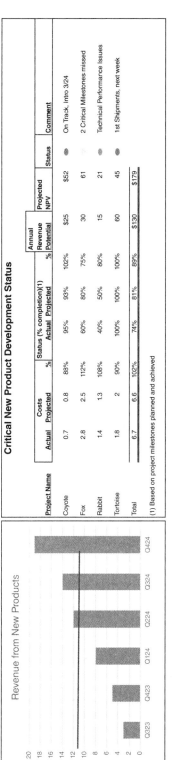

Revenue from New Products

ECN's New Products

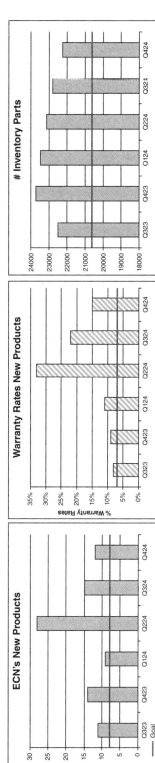

Warranty Rates New Products

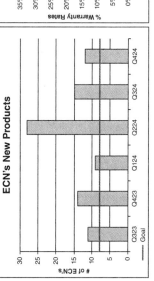

Inventory Parts

FIGURE 16.7 **Revue process/receivable improvement dashboard.**

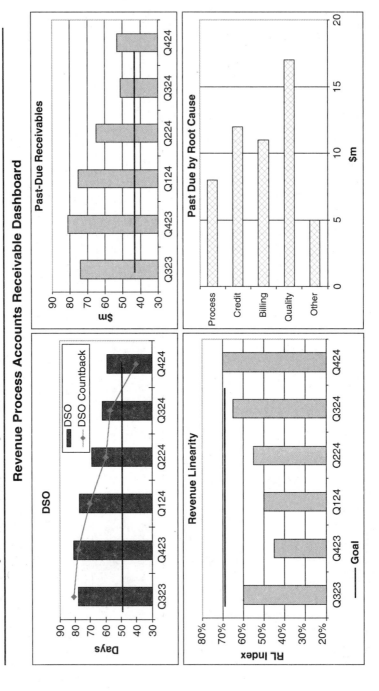

Revenue Process Accounts Receivable Dashboard

Examples include:

Accounts past due.

Sales transactions with excessive discount or low margin.

Retail transactions that may be fraudulent.

Patient vital signs deteriorate.

SAMPLE DASHBOARDS FOR SELECTED INDUSTRIES

It can be insightful to think about KPIs and dashboards for businesses other than our own. What are the key value drivers and performance measures? The sample dashboards in Figures 16.8 through 16.11 are focused on revenue, which is critical to any business. Note how these dashboards focus on leading indicators of performance, including critical assumptions and variables affecting revenue levels. These variables will always include external factors. For example, weather impacts each of these businesses and would be reflected on the revenue dashboard. Lower temperatures and greater snowfall would have a negative impact on many businesses, but not for a ski resort or a retailer selling snow throwers or winter apparel. The dashboard for a regional bank is very different; the focus is on interest rates, deposits, and asset composition.

SUMMARY

Key performance measures and dashboards are two very useful tools in developing effective EPM. However, the selection of measures and development of dashboards are extremely important since they implicitly state priorities and key areas of emphasis for the organization. People and organizations respond to the use of measures. The mere fact that performance is being tracked often leads to improvements in productivity. This is even more dramatic if compensation plans are tied to the measures. As a result, care must be exercised to select appropriate measures. Establishing measures that are not well vetted may lead to behavior changes that have unintended consequences. In addition, it is critically important to achieve a balance in the measures. For example, measuring inventory turns could lead to the unintended consequence of impacting customer deliveries if not balanced with appropriate measures of on-time deliveries and customer satisfaction. The selection of performance measures should be done in the context of building a comprehensive EPM.

FIGURE 16.8 **Dashboard for a specialty retail store: Lawn and garden.**

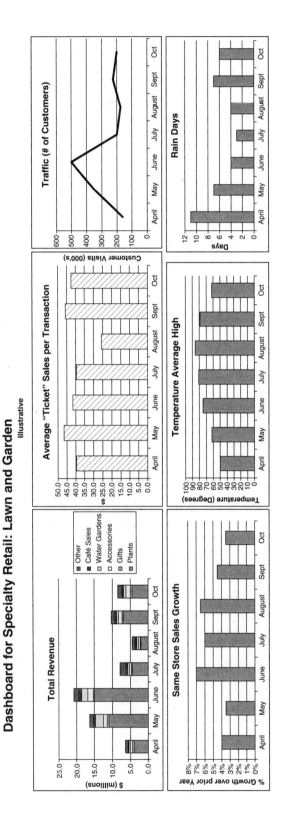

Dashboard for Specialty Retail: Lawn and Garden

Illustrative

FIGURE 16.9 **Dashboard for a ski resort.** 🔲

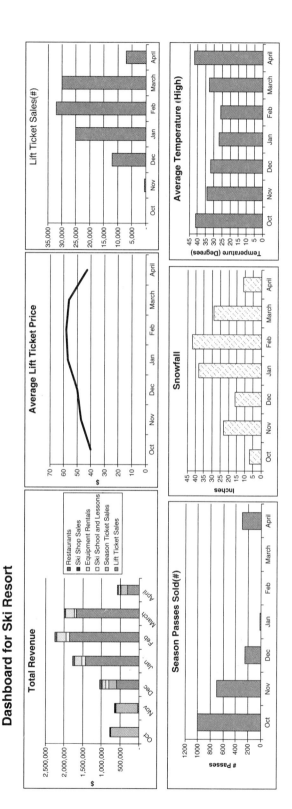

329

FIGURE 16.10 **Dashboard for a medical vendor.** 🔲

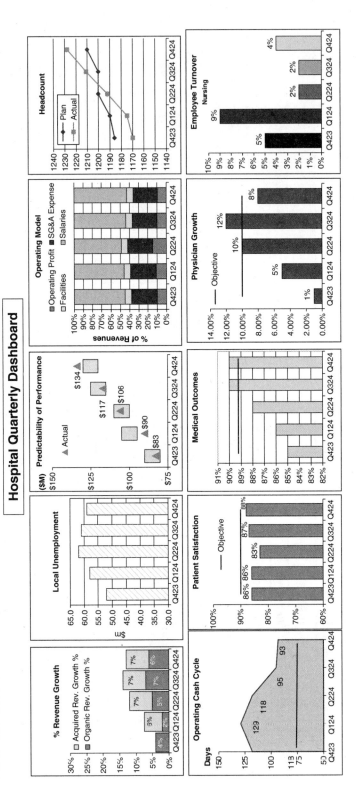

Hospital Quarterly Dashboard

FIGURE 16.11 **Dashboard for s regional bank.**

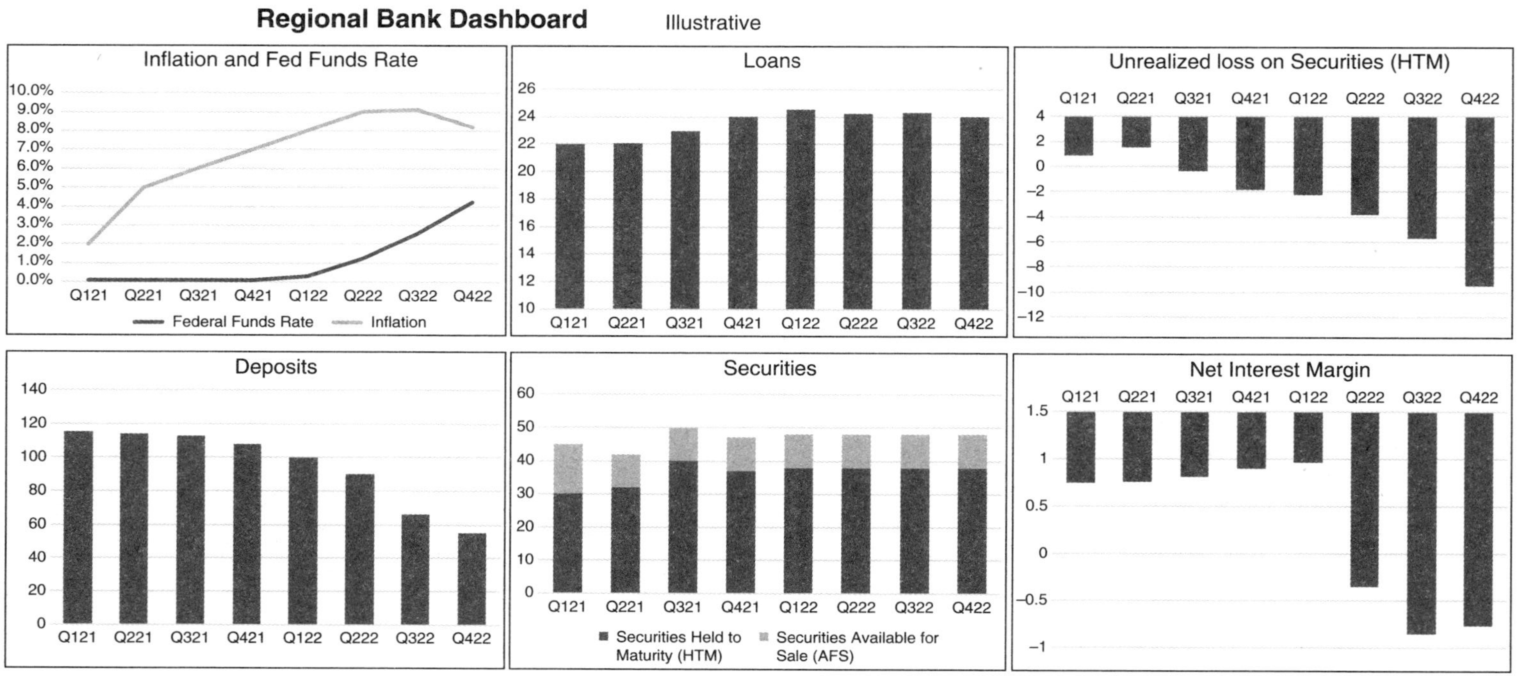

Regional Bank Dashboard   Illustrative

17

Institutionalizing Performance Management

In earlier chapters in this part on enterprise performance management (EPM), we covered the importance of stating objectives and developing a context. We then outlined best practices in selecting key performance indicators (KPIs) and building dashboards. We now turn to the process of *institutionalizing* performance management (PM), that is, successful implementation and integration into all critical management processes. This step is the final, and arguably most important, aspect of successful EPM. If the PM is not integrated with other management processes, it will not be successful.

FIGURE 17.1 **Establishing a Performance Management Framework**

Establishing or Improving Enterprise Performance Management

Identify Objectives	Create Context	Build Framework	Institutionalize
❏ Integrate Financial and Operational Measures ❏ Accelerate Value Creation ❏ Alignment and Execution of Goals	❏ Strategy ❏ Key Initiatives ❏ Assess Performance ❏ Identify Threats and Opportunities ❏ Shareholder Value	❏ Select Key Performance Measures ❏ Build Dashboards and Reports ❏ Build Delivery Mechanisms	❏ Training ❏ Technology Platform ❏ Planning and Forecasting ❏ Performance Evaluation ❏ Compensation ❏ Evaluate/Refresh

GAINING TRACTION

There are several critical steps that are necessary to effectively adopt EPM (see Figure 17.1). These include obtaining executive support, communication and training, using performance improvement tools, and developing a delivery mechanism.

Executive Support

Few initiatives are successful in a company without the passion and support of the CEO, CFO, and other members of the senior management team. Managers and employees are very adept at reading the level of commitment of leadership to any new project. Senior managers must support PM in both word and action. The CEO will determine the ultimate success of PM. Is he insisting on a review of dashboards and key performance metrics at management meetings? Is she using the performance measures as a critical element of evaluating managers' performance? Is PM going to be integrated across all management processes? If the answer is no, then EPM will be an interesting activity, but will fail to achieve its full potential impact on the organization. It is extremely important to win the support and buy-in across the executive suite before proceeding with EPM.

Communication and Training

After selecting and developing the performance measures, it is important to provide managers and employees with appropriate training and other tools to use the measures and make performance improvements.

The effectiveness of a PM system and related initiatives will be greatly enhanced if accompanied by manager and employee training. A substantial part of the value in PM is in connecting the dots between operating performance, financial performance, and value creation. A comprehensive training program for managers and executives should include the following topics:

- ❏ Fundamentals of finance.
- ❏ Valuation and value drivers.
- ❏ Linking performance to value.
- ❏ Developing and using KPIs.
- ❏ Use of dashboards to monitor and improve performance.
- ❏ Use of software products and data management.

The training should be tailored to various levels within the organization. The core concepts can be modified to be appropriate to the executive team, mid-level managers, and other employees.

Managers should also be educated on the development and use of KPIs, the use of dashboards to monitor and improve performance, and the use of any software employed to deliver this vital information. For example, if actual results are falling short of targets, the manager must be able to identify the root causes of the variance and even possible actions to improve performance.

Change Management

As with any initiative that impacts the way humans work and are evaluated, attention to change management is a must. In addition to training and communication initiatives, the organization should anticipate and address likely concerns about changes to, or the adoption of, a new PM framework. These will include changes in the way the organization performs key functions, such as reports, software, and performance evaluation. Senior human capital managers should be included in the project team to address these concerns.

Process Improvement Tools

In order to achieve improvements in performance in critical areas and measures, managers and employees must be provided with tools to evaluate and improve key business processes. In Chapter 22, we will review examples of process evaluation tools for the revenue and supply chain management processes. In addition, there are several very useful process evaluation and quality management tools that work across all business processes, including:

❑ Six Sigma.
❑ Total Quality Management (TQM).
❑ Process assessment and improvement.
❑ "Lean" management.
❑ Benchmarking.

Delivery Mechanism

Many software vendors have developed products that will deliver key performance indicators and financial results in real time to designated managers throughout the organization. Critical information is available on demand and using best practices to present business information, including data visualization. These are effective long-term solutions in many cases. However, many companies become bogged down in attempting to use or even evaluate and procure these technology tools. Often, the introduction of the software solution is done without defining the objectives and context that were described in Chapter 15. Many of the "canned" KPIs and dashboards miss the mark in terms of measuring what is most important and relevant to this specific organization. The performance measures and dashboards that are developed in this way often fail to fully achieve the objectives of implementing PM. In addition, the implementation is often delayed until the technology is procured and installed. In some cases, valuable time is lost in critical performance areas.

While generally not a good long-term, *total* solution, many companies begin producing dashboards on spreadsheet tools such as Microsoft Excel. The advantage in this approach is that a few key dashboards can be produced in hours or days, rather than in weeks or months. This can be a good way to get started, especially in situations where improving business performance is a matter of urgency, for example, in a business turnaround situation. Long-term technology solutions can then be put in place as time permits, and objectives and definition of needs are understood, building on the initial efforts. Due to the power and flexibility of Excel, it or other similar products will always play a role in FP&A and EPM.

Oversight of PM

Who should be responsible for designing, implementing, and overseeing PM? The answer to this question varies from one organization to another depending on several factors, including the skill set and experience of key managers and functions within the organization.

Many organizations that have successful PM initiatives develop a steering committee or PM council to oversee the implementation and ongoing execution of PM. The council should include representation from all critical functions, including strategy, operations, finance, information technology (IT), and sales and marketing. This broad representation will ensure that PM will consider diverse perspectives and will encourage buy-in and acceptance across the organization.

The responsibility for the implementation and direction of PM on a day-to-day basis is usually assigned to a working group or related function. Two obvious functions to lead the working group are the IT and FP&A departments. I have generally found that the director of FP&A or equivalent is usually best suited to lead the working group. PM and FP&A must be fully integrated to be successful. An effective FP&A group is already aware of and analyzing critical areas of performance and understands drivers of financial performance and shareholder value. In addition, their role typically exposes them to all critical functions, strategic issues, and initiatives across the organization. If an IT professional is chosen to lead, that individual must have a business orientation in addition to software and hardware expertise.

INTEGRATING BUSINESS PM WITH OTHER MANAGEMENT PROCESSES

To be effective, the PM framework must be integrated with other key management processes and activities, including planning, management meetings, performance reviews, project management, and evaluating and compensating human resources (see Figure 17.2).

FIGURE 17.2 **Integrating EPM with other Management Processes**

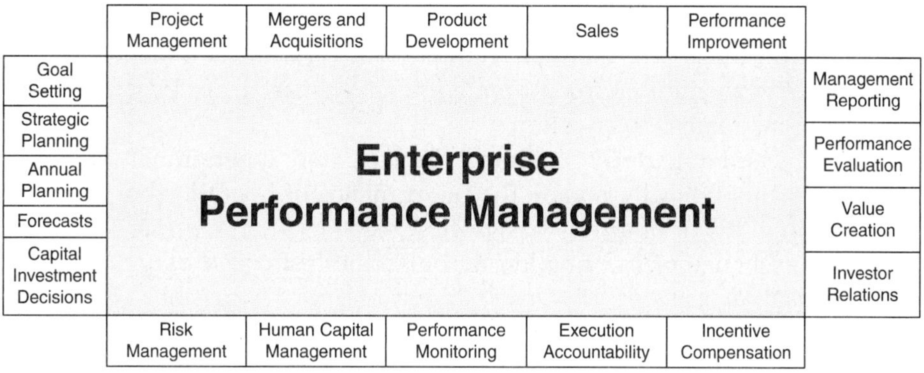

	Project Management	Mergers and Acquisitions	Product Development	Sales	Performance Improvement	
Goal Setting						Management Reporting
Strategic Planning						Performance Evaluation
Annual Planning		Enterprise Performance Management				
Forecasts						Value Creation
Capital Investment Decisions						Investor Relations
	Risk Management	Human Capital Management	Performance Monitoring	Execution Accountability	Incentive Compensation	

Strategic and Operational Planning. Most companies develop strategic and annual operating plans each year. Planning activities will be greatly improved by incorporating the key elements of PM. What level of shareholder value is likely if the planned results are achieved? The financials included in the plan should not be a spreadsheet exercise; rather, they must be grounded by execution plans and projected levels of performance on key operating measures. For example, if a company plans to achieve improved inventory turnover in the future, this goal should be supported by a detailed plan and targets for KPIs that impact inventory levels, such as revenue patterns, production cycle times, past-due deliveries, and forecasting accuracy. Each plan or alternative should be valued, that is, the team should estimate what the likely market value of the company will be if the plan is achieved. Is this an acceptable return to shareholders? Can we identify other actions that will enhance value? Finally, the planning process should identify the measures that will be monitored to track and evaluate assumptions and performance in executing the plan.

Forecasting and Business Outlook. Most companies spend a great deal of time forecasting business performance. In a successful PM framework, companies will place more emphasis on forecasting and tracking key performance drivers and measures that will result in achieving the financial projections. These managers recognize that it is easier to track progress and drive improvement to performance measures that will impact financial results rather than attempt to drive improvement directly to financial results.

Project Management. At any one point in time, most organizations will have hundreds of projects underway. These will include projects in information technology, product development, process improvement, developing plans, and many others that have a direct and significant effect on performance. Project management can be improved by incorporating EPM, including execution planning, monitoring, and visibility. Adopting standard project management dashboards and reports across the organization will ensure utilization of best practices and facilitate reporting and review.

Product Development. As the pipeline for new product and revenue growth, product development is a very important process for value creation. Product development activity includes the evaluation of potential new programs and products and the management of several development projects. Both project evaluation and management lend themselves to EPM and their importance mandates the attention.

Monthly and Quarterly Business, Project, and Operational Reviews. Executive teams typically review the performance of operations of business units on a monthly or quarterly basis. These sessions often represent the most important exchange of information and also the *best opportunity to focus on execution and hold managers accountable for performance*. Discussions at monthly and quarterly management meetings should center on key objectives, critical issues, progress toward goals and targets, KPIs, and the performance dashboards. All too often, these meetings drift away from critical performance objectives aided by long discussions around lengthy slideshow presentations. If the team has implemented the performance framework by developing context and linking to strategic initiatives and value drivers, then the dashboards will provide visibility into performance in critical areas and programs. Meetings will stay focused on key issues and managers can be easily held accountable to the performance tracked by these objective measures.

It's hard to hide from the information on the slide shown in Figure 17.3. When required to be presented, it prevents long-winded, diversionary presentations that mask or fail to address the important elements of performance.

Talent Acquisition, Evaluation, Development, and Compensation (Human Capital Management). It is very unlikely that any PM system will be completely successful unless it is integrated into the talent acquisition, evaluation, development, and compensation processes. Performance objectives should be established for each manager that are consistent with achieving the company's goals for value creation and strategic and operational objectives. Too often, individual and functional objectives and targets are set independently, without adequate linkage to overall corporate objectives. Incorporating the principles from the EPM into the evaluation of managers' performance will increase the effectiveness of the performance reviews and underscore the organization's commitment to PM. Of course, aligning compensation and incentive practices with PM ensures ultimate connectivity.

PM can also be *applied* to overall human capital management (HCM). Since an organization's team of associates may be considered its greatest asset, PM can be used to analyze the workforce and critical HCM processes. The use of KPIs and analytics in HCM was explored in Chapter 7.

Management Reporting. Monthly financial and management reports should be modified to include the KPIs and drivers selected in developing the PM. Typical monthly reports include traditional financial statements, supporting schedules, and spreadsheets that are easily understood by accountants, but are difficult for most nonfinancial managers and employees to understand

FIGURE 17.3 **Business unit accountability dashboard.**

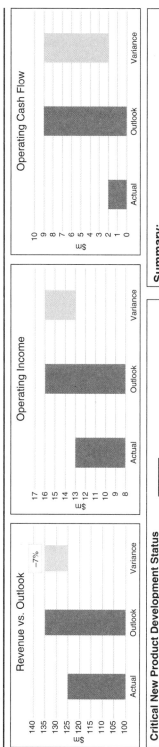

Revenue vs. Outlook

Operating Income

Operating Cash Flow

Critical New Product Development Status

Project Name	Costs			Status (% completion)(1)			Annual Revenue Potential	Status	Comment
	Actual	Projected	%	Actual	Projected	%			
Coyote	0.7	0.8	88%	95%	93%	102%	$25	Green	On Track, Intro 3/24
Fox	2.8	2.5	112%	60%	80%	75%	30	Yellow	2 Critical Milestones missed
Rabbit	1.4	1.3	108%	40%	50%	80%	15	Red	Technical Performance Issues
Tortoise	1.8	2	90%	100%	100%	100%	60	Green	1st Shipments, next week
Total	6.7	6.6	102%	74%	81%	89%	$130		

(1) Based on project milestones planned and achieved

Summary:

- Significant shortfall in revenue and profit

- Delay in new product introductions

- Cash Flow levels also impacted by rising inventories due to revenue shortfall and new product delays

- Corrective action plan developed

and digest. Key trends or exceptions may be buried in the statements and are extremely difficult to identify or act on. More visual content (graphs) should replace pages of financial tables and reports. Focus should shift away from lagging financial results toward providing crisp, predictive leading indicators of future performance. The reports should also focus more attention on revenue drivers and analysis of external factors rather than the traditional measures of internal financial performance.

Board and Investor Communication. For both publicly traded and privately owned firms, communication with investors is a very important activity. Many investors are intensely focused on company performance and the future potential to create shareholder value. Investors will appreciate managers who recognize that a broad set of performance factors drive long-term value creation. They fully understand that successful execution on key strategic initiatives and improvement on value drivers will lead to long-term shareholder returns. Shareholders applaud managers who are focused on execution, accountability, and PM since they know that these are precursors to value creation.

Executives running publicly traded companies should communicate the performance on key business and value drivers, and related performance measures, and not just focus on sales or earnings per share (EPS). Investors who use economic valuation methods such as discounted cash flow (DCF) need inputs for sales and earnings growth as well as capital requirements and cost of capital. Even those investors using multiples of revenue or earnings must consider these factors in selecting an appropriate price-earnings (PE) or revenue multiple to value the company. Presenting and emphasizing the long-term value drivers also encourages investors to focus less attention on short-term quarterly financial results.

Corporate Development. The corporate development function is typically responsible for merger & acquisition (M&A) activity within most companies. The M&A process and resultant deals are important contributors or detractors to performance and value in many companies. For companies that are active in mergers and acquisitions, it is important that M&A activity be viewed as a process and that the key elements of the PM be incorporated into the identification, evaluation, valuation, and integration of acquisitions. The analysis of M&A will be fully explored in Chapter 31.

Periodic Review and Revision

The selection of KPIs and the creation of dashboards will be based on numerous factors, including many that relate to specific issues and opportunities, events, and projects. The KPIs and dashboards should be reviewed periodically to evaluate the ongoing utility of each measure and dashboard. For example, some measures can be eliminated because the underlying issue or project has been addressed or completed. New priorities and challenges arise that may warrant inclusion in the measurement system going forward.

An excellent time to review measures and dashboards is in the later stages of the annual and/or strategic process, when new objectives, initiatives, and targets are established. Of course, measures that are no longer useful can be replaced at any point.

AVOIDING COMMON MISTAKES

Don't Drive the Car by Staring at the Dashboard

You won't keep the car on the road if you stare at the dashboard. Look out the front window and check the rear-view mirror. Pay attention to road conditions, traffic patterns, and aggressive drivers as well as the dashboard. Similarly, pilots seldom fly by staring at the instrument panel. They utilize this visual input, but also rely on their intuition, feel, conditions, and other input. Get out of the office. Talk to employees, customers, and suppliers. Combine this input with your intuition and the objective information from the dashboards.

Don't Make It a Finance or Information Technology Project

Many projects fail because they are driven exclusively by the finance or information technology functions. In order to be successful, PM must be driven from the top and integrated into the fabric of the management systems. Functions such as finance and IT are critical in the development, implementation, and support of PM, but all disciplines must buy into and support this activity to be successful.

Don't Measure Everything

Organizations that follow the process that was outlined in Chapter 15 to define objectives and develop context for PM will develop a framework that focuses the organization's attention on important value and performance drivers. Failure to do so will result in selecting too many measures, and some measures that are not consistent with priorities and performance drivers.

Don't Measure Only What Is Easy and Available

There is a tendency to select KPIs and build dashboards based on the information that is readily available. Examples include financial ratios and trends or certain operational metrics. In many cases, the most important information on key businesses processes, threats and opportunities, intangibles, and other critical drivers is not readily available. While it may be challenging to measure things like innovation, agility, or human capital, their importance to success justifies attempts at measuring and evaluation. Even if the measures are imperfect, they will focus attention and provide insight into these critical areas. These softer performance drivers were explored in Chapters 7 (on human capital) and 14 (on innovation, agility, and resilience).

Don't Attempt to Replace Judgment or Intuition

Some executives resist PM initiatives because they argue that EPM is an attempt to replace or limit their management judgment and intuition. While analysis and PM can significantly improve decision-making and management, many important decisions must incorporate the experience and judgment of the executive. PM can ensure that all relevant information is presented, leading to better decisions, by confusing the discussion with facts!

Don't Measure Too Frequently

New information availability may encourage managers to "take the pulse" of the business and key activities too often. This will lead to frustration for managers and team members alike, and may also result in decisions or actions based on small sample size, cycles, or minor perturbations.

Software Is Not a Silver Bullet

Many organizations look to a software product as the silver bullet in measuring and improving performance. While software can be a helpful contribution to PM, it is at least as important, if not more important, to develop context, select measures, training, and integration with other management processes.

Avoid GIGO (Garbage In, Garbage Out)

Even if an organization implemented the best software, trained associates, and developed thoughtful KPIs and dashboards, if the underlying data is unavailable or of poor quality, the project will crash and burn. Nothing destroys the credibility and potential utility of EPM more than bad data. The project team must assess and address the availability and integrity of the data early in the EPM process.

SUMMARY

PM cannot succeed as a separate and distinct management process. To be successful, it must be integrated into key management processes, including strategic and operational planning, monthly or quarterly business and operational reviews, and talent evaluation and compensation. EPM must also be driven from the top to be successful. The CEO and CFO must demand utilization of PM throughout critical management processes. In order to remain relevant and vital, PM must be evaluated and adjusted periodically to ensure that it remains focused on the critical drivers of performance and value.

18

Benchmarking Performance

Most traditional efforts by finance professionals are directed at the internal aspects of the enterprise, including financial and operational performance. Business partners can extend and expand the value they add by looking outside the enterprise. This chapter will focus on utilizing benchmark information to evaluate performance and to set enterprise goals for performance and value creation.

BENCHMARKING TO EVALUATE PERFORMANCE

Two types of benchmarking can be useful in evaluating performance and identifying improvement opportunities:

1. Process or functional benchmarks.
2. Overall performance.

Process or Functional Benchmarks

For many years consultants and trade organizations have collected cost and performance data on various business processes or functions. Examples include:

- Finance costs as a percentage of sales.
- Cost of processing an invoice.
- Length of time to close books.

- Duration of budget or plan cycle.
- Product development—time to market.
- Revenue process management.
- Supply chain management.
- Information technology.

For example, these studies allow you to compare the cost of finance and key processes in your organization to the costs of companies included in the study. Most surveys emphasize the importance of using consistent definitions since the scope of finance functions may vary from organization to organization. These surveys are very useful in identifying performance gaps and improvement opportunities, especially in transaction processing (e.g., payroll, payments, and revenue). They also should allow you to understand the mix of functions (e.g., transaction processing vs. FP&A) relative to average and best practices companies. The better benchmark surveys enable you to compare organizations of similar size and allow you to ascertain the reasons for gaps between your company's performance and the benchmark averages. In my experience, the most useful aspect of benchmark studies is the identification of best practices and trends. When utilizing benchmark surveys, select one that considers the overall effectiveness, not simply efficiency and cost.

Evaluating Overall Performance   In Chapter 6, the expanded view of the business model was introduced, which is a useful tool to benchmark performance across value drivers. We can compare performance on key elements such as revenue growth, margins, expense levels, and return on investment.

Many managers limit benchmarking to a peer group of similar companies or competitors. Their logic is that it is meaningful to compare performance only across companies in the same industry, so-called "comparables." Companies in the same industry tend to adopt similar business practices. In addition, their financial performance is shaped by the same market forces since they typically would share common customers and suppliers. While benchmarking comparable companies is useful, it does not capture many of the potential benefits of a broader benchmarking process.

The potential for learning can be greatly expanded if the universe of companies in the benchmark is expanded, as shown in Figure 18.1. If you want to identify the best and the most innovative practices in supply chain management, do you want to study a competitor that has achieved a mediocre level of performance or a best practice or wildcard company like Apple or Amazon? While these companies may be in a very different business from yours, understanding the business practices that they have employed and the resultant impact on the business model is very enlightening and may lead to potential improvement opportunities for your business.

FIGURE 18.1 **Expanded benchmarking view.**

Assessing Performance: Expanded Benchmarking View

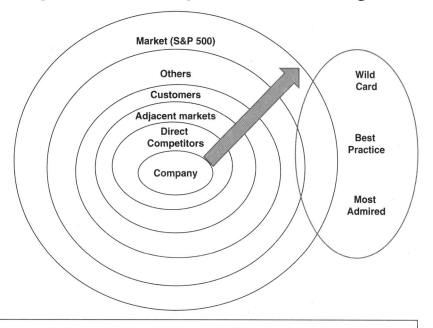

The value (learning) of benchmarking is far greater if the field is expanded beyond "comparable companies"

It is also helpful to look at the performance of key customers and companies in related or adjacent industries. A primary factor in a company's success will be the performance of key customers. How fast are they growing? Are they profitable? Are they cash strapped or cash flush? Comparing your company's performance to these companies on key metrics such as sales growth, operating costs, and capital requirements can be useful in evaluating your performance on a relative basis and in setting future performance targets. In addition, you may find it meaningful to contrast your business to other models. Understanding the different financial results in light of varying business practices may identify potential improvement opportunities as well as potential vulnerabilities. The financial analysis and research into the company's performance can be integrated with a product/service competitive analysis and overall market assessment.

A comprehensive benchmark approach is illustrated in Table 18.1. This one-page summary will allow managers to easily compare critical elements of their company's financial performance and valuation to those of competitors and customers as well as most admired and best practices companies. The summary was prepared using the sources that were identified in Chapter 10, the external view, and analyzed using the assessment model introduced in Chapter 2. This comparative table can be supported by more detailed analysis, illustrated for Microsoft in Figures 10.7 through 10.9. This more detailed analysis includes information and analysis on strategy, competitors, growth strategy, revenue detail, acquisitions, and the company's business segments.

Benchmarking Illustration To illustrate the performance and business model benchmark we utilize a hypothetical company, Gladnor Technologies. The company is a relatively small player in the overall tech industry, dominated by several large players. The executives of the company, traded on a public exchange, feel that the company is missing opportunities to accelerate growth and is undervalued compared to the larger tech firms. The firm has been focused on hardware and most customers are based in the U.S. A number of strategic actions/and alternatives are under consideration, including:

- Sell the company at an expected premium to current valuation.
- Increase revenues by:
  - Redirecting R&D to higher growth opportunities, including "cloud" and AI.
  - Developing complementary software products and service offerings.
  - Transforming product offerings into more recurring, subscription based.
  - Expanding to serve more international customers.
- Acquire a company to accelerate revenue growth opportunities previously identified.

The CEO and board have initiated a comprehensive strategic review. Product and marketing managers are preparing a thorough analysis of product competitiveness and market trends. These findings will be summarized using the framework outlined in Chapter 8. Finance is charged with a comprehensive evaluation of performance and value drivers, including benchmarking performance against notable, successful industry players. The team intentionally selected a diverse group to study a wide variety of best practices and business models.

Analysts have researched the selected players using the process in Chapter 10 on the external view, specifically competitive analysis. The executive team has identified the following companies to benchmark; some are customers and others represent interesting performance and business model characteristics.

HP Inc. (HPQ). Manufacturers of personal computers and printers with high consumable sales (I just replaced the cartridge on my printer!).

Microsoft (MSFT). Known for Office® products, the company has expanded via many other segments, including cloud services and artificial intelligence. Some of this expansion has been accelerated through acquisitions, strategic investments, and partnerships.

Dell Technologies (DELL). Dell started as a PC supplier and then developed an innovative manufacturing and distribution model for PCs. Dell expanded to IT services, infrastructure, and AI. The company went public, then was taken private, and then went public again in 2018. Dell completed the acquisition of EMC Corporation, a leader in digital storage, in 2016.

ServiceNow (NOW). ServiceNow offers subscription-based services to support digital transformation on an integrated platform and has experienced remarkable growth in recent years.

Amazon (AMZN). Amazon is selected because of a long period of sustained growth and the development of Amazon Web Services (AWS), offering cloud and other IT capabilities to corporate clients.

Apple Computer (AAPL). While this company does not participate in any of Gladnor's direct markets, it is selected because of its innovative practices, and extraordinary growth and value creation.

IBM (IBM). Big Blue is included in the analysis. The old-guard technology company has been transforming itself, spinning off its IT infrastructure business to focus on cloud and AI.

Oracle (ORCL). Oracle offers network products and services worldwide, including ERP.

Salesforce, Inc. (CRM). Salesforce offers customer relationship management software (CRM) and has expanded with acquisitions of Slack, Tableau, and other companies. Founded in 1999 by a former Oracle executive, revenues grew to over $30 billion in fiscal year 2023. CRM is a component of the Dow Jones Industrial Average.

The results of the analysis of each company have been summarized in Table 18.1 and Figure 18.2. The combination of tabular and graphic presentation aids in making comparisons.

Even in this simple example, several takeaways are evident, as summarized in the takeaways from performance and value benchmarking in Figure 18.3.

While this top-level benchmarking provides a view into the performance of all companies selected, it does not always provide detailed insight into the practices and drivers of the financial results. Without an understanding of each of the business's practices and other factors, it provides limited benefit. For example, in the early 2000s, it was useful to observe that Dell turns inventory nearly 100 times per year. But just how did they do that? Are there best practices identified that can be considered for use in your company?

The second and more meaningful method of benchmarking requires us to climb under the numbers to understand the practices and drivers of one firm's performance versus others. This requires detailed knowledge of the

TABLE 18.1 **Comprehensive benchmark analysis.**

Benchmark Summary

	Gladnor	HP Inc.	Microsoft	Dell	ServiceNow	IBM	Oracle	Salesforce	Wild cards Amazon	Apple
Revenue	10,000.0	62,983.0	198,300.0	102,301.0	7,245.0	60,530.0	42,440.0	31,352.0	513,983.0	394,328.0
Revenue CAGR (3 year historical)	5.6%	2.3%	16.4%	6.4%	27.9%	1.6%	2.4%	22.4%	22.4%	14.9%
Gross Margin %	40.0%	19.6%	68.4%	22.2%	78.3%	54.0%	79.1%	73.3%	27.4%	43.3%
SG&A % Revenue	23.0%	8.4%	14.0%	13.8%	49.0%	30.7%	22.1%	51.3%	10.5%	6.4%
R&D % Revenue	7.0%	2.5%	12.4%	2.7%	24.4%	10.8%	17.0%	16.1%	14.2%	6.7%
Operating Profit	1,000.0	4,676.0	83,383.0	5,771.0	355.0	5,992.0	10,926.0	1,030.0	12,248.3	119,437.0
Operating Profit % Revenue	10.0%	7.4%	42.0%	5.6%	4.9%	9.9%	25.7%	3.3%	2.4%	30.3%
EBITDA $	1,100.0	5,456.0	97,883.0	8,927.0	788.0	10,794.0	14,048.0	4,816.0	54,169.0	130,541.0
EBITDA %	11.0%	8.7%	49.4%	8.7%	10.9%	17.8%	33.1%	15.4%	10.5%	33.1%
Net Income	800	3,203	72,738	2,422	325	1,639	6,717	208	(2,722)	99,803
Net Income % Revenue	8.0%	5.1%	36.7%	2.4%	4.5%	2.7%	15.8%	0.7%	-0.5%	25.3%
Asset Utilization and Returns										
Days Sales Outstanding (DSO)	54.8	26.3	81.5	44.5	86.9	39.4	51.2	125.2	30.1	26.1
Days Sales Inventory (DSI)	109.5	54.7	71.6	26.4		88.9			33.7	9.0
Goodwill and Intangibles % Revenue	1.5%	13.6%	5.7%	25.6%	14.6%	110.9%	106.6%	177.6%	3.0%	0.3%
Asset Turnover	1.43	1.63	0.54	1.14	0.54	0.48	0.39	0.32	1.11	1.12
ROIC	17.3%	41.7%	33.5%	16.3%	4.4%	9.3%	13.7%	0.5%	4.2%	62.3%
Enterprise Value	11,900	37,410	2,244,024	54,491	89,413	112,796	315,765	196,493	1,013,262	2,655,960
Value Metrics:										
EV/Revenue	1.2	0.6	11.3	0.5	12.3	1.9	7.4	6.3	2.0	6.7
EV/EBITDA	10.8	6.9	22.9	6.1	113.5	10.4	22.5	40.8	18.7	20.3

Note: Analysis are based on results reported in financial statements and have not been adjusted for non recurring items or other adjustments.

Source: Compiled from annual and other reports.

FIGURE 18.2 **Benchmark graphic summary.**

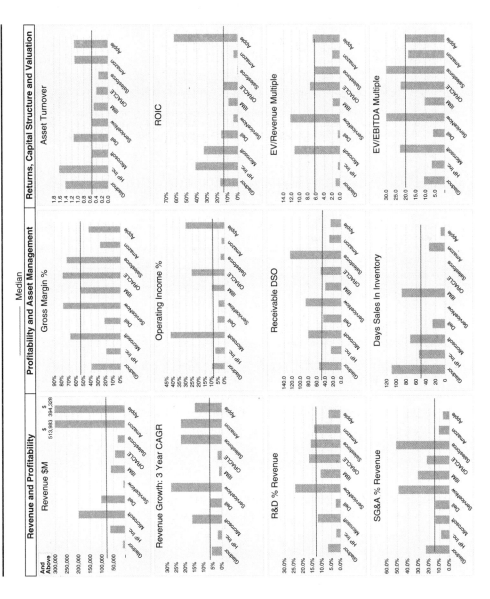

FIGURE 18.3 **Benchmark takeaways.**

Takeaways from Performance and Value Benchmarking

Observations

- The group as a whole has experienced growth over an extended period and most are highly profitable with strong cash flow from operations.
- Many of the companies have very different revenue mix profiles from Gladnor. Specifically, a greater percentage of revenues from geographies outside the U.S., and significantly higher revenues from the sale of software and systems. In addition, many benefit by providing services in addition to products. Others have developed recurring revenue models with licensing and subscription-based offerings.
- Rapid growth requires significant investment.
- Scale is important. Most of the companies are significantly larger than Gladnor, impacting manufacturing, distribution and development costs as a percentage of revenue.
- There is a wide range of performance and a variety of different business models employed by these benchmarks.
- Gladnor is valued at a discount to the other companies. This is due to a number of factors including brand awareness, lower growth and financial performance.
- The group, especially Apple and Microsoft have accumulated huge stockpiles of cash and marketable investments.
- Apple utilizes an innovative supply chain, and distribution model. This results in very low receivables, inventories and fixed assets.
- Several large technology companies are making strategic acquisitions, as evidenced by high Goodwill and Intangible Assets for selected companies.
- Valuation Multiples are highly influenced by growth and profitability.

Recommendations:

- Company should evaluate several opportunities to accelerate growth:
  - Add software and service to product mix
  - Geographic expansion
  - Explore recurring revenue opportunities
- Gladnor should evaluate the attractiveness of the business and consider selling in the context of maximizing overall shareholder value. With improvements in operating performance and growth, the company may be an attractive acquisition candidate.
- While valuation is driven by performance expectations, the company should enhance Investor Relations to showcase performance opportunities and characteristics shared with the broader tech industry.

---

market, business model, processes, and practices of the firm. For example, Dell's performance in inventory management is a result of creating a breakthrough business model with significant attention to managing the supply chain, assembly, order fulfillment, and distribution processes. Apple has outsourced most of its manufacturing and supply chain to Asia. While this has the observed benefits (e.g., low inventory balances), it also introduces risk, such as the challenges of managing the supply chain during a pandemic or geopolitical tensions.

Much has been written and published about the best practices at Dell, Apple, Amazon, and other innovative companies. It is also possible to enhance insight by reviewing the disclosures in the company's reports and investor presentations. Many of these companies have also been open about sharing the methods they employed in achieving breakthrough performance in a particular area. In addition, many consulting firms have developed a practice in this area or offer training courses in implementing best practices in various business processes. Additional insight can be derived by integrating the financial performance benchmark with the strategic and competitive analysis performed by marketing, product management, or segment leadership. By comparing your performance to competitors as well as best practice companies, it is possible to identify gaps in your performance that represent significant opportunities to increase shareholder value. Understanding the best practices that lead to extraordinary performance provides a roadmap to closing these performance gaps.

There are many different business models and combinations of value drivers that will lead to building long-term shareholder value. For example, some companies operate with very low operating margins, but earn respectable levels of return on invested capital (ROIC) based on effective utilization of assets. Others earn high margins but are very capital intensive. Companies that have built and sustained shareholder value over an extended time period have blended a mix of the two critical ingredients for value creation: revenue growth and return on invested capital.

Most Admired or Wild Card Benchmarks

Understanding the performance and shareholder value created by most admired or wild-card companies can be inspiring and identify opportunities that a company can evaluate for its own use.

Apple has developed one of the most recognized brands and enjoys customer loyalty approaching cult-like obsession (Figure 18.4). The company has

FIGURE 18.4 **Apple performance trends.**

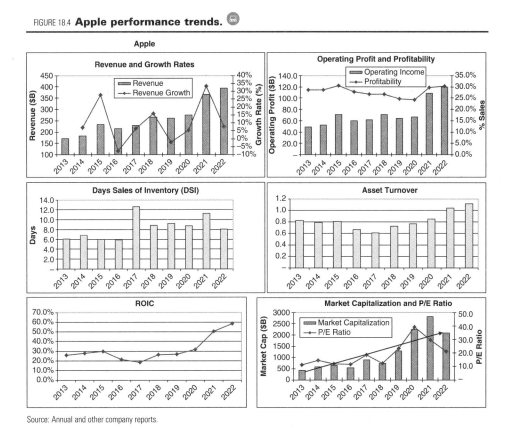

Source: Annual and other company reports.

developed a steady pipeline of both revolutionary and evolutionary products. Apple has worked at developing an internal culture that fosters innovation. The results are reflected in high sales growth over an extended period, very high margins, and outstanding performance in creating shareholder value.

FIGURE 18.5 **Amazon revenue and EBITDA performance.**

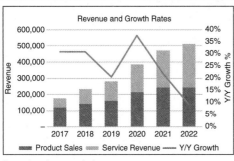
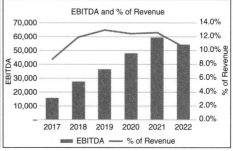

Source: Annual reports and other company reports.

Starting as a purveyor of books and related products on-line, Amazon has leveraged its investment in technology and fulfillment to many other markets. It has chosen to reinvest most profits into future growth opportunities. Amazon has disrupted many retail markets, and continues to test and expand to other markets. The company built on its IT prowess to start Amazon Web Services (AWS), a line of business that leverages the competencies Amazon has developed in technology that contribute significantly to growth and profitability for Amazon as reflected in Figure 18.5.

USING BENCHMARKS TO SET ENTERPRISE GOALS FOR PERFORMANCE AND VALUE CREATION

The business model is a decomposition of various performance and value drivers. Benchmarking the organization by comparing it to competitors, customers, and most admired and wild-card companies can be part of an overall assessment of performance, establishing goals and estimating potential value creation.

Based on the performance assessment described earlier, the management team can begin to set preliminary goals and targets. Table 18.2 provides a simple but effective benchmark summary and target setting worksheet. In this summary, key elements of Gladnor Technology's financial performance are compared to benchmark results, including range, median, and mean. It may also be useful to include a column for best practice or wildcard to highlight exceptional performance in each measure. This analysis can lead to productive discussions to evaluate the company's performance on an objective basis and provide a basis for establishing credible targets for future performance. While

TABLE 18.2 **Benchmarking summary and target worksheet.** 🌐

Benchmarking Summary and Target Worksheet							
	Gladnor	Range		Mean	Median	Performance	Key Initiatives
		Low	High			Target	
Revenue Growth (3 year CAGR)	5.6%	1.6%	27.9%	13.0%	14.9%	8.0%	Introduce software and service offerings
Gross Margin %	40.0%	19.6%	79.1%	51.7%	54.0%	45.0%	Supply chain management (SCM) initiative
R&D % Revenue	7.0%	2.5%	24.4%	11.9%	12.4%	9.0%	Increased investment for growth
SG&A % Revenue	23.0%	6.4%	51.3%	22.9%	14.0%	18.0%	Rationalize distribution channels
Operating Margins	10.0%	2.4%	42.0%	14.6%	7.4%	19.0%	Result
Asset Turnover	1.43	0.32	1.63	0.81	0.54	2.40	Reduce Inventory with SCM
ROIC	17.3%	0.5%	62.3%	20.6%	13.7%	40.0%	Result
Valuation:							
EV/Revenue	1.19	0.50	12.30	5.45	6.27	2.50	
EV/EBITDA	10.82	6.10	113.50	29.13	20.35	12.00	

a potentially useful tool, it should not be viewed as simply a quantitative exercise without consideration to the underlying process changes, investments, and programs to achieve the results.

In the case of Gladnor, specific initiatives are planned to improve supply chain management and distribution to reduce costs and inventory requirements. Service and software offerings are planned, resulting in higher R&D levels. The company expects to see increased valuation multiples based on the expected future performance. While not reflected in Table 18.2, the company is open to acquiring firms that accelerate strategic growth opportunities.

Combining this perspective with other assessment tools can facilitate the development of performance targets. By utilizing the tools to estimate the value of a company and value drivers in Chapter 30, the company can quantify the potential effect of achieving these targets on shareholder value.

SUMMARY

An external view is also a terrific way to evaluate the company's performance. Benchmarking is a very useful way to evaluate performance and to identify potential improvement opportunities. By monitoring and analyzing the performance of competitors and customers, analysts can also provide insight into critical performance trends, events, and relative performance of those companies.

Part Four

Business Projections and Plans

19

Business Projections and Plans—Introduction and Best Practices

The most challenging aspect of financial planning and analysis (FP&A) centers on the need to develop and evaluate projections of *future* financial performance. Almost every important managerial decision requires some estimation of future financial results. Owing to the dynamic nature of the world in which we now operate, the task of predicting future performance has become very challenging. Many finance teams have stepped up to this challenge and made significant changes to planning, budgeting, and forecasting processes over the last 30 years. In this chapter, we will provide an overview of financial projections. Succeeding chapters in Part IV, "Business Projections and Plans," will cover planning and budgeting, forecasts and outlooks, and long-term financial projections. Planning and estimating specific areas such as revenues and gross margins, operating expenses, and working capital will be covered in Part V, "Planning and Analysis for Critical Business and Value Drivers."

OVERVIEW OF BUSINESS PLANNING AND PROJECTIONS

Historical Perspective

Budgets, in some form, were originally used by the British Empire and other governments hundreds of years ago. They were in common use by commercial enterprises in the late 19th century. Budgeting became very popular in the 20th century and was adopted as a key part of managing the business by most companies and organizations. Incremental improvements were made to the process and significant gains in information technology facilitated the preparation of budgets.

Typically, the organization would prepare a budget once each year, several months before the new fiscal year began. For example, the budget for 1954 would likely have been prepared in the fall of 1953. This process served most businesses well during this time. Revenues were relatively stable and predictable. Costs and expenses were, for the most part, easily controlled and estimated on a detail basis. The pace of change and innovation was far slower than recent experience. The process typically included four steps, as illustrated in Figure 19.1.

FIGURE 19.1 **Historical budget and control process.**

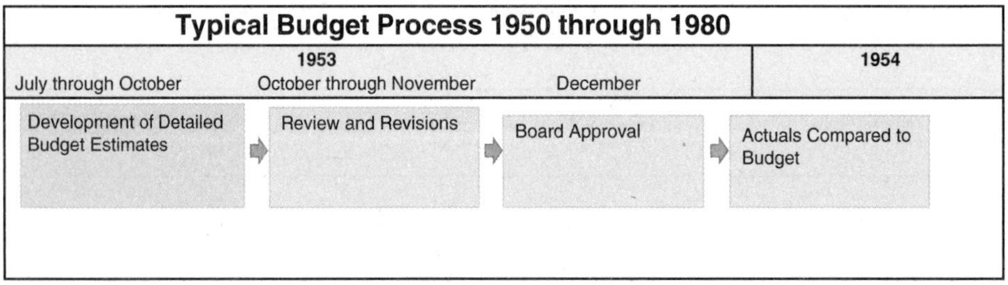

Typical Budget Process 1950 through 1980			
July through October	1953 October through November	December	1954
Development of Detailed Budget Estimates	Review and Revisions	Board Approval	Actuals Compared to Budget

Evolution of Financial Projections

Over time, deficiencies in the annual budget process were recognized. As a result of economic, political, technological, and global developments, the pace of change increased, often resulting in the budget being obsolete or at least dated soon after it was prepared. Many organizations began updating the budget or re-forecasting the expected performance several times each year. In addition, pressure from the capital markets for updates to forecasts of earnings (and severe and disproportionate reactions to missed forecasts) drove many finance teams to update and monitor projections frequently. This phenomenon was greatly accelerated during and immediately following the Covid-19 epidemic, requiring additional process changes.

Organizations began preparing strategic plans in the 1970s, which required the ability to produce estimates of financial performance over an extended time period.

Actual Results Often Fall Short of Projections

Actual results often vary significantly from plans and forecasts. Most variances represent *shortfalls* from projected results. There are several causes of this bias. First, most humans, and particularly managers, are inherently optimistic. Second, many plans or projections are incorrectly prepared as goals rather than probable outcomes. Third, less attention is paid to identifying and managing potential risks and downsides to the plan. Fourth, the projections are often not supported by execution plans. This gap in actual results from projections is particularly evident in long-term projections due to the long period between developing the projections and the day of reckoning. This makes it difficult to hold managers accountable for long-term projections, even if they are still in the chair several years later.

Improved practices in planning and developing projections as well as integration of performance management can significantly raise the effectiveness of planning. Specifically, identifying and testing critical assumptions, identifying risks and upside events, and developing scenarios will greatly improve the effectiveness of determining projections. In addition to the general practices and techniques advocated in Part IV's chapters, the optimistic bias of plans can be countered with stated guidelines, identification and evaluation of critical assumptions, development of multiple scenarios, focus on execution and accountability, execution plans, and measurement of forecast variances.

Types of Financial Projections

Financial projections are utilized in a multitude of applications in managing and optimizing performance. Because of this wide usage, it is important to hone projection skills within an enterprise. This can be facilitated by adopting best practices detailed later in this chapter as well as in succeeding chapters. A few of the most common FP&A and management uses of projections follow.

Budgeting Budgeting continues to be employed by many organizations. In some cases, detailed budgets are required by customers or for statutory purposes. Some organizations continue to significantly reduce or even eliminate the detailed budget process by developing rolling forecasts or on-demand business outlooks (DBOs). Some organizations that continue to prepare budgets have implemented changes to the process to address deficiencies. Budgeting will be more fully explored in Chapter 20.

Annual Operating Plan I define the *annual operating plan* as a broader and evolved form of the budget. The term *budget* typically has negative connotations and is viewed as a financial drill without substantive value to many other functions in the enterprise. Labels are important, and shifting the focus from financial projections to the development of a game plan for the organization can be significant.

As a game plan, the organization must develop a framework to operate the business in the coming year. The financial projections for the coming year are an important element of the operating plan and are a primary way to measure actual results of the operating plan. Operating plans will also be addressed in Chapter 20.

Forecast or Business Outlook   Due to the rate of change experienced in the late 20th and early 21st centuries, the need for frequent updates to the budget or operating plan became necessary. Early efforts involved replicating much of the annual process more frequently, or alternatively, preparing high-level estimates of financial performance. Neither is a very good solution.

In recent years the rolling forecast (or "on-demand business outlook" as I like to call it) has become an important part of the overall management process. It represents a more effective and efficient means to develop and update projections by focusing on *important* drivers and assumptions. Forecasts and business outlooks will be covered in Chapter 20.

Long-Range Projections   Long-range projections are required to evaluate investment and business decisions, acquisitions of businesses, and the evaluation of strategic plans and alternatives. Depending on the objective, these projections will have a horizon of two to seven or more years. Occasionally, for projects with long investment and life cycles, the horizon may be extended to 20 years, or longer. We will explore long-range projections in Chapter 21.

Capital Investment Decisions (CIDs)   Projections are required to evaluate the economic case of investing in equipment, product development, new business, and business acquisitions. The projections are of vital importance in these capital investment decisions (CIDs) because they are the basis for determining whether the project will create value for shareholders. Additional techniques for evaluating projections as part of CID and integrating them with decision criteria will be covered in Chapters 28 and 29.

Special Purpose Projections   Projections are implicit in nearly all business decisions. Decisions such as lease versus buy, produce in house versus outsource, and many other decisions are based on expectations of future revenues, costs, and capital requirements. Tools, techniques, and best practices for projecting revenue, working capital, other assets, and cash flow are covered in detail in Part V.

BEST PRACTICES IN PROJECTING FUTURE FINANCIAL RESULTS

Whether predicting financial performance for the next quarter or the next 20 years, there are several considerations and best practices that should be employed in most projections.

The projections used in estimating value, evaluating a capital project, and evaluating financing alternatives will be a significant input to the decision-making process. There are a few concepts and elements that apply across all financial projections.

Projections Are Not a Finance Exercise!

While the finance team is typically the facilitator and process owner, it is important that all projections must reflect the best estimate of the manager, executive, or team responsible for achieving them. Unfortunately, in many organizations, the "ownership" of the projections is often inadvertently transferred to finance. Operating managers must be fully engaged in developing projections, including assumptions, estimates, decisions, risks, upsides, and the execution plan to achieve the results. The executives with overall responsibility for achieving the results should also formally approve the final plan. Labels are also important! Changing *Forecast* to *Business Outlook*, and *Budget* to *Operating Plan* can help to shift the perception of these exercises from financial to operational.

Trend Analysis and Extrapolation

Most financial projections for established businesses contain some element of extrapolation, that is, basing the projections on recent financial performance trends. We could start with recent financial statements and extrapolate financial trends into the future. Recent sales growth rates can be extended into the future. We could assume gross margins, expenses, and asset levels maintain a constant percentage of sales. This method is reasonable in very stable environments, which are increasingly becoming the exception rather than the rule.

This practice is generally not the best way to project financial performance. Most businesses are dynamic, and key variables will change over time. However, it may provide a useful view in serving as one potential scenario, that is, assuming that recent trends will continue into the future. This can be very useful in cases where other scenarios appear optimistic relative to historical performance. Extrapolation can also be used for certain areas that are stable or unlikely to vary over time.

Strike a Balance between Bottom-Up and Top-Down

The traditional budget process started at the lowest level of revenue, costs and expenses. My first exposure to a budget process in the early 1980s highlights many of the pitfalls with this approach. The entire organization, which was very profitable but slow growing (after many years of high growth), embarked on the process with little direction. The result was a huge effort, spanning six weeks and involving hundreds of work hours across the organization.

When the results were processed and tabulated, we presented a projection that included a modest growth in revenues, 40% increase in staffing, 30% increase in other expenses, and a tripling of capital expenditures, turning a profitable business unit into a substantial loss. Since the management team had not developed a game plan or macro view of expected performance, department managers submitted a "wish list" of investments, staffing, and expenses. There were five iterations of this bottom-up detail process spanning a total of four months before it approached a reasonable plan.

Other organizations operate at the other end of this spectrum, essentially dictating performance expectations for the coming year from the top. They may or may not consider fundamental drivers, changes, risks, and upsides in this process.

The best solution, in my experience, is a combination of realistic guidelines, boundaries, and targets in the form of planning guidelines. These should be the result of analysis and discussions about the current performance level and market conditions. Of course, managers should always be encouraged to present additional opportunities and risks. If the organization is effectively using rolling forecasts or DBOs, the process is more efficient and effective since a view into next year's performance is already on the table.

Go Beyond the Numbers

For most significant decisions, managers should prepare well–thought-out financial projections. A well-developed planning process will have less detail than the bottom-up approach and will focus attention on the most critical drivers of performance. In addition to historical performance and trends, the projections should consider the impact of several factors, including:

- Strategic objectives.
- Actions and potential actions of customers and competitors.
- Anticipated changes in prices, costs, and expense levels.
- Investments required to achieve the strategic objectives.
- Economic variables (i.e., interest rates, inflation, growth, or recession).

Managers must carefully address several questions in order to estimate future performance on key value drivers. We discuss key financial inputs to each value driver in Part V. A few examples are provided here.

Revenue:
- How fast is the market growing?
- Is our market share expected to increase or decrease? Why?
- Will we be able to increase prices?
- What new products will be introduced (by our company and competitors)?

- What products will post declining sales due to product life cycles or competitive product introductions?
- What general economic assumptions are contemplated in the plan?
- What technology or geopolitical and social trends or events may impact our market and demand for our products and services?

Costs and Expenses:

- What is the general rate of inflation? Are there underlying forces that could give rise to inflation (e.g., excess government spending, supply or labor shortages, etc.)?
- What will happen to significant costs such as key raw materials, energy, and labor and related expenses such as employee healthcare?
- What increases to headcount will be required to execute the plan?
- What operating efficiencies and cost reductions can be achieved?

Asset and Investment Levels:

- What level of receivables and inventories will be required in the future?
- Will we need to increase production capacity to achieve the planned sales levels?

Financing and Cost of Capital:

- Will we need additional financial resources to execute the plan?
- How much financial flexibility do we have?
- Are we operating at an appropriate and well-considered capital structure?
- Do we plan to change the mix of debt and equity in the capital structure?
- Will we have to refinance any existing loans during the plan horizon?
- Is our business profile becoming more or less risky?
- What is likely to happen to interest rates over the plan horizon?

Identify and Test Assumptions

Developing projections of any type requires the use of assumptions. Critical assumptions should be identified, evaluated, and "flexed" to determine a range of potential outcomes and sensitivity. Managers should test the sensitivity of the projections and the decision criteria of each critical assumption. Once identified, these critical assumptions can be closely monitored as leading indicators of the firm's ability to achieve the plan.

Link to Performance Management

Most projections are presented and evaluated through a financial lens with a focus on outcomes. Cost center reports, profit and loss statements, and working capital and cash flow projections are all financial tools and reports that are based on expected performance of people, processes, projects, and other activities. With the possible exception of a few acceptable areas, you *cannot* directly manage financial outcomes; you *can* only manage people, processes, and activities that result in those outcomes. Many organizations utilize key performance indicators (KPIs) and dashboards as part of an overall performance management framework (Part III). By integrating these KPIs into the planning process, we directly link the financial results to business processes and activities.

A simple example is the projection of accounts receivable. Many organizations plan the receivables level based on past days sales outstanding (DSO) levels. However, receivables balances and DSO are the financial result of several important drivers, including:

- Credit terms and creditworthiness.
- Timing and pattern of revenues.
- Product and revenue process quality.
- Customer service, problem resolution, and collection activities.

It is far more effective to model future receivables levels based on these drivers and assumptions. Any projected improvements in DSO will be based on achieving improved performance on these drivers. These activities are leading indicators of future receivables levels and DSO. They can be monitored against plan assumptions to ascertain that the projected outcome is likely or that some management intervention is required.

Evaluating Financial Projections (Note: Nearly All Projections Are Wrong!)

It is important to recognize that it is difficult to predict the future and that all projections incorporate a large number of assumptions about an uncertain future. Therefore, nearly all projections of performance will be incorrect. However, there are several things that managers can do to improve the financial projections, their understanding of the dynamics affecting future performance, and the probability of achieving planned results. Multiple scenarios and sensitivity analyses of financial projections will provide an understanding of how the key decision variables will be impacted under various scenarios and assumptions. Scenario analysis and planning have become a critical part of business planning and enterprise management and were covered in detail in Chapter 13. In addition to improving the overall plan process, these tools serve to prepare the organization to address upside and downside events.

Another useful way to evaluate projections is to simply compare them to recent performance trends. For long-term projections, it is always useful to compare projected results to an extrapolation of recent history. This is not to say that future performance cannot depart from historical trends, but it clearly presents the issue and would lead to identifying and reviewing the factors that would lead to the projected reversal. In the example provided in Figure 19.2, a slow decline in revenues is projected to reverse in the future. Notice how effectively the graph presents this comparison as compared to the table. Evaluation of this forecast should focus on the factors that will lead to this sudden and dramatic change in performance. If we don't soon change our direction, we will wind up where we are headed!

FIGURE 19.2 **Historical versus plan trends.**

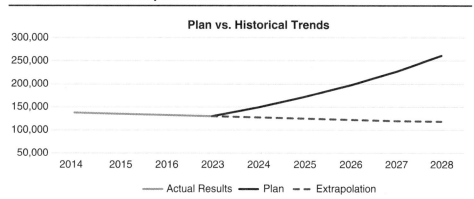

Short-term projections can be compared to recent trends and against last year's results. In Figure 19.3, we compare the weekly run rate of revenues year to date (YTD) to last year (YTD-LY) and to the plan (YTD-Plan), and compare

FIGURE 19.3 **Revenue run-rate analysis.**

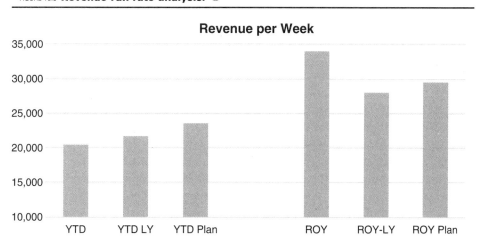

the rest of year forecast (ROY) to last year (ROY-LY) and to the plan (ROY-Plan). This year's run rate of *actual* revenues is slightly below last year's, but the *forecast* projects a significant increase over the same period last year and the plan. Again, what are the specific drivers that support the dramatic change from the past?

Another useful tool to evaluate forecast performance is to track actual performance against forecast amounts. Figure 19.4 shows the actual revenue level achieved compared to the forecast range for recent quarters. The use of a forecast range is an effective technique to reinforce uncertainty and reflect known upsides and downsides to a single point projection. This analysis shows that actual revenues have been within the forecast range 5 of 8 quarters, with two shortfalls and one quarter exceeding ranges. The outliers can be analyzed to determine why the actual performance fell outside the projected range, and if necessary, make revisions to the process in future periods.

FIGURE 19.4 **Actual revenue versus forecast range.**

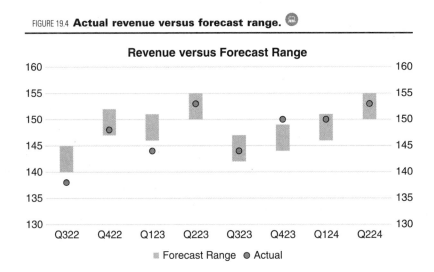

Identify Assumptions, Risks, and Upsides to the Projection

Unless otherwise intended, managers should set the expectation that a projection should be the "best estimate" of the outcome under the present strategy and expected market and economic conditions. Some organizations clarify this expectation by using language such as "most probable" or establishing desired confidence levels such as 80% confidence levels. This base plan includes numerous assumptions, such as the probability and estimated impact of many potential events. It is useful to identify and present how these potential events have been reflected in the plan. For example, if the plan assumes a continued favorable economic expansion, then a potential downside would be an economic recession. Other possible downside events may include competitive threats, or loss of a major customer or contract. A summary of upside and downside events is presented in Table 19.1.

In addition, assessing the potential impact on the financial projections, this analysis allows management to monitor these potential factors and to develop preliminary contingency and response plans.

TABLE 19.1 **Upside and downside event summary.**

$M Event Description	Leading Indicators	Event Criteria	Potential Impact on Projections(PAT)	Probability this Plan Horizon	Probability Weighting	Management Action
Upside and Downside Summary						
Upsides (U)						
Project XYZ Extension	Customer initiates extension	Extension signed	1.2	20%	0.24	(1) Monitor
						(2) Revise/extend termination plan
Contract Win Tonk Corp	Selected as finalist	Award	__5__	__10%__	0.5	
Total Upsides			6.2		0.74	
Downsides (D)						
Loss of Donaldson Contract	Feedback on proposal	Award notification	−5.2	60%	−3.12	(1) Monitor
						(2) Develop contingency plan
Recession	Backlog	Backlog down 10%	−3.2	50%	−1.6	(1) Monitor and develop contingency plan
Product Licensing Lawsuit			−4.2	20%	−0.84	(1) Monitor, consider appeal
						(2) Develop plan for technology alternative
Total Downsides			−12.6		−5.56	
Total of U and D Events			−6.4		−4.82	

The summary presented in Table 19.1 raises several concerns. First, the absolute value of downside risks is two times greater than potential upsides. Second, the probability of two downside events is quite high, 50% and 60%. This suggests the plan is unbalanced, with greater downside exposure than upside. Since two of the downside risks have at least a 50% probability, these risks should be further evaluated and perhaps incorporated into the base plan.

Scenario and Sensitivity Analysis

Multiple scenarios and sensitivity analyses provide context and insight into the dynamics of expected performance.

Sensitivity Analysis. This technique determines the sensitivity of an outcome (e.g., profit projection) to changes in key assumptions used in a base or primary case. Any projection or estimated value must be viewed as an estimate based on many inherent assumptions. Sensitivity analysis is very useful to understand the dynamics of a projection or decision and to highlight the importance of testing assumptions. For example, Figure 19.5 presents the estimated sensitivity of a company's profit projection to changes in a key assumption, the price of fuel.

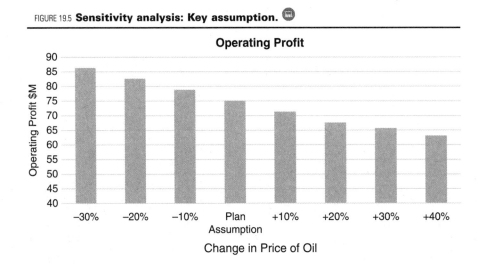

FIGURE 19.5 **Sensitivity analysis: Key assumption.**

Scenario Analysis. While a sensitivity analysis provides insight into the importance of one variable, a scenario analysis contemplates the effect of an event or change in circumstances. The scenario will typically require reevaluation of several different variables in the plan. For critical projections, including plans, it is essential to run several different versions of financial projections, for example:

- Base Case: This is the most likely outcome.
- Extrapolation of Recent Performance: Provides a reference point to evaluate other scenarios.
- Conservative Scenario: A scenario reflecting lower expectations or downsides.

- Upside or Stretch Scenario: A scenario reflecting the potential of certain upside events.
- Recession Scenario: What will happen to the projections if a recession occurs?
- Competitive Attack.

Once scenarios are identified, projections are developed for each specific scenario. This is a critical aspect of scenario planning. Unlike sensitivity analysis, where we simply flex selected variables, we will revise the base projections for expected changes under the scenario. For example, in a recession, a company may experience price pressure and lower demand. That company may also experience different interest rates, labor rates, and commodity pricing.

Once alternative scenario plans are developed, these can be used to determine a range of potential outcomes. A "most probable" estimate can be calculated by weighting each estimated outcome by the probability of occurrence. Figure 19.6 presents a recap for various scenarios. This analysis is very useful in presenting the range of potential outcomes.

FIGURE 19.6 **Scenario recap.**

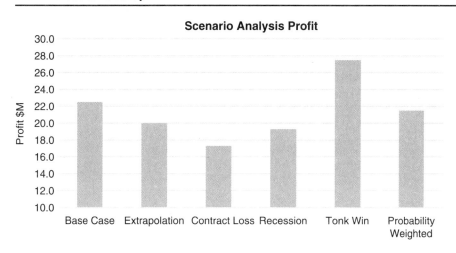

In Table 19.2, we illustrate the use of weighting a range of revenue levels by the estimated probability of each occurring to compute an expected value or probability weighted estimate. In this case, the analysis shows that there appears to be more downside than upside to the base forecast of $115,000.

Due to the level of uncertainty and the extreme rate of change in today's environment, scenario analysis should be integrated into all planning and management activities. Scenario analysis was covered in detail in Chapter 13.

TABLE 19.2 **Revenue probability analysis.** 🔊

**Revenue Projection
Probability Analysis**

	Expected Revenue Level	Probability	Weighting
Upside 1	125,000	5%	6,250
Upside 2	120,000	5%	6,000
Base Plan	115,000	45%	51,750
Downside 1	110,000	25%	27,500
Downside 2	105,000	20%	21,000
Probable Outcome		100%	112,500

Building on the Business Model

Chapter 6 introduced the business model as an analytical tool. Using this conceptual framework, managers will set prices, establish business plans, evaluate business proposals, set expense levels, and make other critical business decisions. For example, a company that is developing a product with a cost of $450 would likely set a target selling price of $1,000 to maintain a 55% margin. In establishing the research and development (R&D) budget, the company may target spending at 8% of projected sales.

The business model can be a useful way to initiate or to set high-level targets for the operating plan as illustrated in Figure 19.7. Starting with the actual or forecast results for the current year (2023), a preliminary model for 2024 can be estimated by maintaining key ratios and measures. Executives can then adjust this preliminary result for known or anticipated changes for 2024, for example, increased revenue growth and expenses related to new product introductions.

The considered estimate can be used as a starting point or basis for setting targets and boundaries for the development of the 2024 operating plan.

Comprehensive Financial Picture

There is a tendency to evaluate business decisions solely based on the effect on profit and loss (P&L) or earnings per share (EPS). In order to provide a complete summary of expected financial performance financial projections should include the P&L, Balance Sheet, and Statement of Cash Flows. Exceptions would include limited scope exercises such as a forecast of quarterly EPS or expense savings.

Many decisions should be based on the economic analysis of projected results, including measures such as net present value and return on investment, capital requirements and cash flow. In addition, many projections will result in additional financing requirements or may test and even exceed existing debt covenants. Where important, these should be incorporated into the projections model and presentations.

FIGURE 19.7 **Using business model to develop projections.**

Business Model Illustration
Comprehensive View

LSA Company

	2023	% of Sales	Prelim 2024	% of Sales	Considered 2024	% of Sales	Notes
Historical Sales Growth Rate:	8.0%		8%		10%		
Profitability Model							
Sales	$100,000	100.0%	$108,000	100.0%	$110,000	100.0%	New Product Introduction
Cost of Sales	45,000	45.0%	48,600	45.0%	50,600	46.0%	Lower margin on new product
Gross Margin	55,000	55.0%	59,400	55.0%	59,400	54.0%	
SG&A	32,000	32.0%	34,560	32.0%	35,200	32.0%	
R&D	8,000	8.0%	8,640	8.0%	9,500	8.6%	Increased R&D, large development project
Total Expenses	40,000	40.0%	43,200	40.0%	44,700	40.6%	
Operating Income	15,000	15.0%	16,200	15.0%	14,700	13.4%	
Other (Income) Expense	605	0.6%	653	0.6%	666	0.6%	
Taxes 32%	4,894	4.9%	5,327	4.9%	0	0.0%	
Net Income	9,501	9.5%	10,219	9.5%	14,035	12.8%	
Asset Utilization							
Days Sales Outstanding	73.0		73.0		65.0		Revenue Process Project
Days Sales Inventory	146.0		146.0		140.0		Supply Chain Initiative
Operating Capital Turnover	3.4		3.4		3.4		
Fixed Asset Turnover	5.0		5.0		5.0		
Intangible Turnover	9.1		9.1		9.1		
Total Asset Turnover	1.3		1.3		1.4		
Leverage							
Debt to Total Capital	1.4	15.3%	1.4	15.3%	1.4	15.3%	
Returns							
ROE	17.2%		17.2%		22.0%		
ROIC	15.2%		15.2%		19.0%		

The Value Is in the Planning, Not the Plan

While developing a plan is important, the far greater value is likely in the assessment of factors impacting the organization, critical thinking, and the ability to monitor performance against the plan. While financial projections are an important element of all decisions and plans, it can be argued that there is even more value created by the thinking necessitated in developing the financial projections. For example:

- Identifying critical assumptions that can be tested and monitored (an important management activity).
- Identifying and thinking through different scenarios and developing contingency plans.
- Understanding how critical management decisions impact the financial model and shareholder value.

Presenting and Communicating Projections   Too often, the presentation and review of projections, including operating plans and capital investment decisions, center on the financial outcomes as represented in the P&L statement. To effectively present and review significant plans and projections, a comprehensive package should be developed, including the following:

- ❏ Strategic issues.
- ❏ Market forces, including customer and competitors.
- ❏ Critical business assumptions.
- ❏ Critical success factors.
- ❏ Execution plan.
- ❏ Execution risks.
- ❏ Comprehensive financial evaluation (P&L, Balance Sheet, Statement of Cash Flows, returns).
- ❏ Sensitivity analysis.
- ❏ Recap of possible scenarios.

Examples of plans and recaps are included in the chapters on plans and budgets (Chapter 20), long-term projections (Chapter 21), capital investment decisions (Chapters 28 and 29), and mergers and acquisitions (Chapter 31).

The Future Is Now: Artificial Intelligence, Machine Learning in Developing Projections

In Chapter 12, "Leveraging and Promoting Technology Investments," we introduced the emerging use of artificial intelligence (AI) and machine learning

(ML). In its simplest form, AI is using computer power to perform many of the functions we have described in this chapter, the remaining chapters in Part V on planning, and in Chapter 22, specifically on revenues. ML is the ability of digital technology to learn autonomously without human assistance.

A core part of AI is the use of statistical tools at a scale that humans cannot perform. These include trend (time-series) analysis, regression analysis, decision trees, probability, Monte Carlo simulation, expected value, and predictive analytics. These techniques have been used in business over time and are discussed throughout this book, but the technology now enables their application to large data sets. Recent progress has been enabled by the development of sophisticated software algorithms and an explosion of digital data generation and storage. AI has already been utilized to develop projections by early adopters:

Revenue Projections. Developing revenue projections is generally the most challenging estimate in financial planning. These involve many drivers, complex relationships, and enormous amounts of potentially relevant data sets. At present, the use of AI is in early stages in companies and is often used to generate an "AI or machine version" of a projection. This version is then reviewed and compared to projections generated by traditional methods. The AI projection is typically adjusted (by humans) for errors or anomalies that are not presently considered by the machine, for example, the bankruptcy of a major customer, a geopolitical or economic shock, a one-time or nonrecurring activity, new product introductions, and so on. Finally, the development of projections in an uncertain and rapidly changing world is challenging even if AI and ML are utilized effectively. Undue confidence and reliance in the machine-generated projections may be unwarranted and even dangerous. It is easier to envision the use of AI in situations where there are a large number of transactions, customers, and other data points.

P&L Projections. Some organizations have initiated projects to use AI to develop complete P&L forecasts, by prefilling a prelim forecast version based on trends and other factors included in the data sets and auto-generated by AI. Once a revenue projection is developed, it possible to imagine that cost of sales and operating expenses could be "machine" computed based on trend analysis and examining other drivers such as material requirements, open personnel requisitions, and other changes. Essentially, the software would perform the same functions that the human analyst performs, gathering relevant information, developing estimates based on key assumptions. Again, this would likely be considered the *machine version*, requiring review and potential adjustment by humans for factors that may be outside the data sets considered by the projection's software. For example, a human would likely have to adjust for a projected legal settlement, decision to sell a business segment, or planned restructuring, items that would not be visible to the machine process.

Comprehensive Projections Model. Could AI generate a comprehensive financial model including a P&L, Balance Sheet, Statement of Cash Flows, and financial metrics? Some pundits argue that they do not envision AI generating a comprehensive financial model. I disagree since projecting costs and expenses may be relatively simpler to automate than revenue projections and the P&L. Algorithms to project the Balance Sheet and cash flow can be based on several decision rules and the relationship of various accounts in the financials (e.g., accounts receivable and revenue) as presented in Chapters 20 and 21.

Implementing an AI solution to develop projections requires substantial effort. In summary, these include:

- High-quality, structured digital data sets are essential. These do not exist in many organizations.
- A competency in data science (essentially data management and statistics).
- Selection and implementation of software to manage data and develop projections.
- Addressing the potential impact on employment, changes to roles, and overall change management issues.

Finance professionals should stay abreast of progress in using AI in finance, and particularly in developing projections. If digital data availability or accuracy is an issue, these should be addressed prior to initiating AI. Many of the elements of AI can be initiated with human intelligence at a smaller scale, including trend analysis, extrapolation, regression analysis, scenario development, and probability analysis. Introducing the utilization of these tools will serve to demystify AI and accelerate future adoption.

SUMMARY

Projections and plans are an essential aspect of managing any enterprise. Projections are utilized in most business decisions. Owing to the rapid level of change, increased uncertainty, and variability in business and economic activity, additional measures must be taken to develop financial projections. Firms should employ best practices that fit their specific circumstances to develop high-quality and robust projections. All organizations should assess the potential use of AI and ML, and lay the foundation for possible use in the future. In Chapter 20 we will cover budgets, operating plans, forecasts, and business outlooks. In Chapter 21, we will turn our attention to unique aspects of developing long-term projections.

20

Budgets, Operating Plans, and Forecasts

This chapter will focus on projections that estimate performance over a 3- to 18-month period, including budgets, operating plans, and forecasts. Many of the techniques and practices utilized in this chapter were introduced in Chapter 19.

THE BUDGETING PROCESS

In spite of its shortcomings, the budgeting process lives on in many organizations. In some cases, it is required by charter or statute. In other cases, it either suffices or has not been evaluated against new tools, and against best practices and techniques in financial management. In this section, we will review the typical budget process and tools to serve as a foundation for improved planning tools for the 21st century.

The Traditional Budgeting Process

The traditional budget process that became a cornerstone of management systems in the 21st century was described in Chapter 19. While many organizations have adopted more evolved methods of developing business projections explored later in this chapter, others continue to use the traditional budget process.

The traditional budget process follows an annual cycle. The budget for next year would be developed several months before the new year begins.

It is characterized by a very detailed and financially oriented process illustrated in Figure 20.1.

FIGURE 20.1 **Traditional budget and control process.**

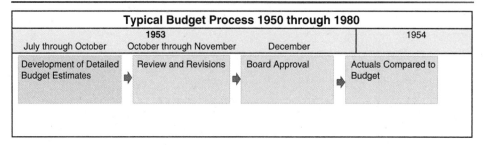

Typical Budget Process 1950 through 1980			
1953			1954
July through October	October through November	December	
Development of Detailed Budget Estimates	Review and Revisions	Board Approval	Actuals Compared to Budget

The first step required departmental managers to complete budget forms for their area of responsibility as illustrated in Table 20.1.

These departmental budgets are then rolled up into cost summaries, and ultimately, Profit and Loss (P&L) projections as shown in Figure 20.2. After a series of reviews and revisions, the budget would be presented to senior executives and the board of directors for approval. The budget then served as the basis for operating and evaluating actual performance against these budget expectations.

Problems with Traditional Budgeting   Annual plans and budgets have been the subject of criticism for years. While many organizations have made substantial improvements, most organizations do not extract the potential utility out of this very time-consuming activity.

One of the major problems with budgeting is the financial orientation, including general ledger accounts and financial statement captions, rather than processes, activities, customers, projects, and critical assumptions. Department managers often had to create "shadow" planning tools to develop budget estimates from an operating perspective and link to their processes and activities.

The output of a traditional budget process would often lock into a single scenario document and the emphasis was on the "document" rather than the potential value of the process. As President Dwight Eisenhower said: "Plans are useless, but planning is essential."[1] In other words, the value is not in the plan document itself or in a single course of action set forth in the plan. Once the battle begins, the conditions and circumstances will depart from those

[1] Several variations of this quote are widely attributed to General (and subsequently, President) Dwight Eisenhower. He attributes it to a long-held view in the army about planning for battle and the recognition of unexpected aspects, that is, battles (and business) will not play out the way people have planned. The only official documentation of these remarks is in a speech to the National Defense Executive Reserve Conference in Washington, D.C. (November 14, 1957); in *Public Papers of the Presidents of the United States, Dwight D. Eisenhower, 1957*, National Archives and Records Service (Washington D.C.; Government Printing Office), 818.

TABLE 20.1 **Traditional departmental budget.** 🔊

Company:	Mangham Distributors $000's	Inside Sales				
		Q1	Q2	Q3	Q4	Year
Labor and Related Costs						
	Salary	145.0	145.0	145.0	160.0	595.0
	Bonus				40.0	40.0
	Commissions					0.0
	Total	145.0	145.0	145.0	200.0	635.0
	Fringe Benefits	36.3	36.3	36.3	40.0	148.8
	% to Total Labor	25%	25%	25%	20%	23%
	Total Labor and Related Costs	181.3	181.3	181.3	240.0	783.8
Other	Travel	4.0	4.0	4.0	4.0	16.0
	Meetings	2.0	2.0	2.0	2.0	8.0
	Consultants	2.0	2.0	2.0	2.0	8.0
	Professional Services	2.0	2.0	2.0	2.0	8.0
	Telecommunications					0.0
	Materials	8.0	8.0	8.0	8.0	32.0
	Contract services					0.0
						0.0
						0.0
	Depreciation					0.0
	Allocations In	5.0	5.0	5.0	5.0	20.0
	Other	2.0	8.0	30.0	35.0	75.0
	Total Other Expenses	25.0	31.0	53.0	58.0	167.0
	Total Expense	206.3	212.3	234.3	298.0	950.8
	Sales	2,850.0	3,300.0	3,150.0	5,700.0	15,000.0
	Selling % of Sales	7.2%	6.4%	7.4%	5.2%	6.3%
Labor Detail (000's)						
	Manager	38.0	38.0	38.0	38.0	152.0
	Admin	10.0	10.0	10.0	10.0	40.0
	New Hire				15.0	15.0
	Lead Internal Sales	25.0	25.0	25.0	25.0	100.0
	Sales Assistant	35.0	35.0	35.0	35.0	140.0
	Internal Sales (3)	37.0	37.0	37.0	37.0	148.0
						0.0
	Total ($000's)	145.0	145.0	145.0	160.0	595.0
	Year to Year Growth %	9.8%	9.0%	8.2%	8.1%	8.8%
	Year to Year Growth $	13.0	12.0	11.0	12.0	48.0

used in developing the plan. The value in planning lies in the thought process, including assessing strengths and weaknesses, evaluating critical assumptions, and developing potential scenarios and contingency plans. Budgets tend to be numbers-driven and tend not to focus attention on issues and opportunities, on risks and upsides, or on execution planning.

FIGURE 20.2 **Budget roll-up illustration.**

Company: Mangham Distributors
$000's

Inside Sales

	Q1	Q2	Q3	Q4	Year
Labor and Related Costs					
Salary	145.0	145.0	145.0	160.0	595.0
Bonus				40.0	40.0
Commissions					0.0
Total	145.0	145.0	145.0	200.0	635.0
Fringe Benefits	36.3	36.3	36.3	40.0	148.8
% to Total Labor	25%	25%	25%	20%	23%
Total Labor and Related Costs	181.3	181.3	181.3	240.0	783.8
Other					
Travel	4.0	4.0	4.0	4.0	16.0
Meetings	2.0	2.0	2.0	2.0	8.0
Consultants	2.0	2.0	2.0	2.0	8.0
Professional Services	2.0	2.0	2.0	2.0	8.0
Telecommunications					0.0
Materials	8.0	8.0	8.0	8.0	32.0
Contract services					0.0
Depreciation					0.0
Allocations In	5.0	5.0	5.0	5.0	20.0
Other	2.0	8.0	30.0	35.0	75.0
Total Other Expenses	25.0	31.0	53.0	58.0	167.0
Total Expense	206.3	212.3	234.3	298.0	950.8
Sales	2,850.0	3,300.0	3,150.0	5,700.0	15,000.0
Selling % of Sales	7.2%	6.4%	7.4%	5.2%	6.3%

Company: Mangham Distributors

Selling Expense

	Q1	Q2	Q3	Q4	Year
Field Sales					
Sales Region 1	50.0	50.0	54.0	56.0	210.0
Sales Region 2	49.0	50.0	54.0	55.0	208.0
Sales Region 3	50.0	50.0	54.0	53.0	207.0
Sales Region 4	51.0	50.0	54.0	55.0	210.0
Sales Region 5	0.0	0.0	54.0	55.0	109.0
Total	200	200	270	274	944.0
Office					
Inside Sales	206.3	212.3	234.3	298.0	950.8
Sales Management	60.0	50.0	54.0	62.0	226.0
Order Processing	32	35	36	37	140.0
Total Selling Expense	498	497	594	671	2,261

Profit & Loss	2024 Budget
Sales	15,000
Cost of Goods Sold	7,600
Gross Margin	7,400
%	49%
Operating Expenses:	
R&D	800
Marketing	1,600
Selling	2,261
G&A	1,100
Total Operating Expenses	5,761
Income from Operations	1,639
%	10.9%

Traditional budgets do not adequately identify and test critical assumptions and performance drivers. The financial focus often means that assumptions are buried in the details and not adequately identified and tested.

Budgets were useful for a time when business was more static. Their utility has declined significantly, resulting from the development of the global economy, the accelerated rate of change, and significant geopolitical events that reshape markets dramatically and frequently. Traditional budget processes are also very labor intensive. Due to the level of detail and the typical need for multiple revisions, the budget process can often lead to a substantial investment (or waste) of time by finance and operating managers alike. Many companies issue planning guidelines and boundaries (which was discussed in Chapter 19) to establish goals and targets in order to create a starting point and to minimize the number of revisions.

In most cases, the organization would be better served by developing an operating plan as is described in the next section.

THE OPERATING PLAN

A key distinction between a budget and an operating plan is that the latter is a complete operating and execution plan for the coming year, whereas the former has a focus on the *financial* projections. The financial projections are an essential aspect of the plan, but should not be the only objective or the focus of the process. An effective operating plan will:

- Assess the current situation.
- Analyze current operations and spending.
- Review strategic objectives and initiatives.
- Establish performance goals and targets.
- Identify business drivers and critical assumptions.
- Develop the game plan for next 12 months.
- Develop multiple scenarios.

Assess Current Situation

Before a plan can be effectively developed for the coming year, management must assess the current situation. Has the external environment changed? Has the competitive landscape changed? Are we on course to meet or exceed strategic goals? Are we meeting current performance targets? This assessment should include a review and evaluation of recent financial results as well as leading indicators of performance. Many organizations find it useful to benchmark competitors and customers (refer to Chapter 18, "Benchmarking Performance") as part of this situational analysis.

Analyze Current Operations, Profitability, and Spending

The annual planning cycle presents a terrific opportunity to analyze current operations, profitability, and spending levels. The plan process will be better informed by performing the following types of analysis:

Customer profitability.

Product/business unit profitability.

Activity-based costing.

Zero-based cost analysis (ZBCA).

The first three of these analytical tools were introduced in Chapter 11. We now take a closer look at ZBCA here.

Zero-Based Cost Analysis (ZBCA)   Zero-based budgeting has recently regained popularity among consultants and FP&A professionals. I believe it is a very useful approach, but find the term misleading. It implies that the entire plan process should be driven by ZBB. It can be a useful and insightful tool as *part* of the overall operational planning process.

One of the deficiencies in most operational planning processes is that the spend rate for next year is based on, or at least influenced by, the spending in the current year. For example, the budget for next year may be set at 5% increase over the current year. Over time, various costs are added to an organization for a specific reason or purpose, originally intended to have a limited duration. Often these programs become part of the base expense if they are not challenged.

FIGURE 20.3 **Cost growth over time.**

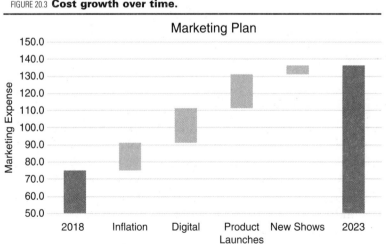

In the example in Figure 20.3, the marketing spend has increased from $75 million to $125 million over a five-year period. The growth includes the impact of inflation in addition to several large spending increments due to specific initiatives or projects. If a *base-plus* approach (Figure 20.4) is employed, the organization is likely to set the next year's marketing spend at $143 million, a 5% growth over the prior year.

FIGURE 20.4 **Base-plus budgeting.**

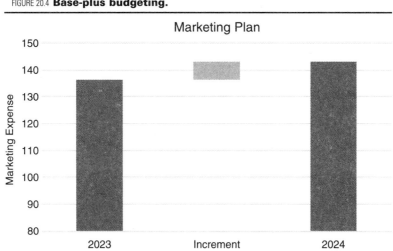

In its simplest form, ZBCA is a thorough review of all spending, challenging every position, cost, function, project, investment, and program in the organization. A critical evaluation of each expense is conducted, focusing on why the cost is incurred, what value is derived, and what would happen if the cost were eliminated. Some companies use a scoring or ranking convention, for example, mission critical, strategic investment, statutory requirement, or "up for grabs."

Figure 20.5 is a simple analysis to start the ZBCA process. The recap includes:

- Five-year historical cost trend and percentage of revenue.
- Year-to-year growth and percentage growth.
- High-level schedule of costs by major category.
- Compound annual growth rates (CAGR) of revenue and major expense categories.

A few high-level observations warrant further analysis and evaluation:

- Marketing expense in total and several major cost lines have risen faster than the rate of revenue growth.

- Headcount and costs for Project X, a large investment in market and technical research, have risen rapidly over the last several years. What are the prospects for this endeavor? Can the costs be reduced?
- Costs for the website, internet, and digital projects have resulted in a large increase over the last five years. Can these costs be reduced since the start-up and development activities are now complete? Can costs in other marketing efforts be reduced in recognition of the transition to digital spend?
- What function is performed by each of the headcount groups?

FIGURE 20.5 **ZBCA summary.**

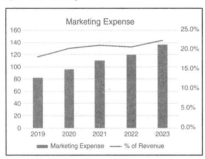

Zero-Based Cost Analysis

Department: Marketing

				75	82	96	110	120	136			
											% of Total	
Historical Cost Trends				**2018**	**2019**	**2020**	**2021**	**2022**	**2023**	**CAGR**	**2023**	**Drivers**
Headcount and Related				20.9	24.7	28.7	30.5	31.3	43.2	15.6%	31.7%	Revenue growth, new product introductions, inflation
Office Space				7.0	7.3	7.6	7.9	8.2	8.5	4.0%	6.3%	
Literature				8.0	8.3	8.7	9.0	9.4	9.7	4.0%	7.1%	
Consulting/Contract Services				2.0	1.2	8.5	13.4	11.5	20.0	58.5%	14.7%	Product Launch, Digital Marketing and transactions
Advertising				15.0	12.0	12.5	13.0	13.5	14.0	-1.3%	10.3%	
Travel				10.0	11.0	5.0	5.0	9.0	10.0	12.0%	7.3%	
Trade Shows				8.0	8.3	4.0	4.2	9.0	9.4	3.2%	6.9%	
Digital and Website				3.0	8.0	10.0	11.0	12.0	11.0	29.7%	8.1%	
Project X Direct Costs				0.1	0.1	10.0	15.0	15.0	7.0	133.9%	5.1%	
All other				1.0	1.0	1.1	1.1	1.2	3.4	27.7%	2.5%	
Total				75.0	82.0	96.0	110.0	120.0	136.2	12.7%	100.0%	
Y/Y Increase				6.0	7.0	14.0	14.1	10.0	16.2			
Y/Y Increase %				8.0%	9.3%	17.1%	14.6%	9.1%	13.5%			
% of Revenue				30%	18%	20%	21%	21%	22%			
Headcount												
Revenue				250.8	450.0	472.5	520.0	580.0	609.0	19.4%		
Y/Y Increase				6.0	199.2	22.5	47.5	60.0	29.0			
Y/Y Increase %				8.0%	79.4%	5.0%	10.1%	11.5%	5.0%			

Headcount Summary						
Marketing Management	3	3	4	4	4	5
Literature prep and management	5	5	5	5	5	5
Trade Shows Administration	3	3	3	3	3	3
Strategic Planning	2	2	2	2	2	2
Website and Internet	3	4	12	13	13	14
Product Launch Support	3	10	10	11	11	11
Product Line Management	20	22	24	26	28	30
Technical Support	30	31	40	55	55	55
Project X	0	0	20	30	32	30
Other	12	13	12	14	15	16
Total	81	93	132	163	168	171
Average Comp ($000's)	258.02	265.59	217.42	187.12	186.31	252.63

Progressive organizations implement ongoing cost management programs as part of their operational planning process. Companies employing ZBCA do not have to evaluate every cost, every year. Pareto analysis can be employed to identify the most significant costs and drivers to review. Alternatively, the ZBCA can be focused on specific departments on a rotating basis.

Review Strategic Objectives

The annual operating plan should be an installment of the company's strategic plan. The operating plan process should include a review of the strategy. Are the critical assumptions supporting the strategic plan still valid? Where do we stand on the implementation or attainment of strategic objectives?

The operating plan is an opportunity to develop an execution plan for the strategic objectives for the next year. It should ensure that the objectives are still valid and plan for human and financial resources to execute and achieve those objectives.

Establish Performance Goals and Targets

Prior to turning the troops loose on developing the operating plan, the leadership team and board should develop performance goals and targets. In establishing goals and targets, the organization should consider the following:

- ❑ Strategic plan.
- ❑ Business model.
- ❑ Recent performance trends.
- ❑ Analysis of current performance.
- ❑ Benchmarking and competitor analysis.
- ❑ Objectives for value creation.

Develop a Game Plan

Next, managers should develop a preliminary execution or game-plan for the coming year. This should be based on the situational analysis and preliminary goals. In order to prevent the chaos of a bottom-up wish list, it is useful to establish parameters or high-level targets of revenue growth and expense and investment levels as well as communicate to all involved in developing the plan.

Develop Preliminary Financial Projections

The organization should develop a preliminary model of projections for the plan year. Not all revenues, costs, and expenses are created equal. The team should focus on the most significant and most variable, using the Pareto rule that was introduced in Chapter 11.

This phase will be very easy if the organization uses rolling forecasts or an on-demand business outlook (DBO), which is discussed later in this chapter, since the team has already developed and evaluated projections for the plan year. In fact, most leading-edge organizations utilize the DBO model to develop the preliminary projections for the operating plan. These preliminary projections must identify and present key assumptions.

Identify Critical Assumptions and Key Actions

The operating plan for next year has hundreds of assumptions. These assumptions likely include everything from general economic conditions to weather, from inflation to pricing, and from the availability of critical materials to their cost. The plan may also include implicit assumptions about the absence of geopolitical or other black swan events. In many plans, these assumptions are buried in the details and are not explicitly identified. Key assumptions should be identified and reviewed. Managers should understand how sensitive the planned results are to changes in these critical assumptions. These assumptions should be tracked over the plan horizon, and any signals indicating that the assumptions may not be valid should trigger a review and a response. Identifying and reacting to changes in significant assumptions early will allow you to minimize the impact of downside events and trends, and to fully capitalize on the upsides.

Successful plans place significant attention on the activities required to achieve the planned results. For example, sales growth arising from the introduction of a new product in the next year requires a series of activities related to the development, production, marketing, and selling of the product. Each of these activities must be thoroughly planned out and adequately resourced to ensure that the planned sales are achieved. In addition, each of the responsible managers must be committed to the completion dates to support the product introduction and revenue plan.

Identify Upside and Downside Events, and Develop Multiple Scenarios

Owing to the rate of change and uncertainty that exists in the current environment, the use of a single-point plan generally is not valid or useful. A single plan estimate, by definition, must reflect a position on the probability and estimated impact of numerous events, transactions, and conditions. Managers should set the expectation that a base projection should be the "best estimate" of the outcome under the present strategy and expected market and economic conditions. Some organizations clarify this expectation by using language such as "most probable" or establishing desired confidence levels. This base plan includes a multitude of assumptions, including the probability and estimated impact of potential events. It is useful to identify and present how these potential events have been reflected in the plan. For example, if the plan assumes a continued favorable economic expansion, then a potential downside would be an economic recession. Other downside events may include competitive threats, loss of a major customer or contract, or geopolitical event.

In addition to assessing the potential impact on the financial projections, this analysis allows management to monitor these potential factors and to develop preliminary contingency and response plans. The developments of multiple scenarios and upside/downside events were discussed in detail in Chapter 13.

Communicate Plan Objectives and Targets

The objectives and targets set during the plan process must be communicated throughout the organization. Failure to communicate is the equivalent of a coach not sharing the game plan with the team prior to the start of the game. Of course, the specific content shared will depend on several factors, such as the need for confidentiality and the level and role within the organization.

A good test of the organization's understanding of the plan is to ask: Can our managers and employees list the five critical priorities for the coming year? Significant leverage is possible by communicating key objectives and activities included in the plan. For example, imagine the potential benefits to a critical project if all finance, human resources, and procurement teams recognized and supported the project as the No. 1 priority for the company. Even more effective results can be achieved if the objective setting and performance management process for individual managers and employees is a part of the annual planning process instead of an independent, subsequent drill.

Develop a Process to Monitor Key Assumptions and Track Progress

In many companies, performance tracking and monitoring are focused on financial results. This is problematic since financial results are lagging measures of business activities and processes. If you wait until trends or problems are visible in the financials, it is already too late to correct for that period. Many problems are easily addressed at an early stage, but grow and compound as time passes. Dashboards should be developed to track performance on leading indicators that will alert managers to unfavorable trends in near real time so that corrective action can be taken.

You can't manage financials; you can manage people, processes, transactions, and projects. The financials are a result of these business activities and inputs. For example, if you want to improve accounts receivable days sales outstanding (DSO) from 75 to 60 days, it won't happen unless you focus on the critical business processes that impact receivables. This requires creating a plan that identifies improvement opportunities on critical drivers of receivables: revenue patterns, improving quality and on-time delivery, and resolving customer problems faster. Establish targets and then monitor KPIs covering revenue linearity, quality, past-due orders and collections, and problem resolution. KPIs were discussed in greater detail in Chapter 16, "Dashboards and Key Performance Indicators."

Evaluate the Annual Plan Process

Each year, the annual plan process should be evaluated to identify potential improvement opportunities. Start by reviewing the current planning and forecasting processes and products. Measure the duration of the entire planning process. Document the process flow, including required inputs, processing, review and revision, and presentation. Identify the most critical assumptions and most significant revenue and cost drivers. Identify time spent in major stages of the process. Review the critical output/presentations of the plan. Do a post-review of the planning process, identifying impediments, issues, and improvement opportunities. Also review actual performance against the original plans, identifying the root cause of any variances. This will highlight bottlenecks, identify redundant and inefficient aspects, and a provide recap of critical assumptions and performance drivers.

Figure 20.6 is a dashboard summarizing KPIs for the planning process. This team started with some significant issues, including a long plan duration,

FIGURE 20.6 **Dashboard: Evaluation of operating plan.**

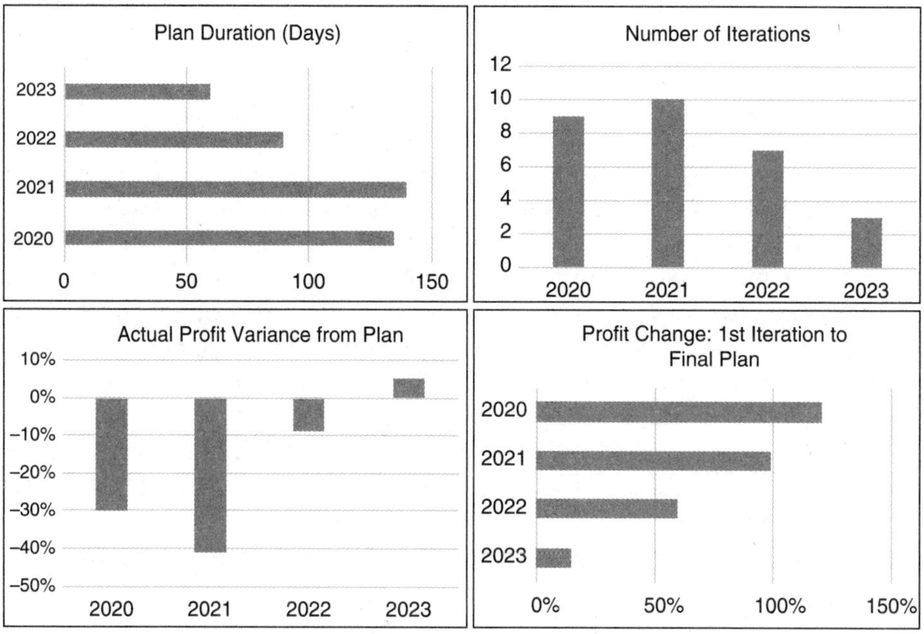

multiple revisions, and ineffective results in the form of large variances to plan. By identifying and addressing root causes, the team implemented changes to make the process both more efficient and effective. The two most important changes were the use of planning guidelines and boundaries at the start of the process, and the implementation of a rolling forecast.

BUSINESS FORECASTS AND OUTLOOKS

Due to rapidly changing business conditions and increasing uncertainty, it has become increasingly important to be able to recast expected performance periodically during the year, and even on demand. In many progressive organizations, the rolling forecast or business outlook has become the cornerstone of the planning, projecting, and management control activities. The forecast or outlook model must be robust enough to easily reflect changes in key assumptions, performance trends, events, or management decisions.

Historical Evolution of Forecasts

Forecasts originally emerged because of the need to update or recast the budgets. As business became more complex and the pace of change increased, the original budgets often were outdated early in the year. These updates were often done at a higher level than the original budget projections.

Many organizations began preparing an update to the budget on a monthly or quarterly basis. As the actual results were available, the remaining forecast period was evaluated to reflect known trends and any additional information that had surfaced since the original plan or budget had been prepared. Companies with stock owned by the public were pressured to confirm or adjust annual estimates. The forecast horizon ended abruptly at the end of the company's fiscal year (see Figure 20.7).

In the 1980s, a number of companies began extending the forecast horizon as they progressed through the year. For example, as the first quarter actual results were known, the forecast was extended to include the first quarter of the following year. Described as a "rolling forecast" this methodology provided a full-year, future outlook on the financial results as illustrated in Figure 20.8. This became extremely helpful in the final several months of a fiscal year, providing a view into the next year before the budget process had been complete.

My first encounter with rolling forecasts occurred in 1985. At that time, I was a division CFO of a technology unit of a large publicly traded company, and the corporation began requiring us to provide rolling forecasts. At first, this was simply a mechanical exercise by the folks in finance to extrapolate or extend the current forecast one additional quarter. The projections were based

FIGURE 20.7 **Traditional forecast horizon.**

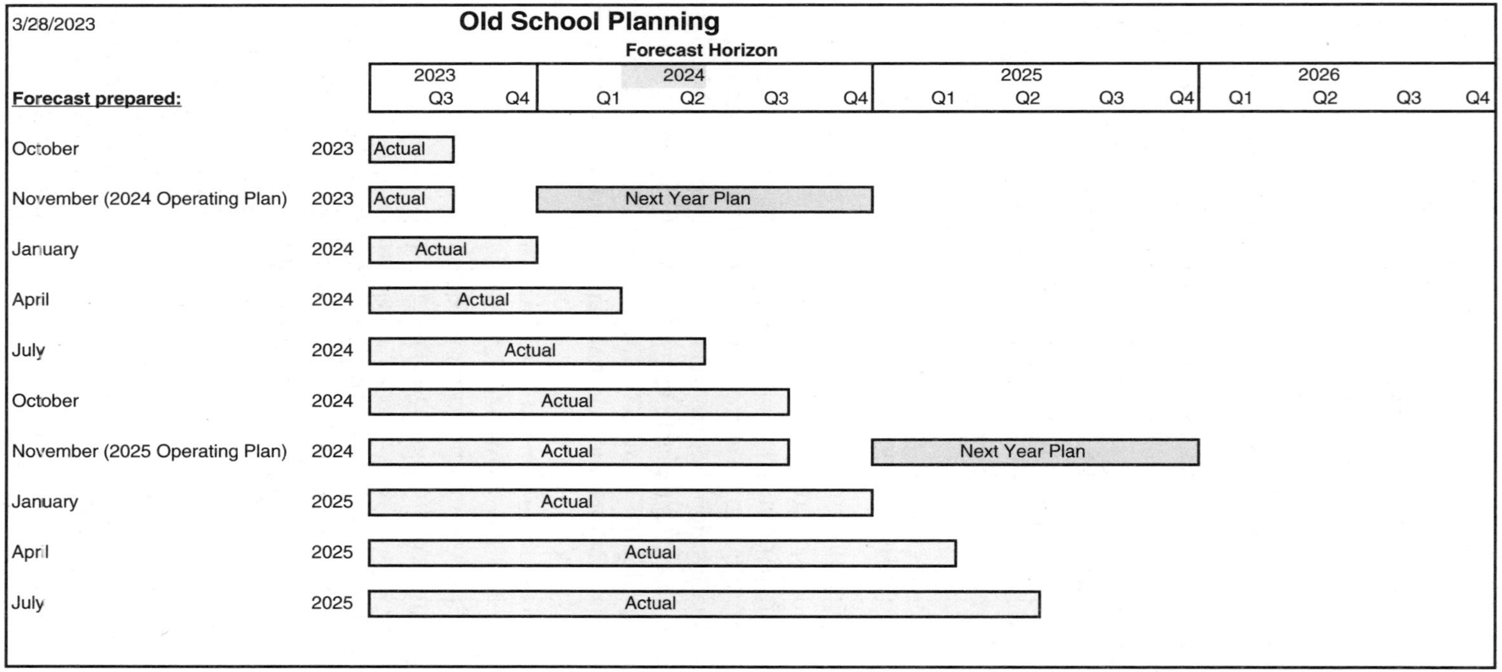

3/28/2023

Old School Planning

Forecast Horizon

Forecast prepared:		2023 Q3	Q4	2024 Q1	Q2	Q3	Q4	2025 Q1	Q2	Q3	Q4	2026 Q1	Q2	Q3	Q4
October	2023	Actual													
November (2024 Operating Plan)	2023	Actual		Next Year Plan											
January	2024	Actual													
April	2024		Actual												
July	2024		Actual												
October	2024			Actual											
November (2025 Operating Plan)	2024			Actual				Next Year Plan							
January	2025			Actual											
April	2025				Actual										
July	2025				Actual										

FIGURE 20.8 **Rolling forecast—Business outlook horizon.**

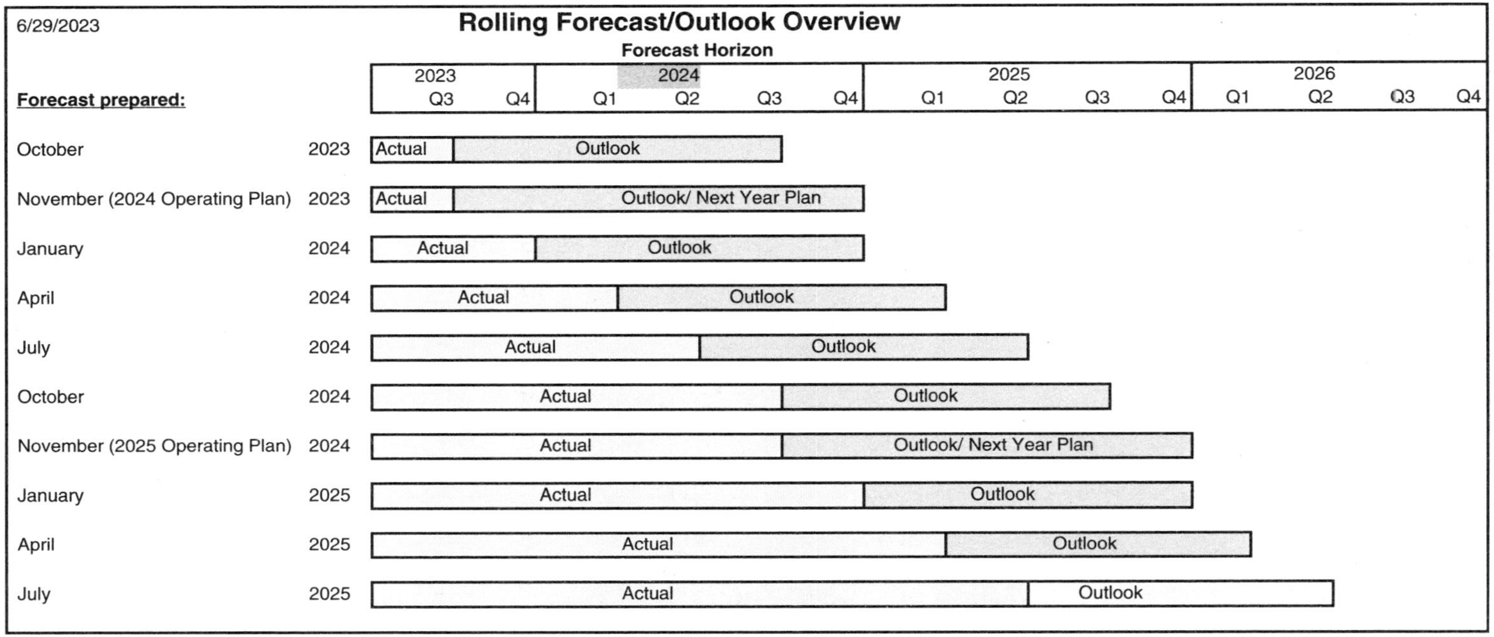

Rolling Forecast/Outlook Overview

on the prior-year actuals and adjusted for any significant expected changes. Of course, we were not excited by the additional work and the perceived difficulty in developing an extended estimate of performance.

The true value of the rolling forecast became apparent after several months. A few major changes to our business had become apparent. We had several major, nonrecurring sales that needed to be reflected as "one-timers" and not built into our run rate or trend for setting expectations for the following year. We also recognized a serious competitive threat that would have a significant impact on our performance in the next fiscal year, now seven to eight months away. We included our initial estimated impact of these factors into our extended projections. More important, the management team developed a plan to address the threats, including the introduction of new products, revisions to pricing, and other actions to respond to the competitive threat well ahead of the annual planning timeline.

Additional value was realized during the annual planning process for the subsequent year. When we began this process in August, we had already begun to internalize and estimate these factors into projections for the first six months of the following year. This greatly simplified the preparation of our annual plan.

Some organizations find the rolling addition of individual quarters to be confusing and prefer to adopt an "extended outlook horizon." Rather than adding individual quarters, the forecast horizon always includes the current year plus the next fiscal year (Figure 20.9). Viewing the projections in the context of a full year is more intuitive for many managers.

The rolling/extended forecast has gained wide acceptance and serves as the cornerstone of planning and projections for many organizations. It provides a good starting point for a more rigorous annual planning process, long-term projections, and scenario and "what if?" analysis. By far, its greatest value is in providing an early view into future trends, upsides, and risks, thereby affording management more time to react to changes and drive performance.

Continuous Business Outlook/On-Demand Business Outlook (DBO)

Many organizations think of the forecast as a business outlook or continuous business outlook. Describing the forecast as a business outlook changes the perception from a financial exercise to a business or operating process. Adding "continuous" or "on-demand" signifies that it can be updated as required by the organization. We explore the use of rolling forecasts and on-demand business outlooks (DBOs) in the remainder of this chapter.

Implementing Rolling Forecasts/Business Outlooks

Despite the compelling case for using some form of rolling forecast/business outlook, surveys indicate many organizations have not adopted them. These organizations cite limited resources, capabilities, or enabling software. Many organizations envision the need to repeat the annual planning process four

FIGURE 20.9 **Extended outlook.**

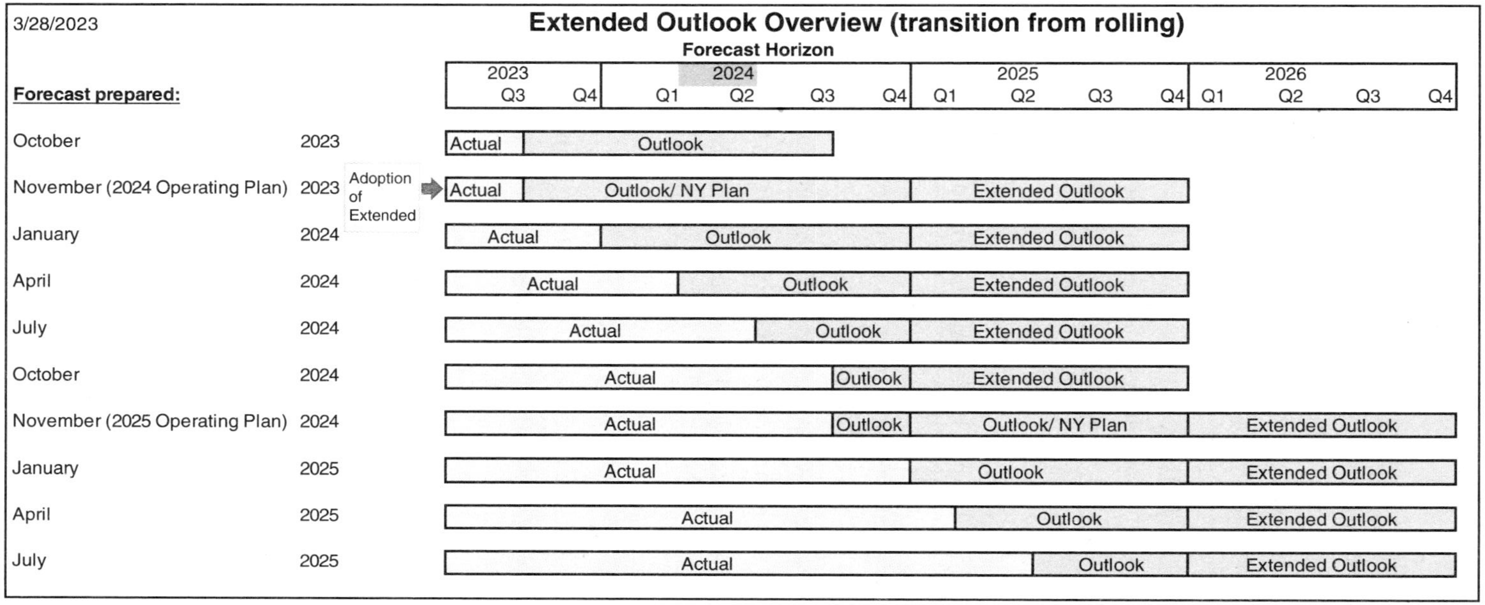

times per year! Getting started with rolling forecasts is much less formidable than most imagine.

Getting Started: A Practical Approach   To overcome the inertia inherent in starting a DBO initiative, I have found that a practical, phased approach is the best way to get started. Utilizing Microsoft Excel is a great way to get started, especially since it is hard to define needs, evaluate, and procure other software products without prior experience in using DBO models.

Articulate the Objectives of Developing the On-Demand Business Outlook
A clear statement of objectives will focus attention on developing a process that meets important needs and requirements. Most organizations point to one or more of the following objectives:

- ❏ Provide a view into expected performance for the next 12 months. This will engage the organization more frequently and reduce surprises that arise in one-year planning cycles.
- ❏ Provide a timely basis for setting future expectations with executives, board of directors, and investors.
- ❏ Identify performance trends and estimate future impact.
- ❏ Identify issues and opportunities that will impact future performance.
- ❏ Afford the greatest lead time possible to address problems and opportunities.
- ❏ Reduce inefficiencies and effort in the annual planning process.

Document and Review Current Operating Plans, Budgets, and Forecasts
Start by reviewing the current planning and forecasting activities and products as described earlier in the chapter. What are the major problems and improvement opportunities? What are the most significant performance drivers? What issues give rise to variances from the plan?

Implementing a Rolling Forecast/Business Outlook

1. Articulate objectives of rolling forecast/business outlook model.
2. Review current operating plans and management reports.
3. Identify critical business drivers.
   - ❏ *Most significant (Pareto's 80/20 rule).*
   - ❏ *Most variable.*
   - ❏ *Critical assumptions.*

4. Design architecture.
   - ❏ *Focus on critical business drivers.*
   - ❏ *Optimize trade-off: detail versus summary.*
   - ❏ *Explicitly incorporate assumptions.*
   - ❏ *Layout flow.*
   - ❏ *Develop an integrated model.*
   - ❏ *Identify analysis and presentation objectives.*
5. Practical implementation path
   - ❏ *Step 1: Start with 12-quarter trend schedule (eight quarters of history, and four quarters of projections).*
   - ❏ *Step 2: Develop high-level, one-page summary for each financial statement caption.*
   - ❏ *Step3: Revise based on experience; intensify focus on drivers.*

Identify Critical Business Drivers

Identification of critical business drivers is a critical step in developing a more effective and efficient forecast process, with the intent to extend the horizon of the projections. The key is to move away from a process that affords equal attention to all costs, expenses, and revenues. Identify the most significant drivers of performance. Here, we can apply the 80/20 rule: 20% of the line items will represent 80% of the value. For example, the top 20% of products or programs will typically account for 80% of total revenues. The top 20% of line-items of expenses (labor, facilities, materials, etc.) will typically account for 80% of all expenses.

Another important analysis is to identify those significant drivers that are most likely to fluctuate, that is, are most variable. Examples include revenues from new products or contracts, contract services, commodity prices, foreign currency fluctuations, and new home starts. These can be contrasted with drivers that are relatively stable and are more easily predicted by aggregation and extrapolation using trend analysis, such as salaries, facilities, and other costs. Critical assumptions should also be identified, including macroeconomic factors such as gross domestic product (GDP), political policy, inflation, and interest rates.

As we construct a DBO process and model, we ensure that these critical drivers and assumptions are fully considered and emphasized, and that less important factors are deemphasized. Figure 20.10 highlights typical drivers that are emphasized in the development of business outlooks.

FIGURE 20.10 **Reflect critical drivers in business outlook.**

Drivers-Based Planning: Focus on Key Performance Drivers
Typical Areas of Emphasis

Revenue and Margins:	Significant Cost Drivers	Macroeconomic Factors
❏ Pricing ❏ Product/program life cycles ❏ New product introductions ❏ New contracts/programs ❏ Macroeconomic factors ❏ Market and competitive forces ❏ Currency	❏ Human resources ❏ Commodities ❏ Significant inputs	❏ GDP ❏ Inflation ❏ Interest rates ❏ Geopolitical ❏ Public policy ❏ Demographics
Major Investments	**Human Capital Plan**	**Risks and Upsides**
❏ New products, programs ❏ Information technology ❏ Major expansion ❏ Acquisitions	❏ Headcount ❏ Retention/turnover ❏ New hires, recruiting ❏ Incentives, COLA ❏ Healthcare and other benefits	❏ New product or program delays ❏ Loss of contract ❏ Major expansion ❏ Acquisitions

❏ For most organizations, 80% of attention should be focused on revenue and margins
❏ The level of detail should vary according to the type of projection
❏ Every business has unique drivers, and projections should be tailored to specific circumstances

Design Process and Model Architecture

After stating the objectives and identifying critical performance drivers, we can begin to visualize an overview of the model. Most organizations should define the product (output) of the model to include the three basic financial statements (Income Statement, Balance Sheet, and Statement of Cash Flows), analysis, and a presentation summary. Beginning with this end in mind, we can lay out the supporting schedules to forecast key elements of finacial performance. For example, the revenue and product (or service) margin projections are of critcal importance in all organizations. These supporting schedules should be constructed to incorporate the most significant and most variable business drivers and assumptions.

This is a critical step in the process. We must be careful not to replicate the annual planning process here. Instead, we need to be disciplined and thoughtful to construct a working model that incorporates the key drivers and assumptions without resorting to the lowest level of detail (see Figure 20.11).

Practical Implemenation Path

At the center of any outlook is a performance trend schedule (typically quarterly). This trend schedule should include prior-year history, the current year plan/

FIGURE 20.11 **Business outlook architecture map.**

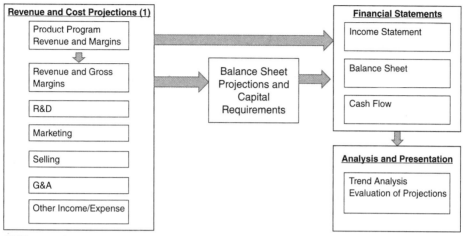

Business Outlooks/Rolling Forecasts
Illustrative Architecture

(1) Where possible, create one-page summaries

outlook, and provision for the next year's outlook. Table 20.2 illustrates a trend schedule for Thomas Technologies, Inc. The company has just closed out the second quarter of 2024. Under a traditional approach, the forecast horizon is compressed to the rest of 2024 (i.e., Q3 and Q4). To implement a rolling outlook, we simply need to extend the projections to include Q1 and Q2 for the subsequent year (2025). What is the minimal information we need to make reasonable estimates? We can start by reviewing the actual results of Q1 and Q2 of 2024. What items can be extrapolated from the previous periods or trends? What significant factors will shape the performance for these future periods? For example, for revenue, the projection must consider major product introductions and contract wins and losses.

For each Income Statement caption, I like to start by constructing a one-page supporting schedule that provides a capsule of information, including actual and projected financial results (presented in a way that is meaningful to the responsible operating manager) and includes all major assumptions and key drivers. By focusing on a one-page summary at this level, we are forced to identify the most signicant factors and drivers. It is important to tailor these schedules to each specific situation. Supporting schedules for product margins, gross margins, and marketing are illustrated in Tables 20.3–20.5. A complete, fully integrated forecast model is illustrated in the book's companion website.

The supporting schedules "roll up" to an Income Statement presenting the forecast for the extended forecast horizon in Table 20.6.

TABLE 20.2 **Rolling forecast method.**

Thomas Technologies, Inc.
Income Statement

	2023				2024				2025	
	Q1	Q2	Q3	Q4	Q1	Q2	Q3	Q4	Q1	Q2
Revenue	28,642,500	28,571,250	28,575,000	35,858,750	30,071,250	31,910,000	32,867,500	39,786,250	33,801,250	35,621,250
Cost of Revenue	14,848,000	14,805,600	14,804,400	18,568,000	15,347,000	16,303,700	16,817,100	20,377,400	17,721,600	18,758,000
Gross Margin	13,794,500	13,765,650	13,770,600	17,290,750	14,724,250	15,606,300	16,050,400	19,408,850	16,079,650	16,863,250
Gross Margin %	48.2%	48.2%	48.2%	48.2%	49.0%	48.9%	48.8%	48.8%	47.6%	47.3%
R&D	3,750,400	3,756,400	3,757,900	4,240,400	3,956,850	4,352,934	4,538,347	4,928,330	5,149,837	5,364,475
Selling	4,255,500	4,255,500	4,256,500	4,357,500	4,427,200	4,428,200	4,428,200	4,518,200	4,603,648	4,603,648
Marketing	1,665,050	1,682,050	1,681,550	2,060,050	1,773,383	1,773,649	1,757,649	2,312,699	2,114,887	2,094,891
G&A	2,185,300	2,185,300	2,185,300	2,625,300	2,292,715	2,292,715	2,292,715	2,762,715	2,405,501	2,405,505
Operating Expenses	11,856,250	11,879,250	11,881,250	13,283,250	12,450,148	12,847,498	13,016,911	14,521,945	14,273,872	14,468,520
Operating Income	1,938,250	1,866,400	1,889,350	4,007,500	2,274,103	2,758,802	3,033,489	4,886,905	1,805,778	2,394,730
Operating Income %	6.8%	6.6%	6.6%	11.2%	7.6%	8.6%	9.2%	12.3%	5.3%	6.7%
Interest Income (Expense)	(3,500)	(3,500)	(3,500)	(3,500)	(3,500)	(3,500)	(3,500)	(3,500)	(3,500)	(3,500)
Other Income (Expense)	2,000	1,800	1,800	1,500	2,000	1,800	1,800	1,500	2,000	1,800
Profit Before Tax	1,936,750	1,884,700	1,887,650	4,005,500	2,272,603	2,757,102	3,031,789	4,884,905	1,804,278	2,393,030
Tax 30.0%	(581,025)	(565,410)	(566,295)	(1,201,650)	(681,781)	(827,131)	(909,537)	(1,465,472)	(541,283)	(717,909)
Net Income	1,355,725	1,319,290	1,321,355	2,803,850	1,590,822	1,929,971	2,122,252	3,419,434	1,262,994	1,675,121
Yr										
Revenue	10.0%	12.0%	14.0%	15.0%	5.0%	11.7%	15.0%	11.0%	12.4%	11.6%
Operating Expenses	5.0%	6.0%	7.0%	8.0%	5.0%	8.2%	9.6%	9.3%	14.6%	12.6%
Operating Income	12.0%	14.0%	13.0%	12.0%	17.3%	46.2%	60.6%	21.9%	-20.6%	-13.2%

% of Sales

Revenue	100.0%	100.0%	100.0%	100.0%	100.0%	100.0%	100.0%	100.0%	100.0%
Cost of Revenue	51.8%	51.8%	51.8%	51.0%	51.1%	51.2%	51.2%	52.4%	52.7%
Gross Margin	48.2%	48.2%	48.2%	49.0%	48.9%	48.8%	48.8%	47.6%	47.3%
R&D	13.1%	13.2%	11.8%	13.2%	13.6%	13.8%	12.4%	15.2%	15.1%
Selling	14.9%	14.9%	12.2%	14.7%	13.9%	13.5%	11.4%	13.6%	12.9%
Marketing	5.8%	5.9%	5.7%	5.9%	5.6%	5.3%	5.8%	6.3%	5.9%
G&A	7.6%	7.6%	7.3%	7.6%	7.2%	7.0%	6.9%	7.1%	6.8%
Operating Expenses	41.4%	41.6%	37.0%	41.4%	40.3%	39.6%	36.5%	42.2%	40.6%
Operating Income	6.8%	6.6%	11.2%	7.6%	8.6%	9.2%	12.3%	5.3%	6.7%

TABLE 20.3 **DBO supporting schedule-product margins.** 🖥

Thomas Technologies, Inc.
Product Margins

Trend Schedule

Product/Product Line	2023 Q1	2023 Q2	2023 Q3	2023 Q4	2024 Q1	2024 Q2	2024 Q3	2024 Q4	2025 Q1	2025 Q2	2025 Q3	2025 Q4
Product 1												
Average Selling Price	4,850	4,850	4,850	4,850	4,900	4,900	4,900	4,900	4,900	4,900	4,900	4,999
Product Cost	2,500	2,500	2,500	2,500	2,517	2,517	2,517	2,517	2,532	2,532	2,532	2,532
Unit Volume	800	1,000	1,100	2,000	1,000	1,100	1,300	2,200	1,300	1,500	1,600	2,300
Revenue	3,880,000	4,850,000	5,335,000	9,700,000	4,900,000	5,390,000	6,370,000	10,780,000	6,370,000	7,350,000	7,840,000	11,497,700
Product Costs	2,000,000	2,500,000	2,750,000	5,000,000	2,517,000	2,768,700	3,272,100	5,537,400	3,291,600	3,798,000	4,051,200	5,823,600
Product Margin	1,880,000	2,350,000	2,585,000	4,700,000	2,383,000	2,621,300	3,097,900	5,242,600	3,078,400	3,552,000	3,788,800	5,674,100
%	48.5%	48.5%	48.5%	48.5%	48.6%	48.6%	48.6%	48.6%	48.3%	48.3%	48.3%	49.3%
Product 2												
Average Selling Price	5,600	5,600	5,600	5,600	5,800	5,800	5,800	5,800	6,000	6,000	6,000	6,000
Product Cost	2,912	2,912	2,912	2,912	2,950	2,950	2,950	2,950	3,200	3,200	3,200	3,200
Un t Volume	4,000	3,800	3,700	4,000	3,600	3,700	3,500	3,800	3,050	3,000	3,100	3,050
Revenue	22,400,000	21,280,000	20,720,000	22,400,000	20,880,000	21,460,000	20,300,000	22,040,000	18,300,000	18,000,000	18,600,000	18,300,000
Product Costs	11,648,000	11,065,600	10,774,400	11,648,000	10,620,000	10,915,000	10,325,000	11,210,000	9,760,000	9,600,000	9,920,000	9,760,000
Product Margin	10,752,000	10,214,400	9,945,600	10,752,000	10,260,000	10,545,000	9,975,000	10,830,000	8,540,000	8,400,000	8,680,000	8,540,000
%	48.0%	48.0%	48.0%	48.0%	49.1%	49.1%	49.1%	49.1%	46.7%	46.7%	46.7%	46.7%
Product 3												
Average Selling Price	1,575	1,575	1,575	1,575	1,575	1,575	1,575	1,575	1,575	1,575	1,575	1,575
Product Cost	800	800	800	800	800	800	800	800	800	800	800	800
Unit Volume	1,500	1,550	1,600	1,650	1,550	1,600	1,700	1,750	1,950	1,950	2,100	2,050
Revenue	2,362,500	2,441,250	2,520,000	2,598,750	2,441,250	2,520,000	2,677,500	2,756,250	3,071,250	3,071,250	3,307,500	3,228,750
Product Costs	1,200,000	1,240,000	1,280,000	1,320,000	1,240,000	1,280,000	1,360,000	1,400,000	1,560,000	1,560,000	1,680,000	1,640,000
Product Margin	1,162,500	1,201,250	1,240,000	1,278,750	1,201,250	1,240,000	1,317,500	1,356,250	1,511,250	1,511,250	1,627,500	1,588,750
%	49.2%	49.2%	49.2%	49.2%	49.2%	49.2%	49.2%	49.2%	49.2%	49.2%	49.2%	49.2%

Product 4											
Average Selling Price	-	-	2,900	2,900	2,900	2,900	2,900	3,000	3,000	3,000	3,000
Product Cost	-	-	1,500	1,500	1,500	1,500	1,500	1,500	1,600	1,600	1,600
Unit Volume	-	-	400	500	600	800	900	900	1,000	1,300	1,500
Revenue	-	-	1,160,000	1,450,000	1,740,000	2,320,000	2,610,000	2,700,000	3,000,000	3,900,000	4,500,000
Product Costs	-	-	600,000	750,000	900,000	1,200,000	1,350,000	1,350,000	1,600,000	2,080,000	2,400,000
Product Margin	-	-	560,000	700,000	840,000	1,120,000	1,260,000	1,350,000	1,400,000	1,820,000	2,100,000
%	-	-	48.3%	48.3%	48.3%	48.3%	48.3%	50.0%	46.7%	46.7%	46.7%
Product 5											
Average Selling Price	-	-	-	4,000	4,000	4,000	4,000	4,200	4,200	4,200	4,200
Product Cost	-	-	-	2,200	2,200	2,200	2,200	2,200	2,200	2,200	2,250
Unit Volume	-	-	-	100	200	300	400	800	1,000	1,100	1,500
Revenue	-	-	-	400,000	800,000	1,200,000	1,600,000	3,360,000	4,200,000	4,620,000	6,300,000
Product Costs	-	-	-	220,000	440,000	660,000	880,000	1,760,000	2,200,000	2,420,000	3,375,000
Product Margin	-	-	-	180,000	360,000	540,000	720,000	1,600,000	2,000,000	2,200,000	2,925,000
%	-	-	-	45.0%	45.0%	45.0%	45.0%	47.6%	47.6%	47.6%	46.4%
Total											
Revenue	28,642,500	28,571,250	28,575,000	30,071,250	31,910,000	32,867,500	39,786,250	33,801,250	35,621,250	38,267,500	43,826,450
Product Cost	14,848,000	14,805,600	14,804,400	15,347,000	16,303,700	16,817,100	20,377,400	17,721,600	18,758,600	20,151,200	22,998,600
Product Margin	13,794,500	13,765,650	13,770,600	14,724,250	15,606,300	16,050,400	19,408,850	16,079,650	16,863,250	18,116,300	20,827,850
%	48.2%	48.2%	48.2%	49.0%	48.9%	48.8%	48.8%	47.6%	47.3%	47.3%	47.5%
Y/Y Growth Rate				5.0%	11.7%	15.0%	11.0%	12.4%	11.6%	16.4%	10.2%

TABLE 20.4 **DBO supporting schedule-gross margins.**

Thomas Technologies, Inc.
Gross Margin

		2023				2024				2025			
		Q1	Q2	Q3	Q4	Q1	Q2	Q3	Q4	Q1	Q2	Q3	Q4
Sales		28,642,500	28,571,250	28,575,000	35,858,750	30,071,250	31,910,000	32,867,500	39,786,250	33,801,250	35,621,250	38,267,500	43,826,450
Product Cogs		14,848,000	14,805,600	14,804,400	18,568,000	15,347,000	16,303,700	16,817,100	20,377,400	17,721,600	18,758,000	20,151,200	22,998,600
Product Margin		13,794,500	13,765,650	13,770,600	17,290,750	14,724,250	15,606,300	16,050,400	19,408,850	16,079,650	16,863,250	18,116,300	20,827,850
% to Sales		48.2%	48.2%	48.2%	48.2%	49.0%	48.9%	48.8%	48.8%	47.6%	47.3%	47.3%	47.5%
Other Costs													
Production Variances		25,000	25,000	25,000	25,000	25,000	25,000	25,000	25,000	25,000	25,000	25,000	25,000
Warranty	1.0%	286,425	285,713	285,750	358,588	300,713	319,100	328,675	397,863	338,013	356,213	382,675	438,265
Inventory Provisions		5,000	5,000	5,000	5,000	5,000	5,000	5,000	5,000	5,000	5,000	5,000	5,000
Royalty		750	750	750	750	750	750	750	750	750	750	750	750
Scrap		1,200	1,200	1,200	1,200	1,200	1,200	1,200	1,200	1,200	1,200	1,200	1,200
Sustaining Engineering		800	800	800	800	800	800	800	800	800	800	800	800
Other		24,535	24,392	24,400	38,967	27,392	31,070	32,985	46,822	34,852	38,492	44,285	54,902
Total Other COGS		343,710	342,855	342,900	430,305	360,855	382,920	394,410	477,435	405,615	427,455	459,710	525,917
% to Sales													
Total COGS		15,191,710	15,148,455	15,147,300	18,998,305	15,707,855	16,686,620	17,211,510	20,854,835	18,127,215	19,185,455	20,610,910	23,524,517
Gross Margin		13,450,790	13,422,796	13,427,700	16,860,446	14,363,396	15,223,380	15,655,990	18,931,416	15,674,036	16,435,796	17,656,590	20,301,934
% to Sales		47.0%	47.0%	47.0%	47.0%	47.8%	47.7%	47.6%	47.6%	46.4%	46.1%	46.1%	46.3%
Headcount		2,864	2,857	2,858	3,586	3,007	3,191	3,287	3,979	3,380	3,562	3,827	4,383

TABLE 20.5 **DBO supporting schedule-marketing.**

Thomas Technologies, Inc.
Marketing — Trend Schedule

	2023 Q1	2023 Q2	2023 Q3	2023 Q4	2024 Q1	2024 Q2	2024 Q3	2024 Q4	2025 Q1	2025 Q2	2025 Q3	2025 Q4
People Costs												
Salary	745,000	745,000	745,000	745,000	782,250	785,138	785,138	900,138	939,395	939,397	939,397	939,397
Bonus				195,000				150,000				221,000
Other												
Total	745,000	745,000	745,000	940,000	782,250	785,138	785,138	1,050,138	939,395	939,397	939,397	1,160,397
Fringe Benefits 17%	126,650	126,650	126,650	126,650	132,983	133,473	133,473	153,023	159,697	159,697	159,697	159,697
Total Labor and Related Costs	1,616,650	1,616,650	1,616,650	2,006,650	1,697,483	1,703,749	1,703,749	2,253,299	2,038,487	2,038,491	2,038,491	2,480,491
Travel	6,000	6,000	6,000	6,000	8,500	8,500	10,000	12,000	12,000	12,000	12,000	12,000
Meetings	1,500	1,500	1,500	1,500	1,500	1,500	1,500	1,500	1,500	1,500	1,500	1,500
Consultants		2,000	1,500	5,000		2,000	1,500	5,000		2,000	1,500	5,000
Professional Services	2,000	2,000	2,000	2,000	2,000	2,000	2,000	2,000	2,000	2,000	2,000	2,000
Materials	4,200	4,200	4,200	4,200	4,200	4,200	4,200	4,200	4,200	4,200	4,200	4,200
Contract services	1,200	1,200	1,200	1,200	1,200	1,200	1,200	1,200	1,200	1,200	1,200	1,200
Advertising	5,000	5,000	5,000	5,000	5,000	5,000	5,000	5,000	5,000	5,000	5,000	5,000
Trade Show		15,000	15,000			17,000			22,000			
Product Launch					25,000							
Depreciation	6,000	6,000	6,000	6,000	6,000	6,000	6,000	6,000	6,000	6,000	6,000	6,000
Allocations In	15,000	15,000	15,000	15,000	15,000	15,000	15,000	15,000	15,000	15,000	15,000	15,000
Other	7,500	7,500	7,500	7,500	7,500	7,500	7,500	7,500	7,500	7,500	7,500	7,500
Total Other Expenses	48,400	65,400	64,900	53,400	75,900	69,900	53,900	59,400	76,400	56,400	55,900	59,400
Total Marketing	1,665,050	1,682,050	1,681,550	2,060,050	1,773,383	1,773,649	1,757,649	2,312,699	2,114,887	2,094,891	2,094,391	2,539,891

TABLE 20.5 *(Continued)*

Thomas Technologies, Inc.
Marketing
Trend Schedule

		2023				2024				2025			
		Q1	Q2	Q3	Q4	Q1	Q2	Q3	Q4	Q1	Q2	Q3	Q4
Year to Year Growth						6.5%	5.4%	4.5%	12.3%	19.3%	18.1%	19.2%	9.8%
Sales		28,642,500	28,571,250	28,575,000	35,858,750	30,071,250	31,910,000	32,867,500	39,786,250	33,801,250	35,621,250	38,267,500	43,826,450
Marketing % of Sales		5.8%	5.9%	5.9%	5.7%	5.9%	5.6%	5.3%	5.8%	6.3%	5.9%	5.5%	5.8%
Salaries													
CMO	1	145,000	145,000	145,000	145,000	152,250	152,250	152,250	152,250	159,863	159,863	159,863	159,863
Advertising Manager	1	125,000	125,000	125,000	125,000	131,250	131,250	131,250	131,250	137,813	137,813	137,813	137,813
Web techs	2	180,000	180,000	180,000	180,000	189,000	189,000	189,000	189,000	198,450	198,450	198,450	198,450
Advertising Manager	1	125,000	125,000	125,000	125,000	131,250	131,250	131,250	131,250	137,813	137,813	137,813	137,813
Marketing Manager	1	115,000	115,000	115,000	115,000	120,750	120,750	120,750	120,750	126,788	126,788	126,788	126,788
Admin	1	55,000	55,000	55,000	55,000	57,750	60,638	60,638	60,638	63,670	63,670	63,670	63,670
New Hire Web manager	1								115,000	115,000	115,000	115,000	115,000
Total Salaries		745,000	745,000	745,000	745,000	782,250	785,138	785,138	900,138	939,395	939,397	939,397	939,397
Headcount	8	7	7	7	7	7	7	7	8	8	8	8	8

TABLE 20.6 **DBO income statement.**

Thomas Technologies, Inc.
Income Statement

		2023				2024				2025	
		Q1	Q2	Q3	Q4	Q1	Q2	Q3	Q4	Q1	Q2
Revenue		28,642,500	28,571,250	28,575,000	35,858,750	30,071,250	31,910,000	32,867,500	39,786,250	33,801,250	35,621,250
Cost of Revenue		14,848,000	14,805,600	14,804,400	18,568,000	15,347,000	16,303,700	16,817,100	20,377,400	17,721,600	18,758,000
Gross Margin		13,794,500	13,765,650	13,770,600	17,290,750	14,724,250	15,606,300	16,050,400	19,408,850	16,079,650	16,863,250
Gross Margin %		48.2%	48.2%	48.2%	48.2%	49.0%	48.9%	48.8%	48.8%	47.6%	47.3%
R&D		3,750,400	3,756,400	3,757,900	4,240,400	3,956,850	4,352,934	4,538,347	4,928,330	5,149,837	5,364,475
Selling		4,255,500	4,255,500	4,256,500	4,357,500	4,427,200	4,428,200	4,428,200	4,518,200	4,603,648	4,603,648
Marketing		1,665,050	1,682,050	1,681,550	2,060,050	1,773,383	1,773,649	1,757,649	2,312,699	2,114,887	2,094,891
G&A		2,185,300	2,185,300	2,185,300	2,625,300	2,292,715	2,292,715	2,292,715	2,762,715	2,405,501	2,405,505
Operating Expenses		11,856,250	11,879,250	11,881,250	13,283,250	12,450,148	12,847,498	13,016,911	14,521,945	14,273,872	14,468,520
Operating Income		1,938,250	1,886,400	1,889,350	4,007,500	2,274,103	2,758,802	3,033,489	4,886,905	1,805,778	2,394,730
Operating Income %		6.8%	6.6%	6.6%	11.2%	7.6%	8.6%	9.2%	12.3%	5.3%	6.7%
Interest Income (Expense)		(3,500)	(3,500)	(3,500)	(3,500)	(3,500)	(3,500)	(3,500)	(3,500)	(3,500)	(3,500)
Other Income(Expense)		2,000	1,800	1,800	1,500	2,000	1,800	1,800	1,500	2,000	1,800
Profit Before Tax		1,936,750	1,884,700	1,887,650	4,005,500	2,272,603	2,757,102	3,031,789	4,884,905	1,804,278	2,393,030
Tax	30.0%	(581,025)	(565,410)	(566,295)	(1,201,650)	(681,781)	(827,131)	(909,537)	(1,465,472)	(541,283)	(717,909)
Net Income		1,355,725	1,319,290	1,321,355	2,803,850	1,590,822	1,929,971	2,122,252	3,419,434	1,262,994	1,675,121
Y/Y											
Revenue		10.0%	12.0%	14.0%	15.0%	5.0%	11.7%	15.0%	11.0%	12.4%	11.6%
Operating Expenses		5.0%	6.0%	7.0%	8.0%	5.0%	8.2%	9.6%	9.3%	14.6%	12.6%
Operating Income		12.0%	14.0%	13.0%	12.0%	17.3%	46.2%	60.6%	21.9%	-20.6%	-13.2%

403

TABLE 20.5 *(Continued)*

Thomas Technologies, Inc.
Income Statement

	2023				2024				2025	
	Q1	Q2	Q3	Q4	Q1	Q2	Q3	Q4	Q1	Q2
% of Sales										
Revenue	100.0%	100.0%	100.0%	100.0%	100.0%	100.0%	100.0%	100.0%	100.0%	100.0%
Cost of Revenue	51.8%	51.8%	51.8%	51.8%	51.0%	51.1%	51.2%	51.2%	52.4%	52.7%
Gross Margin	48.2%	48.2%	48.2%	48.2%	49.0%	48.9%	48.8%	48.8%	47.6%	47.3%
R&D	13.1%	13.1%	13.2%	11.8%	13.2%	13.6%	13.8%	12.4%	15.2%	15.1%
Selling	14.9%	14.9%	14.9%	12.2%	14.7%	13.9%	13.5%	11.4%	13.6%	12.9%
Marketing	5.8%	5.9%	5.9%	5.7%	5.9%	5.6%	5.3%	5.8%	6.3%	5.9%
G&A	7.6%	7.6%	7.6%	7.3%	7.6%	7.2%	7.0%	6.9%	7.1%	6.8%
Operating Expenses	41.4%	41.6%	41.6%	37.0%	41.4%	40.3%	39.6%	36.5%	42.2%	40.6%
Operating Income	6.8%	6.6%	6.6%	11.2%	7.6%	8.6%	9.2%	12.3%	5.3%	6.7%

Comprehensive Financial Picture   To provide a complete view of expected financial performance, financial projections in the rolling forecast should include the P&L statement, Balance Sheet, and Statement of Cash Flows. Many forecasts focus only on the P&L, which does not provide a complete picture of the financial performance of the organization.

There are two reasons for this. First, the focus for many companies is on earnings per share (EPS), and therefore, all attention is directed to the P&L. Even where the CEO is primarily focused on the P&L and EPS, finance should continue to prepare and present the key Balance Sheet and cash flow projections. Most competent finance and general managers understand that profit must be evaluated in the context of the investment levels required. Therefore, measures such as asset turnover and return on investment should be presented. Attention to cash balances, liquidity, intermediate financing, and loan covenants are all important responsibilities of financial management and should be incorporated into all projections.

The second reason is that finance teams are much more comfortable in the mechanics of revenue and expense projections. However, once key models are established, it is relatively easy to project key Balance Sheet and cash flow information. An illustration of a Balance Sheet and cash flow model is provided in Table 20.7. Techniques to project the Balance Sheet and cash flow are found in Chapters 24 and 25.

Summarizing and Presenting Business Forecasts and Outlooks   The most effective way to review and present the results of a revised forecast or outlook is to incorporate a presentation summary directly into the forecast model. This will facilitate review, discussions with managers, and revisions. It enables a high-level quality control review of the projections since the presentation summary will include key variables. Key items that are typically included are major assumptions, changes from prior outlook, key performance metrics, and major risks and upsides. An example of a presentation summary is provided in Figure 20.12.

Frequency and Timing of Forecasts   The frequency and timing of forecasts will depend on several factors. A very dynamic environment will require more frequent updates than a stable environment. Companies that report earnings and provide earnings or other guidance to public capital markets typically use a quarterly cycle. Private companies typically update the outlook around management or board of director meetings. Significant events, such as contract awards or losses, may dictate a special revision to the business outlook.

Analysis and Evaluation of Financial Projections   Chapter 19 introduced tools for analyzing and evaluating projections. These tools should be incorporated into the DBO model. For short-term projections, revenue and expense levels

TABLE 20.7 **DBO supporting schedule: Balance Sheet and cash flow.**

Thomas Technologies, Inc.
Balance Sheet Cash Flow

		2023				2024				2025			
		Q1	Q2	Q3	Q4	Q1	Q2	Q3	Q4	Q1	Q2	Q3	Q4
Cash		3,200,000	5,357,998	7,766,628	1,424,420	11,386,158	11,388,505	12,720,574	7,591,316	16,594,076	16,246,931	15,631,502	12,252,044
Receivables	90.0	28,642,500	28,571,250	28,575,000	35,858,750	30,071,250	31,910,000	32,867,500	39,786,250	33,801,250	35,621,250	38,267,500	43,826,450
Inventories	3.0	19,797,333	19,740,800	19,739,200	24,757,333	20,462,667	21,738,267	22,422,800	27,169,867	23,628,800	25,010,667	26,868,267	30,664,800
Other													
Current Assets		51,639,833	53,670,048	56,080,828	62,040,503	61,920,075	65,036,771	68,010,874	74,547,432	74,024,126	76,878,847	80,767,269	86,743,294
PP&E		25,000,000	25,750,000	26,150,000	27,250,000	28,250,000	29,250,000	30,250,000	31,250,000	32,250,000	33,250,000	34,250,000	35,250,000
Accumulated Depreciation		12,000,000	13,000,000	14,000,000	15,000,000	16,000,000	17,000,000	18,000,000	19,000,000	20,000,000	21,000,000	22,000,000	23,000,000
Net Fixed Assets		13,000,000	12,750,000	12,150,000	12,250,000	12,250,000	12,250,000	12,250,000	12,250,000	12,250,000	12,250,000	12,250,000	12,250,000
Net Goodwill and Intangibles		24,000,000	23,500,000	23,000,000	22,500,000	22,000,000	21,500,000	21,000,000	20,500,000	20,000,000	19,500,000	19,000,000	18,500,000
Other Non Current Assets													
Total Assets		88,639,833	89,920,048	91,230,828	96,790,503	96,170,075	98,786,771	101,260,874	107,297,432	106,274,126	108,628,847	112,017,269	117,493,294
Accounts Payable	20.0%	5,728,500	5,714,250	5,715,000	7,171,750	6,014,250	6,382,000	6,573,500	7,957,250	6,760,250	7,124,250	7,653,500	8,765,290
Notes Payable, Bank		1,000,000	1,000,000	1,000,000	1,000,000	1,000,000	1,000,000	1,000,000	1,000,000	1,000,000	1,000,000	1,000,000	1,000,000
Accrued Expenses & Taxes	18.0%	5,155,650	5,142,825	5,143,500	6,454,575	5,412,825	5,743,800	5,916,150	7,161,525	6,084,225	6,411,825	6,888,150	7,888,761
Current Liabilities		11,884,150	11,857,075	11,858,500	14,626,325	12,427,075	13,125,800	13,489,650	16,118,775	13,844,475	14,535,075	15,541,650	17,654,051
Long Term Debt		12,000,000	12,000,000	12,000,000	12,000,000	12,000,000	12,000,000	12,000,000	12,000,000	12,000,000	12,000,000	12,000,000	12,000,000
Other		257,025	257,025	257,025	257,025	257,025	257,025	257,025	257,025	257,025	257,025	257,025	257,025
Stockholders Equity		64,498,658	65,805,948	67,115,303	69,907,153	71,485,975	73,403,946	75,514,198	78,921,632	80,172,626	81,835,747	84,218,594	87,582,218
Total Liabilities and Equity		88,639,833	89,920,048	91,230,828	96,790,503	96,170,075	98,786,771	101,260,873	107,297,432	106,274,126	108,628,847	112,017,269	117,493,294
Proof		0	0	0	0	0	0	0	0	0	0	0	0
Operating Capital		37,555,683	37,454,975	37,455,700	46,989,758	39,106,842	41,522,467	42,800,650	51,837,342	44,585,575	47,095,842	50,594,117	57,837,199
Total Debt		13,000,000	13,000,000	13,000,000	13,000,000	13,000,000	13,000,000	13,000,000	13,000,000	13,000,000	13,000,000	13,000,000	13,000,000
Invested Capital													

Cash Flow

Net Income	1,355,725	1,319,290	1,321,355	2,803,850	1,590,822	1,929,971	2,122,252	3,419,434	1,262,994	1,675,121	2,394,847	3,375,624
D&A	1,400,000	1,500,000	1,500,000	1,500,000	1,500,000	1,500,000	1,500,000	1,500,000	1,500,000	1,500,000	1,500,000	1,500,000
Capital Expenditures	600,000	(750,000)	(400,000)	(1,100,000)	(1,000,000)	(1,000,000)	(1,000,000)	(1,000,000)	(1,000,000)	(1,000,000)	(1,000,000)	(1,000,000)
(Inc) Decrease in OC	500,000	100,708	(725)	(9,534,058)	7,882,917	(2,415,625)	(1,278,183)	(9,036,692)	7,251,767	(2,510,267)	(3,498,275)	(7,243,082)
OCF	3,855,725	2,169,998	2,420,630	(6,330,208)	9,973,738	14,346	1,344,069	(5,117,258)	9,014,761	(335,146)	(603,428)	(3,367,458)
Dividends	(2,000)	(2,000)	(2,000)	(2,000)	(2,000)	(2,000)	(2,000)	(2,000)	(2,000)	(2,000)	(2,000)	(2,000)
Share Proceeds (Repurchases)	(10,000)	(10,000)	(10,000)	(10,000)	(10,000)	(10,000)	(10,000)	(10,000)	(10,000)	(10,000)	(10,000)	(10,000)
Other												
Debt (Payments) Borrowing												
Cash Flow	3,843,725	2,157,998	2,408,630	(6,342,208)	9,961,738	2,346	1,332,069	(5,129,258)	9,002,761	(347,146)	(615,428)	(3,379,458)
Sales	28,642,500	28,571,250	28,575,000	35,858,750	30,071,250	31,910,000	32,867,500	39,786,250	33,801,250	35,621,250	38,267,500	43,826,450
DSO	90.0	90.0	90.0	90.0	90.0	90.0	90.0	90.0	90.0	90.0	90.0	90.0
Inv Turns	3.0	3.0	3.0	3.0	3.0	3.0	3.0	3.0	3.0	3.0	3.0	3.0
DSI	121.7	121.7	121.7	121.7	121.7	121.7	121.7	121.7	121.7	121.7	121.7	121.7
Asset Turnover	1.3	1.3	1.3	1.5	1.3	1.3	1.3	1.5	1.3	1.3	1.4	1.5
Debt to Total Capital (book)	16.8%	16.5%	16.2%	15.7%	15.4%	15.0%	14.7%	14.1%	14.0%	13.7%	13.4%	12.9%

FIGURE 20.12 **DBO presentation summary.**

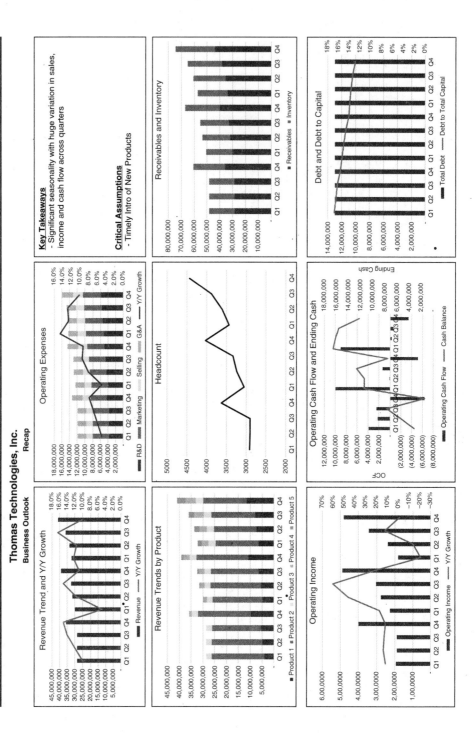

408

can be compared to current run rates and results from the prior period. It is vital to identify and evaluate critical assumptions included in the projections.

SUMMARY

The pace of change in the world today requires most organizations to create more effective planning and forecasting processes. Most organizations have developed an operating plan to replace the financially focused budget process of old. Due to the pace of change, organizations must frequently update business projections. Organizations need a process to project financial performance periodically, as well as on demand, to perform "what if" analysis to evaluate the impact of potential changes and strategic alternatives.

The on-demand business outlook is yet another evolution in planning and forecasting. On-demand refers to the ability to update the business projections at any time. The term *business outlook* shifts the perception from a financial drill to an outlook of business trends and factors.

21

Long-Term Projections

In this chapter, we will focus on developing projections over the long term. We will build on the practices and techniques introduced in Chapter 19, "Business Projections and Plans—Introduction and Best Practices." Long-term projections (LTPs) are required to evaluate new products, acquisitions, capital investments, and strategic plans. In simpler times, LTPs could be easily developed by extrapolating historical performance trends or extending static business models. Over the past 30 years, factors such as globalization, technology developments, geopolitical events, demographics, and economic factors have significantly impacted markets and businesses.

Developing projections of performance over an extended period introduces some unique challenges that require a robust process to overcome. Uncertainty about the future should imply that most LTPs should include identification, testing, and evaluation of underlying assumptions and multiple scenarios.

UNIQUE CHALLENGES IN ESTIMATING LONG-TERM PERFORMANCE

Longer Forecast Horizon

LTPs will have an extended time horizon, ranging from two to five or more years. The methods and considerations used for short- to mid-term projections are usually not well suited to LTPs. There should be less emphasis on performance details and more understanding of strategic issues, market forces, and long-term performance drivers.

Greater Uncertainty

The longer the horizon of our plan or projections, the greater the uncertainty. Few of us standing here now could have reasonably expected many of the events and changes experienced in just the past several years. Many of the strategic plans developed five years ago may appear naive or even absurd in hindsight, given the changes that could not have been anticipated. Even before the Covid-19 pandemic and government responses, there were a multitude of factors limiting our ability to project future business outcomes. So why plan? Again, the value is in the planning not the plan itself. If these organizations identified risks and opportunities and developed alternative scenarios, then they likely were better prepared to react to unforeseen changes that have unfolded.

Capability Required to Model Strategic Alternatives and Scenarios

The value in any plan is not the document or a single projection. The value is the critical thinking, anticipation, and identification of critical assumptions, critical success factors (CSFs), and performance drivers.

The model must be robust to consider radical changes to an organization's market, distribution channel, business model, and cost structure over a three- to five-year period. One scenario should be a simple extrapolation of recent performance trends. Other scenarios should flex key assumptions about the economy, market drivers, key cost drivers, and other factors. An important aspect of strategic planning is the identification of alternative courses of action. The long-term model must be able to portray the financial implications and results of various alternatives. Scenario analysis was covered in greater detail in Chapter 13.

The key lies in the critical thinking the management team steps through in thinking about a range of potential scenarios.

Comprehensive View of Performance

Many organizations limit the content of long-term projections to the income statement. Long-term projections *must* include a complete view of the expected performance, including the Balance Sheet, cash flow, and investment returns and valuation. Any evaluation of future decisions or alternatives must include expected capital requirements, liquidity, a determination of the economic value created, and an evaluation of the investments contemplated in the plan. Why would any responsible executives embark on a plan that, if achieved, does not create value or cannot be financed by the firm?

APPLICATIONS OF LONG-TERM PROJECTIONS

Long-term projections are developed and utilized for a number of applications. The format and content of the projections must be tailored to the specific application.

Strategic Planning

LTPs must be developed as part of any strategic planning process. These projections will estimate the results of a certain strategy and allow for the evaluation of strategic alternatives. The LTPs must be developed using a robust model that can project financial results over several years (the planning horizon). Chapter 8 provided a comprehensive view into strategic analysis and planning.

New Product Development

The evaluation of potential new products should include a comprehensive plan containing strategic plan, execution plan, financial projections, and economic evaluation. New product development activities are investments and should be analyzed as such. The financial projections must include all investments in development and capital as well as projected sales and expenses. New product development projections will be covered in Chapters 28 and 29.

New Business Creation

The evaluation of potential new businesses should also include a complete plan containing strategic plan, execution plan, financial projections, and economic evaluation. New business creation efforts are investments and should be analyzed as such. The financial projections must include all investments in development and capital as well as projected sales and expenses. Projections for new business plans will be covered in Chapters 28 and 29, and the valuation of businesses will be covered in Chapter 30.

Mergers and Acquisitions

Mergers and acquisitions (M&A) represent substantial investments that must yield a return in the form of future financial results. The evaluation of potential acquisitions should also include a comprehensive plan containing strategy, execution, financial projections, and valuation. The investment in an acquisition includes the purchase price, associated costs, and costs to implement synergies. Future projections must consider the standalone results of the acquirer and the target, and the projected synergies resulting from the combination. M&A will be covered in detail in Chapter 31.

Other Capital Investment Decisions

In addition to new products, new business, and M&A decisions, many other capital investment decisions will require long-term projections. Examples include geographic expansion, purchases of manufacturing equipment, and plant expansions, which will all require the development of long-term projections.

DEVELOPING LONG-TERM PROJECTIONS

The process of developing an LTP is not simply a number crunching exercise. The analyst must work closely with key managers and become extremely familiar with the strategic issues and opportunities of the organization. Significant consideration of strategic issues, opportunities, markets, and competitors must be reflected in the LTP. Best practices such as market analysis; benchmarking; competitor analysis; and strengths, limitations, opportunities, and threats (SLOT) analysis should be employed.

Assess Current Situation

As with any projection, LTPs must start with an assessment of the current situation and environment. This is particularly true with long-term projections. This process must include an assessment of the organization's strengths, limitations (or weaknesses), opportunities, and threats (SLOT), illustrated in Figure 21.1. The external environment must be monitored and reflected in the plan. The analyst must also be familiar with the strategic plan. A determination of the status of previous strategic objectives must be made. Recent performance trends must be identified and their impact on future performance considered. Assessing the current situation was covered in more detail in Chapter 8, "Strategic Analysis and Planning."

FIGURE 21.1 **SLOT analysis.**

SLOT Analysis

Strengths	**Limitations (Weaknesses)**
❑ Significant market share ❑ Products with strong competitive advantages	❑ High debt levels ❑ Reduced cash flow ❑ Aging workforce
Threats	**Opportunities**
❑ Emerging competitor ❑ Key customer evaluating in-sourcing ❑ Potential (disruptive) technology possible	❑ Several acquisition opportunities ❑ Potential to extend current products to new market

Incorporate and Review Historical Results

In developing the model for use in developing LTPs, it is important to incorporate history. I recommend presenting three to four years of history. This has two advantages. First, the inclusion of history helps to identify key drivers and assumptions that are critical to projecting future projections. Second, it provides confidence in the relationship between these drivers and the actual financial results posted in prior years represented in the LTP model.

Identify Strategic Issues

Strategic issues must be considered in the development of LTPs. These may include changes in the overall market, competitive threats, weaknesses, human capital gaps that must be overcome, and many other issues that will impact future financial performance.

Identify and Model Critical Assumptions, and Business Drivers

Critical assumptions and business drivers that will affect future performance must be explicitly identified. Too often, these are buried in formulas in a model that prevent review and testing. These items will vary for each individual business. In some cases, market forces will be the most important. In others, product life cycles and introduction plans are critical. Key costs drivers must be identified and incorporated into LTP models. Critical assumptions must be documented, reviewed, and tested. Sensitivity and scenario analysis should be integral elements of the plan.

Evaluate Strategic Alternatives and Scenarios

One of the objectives of strategic planning is to consider alternatives to the company's existing or primary strategic direction. This may be the most important contribution of the strategic planning and LTP process. Examples of strategic alternatives include alternative distribution channels, entering new product or geographic markets, acquisitions, or exiting a business. Other scenarios that are often explored are competitive threats, disruptive technologies, or flexing broad economic assumptions. The LTP model must be flexible enough to develop these alternative scenarios efficiently.

Projecting Key Performance Drivers

This section briefly covers techniques for projecting key areas of financial performance. These will be illustrated with two models in this chapter. Of course, any model must be tailored to the specific situation of each organization. Additional models and best practices are included in Part V, "Planning and Analysis for Critical Business and Value Drivers."

Revenue   Revenue is typically the most important driver and generally the most difficult to predict, both in the long term and in the short term. Accordingly, it warrants the most thought and attention. The drivers that are most important will vary greatly from company to company and may vary over time. In some cases, key revenue drivers will be product related and must consider new product introductions and product life cycles. This would certainly be important for Apple and other technology device providers. Other drivers may include market and competitive forces, foreign currency rates, and macroeconomic trends. Table 21.1 focuses on product drivers and market and competitive share.

Gross Margins   Gross margins are impacted by several factors, including product mix, margins on new products, production and commodity costs, transportation costs, and currency. In our example in Table 21.1, the gross margin projection is incorporated into the revenue plan.

Costs and Expenses   Projecting costs and expenses over several years presents some unique challenges. Many organizations start with a simple extrapolation of historical cost trends. For some types of expenses this a practical approach. However, for significant expenses, or those subject to high volatility, this approach is too simplistic, especially over a term of three to five years. Some expenses will vary with revenue levels. Others are driven by projects or investments that are incurred long before the associated revenue. Many others are highly volatile, including healthcare, commodity prices, and staffing. For these volatile and unpredictable costs, different scenarios or sensitivity analysis should be incorporated into the plan. They also should be reviewed for potential mitigating actions over the course of the plan. Table 21.2 is an illustration of LRP costs and expenses.

Capital Requirements   In developing LTPs, we must consider two types of capital requirements: (1) working capital and (2) property, plant, and equipment.

Working Capital. Working capital requirements can be a significant cash requirement, especially for enterprises experiencing rapid growth. These can easily be estimated in the future by using key metrics such as days sales outstanding (DSO) and inventory turns to project receivable and inventory balances in the future. However, these metrics may change in the future owing to changes in distribution channels, markets, manufacturing, and integration decisions.

Table 21.4, "Capsule Financial Summary," includes projected working capital based on historical measures for DSO, days sales of inventory (DSI), and accounts payable and accrued as a percentage of sales.

Property, Plant, and Equipment (PP&E). If significant, future estimates of PP&E should be based on the existing bases of assets and future capital requirements. Depreciation and accumulated depreciation should be based on the anticipated additions.

TABLE 21.1 **LTP: Revenue and margin projections.**

Revenue and Margins — LRP

	History			CY	Projections					CAGR		Assumptions/Notes
	2021	2022	2023	2024	2025	2026	2027	2028	2029	History	Future	
Sales Product 1200	500	495	485	475	469	450	430	420	400	−1.5%	−3.4%	Successful model slowly showing lower volume
Gross Margin	250	245	237.65	232.75	225.12	211.5	197.8	189	180			
%	50%	50%	49%	49%	48%	47%	46%	45%	45%			
Sales Product 1250	0	15	50	100	125	130	132	130	125		4.6%	Introduced 2022
Gross Margin	0	8.25	27.5	55	68.75	70.2	71.28	68.9	65			
%		55%	55%	55%	55%	54%	54%	53%	52%			
Sales Product 1300	300	250	200	150	100	20	0	0	0	−18.4%	−100.0%	Older model at tail end of product life cycle
Gross Margin	150	125	100	75	50	10	0	0	0			
%	50%	50%	50%	50%	50%	50%						
Sales Product 1400	50	52	48	47	53	58	62	66	70	−2.0%	8.3%	
Gross Margin	24	26	24	23.5	26.5	29	31	33	35			
%	48%	50%	50%	50%	50%	50%	50%	50%	50%			
Sales Product 2000	0	0	0	25	75	200	300	500	600	-	88.8%	Introduced 4th quarter of 2024
Gross Margin	0	0	0	12.5	37.5	80	120	200	240			
%				50%	50%	40%	40%	40%	40%			
Sales Total	850.0	812.0	783.0	797.0	822.0	858.0	924.0	1,116.0	1,195.0	−4.0%	8.4%	
Gross Margin	424.0	404.3	389.2	398.8	407.9	400.7	420.1	490.9	520.0			
%	50%	50%	50%	50%	50%	47%	45%	44%	44%			
Revenue Growth Y/Y ($M)	−10	−38.0	−29.0	14.0	25.0	36.0	66.0	192.0	79.0			
Revenue Growth Y/Y %	2%	−4.5%	−3.6%	1.8%	3.1%	4.4%	7.7%	20.8%	7.1%			

TABLE 21.1 (*Continued*)

		Revenue and Margins						LRP					
	History		CY		Projections					CAGR		Assumptions/Notes
	2021	2022	2023	2024	2025	2026	2027	2028	2029	History	Future	
Market Size and Share												
This Company	850.0	812.0	783.0	797.0	822.0	858.0	924.0	1,116.0	1,195.0	−4.0%	8.4%	
Competitor 1	50.0	50.0	50.0	50.0	50.0	50.0	50.0	50.0	50.0	0.0%	0.0%	
Competitor 2	500.0	600.0	700.0	800.0	900.0	950.0	1,050.0	1,125.0	1,250.0	18.3%	9.3%	
Competitor 3	145.0	159.5	175.5	193.0	200.0	220.0	242.0	266.2	292.8	10.0%	8.7%	
Competitor 4	200.0	175.0	150.0	100.0	75.0	50.0				−13.4%	−100.0%	
Total Market	1,745.0	1,796.5	1,858.5	1,940.0	2,047.0	2,128.0	2,266.0	2,557.2	2,787.8	3.2%	7.5%	
Market Share	48.7%	45.2%	42.1%	41.1%	40.2%	40.3%	40.8%	43.6%	42.9%			
Market Growth		51.5	62.0	81.5	107.0	81.0	138.0	291.2	230.6			
Market Growth Rate		3%	3%	4%	6%	4%	6%	13%	9%			
Our Share of Market Growth		−74%	−47%	17%	23%	44%	48%	66%	34%			

TABLE 21.2 **LTP operating expense projections.**

	Operating Expenses					LRP						
	History			CY	Projections					CAGR		Assumptions/Notes
	2021	2022	2023	2024	2025	2026	2027	2028	2029	History	Future	
Research and Development												
Base	75.0	79.5	84.3	89.3	94.7	100.4	106.4	112.8	119.5	6.0%	6.0%	
Incremental Project Expenses												
Product 1250	12.0	7.0	4.0									Competed 2023
Product 2000				10.0	40.0	20.0		12.0	17.0			Product development started 2024
All Other		5.0	7.0									
Total R&D	87.0	91.5	95.3	99.3	134.7	120.4	106.4	124.8	136.5	4.6%	6.6%	
Y/Y Growth ($m)	0.05	5%	4%	4%	36%	−11%	−12%	17%	9%			
% of Sales	10%	11%	12%	12%	16%	14%	12%	11%	11%			
Marketing												
Base	50.0	53.0	56.2	59.6	63.1	66.9	70.9	75.2	79.7	6.0%	6.0%	Launch costs based on product development
Product Launch 1250		12.0										
Product Launch 2000					5.0	22.0						
Product Launch Other			1.5						1.0			
Total Marketing	50.0	65.0	57.7	59.6	68.1	88.9	70.9	75.2	80.7	7.4%	6.3%	
Y/Y Growth ($M)	0.05	30%	−11%	3%	14%	31%	−20%	6%	7%			
% of Sales	6%	8%	7%	7%	8%	10%	8%	7%	7%			
Selling, General and Administrative												
Base	115.0	121.9	129.2	137.0	145.2	153.9	163.1	172.9	183.3	6.0%	6.0%	
Initiatives - Cyber Security Program	2.0			2.0		5.0	3.0	3.0	3.0			
Legal Settlement			12.0		12.0							
Consultant Strategic Plan				4.0								
IT New System	1.0	4.0										
Total SG&A	118.0	121.9	141.2	143.0	157.2	158.9	166.1	175.9	186.3	9.9%	5.4%	
Y/Y Growth ($M)	5%	4%	16%	1%	10%	1%	5%	6%	6%			
% of Sales	14%	15%	18%	18%	19%	19%	18%	16%	16%			
Total Operating Expenses	254.0	278.4	294.2	301.8	360.0	368.2	343.4	375.9	403.5	7.6%	6.0%	
% of Sales	29.9%	34.3%	37.6%	37.9%	43.8%	42.9%	37.2%	33.7%	33.8%			
Y/Y Growth ($m)		24.4	15.8	7.7	58.2	8.2	−24.7	32.4	27.7			
Y/Y Growth %		10%	6%	3%	19%	2%	−7%	9%	7%			

Most organizations have a base level of expenditures to support general business and replacement requirements. To this base level of capital expenditures, we must estimate any large expenditures to support strategic initiatives or other requirements, for example, manufacturing facilities to support new product introductions and also to expand manufacturing facilities.

Once the capital plan is developed, depreciation expense can be estimated using a model similar to Table 21.3.

Balance Sheet and Cash Flow   The LTP model should include Balance Sheet and cash flow projections. In addition to working capital and PP&E, other important Balance Sheet captions can be incorporated into the model. For many captions such as prepaids, other assets, or accruals, these can be estimated using the historical percentage to sales. Each should be examined for any unique driver that would warrant further analysis and thought.

After estimating these future asset and liability levels (and profit and loss), we can model the financing and capital requirements, and cash balances or shortages. Some strategic plans will result in self-financing scenarios, whereas others will require significant additional capital to fund future growth and investments. By developing an integrated model, we can estimate the cash generation or requirements of executing the plan. We can also project and evaluate any potential conflicts with existing financing restrictions or loan covenants.

Our simple model effectively projects cash flow, cash balances, and financing requirements in Table 21.4.

Returns and Value Creation   For most organizations, the overall objective is to create value for shareholders. It would be inappropriate to prepare a strategy and an LTP that do not estimate and evaluate the levels of returns (e.g., ROIC) and value creation (estimated share price or value of business). The weak results for ROIC and shareholder value in Table 21.4 would certainly provide cause for reevaluating this plan!

PRESENTATION OF LONG-TERM PROJECTIONS

The models used to develop projections of performance well into the future are likely to be complex. The results of the LTP model must be summarized and presented for effective communication and presentation. The best way to accomplish this is to prepare a well-designed presentation summary (see Figure 21.2) and integrate it directly into the LTP model. This will facilitate presenting the outcome of revisions and scenario analysis.

TABLE 21.3 LTP: Capital assets and depreciation.

Property, Plant, & Equipment Capital Requirements

Capital Expenditures		History			CY	Projections				
		2021	2022	2023	2024	2025	2026	2027	2028	2029
Prior		45.0								
General	2021	7.0								
General	2022		12.0							
General	2023			13.0						
General	2024				15.0					
Fabrication Plant New Product	2025					30.0				
General	2025					15.0				
General	2026						17.0			
Plant Expansion-Growth	2027							45.0		
General	2027							18.0		
General	2028								19.0	
General	2029									21.0
Total Capital Expenditures		7.0	12.0	13.0	15.0	45.0	17.0	63.0	19.0	21.0

Depreciation Expense*

		History			CY	Projections				
		2021	2022	2023	2024	2025	2026	2027	2028	2029
Prior		7	5	3	2					
General	2021	1.4	1.4	1.4	1.4	1.4				
General	2022		2.4	2.4	2.4	2.4	2.4			
General	2023			2.6	2.6	2.6	2.6	2.6		
General	2024				3.0	3.0	3.0	3.0	3.0	
Fabrication Plant New Product	2025					1.5	1.5	1.5	1.5	1.5
General	2025					3.0	3.0	3.0	3.0	3.0
General	2026						3.4	3.4	3.4	3.4
Plant Expansion-Growth	2027							2.3	2.3	2.3
General	2027							3.6	3.6	3.6
General	2028								3.8	3.8
General	2029									4.2
		8.4	8.8	9.4	11.4	13.9	15.9	19.4	20.6	21.8

* Assumes 5 year straight line depreciation, except for Fab Plant and Plant Expansion (20 years)

TABLE 21.3 *(Continued)*

Property, Plant & Equipment Recap	History			CY	Projections				
	2021	2022	2023	2024	2025	2026	2027	2028	2029
Property Plant and Equipment									
Beginning Balance	45.0	52.0	64.0	77.0	92.0	137.0	154.0	217.0	236.0
Capital Expenditures	7.0	12.0	13.0	15.0	45.0	17.0	63.0	19.0	21.0
Retirements									
Ending Balance	52.0	64.0	77.0	92.0	137.0	154.0	217.0	236.0	257.0
Accumulated Depreciation									
Beginning Balance	30.0	38.4	47.2	56.6	68.0	81.9	97.8	117.2	137.7
Depreciation	8.4	8.8	9.4	11.4	13.9	15.9	19.4	20.6	21.8
Retirements									
Ending Balance	38.4	47.2	56.6	68.0	81.9	97.8	117.2	137.7	159.5
PP&E, net of depreciation	13.6	16.8	20.4	24.0	55.1	56.2	99.9	98.3	97.6

TABLE 21.4 **LTP capsule financial summary.** 🔒

Capsule Financial Summary

| | 2021 | History | | CY | | | Projections | | | Historical | Future |
		2022	2023	2024	2025	2026	2027	2028	2029	CAGR	CAGR
Income Statement											
Sales	850.0	812.0	783.0	797.0	822.0	858.0	924.0	1,116.0	1,195.0	−2%	8%
Gross Margin	424.0	404.3	389.2	398.8	407.9	400.7	420.1	490.9	520.0		
%	50%	50%	50%	50%	50%	47%	45%	44%	44%		
Operating Expenses	254.0	278.4	294.2	301.8	360.0	368.2	343.4	375.9	403.5		
Income from Operations	170.0	125.9	95.0	96.9	47.9	32.5	76.6	115.0	116.5	6%	6%
%	20.0%	15.5%	12.1%	12.2%	5.8%	3.8%	8.3%	10.3%	9.7%		
Other Income (Loss)	1.0	−1.0	1.5	0.7	0.5	0.7	0.8	0.6	0.5		
Profit before Taxes	171.0	124.9	96.5	97.6	48.4	33.2	77.4	115.6	117.0		
Net Income	111.2	81.2	62.7	63.4	31.4	21.6	50.3	75.2	76.0		
%	13.1%	10.0%	8.0%	8.0%	3.8%	2.5%	5.4%	6.7%	6.4%		
Balance Sheet											
Cash	47.8	83.9	134.0	161.6	139.0	130.9	107.2	125.9	169.8		
Receivables	158.0	175.0	170.0	174.7	168.9	176.3	189.9	229.3	245.5		
Inventory	120.0	145.0	140.0	147.3	153.2	169.1	186.4	231.2	249.7		
Property, Plant, and Equipment	52.0	64.0	77.0	92.0	137.0	154.0	217.0	236.0	257.0		
Accumulated Depreciation	−38.4	−47.2	−56.6	−68.0	−81.9	−97.8	−117.2	−137.7	−159.5		
Other											
Total Assets	339.4	420.7	464.4	507.5	516.1	532.5	583.3	684.7	762.6		
Accounts Payable	125.0	132.0	141.0	119.6	98.6	103.0	110.9	133.9	143.4		
Accrued Liabilities	60.0	68.0	51.0	63.8	74.0	77.2	83.2	100.4	107.6		
Other	4.4										
Long-term Debt	0.0	0.0	0.0	0.0	0.0	0.0	0.0	0.0	0.0		
Other	0.0										
Capital	40.0	40.0	40.0	40.0	40.0	40.0	40.0	40.0	40.0		
Retained Earnings	110.0	180.7	232.4	284.2	303.5	312.4	349.3	410.4	471.6		
Total Liabilities and Equity	339.4	420.7	464.4	507.5	516.1	532.5	583.3	684.7	762.6		
Proof	0.0	0.0	0.0	0.0	0.0	0.0	0.0	0.0	0.0		
Operating Capital	88.6	120.0	118.0	138.7	149.5	165.3	182.2	226.2	244.3		

TABLE 2.4 **(Continued)**

Capsule Financial Summary

	History			CY	Projections					Historical CAGR	Future CAGR
	2021	2022	2023	2024	2025	2026	2027	2028	2029		
Cash Flow											
Net Income	111.2	81.2	62.7	63.4	31.4	21.6	50.3	75.2	76.0		
Add D&A	8.4	8.8	9.4	11.4	13.9	15.9	19.4	20.6	21.8		
Capital Expenditures	-7.0	-12.0	-13.0	-15.0	-45.0	-17.0	-63.0	-19.0	-21.0		
(Increase) Decrease in Operating Capital	-5.0	-31.4	2.0	-20.7	-10.8	-15.8	-16.9	-44.0	-18.1		
Operating Cash Flow	107.6	46.6	61.1	39.2	-10.4	4.7	-10.3	32.8	58.7		
Debt Borrowings (Payments)											
Dividends	-10.0	-10.5	-11.0	-11.6	-12.2	-12.8	-13.4	-14.1	-14.8		
Cash Flow	97.6	36.1	50.1	27.6	-22.6	-8.1	-23.7	18.7	43.9		
Key Metrics											
Y/Y Revenue Growth	29.9%	-4%	-4%	2%	3%	4%	8%	21%	7%		
Operating Expense % of Sales		34.3%	37.6%	37.9%	43.8%	42.9%	37.2%	33.7%	33.8%		
Tax Rate	35%	35%	35%	35%	35%	35%	35%	35%	35%		
Days Sales Outstanding	68	79	79	80	75	75	75	75	75		
Days Sales Inventory	103	130	130	135	135	135	135	135	135		
Accounts Payable % Sales	14.7%	16.3%	18.0%	15.0%	12.0%	12.0%	12.0%	12.0%	12.0%		
Accrued Expenses % Sales	7.1%	8.4%	11.0%	8.0%	9.0%	9.0%	9.0%	9.0%	9.0%		
Debt to Total Capital	0	0	0	0	0	0	0	0	0		
Return on Assets	32.7%	19.3%	13.5%	12.5%	6.1%	4.1%	8.6%	11.0%	10.0%		
Return on Equity	74.1%	36.8%	23.0%	19.6%	9.2%	6.1%	12.9%	16.7%	14.9%		
Return on Invested Capital	73.7%	37.1%	22.7%	19.4%	9.1%	6.0%	12.8%	16.6%	14.8%		
Estimated Enterprise Value (Multiple of Revenue)	1,275.0	1,218.0	1,174.5	1,195.5	1,233.0	1,287.0	1,386.0	1,674.0	1,792.5		1.5
Estimated Value of Equity	1275.0	1218.0	1174.5	1195.5	1233.0	1287.0	1386.0	1674.0	1792.5		
Growth (Decrease) in Value		-57.0	-43.5	21.0	37.5	54.0	99.0	288.0	118.5		

FIGURE 21.2 **LTP presentation summary.**

Critical Assumptions

Significant growth over horizon of plan, primarily due to introduction of Model 2000.

Gross margins decline from 50% to 44% due to lower margins on Model 2000.

Strong balance sheet and cash flow maintained over plan horizon.

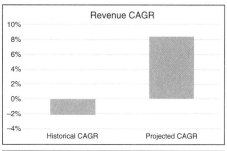

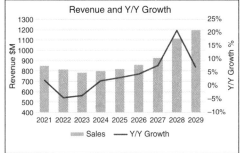

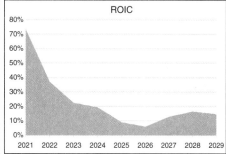

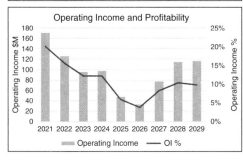

Strategic Model for Tumultuous Industries

Many organizations are facing significant changes in their market or disruptive forces such as technology or nontraditional competitors. Such is the fate of traditional brick-and-mortar retailers as ecommerce retailers continue to drastically cut into their market share.

In the past, a projections model for a retailer would focus on maintaining/ growing sales for existing stores, merchandise mix, and opening new stores. Table 21.5 is a high-level summary of the key drivers for Lienna's Fashion Outlet stores. Revenue growth would be driven by opening new stores and increasing sales per store.

Now these retailers are faced with declining sales in their stores and are forced to offer more promotions and discounts to retain customers. Some are attempting to change the product offerings and store experience to stem the tide. Many traditional retailers are also attempting to build on-line

TABLE 21.5 **Traditional retail model.** 🖲

Existing Stores		2018	2019	2020	2021	2022	2023	2024	2025
		Retailer Traditional Model							
		Lienna's Fashion Outlet							
# of Stores		865	911	957	1008	1064	1120	1181	1242
Average Revenue per Store ($M)		12.5	12.6	12.7	12.8	12.9	12.9	12.9	12.9
Revenue Existing Stores		10,813	11,479	12,154	12,902	13,726	14,448	15,235	16,022
Total Store Margin		2,163	2,296	2,431	2,580	2,745	2,890	3,047	3,204
%		20.0%	20.0%	20.0%	20.0%	20.0%	20.0%	20.0%	20.0%
Store Closings		4	4	4	4	4	4	4	4
New Store Openings									
# of Stores		50	50	55	60	60	65	65	70
1st Year Revenue per Store ($m)		4.0	4.0	4.0	4.0	4.0	4.0	4.0	4.0
Revenue from New Stores		200.0	200.0	220.0	240.0	240.0	260.0	260.0	280.0
Capital Investments									
Capital Investment New Store	1.2	60.0	60.0	66.0	72.0	72.0	78.0	78.0	84.0
Capital Investment Store Refurb*	0.5	43.3	45.6	47.9	50.4	53.2	56.0	59.1	62.1
Total Capital Investment Stores		103.3	105.6	113.9	122.4	125.2	134.0	137.1	146.1
* Remodel/Update 10 % of stores per year									
Total Store Operations									
# of Stores, end of year		915	961	1012	1068	1124	1185	1246	1312
Total Revenue		11,013	11,679	12,374	13,142	13,966	14,708	15,495	16,302
Store Margins		2,163	2,296	2,431	2,580	2,745	2,890	3,047	3,204
%		20%	20%	20%	20%	20%	20%	20%	20%
Capital Investments		103.3	105.6	113.9	122.4	125.2	134.0	137.1	146.1
Y/Y Growth			6.0%	6.0%	6.2%	6.3%	5.3%	5.4%	5.2%

businesses to participate directly in this new retail segment. Consider how these dynamics would be represented in a long-term projections model (Table 21.6).

This simple model allows us to consider the dynamics of the new reality for retailers, including:

❑ Lower sales per store.

❑ Reduce rate of new store openings.

❑ Store closings.

❑ Investments in existing stores to change experience and format.

❑ Investments in an ecommerce platform, including technology, distribution, and other infrastructure.

Figure 21.3 provides a comparison of the traditional retail environment to the new reality. This comparison of the traditional versus the new reality retail environment clearly demonstrates the challenge faced by brick-and-mortar retailers, and the significant change in their business models going forward.

TABLE 21.6 **New reality for established retailers.**

The New Reality for Retailers
Lienna's Fashion Outlet

Existing Stores		2018	2019	2020	2021	2022	2023	2024	2025
# of Stores		865	911	957	987	967	932	904	900
Average Revenue per Store ($M)		12.5	12.6	12	11	10.5	10.5	10	9
Revenue Existing Stores		10,813	11,479	11,484	10,857	10,154	9,786	9,040	8,100
Total Store Margin		2,163	2,296	2,297	2,171	2,031	1,957	1,808	1,620
%		20.0%	20.0%	20.0%	20.0%	20.0%	20.0%	20.0%	20.0%
Store Closings		4	4	10	25	40	40	16	16
New Store Openings									
# of Stores		50	50	40	5	5	12	12	12
1st Year revenue per store ($m)		4.0	4.0	4.0	4.0	4.0	4.0	4.0	4.0
Revenue from New Stores		200.00	200.00	160.00	20.00	20.00	48.00	48.00	48.00
Capital Investments									
Capital Investment new store	1.2	60.0	60.0	48.0	6.0	6.0	14.4	14.4	14.4
Capital Investment Store refurb*	0.5	43.3	45.6	95.7	98.7	96.7	93.2	90.4	90.0
Total Capital Investment Stores		103.3	105.6	143.7	104.7	102.7	107.6	104.8	104.4
* Remodel/Update 20 % of stores per year									
Total Store Operations									
# of Stores, end of year		915	961	997	992	972	944	916	912
Total Revenue		11,013	11,679	11,644	10,877	10,174	9,834	9,088	8,148
Store Margins		2,163	2,296	2,297	2,171	2,031	1,957	1,808	1,620
%		20%	20%	20%	20%	20%	20%	20%	20%
Capital Investments		103.3	105.6	143.7	104.7	102.7	107.6	104.8	104.4
Y/Y Growth			6.0%	−0.3%	−6.6%	−6.5%	−3.3%	−7.6%	−10.3%
Same store sales growth									
E-Commerce									
Invest in Ecommerce Platform				100					
Sales				50.0	250.0	500.0	1,000.0	1,700.0	2,500.0
Margin	0.15			7.5	37.5	75.0	150.0	255.0	375.0
%				15%	15%	15%	15%	15%	15%
Total Retail Operations									
Revenue		11,013	11,679	11,694	11,127	10,674	10,834	10,788	10,648
Margins		2,163	2,296	2,304	2,209	2,106	2,107	2,063	1,995
%		20%	20%	20%	20%	20%	19%	19%	19%
Y/Y Growth			6.0%	0.1%	−4.8%	−4.1%	1.5%	−0.4%	−1.3%
Capital Investment		103.25	105.55	243.70	104.70	102.70	107.60	104.80	104.40

FIGURE 21.3 **Comparison of traditional versus new reality retail.**

Lienna's Fashion Outlet

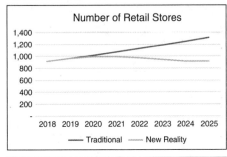

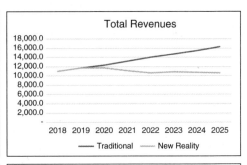

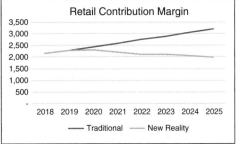

SUMMARY

LTPs are utilized to evaluate a wide range of business decisions. The longer horizon introduces more risk and greater uncertainty in the projections. The models need to focus on critical assumptions and performance drivers and allow the user to flex these assumptions and easily estimate performance under various scenarios. Due to uncertainty and rate of change, it is imperative that underling drivers, assumptions, and events be identified and monitored.

LTPs should present a comprehensive view of performance, extending beyond the Income Statement to investment requirements, cash flow, returns, and valuation.

#### Part Five

Planning and Analysis
for Critical Business and
Value Drivers

22

Revenue and
Gross Margins

Revenue growth is one of the most important drivers in building and sustaining shareholder value. Understanding the drivers of revenue growth, estimating future revenue levels, and achieving sustainable growth rates are some of the most difficult challenges that managers face. The objective of this chapter is to enable more discipline and analysis in predicting, driving, and evaluating future revenue projections.

Gross margins are an important indicator of efficiency and competitive position. Product and service pricing, discounting, new product introductions, and competitor challenges all impact gross margins. Design effectiveness, and material, manufacturing, and supply chain effectiveness impact the costs of products or services and therefore gross margins.

REVENUE GROWTH: KEY DRIVERS

Figure 22.1 presents a summary of key drivers of revenue growth. Revenue growth arises from two sources: growth resulting from internal development activities and growth resulting from acquisitions. Growth resulting from internal activities is often referred to as "organic growth." Growth resulting from acquisitions will have very different drivers and economic characteristics from organic growth. The economics of acquired growth will be covered in detail in Chapter 31, "Analysis of Mergers and Acquisitions." We will focus on organic growth for the remainder of this chapter. Organic growth may result from growth in the overall size of the market, by gaining share from competitors within the market, or by entering new markets.

FIGURE 22.1 **Drill-down illustration: Revenue growth drivers.**

Link Value & Value Drivers to Business Processes & Activities

Drill Down: Revenue Growth

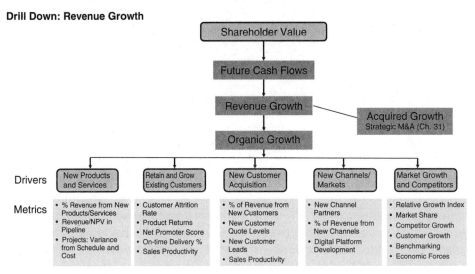

Market

Whether chosen by luck or as a result of great strategic thinking, the market that a company serves will be a key driver in determining potential revenue growth. Some markets are mature and will grow at slow rates. Others are driven by external forces or developments that will result in high growth rates for a number of years. In markets with high growth rates, even marginal competitors may thrive as all market participants are raised by the rising tide.

Competitive Position

Within a market, the competitive environment and the competitive position of a particular company will determine its ability to grow by increasing market share. A number of factors will determine a company's competitive position, including: innovation, intellectual property customer satisfaction and service, cost and pricing, and the number and size of competitors. Analysis of competitive position should be performed from a customer's perspective. What are the key decision criteria that drive a customer's purchase evaluation and decision? Analysis of competitive position is a relative concept; it is the performance of a company on key factors relative to another firm's offering similar products or services.

   Innovation. Innovation can be a leading source of competitive position and should be considered in broad terms and not simply limited to product innovation. In addition to product innovation, firms such as Dell and Amazon have differentiated themselves by radically changing the customer fulfillment and supply chain processes to redefine the business model within an industry. Innovations in marketing or packaging can also produce a significant advantage, leading to revenue gains. Innovation was covered in more detail in Chapter 14.

Customer Satisfaction. Customer satisfaction plays a vital role in revenue growth in three ways. First, customer satisfaction will always be a key factor in retaining existing customers. Second, customers that are satisfied with a supplier's performance are likely to offer additional opportunities to that supplier. Third, a strong reputation for customer satisfaction and underlying performance will also lead to opportunities with new customers. Most markets are "small worlds" with key customer personnel changing companies. A satisfied customer will likely pull a high-performing company along with them.

Customer Service. Many companies compete by providing outstanding service beyond the traditional customer satisfaction areas such as delivery and quality performance. Working with customers to solve their problems and participating in joint development programs are both examples of investments that build long-term customer loyalty.

Cost or Pricing Advantages. Price is nearly always a key factor in a customer's procurement decision. The price of a product or service will be driven by the cost of the product, profit targets, and market forces.

The cost of a product or service includes direct and indirect costs. Prices are often set by marking up or adding a profit margin to the cost to achieve a targeted level of profitability or return on invested capital (ROIC). The actual price will have to be set in the context of market forces, including price-performance comparisons to competitor offerings.

Suppliers can attain a cost advantage in a number of ways, including achieving economies of scale, process efficiencies, or improvements in quality. Most sophisticated customers look at the total life cycle cost of a procurement decision, of which the product selling price is one component. Other elements of life cycle cost may include installation and training, service, maintenance, and operating and disposal costs. Suppliers that can demonstrate a lower life cycle cost can achieve an advantage over competitors, even if the product price component is more expensive.

Competitor Attributes and Actions. The performance of competitors in the areas that are important to customers will have big impact on a company's ability to grow or even maintain sales. It is not meaningful to project or evaluate revenue projections without a view of competitor intentions, tendencies, and actions. What is the competitor's strategy? How will its financial performance impact its performance in the market? If the competitor has other related businesses, how does that impact its ability to serve this market? What new product or service will the competitor introduce? How will the competitor respond to the introduction of a new product? Do competitors define the market differently? What new competitors may enter the market?

Many revenue projections are prepared without fully considering the answer to these questions. Revenue from new products is assumed to gain market share, without reflecting the competitor response. Again, the value in planning is not the precise quantitative values on the spreadsheet, but rather in the evolution in thinking as a result of the planning process.

Entering New Channels or Markets   Many companies have been successful at growing over extended periods of time. In addition to growing with their primary market and gaining share within that market, companies have found ways to expand the size of the market they serve by moving into adjacent markets. Amazon, for example, leveraged its competencies in distribution and supply chain management to expand its market from books to just about everything (and then leveraging IT competencies to start Amazon Web Services)!

PROJECTING AND TESTING FUTURE REVENUE LEVELS

Since revenue growth is an important driver of economic value, it is critical for managers and investors to fully identify, understand, and evaluate the factors impacting future revenues. Despite the relative importance of revenue compared to other drivers, it often suffers from less disciplined analytical approaches than other drivers such as cost management and operating efficiency. This is due, in part, to the complexity of the revenue drivers and to the significant impact of external forces such as customers, competitors, and economic factors. Managers should develop and improve tools and practices for projecting future revenues and monitor leading indicators of revenue levels. Best practices include:

- ❏ Improve revenue forecasting process.
- ❏ Prepare multiple views of revenue detail.
- ❏ Measure forecast effectiveness.
- ❏ Deal effectively with special issues.

Improve Revenue Forecasting Process
Forecasting. In addition to providing a projection of future performance for planning, budgeting, and investor communication, the revenue forecast typically drives staffing, procurement, and manufacturing schedules and activities. Forecasting revenue is an extremely important activity within all enterprises. Forecasting future business levels is also generally a significant challenge!

Predicting the future is inherently difficult. Having said that, there are a number of things managers can do to improve the forecasting process. First, it is of vital importance that all managers understand the importance of forecasting as a business activity. It impacts customer satisfaction and service levels, costs and expenses, pricing, inventories, and investor confidence to name a few. Businesses that operate in a predictable and consistent level of operating performance will have lower perceived risk, leading to a lower cost of capital. Second, huge gains can be made by measuring forecast effectiveness and assigning responsibility and accountability to appropriate managers. Third, there are a number of techniques that can be applied to improve the effectiveness of forecasts, such as using ranges of expected performance, identifying significant risks and upsides, and developing contingency plans. However, because forecasting involves an attempt to predict the future, it will always be an imperfect activity.

Forecast Philosophy and Human Behavior. The starting point in improving forecasting is to recognize tendencies in human behavior. Most managers are optimistic. They are positive thinkers. They are under pressure to achieve higher levels of sales and profits. They are reluctant to throw in the towel by lowering performance targets. They recognize that decreasing the revenue outlook may result in a decrease in value and necessitate cost and staff reductions or even the loss of their job. Managers who are ultimately responsible for the projections, in most cases the CEO and CFO, must recognize these soft factors and their impact on projections. They must communicate and reinforce the need for realistic and achievable forecasts.

Base Forecast. Many companies have improved their ability to project revenues by using multiple scenarios. A base forecast is developed, which is often defined as the most probable outcome. Managers find it helpful to define an intended confidence level for the base forecast. Is it a 50/50 plan or 80/20? The former would indicate that there is as much chance of exceeding the forecast as falling short. The latter confidence level implies a greater level of confidence in achieving the forecast: there is an 80% chance of meeting or exceeding the forecast. A practical way of defining this would be that 8 out of 10 forecasts would be met or exceeded.

Identify, Document, and Monitor Key Assumptions. As with any projection, it is important to identify and document key assumptions that support the revenue forecast. Projecting revenues is typically the most difficult element of business planning and involves many assumptions, including factors external to the organization. Key assumptions for revenue projections typically include:

- Market size and growth rate.
- Pricing.
- Product mix.
- Geographic mix.
- Competitor actions/reactions.
- New product introductions.
- Product life cycle of existing products.
- Macroeconomic factors, including inflation, interest rates, GDP growth, and other.
- Geopolitical forces, including trade policies, conflicts, and so on.

After identifying and documenting these key assumptions supporting revenue projections, these factors must be monitored. Any changes in assumptions must be identified and the potential impact on sales must be quantified and addressed. Critical assumptions should be included on the performance dashboard for revenue growth as illustrated later in this chapter.

Upsides and Downsides. After planning the base case, upside and downside events can be identified. These can be economic factors, competitor actions, or acceleration or delays in new product introductions. For each possible event, managers should identify how they will monitor the possible event and the probability of the event occurring during the plan horizon. In most cases, upside and downside events with high probabilities should be built into the base forecast.

Development of Aggressive and Conservative Forecast Scenarios. Using the base case scenario and potential upside and downside events, managers can prepare an aggressive scenario and a conservative scenario. The aggressive scenario can be achieved if some or all of the upside events materialize, for example, if product adoption rates exceed the estimates incorporated into the base case. The conservative scenario contemplates selected downside events. What actions will we take if it becomes apparent that we are trending toward either the aggressive or the conservative scenarios? If trending to the aggressive scenario, do we need to accelerate production, hiring, and other investments? If trending to the downside scenarios, do we need to reduce or delay investments or hiring? Pedal harder to close the gap?

Prepare Multiple Views of Revenue Detail

Key dynamics of revenue projections can be identified by reviewing trend schedules of revenue from various perspectives. Table 22.1 is a sample summary of revenue by product. This level of detail identifies contributions from key products and provides visibility into dynamics such as product introduction and life cycles. Other views may be sales by region or geography, customers, and end-use market.

Another insightful analysis is to evaluate the projections in light of recent performance and comparisons to the plan and to prior year results. Table 22.2 compares year to date (YTD) actual and rest of year (ROY) projected performance to last year and the plan. Since it is comparing the same periods, seasonality is accounted for in the analysis. This forecast needs some explaining! On a year-to-date basis, revenues are 99% of last year and 92% of plan. However, the forecast revenue for the remainder of the year is 113% of last year and 107% of plan. Coincidentally, the forecast projects that the total year plan will be achieved. There may be some very good reasons for this inconsistency. I sure would like to hear and evaluate them!

TABLE 22.1 **Revenue planning worksheet: Product detail.**

Revenue Planning Illustration

	Actual		Projected		
Existing Products	**2023**	**2024**	**2025**	**2026**	**2027**
1	100	90	80	60	50
2	100	100	100	100	100
3	50	40	20	10	0
4	30	60	70	90	110
Subtotal	280	290	270	260	260
New Product Pipeline					
5			20	35	60
6			5	20	35
7				20	45
8					
Subtotal	0	0	25	75	140
Total Sales Projection	280	290	295	335	400
Year over Year Growth		3.6%	1.7%	13.6%	19.4%
CAGR 2023: 2027P					9.3%

TABLE 22.2 **Forecast evaluation worksheet.**

Forecast Evaluation Worksheet

Revenue ($m)	YTD			ROY			Year		
		Last			Last			Last	
	Actual	**Year**	**Plan**	**Forecast**	**Year**	**Plan**	**Forecast**	**Year**	**Plan**
Product 1	1,175	1,208	1,300	1,525	1,325	1,400	2,700	2,533	2,700
Product 2	950	985	1,100	1,350	1,102	1,200	2,300	2,087	2,300
Product 3	1,250	1,310	1,400	1,650	1,433	1,500	2,900	2,743	2,900
Product 4	850	825	900	1,000	879	950	1,850	1,704	1,850
Product 5	733	715	750	800	775	800	1,533	1,490	1,550
Product 6	1,650	1,612	1,700	1,860	1,725	1,800	3,510	3,337	3,500
Total	6,608	6,655	7,150	8,185	7,239	7,650	14,793	13,894	14,800

Revenue %	YTD		ROY		Year	
	Last		Last		Last	
	Year	**Plan**	**Year**	**Plan**	**Year**	**Plan**
Product 1	97%	90%	115%	109%	107%	100%
Product 2	96%	86%	123%	113%	110%	100%
Product 3	95%	89%	115%	110%	106%	100%
Product 4	103%	94%	114%	105%	109%	100%
Product 5	103%	98%	103%	100%	103%	99%
Product 6	102%	97%	108%	103%	105%	100%
Total	99%	92%	113%	107%	106%	100%

The graphic presentation in Figure 22.2 vividly portrays the inconsistency between actual year-to-date performance relative to plan and last year, compared to projections for the remainder of the year.

FIGURE 22.2 **Revenue variance.**

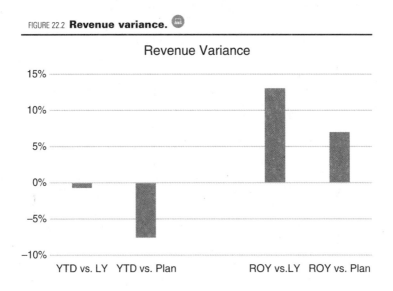

Revenue Change Analysis. A useful way to evaluate revenue projections is to compare them to the prior year and identify significant changes. Each source of significant change can be evaluated and tested. There is a tendency to project future revenues by identifying future sources of revenue growth and adding these increments to existing revenue levels. For example, additional revenues may result from new product introductions or geographic expansion. It is also important to identify factors that will decrease revenues. For example, many industries will experience decreases in average selling prices (ASPs) over time. In addition, all products are subject to life cycles with the eventuality of declining sales levels at some point. Figure 22.3 provides a good visual summary of significant changes in sales from 2023 to 2024.

FIGURE 22.3 **Revenue change analysis.**

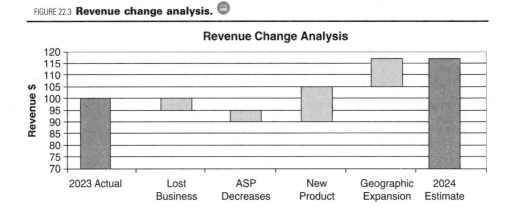

Market Size and Share Summary. Another view that is useful for evaluating revenue projections is to consider them in the context of the overall market size and growth, and market share. Table 22.3 presents the market for Steady Co. For each year, the size of the market is estimated and the growth rate is provided. Sales for each competitor are also estimated, forcing a consideration of competitive dynamics and identification of share gains. In this case, we see that Steady Co.'s 8% growth projected for each year is higher than the market growth. Who will the company take market share from? Why? Is 8% growth each year possible? Is it consistent with the real-life market dynamics such as product introductions and life cycles, economic factors, and competitive factors?

TABLE 22.3 **Market size and share analysis.**

				Market Size and Share Analysis						CAGR
	2017	**2018**	**2019**	**2020**	**2021**	**2022**	**2023**	**2024**	**2025**	**2017–2025**
Market Size	1500	1550	1600	1650	1710	1770	1825	1900	1975	3.5%
Growth rate	4.0%	3.3%	3.2%	3.1%	3.6%	3.5%	3.1%	4.1%	3.9%	
Sales										
BigandSlo Co.	700	705	710	712	705	700	680	660	640	−1.1%
Complex Co.	390	400	420	430	450	475	480	500	510	3.4%
Steady Co.	100	108	117	126	136	147	159	171	185	8.0%
Fast Co.	10	30	50	100	150	200	250	300	370	57.0%
Other	300	307	303	282	269	248	256	269	270	−1.3%
Total	1500	1550	1600	1650	1710	1770	1825	1900	1975	3.5%
Market Share										
BigandSlo Co.	46.7%	45.5%	44.4%	43.2%	41.2%	39.5%	37.3%	34.7%	32.4%	
Complex Co.	26.0%	25.8%	26.3%	26.1%	26.3%	26.8%	26.3%	26.3%	25.8%	
Steady Co.	6.7%	7.0%	7.3%	7.6%	8.0%	8.3%	8.7%	9.0%	9.4%	
Fast Co.	0.7%	1.9%	3.1%	6.1%	8.8%	11.3%	13.7%	15.8%	18.7%	
Other	20.0%	19.8%	18.9%	17.1%	15.7%	14.0%	14.0%	14.2%	13.7%	
Total	100%	100%	100%	100%	100%	100%	100%	100%	100%	
Growth Rate										
BigandSlo Co.		0.7%	0.7%	0.3%	−1.0%	−0.7%	−2.9%	−2.9%	−3.0%	
Complex Co.		2.6%	5.0%	2.4%	4.7%	5.6%	1.1%	4.2%	2.0%	
Steady Co.		8.0%	8.0%	8.0%	8.0%	8.0%	8.0%	8.0%	8.0%	
Fast Co.		200.0%	66.7%	100.0%	50.0%	33.3%	25.0%	20.0%	23.3%	
Other		2.3%	−1.3%	−6.9%	−4.6%	−7.8%	3.2%	5.1%	0.4%	
Total		3.3%	3.2%	3.1%	3.6%	3.5%	3.1%	4.1%	3.9%	

Measuring Forecast Effectiveness A very effective way to improve the forecast effectiveness is to monitor and track actual performance against the forecasts. I prefer not to call this forecast accuracy since forecasting future performance is inherently inaccurate. Table 22.4 presents the changes made to each quarterly projection over the course of 12 months. It is very effective in identifying biases and forecast gamesmanship. In this example, the analysis surfaces a number of concerns and questions. Note that the actual revenue achieved for each quarter is consistently under the forecast developed at the beginning of that quarter. In addition, shortfalls in one quarter are pushed out into subsequent quarters. However, the team does seem to be able to forecast revenues within one month of the quarter end.

Figure 22.4 tracks the evolution of the total year forecast over a 12-month period. Note that the forecast for the year was not decreased until two quarterly shortfalls were posted.

TABLE 22.4 **Revenue forecast Progression.**

Revenue Forecast Progression

Month Forecast Submitted:	Q1	Q2	Q3	Q4	Year
January	7,500	8,000	8,700	9,200	33,400
February	7,200	8,300	8,700	9,200	33,400
March	7,000	8,500	8,700	9,200	33,400
April	7,045	8,400	8,800	9,200	33,445
May		8,400	8,800	9,200	33,445
June		8,000	9,200	9,200	33,445
July		7,076	9,200	9,200	32,521
August			9,100	9,200	32,421
September			8,700	9,600	32,421
October			8,725	9,600	32,446
November				9,600	32,446
December				9,200	32,046
January (Final)				9,250	32,096
Variance, from beginning of quarter ($)	(455)	(1,324)	(475)	(350)	(1,304)
Variance, from beginning of quarter (%)	−6.1%	−15.8%	−5.2%	−3.6%	−4.1%

FIGURE 22.4 **Forecast progression analysis.**

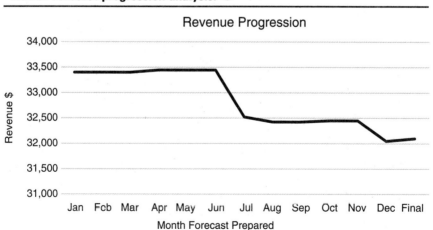

Artificial Intelligence   In recent years, many organizations have started to employ artificial intelligence (AI) to generate or assist in the development of revenue projections. The use of AI was introduced in Chapter 12, "Leveraging and Promoting Technology Investments," and Chapter 19, "Business Projections and Plans." As discussed earlier in this chapter, the development of revenue projections is the most important and complex part of financial planning. One of the strongest applications for AI in finance is in the development of revenue projections.

AI has the potential to automate many of the techniques presented in this book, including trend analysis and extrapolation, regression analysis, expected value, and Monte Carlo simulations. By leveraging technology to apply statistical and other analysis to large data sets, AI can identify patterns, relationships, and trends that may be undetectable by human review. These findings can then be used to project future revenues.

Most companies currently use AI to autogenerate or pre-fill projections templates to develop preliminary versions, subject to review and adjustment by humans. For example, an AI-generated revenue projection likely will not reflect a bankruptcy of a major customer, an economic or geopolitical event, or a recent competitor action.

AI may have more utility in certain businesses and less in others. Some businesses, such as those with a small number of large transactions, may not benefit as greatly as those with high volume transactions.

At the present time, the AI-generated projections are generally used as one version. This version can be compared to the traditional projections developed by human-generated processes to identify reasons for differences inform. AI-generated projections must not be a black box. They should be generally understood by executives and FP&A professionals. Critical assumptions should be presented and the projections should be supported by the key drives impacting revenues.

Requirements for effective use of AI:

Data availability. In order to be effective, AI must have access to relevant data from transaction and other enterprise systems, for example, enterprise (ERP) and customer relationship management (CRM) systems. The data must be structured and available to the software applying AI.

Quality of data. AI will add value by processing and analyzing large volumes of data. If the data contains errors, the output of AI will be "garbage" (as in "garbage in-garbage out").

AI technology. The organization must deploy data management and analytical tools to effectively use AI.

Understanding and competency in data science. The organization must have competencies in data acquisition, structure, and analysis as well as decision sciences and statistics.

The use of AI in developing revenue projections is in early stages. As executives and managers adopt and invest in data and AI tools, their utility and effectiveness will increase exponentially. Financial managers must stay abreast of new developments and tools in applying AI to improve revenue projections.

Additional Tools for Projecting Revenue   There are additional tools that can be effectively utilized in developing and evaluating revenue projections. These topics are covered in several other chapters, principally in Part IV, "Business Projections and Plans," and in Chapter 29, "Capital Investment Decisions—Advanced Topics."

Special Issues   There are a number of special circumstances that present challenges in developing and evaluating revenue projections. These include sales projections for new products, chunky or lumpy businesses with uneven sales patterns, and large programs.

Sales Projections for New Products. The development and introduction of new products are always a factor in growing or maintaining sales. Revenue plans for new products must be directly linked to new product development schedules. These schedules must be monitored closely and any changes in the development timeline must be considered in the related revenue projections. A delay in the product schedule will almost certainly delay introduction and the revenue ramp. Product introduction plans must be broad, expanding beyond product development to incorporate key marketing and customer activities. Critical assumptions should be reviewed as well. Any changes in these underlying assumptions should be tested to support revenue plans and even project viability. Examples include changes in key customer performance, economic conditions, and competitor actions.

Chunky and Lumpy Businesses. Some businesses are characterized by large orders resulting in lumpy business patterns from the presence or absence of these orders. These chunks wreak havoc in trend analysis and short-term projections. Depending on the cost structure and degree of operating leverage, these swings in revenue can result in extremely large fluctuations in profits. Care must be taken in setting expense levels in these situations. It may be appropriate to set expectations and expense levels for a base level of revenue and consider these lumps as upsides. Communicating with investors and other stakeholders about the business variability and disclosing the inclusion of lumpy business are essential to avoid significant fluctuations in the company's valuation and loss of management credibility.

Large Programs and Procurements. In many industries, large procurements, programs, or long-term contracts are awarded periodically, for example, every three years. Revenue changes in these situations are often binary and significant: if the contract is awarded to your firm, significant sales growth will be achieved for the contract period. If unsuccessful, your firm loses the opportunity to obtain that business for that contract period. If a firm loses that business at the end of the contract period, there is a significant decrease to sales. This presents a number of management, financial planning, and stakeholder communication issues.

When pursuing a large procurement opportunity, it is useful to prepare a base forecast without the inclusion of the large procurement and prepare an upside forecast reflecting the award. If a company's existing contracts are up for grabs, consideration should be given to a downside scenario, reflecting conditions if the contract is lost. Investors should have visibility into the presence and expiration dates of significant contracts.

KEY PERFORMANCE MEASURES: REVENUE GROWTH

A number of key performance measures can provide insight into historical trends and future revenue potential.

Sales Growth: Sequential and Year over Year

A critical measure of business performance is simply to measure the rate of growth in sales from one period to another. Table 22.5 illustrates a typical presentation of sales growth rates. Two different measures are frequently used. The first is simply to compute the growth from the previous year. The second measure computes sequential growth rates, that is, from one quarter to another. The year-over-year measure is more relevant for organizations with seasonal revenue patterns.

TABLE 22.5 **Quarterly sales trend.**

$m	Quarterly Sales Trend									
	2023					2024				
	Q1	Q2	Q3	Q4	Year	Q1	Q2	Q3	Q4	Year
Sales	62	64	60	75	261	65	70	58	82	275
Year-over-Year Growth	5.1%	6.7%	11.1%	8.7%	7.9%	4.8%	9.4%	-3.3%	9.3%	5.4%
Sequential Growth	−10.1%	3.2%	−6.3%	25.0%		−13.3%	7.7%	−17.1%	41.4%	

While these growth rate measures are important top-level performance measures, they are of limited usefulness without additional insight and analysis. Some managers and investors will extrapolate past sales growth rates into the future. This works in certain circumstances for a period of time; however, it does not take into consideration the underlying dynamics that will drive future revenues. These factors include market forces, competitive position, innovation, and customer satisfaction discussed earlier in this chapter.

Customer/Competitor Growth Index

The evaluation of a company's performance is best done in the context of competitors, customers, and overall market performance. This is very important in assessing a company's performance in growing sales. For example, if Steady Co. grew 8% last year, the market grew by 3%, and one of the competitors grew 25%, would we consider this acceptable performance?

Comparing growth to rates experienced by key competitors and customers places the company's performance in an appropriate context. It can also be important input to strategic analysis. For example, what are the causes and implications of customer growth exceeding our own? Are we missing potential opportunities to grow with our customers? A summary of comparative growth rates is provided in Figure 22.5. In this case, Steady Co. is growing faster than the market, and at a rate between the company's two largest customers. Steady Co.'s growth rate is ahead of two competitors' rates, but is significantly under Fast Co.'s rate.

FIGURE 22.5 **Year-over-year growth.** 🖥

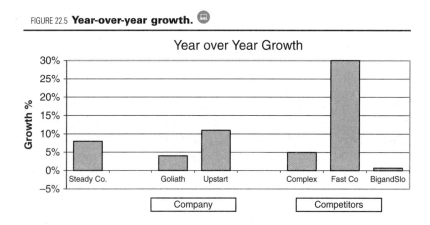

Percentage of Revenue from New Products

Most companies seek to maintain and grow sales by developing and introducing new products. An important indicator of the success of the new product development and introduction activities is the percentage of revenue from products recently introduced. Some companies would define *recently* as within two years. Others may shorten the period to reflect shorter product life cycles. This measure is highly susceptible to gaming, so it is critical to have considered definitions, including "What is a new product?" Does it include product updates or minor modifications or only new products with significant performance and functionality improvements?

Customer Retention, Churn Rate, and Lost Customers

Given the cost and difficulty in obtaining new customers, companies must go to great lengths to retain existing customers. Identifying the loss or potential loss of a customer on a timely basis provides immediate visibility into the revenue impact of losing that customer and may afford the company an opportunity to take corrective action. Of course, the reason for losing a customer should be understood, contemplated, and acted upon.

Lost Orders

Companies should track the value and number of orders lost to competitors. Significant trends may signal some change in the competitive environment. Drilling down into lost orders to identify the root cause can also be enlightening. Most companies expect to lose some orders. For example, a high-end equipment supplier expects to lose some orders to a low-end supplier where price is a driving factor in the customer's buy decision. However, if the company began to lose orders based on performance or service, the alarm should sound.

Revenue from New Customers

Companies may expect future growth by acquiring new customers. In these cases, it would be useful to track revenue derived from sales to new customers. *New* is defined by individual circumstance, but is frequently defined as revenue derived from customers acquired over the prior 12 months.

Customer Satisfaction

An important factor in maintaining current sales levels and in growing sales is customer satisfaction. An increasing number of companies periodically solicit overall performance ratings from their customers. Many customers have sophisticated supply chain processes that include the evaluation of overall vendor performance. These performance ratings are used as a basis for selecting and retaining vendors.

Key elements of the customer's total experience will include price, quality, delivery performance, and service. Therefore, management should measure these factors frequently. It is important to measure these factors from the customer's viewpoint. For example, the customer may measure quality or service levels differently than the supplier. What matters, of course, is only the customer's perspective.

Past-Due Orders

Monitoring the number and value of past-due orders can provide important insight into customer satisfaction. An increase in the level of past-due orders may indicate a manufacturing or supply problem that resulted in delayed shipments to customers. In addition to tracking (and attacking) the level of past-due orders, much can be learned by identifying and addressing recurring causes of past-due orders. Many companies actively "work" past-due orders. Reducing the level of past-due sales orders will increase sales and customer satisfaction and reduce inventories and costs.

On-Time Delivery

On-time delivery (OTD) is a very important determiner of customer satisfaction. Some companies measure delivery to "quoted delivery dates." Progressive companies measure delivery performance against the date the customer originally requested since that is the date the customer originally wanted the product. This is another measure that can be gamed. Extending the original delivery dates or updating the delivery date is counterproductive, but results in a higher OTD performance if the measure is not properly established.

Quality

Measuring the quality of product and other customer-facing activities is an important indicator of customer satisfaction. Examples include: product returns, warranty experience, and the volume of sales credits issued.

Projected Revenue in Product Pipeline

If future growth is highly dependent on new product development and introduction, then management should have a clear view of the revenue potential and project status in each product in the development pipeline. Figure 22.6 is an example of a summary of revenue in the product development pipeline.

FIGURE 22.6 **Revenue in product development pipeline.**

Revenue in Product Development Pipeline						
$m				Annual Revenue		
Project Name	2023	2024	2025	2026	Potential	Status	Comment
Coyote	0	7	18	24	$25	Green	On Track, Intro 3/24
Fox	0	12	26	30	30	Yellow	2 Critical Milestones missed
Rabbit	0	15	15	12	15	Red	Technical Performance Issues
Tortoise	0	20	30	50	60	Green	1st Shipments, next week
Total	$0	$54	$89	$116	$130		

A key benefit to this summary is that development, marketing, sales, and other personnel involved in the introduction of new products have clear visibility of the connection of their activities to future revenue targets. This helps to create linkage in many enterprises where product development teams may not be acutely aware of the timing and potential magnitude of the projects they are supporting. The impact of any delay or acceleration in the development timeline on revenue expectations is easily understood.

Revenue per Transaction

Tracking revenue per transaction can provide important insight into sales trends. Is average transaction or order value increasing or decreasing? Can we capture more revenue per order by selling supplies, related products, service agreements, or consumables? In retail industries, revenue per customer visit ("ticket") is a key revenue metric and retailers put substantial effort into increasing customer spend per visit by offering related products, cross merchandising, and impulse-buy displays.

Revenue per Customer

Reviewing the revenue per customer in total and for key customers can identify important trends. Identifying and tracking sales to top customers is useful in understanding revenue trends, developing future projections and maintaining an appropriate focus on satisfying and retaining these key customers. Analysts must be thoughtful in defining the *customer*. Many order processing systems fragment customers by plant or ship-to addresses or divisions, resulting in a less than complete view of the customer's total revenue and activity.

Quote Levels

For certain businesses with long purchasing cycles, tracking the level of open quotes over time can be a leading indicator of future revenue levels. However, not all quotes are created equal. Some may be for budgetary purposes, indicating a long-term purchase horizon. Others may indicate order potential in the short term. For this reason, quote levels are often summarized by key characteristics to enhance the insight into potential order flow.

Order Backlog Levels

Some businesses have long lead times or order cycles. Customers must place orders well in advance of requested delivery dates. Examples include aircraft, shipbuilding, and large equipment industries. In these industries, the order backlog levels are an important leading indicator of revenue and general business health.

FIGURE 22.7 **Backlog analysis.**

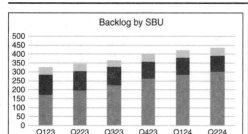
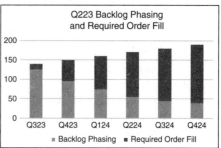

Figure 22.7 provides two views of backlog. In the chart on the left, the backlog by SBU at the end of each quarter is presented. The graph on the right presents a phasing of the backlog at Q223 into the future quarter when the revenue is projected to be recorded.

Anecdotal Input

Nothing beats customer letters or survey responses containing specific feedback. Post them with the quantitative measures and watch the reaction of employees. Many include points actionable by employees at various levels in the company. A few examples:

> "Customer Service never answers the phone. Voice mail messages are not returned for several days."
> "Service levels have declined. We are contemplating an alternative supplier."
> "The delay in scheduling installation and training is unacceptable."

Comprehensive Analysis of Revenue Measures   Collecting and analyzing a broad set of measures supporting revenue growth, lost customers, new product introductions, and other revenue drivers can provide a comprehensive picture into underlying trends and identify issues and opportunities. Table 22.6 illustrates a tool used to collect data that may be useful in the analysis of revenues.

REVENUE DASHBOARDS

Based on the most important drivers and issues impacting current and future revenue growth, a performance dashboard can be created to track and present these measures to managers (Figure 22.8). The selection of the individual measures to include in the dashboard is an extremely important process. There should be an emphasis on leading and predictive indicators of revenue growth. The measures should focus on the most important drivers and should be changed out over time as appropriate. Properly constructed, this one-page summary of critical factors is sure to focus the team's attention to appropriate issues and opportunities. A supplemental revenue analysis, with additional details and trends of revenue performance, is illustrated in Figure 22.9.

TABLE 22.6 **Comprehensive revenue measures.**

Performance Measure Collection Worksheets

Revenue

		2024		2025				Illustrative 2026			
		Q3	Q4	Q1	Q2	Q3	Q4	Q1	Q2	Q3	Q4
Revenue		21	26	18	18.7	21	28	20	20	22	30.6
	Seq growth		24%	-31%	4%	12%	33%	-29%	0%	10%	39%
	Y/Y Growth	3%	4%	4%	2%	0%	8%	11%	7%	5%	9%
	Year		79.4				85.7				92.6
	Y/Y Growth		4%				8%				8%
Lost Orders											
	#	15	16	14	12	11	15	11	7	6	5
	$	1.2	1.5	2	1.5	1.7	1.8	0.5	0.9	1.5	1.2
	% of Sales	5.7%	5.8%	11.1%	8.0%	8.1%	6.4%	2.5%	4.5%	6.8%	3.9%
Lost Customers											
	#	15	16	14	12	11	15	11	7	6	5
	$	1.3	1.7	2	1	4	2	3	1.5	0.8	1.8
	% of Sales	6.2%	6.5%	11.1%	5.3%	19.0%	7.1%	15.0%	7.5%	3.6%	5.9%
New Product Sales		3	2	2	2	2	3.5	3.8	3.9	4.5	4.7
	% of Total	14%	8%	11%	11%	10%	13%	19%	20%	20%	15%
New Customer Sales		2	2.5	3	3.2	3	3.5	3.6	3.8	2.2	0.5
	% of Total	10%	10%	17%	17%	14%	13%	18%	19%	10%	2%
On Time Delivery %		88%	75%	89%	91%	84%	87%	91%	92%	91%	89%
Past Due Orders $		1.7	2.2	3.2	2.8	2.7	2.5	2.6	2.3	2.1	1.9

449

Customer Concentration Trend

	2024 Customer	2024 $	2025 Customer	2025 $	2026 Customer	2026 $
1	Goliath	11.0	Goliath	12.0	Goliath	12.6
2	DEG	10.5	DEG	11.0	DEG	12.0
3	XYZ	5.6	XYZ	7.0	XYZ	9.0
4	PQR	4.8	PQR	5.0	PQR	8.0
5	MNO	2.2	MNO	3.0	MNO	7.0
6	Upstart	1.1	Upstart	1.2	Upstart	1.3
7	HIJ	0.8	HIJ	0.9	HIJ	4.0
8	TUV	0.7	TUV	0.8	TUV	3.0
9	RST	0.6	RST	0.8	RST	2.0
10	ZAB	0.5	ZAB	0.7	ZAB	1.0
Total	0	37.8	0	42.3	0	59.9
% Total revenue		47.6%		49.4%		64.7%

Historical annual revenue

	2016	2017	2018	2019	2020	2021	2022	2023	2024	2025	2026
	57	58	60	62	63	64	68	73.5	79.4	85.7	92.6
Year over Year Growth	4.0%	1.8%	3.4%	3.3%	1.6%	1.6%	6.3%	8.1%	8.0%	7.9%	8.1%

CAGR (through 2026)

2 Year	8.0%
3 Year	8.0%
5 Year	7.7%
10 Year	5.0%

Shading Indicates Input Area

FIGURE 22.8 **Revenue growth and innovation dashboard.**

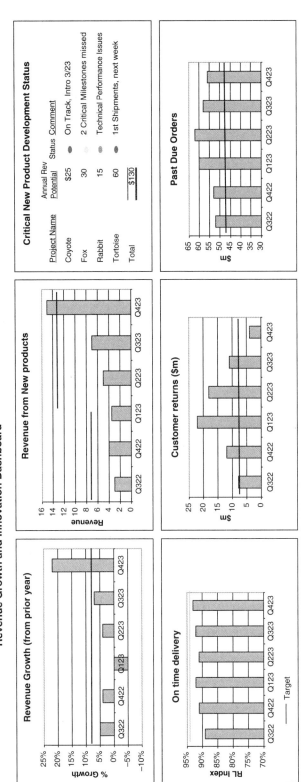

451

FIGURE 22.9 **Supplemental revenue analysis.**

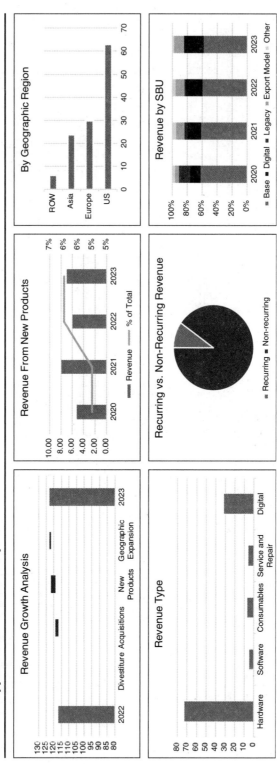

GROSS MARGINS AND RELATIVE PRICING STRENGTH

It is easy to look at a company with high gross margins and profitability and assume that it is highly efficient from an operating perspective. However, a company may be inefficient but still achieve high margins on the basis of a strong competitive advantage that affords it a premium price. This relative pricing advantage can mask operating inefficiencies and high costs, which can be a source of competitive vulnerability. Over time, relative pricing advantages tend to dissipate, leading to margin erosion unless cost and operating efficiencies are achieved.

Gross margins are primarily a function of two variables, cost of goods sold and pricing (see Figure 22.10). Pricing will be driven by a combination of cost and market forces. What typically drives relative pricing strength for a company is a unique product or service offering or an offering with significantly higher performance attributes than competitors' offerings. The leading market indicators for pricing will center on the competitive position and landscape. Factors such as overall industry demand and capacity, aggressive competitor strategies to gain share, and industry health also will play a role.

FIGURE 22.10 **Gross margins and relative pricing strength.**

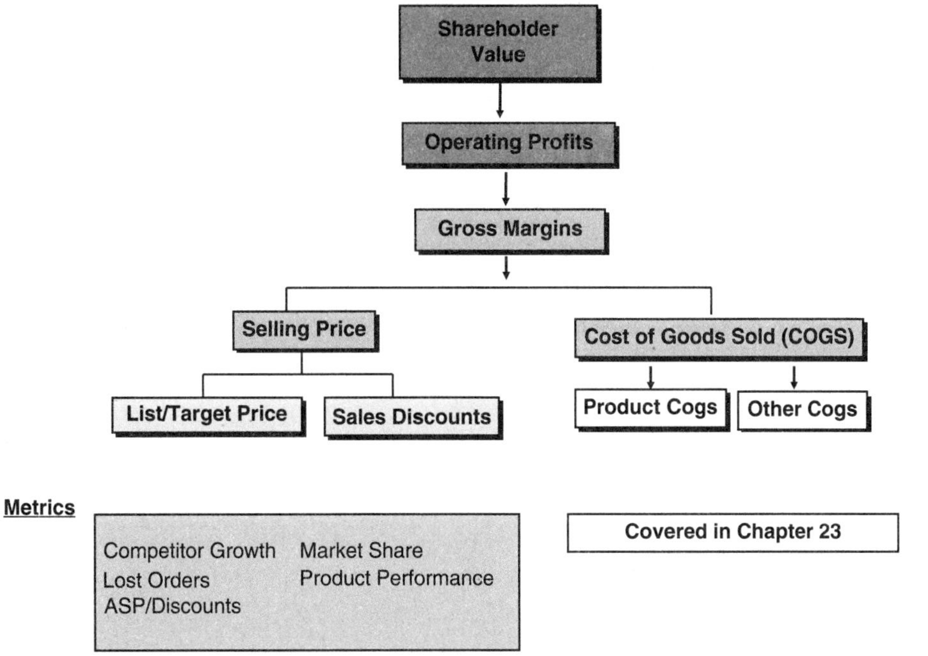

Cost of Goods Sold or Cost of Revenues

Costs and operating effectiveness are covered in greater depth in Chapter 23. Costs are comprised of direct or product cost of goods sold (COGS) and other COGS. Product or service COGS generally include those costs that are directly associated with the product or service. For example, product costs will include the cost of materials, labor, and overhead to assemble or manufacture that product. Other or indirect COGS include items such as warranty, manufacturing variances, and cost overruns. Service costs include time, materials, and overhead.

Gross margin analysis is also impacted by other factors, including changes in product mix and foreign currency fluctuations. Most well-run companies examine gross margin trends carefully and identify the factors accounting for changes between periods, as illustrated in Table 22.7.

TABLE 22.7 **Gross margin analysis.**

| | Gross Margin Analysis | | | Variance Analysis | | | | | | |
	2023	2024	Variance	Volume Increase	Pricing Changes	Mix	Cost Increases	Quality Savings	Other	Total
Sales	125,000	126,000	1,000	2,500	−1,500					1,000
Cost of Sales	78,000	82,000	−4,000	−1,560		−1,500	−820	280	−400	−4,000
Gross Margin	47,000	44,000	−3,000	940	−1,500	−1,500	−820	280	−400	−3,000
Gross Margin %	37.6%	34.9%	−2.7%	0.0%	−0.8%	−1.2%	−0.7%	0.2%	−0.3%	−2.7%

Figure 22.11 presents the analysis in graphical form, highlighting the major changes in gross margin between the two years. This visual presentation enables the viewer to absorb the direction and relative size of each factor contributing to the change.

FIGURE 22.11 **Gross margin reconciliation.**

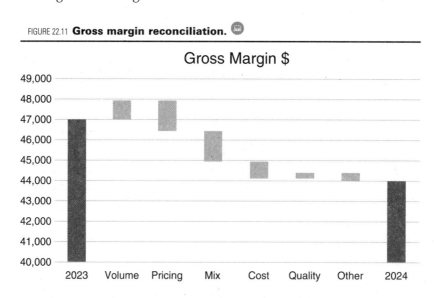

Measures of Relative Pricing Strength   A number of measures can provide visibility into a company's pricing strength.

Average Selling Prices

Tracking and monitoring the average selling prices (ASP) of products over time is a good indicator of the relative pricing strength of a product in the market. ASP will decline, often rapidly, in highly competitive situations. In many markets, customers expect lower pricing over time as a result of expected efficiencies and savings.

Value of Discounts or Discounts as a Percentage of List Price

Tracking the value of pricing discounts or discounts as a percentage of list price are useful indicators of pricing strength that also quantifies the magnitude of any pricing erosion.

Lost Orders

Measuring the value of lost orders provides insight into future revenue, pricing, and margin trends. Orders lost on the basis of pricing are of particular concern since they foreshadow a decrease in both revenue and margins. Orders lost on the basis of product or service performance may point to a weakening competitive position.

Product Competitive Analysis

Capturing and monitoring price and performance characteristics of competitive products is a good way to anticipate changes in relative pricing strength. If a competitor introduces a product with better performance attributes, the pricing dynamics in the market are likely to change in very short order.

Market Share

The pricing and performance measures previously described can be combined with the market share analysis and other measures discussed under revenue growth to help form a complete view of the competitive landscape in the context of pricing and gross margins. For example, it is possible that a company is holding firm on pricing, but losing market share to lower priced competitors.

Gross Margin and Pricing Strength Dashboard

Based on the most important drivers and issues impacting current and future pricing and gross margins, a performance dashboard as shown in Figure 22.12

FIGURE 22.12 **Dashboard: Gross margin and pricing strength.**

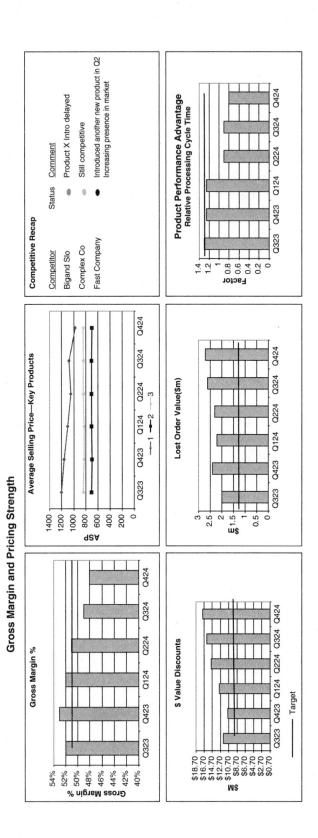

could be created to provide visibility and focus for managers. Again, the selection of the individual measures to include in the dashboard is extremely important. There should be an emphasis on leading and predictive indicators of competitive forces and pricing. The measures should focus on the most important drivers and should be modified over time as appropriate.

SUMMARY

Revenue growth and relative pricing strength are among the most important value drivers. Yet in spite of this importance, managers often do a better job in measuring and managing other value drivers. Revenue planning is inherently difficult owing to the complexity of drivers and the impact of external factors. However, managers can greatly increase their ability to build and sustain shareholder value by improving their discipline over projecting, measuring, and growing revenue. AI will play an increasing role in the development of revenue projections and analysis.

Relative pricing strength is a key driver of value and is realized by holding a strong competitive advantage. Companies that enjoy a strong competitive advantage or have a unique product offering will enjoy strong product margins. It is important to distinguish between strong operating margins resulting from pricing strength and those due to operational efficiency. Over time, competitive advantage and pricing strength often dissipate. This unfavorable impact to margins can be offset by improving operational effectiveness, our topic for Chapter 23.

23

Operating Effectiveness— Costs and Expenses

In this chapter, we will focus on another critical value driver: *operating effectiveness*. Managers and consultants often debate about their preference for either the word *effectiveness* or *efficiency* in this context. While *effectiveness* is often interpreted as doing things well or selecting the right things to address, *efficiency* connotes doing things faster and more cheaply. We will use the term *effectiveness* to encompass both interpretations. Obviously, managers do not want to become highly efficient in an unimportant process or activity. On the other hand, improving efficiency by reducing cycle time, costs, and errors can be a tremendous source of value.

Many observers look to profitability as a key indicator of operating effectiveness. It is a good start, but we recognize that it is possible for a highly inefficient organization to post high profit margins if it possesses a strong competitive advantage leading to pricing strength. In this case, it can pass along high costs arising from their inefficiencies to its customers. This is rarely a sustainable position over the long term, however, since potential competitors are attracted to these opportunities. Additionally, profitability does not directly account for the asset levels required to support a business. Return on invested capital (ROIC) and return on equity (ROE) are considered better overall measures of management effectiveness since they reflect both profitability and asset effectiveness measures.

There is significant crossover between operating effectiveness and capital effectiveness. While working capital has some independent critical drivers, accounts receivable and inventories are directly related to the effectiveness of the revenue and supply chain processes, respectively. We will discuss these two processes in this chapter and again in more detail in Chapter 24, "Capital Management and Cash Flow—Working Capital."

DRIVERS OF OPERATING EFFECTIVENESS

Operating effectiveness has a significant impact on cost, and therefore, value. Even a highly profitable company recording 15% operating margins is "high cost" since the company incurs costs and expenses equal to 85% of the company's revenue. This represents a tremendous pool of opportunity for value creation (Figure 23.1).

FIGURE 23.1 **Operating effectiveness diagram.**

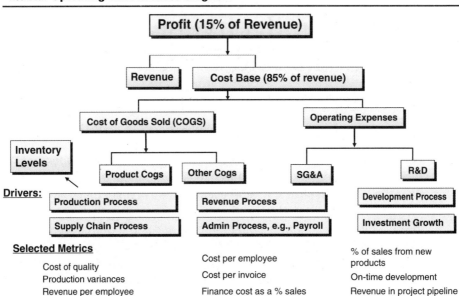

A primary driver of operating effectiveness and profit margins is the effectiveness of business processes. Figure 23.2 identifies critical business processes, including supply chain management, revenue process management, and new product development (NPD), that will impact key financial factors such as costs, revenue levels, working capital requirements, and cash flow.

Typically, a given process will cross several functional areas. For example, new product development may start in marketing with product managers for conceptual definition, then move to research and development for product design. During product development, procurement, and manufacturing will begin purchasing materials and developing the manufacturing process for the product. Marketing and sales will become engaged in the promotion and distribution of the product. The effectiveness of this new product development process will impact costs in each of these functional areas. Mistakes made early in the process, in product conceptualization and design, will often have a significant impact on subsequent steps in the process. Further, the process will contribute to sales growth, pricing strength, and working capital requirements.

FIGURE 23.2 **Process view.**

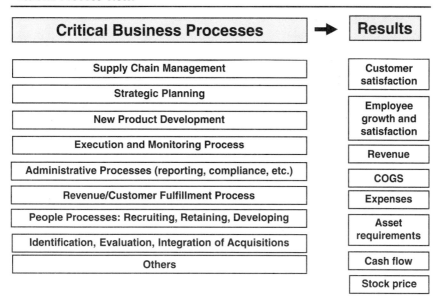

The process view appropriately recognizes cross-functional interaction versus functional silos. In order to improve performance in most critical processes, cross-functional cooperation and teaming are required.

It is typically far more effective to evaluate the performance of a complete process rather than by income statement classification (e.g., SG&A) or function (e.g., sales).

Another critical driver of operational effectiveness is simply a strong focus on execution and cost management. If the CEO, CFO, and other senior managers do not have a focus on operational effectiveness, the organization will drift to follow their other priorities. Even organizations with a history of operational effectiveness can regress quickly when executive leadership shifts emphasis away from this important driver. Managers must achieve a balance between operating effectiveness and other value drivers in order to be successful over the long run.

The specific industry or market served by a company will also impact operational effectiveness. Mature, highly competitive industries such as the automotive industry must relentlessly pursue cost reductions and operational improvements. Other industries, such as aerospace and medical, place a great deal of emphasis on quality due to the nature of the use of their products. Operational effectiveness may be less important for a technology company with products offering significant performance advantages. However, over time, this advantage is likely to dissipate and operational effectiveness is likely to become more important.

Most businesses must anticipate future demand so that product can be ordered or manufactured, human resources can be hired and trained, in order for the product to be available for customers at the time of purchase or service. Ineffective forecasting can increase manufacturing costs, including write-offs, labor, and expediting costs, and can affect quality, customer satisfaction, and working capital levels. However, because forecasting involves an attempt to predict the future, it will always be an imperfect activity. Therefore, in addition to improving the forecasting process, managers should also strive to increase flexibility and response times, for example, by reducing lead times. Forecasting future revenue levels was covered in detail in Chapter 22.

KEY PERFORMANCE INDICATORS: OPERATING EFFECTIVENESS

We will review selected measures covering several areas, including overall measures of operating effectiveness, operating leverage and variability, factory and asset utilization, revenue patterns, key business processes, and people management. For additional background and explanation on the financial statement ratios that follow, please refer to Chapter 2, "Fundamentals of Finance."

Overall Measures of Operating Effectiveness The following measures represent top-level indicators of overall operating effectiveness.

Return on Invested Capital (ROIC). ROIC is one of the best overall measures of operating effectiveness since it reflects both profitability and investment levels. ROIC is covered in greater detail in Chapter 6. ROIC is computed as:

$$= \frac{\text{EBIAT (Earnings before Interest after Tax)}}{\text{Invested Capital}}$$

Asset Turnover. This measure reflects the level of investment in all assets, including working capital; property, plant, and equipment; and intangible assets relative to sales. It reflects each of the individual asset utilization factors discussed in Chapter 2. This measure and underlying drivers will be covered in detail in Chapters 24 and 25.

$$= \frac{\text{Sales}}{\text{Total Assets}}$$

Profitability: Operating Income as a Percentage of Sales. This is a broad measure of operating performance. In addition to operating effectiveness, it will reflect other factors, including pricing strength, and the level of investments for future growth. Profitability is computed as follows:

$$= \frac{\text{Operating Income}}{\text{Sales}}$$

Gross Margin Percentage. Gross margin percentage is simply the gross margin as a percentage of total revenues, computed as:

$$= \frac{\text{Gross Margin}}{\text{Sales}}$$

The gross margin percentage will be impacted by many factors, and therefore, will require comprehensive analysis. The factors affecting gross margin include operating effectiveness and other factors:

Operational effectiveness:

❑ Composition of fixed and variable costs.

❑ Product costs.

❑ Production variances.

❑ Material and labor costs.

Other:

❑ Industry.

❑ Competition and pricing.

❑ Product mix.

R&D Percentage of Revenue. Research and development (R&D) as a percentage of revenue is computed as follows:

$$= \frac{\text{R \& D}}{\text{Revenue}}$$

This ratio determines the level of investment in research and development compared to the current period revenue. R&D as a percentage of revenue ratio will vary significantly from industry to industry and from high-growth to low-growth companies. Objective analysis is required to determine if a high R&D percentage of revenue is due to ineffective processes or large investments to drive future revenues.

Selling, General and Administrative (SG&A) Percentage of Revenue (or Sales). Since this measure compares the level of SG&A spending to sales, it provides a view of spending levels in selling and distributing the firms' products, and in supporting the administrative affairs of the business. The measure will reflect the method of distribution, process efficiency, and administrative overhead. SG&A will also often include costs associated with initiating or introducing new products. Recall that SG&A percentage to revenue is computed as follows:

$$= \frac{SG\,\&\,A}{Revenue}$$

Customer Acquisition Cost (CAC). The cost of acquiring a new customer, including sales, marketing, promotion, and discounts divided by the number of new customers acquired during the period. CAC is useful in subscription or recurring revenue business models and is often compared to the Lifetime Value of a Customer (CLV) to evaluate the efficiency and effectiveness of acquiring new customers. CLV is essentially the total revenue expected from a customer over the life of the relationship, less the cost of acquiring new customers.

Revenue per Employee. This measure is often used as a high-level ratio to measure employee productivity. It is computed as:

$$= \frac{Revenue}{\#\,Employees}$$

The problem with sales per employee is that the measure is very dependent on the business model of a company. If a company outsources a substantial part of manufacturing, for example, the revenue per employee may be much higher than it is for a company that is vertically integrated. This makes it difficult to compare performance to other companies or industries. For example, most retail companies have a high ratio of revenue per employee since they typically purchase, not manufacture, all products in a finished state. Certain manufacturing companies, in contrast, purchase a relatively small level of raw materials and manufacture or transform these materials with substantial labor into finished products, resulting in a lower revenue per employee. Nevertheless, it is useful to look at trends over time and to benchmark performance and business models.

Value Added per Employee. This measure attempts to address the major criticism of the sales per employee measure. Instead of computing the sales per employee, we estimate the value added per employee. Value added would be computed by subtracting purchased labor and materials from sales. The example in Table 23.1 illustrates the difference between the two employee productivity methods.

Operating Leverage and Variability   An important driver of profitability, return on invested capital (ROIC) and variability is the composition of costs in terms of fixed and variable costs. This analysis for LSA Company is presented in Table 23.2. The analysis starts with the basic P&L model introduced in Chapter 2. Then costs can be classified into one of two groups: fixed costs and those that vary with changes in sales levels. The schedule also estimates

TABLE 23.1 **Revenue and value added per employee.** 🔄

Employee Productivity Measures

$ 000's	
Revenue	$ 100,000
External (Purchased or Contract) Costs	
Purchased product	15,000
Purchased Labor	12,000
Outside processing	5,000
Other	7,000
Total	39,000
Internal Costs	
Salaries	30,000
Labor	10,000
Rent	5,000
Other	2,000
Total	47,000
Operating Profit	14,000
Employees	900
Sales per Employee	111
Total Value Added (Revenue-External Costs)	61,000
Value Added per Employee	68

the variable contribution margin representing the additional margin realized on each additional sales dollar.

With these estimates of fixed and variable components of the cost structure, managers can significantly improve their understanding of the business model and the relationship of costs and profitability to sales volume. Given this information, they can estimate the breakeven point in sales and project profit levels at various sales levels.

The breakeven level in sales can be estimated as follows:

$$\frac{\text{Total Fixed Costs}}{\text{Variable Contribution Margin}} = \frac{\$60,000}{75\%} = \$80,000$$

At $80,000, LSA Company's operating income would be $0.00, or at breakeven. For every dollar of sales above this level, operating income will increase by 75 cents. Similarly, for every dollar below $80,000, LSA will lose 75 cents. A summary of this analysis is presented in Table 23.3.

Companies in cyclical industries often attempt to reduce the fixed component of the cost structures in favor of variable costs. If LSA is in a cyclical

TABLE 23.2 **Cost and breakeven analysis.**

Cost and Breakeven Analysis

LSA Company			2023		
			Variable		
	Fixed	Variable	% Sales	Total	% of Sales
Sales				100,000	100.0%
Cost of Sales					
Material		20,000	20.0%	20,000	20.0%
Direct Labor	12,000	1,000	1.0%	13,000	13.0%
Overhead	11,000	1,000	1.0%	12,000	12.0%
Total Cost of Sales	23,000	22,000	22.0%	45,000	45.0%
Operating Expenses					
R&D	8,000			8,000	8.0%
Selling Expense	20,000			20,000	20.0%
Commission Expense		3,000	3.0%	3,000	3.0%
Marketing Expense	4,000			4,000	4.0%
G&A	5,000			5,000	5.0%
Goodwill Amortization					0.0%
Total Operating Expenses	37,000	3,000	3.0%	40,000	40.0%
Total Costs	60,000	25,000	25.0%	85,000	85.0%
Operating Profit				15,000	15.0%
Variable Contribution Margin			75.0%	-	
Breakeven Point Sales per Year				$ 80,000	80.0%
Breakeven Point Sales per Week				1,538	

Note: Fixed costs are defined as costs fixed for the short term (i.e., 90–180 days).

TABLE 23.3 **Operating leverage illustration: Current situation.** ⊙

Operating Leverage Illustration

Current		−60%	−40%	−20%	Base	+20%	+40%	+60%
Sales		40,000	60,000	80,000	100,000	120,000	140,000	160,000
Fixed Costs	60,000	−60,000	−60,000	−60,000	−60,000	−60,000	−60,000	−60,000
Variable Costs	25.0%	−10,000	−15,000	−20,000	−25,000	−30,000	−35,000	−40,000
Operating Profit		−30,000	−15,000	0	15,000	30,000	45,000	60,000
%		−75.0%	−25.0%	0.0%	15.0%	25.0%	32.1%	37.5%
Breakeven Sales Level	80,000							

market with significant variation in sales levels, management may wish to lower the breakeven point or "variablize" more of the costs. As illustrated in Table 23.4, managers could consider reducing the fixed component of the cost model from $60,000 to $40,000, converting these costs to variable. Management may accomplish this in a number of ways, for example, by outsourcing manufacturing or by using outside distributors rather than internal sales employees. Note that the profits and profitability are unchanged at the base sales plan from the levels projected under the current situation in Table 23.3.

TABLE 23.4 **Operating leverage illustration: Revised cost structure.**

Operating Leverage Illustration

Reduce Breakeven

		−60%	−40%	−20%	Base	+20%	+40%	+60%
Sales		40,000	60,000	80,000	100,000	120,000	140,000	160,000
Fixed Costs	40,000	−40,000	−40,000	−40,000	−40,000	−40,000	−40,000	−40,000
Variable Costs	45.0%	−18,000	−27,000	−36,000	−45,000	−54,000	−63,000	−72,000
Operating Profit		−18,000	−7,000	4,000	15,000	26,000	37,000	48,000
%		−45.0%	−11.7%	5.0%	15.0%	21.7%	26.4%	30.0%
Breakeven Sales Level	72,727							

The revision to the company's cost structure has several benefits. LSA will achieve profitability at a lower sales level ($72,727) compared to $80,000 in the current situation. Operating losses will be reduced from the current situation under any sales shortfall scenarios. This will also reduce risk since the firm is more likely to avoid operating losses and resultant liquidity and cash flow problems. It is important to note that converting fixed costs to variable costs is not without downsides. One downside visible from this analysis is that profits will be reduced at the higher ends of the sales range under the revised model. Other downsides may include reduced control over key business processes, such as outsourcing manufacturing, potentially resulting in reduced information flow, longer cycle times, or even supply chain disruptions.

Fixed Costs per Week. In Table 23.2, we estimated the annual level of fixed costs. It can be helpful to compute the weekly (divide by 52) fixed cost level and track over time. In doing so, the organization will become sensitive to the level of fixed costs and to any changes in the fixed costs levels on a timely basis. The impact of increasing staffing levels or committing to additional space will be reflected in real time in this measure.

Breakeven Revenue Levels per Week or Month. Breakeven revenue levels can also be easily estimated and tracked on a weekly or monthly basis. This measure translates any changes to the cost model immediately into required increases in sales to breakeven. It also tends to subliminally influence the organization to level shipments within a given quarter.

Factory or Asset Utilization   In many businesses, there is a substantial fixed cost in factories, stores, or other assets, including people. The extent to which these assets are utilized in a period is a significant driver of breakeven levels and profitability. Until the facility reaches a breakeven level of utilization, these fixed costs will not be covered. Once production exceeds these levels, there is usually a significant increase in profitability since a substantial part of the costs are fixed and do not increase with production.

Factory Utilization. Depending on the nature of the business, factory utilization may be measured on the basis of labor hours, material, process throughput, or production output. If a factory has resources in place with a capacity to work a certain number of hours, then you can measure the utilization of these resources based on the amount of time spent working on product as a percentage of total available hours. Similarly, it would be critical to understand the capacity, breakeven level, and utilization of a refinery operation on a continuous basis. Actual production levels would be closely monitored since they would be a very significant driver of the operating performance.

Professional Services—People Utilization. A significant driver of revenue and profitability for a professional services firm would be the level of professional staff hours that can be billed to clients. Typically, the total billable hours for a professional would be estimated by taking total available hours for a year (40 hours per week × 52 weeks = 2,080 hours per year), and then subtracting time for holidays, vacations, company meetings, professional development, and the like. Partners and managers in these firms may also be expected to spend a significant time in business development and administrative activities. The utilization rate would be computed as follows:

$$\frac{\text{Hours Billed to Clients}}{\text{Billable Hours}}$$

Space Utilization. For businesses that incur significant occupancy costs, measures are often put in place to monitor the utilization of space. These can range from sales per square foot in a retail setting to headcount per square foot for manufacturing and office space. Headcount per square foot can vary significantly between manufacturing, research, office, and other uses. Standards have been developed that allow companies to compare their density levels to other companies.

Headcount Analysis. People-related costs are typically a significant percentage of total costs. Tracking headcount levels is essential to cost management. Significant changes to the cost model will result from additions or deletions to headcount. Tracking headcount by department over time can provide significant insight into changes in costs. Some companies include the full-time equivalent (FTE) of part-time, temporary, or contract employees in the analysis to provide a comprehensive view and to prevent gaming the measure by using resources that may fall outside the employee definition. In addition, tracking open employment requisitions, new hires, and terminations provides a leading indicator of future cost levels. An example of a headcount analysis is presented in Table 23.5.

TABLE 23.5 **Headcount analysis.**

Headcount Analysis

Department	2022 Q4	2023 Q1	2023 Q2	2023 Q3	2023 Q4	2024 Q1	2024 Q2	2024 Q3	2024 Q4	Increase (Decrease) Q424–Q423
Operations										
Manufacturing	125	123	126	135	126	127	125	140	132	6
Quality Control	7	7	7	7	7	7	7	7	7	0
Inspection	3	3	3	3	3	3	3	3	3	0
Procurement	8	8	8	8	8	8	8	8	8	0
Other	9	9	9	9	9	9	9	9	9	0
Total	152	150	153	162	153	154	152	167	159	6
R&D										
Hardware Engineering	15	15	15	15	15	15	15	15	15	0
Software Engineering	17	17	17	17	17	19	23	25	30	13
Other	2	2	2	2	2	2	2	2	2	0
Total	34	34	34	34	34	36	40	42	47	13
SG&A										
Management	7	7	7	7	7	7	7	7	7	0
Sales	15	15	15	15	15	15	15	15	15	0
Finance	11	11	12	12	14	14	14	14	14	0
Human Resources	4	4	4	4	4	4	4	4	4	0
Total	37	37	38	38	40	40	40	40	40	0
Company Total	223	221	225	234	227	230	232	249	246	19
Increase (Decrease)		−2	4	9	−7	3	2	17	−3	

Open Requisitions	Number	Annual Cost (000's)
Operations	3	$ 150
R&D	6	750
Finance	1	95
Human Resources	1	75
Total	11	$ 1,070

Revenue Patterns   Many companies have revenue patterns that are significantly skewed to the end of the quarter or the end of the fiscal year. Revenue patterns impact such areas as receivables, inventories, costs, and risk. Some firms are successful in "leveling" production and revenue evenly throughout a quarter; others ship as much as 60% or more in the final two weeks of a

13-week quarter. This latter pattern is often described as a "hockey stick" based on the shape of the curve of weekly shipments shown in Figure 23.3.

FIGURE 23.3 **Revenue patterns.**

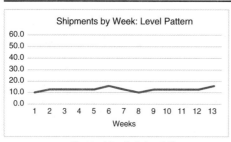
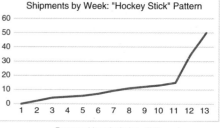

This graph is a presentation of revenue patterns within a quarter. The revenue linearity index can be used to track revenue patterns over time, computed as follows:

$$\frac{\text{Shipments Last 45 days}}{\text{Shipments First 45 days}}$$

Hockey stick = $\$140.5m / \$28.0m = 5.02$

Level = $\$84.25m / \$84.25m = 1.00$

Revenue patterns can have a significant impact on cost, quality, and risk. Revenue patterns that are skewed to the end of a quarter result in higher costs since overtime and other costs to match product with demand are likely to be incurred. Quality may suffer as the flurry at the end of a quarter can lead to errors in building, testing, documenting, and shipping product. "Hockey sticks" increase the risk that a problem or event leads to a significant shortfall in revenue for a given period. Revenue patterns also have a significant impact on working capital levels, specifically accounts receivable and inventory. This aspect will be addressed in detail in Chapter 24.

Key Business Processes

Forecast Accuracy   Measuring and improving the accuracy of sales forecasts compared to actual demand levels will provide visibility into a key performance driver and serve to establish accountability for sales projections. Inaccurate forecasts lead to operating inefficiencies and higher levels of working capital. The measurements presented in Chapter 22 for measuring revenue forecast accuracy can be easily adapted to other variables, including costs, expenses, and profits.

Revenue Process   The revenue process covers all activities around a customer order, from the pre-sales activities to order entry, shipping, invoicing, and collections. This process was covered in detail in Chapter 22. A few additional measures that focus on efficiency of the revenue process are covered next.

Cost per Revenue Transaction. What is the total cost to process a revenue transaction, including order processing, shipping and handling, billing, and collections? This measure can be computed by estimating the cost incurred in each department and dividing by the number of transactions. The cost is typically higher than expected and may lead to further analysis to identify process or technology issues. This measure may also lead to the consideration of minimum order levels necessary to cover the cost of transaction processing.

Invoice Error Rate. Invoicing errors can result in a number of problems. They are costly to correct, requiring the issuance of credit memos or additional invoices. They impact customer satisfaction since the customer must also address invoicing errors in their systems. Invoicing errors will delay collection, resulting in higher levels of accounts receivable. They may also go undetected, likely affecting margins and profitability.

New Product Development Process   Key elements of R&D performance include innovation, cost, time to develop, and impact of design on downstream process activities, for example, manufacturing. Measuring R&D effectiveness presents a number of challenges. New product development (NPD) often involves planning for new projects that contain tasks that haven't been performed before. Another challenge is that some engineering professionals resist performance measures in a creative environment. However, there are many aspects of the process that are repeatable and for which feedback on past projects can be extremely useful in planning and managing future projects. In addition, some aspects may be compared to the performance at other companies, for example, the time and cost to develop a printed circuit board with certain capacity or performance characteristics.

Key performance indicators (KPIs) for new product development were also discussed in Chapter 22, "Revenue and Gross Margins," and include percentage of revenue from new products and projected revenue in the R&D project pipeline. Additional measures that should be considered to evaluate the effectiveness of the new product development process are actual performance versus target development schedule and cost, and target product cost. To measure the broad effectiveness of new product development, other measures should also be considered, including production yields, engineering change notices/orders (ECNs), and warranty costs for new products.

Actual versus Target Development Costs. This measure compares actual costs incurred to the costs estimated for each project. This can be done at the conclusion of the project, but is more useful if it is also examined periodically

TABLE 23.6 **Critical new product development status.** 🔲

Critical new product development status

Project Name	Costs			Status (% completion) *			Annual Revenue Potential	Status	Comment
	Actual	Projected	%	Actual	Projected	%			
Coyote	0.7	0.8	88%	95%	93%	102%	$25	● Green	On track, intro 3/24
Fox	2.8	2.5	112%	60%	80%	75%	30	● Yellow	2 critical milestones missed
Rabbit	1.4	1.3	108%	40%	50%	80%	15	● Red	Technical performance issues
Tortoise	1.8	2	90%	100%	100%	100%	60	● Green	1st shipments, next week
Total	6.7	6.6	102%	74%	81%	89%	$130		

* Based on project milestones planned and achieved

during the project. Under-spending is not necessarily a good thing if it is the result or cause of delays in the development process. This issue can be addressed by combining the cost evaluation with a measure of project progress. This requires disciplined project planning that details key project phases and checkpoints in addition to cost. This type of discipline could result in the analysis shown in Table 23.6.

Actual Product Costs versus Target Costs. Even if the product is developed on time and within the development cost estimate, it is unlikely to be a successful project unless the product can be manufactured at a cost approximating the cost target developed in the project proposal. Adopting this measure will help to ensure that the product managers and development team will be attentive to estimating and achieving target costs.

Production Yields on New Products. It is understandable that a new product may incur some problems in the first few production runs. The learning curve and process efficiencies will typically kick in over time. However, if manufacturing incurs large cost overruns, rework, or excessive production variances on new products, it may be an indication of design problems or a failure to design the product for manufacturability.

Engineering Change Notices/Orders (ECNs) on New Products. After a product is designed and released to manufacturing for production, any subsequent changes to the design or manufacture process are initiated by ECNs. ECNs are very expensive in terms of time, rework, and inventory costs. An excessive level of ECNs on new products may indicate process issues or premature release to manufacturing.

Warranty and Return Levels. The new product development (NPD) process has a significant impact on downstream activities in manufacturing and in quality and customer service levels. These measures are typically tracked for other reasons, but should be included in the NPD dashboard since these measures will be affected by the development process.

Supply Chain Management and Production   Supply chain management will be covered in detail in Chapter 24 since it is a critical driver of inventory. Additional measures related directly to operating effectiveness will be discussed here.

Cycle Time. A very effective measure of supply chain and inventory management is the amount of time required to produce a unit of inventory. The shorter the cycle time for a product, the less time the product spends in the factory. Reducing cycle times typically leads to lower manufacturing costs, lower inventory balances, and increased flexibility. Cycle time can be estimated by using the days in inventory for the company in total or by looking at days in inventory for specific products or processes. Specific cycle times can be measured by tracking the flow of material through the factory until completion. This detailed method is likely to identify opportunities to reduce the cycle time by exposing bottlenecks and dead time in the process.

First Time Production Yield. During most manufacturing or process activities, there are critical steps where the product must be tested for conformity to specifications, including performance, appearance, and other characteristics. Significant costs will be incurred if there is a large percentage of product that must be scrapped or reworked. Measuring the yield rate of products that pass inspection and reviewing the root causes of failures will provide good visibility into critical production processes.

Number of Vendors. There is a significant cost in dealing with vendors. Each buyer can deal only with a certain number of vendors. Contracts must be negotiated. Vendor performance must be assessed. Many companies have reduced procurement, and overhead costs and inventory levels by reducing the number of vendors, subject to good business sense on maintaining alternative suppliers.

Number of Unique Parts. The number of unique parts a company carries in inventory is a significant driver of both costs and inventories. Each part number must be ordered, received, paid, stored, and counted. Each part is susceptible to obsolescence and forecasting errors. Companies with a focus on supply chain management attempt to reduce the number of parts. They often start by identifying low-volume or redundant parts. This may lead to decisions to prune the product line of old or low-volume products and drive the development team to use common components, where possible.

Vendor Performance Assessment. Companies with an effective supply chain management process will monitor vendor performance and typically evaluate performance formally at least once per year. Underperforming vendors may be counseled or terminated in favor of suppliers that consistently meet or exceed pricing, delivery, and quality expectations.

Quality   Quality is an important factor in business performance. It will affect costs and expenses, revenues, receivables, inventories, and customer satisfaction. Corporations have focused significant attention on quality over the past 30 years. The following are a few additional measures not covered in other areas.

Cost of Quality (or Cost of Quality Failures). This measure can be a very effective way to estimate the cost of quality issues across the organization. Typical costs that should be considered for inclusion in this measure include:

❑ <u>Manufacturing.</u> Include any costs arising from quality problems or that are incurred because of the need to test for frequent quality lapses. Examples are:

- Warranty costs.
- Rework.
- Scrap.
- Inventory write-offs.
- Customer returns.
- Inspection.
- Quality control.

❑ <u>Back office.</u> The quality of back-office activities should also be considered. Examples include:

- Billing errors.
- Accounts receivable problem resolution.
- Cost of issuing credit memos.
- Cost of journal entries to correct mistakes.

❑ <u>Revenue.</u> Quality issues can have a significant impact on customer satisfaction and may result in lost customers and revenue.

These costs can be aggregated and used to track the dollar level of quality failures and the cost of quality measures as a percentage of sales or revenue:

$$\frac{\text{Total Cost of Quality Failures}}{\text{Sales}}$$

Defined broadly, the cost of quality failures can easily exceed 10% for many companies. It will typically identify significant opportunities to address the root cause of these failures and can lead to improved profitability, inventory, receivables, and customer satisfaction.

Error or Defect Rates. We have covered error rates in a number of areas, including invoicing errors and production failures. Many companies have achieved great success with initiatives to measure error rates, including Six Sigma. This program has an objective of decreasing error or failure rates to an extremely low level. Care must be exercised to select and focus on critical activities and processes so that the level of effort in driving to Six Sigma performance will impact important performance drivers.

People Management   Many CEOs are often quoted as saying that people are their company's greatest asset and resource. Progressive companies treat these assets well and measure the effectiveness of people related processes. Human capital management (HCM) and related measures were more fully explored in Chapter 7. In addition to KPIs for human capital management, that chapter introduced a "portfolio analysis" of these important assets. Examples of important HCM measures include:

❑ Associate turnover.
❑ Associate satisfaction/engagement.
❑ Days to fill open positions.
❑ Training days per associate.

Functional Perspective   While it is better to look at process measures in general, some measures of functional performance are useful, particularly where an entire process falls within that function. For example, closing the books of the company is primarily an accounting activity. Functional managers should strive to ensure that their organizations are competitive and incorporate best practices in key activities. Consulting firms developed comprehensive benchmarks and best practices for certain functions for this purpose beginning in the 1990s. Many consulting firms and professional and trade associations also conduct and publish benchmark surveys. Examples of measures that can be used to evaluate performance of functional areas are discussed next.

Finance-Budget Cycle. Preparing the annual operating plan or budget can be a time-consuming and inefficient process in many organizations. The cost and time involved in preparing the budget go well beyond the finance organization since nearly every function in the organization is involved in the process. The budget cycle can be measured in terms of days, from initial planning through management or board approval.

Financial Closing Cycle. The "closing cycle" can be a time when accounting folks work excessive hours and are unavailable to support the business. The closing cycle begins some time before the end of the accounting period (e.g., quarter end) and ends with the review of financials with the CEO or audit committee. Many organizations have reduced this cycle significantly while maintaining or improving quality by implementing process and technology improvements. This reduces time spent in this activity and provides the management team with critical business information sooner.

Finance: Percentage of Time Spent in Transaction Processing and Compliance Activities. During the 1990s, many finance organizations began to measure the percentage of time spent on transaction and compliance versus value-adding activities such as decision support and financial analysis. The objective was to become more efficient (but not less effective) in the areas of compliance and processing in order to devote more time to business support.

Human Resources (HR): Costs per Employee. How efficient is the human resource (HR) department? What are the costs incurred in recruiting, providing benefits, employee development, and evaluating performance? How do these costs compare to those of other companies in our industry? To best practice companies?

HR: Average Days to Fill Open Positions. This measure captures the speed in filling vacant positions. This is a good productivity measure as long as it is balanced by a measure of hiring effectiveness.

HR: Successful Hire Rate Percentage. While it is important to fill open positions on a timely basis, it is obviously more important to fill the positions with capable people who will be compatible with the organization. This measure tracks the success rate in hiring new employees, including managers. The percentage of new employees retained for certain periods, or achieving a performance rating above a certain level will be a good indication of the effectiveness of the recruiting and hiring process.

Information Technology (IT) Costs as a Percentage of Sales. Information technology (IT) has become both a significant asset and a major cost to most businesses. Measures should be used to monitor both effectiveness and efficiency of this critical function. IT costs as a percentage of sales have risen sharply over the past 10 years. Capturing this spending rate and evaluating benefits is a necessity.

IT: Network Uptime. Nearly all business functions are dependent on the reliability of the IT network. Measuring the percentage of time that the network is up and running is an important indicator of service levels and performance.

IT Help Desk: Request Levels and Response Times. How many requests are received by the help desk for application or desktop support? What are the root causes of these requests? They may be due to inadequate training, software problems, user errors, or equipment problems that indicate needed action. How fast and effective are we in responding to help desk requests?

Other Measures   Over time, there may be certain specific issues or challenges that warrant special consideration and visibility. These may be due to a dramatic shift in the market or increased regulatory pressure, for example, the costs associated with being a public company.

Costs Associated with Being a Public Company. There has always been a focus on the cost of public versus private ownership of a firm. With the enactment of the Sarbanes-Oxley Act and subsequent attempts to comply with the new requirements implied in the legislation, the cost of compliance has risen significantly. These costs should be captured and be part of an overall evaluation of whether a company should be taken (or remain) public. The costs of being a public company fall into two categories: obvious and subtle.

Obvious:
❏ Investor relations program.
❏ Professional fees (legal and audit) associated with public company filings and compliance.
❏ Cost of annual reports and meetings.
❏ Increased directors' and officers' insurance premiums.
❏ Potential costs associated with shareholder suits and actions.
❏ Cost of evaluating and certifying internal controls.

Subtle:
❏ Cost of maintaining a public company board.
❏ Executive time spent in public company compliance and investor relations.
❏ Compensation consultants for proxy documentation.
❏ The cost and impact of the focus on short term and quarterly performance.

TOOLS FOR ASSESSING AND IMPROVING OPERATING EFFECTIVENESS

In addition to the performance measures covering operating effectiveness, two other tools may be used to understand costs and business processes: the natural expense code analysis and business process assessment.

Natural Expense Code Analysis

While it is generally better to focus on costs and efficiency from a process perspective, another helpful view is what accountants call the "natural" expense accounts. Instead of looking at expenses based on the typical income statement classifications such as R&D or SG&A, we look at the type of spending, for example, salaries, wages, and fringe benefits across the entire company. A top-level summary of natural expense codes is presented in Table 23.7. Note that it is essentially a "roll-up" of information typically presented on a department or cost center report.

TABLE 23.7 **Natural expense code analysis.**

| | Cost of Sales | | | | | $M | Illustrative | | |
	Product	Other	R&D	Selling	Marketing	General	Other	Total	%
Salaries and Wages	175.0	10.0	15.0	10.0	6.0	15.0	2.0	233.0	32%
Fringe Benefits	35.0	2.0	3.0	2.0	1.2	3.0	0.4	46.6	6%
Travel	4.0	0.5	0.8	2.0	1.5	2.0		10.8	1%
Telecommunications	4.0	0.5	1.0	2.0	1.5	3.0		12.0	2%
Rent	15.0	1.0	1.0	1.4	0.5	0.7		19.6	3%
Depreciation	15.0	1.0	3.0	2.0	3.0	4.0		28.0	4%
Purchased Materials	275.0	4.0	2.0			1.0		282.0	39%
Purchased labor	55.0	3.0	4.0	1.0				63.0	9%
Consultants	3.0		2.0		1.0	6.0		12.0	2%
Other	4.0	1.0	3.0	2.0	4.0	3.0	1.0	18.0	2%
Total	585.0	23.0	34.8	22.4	19.7	36.7	3.4	725.0	100%

This view provides a great way to examine costs. If we are attempting to control or reduce costs, it is important to understand the largest cost categories. The 80/20 rule typically applies here. A small number of expense categories are likely to account for 80% of the total cost. For example, if people and related costs approximate 40% of the total cost base, then these expenses would likely have to be addressed in order to have an impact on total costs. If purchased materials are significant, then we must look at our procurement practices, vendor pricing, and perhaps, alternative sources. Can we attack the cost of healthcare premiums? Can we negotiate better terms with travel vendors to reduce costs? These opportunities do not come into sharp focus if expense analysis is limited to either Income Statement classification or process view. The results of the natural expense code analysis can then be graphically presented as in Figure 23.4, sorted in descending order to highlight the most significant costs. This analysis is at a summary level. Each of the categories can be broken down into more detail. For example, fringe benefits can be further broken down into medical costs, retirement contributions, and payroll taxes, including Social Security.

FIGURE 23.4 **Natural expense code analysis histogram.**

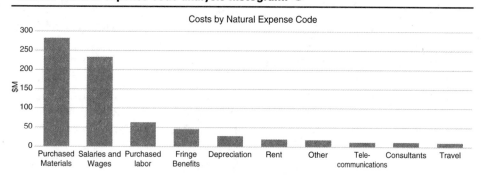

Zero-Based Cost Analysis   Zero based cost analysis (ZBCA), a refinement of zero-based budgeting, is an effective tool to challenge the overall expense base and the creep of expenses levels over time. ZBCA was covered in detail in Chapter 11.

Business Process Assessment

Each significant business process can be reviewed to assess the effectiveness and the efficiency of the process. The following critical business processes are likely to have a significant impact on overall business performance, and therefore, should be assessed periodically:

❑ New product development.
❑ Supply chain management.
❑ Revenue/customer fulfillment.
❑ Strategic and operational planning.
❑ Mergers and acquisitions.

Examples of process assessment tools for the revenue process and supply chain management processes will be reviewed in Chapter 24.

OPERATING EFFECTIVENESS DASHBOARDS

Sample dashboards are shown for overall operating effectiveness (Figure 23.5), new product development (Figure 23.6), and supply chain management (Figure 23.7). The measures selected by an individual company should be based on their specific circumstances and priorities.

FIGURE 23.5 **Overall operating effectiveness dashboard.**

Operational Effectiveness Dashboard

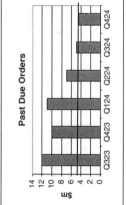

Value Added per Employee

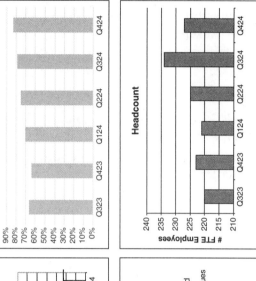

Past Due Orders

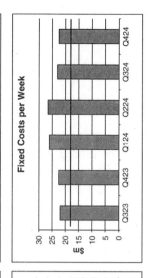

On-time Delivery

Headcount

Fixed Costs per Week

Critical New Product Development Status

Project Name	Costs			Status (% completion)(1)			Status	Comment	Annual Rev Potential
	Actual	Projected	%	Actual	Projected	%			
Coyote	0.7	0.8	88%	95%	93%	102%	●	On Track, Intro 3/17	$25
Fox	2.8	2.5	112%	60%	80%	75%	○	2 Critical Milestones missed	30
Rabbit	1.4	1.3	108%	40%	50%	80%	◐	Technical Performance Issues	15
Tortoise	1.8	2	90%	100%	100%	100%	●	1st Shipments, next week	60
Total	6.7	6.6	102%	74%	81%	89%			$130

(1) Based on project milestones planned and achieved

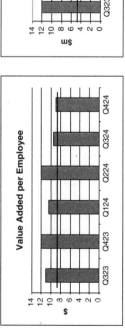

Revenue Linearity

——— Goal

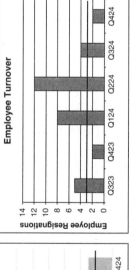

Employee Turnover

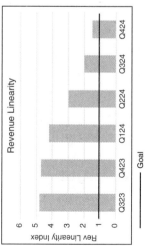

FIGURE 23.6 **New product development process dashboard.**

New Product Development Dashboard

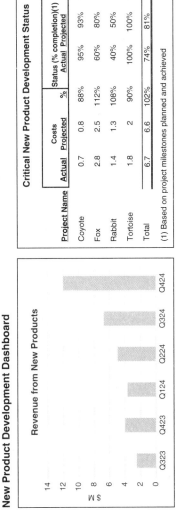

Critical New Product Development Status

Project Name	Costs			Status (% completion)(1)			Annual Revenue Potential %	Projected NPV	Status	Comment
	Actual	Projected	%	Actual	Projected	%				
Coyote	0.7	0.8	88%	95%	93%	102%	$25	$52	●	On Track, Intro 3/24
Fox	2.8	2.5	112%	60%	80%	75%	30	61		2 Critical Milestones missed
Rabbit	1.4	1.3	108%	40%	50%	80%	15	21	●	Technical Performance Issues
Tortoise	1.8	2	90%	100%	100%	100%	60	45	●	1st Shipments, next week
Total	6.7	6.6	102%	74%	81%	89%	$130	$179		

(1) Based on project milestones planned and achieved

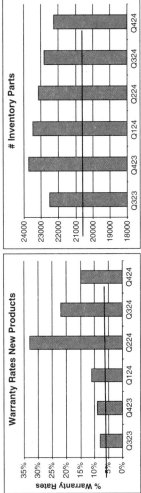

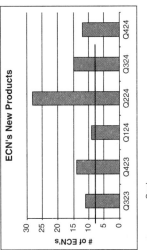

— Goal

FIGURE 23.7 **Supply chain management dashboard.**

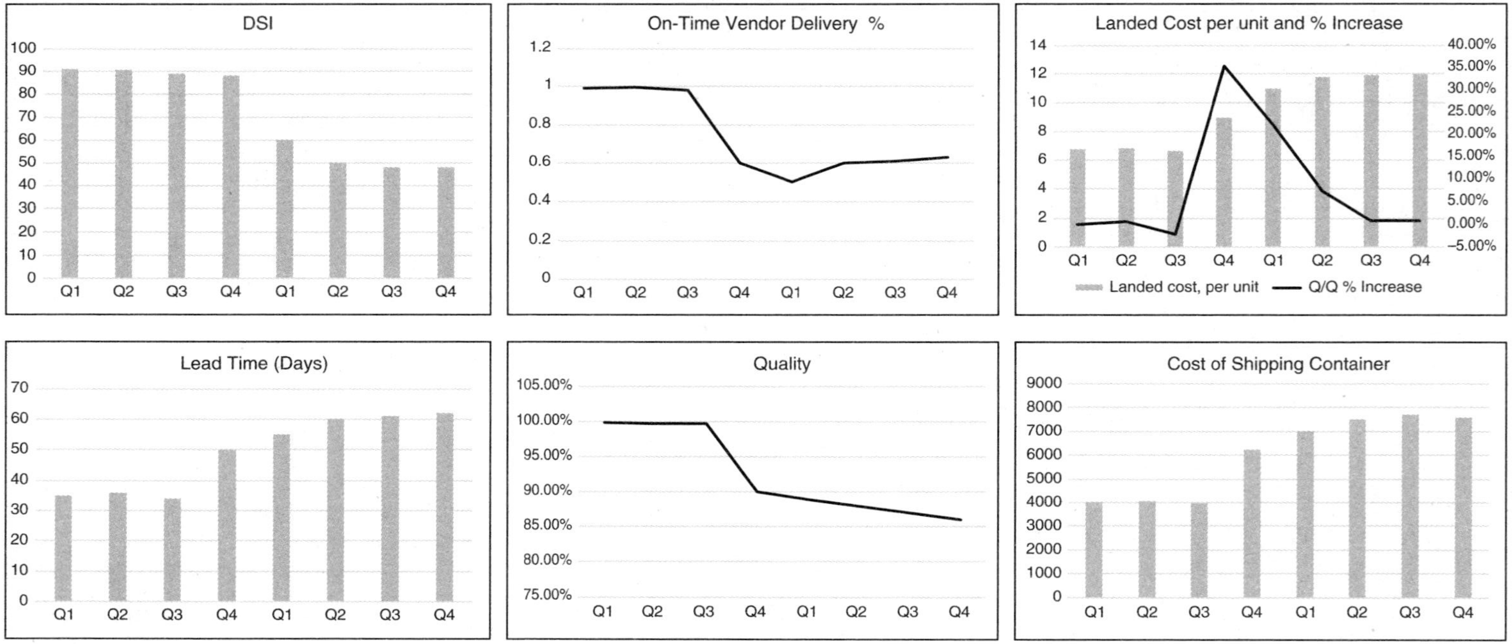

SUMMARY

Operating effectiveness is a tremendous source of potential shareholder value. Operating effectiveness has an impact on profitability, revenue growth, and asset requirements. There are hundreds of potential measures to choose from to measure different aspects of operating effectiveness. Great care must be exercised in selecting the measures that are most appropriate to a firm at a specific point in time. The performance dashboards must reflect key business priorities. The measures should be evaluated periodically and revised to reflect ever-changing priorities and conditions. It is also critical to provide balance to ensure that a focus on efficiency is not achieved at the expense of quality, customer satisfaction, or growth.

24

Capital Management and Cash Flow— Working Capital

Capital efficiency is an important driver of shareholder value. Improving the management and turnover of assets can significantly improve cash flow and returns. Unfortunately, due to the emphasis on sales and earnings per share growth at many companies, capital management often doesn't get the attention it deserves. Managers and investors who understand the importance of working capital in cash flow appreciate the role that effective capital management plays in value creation. Figure 24.1 drills down into the key drivers of capital efficiency and asset management, and highlights the major components of capital employed in a typical business:

❑ Operating capital.
❑ Capital assets: property, plant, and equipment.
❑ Intangible assets, including goodwill.

The Balance Sheet is a snapshot of transactions in process. Therefore, it stands to reason that a company with greater process efficiency will have a leaner Balance Sheet than a company that is less efficient. This leaner Balance Sheet is evident by better performance on measures of asset utilization and turnover such as accounts receivable days sales outstanding (DSO), inventory turns, and asset turnover. In addition to eroding returns and decreasing cash flow, companies that have bloated balance sheets (i.e., excessive inventories or receivables) are also inherently more risky than their leaner counterparts. A company with excess inventory or slow-paying

FIGURE 24.1 **Drill-down illustration: Capital efficiency and asset management.**

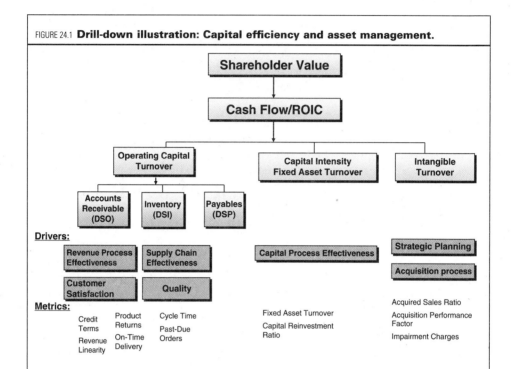

customers is more likely to have future write-offs. A wise CFO once told me, "There are only two things that happen to inventory; you either sell it to a customer or write it off." A rising DSO may indicate a number of problems, including potential collection problems, aggressive revenue recognition policies, or a delay of shipments to the end of the quarter. Key asset utilization and turnover measures described later in the chapter can also be used to identify potential risks due to excessive asset levels.

In Chapter 6, we noted that different businesses will have distinct operating or business models. Among other differences, capital requirements and asset turnover will vary significantly across businesses. Some will require large capital outlays for manufacturing plants; others will require little capital for this purpose. For example, a consulting firm typically requires little in the way of capital assets since people and intellectual property are the firm's primary assets. These firms do not require large expenditures for plants, warehouses, and the like that other firms may need. Some businesses will sell products or services on credit and will carry large accounts receivables. Others will collect the money up front in cash or credit card sales. Each of these extremes must be considered in developing the overall business model in order to earn an acceptable to superior return for shareholders. Within specific industries, there is also a wide range of asset and turnover levels. Effective operating capital management is driven by several factors, including management attention and process efficiency.

CRITICAL SUCCESS FACTORS

The critical success factors for achieving improved capital management include management attention, performance visibility, process efficiency, context creation, and accountability.

Management Attention   The extent to which managers emphasize and attend to any specific process, project, or measure will have a large impact on the effort and result of that endeavor. This is very true in capital management. If a manager is only sales or earnings driven, it will follow that operating capital levels will be higher. Conversely, if a manager recognizes the importance of working capital and actively drives and monitors performance, operating capital levels will be lower. In addition, a well-designed management compensation plan that includes capital utilization (or uses a broad measure such as ROIC that reflects capital) will ensure focus in this important area.

Performance Visibility   Capital management will be improved if managers have appropriate visibility into key performance indicators (KPIs) on a timely basis. Well-designed performance dashboards provide managers with key process measures and leading indicators of capital efficiency.

Process Efficiency   Capital requirements are very closely associated with process efficiency. Companies that have well-established process and quality programs will typically require less capital to support the business. Conversely, a manufacturing process that is not efficient and has a high level of rejected products will result in high inventories (and costs).

Context Creation: Understanding the Importance of Capital Management
When managers and employees fully understand the dynamic impact of capital in creating value, more attention is paid to this driver and related processes. However, organizations with an exclusive focus on sales or earnings growth will often view capital as "free," with the result of higher than required asset levels, poor overall utilization, and ultimately, risk of valuation write-down.

Accountability   Assigning appropriate accountability for assets such as inventory and receivables is difficult. Out of convenience, many companies look at the functional area responsible for the last step in the related process. For example, manufacturing is often held responsible for inventory and finance is held responsible for receivables levels since finance staff are typically involved in collections. However, most financial measures and other outcomes are the result of a business process that crosses a number of functional areas. For example, inventory levels are certainly a result of manufacturing activities. But they are also a result of the design of products and the product demand forecasts typically furnished by sales or marketing management. Each driver must be disaggregated and assigned to the appropriate process team and leader.

The remainder of this chapter will focus on measuring and improving the management of operating capital. We will explore the other components of capital investment, fixed assets, and intangibles in Chapter 25.

OPERATING CAPITAL MANAGEMENT

We will focus on measuring and improving the operating components of working capital, primarily accounts receivable, inventories, and accounts payable. We are treating the remaining components of working capital, cash, and short-term debt, as "nonoperating" or financing accounts. Table 24.1 presents the major components of operating capital and includes key activity measures for these accounts. Operating capital assets such as receivables and inventories represent a past investment in cash or a future claim to cash. Reducing either of these balances will increase cash and improve returns.

Accounts payable and accrued liabilities offset these "investments" and reduce the total cash required to support the business. Although increasing accounts payable by delaying payments to vendors will reduce the total investment and improve returns, caution must be exercised with this tactic. It runs counter to developing a partnership with vendors and is inconsistent with motivating vendors to higher performance and service levels. Vendors may seek compensation for delayed payment in the form of higher prices or in other subtle ways.

TABLE 24.1 **Operating capital (working capital less cash and debt).**

Operating Capital (Working Capital excluding cash and debt)					
LSA Company					
		Measure			Sales
Component	2023	Description	Result	% of Sales	Turnover
Receivables	20,000	DSO	73	20.0%	5.0
Inventory	18,000	Inventory Turns	2.5	18.0%	5.6
Other	900			0.9%	111.1
Payables	−4,500	DSP	−16.4	−4.5%	−22.2
Accrued Liabilities	−5,000			−5.0%	−20.0
Operating Capital (OC)	29,400	OC Turnover	3.4	29.4%	3.4
Sales	100,000				
COGS	45,000				

UNDERSTANDING THE DYNAMICS OF OPERATING CAPITAL

In order to understand the dynamics of working capital and to be able to predict future levels of operating capital and cash flows, managers should employ the operating capital forecast, illustrated in Table 24.2. This tool is very helpful in understanding the inputs and outputs to receivables and inventories. The basic idea is to start with a projected profit and loss by month. Then, based on

TABLE 24.2 **Operating capital forecast—Thomas Industries.**

Operating Capital Forecast		History			Projections		
	Oct	Nov	Dec	Jan	Feb	March	April
Income Statement							
Sales	600.0	660.0	1000.0	400.0	500.0	550.0	600.0
Cogs	420.0	462.0	700.0	280.0	350.0	385.0	420.0
Gross Margin	180.0	198.0	300.0	120.0	150.0	165.0	180.0
GM % Sales	30.0%	30.0%	30.0%	30.0%	30.0%	30.0%	30.0%
Operating Expenses	165.0	174.0	225.0	135.0	150.0	157.5	165.0
Operating Profit	15.0	24.0	75.0	−15.0	0.0	7.5	15.0
Tax Expense	6.0	9.6	30.0	−6.0	0.0	3.0	6.0
Net Income	9.0	14.4	45.0	−9.0	0.0	4.5	9.0
Accounts Receivable							
Beginning Balance	950	1,150	1,310	1,810	1,452	1,310	1,285
Sales	600	660	1,000	400	500	550	600
Collections	(400)	(500)	(500)	(758)	(642)	(575)	(510)
Other							
Ending Balance	1,150	1,310	1,810	1,452	1,310	1,285	1,375
DSO	57.5	59.5	54.3	108.9	78.6	70.1	68.8
% sales (annualized)	16.0%	16.5%	15.1%	30.3%	21.8%	19.5%	19.1%
Collections CM	M+1	M+2	M+3				
Assumptions 10.0%	40.0%	30.0%	20.0%				
Inventories							
Beginning Balance	1,300	1,220	1,112	832	762	902	1,077
Purchases	140	154	168	84	196	224	280
Labor	100	100	168	84	196	224	280
OH	100	100	84	42	98	112	140
COGS	(420)	(462)	(700)	(280)	(350)	(385)	(420)
Ending balance	1,220	1,112	832	762	902	1,077	1,357
Inventory turns	4.1	5.0	10.1	4.4	4.7	4.3	3.7
DSI	87.1	72.2	35.7	81.6	77.3	83.9	96.9
% sales	16.9%	14.0%	6.9%	15.9%	15.0%	16.3%	18.8%
Accounts Payable							
Beginning Balance	160	170	184	198	114	226	254
Purchases	140	154	168	84	196	224	280
Payments	−130	−140	−154	−168	−84	−196	−224
Other							
Ending Balance	170	184	198	114	226	254	310
% of annualized sales	2.4%	2.3%	1.7%	2.4%	3.8%	3.8%	4.3%

past experience and management practices, receivables, inventories, and payables can be projected. Let's take a look at the projected levels and activity for accounts payable. We will discuss receivables and inventories in each respective section later in the chapter.

Payables represent amounts due to vendors. When inventory is received by a company, an addition to the company's inventory and payables is recorded. When the invoice is paid, the payment is subtracted from the balance. In Table 24.2, payables will increase by the amount of inventory purchases each month. In January, the company received $84 million worth of inventory and typically pays vendors in 30 days. This transaction will increase both inventory and payables by $84 million. Payables will be reduced in February when the company pays vendors $84 million for deliveries received in the prior month.

It is also necessary to develop estimates of working capital levels for long-term projections. Projecting operating capital requirements for long-term projections for strategic plans, valuations, and capital investments was covered in Chapter 21, "Long-Term Projections."

Projecting working capital requirements and cash flow is a potential application for artificial intelligence (AI), where algorithms could be developed to perform human estimates of collections, purchase requirements, and so on based on historical data and analysis.

UNLEASHING THE VALUE TRAPPED IN OPERATING CAPITAL

It is not uncommon to find companies that have operating capital levels between 20% and 30% of annual sales levels. Many companies have been able to improve on these levels and achieve ratios of 5% to 10%, and in some cases, even negative operating capital levels. In other words, companies have created business models that provide for payables and accrued liabilities that exceed receivable and inventory levels. The potential value associated with dramatic improvements is significant. Table 24.3 presents a summary of the benefits of a company reducing operating capital levels by 10%, 20%, and 30%. An Income Statement, Balance Sheet, and key activity ratios are presented. To fully understand the benefits, key measures of operating and financial performance are also shown on the analysis, including earnings per share, asset turnover, return on equity (ROE), and economic profit.

Most attention should be focused on reducing receivables and inventories rather than increasing accounts payable or other liabilities. A focus on receivables and inventories will reduce investment levels and can lead to improvements in the revenue and supply chain management processes, customer service, and profitability.

TABLE 24.3 **Working capital improvement illustration.**

		Base		Improvement Scenario						
				10%		20%		30%		
	$m	$	% Sales	$	% Sales	$	% Sales	$	% Sales
P&L									
Sales		1,200.0	100.0%	1,200.0	100.0%	1,200.0	100.0%	1,200.0	100%
COGS		600.0	50.0%	600	50.0%	600	50.0%	600.0	50%
Operating Profit		240.0	20.0%	240	20.0%	240	20.0%	240.0	20%
Interest Expense		14.0	1.2%	10.9	0.9%	7.7	0.6%	4.6	0%
Profit before Taxes		226.0	18.8%	229.2	19.1%	232.3	19.4%	235.5	20%
Taxes	40%	90.4	7.5%	91.66	7.6%	92.92	7.7%	94.18	8%
Net Income		135.6	11.3%	137.5	11.5%	139.4	11.6%	141.3	12%
Balance Sheet									
Cash		100.0	8.3%	100.0	8.3%	100.0	8%	100.0	8%
Accounts Receivable		250.0	20.8%	225.0	18.8%	200.0	17%	175.0	15%
Inventory		200.0	16.7%	180.0	15.0%	160.0	13%	140.0	12%
Net Fixed Assets		100.0	8.3%	100.0	8.3%	100.0	8%	100.0	8%
Total Assets		650.0	54.2%	605.0	50.4%	560.0	47%	515.0	43%
Accounts Payable		75.0	6.3%	75.0	6.3%	75.0	6.3%	75.0	6.3%
Accrued		50.0	4.2%	50.0	4.2%	50.0	4.2%	50.0	4.2%
Debt		200.0	16.7%	155.0	12.9%	110.0	9.2%	65.0	5.4%
Equity		325.0	27.1%	325.0	27.1%	325.0	27.1%	325.0	27.1%
Total Liabilities & Equity		650.0	54.2%	605.0	50.4%	560.0	46.7%	515.0	42.9%
Cost of Capital	12%								
Interest Rate	7.0%								
Key Measures									
DSO		76.0		68.4		60.8		53.2	
Inventory Turns		3.0		3.3		3.8		4.3	
Asset Turnover		1.8		2.0		2.1		2.3	
Working Capital		425	35.4%	380.0	31.7%	335.0	27.9%	290.0	24.2%
Net Operating Assets		525	43.8%	480.0	40.0%	435.0	36.3%	390.0	32.5%
Invested Capital		525	43.8%	480.0	40.0%	435.0	36.3%	390.0	32.5%
ROE Analysis		41.7%		42.3%		42.9%		43.5%	
Profitability		11.3%		11.5%		11.6%		11.8%	
Asset Turnover		1.85		1.98		2.14		2.33	
Leverage		2.00		1.86		1.72		1.58	
ROIC		27.4%		30.0%		33.1%		36.9%	
Additional Cash Generated				45		90		135	
Increase in Net Income				1.9	1%	3.8	3%	5.7	4%

The base case presents a company with $1,200 million in sales and net income of $135.6 million. The company has accounts receivable of $250 million (76 DSO) and inventories of $200 million (3.0 turns). Let's look at the 20% improvement scenario. What would be the benefit of reducing receivables to

$200 million (60.8 DSO) and inventories to $160 million (3.8 turns)? The following changes would result:

$90 million additional cash is generated.

The additional cash could be used to repurchase shares, pay down debt, or make strategic investments, including acquisitions. In this case, the company pays down debt from $200 million to $110 million.

Reducing debt also reduces annual interest expense from $14.0 million to $7.7 million. Net income increases from $135.6 million to $139.4 million.

Asset turnover increases from 1.85 to 2.14.

ROIC increases from 27.4% to 33.1% (a 21% improvement).

ACCOUNTS RECEIVABLE

Figure 24.2 presents a drill down into the drivers and critical measures for accounts receivable. Key among these drivers are credit terms, quality of products, and paperwork, effectiveness of the revenue process, and revenue patterns.

FIGURE 24.2 **Drill-down illustration: Accounts receivable.**

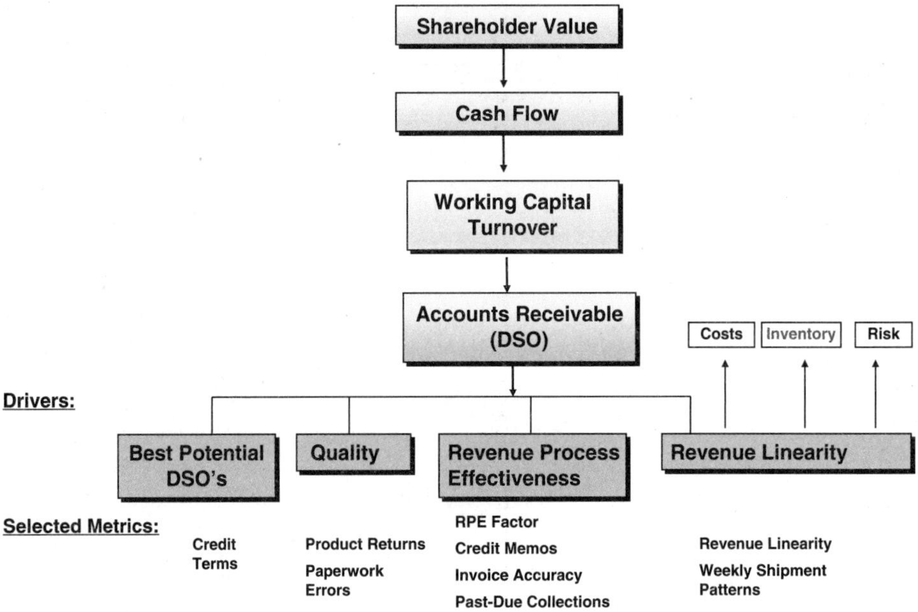

Best Potential DSOs   A significant determiner of a company's actual DSOs is the credit terms extended to customers. There tends to be wide variation in credit terms by industry, country, and competitive situation. Even within a company, it is fairly typical to see a wide range of terms extended to customers for different products, channels, and regions. A useful way to evaluate receivable management is to compare actual DSO to the "best possible DSO" (BPDSO). This computation estimates the DSO level if all customers paid invoices on the contractually agreed date. It is computed by weighting the credit terms for each type of customer, region, or business line by annual sales, and is illustrated later in this chapter in Table 24.5, "Best Possible DSO Estimate." Companies should also consider the possibility and merits of reducing credit terms to customers, resulting in a reduction to the best possible DSO.

Quality   It stands to reason that receivable collections will be affected by the quality of products and services, and customer-facing processes such as billing. The typical customer is not anxious to part with cash in the first place. Obviously, if the product is not performing, the customer will not pay. The same is true for nonconforming or incomplete paperwork. If the invoice does not match the customer purchase order or does not provide required supplemental information, the payment cannot be processed without additional action.

We all recognize that the impact of quality problems goes far beyond slow collections. It reduces customer satisfaction and loyalty, increases costs for both you and your customer, and may jeopardize future sales. By examining slow-paying accounts and identifying underlying reasons, managers can learn a great deal about any customer dissatisfaction and take steps to deal with underlying product or process problems.

Effectiveness of the Revenue Process   The effectiveness of the revenue process is a key driver of accounts receivable. The timeline of the revenue process for a typical company is summarized in Figure 24.3. The process starts long before a product is shipped, when the company is engaged in the product design and pre-selling activities with the customer. In addition, the setup of the order processing software and product definitions can also facilitate or encumber later stages of the revenue process.

Other activities preceding shipment include order processing and manufacturing and quality control. Imagine the downstream process implications of botching the order entry step by entering an incorrect part number or shipping address. The wrong product will be shipped to the customer or the product will be shipped to an incorrect location. The ability to reduce defects at this stage in the process can save a great deal of time, money, and customer goodwill.

FIGURE 24.3 **Revenue process timeline from order to collection.**

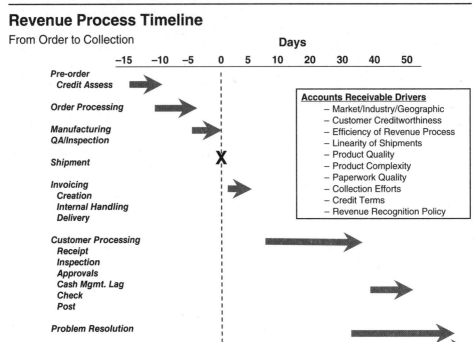

Revenue Process Timeline

When available, the product is shipped and an invoice is generated and delivered to the customer by post or electronic means. Understanding what happens at the customer's facility to process purchases and payments is essential to speed collections. What process and system does the customer employ to receive the product, test that it works properly, review the transaction, and initiate payment? Does the customer require special paperwork to facilitate processing? How does the customer identify and resolve problems and discrepancies? Does the customer pay on negotiated terms or routinely delay payment to help its own cash flow (often called the cash management lag [CML])?

A best practice is for customer service to contact the customer shortly after delivery to ensure that the customer has received and is satisfied with the product and has everything necessary to pay the invoice. If any issues exist, they are identified early and can be addressed at this time. Unfortunately, many companies wait until the receivable is past due to contact the customer. They may be unaware that there is a problem with the product or paperwork, preventing payment. Under even the best of circumstances, this situation results in an unsatisfied customer and delayed payment for 40 days or more.

KEY PERFORMANCE INDICATORS FOR THE REVENUE PROCESS AND ACCOUNTS RECEIVABLE

The specific measures utilized will vary based on the individual circumstances. However, there are some common measures that are useful in evaluating and measuring improvements in this area.

Days Sales Outstanding (DSO). DSO is a measure of the length of time it takes to collect from customers. It will be affected by the industry in which the firm participates, the creditworthiness of customers, and even the countries in which the firm does business. In addition, DSO is affected by the efficiency and effectiveness of the revenue process (billing and collection), by product quality, and even by the pattern of shipments within the quarter or the year.

The basic DSO formula is:

$$= \frac{\text{Receivables} \times 365}{\text{Revenue}}$$

In Chapter 2, we computed the DSO for LSA Company as follows:

$$= \frac{\$20,000 \times 365}{\$100,000}$$
$$= 73 \text{ days}$$

The basic formula can be adjusted for use as a quarter or monthly measure by annualizing sales for the period. For example, DSO for a quarter would be computed as follows:

$$= \frac{\text{Receivables} \times 365}{\text{Quarterly Sales} \times 4}$$

Assuming that Q4 sales for LSA were $35 million, the quarterly DSO would be computed as follows:

$$= \frac{\$20,000 \times 365}{\$35,000 \times 4}$$
$$= 52.1 \text{ days}$$

Many financial and operating managers prefer to examine DSOs based on average levels of receivables throughout the year since year-end receivable levels may be large due to the year-end push (hockey stick):

$$= \frac{\text{Average Monthly Receivables} \times 365}{\text{Annual Sales}}$$

DSO Count-Back Method. This measure is a terrific variation of the basic DSO concept that considers variations in shipment patterns. The traditional DSO measure described earlier can be significantly impacted by

shipment or billing patterns during a period. For example, if a disproportionate level of shipments are made at the end of the quarter, DSO will rise
since it is very unlikely that these invoices will be collected within 10 to
15 days after shipment.

The DSO count-back method accumulates sales starting with the last day
of the quarter and continuing backward until the total equals the receivables
balance as illustrated in Table 24.4. The number of days counted results in the
DSO count-back.

TABLE 24.4 **DSO count-back illustration.**

DSO Count-back Illustration			
October	Sales	Cumulative Countback	Days
Week 1	700.0	35,000.0	
Week 2	900.0	34,300.0	
Week 3	1,200.0	33,400.0	
Week 4	2,000.0	32,200.0	
November			
Week 1	2,200.0	30,200.0	
Week 2	2,300.0	28,000.0	
Week 3	2,700.0	25,700.0	
Week 4	3,000.0	23,000.0	
December			
Week 1	3,800.0	20,000.0	7.0
Week 2	3,200.0	16,200.0	7.0
Week 3	3,700.0	13,000.0	7.0
Week 4	3,800.0	9,300.0	7.0
Week 5	5,500.0	5,500.0	7.0
Total Sales	35,000.0		
Ending Receivables	20,000.0		
DSO, Quarterly Basis	52.1		
DSO, Count-back			35.0

The count-back method results in a DSO of 35 days, approximately 17 days
lower than the traditional DSO computation. The difference is a good estimate
of the impact of a nonlinear revenue pattern during the quarter.

Best Potential DSOs. A useful way to evaluate the actual DSO performance
is to compute the best possible DSO (BPDSO) (see Table 24.5). This computation estimates the DSO level if all customers paid invoices on the contractually agreed date. It is computed by weighting the credit terms for each type of
customer, region, or business line by annual sales. This is a key step in understanding an important variable in receivables management and in setting realistic targets for DSO levels.

Past-Due Collections. Receivables that are not collected in a reasonable
period (a cushion beyond agreed-upon terms) will obviously have a significant
impact on DSOs. Tracking this level of past-due receivables on a monthly,

TABLE 24.5 **Best possible DSO estimate.**

	Best Possible DSO Estimate			
Geography/Channel	Credit Terms	Estimated Revenue($m)	% of Total	Weighted(A)
Product Line 1 Direct	30	30.5	31%	9.2
Product Line 1 Distributor	45	7.5	8%	3.4
Product Line 1 Export	60	15.0	15%	9.0
Product Line 2 Direct	30	30.0	30%	9.0
Product Line 2 Distributor	50	5.0	5%	2.5
Product Line 2 Export	60	12.0	12%	7.2
Total		100.0	100%	40.2
				Best Possible DSO's

(A) Weighting is computed as: Credit Terms × % of total

weekly, and even daily basis allows for timely identification and faster resolution of emerging problems, and is a leading indicator of accounts receivable performance.

Returns. Product that is returned by customers represents a costly transaction on a number of fronts. Performance problems culminating in product returns are likely to have a significant negative impact on customer satisfaction. By identifying the root cause of these returns, process failures and problems can be identified and addressed. There is also a significant transaction cost of shipping, receiving, and carrying the returned product. Depending on the specific circumstance, some companies choose to track the dollar value of returns; others prefer to measure the number of transactions.

Revenue Patterns. In Chapter 23, the impact of revenue patterns on operating efficiency was discussed. Revenue patterns, especially those with revenue skewed toward the end of the quarter also impact working capital requirements. As evident in the count-back method, accounts receivable will be higher if the revenue pattern is a hockey stick since a greater percentage of revenue will be uncollected at the end of the period. Inventories will likely be higher since more inventory must be carried to meet last-minute orders.

Revenue patterns within a quarter can be plotted as shown in Figure 23.3 in Chapter 23. The revenue linearity index is a useful measure to track revenue patterns over time.

Revenue Process–Accounts Receivable Dashboard Depending on the specific facts and circumstances, several of these measures should be selected and combined to create a dashboard for the revenue process and accounts receivable, illustrated in Figure 24.4.

FIGURE 24.4 **Revue process–Accounts receivable dashboard.**

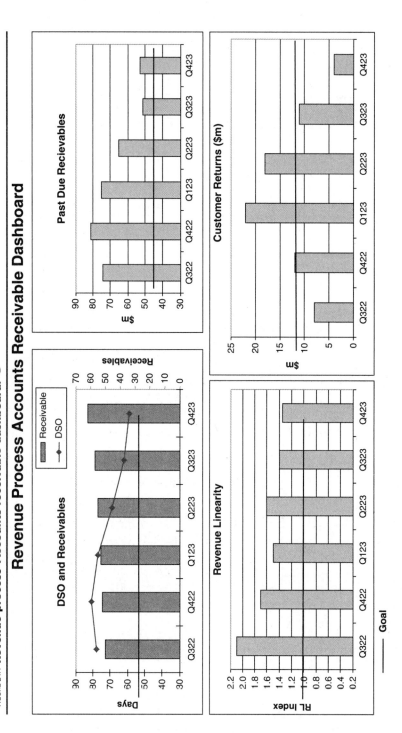

Revenue Process Accounts Receivable Dashboard

Tools for Assessing and Improving Revenue Process and Accounts Receivable
A number of tools can be employed to help in assessing and improving the
revenue process and accounts receivable management.

Accounts Receivable–DSO Drivers Chart. The chart in Figure 24.5 presents a high-impact visual summary of DSOs. We begin with the best possible
DSOs (BPDSOs) of 40 days and then identify the number of days associated
with significant factors, resulting in an actual DSO of 64 days. In this illustration, three factors account for most of the 24 days: customer cash management
lag, revenue linearity, and past-due collections. Each of these items represents
high-leverage improvement opportunities for managers to address.

FIGURE 24.5 **DSO drivers.**

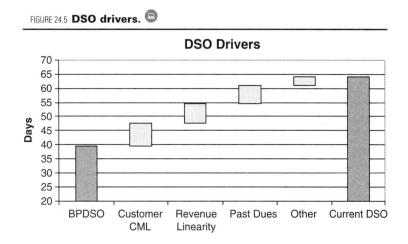

Accounts Receivable Aging Schedule. A useful tool for managing accounts
receivable, customer satisfaction, and the revenue process is the standard
accounts receivable aging report. An example of an accounts receivable aging
report is presented in Table 24.6. This report simply details the current accounts
receivable balance for each customer by age of invoice. Invoices issued in the
last 30 days would be included in the 0–30 days column. Invoices issued in
the previous month would be reported in the 31 to 60 day column, and so on.
This report allows the identification of macro payment patterns, such as slow
to pay customers, but will also identify specific overdue invoices for review
and follow-up. The report is used by accounts receivable and collections staff,
but is so rich in information about customers and payment delays that it may
also be useful for managers to review from time to time.

Root Cause Analysis: Past-Due Collections. A very effective way of assessing key aspects of the revenue process and accounts receivable management
is to perform a root cause analysis of any invoice exceeding a certain dollar
level and past due for a certain period of time. This also serves as an extremely
important tool to identify customer service problems since an unsatisfied
customer will not pay the invoice. Once identified, overdue invoices can be

TABLE 24.6 **Accounts receivable aging schedule for Morehouse Company.**

Customer	Total	Current	31-60	61-90	91-120	>120
		Accounts Receivable Aging Schedule				
		Morehouse Company				
A	83,000	50,000	20,000	10,000	-	3,000
B	54,000	20,000	20,000	10,000	2,000	2,000
C	40,000	10,000	20,000	10,000	-	-
Others	50,000	30,000	20,000			
Totals	227,000	110,000	80,000	30,000	2,000	5,000
Sales	1,500,000					
DSO Impact	55.2	26.8	19.5	7.3	0.5	1.2
Aging % of Total Balance:						
%	100.0%	48.5%	35.2%	13.2%	0.9%	2.2%
Last Month %	100.0%	60.0%	30.0%	5.0%	5.0%	0.0%

reviewed to determine the root cause for the delay. Overdue receivables generally will fall into one of several root causes categories. For example, key process problems such as invoicing errors or poor quality associated with a particular product may be contributing to overdue receivables. An example of a simple root cause analysis is shown in Table 24.7.

TABLE 24.7 **Accounts receivable past due analysis.**

Invoice	Date	Division	Customer	Product	Amount	Root Cause
			Accounts Receivable Past Due Analysis			
220921	11/3/2024	A	Mangham	'M-1	22,000	Dead on arrival
230073	10/4/2024	B	Rhodes	B-1	15,000	Installation problem
223578	9/30/2024	B	Webster	C-1	140,000	Paperwork discrepancy

The analysis can then be summarized to provide useful insight into the root cause of problems that can lead to the development of a corrective action plan as shown in Figure 24.6.

FIGURE 24.6 **Past due by root cause.**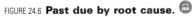

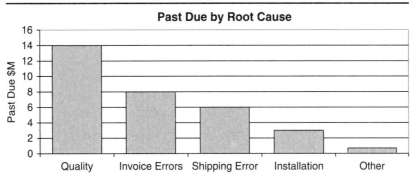

Accounts Receivable Roll-Forward Summary. This tool is a subset of the operating capital budget tool discussed earlier in the chapter. It is a great way to understand and communicate the dynamics of accounts receivable. Accounts receivable represents amounts due from customers for product delivered or services rendered. Receivables are increased by sales and reduced by amounts collected from customers. Sales for each month are taken from the profit and loss (P&L) forecast. Collections will be estimated based on past and projected payment patterns. In the example in Table 24.8, it is estimated that 10% of sales will be collected in the current month, 40% in the next month, and then 30% and 20% in months 2 and 3, respectively.

TABLE 24.8 **Accounts receivable roll-forward summary.**

Accounts Receivable Roll-forward

Accounts Receivable		Oct	Nov	Dec	Jan	Feb	Mar	Apr
Beginning Balance		950	1150	1310	1810	1452	1310	1285
Sales		600	660	1000	400	500	550	600
Collections		−400	−500	−500	−758	−642	−575	−510
Other								
Ending Balance		1150	1310	1810	1452	1310	1285	1375
DSO		57.5	59.5	54.3	108.9	78.6	70.1	68.8
% sales (annualized)		16.0%	16.5%	15.1%	30.3%	21.8%	19.5%	19.1%
Collections	CM	M+1	M+2	M+3				
Assumptions	10.0%	40.0%	30.0%	20.0%				

For example, collections in January of $758 million are estimated as follows:

January shipments: 10% of $400m	$40m
December shipments: 40% of $1,000m	400m
November shipments: 30% of $660m	198m
October shipments: 20% of $600m	120m
Total estimated January collections	$758m

Assess Effectiveness of Revenue Process. Before embarking on a project to establish measures and improve the revenue process and accounts receivables, many companies first assess the effectiveness of the process by evaluating each segment of the process and identifying high leverage improvement opportunities. Using tool kits or best practices surveys for the revenue process, a rating (on a scale of 1to 5) can be assigned to each stage as illustrated:

Pre-order	3.0
Credit assessment	4.0
Manufacturing	4.0
Quality	4.5
Invoicing	2.5
Follow-up	2.0
Problem resolution	4.0
Visibility: metrics and reporting	<u>1.5</u>
Overall rating	<u>25.5</u> (out of 40)

This evaluation will set the focus on weak segments of the process, in this case, invoicing, follow-up, and visibility.

Inventories   Many businesses must build, manufacture, or hold products for resale to customers. Inventory levels are the result of several key drivers and the effectiveness of the procurement and conversion process as shown in Figure 24.7.

FIGURE 24.7 **Procurement and conversion processes.**

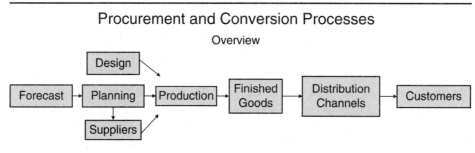

Procurement and Conversion Processes
Overview

Inventory Drivers
- Market/Industry
- Efficiency of Procurement and Conversion Process
- Linearity of Shipments
- Product Quality
- Design for Manufacturability
- Product Complexity

- Paperwork Quality
- Inventory Valuation Policy
- Breadth of Product Lines
- Degree of Vertical Integration
- Stability and Predictability of Demand

Drivers of Inventory Levels

Market and Industry. The very nature of certain businesses and industries often determines the level of inventory required. For example, retailers must purchase and hold inventories for resale to consumers. Manufacturing companies must acquire materials, assemble product, and distribute finished goods to their customers. However, service companies, including consulting firms, do not have to hold significant levels of inventory.

Effectiveness of Procurement and Conversion Processes. Inventories as well as manufacturing costs can be reduced by improving procurement and manufacturing or conversion processes. For example, by evaluating and then improving vendor quality and delivery performance, the company can reduce lead times and inventory levels. Over the past 25 years, tremendous improvements have been made by many companies in improving the flow and efficiency of the manufacturing process.

Product Life Cycle Issues. The evolution of a product from conception to full-scale production and to end of life has significant impact on inventory levels. Two critical phases in the product life cycle are new product introduction and the end of the product's life.

1. *New Product Introduction.* Many companies carry high inventory levels associated with problems in the design and introduction of new products. If a new product is transferred to manufacturing before all design issues are resolved, there are likely to be high inventory levels associated with the product. In addition to tying up excess capital, this inventory may be at risk for obsolescence if the design of the product is changed.

2. *End of Life.* The company must carefully plan and manage the end of a product's life cycle. If this is not done effectively, the company may carry, and ultimately, have to write off inventories that are no longer saleable to customers.

Design for Manufacturability. Many companies have reduced costs and inventory requirements by designing products that are easier to manufacture. Examples include using common components and requiring fewer complex assembly steps. These types of improvements reduce costs and inventories, improve quality, and prevent delays associated with introducing products to market.

Product Quality. If a company manufactures a quality product, inventory levels will be lower than for a similar product with quality problems. A firm with high-quality manufacturing processes will require lower levels of material input; less time and inventory in test, repair, and rework; and lower levels of inventory returned from customers.

Breadth of Product Line. The company that offers a broad selection of products will typically require higher inventory levels. Conversely, a firm with limited product alternatives will typically have less inventory. Many firms have reduced inventory levels by limiting product variety to fewer options and choices (e.g., color, size, configurations, and power).

Vertical Integration/Outsourcing. Companies that are highly vertically integrated will carry higher inventory balances than a firm that outsources a substantial part of the manufacturing process to other firms. Many companies have outsourced manufacturing or other elements of their supply chain over the last 20 years, notably to China and other low-cost regions. While this has resulted in lower costs and inventories, it can and has introduced risks due to geopolitical, health, transportation, and other disruptions.

Forecasting. In Chapter 22 we discussed that most businesses must anticipate future demand for their products so that product can be ordered or manufactured and be available for customers at the time of purchase. The revenue forecast typically drives procurement and manufacturing schedules and activities. The accuracy of forecasts will have a significant impact on inventory levels. If demand is overestimated, excess inventory will result. Even if the total revenue forecast is accurate, if the mix of product is different than projected, the company may miss sales and build products that were not ordered, leading to an increase in inventory. In Chapter 22, we outlined several measures that can be taken to improve the revenue forecasting process. In addition to improving the forecasting process, managers should also strive to increase flexibility and response times, for example, by reducing lead times.

Key Performance Indicators for Supply Chain Management and Inventory

There are several performance measures that can be developed and tracked to provide visibility into key drivers of supply chain and inventory management.

Inventory Turns. In Chapter 2, we computed inventory turns and DSI for LSA, as follows:

$$= \frac{\text{Cost of goods sold (COGS)}}{\text{Inventory}}$$

$$= \frac{\$45,000}{\$18,000}$$

$$= 2.5 \text{ times (turns)}$$

Inventory turns measure how much inventory a firm holds compared to sales levels. Factors that will affect this measure include: effectiveness of supply chain management and production processes, product quality, breadth of product line, degree of vertical integration, and predictability of sales.

Days Sales of Inventory (DSI). This measure is a derivative of inventory turns and is computed as follows:

$$= \frac{365}{\text{Inventory turns}}$$

$$= \frac{365}{2.5}$$

$$= 146 \text{ days}$$

This measure is driven by the same factors as inventory turns. The advantage to this measure is that it can be easier for people to relate to the number of days of sales in inventory. As a result, it may be easier to conceptualize the appropriateness (or potential improvement opportunity) of carrying 146 days'-worth of sales in inventory than to conceptualize 2.5 inventory turns.

Slow Moving and Obsolete Inventory Levels. It is important to identify and manage excess and obsolete inventory. Excess inventory is the inventory on hand in excess of foreseeable demand over a defined period such as 12 months. Excess inventory results from overestimating demand or from radical changes in demand patterns. Obsolete inventory results from holding inventory that is no longer saleable or usable in the ordinary course of business. A useful summary of excess and obsolete inventory is illustrated in Figure 24.8. A good first step in managing excess and obsolete (E&O) inventory is to trend the levels over time. Measuring levels of E&O inventory will provide visibility and identify trends. This measure is complemented by a "root cause analysis" that provides insight into the underlying causes of E&O inventory. Typical causes include product life cycle issues (end of life issues, new product introductions) and forecasting errors.

FIGURE 24.8 **Excess and obsolete inventory summary.**

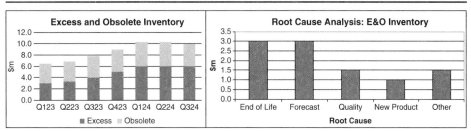

Number of Unique Inventory Parts. Tracking the number of unique inventoried parts may provide insight into a key driver of inventory management. The company may be able to reduce inventory levels by reducing the number of unique inventory parts. This objective may take time to achieve and must consider supplier, customer, and manufacturing issues.

Past-Due Customer Orders. If customer orders are delayed past the requested delivery date, the inventory must be carried until the order can be completed. Perhaps the inventory for an order is completed except for a single, integral part that is out of stock. Obviously, past-due orders are likely to negatively affect customer satisfaction as well.

Supplier Performance. Companies should measure the quality of parts supplied by vendors. Poor quality of incoming parts will delay internal processes and result in higher inventories. Late deliveries from suppliers will also wreak havoc with production schedules, resulting in higher inventories and potential delays in shipments to customers.

Forecast Accuracy. Measuring the accuracy of sales forecasts compared to actual demand levels will help to explain inventory shortages and excesses. It will also provide visibility into a key performance driver and serve to establish accountability for sales projections. Measures of forecast accuracy were presented in Chapter 22.

Cycle Time. A very effective measure of supply chain management and inventories is the amount of time required to produce a unit of inventory. The shorter the cycle time for a product, the less time the product spends in the factory. Reducing cycle times typically leads to lower manufacturing costs, lower inventory balances, and increased flexibility. It can also lead to higher levels of customer satisfaction.

Additional measures for supply chain management were discussed in Chapter 23.

Supply Chain Management and Inventory Dashboard   The most relevant of these measures just presented can be displayed on a dashboard for supply chain management and inventory. See Figure 24.9.

Tools for Understanding and Assessing Inventory and Related Processes
Assess Related Business Process. Similar to the approach suggested for accounts receivable earlier in the chapter, it may be helpful to assess the supply chain and related processes before selecting performance measures. Using tool kits or best practice surveys for the supply chain management process, a rating (on a scale of 1 to 5) will be assigned to each stage as illustrated:

Product design and new product introduction	2.0
Forecasting and production planning	3.0
Manufacturing	3.5
Quality	4.5
Management of end of life, excess and obsolete inventory	2.5
Visibility: metrics and reporting	3.5
Overall assessment	19 (of 30)

FIGURE 24.9 **Supply chain and inventory dashboard.**

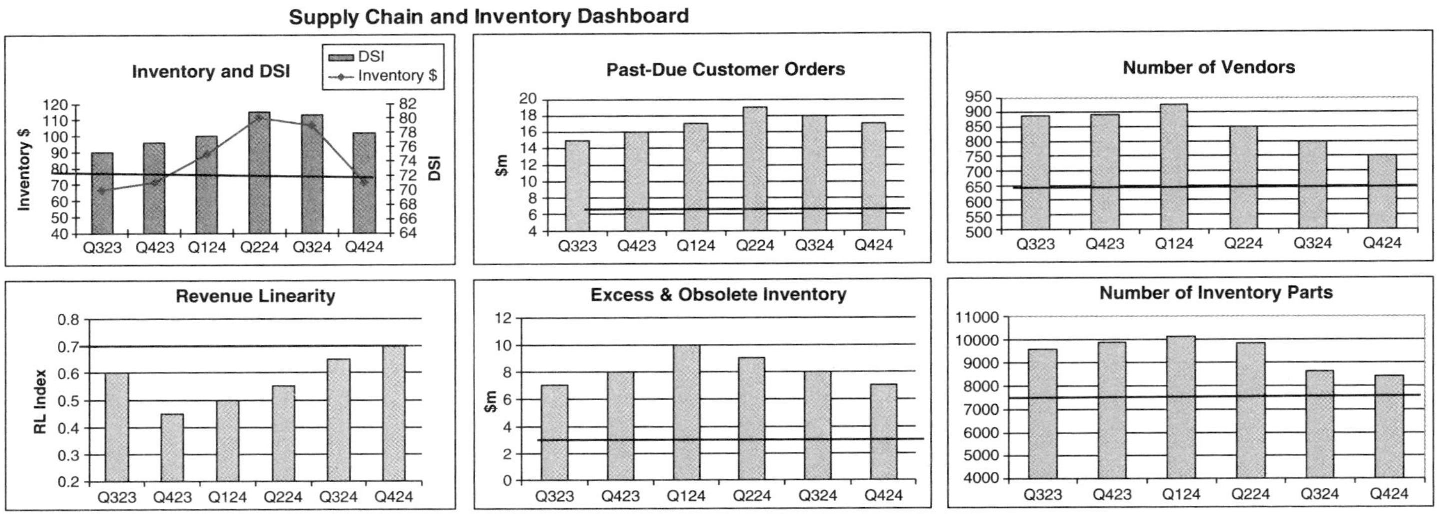

This assessment will focus attention on weak segments of the process, in this case, product design and new product introduction, forecasting, and management of excess and obsolete inventory.

Improving Visibility: Useful Analytical Reports   In addition to the dashboard and assessment, there are a number of reports and tools that are very useful in identifying trends and providing visibility into key drivers of inventory.

Inventory Trend Schedule by Major Category. Much can be learned by drilling down into the major components of inventory and tracking trends in each over time (see Table 24.9). It is also useful to compute turnover for each significant category of inventory.

This schedule includes outstanding purchase commitments to provide visibility into the inventory that the company has ordered and is contractually obliged to take in the near term. Tracking and managing the purchase commitments and the total inventory commitment provides a leading indicator of future inventory levels.

Inventory Roll-Forward Summary. Similar to the schedule presented for receivables, the inventory roll-forward summary shown in Table 24.10 displays the transactions projected for each month that will increase or decrease the inventory balance. Inventory will be increased by purchases, manufacturing labor, and overhead applied to inventory. It will be reduced by cost of sales (COGS), including cost of product sold, write-offs, and so on.

This schedule is a great tool for tracking and communicating the key variables that will affect inventories. It also allows us to identify specific reasons why inventories are higher or lower than we projected they would be as shown in Table 24.11. Did we purchase more material than projected? If so, inventories will be higher than expected. Did we sell less product, resulting in lower cost of sales relief from inventory? If so, then inventories would also be higher.

Tracking Top 20 to 50 Inventory Items. Focusing attention on the inventory items that have the greatest value can provide insight into inventory performance and allow managers to focus on specific items that account for the lion's share of the inventory value. It is common for the top 20 to 50 line items to account for 50% to 80% of the total inventory value, consistent with the Pareto (80/20) rule.

TABLE 24.9 **Inventory trend schedule by category.** ⊕

Inventory Trend Schedule by Category					
$m					
	Jan	Feb	Mar	April	May
Raw Material					
Incoming inspection	2	2	5	7	7
Supplies	6	6	6	6	6
Electronic components	22	25	27	22	22
Total	30	33	38	35	35
Work In Process					
Fabrication	4	4	4	4	4
Assembly	12	13	14	18	18
Burn in	1	1	1	1	1
Rework	3	3	3	3	3
Test	1	1	1	1	1
Final Inspection	4	4	4	4	4
Total	25	26	27	31	31
Finished Goods					
Manufacturing plants	5	4	6	4	5
Warehouse	7	7	7	7	7
International locations	12	12	13	12	10
Sales offices	6	6	6	6	6
Total	30	29	32	29	28
Total Gross Inventory	85	88	97	95	94
Less: Inventory reserves	−15	−15	−16	−16	−17
Net Inventory	70	73	81	79	77
Purchase Commitments	15	17	22	25	30
Total Inventory Commitments	85	90	103	104	107
Key Performance Indicators					
Inventory Turns	2.9	2.7	2.5	2.5	2.6
Days Inventory	127.8	133.2	147.8	144.2	140.5
% of Total					
Raw Materials	35.3%	37.5%	39.2%	36.8%	37.2%
Work In Process	29.4%	29.5%	27.8%	32.6%	33.0%
Finished Goods	35.3%	33.0%	33.0%	30.5%	29.8%
Inventory Reserves % of total	17.6%	17.0%	16.5%	16.8%	18.1%
Committed Inventory % Cost of Sales	43%	45%	52%	52%	54%
Cost of Sales (annual)	$ 200				

TABLE 24.10 **Inventory roll-forward summary.**

Inventory Roll-Forward

Inventories	Oct	Nov	Dec	Jan	Feb	March	April
Beginning Balance	1300	1220	1112	832	762	902	1077
Purchases	140	154	168	84	196	224	280
Labor	100	100	168	84	196	224	280
Overhead	100	100	84	42	98	112	140
COGS	−420	−462	−700	−280	−350	−385	−420
Ending Balance	1220	1112	832	762	902	1077	1357
Inventory Turns	4.1	5.0	10.1	4.4	4.7	4.3	3.7
DSI	87.1	72.2	35.7	81.6	77.3	83.9	96.9
% sales	16.9%	14.0%	6.9%	15.9%	15.0%	16.3%	18.8%

TABLE 24.11 **Inventory forecast analysis.**

Inventory Variance Analysis

Inventories	December Actual	Forecast	Variance
Beginning Balance	1112	1112	0
Purchases	235	168	−67
Labor	185	168	−17
Overhead	93	84	−9
COGS	−710	−700	10
Ending Balance	915	832	−83
Inventory Turns	9.3	10.1	
DSI	38.7	35.7	
% sales	7.5%	6.9%	
Sales	1,021	1,000	
Cogs	710	700	

SUMMARY

The capital required to support a business and the effectiveness of management in managing capital assets are significant drivers of performance and value. Major components of capital include operating capital; property, plant, and equipment; and intangible assets. The level of assets required to support a business is driven by a number of factors, including the nature of the industry, the business model, and the level of efficiency in key business processes such as supply chain management and revenue processes. Significant improvement in asset utilization is possible by improving the effectiveness of the related business processes.

## 25

Capital Management and Cash Flow: Long-Term Capital Assets

In Chapter 24, we described capital efficiency as a key value driver and explored operating capital in detail. This chapter will examine the remaining components of capital effectiveness, including property, plant, and equipment, and intangible assets. Figure 25.1 drills down into the components of capital investment and asset management.

CAPITAL INTENSITY

The term *capital intensity* is used to describe the level of property, plant, and equipment (PP&E; also known as fixed assets) that is required to support a business. Capital intensity will vary significantly from firm to firm, from industry to industry, and from one business model to another. Key among the drivers of capital intensity are the nature of the industry, the effectiveness of capital processes, and the degree of vertical integration.

Nature of Industry   Certain industries, such as automotive manufacturing, refining, and transportation require high levels of capital assets. Others, such as consulting, require very little in the way of capital assets. Other industries fall somewhere in the middle of these two extremes.

FIGURE 25.1 **Drill-down: Capital effectiveness and asset management.**

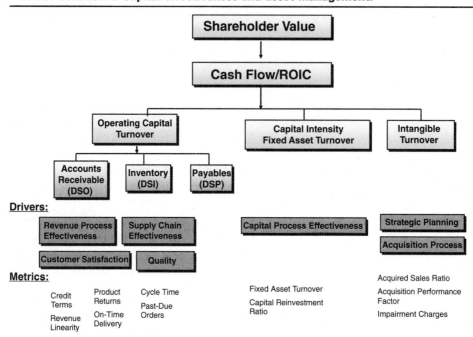

Effectiveness of Capital Process   Companies that require substantial investments in capital assets must develop effective decision and control processes over capital spending and asset management. Key process controls will include review of proposed expenditures to ensure business and economic justification, reviews to monitor project implementation, post-audits, physical control over existing assets, and identification and disposal of under-utilized assets. The process of making capital investment decisions will be discussed in detail in Chapters 28 and 29.

Vertical Integration   *Vertical integration* refers to the extent to which a company directly owns supply chain activities and resources. A company that is considered vertically integrated will produce a substantial part of the final product. An example of a vertically integrated organization would be a company engaged in growing, harvesting, processing, and distributing food products. Other companies, by contrast, will purchase or acquire a substantial part of the product from third parties, commonly referred to as contract manufacturing or outsourcing. In recent years, there has been a strong movement toward outsourcing activities such as manufacturing so that the enterprise can focus attention and resources on core activities such as product design and marketing. A company that outsources a substantial part of its manufacturing will require substantially less plant and equipment (and of course, inventory) than a company that is more vertically integrated.

Depreciation Policy   *Capital assets* are defined as assets with a utility greater than one year. Accounting practices require that these investments be "capitalized" (recorded as assets) and depreciated over an estimated useful life. While there are general guidelines for depreciation methods and periods for each type of asset, companies can adopt either a conservative or an aggressive practice within the acceptable range. Companies that use shorter lives and faster depreciation methods will depreciate assets faster, resulting in higher depreciation expense and lower book values for these assets on the balance sheet.

TOOLS FOR IMPROVING THE MANAGEMENT OF LONG-TERM CAPITAL

Tools and best practices can be employed to improve the utilization and effectiveness of long-term assets. These include developing an effective capital investment process, monitoring projects, and conducting post-implementation reviews.

Effective Capital Review and Approval Process   A fundamental driver of effective utilization of capital is the strength of the capital investment process. Figure 25.2 recaps key steps in an effective capital investment process.

FIGURE 25.2 **Capital investment process overview.**

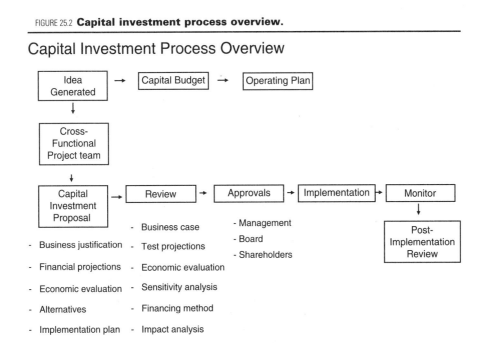

Capital Investment Process Overview

Companies should identify potential capital projects as part of their strategic and annual operating planning activities. The capital budget will be an important element of each plan. For strategic plans, the managers should look out three to five years and anticipate significant capital expenditures to support growth, strategic initiatives, and other requirements. Integrating the capital plan into the financial projections will afford the opportunity to review cash flow projections and determine the adequacy of returns over the strategic planning horizon.

For significant expenditures, a capital investment proposal (CIP) should be prepared to document key aspects of the project, including business justification, economic case, alternatives, and implementation plan. The scope of the CIP and the management approval level should scale with the size and importance of the project. The CIP would typically include:

❑ Business case.

❑ Economic case.

❑ Alternatives.

❑ Implementation plan.

If a capital project has been supported by a well-documented proposal, including a detailed implementation plan, managers can review the progress of the project at various points. Is the project on schedule? If not, why? Have the underlying assumptions changed? If so, is the project still worth doing? The capital investment decision process will be covered in detail in Chapter 28.

Post-Implementation Review   A terrific way to improve the utilization of capital and the capital investment process is to review the actual performance of capital investments compared to the original CIP (see sidebar: "Post-Audit Review of Projects"). While this can be a difficult exercise for many projects, there is great value in the effort. First, managers will know, in advance, that the results of capital projects will be formally evaluated. This will encourage well-thought-out and realistic proposals. Second, even where the results may be difficult to measure, much can be learned about the project results as well as lessons for future projects. Third, the review can identify improvement opportunities in the capital investment process or management issues such as unrealistic projections or inadequate project oversight.

My first attempt at post-implementation reviews of capital projects was both difficult and modest. Managers complained that they didn't have adequate systems to measure the incremental savings for many projects. So we simply met to discuss the project and physically inspected the asset, where appropriate. On one occasion, we discovered that a substantial piece of equipment had been essentially abandoned shortly after purchase. We were able to sell the equipment, generating cash and reducing asset and depreciation levels. We also worked with the managers to ensure that the process to develop capital project proposals was improved to decrease the chances of this occurring in the future.

Post-Audit Review of Projects

- Objectives:
  - Hold managers accountable.
  - Identify indicated actions (project specific):
      Example: Dispose/shut down/stay course.
  - Global feedback on process and execution.
- Feedback:
  - How many projects have met or exceeded planned results?
  - Identify and address estimation bias.
  - What are the root causes of underperforming projects?
  - What are the key ingredients in successful projects?
  - What should we do differently on future projects?
- Post-audit reviews are sometimes difficult to perform.
  - Results are not always easily identifiable.
  - The process is worth the effort.

Asset Inventory and Utilization Review   Periodically, companies should perform a physical inventory of fixed assets and compare to accounting records. This process should be part of a company's internal control framework. The inventory can easily be expanded to review the estimated utilization of significant assets. If certain assets are not utilized, these assets may be sold (or otherwise disposed of), which will generate cash, reducing associated expenses (e.g., taxes, depreciation, maintenance, and insurance), and increase asset turnover.

In some cases, an asset's fair value may appreciate significantly over the value carried in the accounting records. This occurs frequently with real estate assets. Management should consider if the potential value realized by liquidating that asset exceeds the value of continuing to hold and operate that asset. Table 25.1 illustrates an asset utilization recap for the top 10 line items in property, plant, and equipment.

TABLE 25.1 **Asset utilization review.**

Asset Utilization Review						
Asset Description	Acquisition Date	Original Cost	Net Book Value	Estimated Utilization	Market Value	Indicated Action
Machining Station	1998	800,000	0	10%	200,000	Sell and outsource machining
Warehouse 1	1990	2,400,000	160,000	90%	3,700,000	No action
Warehouse 2 (Roberts)	1994	1,600,000	177,778	10%	1,800,000	Consolidate into Warehouse 1, sell
Corporate Headquarters	1997	1,350,000	300,000	80%	1,250,000	Lease excess space
R&D Facility-wet lab	2015	900,000	360,000	0	750,000	Project terminated, Lease or sell
Manufacturing Line 1	1995	600,000	22,000	80%	20,000	No action
Manufacturing Line 2	2020	850,000	340,000	88%	800,000	No action
Land						
Lots - Sheridan Business Park	2004	1,600,000	1,600,000	0%	2,200,000	New complex indefinitely postponed; consider selling

Ensure Key Business Decisions Include Capital Requirements   Frequently, capital requirements are not fully considered in business decisions. This may occur in companies with a narrow focus on sales and earnings per share (EPS) growth and in companies with cash surpluses. Capital is sometimes viewed as "free" in these situations because of the muted effect of capital on EPS (depreciation expense is spread out over several years) and limited alternatives for utilizing excess cash.

PROJECTING CAPITAL INVESTMENTS AND DEPRECIATION

Estimating future capital expenditures, depreciation, and related balance sheet accounts is an important part of developing projected profits, asset requirements, and cash flow.

Estimates of capital expenditures should be integrated with the strategic and operational planning process as well as the short-term forecast or business outlook. Drivers of capital expenditures include growth and expansion; new product development, introduction, and production; replacement and refurbishment; and statutory requirements (e.g., environmental regulations).

There is a tendency to short-cut the process of estimating depreciation expense and accumulated depreciation in the balance sheet. Unlike many other financial elements depreciation generally cannot be trended or extrapolated. It is driven by the timing of acquisitions, depreciation methods, and lives. Significant changes in depreciation occur:

❑ When an asset is acquired or placed in service.
❑ When an asset has been fully depreciated.

Table 25.2 illustrates the methodology for forecasting depreciation expense. The worksheet captures the estimated depreciation for assets already in service, including the timing of reduced depreciation when assets become fully

TABLE 25.2 **Projecting property and equipment and accumulated depreciation.** 💿

Property and Equipment	2023				2024				Total Year	
	Q1	Q2	Q3	Q4	Q1	Q2	Q3	Q4	2023	2024
Beginning Balance	139.0	149.0	161.0	166.0	178.0	203.0	265.0	307.0	139.0	178.0
Additions	10.0	12.0	5.0	12.0	25.0	62.0	42.0	12.0	39.0	141.0
Retirements			-				-			
Other									-	-
Ending Balance	149.0	161.0	166.0	178.0	203.0	265.0	307.0	319.0	178.0	319.0

Accumulated Depreciation	2023				2024				Total Year	
	Q1	Q2	Q3	Q4	Q1	Q2	Q3	Q4	2023	2024
Beginning Balance	70.0	74.7	79.7	84.8	89.6	95.3	103.2	112.3	70.0	89.6
Depreciation Expense	4.7	5.0	5.0	4.8	5.7	7.9	9.1	9.6	19.6	32.3
Retirements										-
Other									-	-
Ending Balance	74.7	79.7	84.8	89.6	95.3	103.2	112.3	121.9	89.6	121.9

Depreciation Estimate	Acquisition	2023				2024				Total Year		Average
Acquisition Period	Cost	Q1	Q2	Q3	Q4	Q1	Q2	Q3	Q4	2023	2024	Life
Prior	40.0	0.8	0.8	0.7	0.7	0.7	0.6	0.6	0.7	3.1	2.6	12
2018	50.0	1.8	1.7	1.6	1.0	1.0	1.0	0.9	0.9	6.0	3.8	7
2019	15.0	0.5	0.5	0.5	0.5	0.5	0.5	0.4	0.4	2.1	1.9	7
2020	10.0	0.4	0.4	0.4	0.4	0.4	0.4	0.4	0.3	1.4	1.4	7
2021	12.0	0.4	0.4	0.4	0.4	0.4	0.4	0.4	0.4	1.7	1.7	7
2022	12.0	0.4	0.4	0.4	0.4	0.4	0.4	0.4	0.4	1.7	1.7	7
Total 2022 and Prior	139.0	4.4	4.2	4.1	3.5	3.5	3.4	3.1	3.2	16.1	13.1	
Q12023	10.0	0.4	0.4	0.4	0.4	0.4	0.4	0.4	0.4	1.4	1.4	7
Q22023	12.0		0.4	0.4	0.4	0.4	0.4	0.4	0.4	1.3	1.7	7
Q32023	5.0			0.2	0.2	0.2	0.2	0.2	0.2	0.4	0.7	7
Q42023	12.0				0.4	0.4	0.4	0.4	0.4	0.4	1.7	7
Q12024	25.0					0.9	0.9	0.9	0.9	-	3.6	7
Q22024	62.0						2.2	2.2	2.2	-	6.6	7
Q32024	42.0							1.5	1.5	-	3.0	7
Q42024	12.0								0.4	-	0.4	7
Total Projected Acquisitions	180.0	0.4	0.8	1.0	1.4	2.3	4.5	6.0	6.4	3.5	19.2	
Total Depreciation	319.0	4.7	5.0	5.0	4.8	5.7	7.9	9.1	9.6	19.6	32.3	

depreciated. The depreciation for expected acquisitions is then estimated based on projected service date, cost, and useful life. Note the dramatic fall-off in depreciation of prior assets and the subsequent increase when new assets are placed in service.

A version of this method for long-term projections was included in Chapter 21.

KEY PERFORMANCE INDCATORS FOR CAPITAL INTENSITY

Managers can utilize performance measures to provide visibility into drivers of capital intensity and the effectiveness of capital management. We will use the financial information introduced in Chapter 2 for LSA Company (LSA).

Capital Asset Intensity (Fixed Asset Turnover)   Capital asset intensity, or fixed asset turnover, is computed as follows:

$$= \frac{\text{Sales}}{\text{Net Fixed Assets}}$$

For LSA in 2023,

$$= \frac{\$100,000}{\$20,000}$$

$$= 5 \text{ turns per year}$$

This measure reflects the level of investment in property, plant, and equipment relative to sales. Some businesses are very capital intensive (i.e., they require a substantial investment in capital), whereas others have modest requirements. For example, electric utility and transportation industries typically require high capital investments. On the other end of the spectrum, software development companies usually require minimal levels of capital.

Capital Asset Intensity-at Cost (Fixed Asset Turnover-at Cost)   This is a variation of the previous formula that uses the original cost of the assets instead of the net book or depreciated value. It may be more useful in those situations where capital remains employed far beyond the original depreciation period, or to level set comparisons across companies with different depreciation policies.

$$= \frac{\text{Sales}}{\text{Fixed Assets}\left(\text{at original cost}\right)}$$

$$= \frac{\$100,000}{\$50,000}$$

$$= 2 \text{ turns per year}$$

Capital Reinvestment Rate   One way of measuring the rate of investment in capital is to compute the ratio of capital spending to depreciation.

$$= \frac{\text{Capital Expenditures}}{\text{Depreciation}}$$

For LSA in 2023,

$$\frac{\$5,000}{3,750} = 1.33$$

Changes in depreciation levels lag capital investment because assets are depreciated over several years. For businesses with little or modest top line growth, a reinvestment index of one or lower may be appropriate. For high-growth businesses, capital expenditures will typically exceed depreciation, resulting in a high-capital reinvestment rate.

Asset Write-Offs and Impairment History   Significant charges to write off or write down assets may indicate an ineffective decision or implementation process for capital investment. Companies that have frequent asset write-offs and impairment charges (and other nonrecurring charges) likely have an opportunity to improve capital investment, strategic, and related processes.

INTANGIBLE ASSETS

Unlike tangible fixed assets, intangible assets are not associated with a specific identifiable asset like property or equipment. Intangible assets typically arise from acquisitions, where the purchase price of an acquisition target exceeds the fair market value of tangible assets. The excess of the purchase price is recorded as goodwill or assigned to other intangible assets as shown in Table 25.3.

A company that has made one or several acquisitions is likely to have a substantial balance in goodwill and intangible assets. Companies that focus exclusively on internal growth will not have goodwill or related intangibles.

Figure 25.3 compares goodwill and intangibles as a percentage of total assets of several well-known companies with a range of acquisition activity ranging from minimal to extensive.

Companies that have done a poor job in evaluating, valuing, and integrating acquisitions will likely have been forced to write off or write down goodwill arising from failed acquisitions. Companies that are successful with mergers and acquisitions (M&A) will continue to carry the goodwill as an asset. Goodwill and certain acquisition intangibles must be evaluated each year to determine if the assets are impaired. Stated simply, the performance of acquisitions

TABLE 25.3 **Acquisition purchase price allocation.** 🌐

Purchase Price Allocation	
Purchase Price	$ 100,000
<u>**Assigned to Tangible Assets:**</u>	
Accounts Receivable	15,000
Inventories	12,000
Property, Plant, & Equipment	17,000
Other Assets	2,000
Accounts Payable	(4,000)
Accrued Liabilities	(6,000)
Net Tangible Assets	36,000
Excess of Purchase Price over Tangible Assets	64,000
Value of Identifiable Intangibles*	15,000
Remainder ("Goodwill")	49,000

*Includes patents, trademarks, customer lists, etc.

FIGURE 25.3 **Goodwill and intangible assets as a percentage of total assets.**

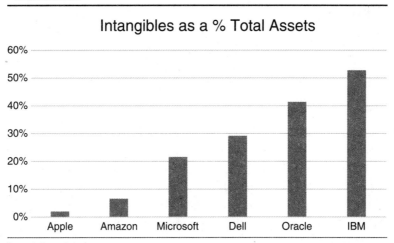

Source: Author analysis of company reports.

is monitored to determine if the purchase price paid, and resulting assets on the balance sheet, are supported by current performance expectations.

The level of goodwill and related intangibles for firms that have completed acquisitions must be evaluated in the context of other value drivers, including sales growth and return on invested capital (ROIC). Refer to the analysis and economics of M&A in Chapter 31 for additional discussion of acquisitions.

KEY PERFORMANCE INDICATORS: GOODWILL AND INTANGIBLE ASSETS

Intangible Asset Turnover Intangible asset turnover is a ratio that helps explain the overall measure of asset turnover. A company that has made significant acquisitions will have a large intangible balance and lower asset turnover than a company that has grown organically. The measure provides an indication of how significant acquisition activity has been relative to sales levels and is computed as:

$$= \frac{\text{Annual Sales}}{\text{Intangible assets}}$$

$$(\text{Intangible Assets} = \text{Goodwill} + \text{Other Intangibles})$$

For LSA, the intangible asset turnover

$$\frac{100,000}{11,000} = 9.1 \text{ times}$$

Goodwill Impairment Charges Goodwill impairment charges result from acquisitions failing to perform to expectations that supported the original purchase price. Significant charges to write-off or write-down assets may indicate an ineffective decision or implementation process for business acquisitions. Companies that have recorded impairment (and other nonrecurring) charges likely have an opportunity to improve acquisition and strategic processes.

Performance of Acquisitions: Synergies and Strategic Objectives One way to determine if the intangibles related to a specific acquisition are "safe" or will be required to be written down in the future is to track key performance indicators on the value drivers that are critical to the success of the acquisition. Examples include key integration milestones such as sales force consolidation, the introduction of new products based on combined technologies, sales growth resulting from distribution synergies, and headcount reductions. Achieving these objectives, as set out in the acquisition plan and reflected in the acquisition pricing, should result in a favorable impairment test result.

EXCESS CASH BALANCES

In Chapter 24, we indicated that we would exclude financing accounts from our discussion of capital efficiency. However, we do need to address the impact of holding excessive levels of cash or short-term investments. What is excess cash? Most businesses need a minimum level of cash to operate the business. The minimum level of cash to operate will be a function of several factors, including business seasonality, cash generation and requirements, life cycle stage, international complexities, and management preference. This minimum level may be reduced if the company has ready access to a short-term credit facility. Many companies hold cash significantly higher than levels necessary to support operations. Typically, this occurs in profitable firms with good returns where investments to support future growth have declined. Many firms retain excess cash as a cushion against unforeseen challenges or as a "war chest" to allow the company to pursue large investments, including acquisitions. In some cases, what appears as excess cash for U.S.-based multinationals is often a result of a surcharge tax that would be due if the cash and earnings were repatriated to the United States. Some of these firms hold on to the excess cash year after year, despite their stated intention to invest the cash. One of the most notable cash hoarders is Microsoft, having amassed a cash and investment balance exceeding $107 billion as of September 30, 2022. The combination of high growth and low cash requirements has created this "challenge" for one of the most successful companies over the past quarter century.

Maintaining this flexibility by holding excess cash dilutes shareholder returns. The interest earned (after tax) on cash and short-term investments is typically much lower than the firm's cost of capital. Table 25.4 illustrates the

TABLE 25.4 **Estimating the economic cost (penalty) of retaining excess cash.**

Estimating the economic cost (penalty) of retaining excess cash

Retainage Inc

Estimate of "Excess Cash"	$m			
Year-end cash balance	600.0			
Assume $100 thousand required to support business	−100.0			
"Excess Cash"	500.0			
Estimate of Impact on Economic Profit				
Earnings (6% interest rate, 30% tax rate)				
After tax interest rate of	4.2%			
Profit after Tax	21.0			
Cost of capital:	15.0%			
WACC	500.0	−75.0		
Excess Cash				
Economic Profit (Loss) on Excess Cash	−54.0			
Estimated Impact on ROA	**Including Cash**	**Excess Cash**	**Excluding Cash**	**% Change**
Net Income	150.0	−21.0	129.0	−14.0%
Assets	1500.0	−500.0	1000.0	−33.3%
ROA	10.0%	4.2%	12.9%	29.0%

impact of retaining excess cash. Retainage Inc. has a $600 million cash balance, of which $100 million is required to support the business. The firm has a net income of $150 million and total assets of $1,500 million. The cash earns 6% and is taxed at 30%. The firm's cost of capital is 15%.

The analysis estimates that retaining excess cash reduces economic profit by $54 million and reduces return on assets by 29.0%.

Managers and boards should carefully evaluate the trade-off involved in retaining excess cash. In some situations, some (or all) of the excess cash should be returned to shareholders in the form of dividends or share repurchases. This methodology can also be used to estimate the economic impact of retaining other underperforming assets, for example, a unit with low profitability or returns.

LONG-TERM CAPITAL DASHBOARD

Based on the specific facts and circumstances, managers can combine several key performance measures into a dashboard to monitor key drivers of long-term capital assets (Figure 25.4).

SUMMARY

The capital required to support a business and the effectiveness of management in managing capital assets are significant drivers of performance and value. Major components of capital include operating capital; property, plant, and equipment; and intangible assets. The level of assets required to support a business is driven by a number of factors, including the nature of the industry, the business model, and the level of efficiency in key businesses processes. Improvements to the capital investment process such as post-implementation and utilization reviews can lead to improved cash flow, profitability, higher asset turnover, and return on equity. Goodwill and intangibles are largely a function of acquisition activity and the effectiveness of the acquisition process, including the evaluation, valuation, and integration of acquisitions. Companies should estimate the economic impact of retaining excess levels of cash and other underperforming assets, and consider this in their evaluation of these assets.

FIGURE 25.4 **Long-term capital dashboard.**

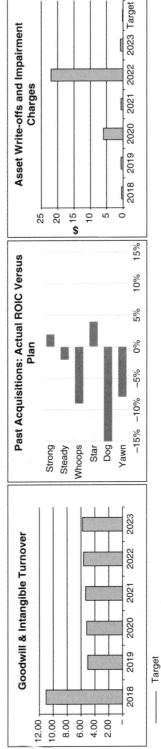

Long-Term Capital Dashboard

Capital Asset Turnover

Capital Reinvestment Rate

Project Evaluation: % Meeting-Exceeding Plan

Goodwill & Intangible Turnover

Past Acquisitions: Actual ROIC Versus Plan

Asset Write-offs and Impairment Charges

— Target

26

Risk, Uncertainty, and the Cost of Capital

Risk and uncertainty impact all projections about future performance that support everything from forecasts and plans to investment decisions and valuations. We will deal with uncertainty in this chapter in the form of discounting future cash flows. Risk and uncertainty are addressed, in part, in two fundamental financial principles: the time value of money and the cost of capital. Additional mechanisms to understand and deal with risk and uncertainty will be addressed in Chapters 28 and 29 covering capital investment decisions.

THE TIME VALUE OF MONEY

The time value of money (TVOM) is an important financial concept. Essentially, the TVOM recognizes that a dollar today is worth more than an expectation of receiving a dollar in the future. Several factors contribute to this:

- Inflation reduces the purchasing power in the future.
- Uncertainty reduces the value of future cash or income payments (you may never get paid in full).
- If you hold or invest a dollar, there is an "opportunity cost" (i.e., you are forgoing other opportunities to use that dollar). If you leave your savings in a bank savings account with very modest interest rates, you have passed on an opportunity to invest in a stock or bond with potentially higher returns. If a company invests in a project, it is passing on the opportunity of investing the capital in another project or financial security (or returning it to shareholders).

We will review the key aspects of TVOM before proceeding to the cost of capital.

Compounding

Compounding is used to estimate the future value of a present sum. This enables us to estimate the future value of an investment, as in compound interest or compound growth rates.

Simple Compounding Illustration   Simple compounding is determining the future value (FV) of a present value (PV) or sum growing at an interest rate (i). The formula for determining the future value of a single cash flow for a single year is:

$$FV = PV + PV(i)$$
$$FV = \$100,000 + \$100,000(.04)$$
$$= \$104,000$$

For multi-year compounding, that is, to determine the future value (FVn) of a sum growing at an interest rate (i) for multiple years (n), the formula is:

$$FV_n = PV(1+i)^n$$
$$= \$100,000(1+0.4)^4$$
$$= \$116,986$$

This growth in value or compounding is illustrated in Figure 26.1. Note an important feature of compounding: the interest earned in prior periods earns interest!

FIGURE 26.1 **Compounding illustration.**

Future Value of a Present Amount					
Original Amount	100,000				
Interest Rate	4.0%				
	Now (year 0)	Year 1	Year 2	Year 3	Year 4
Value	$100,000	104,000	108,160	112,486	116,986
		× 1.04	× 1.04	× 1.04	× 1.04
Growth in Value		4,000	4,160	4,326	4,499

Applications of compounding include:

❑ Calculating how much a $5,000 savings balance will grow to in 10 years.
❑ Estimating sales with a compound annual growth rate (CAGR).

Future Value of an Annuity   An annuity is a stream of equal cash flows that occur at regular intervals over time. Examples of annuities include determining the future value of a regular savings plan, such as contributions to a 401(k) or IRA account. To compute the future value of an annuity (FVAn), with periodic payments (PMT) for (n) years, at a periodic interest rate (i), we use the following formula:

$$FVA_n = PMT \times \frac{([1+i]^n)-1}{i}$$

For example, what is the value in year 5 of annual contributions to an investment earning 10% per annum?

$$FVA_n = \frac{\$1,000 \times [(1+0.10)^5]-1}{0.10}$$

$$FVA_n = \$6,105$$

Figure 26.2 details the growth of each contribution and provides important insight into the TVOM. The initial $1,000 contribution grows to $1,464 over five years, while subsequent contributions have shorter periods to compound.

FIGURE 26.2 **Future value of annuity illustration.**

FV of an annuity (end of each year)						
Annual Contribution	1000					
Growth rate	10%					
Years	5					
		Year 1	Year 2	Year 3	Year 4	Year 5	Value in Year 5
Year 1		1,000					1,464
2			1,000				1,331
3				1,000			1,210
4					1,000		1,100
5						1,000	1,000
							6,105

Applications: How much will my annual IRA contribution be worth in 20 years?

Discounting

Discounting is the methodology we employ to estimate the present value of a future sum or payment. Discounting is a key tool used in business and investment valuation and evaluating capital investments.

Discounting a Future Payment   Let us assume that we will get a $100,000 payment (FV) in four years (n) from today. Based on the risk and opportunity costs, we have determined that a 4% interest (*i*) rate is appropriate. What is the value of this future payment today (PV$_0$), given this risk and opportunity cost? Figure 26.3 shows that the future payment is discounted by 4% per year to arrive at the present value.

FIGURE 26.3 **Discounting illustration.**

Present Value of a Future Amount					
Original Amount	100,000				
Interest rate	4.0%				
Years	4				
	Now (Year 0)	**Year 1**	**Year 2**	**Year 3**	**Year 4**
Present Value	85,480	88,900	92,456	96,154	100,000
		/1.04	/ 1.04	/1.04	/1.04

The formula for computing the present value (PV$_0$) of a future sum (FV*n*) is:

$$PV_0 = FV_n / (1+i)^n$$
$$= \$100,000 / (1+.04)^4$$
$$= \$100,000 / 1.17$$
$$= \$85,480$$

Applications:

How much money do I need to invest today for n years to pay for my kids' college educations?

Discounting Future Cash Flows   In many business decisions, the future cash flows will be realized in several future periods. The cash flow for each of the periods will have to be estimated and then discounted to its present value. We'll start with a simple example, determining the present value of a bond (see Figure 26.4).

Bond Pricing Illustration:

How much should you pay for a $10,000 bond, maturing in two years, with a coupon rate of 7%, paid annually, if the current rate on comparable bonds is 10%?

FIGURE 26.4 **Bond valuation illustration.**

Value of a Bond				
Value at Maturity	10,000			
Interest Rate (Coupon)	7.0%			
Discount rate	10%			

	Now (Year 0)	Year 1	Year 2	Year 3
Maturity Value				10,000
Coupon Payments		700	700	700

Total Cash Flow to Investor					PVF
Year 1	636	700			0.909
Year 2	579		700		0.826
Year 3	526			700	0.751
	7,513			10,000	0.751
Present Value of Cash Flows	9,254				

The Value of an Annuity in Perpetuity An annuity in perpetuity is a fixed payment every year, forever! In practice, these rarely exist, but they provide a basis for valuing long-term payment streams such as the value of annual payments to lottery winners and the terminal, or post-horizon, value in business valuations (which will be covered in Chapter 30).

Example:

What is the PVt on a $100,000 annuity (PMT) in perpetuity if the discount rate is 10% (i)? The present value of an annuity in perpetuity is computed as follows:

$$PV_t = \frac{PMT}{i}$$
$$= \frac{\$100,000}{.10}$$
$$= \$1,000,000$$

Present Value of a Growing Annuity in Perpetuity A growing annuity in perpetuity provides that a periodic cash flow is expected to grow at a constant rate (g) forever. Examples include terminal values in valuation and in valuing stocks using the dividend method.

$$PV_t = \frac{PMT_t + 1}{i - g}$$

where $PMT_t + 1 = $ PMT next year

Example:

What is the PV of a $100,000 annuity growing at 5% per year in perpetuity if the discount rate is 10%?

$$PV_t = \frac{\$100,000(1.05)}{.10-.05}$$
$$= \$2,100,000$$

Note the significant difference from the value computed for the present value of an annuity in perpetuity ($1,000,000). This illustrates the importance of growth as a driver of value.

Present Value of Uneven Cash Flows   Frequently, the application of TVOM involves uneven cash flows over a number of years. This occurs in most real-world business problems such as valuing businesses and acquisitions and capital investment decisions.

Uneven Cash Flows—Illustration:

What is the present value (PV) of a project that requires a $1 million investment now, will generate cash flows of 0 in year 1, $50,000 in years 2 and 3, and $100,000 in year 4 and has an estimated terminal value in year 5 of $1.4 million? Assume a discount rate of 10%. Will the investment in this project create value for the firm? See Table 26.1.

The construction of cash flow timeline by year is the critical first step. Next, we will compute the present value factor (PVF) for each year and multiply the cash flow for each year by the respective PVF. The sum of the PV of cash flows for each year is known as the net present value (NPV).

TABLE 26.1 **Uneven cash flows illustration.**

Year	0	1	2	3	4	5
Cash Flow	(1,000,000)	–	50,000	50,000	100,000	1,400,000
Present Value Factor (PVF)	1.000	0.909	0.826	0.751	0.683	0.621
Formula		$1/(1+.1)^1$	$1/(1+.1)^2$	$1/(1+.1)^3$	$1/(1+.1)^4$	$1/(1+.1)^5$
Present Value (PV)	(1,000,000)	–	41,322	37,566	68,301	869,290
NPV (Sum of Present Value)	16,479					
Discount rate	10%					

As we will fully explore in Chapter 28, "Capital Investment Decisions—Introduction and Key Concepts," this project has a positive NPV, indicating that the project will create value and should be approved and implemented.

Discounting uneven cash flows will be utilized throughout Part VI, "Valuation and Capital Investment Decisions."

THE COST OF CAPITAL

Introduction

The cost of capital is a significant determinant of shareholder value. It is the rate used by investors to discount future cash flows as shown in Figure 26.5. For investors who value companies using multiples of earnings or sales, it is one of the implicit assumptions made in selecting the multiple to use. Value is inversely related to the cost of capital. As the cost of capital declines, the value of the firm will increase and vice versa.

FIGURE 26.5 **Discounted cash flow (DCF).**

Assumptions about Future Performance		
Revenue Growth →	Cash Flow Year 1	Cash Flow Year 2	Cash Flow Year 3...
Pricing Strength →		
Operating Effectiveness →		
Capital Effectiveness →		
Shareholder Value ←	Cost of Capital (discount rate)	

DCF requires explicit assumptions about key value drivers that are utilized to project future cash flows. These cash flow projections are discounted at the firm's cost of capital to determine the value of the firm.

Cost of capital can have a significant impact on the value of a firm. Figure 26.6 plots the relationship between cost of capital and enterprise value for LSA Company based on the DCF model that is used in Chapter 30.

FIGURE 26.6 **Sensitivity of value to cost of capital.**

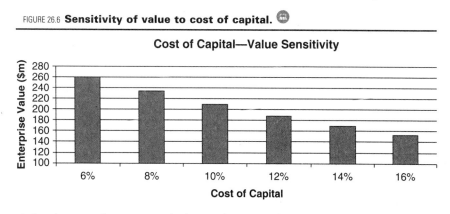

A fundamental aspect underlying the cost of capital is the relationship between risk and return. We all recognize that a riskier investment must have a higher potential return than a safer one, as otherwise we would simply invest in the safer investment. For example, few sensible people would invest in a start-up company that, if successful, was expected to return a rate close to the risk-free rate on U.S. Treasury bonds. Most would invest in the much safer investment providing the same return. We all would expect a risk premium for the higher-risk start-up investment. This risk-return trade-off is pictured in Figure 26.7.

FIGURE 26.7 **Risk and return.**

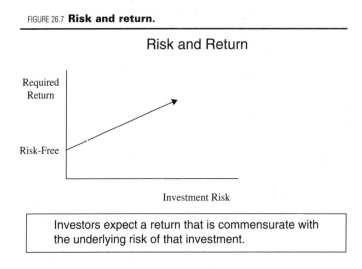

Cost of Capital Drivers

The cost of capital for a firm is driven by several factors as illustrated in Figure 26.8, including interest rates, financial and operating leverage, volatility, and risk.

FIGURE 26.8 **Cost of capital drivers.**

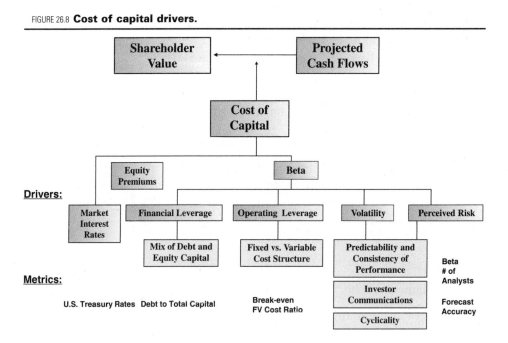

Market Interest Rates   The starting point in determining the cost of capital is typically the risk-free rate of return. Investors have the opportunity to invest in an essentially risk-free investment, U.S. Treasury notes. This rate will form the baseline for setting required rates of return for alternative investments with progressively higher risks.

Financial Leverage   Another significant driver of the cost of capital for a firm is the mix of capital used to run the business. Typically, the cost of debt is lower than the cost of equity as interest rates are generally well below expected rates of return on equity investments. In addition, the cost of debt is reduced by the related tax savings since interest expense is a deduction in computing taxable income in most cases.

Operating Leverage   Operating leverage refers to the composition of costs and expenses for a company and was covered in detail in Chapter 23. A firm that has most of its costs fixed in the short term is said to have a high degree of operating leverage. A change in sales levels will have a dramatic effect on profits for this firm since most of its costs are fixed. By contrast, a company with lower operating leverage has a greater portion of its cost structure as variable. That is, if sales decline, the variable costs will also be reduced. The firm with high operating leverage will experience greater fluctuations in profits and cash flows for a given change in sales, leading to a higher level of volatility and perceived risk.

Volatility and Variability   Companies that have unpredictable or inconsistent business results typically are valued at a discount to companies with predictable and consistent operating performance. Investors that employ multiples to value a highly volatile business will use a lower multiple of sales or earnings. Investors that use discounted cash flow will use a higher weighted average cost of capital (WACC) to discount future projected cash flows.

Perceived Risk   Investors will demand returns commensurate with the risk level they perceive in a business. Examples of additional factors leading to higher perceived risk include:

- Geopolitical factors, for example, developing countries or unstable regions.
- Currency exposure.
- Competitive pressure.
- Technological obsolescence.
- Management transitions.

Estimating the Cost of Capital

The most common method used to estimate the cost of capital is the weighted average cost of capital (WACC) method. The WACC methodology computes a blended or weighted cost of capital, considering that capital is often supplied to the firm in various forms. The most common are equity, provided by shareholders, and debt, provided by bondholders. In addition, there are many other forms that combine elements of both debt and equity. Examples of these hybrid securities include preferred stock and convertible bonds. It is important to emphasize that the cost of capital represents an estimate, or approximation. Recognizing this, we should test the inputs to the WACC formula and use sensitivity analysis to understand the impact of these assumptions on the valuation of a company.

WACC Computation   Following are the steps to compute the WACC:

1. Estimate the cost of equity.
2. Estimate the cost of debt.
3. Weight the cost of equity and debt to compute the WACC.

The information in Table 26.2 will be used to illustrate the WACC computation.

TABLE 26.2 **WACC illustration inputs.**

Market Information	
Current Risk-free rate on U.S. Treasury Notes	4.0%
Historical Market Premium for stocks (vs Risk Free)	5.5%
Company Information:	
Market Value of Equity ($ millions)	90.0
Beta of Company stock (Measure of Volatility)	1.09
Market Value of Debt ($ millions)	10.0
Interest Rate (Yield to maturity*) YTM	6.0%
Tax Rate	40%

*Yield to maturity is used in WACC computation, not coupon rate

Step 1: Estimate the Cost of Equity   The cost of equity represents the estimated return expected by shareholders and potential shareholders. Three components are considered: the risk-free rate, the premium expected for equity investments (market premium), and risk associated with a specific company (beta). The cost of equity for this firm would be computed as follows:

$$\text{Cost of Equity} = \text{Risk-Free Rate} + (\text{Beta} * \text{Market Premium})$$
$$= 4.0\% + 1.09 \, (5.5\%)$$
$$= 10.0\%$$

Step 2: Estimate the Cost of Debt   Since interest expense is generally tax deductible, the cost of debt is reduced by the tax savings and is computed as follows:

$$\text{Cost of Debt} = \text{Yield to Maturity} \times (1 - \text{Tax Rate})$$
$$= 6\% \, (1 - 40\%)$$
$$= 3.6\%$$

Step 3: Weight the Cost of Equity and Debt to Compute WACC   Table 26.3 shows the WACC computation based on levels of debt and equity.

TABLE 26.3 **WACC computation.**

WACC Computation	Cost	Market Value	Market Value %	Weighting
Debt	3.6%	10.0	10%	0.36%
Equity	10.0%	90.0	90%	9.00%
Total/WACC		100.0	100%	9.36%

Figure 26.9 provides a visual summary of how these elements come together in the WACC computation. Investors who invest in equity securities expect a premium over returns obtainable from risk-free securities (U.S. Treasury notes). This market premium results in an expected return for the market (e.g., S&P 500), in the illustration, just above 10%. The cost of capital for a particular security is then computed by adding a premium for the risk of investing in an individual security. The cost of equity is then blended with the after-tax cost of debt to estimate the weighted average cost of capital.

FIGURE 26.9 **WACC visual summary.**

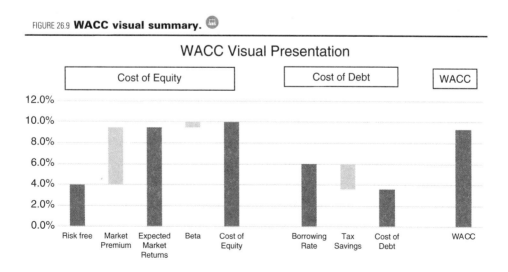

Since the cost of debt is typically lower than the cost of equity, it is easy to conclude that some blend of debt and equity would result in the lowest cost of capital. The combination of debt and equity that results in the lowest cost of capital is called the optimal capital structure. This concept is illustrated in Figure 26.10. A firm with no debt will have a WACC equal to the cost of equity. As the firm adds debt to the mix, the WACC will be reduced to a point. However, at some point, the increased risk associated with high borrowings will increase the required interest rates and will also increase the required cost of equity. The combined effects will increase the WACC above the minimum level projected at the optimum capital structure.

FIGURE 26.10 **Optimal cost of capital and capital structure.**

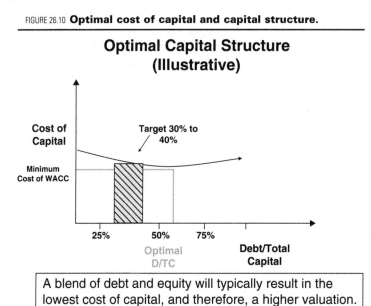

A blend of debt and equity will typically result in the lowest cost of capital, and therefore, a higher valuation.

Most firms do not operate at or near the "optimal capital structure." The capital structure is the result of a number of factors, as will be discussed in Chapter 27.

Key Ways Managers Can Reduce the Cost of Capital

Some of the factors that determine cost of capital are out of the firm's control. For example, market interest rates are the foundation for estimating cost of capital. Unless they have influence over the general economy, inflation, or the chairman of the Federal Reserve Bank, there is little managers can do about interest rates. Here are some specific actions managers *can* take to reduce the cost of capital:

1. Managers can reduce surprises and volatility that will result in a lower beta and cost of capital, and therefore, higher valuation. Managers should strive to improve the predictability and consistency of business

performance for several reasons. In addition to reducing surprises and volatility that affect the cost of capital, improvements in this area will result in lower working capital requirements and operating costs.

2. Managers can consider using a reasonable level of debt in the capital structure. Utilizing a sensible level of debt provides leverage to equity investors and reduces the cost of capital. The level of debt should be lower than the theoretical borrowing capacity to provide for a cushion to service this debt during a business downturn or unforeseen future challenges.

3. Managers can improve communications with investors. To the extent that investors have a full understanding of the business performance and potential they will likely have a better perspective on the business. This better understanding and perspective will result in reducing potential overreactions to expected variations in business performance.

Key ways operating managers can influence perceived risk (and therefore value):

- ❏ Utilize a reasonable level of debt in the capital structure.
- ❏ Reduce surprises and volatility.
- ❏ Improve predictability and consistency of performance.
- ❏ Reduce operating leverage by "variabilizing" costs.
- ❏ Improve communications with investors.

PERFORMANCE MEASURES

A number of measures can be tracked to provide insight into the firm's WACC and identify potential opportunities to reduce the cost of capital.

Financial Leverage: Debt to Total Capital

In Chapter 2, we reviewed key financial ratios that measure financial leverage and capital structure. The mix of debt and equity in the capital structure is an important variable in the cost of capital and valuation. For evaluating financial leverage, the measure is usually computed using book values:

$$\text{Debt to Total Capital} = \frac{\text{Interest-Bearing Debt}}{\text{Total of Interest-Bearing Debt and Equity}}$$

Stock Volatility/Beta

For a public company, the volatility of the company's stock price is an important indicator of the level of risk perceived by investors. Investors attempt to estimate the risk inherent in future performance and cash flows by looking at historical measures of stock volatility or beta. Beta compares the change in the firm's stock price to the change in a broad market measure. Beta, which measures the correlation of an individual stock to the S&P 500 is available in many financial reporting services. Services use different time horizons to calculate beta and stock volatility, often going back several years. Since we want to track Beta or stock volatility to use in estimating a cost of capital for future performance, we must ensure that the historical measure is indicative of future performance. Care should be exercised in circumstances where significant changes have recently occurred, or are anticipated, in the company's market, strategic direction, or competitive environment. In these cases, managers and investors may focus on recent history or expected future stock price volatility or beta as a better indicator of current investor confidence and perceived risk.

Operating Leverage

In Chapter 23 we concluded that the mix of variable and fixed cost components has a significant impact on the earnings and cash flow of a firm as sales levels vary. Where sales volatility is likely, for example, in cyclical businesses, managers should closely monitor and evaluate the cost structure of the company. Fixed cost levels or breakeven sales levels should be measured and evaluated periodically.

Actual versus Projected Performance   Preparing business forecasts is an important activity for most companies. These forecasts will be the basis for making important decisions and in investor communications. For many firms, future estimates of revenue are typically the most important and difficult operating variable to forecast. In Part IV, "Business Projections and Plans," we presented a number of tools to monitor and evaluate the accuracy and effectiveness of forecasts. Forecast variances should also be reviewed in the context of the firm's cost of capital since the predictability and consistency of operating performance will affect stock volatility.

Illustrative Dashboard: Cost of Capital

A dashboard for the cost of capital should be utilized, incorporating key performance indicators appropriate to the specific issues and priorities for each company. An illustrative cost of capital dashboard is presented in Figure 26.11.

FIGURE 26.11 **Cost of capital dashboard.**

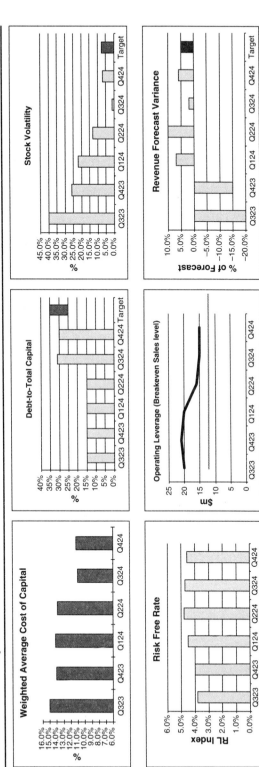

SUMMARY

The time value of money is a core financial concept. Simply stated, a dollar promised in the future is worth less today. The value today must recognize risk and the opportunity cost of not having that dollar today to invest in other alternatives.

The cost of capital for a firm is a significant value driver. Cost of capital is inversely related to the firm's value. Managers should be aware of the sensitivity of the company's valuation to the cost of capital. Management can reduce the cost of capital, thereby increasing value, by reducing risk and volatility, and by using an appropriate mix of debt and equity. Key factors impacting the firm's cost of capital should be identified and measured.

27

Capital Structure and Financial Leverage

The capital structure of a firm is critically important for two reasons. First, it is the source of capital to finance the company's operations. Second, it is a significant factor in determining the firm's cost of capital, which was discussed in Chapter 26. In this chapter, we will explore capital structure and financial leverage in greater detail.

OVERVIEW OF FINANCING AND CAPITAL STRUCTURE

We will use the financial statements of LSA Technology Company to illustrate key aspects of capital structure and financial policy (see Table 27.1).

In Chapter 6, we suggested an alternative presentation to the traditional Balance Sheet as shown in Figure 27.1. This presentation delineates the net operating assets (or invested capital) required to support the business and the sources of this invested capital. The net assets deployed in this business are $64,755 and are funded by $10,000 in debt and $54,755 in equity.

The column on the right represents the capital structure of the firm, and the mix of debt and equity used to finance the capital requirements of the firm.

Capital Structure and Liquidity Measures

Capital structure measures are indicators of the firm's source of capital (debt vs. equity), creditworthiness, ability to service existing debt, and ability to raise additional financing if needed (see Table 27.2). Liquidity measures

TABLE 27.1 **LSA Technology Company financials.**

LSA Technology Company
Historical and Estimated Financials

		2020	2021	2022	2023
P&L					
Net Sales		79,383	84,000	91,000	100,000
Cost of Goods Sold		36,000	38,000	41,000	45,000
Gross Margin		43,383	46,000	50,000	55,000
SG&A		25,403	26,880	29,120	32,000
R&D		6,351	6,720	7,280	8,000
Operating Income		11,630	12,400	13,600	15,000
Interest (Income) Expense		600	600	600	600
Other (Income) Expense		5	7	6	5
Income Before Income Taxes		11,025	11,793	12,994	14,395
Federal Income Taxes		3,748	4,010	4,418	4,894
Net Income		7,276	7,783	8,576	9,501
Balance Sheet					
Cash		25	2,404	4,400	7,944
Receivables		15,877	16,800	18,545	20,000
Inventories		14,400	15,200	16,400	18,000
Other		200	800	975	900
Current Assets		30,502	35,204	40,320	46,844
Net Fixed Assets		15,877	16,800	18,750	20,000
Net Goodwill and Intangibles		14,000	13,000	12,000	11,000
Other Non-Current Assets		200	210	428	205
Total Assets		60,578	65,214	71,498	78,049
Accounts Payable		3,600	3,800	4,100	4,500
Notes Payable, Bank		-	-	-	-
Accrued Expenses & Taxes		4,000	4,500	4,750	5,000
Current Liabilities		7,600	8,300	8,850	9,500
Long-Term Debt		10,000	10,000	10,000	10,000
Other		3,083	2,536	3,194	3,794
Stockholders' Equity		39,895	44,378	49,454	54,755
Total Liabilities and Equity		60,578	65,214	71,498	78,049
Other Information:					
Stock Price		9.22	9.78	10.00	10.59
Shares Outstanding (in millions)		16.7	16.8	16.9	17.0
Market Value of Equity		153,974	164,304	169,000	180,030
Interest Rate	6%				
Income Tax Rate	34%				
Dividends		3,000	3,300	3,500	4,200
Capital Expenditures		3,000	4,200	4,800	5,000
D&A		2,800	3,277	2,850	3,750
Employees		411	450	460	490

examine the ability of the firm to convert assets to cash to satisfy short-term obligations.

Our definition of *debt* includes all interest-bearing obligations. The following measures will include notes payable, current maturities of long-term debt (long-term debt due within one year), and long-term debt.

FIGURE 27.1 **Alternative Balance Sheet illustration.**

Net Operating Assets/Invested Capital Illustration

Net Operating Assets (Invested Capital)		Sources of Capital	
Cash	7,944		
Receivables	20,000		
Inventories	18,000		
Fixed Assets, net	20,000		
Intangibles Net	11,000	Debt	10,000
Other	1,105		
Total Assets	78,049		
Less Operating Liabilities		Shareholders Equity	54,755
Accounts Payable	(4,500)		
Accrued Liabilities	(5,000)		
Deferred Liabilities	(3,794)		
Net Assets	64,755	Total "Invested Capital"	64,755

For LSA Technology Company:

Notes Payable	$0
Current Maturities of Long-Term Debt	$0
Long-Term Debt	$10,000
Total Debt	$10,000

Current Ratio
How Is It Computed?

$$\text{Current Ratio} = \frac{\text{Current Assets}}{\text{Current Liabilities}}$$

$$= \frac{\$46,844}{9,500}$$

$$= 4.93$$

What Does It Measure and Reflect? This measure of liquidity computes the ratio of current assets (that will convert to cash within one year) to current liabilities (that require cash payments within one year). As such, it compares the level of assets available to satisfy short-term obligations.

Quick Ratio
How Is It Computed?

$$\text{Current Ratio} = \frac{\text{Current Assets} - \text{Inventory}}{\text{Current Liabilities}}$$

$$= \frac{\$46,844 - 18,000}{9,500}$$

$$= 3.04$$

TABLE 27.2 **Capital structure analysis.**

Liquidity and Capital Structure Recap

P&L Recap	LSA Technology
Revenue	100,000
Operating Income	15,000
%	
Interest Expense	600
Interest Expense after Tax	396
Net Income	9,501
Balance Sheet Recap	
Current Assets	46,844
Working Capital	37,344
Total Assets	78,049
Debt	10,000
Equity	54,755
Ratio Analysis	
Working Capital % of Revenue	37.3%
Quick Ratio	3.04
Debt to Total Capital	15.4%
Times Interest Coverage	25
ROE Analysis	
Asset Turnover (a)	1.28
Profitability (b)	9.5%
Financial Leverage (c)	1.43
Return on Equity (a × b × c)	17.4%

What Does It Measure and Reflect? The quick ratio is a more conservative measure of liquidity than the current ratio since it removes inventory from other assets that are more readily converted into cash.

Debt to Equity
How Is It Computed?

$$D/E = \frac{\text{Debt}}{\text{Equity}}$$

$$= \frac{\$10,000}{54,755}$$

$$= 18.3\%$$

What Does It Measure and Reflect? Debt to equity measures the proportion of total book capital supplied by bondholders (debt) versus shareholders (equity).

Debt to Total Capital
How Is It Computed?

$$D/TC = \frac{\text{Debt}}{\text{Total Capital}(\text{Debt} + \text{Equity})}$$

$$= \frac{\$10,000}{(\$10,000 + 55,249)}$$

$$= 15.3\%$$

What Does It Measure and Reflect? This measure computes the percentage of total "book" value (as recorded on the books and financial statements) of capital supplied by bondholders. A low debt to total capital percentage indicates that most of the capital to run the firm has been supplied by stockholders. A high percentage, say 70%, would indicate that most of the capital has been supplied by bondholders. The capital structure for the latter example would be considered "highly leveraged." This measure is also computed using market value of debt and equity.

Times Interest Earned (Interest Coverage)
How Is It Computed?

$$TIE = \frac{\text{EBIT (Operating Income)}}{\text{Interest Expense}}$$

$$= \frac{\$15,000}{600}$$

$$= 25 \times$$

What Does It Measure and Reflect? This measure computes the number of times the firm earns the interest expense on current borrowings. A high number reflects slack, indicating an ability to cover interest expense even if income were to be reduced significantly. It also indicates a capacity to borrow more funds if necessary. Conversely, a low number reflects a limited ability to service existing debt levels and borrow additional funds.

These metrics are reviewed by credit rating agencies, banks, and other lenders to assess creditworthiness of companies. They should also be monitored by equity investors. Many of these measures also are incorporated into loan agreements as covenants. In short, the company must report and maintain certain minimum or maximum levels on key metrics. For example, a covenant may require the debt to total capital not exceed 30%. Failure to satisfy the covenants can result in the debt being called or renegotiating the terms of the loan.

Return on Equity   Financial leverage is a key driver of return on equity (ROE). Recall that in Chapter 2 we computed ROE as follows:

$$= \frac{\text{Net Income}}{\text{Equity}}$$
$$= \frac{\$9,501}{\$55,249}$$
$$= 17.2\%$$

In Chapter 2, we examined the ROE of LSA Technology Company using the Dupont formula.

This methodology, also called the return tree, is illustrated here:

$$\text{ROE} = \text{Profitability} \times \text{Asset Turnover} \times \text{Financial Leverage}$$

$$\frac{\text{Net Income}}{\text{Sales}} \times \frac{\text{Sales}}{\text{Assets}} \times \frac{\text{Assets}}{\text{Equity}}$$

For LSA Technology Company:

$$17.4\% = 9.5\% \times 1.28 \times 1.43$$

For our purposes in this chapter, we will focus on financial leverage.

Financial Leverage   Financial Leverage (FL) is a measure of the ratio of total assets to equity. A lower level of borrowings will reduce the financial leverage and return on equity (ROE). Financial leverage can have a substantial effect on ROE. In Table 27.3, we compare the ROE analysis for LSA Technology to Hilever Co. to illustrate the dramatic effect that leverage can have on ROE. Hilever has an ROE of 32.3% compared to 17.4%, due only to the effect of an additional $28,853 in debt resulting in a debt to total capital of 60% (profitability is also lower owing to the higher interest expense after tax). In order to remove the impact of leverage on financial returns, we recommend that we also measure return on invested capital (ROIC).

TABLE 27.3 **Capital structure comparison.** 🔘

Financial Leverage Comparison		
	LSA	**Hilever Co**
Profitability	9.5%	8.4%
Asset Turnover	1.28	1.28
Financial Leverage	1.43	3.0
Return on Equity	17.4%	32.3%
Assets	78,049	78,049
Debt	(10,000)	(38,853)
Other Liabilities	(13,294)	(13,294)
Equity	54,755	25,902
Debt to Total Capital	15.4%	60.0%
Financial Leverage		
Assets/	78,049	78,049
Equity	54,755	25,902
=		
Financial Leverage	1.43	3.01

Capital Requirements and the Company Life Cycle

The need, sources, and uses of capital change significantly over a company's life cycle, as illustrated in Figure 27.2. For start-ups or early-stage ventures, capital is needed to develop products or service frameworks, build a marketing and sales organization, and prove the merits of the underlying business plan. Entrepreneurs often raise money from personal savings, friends and families, angel investors, and often venture capital (VC) firms.

If the firm enjoys initial success and transitions to a high revenue growth stage, the cash requirements typically *increase*. In addition to continued high investments in R&D, marketing, and sales to support growth, the firm must build out infrastructure (e.g., manufacturing, distribution) and also fund working capital requirements. As revenue grows, the firm must build inventory ahead of revenue and will also experience a delay in collecting from customers, resulting in an increase in receivables. In addition, other capital investments to support growth may also be required. Cash flow generated from revenue will be offset by the working capital and investments to support expansion. This reality is often not anticipated by entrepreneurs and results in the need to raise additional funds beyond initial expectations.

Eventually, the rate of growth slows for all enterprises. The rate of investment to support growth also declines as does the need for higher levels of working capital. Profitability and cash flow generally reach peak performance levels. The company will likely consider returning excess cash

FIGURE 27.2 **Company life cycle and financing.**

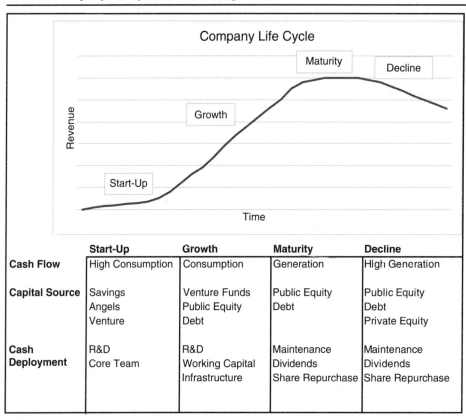

	Start-Up	**Growth**	**Maturity**	**Decline**
Cash Flow	High Consumption	Consumption	Generation	High Generation
Capital Source	Savings Angels Venture	Venture Funds Public Equity Debt	Public Equity Debt	Public Equity Debt Private Equity
Cash Deployment	R&D Core Team	R&D Working Capital Infrastructure	Maintenance Dividends Share Repurchase	Maintenance Dividends Share Repurchase

flow to investors through dividends or share repurchases. If the company is unsuccessful in refreshing the growth curve, revenue levels will flatten and begin to decline.

SHORT-TERM FINANCING

Short-term financing refers to requirements over the next 12 months or operating cycle. There are two elements to short-term financing. First is the management of working capital and projecting short-term cash flows, which was addressed in Chapter 24. The second is to ensure that the company has adequate cash reserves or access to short-term financing to address seasonal variations or surprises.

Types of Short-Term Financing Vehicles

Short-term financing needs can be covered by cash generated from operations, cash reserves, lines of credit, revolving credit facilities, and the issuance of commercial paper.

Cash Flow and Reserves. A company may choose to finance short-term cash requirements, for example, due to seasonality, by building a cash reserve. The maximum requirements can be estimated by projecting maximum cash flow requirements over the next 12 months. Since cash inflows and outflows vary by month and even by week or day, the projections often look at cash flow by week.

Revolving Credit Agreements. A revolving credit agreement, typically with a bank or other financial institution, allows the company to draw down on the credit multiple times as additional cash is required. The agreement typically calls for regular payments on the outstanding balance and is subject to various terms, including covenants. The concept is similar to a credit card for individuals.

Commercial Paper. Firms with strong credit characteristics may be able to borrow by issuing commercial paper, with durations of weeks or months. Commercial paper is unsecured and is used to cover temporary shortfalls in cash.

Other Short-Term Loans. Banks and other lenders may be willing to lend on a short-term basis, especially where the need is due to seasonal requirements. For example, industries such as retail and farming typically have large cash outflows several months before harvest or holiday sales.

LONG-TERM FINANCING

Long-term financing refers to securing the capital required by the firm over the long term. The firm may seek long-term financing from equity investors, lending institutions, or a mix of both.

Equity. Proceeds from issuing stock to investors is recorded as shareholders' equity.

Debt. The firm may borrow from investors or lending institutions for some portion of long-term financing requirement.

Other. There are many "hybrid" securities such as preferred stock or convertible bonds that have features of both debt and equity.

Setting the Capital Structure

We would like to think that the capital structure is set based on a strategic plan and thorough analysis of various alternative structures, arriving at an optimal capital structure. In some cases, it is. However, many firms are heavily influenced by risk-averse managers and boards, the history of the company, the desire to maintain future flexibility, and other considerations.

In Chapter 26, we discussed the optimal capital structure in terms of minimizing the WACC, and therefore, maximizing shareholder value (Figure 27.3).

FIGURE 27.3 **Optimal cost of capital and capital structure.**

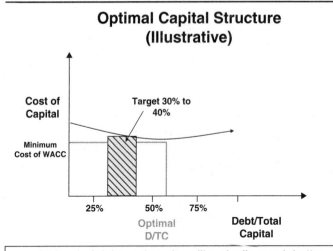

A blend of debt and equity will typically result in the lowest cost of capital, and therefore, a higher valuation.

Most firms do not operate at or near the optimal capital structure. There are several reasons for this. First, some managers do not fully accept the concept of discounted cash flow/cost of capital or WACC. Others are very conservative and are opposed to the risk introduced by using or increasing debt. Even managers that accept the basic concept choose not to add leverage, or will add reasonable levels of debt that leave them far short of the theoretical optimum capital structure. Typically, companies will set a target capital structure, expressed as a range of debt to total capital, for example 30% to 40%. Figure 27.4 captures some of the factors that influence decision-makers in setting a target capital structure. Tolerance for risk, capital requirements, and growth rates are a few examples. Firms will then often deviate from this target capital structure. For example, they may choose to exceed the target range to finance a strategic opportunity such as an acquisition. Typically, the corporation would plan to return to the target range within a couple of years or reset the range to a higher level.

Types of Long-Term Financing Vehicles

Corporations have a number of options for long-term financing. Major considerations include the company's creditworthiness, interest rates, and costs of transactions.

Term Loans. Term loans are direct business loans from banks, insurance companies, and other lenders that specialize in corporate financing, including private equity firms. For large loans, several lenders may form a "consortium"

FIGURE 27.4 **Capital structure and financial policy.**

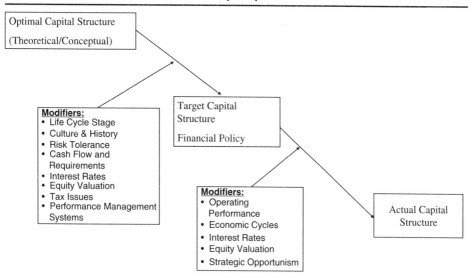

to spread the risk across all members of the group. The terms generally are less than five to seven years and full payment is due at the end of the term.

Private Placement Bonds. Similar to term loans with longer terms offered by insurance companies and pensions.

Bonds Issued in the Public Capital Markets. Firms can also raise money in the public capital markets. This requires filing a comprehensive prospectus with the Securities and Exchange Commission (SEC) and ongoing public reporting requirements.

Special Purpose Financing. The firm may choose to borrow to finance the construction of a large facility or similar investment, obtaining lower interest rates due to collateral of the property.

Financial Flexibility

Competent CFOs and Treasurers maintain a cash reserve and the ability to raise additional funds should needs or opportunities arise. We often refer to this as "keeping your powder dry." Potential sources include excess cash (amount held in excess of expected liquidity needs), additional borrowing capacity, expected future cash flows, and ultimately, changing the target capital structure (Figure 27.5). The exercise is especially important where the firm is considering large investment opportunities such as acquisitions, or significant product or geographic expansion.

FIGURE 27.5 **Financing flexibility.**

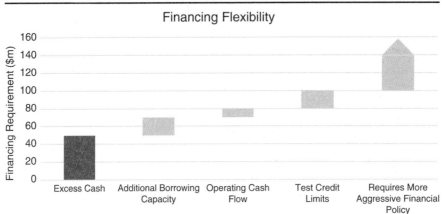

Up to $80.0m requirement easily accommodated
$80-$100m requirement would test credit rating limits
$100.0m and greater requirement would require a significant change to financial policy

CAPITAL RESTRUCTURING

Most firms will explore and likely change their capital structure at some point in their life cycle. This may be due to additional capital requirements or a goal to reduce their cost of capital. Leveraged buy-out transactions (LBOs) represent an extreme restructuring often employed by private equity firms to dramatically increase equity returns (e.g., return on equity).

Restructuring the Capital Base

As discussed earlier in the chapter, many companies operate without debt or with modest debt levels. While this has certain advantages, it results in two suboptimal value drivers: a higher cost of capital and reduced return on equity (ROE). In order to maximize shareholder value, boards and executives often evaluate potential changes to the mix of debt and equity in the company's capital structure.

Often, recaps are part of an overall business restructuring or transformation. In one publicly traded company that I served as CFO, we restructured our capital base to enhance returns. We had operated with relatively low debt levels and financed operating requirements, internal development, and acquisitions from operating cash flows. This restructuring was similar to the illustration in Table 27.4.

TABLE 27.4 **Capital restructuring analysis.**

Liquidity and Capital Structure Recap

P&L Recap	Current	Transaction	Pro forma Restructured
Revenue	100,000		100,000
Operating Income	15,000		15,000
%			
Interest Expense	600	1,344	1,944
Interest Expense after Tax	396	887	1,283
Net Income	9,501	(887)	8,614
Balance Sheet Recap			
Current Assets	46,844		46,844
Working Capital	37,344		37,344
Total Assets	78,049		78,049
Debt	10,000	22,400	32,400
Equity	54,755	(22,400)	32,355
Ratio Analysis			
Working Capital % of Revenue	37.3%		37.3%
Quick Ratio	3.04		3.04
Debt to Total Capital	15.4%		50.0%
Times Interest Coverage	25.00		7.72
Return Analysis			
Asset Turnover (a)	1.28		1.28
Profitability (b)	9.5%		8.6%
Financial Leverage (c)	1.43		2.41
Return on Equity (a × b × c)	17.4%		26.6%
Return on Invested Capital (ROIC)	15.3%		15.3%

Leveraged Recapitalizations and Leveraged Buy-Out Transactions

A leveraged recap or leveraged buy-out transaction analysis (LBO transaction analysis) is a useful exercise for companies evaluating strategic alternatives, maximizing shareholder value or testing optimal capital structures (Table 27.5). This results in a substantial improvement in ROE, but would, of course, increase risk associated with the company's ability to service the debt.

TABLE 27.5 **Leveraged recap analysis.** 🔗

Liquidity and Capital Structure Recap: Leveraged Transaction			
P&L Recap	**Current**	**Transaction**	**Proforma Leveraged**
Revenue	100,000		100,000
Operating Income	15,000		15,000
%			
Interest Expense	600	2,508	3,108
Interest Expense after Tax	396	1,655	2,051
Net Income	9,501	(1,655)	7,845
Balance Sheet Recap			
Current Assets	46,844		46,844
Working Capital	37,344		37,344
Total Assets	78,049		78,049
Debt	10,000	41,800	51,800
Equity	54,755	(41,800)	12,955
Ratio Analysis			
Working Capital % of Revenue	37.3%		37.3%
Quick Ratio	3.04		3.04
Debt to Total Capital	15.4%		80.0%
Times Interest Coverage	25.00		4.83
Return Analysis			
Asset Turnover (a)	1.28		1.28
Profitability (b)	9.5%		7.8%
Financial Leverage (c)	1.43		6.02
Return on Equity (a × b × c)	17.4%		60.6%
Return on Invested Capital (ROIC)	15.3%		15.3%

A traditional LBO analysis is illustrated in Table 27.6. This is an effective, one-page analysis to explore whether a given company is a candidate for such a transaction.

TABLE 27.6 **LBO analysis.**

LBO Analysis

LSA

Illustrative Model

Transaction Summary [1]

Sources:	Amount	% of Total	Int Rates
Bank Debt	65.0	28%	8.00%
Sr. Sub. Notes	97.1	41%	9.00%
Total Debt	162.1	69%	
New Equity	65.0	28%	
Cash on Hand	7.9	3%	
Total	235.0	100%	

Uses: [2]

	Shares	Price	Prem to Market	Amount
Purchase of Equity	17	13.00	22.76%	221.0
Retire Existing Debt				10.0
Purchase Price				231.0
Transaction Costs	1.75%		3.5%	4.0
Total				235.0
Current Market Price		10.59		

Goodwill Estimates [3]

Purchase Price of Equity	231.0	
Book Value	78.0	
Excess	153.0	
Good will	130.0	85%
Intangibles	22.9	15%
Years	10.0	
Annual Amortization	2.3	

Acquisition Price Multiples [4]

Price:	231	2024	2025
Sales		2.1	2.0
EBITDA		11.3	10.2
EBIT		12.7	13.1

Equity Returns Based on Trailing EBITDA Multiple [7]

EBITDA Multiple	5 year Ent Value	Eq Return	7 year Value	Return
6.0	190.4	3.8%	204	8.5%
7.0	222.2	11.1%	238	12.6%
8.0	253.9	16.9%	272	15.9%
9.0	285.6	21.7%	306	18.8%
10.0	317.4	25.9%	340.0	21.3%

Equity Returns Based on Trailing P/E Multiple

PE	5 year Value	Eq Return	7 year Value	Return
14	135.8	15.9%	158.7	13.6%
16	155.2	19.0%	181.3	15.8%
20	194.0	24.4%	226.7	19.5%
22	213.4	26.8%	249.4	21.2%

Financial Projections [5]

P&L	History 2021	2022	2023	Projections 2024	2025	2026	2027	2028	2029	2030	2031	CAGR 2024-2029
Revenue	84.0	91.0	100.0	108.0	116.6	126.0	136.0	146.9	158.7	165.0	170.0	8.0%
% Change Year to Year	8.0%	8.3%	9.9%	8.0%	8.0%	8.0%	8.0%	8.0%	8.0%	4.0%	3.0%	
EBITDA	15.7	16.5	18.8	20.5	22.7	25.2	27.2	29.4	31.7	33.0	34.0	9.1%
% of Sales	18.7%	18.1%	18.8%	19.0%	19.5%	20.0%	20.0%	20.0%	20.0%	20.0%	20.0%	
Depreciation	3.3	2.9	3.8	2.3	2.8	3	2.5	2.5	4	5	5.5	
Amortization of Intangibles				2.3	2.3	2.3	2.3	2.3	2.3	2.3	2.3	
EBIT	12.4	13.6	15.0	18.2	17.7	19.9	22.4	24.6	25.4	25.7	26.2	6.9%
% of Sales	14.8%	14.9%	15.0%	16.9%	15.1%	15.8%	16.5%	16.7%	16.0%	15.6%	15.4%	
Interest Expense												
Bank				5.2	5.2	4.4	3.4	2.7	2.0	1.2	0.3	
Sr. Sub Notes				8.7	8.7	8.7	8.7	8.7	8.7	8.7	8.7	
Total Interest	0.0	0.0	0.0	13.9	13.9	13.2	12.1	11.5	10.7	9.9	9.0	
Earnings Before Taxes	12.4	13.6	15.0	4.3	3.7	6.7	10.3	13.1	14.7	15.8	17.2	
Taxes 34.0%	4.2	4.6	5.1	0.0	0.0	0.0	3.5	4.5	5.0	5.4	5.8	
Net Income	8.2	9.0	9.9	4.3	3.7	6.7	6.8	8.7	9.7	10.4	11.3	
% of Sales	9.7%	9.9%	9.9%	4.0%	3.2%	5.3%	5.0%	5.9%	6.1%	6.3%	6.7%	

TABLE 27.6 *(Continued)*

Capital Structure [6]

Bank Debt		65.0	55.3	42.2	34.0	25.1	14.8	3.7	-7.9
Sr Sub Notes		97.1	97.1	97.1	97.1	97.1	97.1	97.1	97.1
Tot Debt		162.1	152.4	139.3	131.1	122.2	111.9	100.8	89.2
Equity		65.0	68.7	75.5	82.2	90.9	100.6	111.0	122.4
Total Capital		227.1	221.1	214.7	213.4	213.1	212.5	211.8	211.5
Free Cash Flow									
Net Income		4.3	3.7	6.7	6.8	8.7	9.7	10.4	11.3
D&A		2.3	5.1	5.3	4.8	4.8	6.3	7.3	7.8
(Inc) Dec WC	5.0%	-0.4	3.0	4.0	-0.5	-0.5	-0.6	-0.3	-0.3
Capital Expenditures		-2.0	-1.0	-1.5	-2.0	-3.0	-4.0	-5.0	-6.0
Cash Flow		4.2	10.8	14.5	9.1	9.9	11.4	12.4	12.9
Reduction in Debt			-9.7	-13.1	-8.2	-8.9	-10.3	-11.2	-11.6
Credit Statistics									
Interest Coverage	EBITDA/Interest Expense	1.5	1.6	1.9	2.2	2.6	3.0	3.3	3.8
Debt/Bk Capital	Debt/Total Capital	71.4%	68.9%	64.9%	61.5%	57.3%	52.7%	47.6%	42.2%
Debt to Equity	Debt/Equity	249.4%	221.8%	184.6%	159.4%	134.4%	111.2%	90.8%	72.9%
Debt to EBITDA	Debt/EBITDA	7.9	6.7	5.5	4.8	4.2	3.5	3.1	2.6

Equity Returns Based on Trailing Revenue Multiple

Revenue	5 year		7 year	
0.8	126.9	-25.4%	136.0	-4.6%
1.0	158.7	-6.4%	170.0	3.2%
1.2	190.4	3.8%	204.0	8.5%
1.4	222.2	11.1%	238.0	12.6%
1.6	253.9	16.9%	272.0	15.9%
1.8	285.6	21.7%	306.0	18.8%

1. Transaction Summary—Sources. Presents the sources of "new capital," including new borrowings and equity investment.

2. Transaction Summary—Uses. The new capital must purchase outstanding shares and retire existing debt, in addition to covering transaction costs.

3. Acquisition Accounting Estimates. This is a high level and preliminary allocation of the purchase price to determine annual amortizations costs.

4. Acquisition Price Multiples. This section computes the purchase price as a multiple of revenue, EBITDA, and earnings.

5. Financial Projections. Projected operating performance for the next 5–10 years is key to the ultimate success of the LBO process.

6. Cash Flow and Capital Structure Analysis. Due to the significance of optimizing cash flow to service debt, a summary of cash flow, capital structure, and key metrics is presented.

7. Equity Returns. Since the primary objective of the transaction is to provide superior returns to the "new" equity investors, the returns are calculated at possible exit multiples based on the final year estimated performance.

RETURNING CAPITAL TO SHAREHOLDERS

Executives and boards generally develop a policy on deploying any cash flow generated in excess of operating requirements or investment opportunities. This is typically presented as capital deployment policy, for example:

1. Fund operating requirements.
2. Finance strategic investments, including acquisitions.
3. Pay a regular dividend.
4. Pay a special dividend or repurchase outstanding shares.

This policy is typically included in a financial policy summary presented to the board, investors, and lenders and is illustrated in Figure 27.6.

Regular Dividends   Companies that generate cash in excess of operational needs may choose to pay a dividend to shareholders. Desired by many investors, including funds with investment thesis to hold companies with a consistent history of paying dividends and those with a history of growing

FIGURE 27.6 **Illustrative financial policy summary.**

Financial Policy Summary

Capital Structure:
- 20–30% debt to total capital
- Maintain healthy interest coverage
- May exceed temporarily for strategic opportunity

Dividend Policy:
- 20 Year history of increasing dividends
- Target payout ratio: 30% to 40% of net income

Share Repurchases:
- Target repurchases to offset dilutive effect of stock options

Capital Deployment Priorities:
1. Operating requirements
2. Strategic investments, including acquisitions
3. Pay a regular dividend
4. Pay a special dividend or repurchase outstanding shares

---

the dividend. Dividends provide a current stream of income to investors and increase value since expected cash flows to investors include not only the potential capital appreciation, but a stream of dividends over time. One investor (a large mutual fund company) in a company that I served as CFO considered the dividend the primary reason for investing in the company. The company had a long history of paying a consistently increasing dividend. In each meeting with this investment firm, they wanted to confirm that there were no plans to change the dividend policy. Two key metrics are used to evaluate dividends: the dividend payout ratio and the dividend yield.

Payout Ratio. The payout ratio is the percentage of net income distributed to shareholders in the form of a dividend. For LSA Company:

$$= \frac{\text{Dividend}}{\text{Net Income}}$$

$$= \frac{\$4,200}{\$9,501}$$

$$= 44.2\%$$

This is a relatively high dividend payout, enabled by a strong cash flow, without significant reinvestment requirements.

Dividend Yield. The dividend yield computes the level of dividends to the market value of the company. It is similar to the interest rate paid on the value of a bond. The yield is an important investment consideration, especially for income dividend funds. The dividend yield is computed as follows:

$$= \frac{\text{Dividend}}{\text{Market Value of Equity}}$$

$$= \frac{\$4,200}{\$180,030}$$

$$= 2.45\%$$

Over the last decades, the dividend yields on stocks exceed many rates on interest-bearing deposits and bonds, creating a large demand for dividend-focused stocks and funds.

These ratios may be calculated at the company level (previously shown) or on a per-share basis.

Special Dividends   A special dividend is a nonrecurring distribution to shareholders in the form of a dividend. Special dividends can be used to distribute excess cash accumulated over time or to distribute proceeds from the sale of a business unit.

Share Repurchases   Share repurchases are used by most publicly traded companies. A share repurchase is affected by purchasing the company's shares from shareholders. This can be done on the public markets or in a private transaction. One of the most common objectives is to purchase shares to offset the dilution from issuance of stock options to employees. Share repurchases can also be used to return excess cash to shareholders and improve earnings per share by reducing the number of shares outstanding.

Capital Structure and Financial Policy Illustrations

A dashboard for the capital structure and financing should be utilized, incorporating key performance indicators appropriate to the specific issues and priorities for each company. An illustrative capital dashboard is presented in Figure 27.7.

SUMMARY

Financing the corporation is an important value driver and ensures financial resources to fund the needs of the company. Setting financial policy, implementing the strategic capital structure, and providing for short-term financing requirements are fundamental responsibilities of financial executives.

FIGURE 27.7 **Capital structure dashboard.**

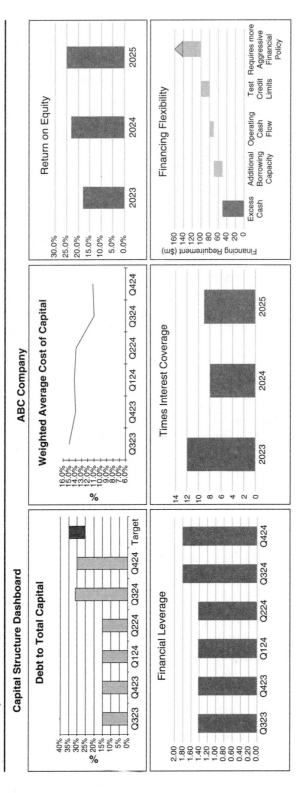

Part Six

Valuation and Capital
Investment Decisions

28

Capital Investment Decisions—Introduction and Key Concepts

Capital investment decisions (CIDs) are some of the most important business decisions that managers make. *Capital decisions* are generally defined as relatively large investments that will have an economic life of several years. We will define *capital investments* broadly, including purchases of equipment, new product development projects, acquiring a product line or a company, building a factory or distribution center, and many others. The capital investment *decision* is a determination of whether the project is likely to create value for shareholders. In this chapter, we will introduce capital investments, evaluation and key decision criteria, and outline the steps required to evaluate CIDs. In Chapter 29, we will cover advanced topics of CIDs, including dealing with risk and uncertainty, monitoring projects, and presenting capital investment decisions.

THE CAPITAL INVESTMENT PROCESS

A strong capital investment process is critical to ensure a thorough evaluation and decision. Figure 28.1 outlines key steps in an effective capital investment process.

Companies should identify potential capital projects as part of their strategic and annual operating planning activities. The capital budget should be an important element of each plan. For strategic plans, the managers should look out three to five years and anticipate significant capital expenditures to

FIGURE 28.1 **Capital investment process overview.**

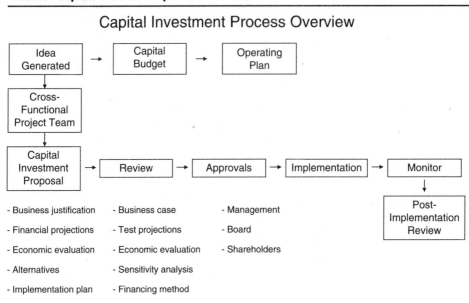

support growth, strategic initiatives, and other requirements. Integrating the capital plan into the financial projections will afford the opportunity to review cash flow projections and determine the adequacy of returns over the strategic planning horizon.

For significant expenditures, a capital investment proposal (CIP) should be prepared to document key aspects of the project, including business justification, economic case, alternatives, and implementation plan. The scope of the CIP and the management approval level should scale with the size and importance of the project.

Business Case. The business case should define the strategic and business objectives that will be achieved or supported with this use of capital. In addition to passing certain economic tests, the project must be clearly linked to a strategic or operational objective. Some projects may make economic sense but may be outside, or even inconsistent with, the strategic direction of the company.

Economic Case. All capital investment projects should be supported by financial projections and an economic evaluation. The financial projections should be based on the business case and implementation plan, and include the following:

- Estimated costs to purchase and start up the project.
- Incremental revenues, costs, and capital requirements that result from undertaking the project.
- Estimated salvage or terminal value at the end of the project life.

Alternatives. Most projects have several alternative courses of action. These should be explored as part of the capital investment decision and documented in the capital investment proposal. Reviewers should test the selection of the recommended plan to ensure that this alternative provides the best balance of technical, business, and economic performance.

Implementation Plan. Execution and implementation are always a critical success factor for any project. Capital projects should be supported with a detailed implementation plan. This plan will provide a roadmap to achieve the objectives of the capital investment. A good implementation plan is a strong indication that the project is well planned, including identification of resource requirements, risks, and alternatives. The implementation plan also provides a basis for monitoring and reviewing progress of the project. Identifying key assumptions, checkpoints, and go/no go decision points will also allow managers to consider redirecting or terminating projects that may be at risk. The characteristics of a good implementation plan are detailed in the sidebar.

Characteristics of Good Implementation Plans

❑ Identify and address obstacles and barriers.

❑ Identify critical success factors.

❑ Identify resource requirements and key assumptions.

❑ Assign responsibility for critical activities.

❑ Include sufficient detail:

- Specific tasks: What should I be doing today?
- Interdependencies/critical path.
- Monitoring and communication value.

❑ Measurable objectives and targets.

- Make sure these link to and support financial targets.

❑ Identify key performance indicators.

Executive Review of Capital Investment Projects   Most companies require management approval for investments over a certain limit. Approval requirements typically escalate to higher levels of management, the board of directors, or even shareholders based on the nature and size of the investment and source of financing. The sidebar ("Executive Review of Capital Projects") highlights key points that executives should consider in their evaluation of significant investments.

Executive Review of Capital Projects
  Key points:

  ❑ Consistency with mission/strategy.
  ❑ Strategic and business case.
  ❑ Economic case:
     • Projections, market size and share, adoption rate, business model, and investment requirements.
  ❑ Identify and test assumptions:
     • What are the critical assumptions? Are they realistic? How will we monitor these over the course of the project?
     • Review scenario and sensitivity analysis: Can we live with downside scenarios?
  ❑ Project management and ownership:
     • Experience/knowledge.
     • Track record.
     • Passion for program.
  ❑ Implementation plan; human and financial resource requirements.
  ❑ Risk identification and mitigation plans.

EVALUATING THE ECONOMIC MERITS OF CAPITAL INVESTMENTS

No matter how simple or complex the project, the same basic three steps should be employed to evaluate and select appropriate capital investments. The three steps are:

1. Estimate relevant cash flows associated with the project.
2. Measure the project's expected performance against investment decision rules.
3. Accept or reject based on decision rules.

These three steps focus on the financial or economic part of the evaluation. Of course, there also needs to be a review of other business issues and to ensure the project is consistent with the firm's strategic direction as described earlier.

Step 1: Estimate Relevant Cash Flows Associated with the Project

Economic evaluations should be based on projected cash flows. The first step will be to estimate the *incremental* investments and profit and loss (P&L) on the project, and then to estimate cash flows, reflecting the capital investment, depreciation, and working capital requirements.

Estimating both the acquisition or development cost and future cash flows of a project is by far the most important and most difficult part of CIDs. There are three categories of cash flow to consider for most projects: the initial cash outflow or investment, the stream of annual cash flows over the project's expected life, and a residual or terminal value at the end of the project (or projected cash flow).

The definition and application of incremental cash flows is a source of confusion in estimating relevant cash flows. Incremental revenues, investments, costs, and expenses should be limited to those that directly result from undertaking the project. The test is to identify those expenses and revenues that are not incurred if the project is not undertaken.

For significant and complex projects, we should utilize the techniques covered in developing long-term projections of future business in Chapter 21.

Initial Investment   We need to estimate the total investment or cash outflows associated with the project. This can be as simple as the purchase cost of a new piece of equipment. However, if the machinery is shipped to us and requires installation, setup, and training, then these costs also must be reflected as the total cost of acquiring the asset.

The project investment can become very complex and extend over several years. For example, the total design, approval, and construction of a new refinery or nuclear plant can extend for a decade or longer. Similarly, the development of a new product, such as a prescription pharmaceutical, can extend over many phases with a high degree of uncertainty of efficacy and approval by regulatory agencies. The investment in these cases may be very difficult to estimate.

All cash outflows must be considered, regardless of the accounting treatment. These include operating expenses (after tax), purchases of property and equipment, development of facilities, and working capital required to support the project.

Cash Flows over Project Life   The second set of cash flows to consider is the estimated annual cash flows over the project's life. For simple projects, such as purchasing a more efficient piece of manufacturing equipment, the savings may be as simple to define as reduced labor or scrap costs. At the other end of the spectrum are complex projects such as new product development or the acquisition of a company. In both these cases, a complete set of financial projections would be required, including a complete P&L, Balance Sheet, Statement of Cash Flows, and supporting schedules (see Chapter 21, "Long-Term Projections").

Residual or Terminal Value   We need to estimate what, if any, value may exist at the end of the project's expected (or projected) useful life. For projects involving manufacturing or transportation equipment, the value at the end of life may be trade-in, salvage, or resale value. For more complex and longer-term programs, such as the acquisition of a business or development of a product line, we must estimate the value of the business at the end of its useful life (or forecast horizon). This value may be a liquidation value if the business would be shut down and the remaining assets sold at liquidation value. If the business could be sold or continue to operate beyond the projected life or forecast horizon, then we need to estimate the terminal or post-horizon value.

Capital Investment Examples

Case Study 1: Automate Manufacturing Process

Roberts Pharmaceuticals is considering automating a key part of its manufacturing process. The equipment will cost $100,000 and is expected to reduce manufacturing cycle time, improve yield, and decrease test costs.

What incremental cash flows are likely to result from undertaking this project? This project will probably involve the following incremental cash flow items, among others:

- Cost of equipment.
- Cost of installation.
- Reduced labor and test costs.
- Reduced material costs due to yield improvement.
- Increased depreciation expense.
- Increased taxes on profit improvement.

Case Study 2: Develop and Introduce New Treatment

Roberts Pharmaceuticals is considering the development of a breakthrough treatment for procrastination. The project will require several years of development and will result in a significant increase in sales. The treatment can be produced in the company's existing facilities.

What *incremental* cash flows are likely to result from undertaking this project? This project will probably include the following incremental cash flows:

- R&D investment.
- Cost of FDA approval.
- Investment in manufacturing process.
- Distribution channel and training.
- Marketing and promotion.
- Revenue and profits.
- Working capital required to support program.
- Increased depreciation expense.
- Increased taxes on profit improvement.

Step 2. Measure the Project's Expected Performance against Investment Decision Rules

A variety of measures or decision criteria are used to evaluate the economic characteristics of the investment. In addition to satisfying these economic tests, the project must also be justified on a business and strategic basis. The three most common measures are net present value (NPV), internal rate of return (IRR), and payback. In special situations, additional measures are utilized. Most of the decision rules are based on the economic principle of the time value of money (TVOM). Refer to Chapter 26 to review TVOM, discount rates, and cost of capital.

We illustrate the measurement criterion with the following simple example:

Project life: 5 years

Initial investment: $24,000

Projected after-tax savings for 5 years: $8,000

Project terminates at end of year 5 with no residual value

Discount rate: 10%

Net Present Value (NPV)   Net present value (NPV) utilizes the discounted cash flow methodology described in Chapter 26 to account for the time value of money and project risk. The cash flow for each year is discounted back to the equivalent value today ("year 1") using a discount or hurdle appropriate for the risk level of the project. NPV is the sum of all discounted cash inflows and outflows. A positive NPV indicates that the project has a rate of return that exceeds the discount rate used, and therefore, should be approved. A negative NPV indicates that the project has a return under the discount rate, and should not be undertaken.

TABLE 28.1 **NPV illustration.**

Discount rate	10%					
	Year 1	**Year 2**	**Year 3**	**Year 4**	**Year 5**	**Year 6**
Project Cash Flows:						
Cash Inflows	−24,000	8,000	8,000	8,000	8,000	8,000
Present Value Factor	0.91	0.83	0.75	0.68	0.62	0.56
Present Value	−21,818	6,612	6,011	5,464	4,967	4,516
Net Present Value (Sum of PV)	5,751					

In the example in Table 28.1, the NPV is +$5,751, indicating that the project has a return above the expected return (discount rate) and should be implemented. Note that we provided the present value factor (PVF) and present value (PV) for each annual cash flow. This provides insight into the TVOM and the dynamics of the project's NPV, which would not be visible if buried in a single cell of a spreadsheet.

Internal Rate of Return (IRR)   The internal rate of return (IRR) of a project is the actual rate of return implied in the project's cash flows. If the IRR exceeds the discount rate (DR), the project should be approved. If the IRR is less than the cost of capital, the project should be rejected. Prior to the widespread availability of spreadsheet and finance application software, the IRR would be computed by trial and error by guessing at the IRR and re-computing until NPV = 0.

TABLE 28.2 **IRR illustration.**

Internal Rate of Return						
	Year 1	**Year 2**	**Year 3**	**Year 4**	**Year 5**	**Year 6**
Project Cash Flows	−24,000	8,000	8,000	8,000	8,000	8,000
Present Value Factor	0.83	0.70	0.58	0.48	0.40	0.34
Present Value	−20,024	5,569	4,646	3,876	3,234	2,698
Sum PV	0					
NPV	0					
IRR	19.9%					

The project in the example in Table 28.2 has an IRR of 19.9%, which is above the 10% discount rate used for the project. Note that IRR and NPV are consistent decision criteria, using estimated cash flows and the discount rate as key inputs. The use of IRR and NPV will result in consistent decisions as follows:

IRR	NPV	Result
R > DR	NPV > 0	Approve
IR < DR	NPV < 0	Reject

Payback   The investment payback is a simple measure that estimates how long (in years and fractions of years) it will take to recover the investment in a project. Investments with shorter payback periods are typically viewed as positive; investments with longer payback periods may be rejected or require additional review. This method does not consider the time value of money (i.e., cash flow in future years does not have the same value as an equivalent cash amount now). Despite this criticism, it has high acceptance and usage because it is easily understood and measures an important characteristic: How long until we recover our initial investment? Many organizations have rules of thumb based on payback, requiring a certain class of investments to have a payback of three years or less.

In this example, the cumulative cash flow for the project becomes positive in year 3. We estimate the payback as shown in Table 28.3.

TABLE 28.3 **Payback illustration.**

Payback	Year 1	Year 2	Year 3	Year 4	Year 5	Year 6
Project Cash Flows:						
Cash Inflows		8,000	8,000	8,000	8,000	8,000
Cash Outflow	−24,000					
Cumulative	−24,000	−16,000	−8,000	–	8,000	16,000
Payback	3.0					

Typically, the payback will not end exactly at the end of a year and will require an estimation of partial-year payoffs, using interpolation.

All three methods should be utilized since they each provide different views into the economic dynamics of the project. Table 28.4 presents a summary of the economic evaluation of this project, reflecting all three measures.

TABLE 28.4 **Combined illustration.**

Discount rate	10%						
		Year 1	**Year 2**	**Year 3**	**Year 4**	**Year 5**	**Year 6**
Project Cash Flows:							
Cash Flows		−24,000	8,000	8,000	8,000	8,000	8,000
Cumulative		−24,000	−16,000	−8,000	-	8,000	16,000
Present Value Factor		0.91	0.83	0.75	0.68	0.62	0.56
Present Value Cash Flow		−21,818	6,612	6,011	5,464	4,967	4,516
Net Present Value		5,751					
IRR		19.9%					
Payback		3.0					

While NPV indicates whether the project should be undertaken based on a given discount rate, IRR provides the precise rate of return on the project. By comparing the IRR to the DR, you can get a sense of the return "slack." Payback complements these measures by estimating the number of years until cash outlays are fully recovered. For example, a project may have a positive NPV and a high rate of return, but the bulk of the cash may be recovered late in the project life, or even in the terminal or salvage value. This long payback should be evaluated in the context of project risks.

We used a discount rate of 10% in the example. The discount rate for each project should be based on the level of risk associated with the project. For practical reasons, companies often set a hurdle rate above the company's cost of capital (covered in Chapter 26) to ensure that projects will earn an acceptable return. If individual projects are perceived as having very low or high risk, the discount rate may be adjusted accordingly, as will be discussed in Chapter 29.

Other Measures   In addition to NPV, IRR, and payback, the following measures are occasionally used to evaluate capital projects. Their primary utility is to relate the level of NPV to the value of the investment or outflow. This can be useful in ranking projects based on their relative return.

Benefit-Cost Ratio (BCR). The BCR is computed as follows:

$$\frac{\text{PV of Cash Inflows}}{\text{PV of Cash Outflows}}$$

For our illustration,

$$\text{BCR} = \frac{\$27,569}{21,818}$$
$$= 1.26$$

Profitability Index (PI). The PI is also used in ranking projects in capital rationing applications. Essentially, it scales the NPV of the investment to each dollar of investment, allowing a ranking by "biggest bang for the buck." The PI is computed as follows:

$$= \frac{NPV}{Initial\ Investment}$$
$$= \frac{\$5,751}{\$24,000}$$
$$= 0.24$$

Step 3: Accept or Reject the Project   Financial theory provides that projects should be approved if the following requirements are met:

- ❏ IRR exceeds the discount rate.
- ❏ NPV is greater than 0.
- ❏ Payback < limit (e.g., 3 years).

Of course, these decision criteria must be applied in a sensible manner. Projects that marginally satisfy these requirements should be subjected to further review, including evaluating the projections and sensitivity and scenario analyses.

What Is a Strategic Investment?   Organizations (and most commonly CEOs) often refer to *strategic investments* as including any investment that is of strategic importance to the enterprise. This may include new products, geographic expansion, or even the acquisition of a firm. Many cynical CFOs jokingly refer to a *strategic investment* as any investment the CEO is firmly committed to that does not meet the economic criteria described previously! As a result, it is ascribed some unquantifiable "strategic value."

In some cases, these projects may indeed have dubious value other than as a favorite initiative of the CEO. In other cases, this dichotomy arises because the analysis does not reflect all potential sources of value. The finance team should persevere to identify and estimate other scenarios and options that may not be reflected in the base case of the investment analysis. More on this will be covered in Chapter 29.

CAPITAL INVESTMENT ILLUSTRATIONS

Two illustrations of capital investment decisions will be presented next. The illustrations include the projected cash flows and the evaluation criteria for each investment. Table 28.5 is an example of an analysis of a project to automate manufacturing. Table 28.6 is an illustration of a new product development

TABLE 28.5 **Capital expenditure: Manufacturing project.**

Roberts Pharmaceuticals
Automate Manufacturing Process

Project Investment Analysis $000's (Unless otherwise noted)

Incremental Changes		2023	2024	2025	2026	2027	2028	2029	2030	Terminal Value
Revenues										
Cost of Revenues										
On Incremental Revenues	30%									
Project Savings		-	-25,000	-40,000	-75,000	-75,000	-75,000	-75,000	-75,000	
Incremental Cost of Revenues		-	-25,000	-40,000	-75,000	-75,000	-75,000	-75,000	-75,000	
Gross Margin Impact		-	25,000	40,000	75,000	75,000	75,000	75,000	75,000	
Operating Expenses:										
On Incremental Revenues	15%									
Project Savings										
Project Costs and Expenses		50,000								
Depreciation on Project Capital			30,000	30,000	30,000	30,000	30,000			
Incremental Operating Expenses		50,000	30,000	30,000	30,000	30,000	30,000	-	-	
Operating Profit		-50,000	-5,000	10,000	45,000	45,000	45,000	75,000	75,000	
Tax	40%	20,000	2,000	-4,000	-18,000	-18,000	-18,000	-30,000	-30,000	
Operating Profit After Tax		-30,000	-3,000	6,000	27,000	27,000	27,000	45,000	45,000	

Operating Cash Flow:								
Depreciation		30,000	30,000	30,000	30,000	30,000	45,000	-
(Inc) Dec in Accounts Receivable		50,000						
(Inc) Dec in Inventories			25,000					
Capital Expenditures	-150,000							
Incremental Cash Flows	-180,000	77,000	61,000	57,000	57,000	57,000	45,000	45,000
Cumulative Cash Flow	-180,000	-103,000	-42,000	15,000	72,000	129,000	174,000	219,000
Present Value Factor	0.909	0.826	0.751	0.683	0.621	0.564	0.513	0.467
Present Value of Cash Flows	-163,636	63,636	45,830	38,932	35,393	32,175	23,092	20,993

NPV	$96,414	
IRR	28%	Discount Rate 10%
Payback	3 years	PH Growth Rate 0%

TABLE 28.6 **Capital expenditure: Pharmaceutical product development.**

Roberts Pharmaceuticals
New treatment for Procrastination

Project Investment Analysis $000's (Unless otherwise noted)

Incremental Changes		2023	2024	2025	2026	2027	2028	2029	2030	Terminal Value
Revenues	25%	-	-	-	25,000	75,000	125,000	200,000	225,000	
Cost of Revenues										
On Incremental Revenues					6,250	18,750	31,250	50,000	56,250	
Project Savings		-	-	-						
Incremental Cost of Revenues		-	-	-	6,250	18,750	31,250	50,000	56,250	
Gross Margin Impact					18,750	56,250	93,750	150,000	168,750	
Operating Expenses:	15%									
On Incremental Revenues					3,750	11,250	18,750	30,000	33,750	
Project Savings		-	-	-						
Project Costs and Expenses		20,000	10,000	10,000	10,000	10,000	10,000			
Depreciation on Project Capital										
Incremental Operating Expenses		20,000	10,000	10,000	13,750	21,250	28,750	30,000	33,750	
Operating Profit		-20,000	-10,000	-10,000	5,000	35,000	65,000	120,000	135,000	
Tax	40%	8,000	4,000	4,000	-2,000	-14,000	-26,000	-48,000	-54,000	
Operating Profit after Tax		-12,000	-6,000	-6,000	3,000	21,000	39,000	72,000	81,000	

Operating Cash Flow:

Depreciation		10,000	10,000	10,000	10,000	10,000	10,000		
(Inc) Dec in Accounts Receivable		-	-	-938	-1,875	-2,813	-4,688	-7,500	-8,438
(Inc) Dec in Inventories		-	-	-1,875	-5,625	-9,375	-15,000	-16,875	-16,875
Capital Expenditures	-50,000								
Incremental Cash Flows	-62,000	4,000	2,125	6,438	18,813	29,313	47,625	55,688	371,250
Cumulative Cash Flows	-62,000	-58,000	-55,875	-49,438	-30,625	-1,313	46,313	102,000	473,250
PV Factor	0.870	0.756	0.658	0.572	0.497	0.432	0.376	0.327	0.284
PV Cash Flow	-53,913	3,025	1,397	3,681	9,353	12,673	17,904	18,204	105,532

NPV	$117,856	Discount Rate	15%
IRR	37%	PH Growth Rate	0%
Payback	6 Years		

577

analysis. These examples were introduced earlier in the chapter to illustrate the identification of incremental cash flows for a project.

In both examples, the shaded part of the worksheet develops the incremental cash flows associated with the project. As discussed earlier in the chapter, each project will have unique characteristics and therefore unique cash flows. In addition to the incremental cash flow per year, we include the cumulative cash flow per year to highlight the timing of cash flows. Note that the cumulative cash flow for the new pharmaceutical remains negative through 2028 (six years), while the cumulative cash flow for the manufacturing project becomes positive in 2025 (three years).

The unshaded portion presents the economic evaluation of each project. In addition to presenting the project NPV, IRR, and payback, we include the present value factor and present value of cash flow for each year. This provides insight into the dynamics of the economic valuation and the importance of accelerating cash flows in any project.

This project has a positive NPV, an IRR that exceeds the discount rate, and a relatively quick payback (three years).

The development project has a positive NPV and an IRR that exceeds the discount rate. As expected, the payback (six years) is longer than the manufacturing example, but certainly acceptable for a product development initiative. Note that the discount rate of 15% is higher than that of the manufacturing project due to the higher level of risk (and therefore, higher expected return) for developing a new product.

Monitoring Capital Investment Projects   After approving capital investment projects, organizations should have a process for tracking and evaluating the progress and re-validating the continued investment in resources. The critical assumptions and implementation progress can be compared to the original assumptions and project plan in the capital investment proposal (CIP).

This is especially important for mid- to long-term projects such as product development. In these times of rapid change, it is entirely possible that the underlying assumptions for a project have changed to an extent that continued investment is not justified. Have market or competitive factors changed significantly? Will the product meet targeted cost and performance attributes? Similarly, implementation may have incurred delays or unforeseen hurdles that need immediate attention or may threaten the success of the project, including economic justification. Are we on schedule to introduce the product as planned? Will the project meet the expectations for revenue, profits, and NPV that were established in the CIP? By monitoring critical projects, early detection is possible, providing the greatest window for consideration and action. If the ongoing project is determined to be dubious, investments can be terminated and resources redirected to other, more promising opportunities. Venture capital firms are masters of using this method. Their continued investment in a firm or project is dependent on progress or the attainment of specific objectives that foretell ultimate success.

Organizations should also evaluate the performance of completed projects and review utilization of assets on a periodic basis. These topics were covered in Chapter 25, "Capital Management and Cash Flow: Long-Term Capital Assets."

SUMMARY

Capital investment decisions are a critical aspect of managing an enterprise. Each CID requires a determination of whether that project will create value for the owners of the firm. Accordingly, firms must establish a rigorous process to allocate capital and evaluate individual uses of capital.

Capital investments include a wide spectrum of projects and purchases, from purchases of equipment to development of new products to acquiring a company. Common economic evaluation measures include payback, net present value, and internal rate of return.

Since CIDs require projections of future results, they incorporate a significant level of risk and uncertainty. Techniques for identifying and addressing risk and uncertainty will be covered in Chapter 29.

29

Capital Investment Decisions— Advanced Topics

In Chapter 28, we introduced key elements of capital investment decisions. In this chapter, we will cover advanced topics, including dealing with risk and uncertainty, capital budgeting and rationing, and methods of evaluating the effectiveness of the capital investment decision process. Finally, we will review best practices in presenting capital investment decisions.

DEALING WITH RISK AND UNCERTAINTY IN CAPITAL INVESTMENT DECISIONS

Since we are dealing with expectations, predictions, and projections of *future* performance, capital investment decisions have an inherent level of risk and uncertainty. The risk and uncertainty can be extreme in projects that extend over a long period, or involve rapidly changing environmental and competitive factors (almost all markets now!). In recent years, the pace of change, level of uncertainty, and frequency of black swan events have exacerbated business risks.

Sources of Risk and Uncertainty

❑ Project-specific risk.

❑ Competitive risk.

❑ Industry risk.

❑ Global and international risk.

❑ Geopolitical risk.

❑ Financial market risk.

❑ Estimation bias.

There are two broad techniques for addressing risk and uncertainty in capital investment decisions:

1. Utilization of an appropriate discount rate for the project risk.
2. Analysis, evaluation, and flexing of financial projections.

Utilization of an Appropriate Discount Rate for the Project Risk   Many firms use a single discount rate for all capital projects. In many cases, the origin and basis of the discount rate is not known or well understood. The discount rate should be reviewed periodically and the appropriateness of using it on a specific project should always be considered.

The starting point for selecting the discount rate should be the firm's overall cost of capital. This weighted average cost of capital (WACC) is a blend of all risk and return factors for the company. The rate for a specific project should be reviewed to determine if it is appropriate for the specific risk characteristics of that project.

Let's begin with the security market line, commonly known as the risk-return graph. While its origin lies in the capital assets pricing model (CAPM) for financial securities, the concept transfers to real investments as well. Investors and managers can choose to invest in a wide range of investment alternatives, each with its own level of risk. As you move down the investment risk axis, the theory holds that investors should have a higher return expectation (Figure 29.1).

The firm's weighted average cost of capital is simply one point on this curve, representing the required return for all investors in the company's debt and equity. The spectrum of potential investments for a firm ranges from low-risk investments, such as replacing equipment on the manufacturing line, to investing in a high-risk venture. Figure 29.2 illustrates typical investments a firm may evaluate; the actual placement and ranking would be very situation and project specific. Replacing the equipment on the manufacturing line

FIGURE 29.1 **Risk and return.**

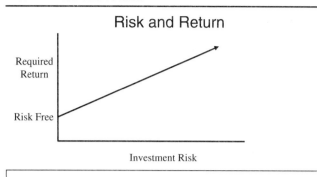

Investors expect a return that is commensurate with the underlying risk of that investment.

FIGURE 29.2 **Risk and expected return.**

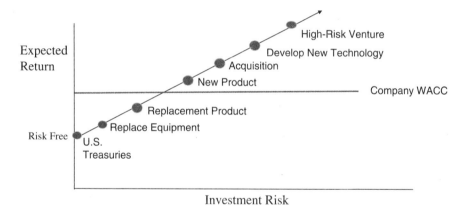

Potential investments have different levels of risk, and therefore, required return.

would generally have low risk since the firm already has experience in this activity and there is little risk of loss since it appears to be needed to support revenue. Replacing an existing product would also likely have lower risk than the firm-wide composite (WACC). However, investments to develop a new product, acquire a business, or develop a new technology would likely be higher than the firm's WACC.

If the firm uses the WACC to evaluate higher risk programs, it runs the risk of approving projects that have higher risk than expected returns. Conversely, if the WACC is used to evaluate projects with lower risk, it may reject projects that should be approved. Refer to Chapter 26 for a more complete discussion on the cost of capital and WACC.

In theory, the firm could research similar investments and develop an expected return (discount rate) for each individual project. This can be time-consuming and difficult. Most firms would develop a practical framework that allows for some recognition of differing risk levels as illustrated in Figure 29.3.

FIGURE 29.3 **Setting hurdle rates based on risk.**

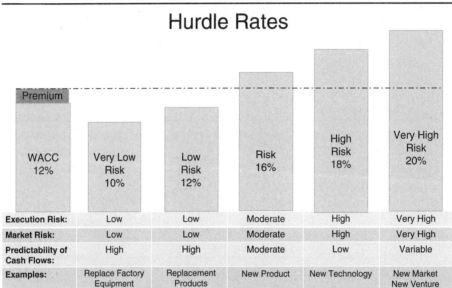

In this example, the firm's WACC is estimated to be 12%. The firm could establish an overall hurdle rate of 14% by tacking on a premium or cushion of 2%. For project categories with lower risks, the hurdle rate would be reduced. For investment categories with higher risks, the hurdle rate would be increased to require a higher expected return to be approved. The firm can override the hurdle rate for any specific project if that is deemed appropriate. The firm's WACC and hurdle rates are typically reviewed and updated if appropriate, on an annual basis. Any significant events that change the risk profile would also warrant reconsideration.

Analysis, Evaluation, and Flexing of Financial Projections   I have always found that understanding and evaluating the financial projections in a capital decision are among the most important *and* difficult aspects of the review process. For significant projects, it may be appropriate to look at several projection scenarios and analyses. The best practices in projecting and evaluating long-term projections discussed in Chapter 21 should be employed in significant projects.

For significant projects with extended time horizons, a thorough plan and financial projection should be developed to support the capital investment decision. The following capital investment decisions would warrant a complete business plan and detailed financial projections:

❑ Developing a new product.

❑ Creating a new business unit.

❑ Entering a new market.

❑ Acquiring another business or company.

There are several tools that have proven effective in dealing with risk and uncertainty in capital investment decisions. We will build on our illustration of the new pharmaceutical development to treat procrastination introduced in Chapter 28.

Base Case. The base case employs a discounted cash flow (DCF) analysis using the most likely estimates for all variables. This case represents a single outcome from a range of potential outcomes and includes many assumptions about future events and performance. The base case is the project investment analysis in Table 29.1.

Sensitivity Analysis. This technique determines the sensitivity of the decision criteria (e.g., NPV) to changes in the assumptions used in the base case. Table 29.2 presents the traditional sensitivity analysis, showing the base case of $117.8 and the resultant NPV values at different assumptions of revenue and development costs.

Table 29.2 shows that this project could have a NPV as low as $77 million to a high of $154 million within the ranges of these assumptions. This provides great context to the decisions-makers, providing insight into the dynamics of the investment over a wide range of potential outcomes.

Breakeven Analysis. Table 29.3 presents a different form of sensitivity analysis that highlights the impact of a 10% change in each variable and determines how far the assumptions can change before resulting in a breakeven NPV value.

Scenario Analysis. This important tool determines projected NPV of the project under specified scenarios (e.g., recession, best case, competitive reaction, etc.). Projections for each specific scenario are developed, and the investment is evaluated under each scenario. Scenario analysis was introduced in Chapter 13.

TABLE 29.1 **Project investment analysis: New procrastination treatment.** 🔄

Roberts Pharmaceuticals		Project Investment Analysis					$000's (Unless otherwise noted)			
New Treatment for Procrastination										
										Terminal
Incremental Changes		**2023**	**2024**	**2025**	**2026**	**2027**	**2028**	**2029**	**2030**	Value
Revenues		-	-	-	25,000	75,000	125,000	200,000	225,000	
Cost of Revenues										
On Incremental Revenues	25%	-	-	-	6,250	18,750	31,250	50,000	56,250	
Project Savings		-								
Incremental Cost of Revenues		-	-	-	6,250	18,750	31,250	50,000	56,250	
Gross Margin Impact		-	-	-	18,750	56,250	93,750	150,000	168,750	
Operating Expenses:										
On Incremental Revenues	15%	-	-	-	3,750	11,250	18,750	30,000	33,750	
Project Savings										
Project Costs and Expenses		20,000								
Depreciation on Project Capital			10,000	10,000	10,000	10,000	10,000			
Incremental Operating Expenses		20,000	10,000	10,000	13,750	21,250	28,750	30,000	33,750	
Operating Profit		−20,000	−10,000	−10,000	5,000	35,000	65,000	120,000	135,000	
Tax	40%	8,000	4,000	4,000	−2,000	−14,000	−26,000	−48,000	−54,000	
Operating Profit After Tax		−12,000	−6,000	−6,000	3,000	21,000	39,000	72,000	81,000	
Operating Cash Flow:										
Depreciation			10,000	10,000	10,000	10,000	10,000			
(Inc) Dec in Accounts Receivable			-	-	−938	−2,813	−4,688	−7,500	−8,438	
(Inc) Dec in Inventories			-	−1,875	−5,625	−9,375	−15,000	−16,875	−16,875	
Capital Expenditures		−50,000								
Incremental Cash Flows		−62,000	4,000	2,125	6,438	18,813	29,313	47,625	55,688	371,250
Cumulative Cash Flows		−62,000	−58,000	−55,875	−49,438	−30,625	−1,313	46,313	102,000	473,250
PV Factor		0.870	0.756	0.658	0.572	0.497	0.432	0.376	0.327	0.204
PV Cash Flow		−53,913	3,025	1,397	3,681	9,353	12,673	17,904	18,204	105,532

NPV	$117,856		Discount Rate	15%
IRR	37%		PH Growth Rate	0%
Payback	6 Years			

TABLE 29.2 **Sensitivity analysis.**

Roberts Pharmaceuticals
Procrastination Treatment
Sensitivity Analysis   NPV

		Revenues (m)				
		175.0	**200.0**	**225.0**	**250.0**	**275.0**
	$ 18.0	88.0	105.0	122.0	137.0	154.0
Development	**19.0**	86.0	103.0	120.0	135.0	152.0
Costs (m)	**20.0**	83.0	101.0	117.8	133.0	150.0
	21.0	81.0	98.0	115.0	131.0	149.0
	22.0	77.0	94.0	111.0	129.0	146.0

TABLE 29.3 **Sensitivity and breakeven analysis.**

Roberts Pharmaceuticals
Procrastination Treatment

Sensitivity and Breakeven Analysis

	Key Assumptions				Breakeven Approx. Value
	Base	**10% Change**	**NPV**	**% Change in NPV**	**NPV=0**
Base			117.9		117.9
Sales (2025)	225.0	202.5	101.8	−13.6%	56.5
Cost & Expense Levels	40%	44.0%	87.9	−25.4%	56.0%
Tax Rate	40.0%	44.0%	103.3	−12.4%	NMF
Initial Outlay	70.0	77.0	114.2	−3.1%	250.0*
Terminal Value	371.3	334.1	107.3	−9.0%	0
Discount Rate	15.0%	16.5%	93.2	−20.9%	30.0%

*Dependent on assumptions capital versus expense.

Steps to develop scenarios:

1. Select potential scenarios (e.g., general economic, price of oil, competitive reaction, adoption rates).

2. Develop projections under each scenario. This is a critical aspect of scenario planning. Unlike sensitivity analysis, where we simple flex selected variables, we will revise the projections for expected changes under the scenario. For example, in a recession, a company may experience price pressure and lower demand. That company may also expect different interest rates, labor rates, and commodity pricing.

3. Measure scenario using: NPV, IRR, payback, and so forth.

4. Use this insight in evaluating the project.

In our example of the development of a procrastination treatment, there are several potential scenarios to consider, including:

❑ Product development efforts fail, and the project is abandoned.

❑ Product development is successful, but revenues do not meet projections because a competitor introduces a similar product.

❑ Revenues exceed the base projections.

❑ Others:

  • Prices are controlled by government.

  • A recession occurs.

The results of each of each scenario can be evaluated and presented to decision-makers (see Figure 29.4). In addition to providing insight into all potential outcomes, an important benefit is that it encourages the identification of important checkpoints and management options. For example, an executive should insist on identifying and monitoring the key drivers that will lead to abandonment of the project. Timely determination of ultimate failure will allow the project to be terminated at the earliest possible time, resulting in minimizing the loss on the project and allowing resources to be deployed to other, more promising projects.

FIGURE 29.4 **Scenario recap.**

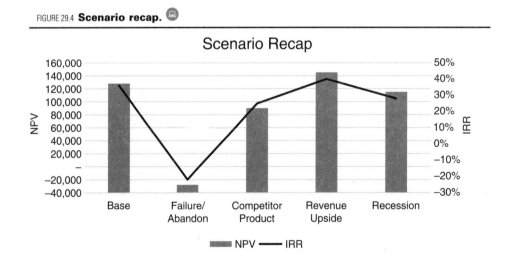

Event, Decision, and Option Trees. Event, decision, and option trees can be very effective tools in evaluating and presenting capital investment decisions. An *event tree* generally refers to a presentation of alternative events or outcomes. *Decision* or *option trees* include future management decisions (options) as one or more possible events in the future. They build on the concept of scenario analysis described earlier. Decision and event trees are a useful way to visualize, communicate, and evaluate various scenarios, especially future projects or other decisions where the outcomes are uncertain (virtually all projects in the 21st century!). Projects may result in several different outcomes (success, failure, delay) and may also be subject to management decisions after the initial project approval (delay, cancel, etc.). For example, a firm may face a choice to replace an existing product with a new product or continue to sell the existing one. This is unlikely to be a single decision point. How successful will the new product be? What will happen to the sales of the existing product if not replaced? What subsequent options will management have to optimize the result? A decision tree identifies and presents decisions and probable outcomes at each stage of a project as illustrated in Figure 29.5.

FIGURE 29.5 **Decision tree.**

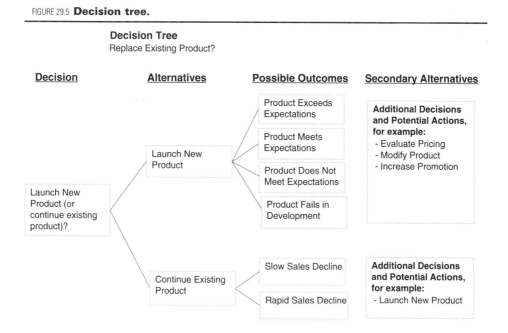

The simple illustration in Figure 29.5 is a very effective way of presenting various management decisions and to describe potential outcomes resulting from each alternative scenario/decision. Each of the six potential outcomes will have a probability of occurrence and an estimated value (e.g., NPV, sales, earnings per share). Each of these six outcomes will also have a second level of management options or decisions.

Simulations. In simulations, decision criteria would be estimated across an entire probability distribution for key variables. For example, revenues, margins, investments, and other key variables would be analyzed to develop a spectrum of potential outcomes and associated probabilities. The biggest downside is the need to develop estimates and probabilities across the entire distribution of potential outcomes for each variable and then to determine value (e.g., NPV) under each combination of variables. Simulation methodologies, including Monte Carlo, can be used for large development projects and are typically used by large consumer product and retail companies where history is readily available to develop estimated outcomes and probabilities.

The output of a simulations would provide a range and probability distribution for a project that can give decision-makers insight on the project dynamics. For many decisions, the scenario and event tree methods just described will get decision-makers close to the same insight with far less effort.

Illustration: Decision Tree for Procrastination Pharmaceutical Treatment
The base case for the development and introduction of the pharmaceutical for the treatment of procrastination presents a single scenario outcome for that project. It includes many assumptions about the timing and success of the development process and also assumes that management has no ability in the future to change the course of development and introduction if circumstances change. Figure 29.6 provides a simple illustration of multiple outcomes for this project. Note that this illustration is a gross oversimplification of the process for developing and obtaining approval for new pharmaceuticals!

This analysis provides several additional insights. First, the base case assumes approval and a solid revenue stream resulting in an NPV of $117, 856. However, there is a 30% chance that the pharmaceutical will not be approved, resulting in a negative NPV of $12,000 ($20,000 research expense less 40% tax savings). Second, it highlights that there are also additional scenarios that revenues will fall short or exceed the base case, with the shortfall resulting in a negative NPV of $2,226.

Clearly the addition of this analysis adds significant insight to the decision. The results of this analysis can be summarized in Figure 29.7, but the decision tree also has outright value in understanding and communicating the dynamics of the investment decision.

Real Options and Option Value   Real options build on the principles of option trees illustrated earlier. Essentially, the advocates of real options apply the option pricing model for securities to "real" investments. While this is a fascinating area for math majors, I find it difficult to effectively utilize in most practice situations. In addition, presenting a value from a complex formula is difficult to explain and doesn't add value in terms of understanding the dynamics of an investment decision.

A related concept that is often used is the option value. An investment may have a positive (or negative) NPV based on the primary opportunity under

FIGURE 29.6 **Event/option tree.**

Event/Option Tree New Pharma

Development and Testing	Success? Proceed?	Invest in Manufacturing	Potential Outcomes	Result 2023	2024	2025	2026	2027	TV	NPV	Probability	Expected Value
			Upside Case 20%	7,413	24,738	39,438	66,675	77,963	519,750	181,900	14%	25,466
		50,000	Base Case 60%	6,438	18,813	29,313	47,625	5,568	371,250	117,856	42%	49,500
			Downside Case 20%	4,609	7,703	10,328	11,906	13,922	92,813	−2,226	14%	−312
		Stop								−12,000	30%	−3,600
										Total	100%	71,054

Invest in Development

−20,000

70%

30%

591

FIGURE 29.7 **Option event summary for procrastination pharmaceutical treatment.**

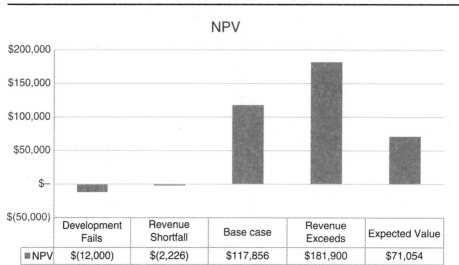

	Development Fails	Revenue Shortfall	Base case	Revenue Exceeds	Expected Value
■NPV	$(12,000)	$(2,226)	$117,856	$181,900	$71,054

evaluation. It may also provide a platform or ability to pursue another opportunity. For example, the procrastination treatment may also be the foundation for another treatment for smart phone attention deficit (SPAD). Another plan and projection can be developed for this new treatment to commence after the procrastination treatment is completed. The potential NPV of this second project can be estimated and considered in the evaluation of the program (see Figure 29.8).

FIGURE 29.8 **Option value illustration.**

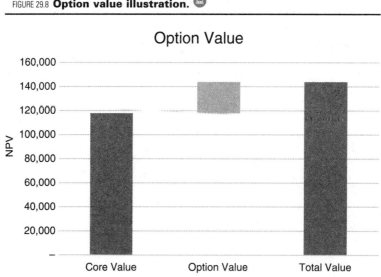

The option value is often used to justify a program that has negative or marginal NPV (prospect for value creation). Of course, this can be abused if not managed properly.

PRESENTING CAPITAL INVESTMENT DECISIONS

Capital investment decisions are a critical aspect of the management process, since it is the determination of what projects should be approved to create value for shareholders. In addition to effectively developing plans and investment evaluations for significant projects, it is important that finance teams also develop effective presentations to management in order to facilitate the overall evaluation and approval of projects.

Many projects, for example, a large developmental project or acquisition, will be accompanied by a complete business plan that supports the economic valuation and analysis described in this chapter.

Figure 29.9 provides an illustration of a recap or approval summary for a capital investment decision. The advantage of this one-page summary is that all relevant information is presented on this single document. Of course, this recap will likely be supported by a detailed presentation and business case.

CAPITAL BUDGETING AND RATIONING

Although in theory we assume that capital is available for any investment opportunity with a positive NPV, as a practical matter, firms must allocate capital and evaluate many potential projects for possible investment. This process often occurs as part of the strategic and operational planning process and product development activities. Typically, operating and business unit executives identify more potential capital projects than the company is able or willing to fund, with reasons ranging from cash or profit constraints to management capacity. Firms employ several techniques to provide insight on which projects should be selected.

Raise the Hurdle or Discount Rate. If the hurdle or discount rate were raised for all projects, some investments would not have positive NPV and would be rejected. However, this has the effect of penalizing all projects.

Profitability Index (PI). The PI is a tool used to measure the value of a project compared to the initial investment.

The Profitability Index is computed as follows:

NPV/Initial Investment.

FIGURE 29.9 **Capital investment summary.**

Capital Investment Summary and Approval

Project Description:

Development of New Pharmaceutical for Treating Procrastination

Critical Assumptions:
o Successful development
o FD&A approval
o No competitive product for 7 years

Key Checkpoints:
o Feasibility
o FD&A approval
o Manufacturing

Alternatives:
o Forgo opportunity
o
o

	Base	10% Change	NPV	% Change in NPV	Breakeven Approx. Value NPV=0
Base			117.9		117.9
Sales(2025)	225.0	202.5	101.8	−13.6%	56.5
Cost & Expense Levels	40%	44.0%	87.9	−25.4%	56.0%
Tax rate	40.0%	44.0%	103.3	−12.4%	NMF
Initial outlay	70.0	77.0	114.2	−3.1%	250.0
Terminal Value	371.3	334.1	107.3	−9.0%	0
Discount Rate	15.0%	16.5%	93.2	−20.9%	30.0%

		Revenues(M)			
		175.0	200.0	225.0	250.0	275.0
	$ 18.0	88.0	105.0	122.0	137.0	154.0
Development	19.0	86.0	103.0	120.0	135.0	152.0
Costs (M)	20.0	83.0	101.0	117.8	133.0	150.0
	21.0	81.0	98.0	115.0	131.0	149.0
	22.0	77.0	94.0	111.0	129.0	146.0

Base Case	
Revenue	
Operating Income	
NPV	
RR	

Approvals	
Preparer	
Operating Executive	
FP&A Analyst	
Controller	
CFO	
CEO	

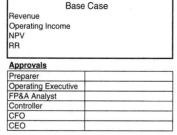

For our drug development example, the PI is computed as follows:

$$PI = \frac{NPV}{Initial\ Investment} = \frac{\$117/856}{\$70,000}$$

$$= 1.68$$

The firm can then rank projects by the index and approve those projects with the highest PI as illustrated in Table 29.4. In this example, if the capital budget for the coming year must be held to $325,000, then the last five projects would not be pursued.

The problem with using only a financial measure to evaluate projects is that many projects have important nonfinancial attributes that must be considered, ranging from executive preferences to statutory requirements. In this case, the casualties of PI ranking would prohibit repairing the roof and addressing the wastewater issue, an apparent Environmental Protection Agency requirement.

TABLE 29.4 **Capital investment allocation.**

Roberts Pharmaceuticals
Capital Investment Allocation

Overall Rank	Project Description	Investment	NPV	IRR	Profitability Index	Cumulative Investment
6	Airplane for CEO	4,000	8,000	60.0%	2.000	4,000
3	Procrastination Drug	70,000	117,856	0.37	1.684	74,000
11	Replace Building 2 Equipment	3,200	2,900	50.0%	0.906	77,200
5	Laziness Treatment	32,000	22,000	17.0%	0.688	109,200
10	Info Technology-Enterprise System	12,000	6,100	15.0%	0.508	121,200
7	Automate Manufacturing	200,000	96,414	28.0%	0.482	321,200
5	Expand Distribution Center	4,875	2,265	18.5%	0.465	326,075
8	All other < 1,000	16000	4200	0.17	0.263	342,075
12	New Corporate Headquarters	4,000	23	0.1%	0.006	346,075
2	New Roof	1,200	−120	−11.0%	−0.100	347,275
4	Info Technology-Security	7,000	−2,100	−7.0%	−0.300	354,275
1	Wastewater Treatment	15,000	−5,260	−15.0%	−0.351	369,275
	Total	369,275	252,278	25%	0.683	

Holistic Approach. To reflect both the financial rankings and other important business issues, leading finance organizations develop a holistic view of all capital investments and rank them taking into account a multitude of factors, including PI, EPS impact, strategic importance, and statutory requirements. Table 29.5 incorporates all factors in a single summary. This presentation will generally facilitate the review and ranking of capital priorities.

Note that the statutorily required projects top the list, since they are mandated by law. Of course, the airplane for the CEO still made the cut!

EVALUATING THE EFFECTIVENESS OF THE CAPITAL INVESTMENT DECISION PROCESS

Firms should evaluate the effectiveness of the CID process. The process should identify any estimation bias, execution failures, root causes, and possible corrective actions. This insight can then be used to revise the current process to improve future results. The process can also be used to identify problematic programs that require management attention and action on a real-time basis. Even in the simple illustration in Table 29.6, it is clear this company has a pattern of poor execution and underestimating costs. These issues should be addressed by improving the CID process.

In Chapter 25, we also discussed the asset utilization process for all prior significant investments in property, plant, and equipment.

TABLE 29.5 **Capital plan ranking.**

Roberts Pharmaceutical
Capital Investment Allocation

Overall Rank	Project Description	Investment	NPV	IRR	Profitability Index	Cumulative Investment	EPS Accretive Year	$0.00	Strategic Importance	Statutory Requirement	Notes
1	Wastewater Treatment	15,000	−5,260	−15.0%	−0.351	15,000			Low	Yes, EPA Requirement	
2	New Roof	1,200	−120	−11.0%	−0.100	16,200				No	Leaking roof jeopardizing FDA License
3	Procrastination Treatment	70,000	117,856	0.37	1.684	86,200	2021	0.11	High		Most Important PD effort
4	Info Technology-Security	7,000	−2,100	−7.0%	−0.300	93,200			High	No, but…	Cyber-threats increasing
5	Laziness Treatment	32,000	22,000	17.0%	0.688	125,200	2024		Yes		
5	Expand Distribution Center	4,875	2,265	18.5%	0.465	130,075			No	Yes	Support sales growth, new products
6	Airplane for CEO	4,000	8,000	60.0%	2.000	134,075	2018		Yes		Expense/Time Savings
7	Automate Manufacturing	200,000	96,414	28.0%	0.482	334,075	2020	0.200	Moderate	No	
8	All other< 1,000	16000	4200	0.17	0.263	350,075					
10	Info Technology-Enterprise System	12,000	6,100	15.0%	0.508	362,075				No	Replace existing/add functionality
11	Replace Building 2 Equipment	3,200	2,900	50.0%	0.906	365,275	2020				
12	New Corporate Headquarters	4,000	23	0.1%	0.006	369,275			Yes	No	Image/Locate in Financial ctr
	Total	369,275	252,278	25%	0.683						

TABLE 29.6 **Review of capital investments.**

Review of Significant Capital Investments

Project	% Complete Status	Cost/Investment			NY Revenue			Net Present Value			Indicated Actions
		Original	Act/Est	Variance	Original	Current	Variance	Original	Act/Est	Variance	
Plant Expansion	Complete	1,400,000	1,480,000	–80,000		N/A		125,000	45,000	–80,000	None, 6% cost overrun
Network Update/Expansion	70% Complete, Delay	2,600,000	2,725,000	–125,000		N/A		54,000	–71,000	–125,000	Cost overrun, delayed. Review needed
Wastewater Treatment Facility	Complete	800,000	875,000	–75,000		N/A			N/A		
Replace Manufacturing Cells 3 to 7	On-schedule	1,200,000	1,175,000	25,000		N/A		67,500	92,500	25,000	On schedule, no action required
New product 1	Complete	950,000	975,000	–25,000	1,200,000	1,135,000	–65,000	1,200,000	1,160,000	–40,000	6-month delay, outlook positive
New product 2	Delay	825,000	962,000	–137,000	750,000	125,000	–625,000	800,000	420,000	–380,000	Design delays, review needed
New product 3	20% Complete, Delay	1,400,000	1,425,000	–25,000	750,000	–	–750,000	1,450,000	265,000	–1,185,000	On schedule but competitor product introduced. Review Needed.

SUMMARY

Capital investment decisions are of critical importance in creating value for shareholders. A CID, by its very nature, involves an extended planning horizon. The future is uncertain and many factors and assumptions can impact the success of the project and the prospect of creating value for shareholders.

Techniques for dealing with uncertainty include:

- Identify, document, and monitor key assumptions.
- Adjust discount (hurdle) rates for risk.
- Utilize sensitivity and scenario analyses, and other tools to understand the dynamics of the investment and projected results.

Owing to the importance and complexity of many CIDs, it is important to thoroughly evaluate and develop comprehensive presentations to decision-makers.

30

Business Valuation and Value Drivers

Nearly all valuation techniques are based on estimating the cash flows that an asset, for example, real estate or a firm, can generate in the future. Two critical points are worth emphasizing. First, the value of any asset should be based on the expected *cash flows* the owner can realize by holding that asset or selling it to another party. Second, only the *future* expectations of cash flows are relevant in determining value. Historical performance and track records are important inputs in estimating future cash flows, but "the market prices forward" based on expectations of future performance.

It is important to recognize that valuation is both an art and a science. While we outline a number of quantitative, objective approaches to valuing a business, many other nonquantitative, and perhaps, even irrational factors do affect the value of the firm, especially in the short term. It is a marvel that each day millions of shares of stock are traded on the public exchanges, with buyers and sellers on both sides of the transaction, one deciding to sell at the same value at which the other has decided to purchase.

Commonly used valuation techniques fall into two major categories: (1) estimating the value by discounting future cash flows, and (2) estimating the value by comparing to the value of other similar businesses. This chapter is not intended to be an exhaustive work on business valuation; that has been the objective of some very well written books.[1] The goal in this chapter is to provide a foundation in key valuation concepts and to highlight key analytical tools and measures.

---

[1] Several very useful books provide a more comprehensive study on valuation concepts and tools, including *Investment Valuation* (3rd edition, 2012) and *Damodaran on Valuation* (2006), both by Aswath Damodaran, and *Valuation: Measuring and Managing the Value of Companies* by McKinsey & Company, Tom Copeland, Tim Koller, and Jack Murrin (3rd edition, 2000), all three from John Wiley & Sons.

ESTIMATING THE VALUE OF A BUSINESS BY DISCOUNTING FUTURE CASH FLOWS

This discounted cash flow (DCF) valuation method is based on sound fundamental economic theory. Essentially, the value of a firm is equal to the present value of expected future cash flows. These future cash flows are "discounted" to arrive at the value today. Since DCF is based on projections of future cash flows, it requires that financial statement projections be prepared. In order to prepare financial statement projections, assumptions must be made about the firm's performance in the future. Will sales grow, and if so, at what rate? Will margins improve or erode? Why? What capital will be required to support the future business levels? Financial projections are covered in more depth in Part IV, "Business Projections and Plans." The DCF technique also allows us to determine the magnitude of improvement in key operating variables necessary to increase the value of the firm by say, 20%.

Figure 30.1 presents an overview of DCF methodology. Estimates of key financial and operating variables result in projected cash flows. These projected cash flows are then discounted to estimate the value of the firm. The discount rate considers a number of factors, including the time value of money and the level of risk of the projected cash flows. The discount rate, or cost of capital, was more fully explored in Chapter 26.

FIGURE 30.1 **Discounted cash flow (DCF).**

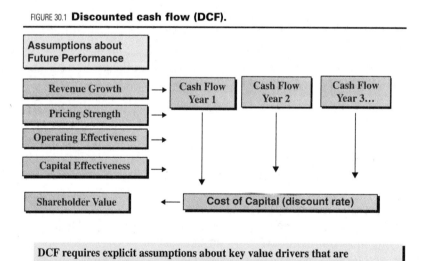

A sample worksheet for a DCF valuation is presented in Table 30.1. This example builds on the LSA Technology Company (LSA) example introduced in Chapter 2, utilizing the financial performance and other information presented in Table 2.7. This DCF valuation worksheet was developed for the primary purpose of understanding the overall dynamics of a firm's valuation and may require modification to be used as a valuation tool for a specific application. For example, the model uses a single estimate of future sales growth and other key variables. Generally, a valuation would be based on estimates of key financial inputs for each period, supported by detailed projections and assumptions.

At first glance, the model presented in Table 30.1 can be overwhelming. We will review the model by breaking it into six key steps:

1. Review and present the firm's financial history.
2. Project future cash flows by estimating key elements of future operating performance.
3. Estimate the terminal or post-planning horizon value.
4. Discount the cash flows.
5. Estimate the value of the firm and equity.
6. Explore the dynamics of the valuation.

Step 1: Review and Present the Firm's Financial History   While the DCF valuation will be based on expected future cash flows, it is essential to review and consider recent history and trends in developing the projected financial results. The DCF model should present three or four years of history alongside the projections. In addition to providing a "base" from which the preparer estimates future cash flows, it provides a basis for others to evaluate the future projections in the context of recent performance. For example, if sales had grown at 3% to 5% over the past several years, why are we projecting 8% growth over the next several years?

Step 2: Project Future Cash Flows by Estimating Key Elements of Future Operating Performance   After reviewing the historical performance and identifying the key drivers of current and future performance, the analyst or manager can project the expected future financial performance. It is deceptively easy to "plug in" estimated sales, margins, expenses, and so forth to arrive at financial projections and estimated cash flows. However, significant analysis, understanding, and thought are required to project key variables such as revenue or gross margins. For example, to predict revenue for a firm, multiple factors must be considered, including:

- Economic factors (growth, recession, inflation, interest rates, etc.).
- Market size and growth.
- Competitive factors.
- Unit volume.

TABLE 30.1 **DCF valuation model.**

LSA Technology Company   DCF Valuation Model

($m)

	2020	2021	2022	2023	Estimates	2024	2025	2026	2027	2028	2029	2030	2031	Terminal Value
Revenues	$79,383	$84,000	$91,000	$100,000		$108,000	$116,640	$125,971	$136,049	$146,933	$158,687	$171,382	$178,238	
Year over Year Growth		6%	8%	10%	8.0%	8%	8%	8%	8%	8%	8%	8%	4%	
Cost of Good Sold	36,000	38,300	41,000	45,000										
Gross Margin	43,383	46,000	50,000	55,000	55.0%	59,400	64,152	69,284	74,827	80,813	87,278	94,260	98,031	
% Sales	55%	55%	55%	55%		55%	55%	55%	55%	55%	55%	55%	55%	
Operating Expenses	31,753	33,600	36,400	40,000	40.0%	43,200	46,656	50,388	54,420	58,773	63,475	68,553	71,295	
% Sales	40%	40%	40%	40%		40%	40%	40%	40%	40%	40%	40%	40%	
Operating Income (EBIT)	11,630	12,400	13,600	15,000		16,200	17,496	18,896	20,407	22,040	23,803	25,707	26,736	
% Sales	14.7%	14.8%	14.9%	15.0%		15.0%	15.0%	15.0%	15.0%	15.0%	15.0%	15.0%	15.0%	
- Taxes	-3,748	-4,010	-4,418	-4,894	-32.0%	-5,184	-5,599	-6,047	-6,530	-7,053	-7,617	-8,226	-8,555	
OPAT	7,882	8,391	9,182	10,106		11,016	11,897	12,849	13,877	14,987	16,186	17,481	18,180	
+ Depreciation/Amortization	2,800	3,277	2,850	3,750		5,000	5,400	5,832	6,299	6,802	7,347	7,934	8,569	
- Capital Expenditures	-3,000	-4,200	-4,800	-5,000	-5.0%	-5,400	-5,832	-6,299	-6,802	-7,347	-7,934	-8,569	-7,130	
(Increase) Decrease in OC		-1,623	-2,570	-2,330	30%	-2,400	-2,592	-2,799	-3,023	-3,265	-3,526	-3,808	-2,057	
Free Cash Flow	7,682	5,844	4,662	6,526		8,216	8,873	9,583	10,350	11,178	12,072	13,038	17,563	
						0								

	2024	2025	2026	2027	2028	2029	2030	2031	Terminal Value
+ Terminal Value	8,216	8,873	9,583	10,350	11,178	12,072	13,038	17,563	228,324 / 228,324
Present Value Factor	1.000	0.893	0.797	0.712	0.636	0.567	0.507	0.452	0.452
Present Value of Cash Flow (PVCF)	8,216	7,923	7,640	7,367	7,104	6,850	6,605	7,945	103,282

Sum PVCF   59,650
Present Value of Terminal Value   103,282
Estimated Value of Firm (Enterprise Value)   162,932
Add: Excess Cash and non Operating Assets   7,944
Subtract: Value of Debt   10,000
Estimated Value of Equity   160,876
Number of Shares Outstanding   17,000
Estimated Value per share $9.46

Cost of Capital   12.00%

Terminal Value(TV) Assumptions

	Multiple/Rate	TV
Multiples of Earnings (PE)	12.0	218,165
	16.0	290,886
	20.0	363,608
Multiples of Revenue	1.0	178,238
	2.0	356,475
Perpetuity No Growth	0%	146,362
Perpetuity Growth	4%	228,324
Use **Perpetuity Growth**	4.0%	228,324

- Pricing trends.
- Product mix.
- Customer success.
- New product introduction.
- Product obsolescence.

It is extremely important to document the critical assumptions about revenue and all other key elements of financial performance. These assumptions can then be evaluated, changed, monitored, and "flexed" to understand the significance of each on the estimated value of the firm. Since no one has a crystal ball, we know that actual results will vary from our projections. Much of the value in business planning results from the *process* of planning, as opposed to the plan or financial projection itself. Additional information on developing long-term projections is contained in Chapter 21.

Another critical decision in DCF valuations is to determine the *forecast horizon*, the period for which we project future financial performance in detail. In theory, a company has an extended, if not infinite, life. However, it typically is not practical or necessary to attempt to forecast financial results for 20 or 30 years. The forecast horizon selected should vary according to the individual circumstances. Most discounted cash flow estimates for ongoing businesses will determine the value of the projected cash flows for the forecast horizon (5 to 10 years) and will then add to that an estimate of the value of the business at the end of that period, called the "terminal value" (TV) or "post-horizon value."

Two key factors should be considered in setting the forecast horizon. First, ensure that there is a balance between the value of the cash flows generated during the forecast horizon and the estimated terminal value. If substantially all of the estimated value is attributable to the terminal value, the forecast horizon should be extended. The second and related consideration is to extend the forecast horizon to a point where the financial performance reaches a sustainable or steady-state basis. For example, if a firm is in a period of rapid growth, the cash flows at the end of the horizon will still reflect significant investments in expenses, working capital, and equipment. The forecast horizon should extend beyond this rapid growth phase to a point beyond where it reaches a long-term sustainable growth rate. This will ensure that the key variables impacting cash flow reach a steady state, allowing this to be used as a base for estimating the terminal value. In this illustration, we moderate revenue growth in 2031 to 4% to provide a better base for use in computing the terminal value.

Step 3: Estimate the Terminal or Post-Planning Horizon Value   The use of a terminal value or post-horizon value is an effective practical alternative to very long forecast horizons, subject to proper application. First, the factors in setting the forecast horizon as just described must be utilized. Second, care must be exercised in selecting the multiple or valuation technique utilized in calculating the terminal value. The terminal value is usually estimated by using one of two methods:

1. Taking the base performance in the last year (or average of the past several years) and estimating the value of the firm by applying a multiple to earnings or sales. For example, taking the final estimated earnings in year 2031 of $18,180 and applying a multiple of 12× to arrive at an expected terminal value of $218,165. Multiples could be applied in this manner to EBIT, EBITDA, and revenues as well as cash flow.

2. Determining the economic value of cash flows beyond the forecast horizon by assuming that the cash flows will continue to be generated at the level of the last projected year, forever. More common is to assume that the future cash flows will continue to grow from the last projected year at some level, say 3% to 5% in perpetuity.

   Assuming no future growth beyond 2030, the estimated value of annual cash flows of $17,563 continuing in perpetuity is:

$$TV = \text{Cash Flow}_{\text{Final Year}} / \text{Discount Rate}$$

$$TV = \$17,563/12\%$$

$$TV = \$146,362$$

Assuming future growth after 2031 at $g\%$:

$$TV = \left(\text{Cash Flow}_{\text{Final Year}} (1+g)\right) / \left(\text{Discount Rate} - g\right)$$

$$TV = \left(\$17,563 \times 1.04\right) / \left(12\% - 4\%\right)$$

$$TV = \$228,324$$

Note the significant difference in valuation between flat cash flow and just a 4% growth rate!

Since a case can be made supporting both methods, I recommend computing a range of estimated terminal values using both multiples and economic value. Understanding the underlying reasons for the different values is informative and should be explored. One of the estimates must ultimately be selected and used for the terminal value. Since the estimate of TV is usually significant to the overall valuation, a sensitivity analysis using multiple estimates of the terminal value should be created. This analysis should provide a more comprehensive understanding of the impact of key assumptions on the valuation of the company.

Common mistakes in estimating the terminal value include using inappropriate multiples or unrealistic post-horizon growth rates. The multiple used in the TV estimate should be consistent with the performance estimated for the post-horizon growth period. This may be significantly different from current multiples reflecting current performance. Post-horizon growth rates should be modest since perpetuity means forever! Few companies achieve high levels of growth over extended periods and many companies' growth rates slow to overall economic growth levels or even experience declines in sales over time.

Step 4: Discount the Cash Flows   Discounted cash flow (DCF) can be utilized to estimate the total value of the firm or the value of equity. Typically, we will estimate the total value of the firm by projecting total cash flows available to all investors, both equity and debt. We will then discount the cash flows at the weighted average cost of capital (WACC), which is an estimate of the returns expected by all investors. The alternative method, free cash flow to equity (FCFE), is presented later in this chapter. Discount rates and the cost of capital were explored in greater detail in Chapter 26. Note that we have displayed the present value of each individual year's cash flow, as opposed to presenting a single "present value" of all years. This allows the analyst to review the contribution of each year to the present value, reinforcing the time value of money.

Step 5: Estimate the Value of the Firm and Equity   The resultant discounted cash flow is the *total* value of the firm, also referred to as the *enterprise value (EV)* as shown in Figure 30.2. To compute the value of equity, two adjustments must be considered. First, if the firm has a substantial cash reserve, this

FIGURE 30.2 **Enterprise versus equity value.**

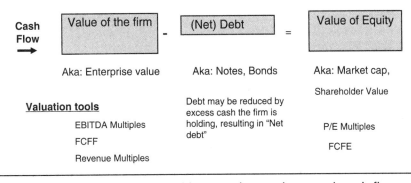

Enterprise versus Equity Value

adjustment is added to the discounted value of projected cash flows. Second, in order to compute the value of equity, we deduct the value of the debt. The estimated value of an individual share can then be determined by dividing the market value of equity by the number of shares outstanding. Where there are significant stock options or other common stock derivatives outstanding, these should also be considered in the share count. In some cases, analysts may also make an adjustment to reflect the absence of ready liquidity, for example, for smaller privately owned enterprises.

Step 6: Explore the Dynamics of the Valuation   Arguably the most important part of valuing a business is to explore, evaluate, and communicate the dynamics of the valuation. This can be accomplished by performing sensitivity analysis, scenario analysis, and value decomposition using DCF. One of the criticisms of discounted cash flow valuation is that it requires assumptions about the future. In my view, this is a major strength of DCF analysis. We all recognize that it is not possible to predict the future, including specific projections of sales, costs, and numerous additional variables required for completing a thorough DCF analysis.

Sensitivity Analysis. By using sensitivity analysis, we can identify and quantify the sensitivity of shareholder value to key assumptions. The analysis allows us to identify the most critical factors impacting the value of a firm, such as revenue growth and profitability. Using the DCF worksheet, the analyst can change or flex key assumptions such as sales growth and profitability, and record the resultant value. The results can then be summarized as illustrated in Table 30.2.

TABLE 30.2 **DCF sensitivity analysis.**

			DCF Value Sensitivity Analysis			
					Stock Price	
LSA Technology Company			Sales Growth Rate			
		4%	6%	8%	10%	12%
	20.0%	$10.88	$11.93	$13.08	$14.36	$15.77
Operating	17.5%	9.43	10.30	11.27	12.35	13.53
Income %	15.0%	7.97	8.68	9.46	10.33	11.29
	12.5%	6.52	7.06	7.65	8.32	9.05
	10.0%	5.06	5.43	5.85	6.31	6.81

Scenario Analysis. While sensitivity analysis is simply a math exercise to determine the effect of changing specific assumptions, scenario analysis requires that a different "story" be told. The base or primary case undoubtedly contains critical assumptions about product introductions, competitor and customer actions and performance, the economy, and many others.

Under each scenario, multiple assumptions must be revisited. For example, a recession might affect sales volume and pricing and may also reduce material and labor costs.

For LSA, additional scenarios could be created. Each scenario would be supported by a financial projection that would be used to re-value the enterprise.

Value Decomposition. Using our DCF model, we can "decompose" or estimate the contribution to total value of any specific variable. For example, I find it useful to highlight the value of current performance for an enterprise versus the value associated with improvements to performance, including future growth and profitability improvements (Figure 30.3). The value of current performance levels (i.e., assuming that the current cash flow remains constant in perpetuity) can be estimated using the formula for an annuity in perpetuity that was introduced in Chapter 26.

$$\text{Value} = \frac{\text{Cash Flow Year 2024}}{\text{Cost of Capital}}$$

$$\$68,468 = \frac{\$8,216}{0.12}$$

This value compares to our DCF valuation of $162,932, indicating that a disproportionate amount of the valuation is associated with assumptions about improved performance in the projections (Figure 30.2). In the case of LSA, this improvement is due to the assumption of 8% growth per year (all other assumptions are held constant).

FIGURE 30.3 **Value decomposition.**

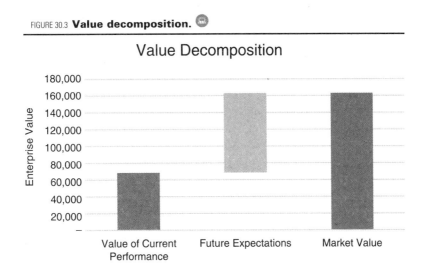

Free Cash Flow to Equity   The discounted cash flow methodology presented earlier in this chapter is based on the free cash flow to the firm (FCFF), available to all investors, discounted at the weighted average cost of capital (WACC).

An alternative method is the free cash flow to equity (FCFE) investors, discounted at the cost of equity. The FCFE is generally used in valuing enterprises or projects with substantial leverage, including many real estate transactions and leveraged buy-out transactions, where the blended WACC may distort the returns to equity. In these cases, the equity investors are concerned with maximizing the return to *equity* investors.

Comparing Free Cash Flow to the Firm (FCFF) and to Equity (FCFE)

Method	FCFF	FCFE
Aliases	DCF Valuation	Residual Cash Flow
Cash Flow available:	To all Investors	To Equity Investors
Result	Enterprise Value	Equity Value
Applications	General Valuation	Direct Financing (e.g., real estate)
		High Leverage (e.g., LBO)
Calculation	Operating Profit after Tax	Net Income (includes interest expense)
	+ D&A	+ D&A
	+– Working Capital	+– Working Capital
	– Capital Expenditures	– Capital Expenditures
		+ New Borrowings
		– Debt Payments
	= Free Cash Flow Firm	= Free Cash Flow Equity

An illustration of a FCFE approach is shown in Table 30.3. This illustration highlights the emphasis on cash flows and returns to equity investors for a leveraged buy-out transaction of Emmy's Cookies. Note the values of equity and equity returns are based on residual cash flows, after interest and debt service.

Estimating the Value of Firms by Using the Valuation of Similar Firms: Multiples of Revenues, Earnings, and Related Measures

The other commonly used valuation technique is based on using measures of revenues, earnings, or cash flow, and capitalizing these amounts using a multiplier that is typical for similar companies. These methods are essentially shortcuts or rules of thumb based on economic theory. Users of these methods tend to establish ranges for certain industries. For example, retail companies

TABLE 30.3 **FCFE illustration: Leveraged buy-out investment.** 🖲

| Leveraged Buy-Out | Transaction | Free Cash Flow to Equity Illustration Emmy's Cookies | | | | | |
		2024	2025	2026	2027	2028	2029
Profit and Loss							
Revenue		1,100.0	1,200.0	1,325.0	1,475.0	1,600.0	1,800.0
Operating Income		137.5	135.6	185.5	221.3	240.0	270.0
Interest Expense		(126.0)	(123.8)	(119.3)	(114.8)	(110.3)	(105.8)
Profit Before Tax		11.5	11.9	66.3	106.5	129.8	164.3
Tax		–	(3.0)	(16.6)	(26.6)	(32.4)	(41.1)
Net Income		11.5	8.9	49.7	79.9	97.3	123.2
Residual Cash Flow							
Net Income		11.5	8.9	49.7	79.9	97.3	123.2
D&A		25.0	25.0	25.0	25.0	25.0	25.0
Capital Expenditures		(10.0)	(25.0)	(25.0)	(25.0)	(25.0)	(25.0)
(Increase) Decrease in Working Capital		(5.0)	(10.0)	(12.5)	(15.0)	(12.5)	(20.0)
New Borrowings	1,400.0						
Debt Repayments		(25.0)	(50.0)	(50.0)	(50.0)	(50.0)	(1,175.0)
Acquire Firm	(2,000.0)						
Net Proceeds from Anticipated Sale							4,000.0
Residual Cash Flow	(600.0)	(3.5)	(51.1)	(12.8)	14.9	34.8	2,928.2
PV Factor	1.0	0.833	0.694	0.579	0.482	0.402	0.335
PV Cash Flow	(600.0)	(2.9)	(35.5)	(7.4)	7.2	14.0	980.6
Value of Equity							
Present Value of Residual Cash Flows	$956.0						
Return to Equity Investors							
IRR on Equity	29%						
NPV on Equity Investment	356.0						
Transaction							
Acquisition	2,000.0						
Equity Investment	600.0						
Debt	1,400.0	1,375.0	1,325.0	1,275.0	1,225.0	1,175.0	-
Interest Rate	9%						
Cost of Equity	20%						

may trade at a multiple of 0.5 to 1.0 times revenues, while technology companies may trade at 4 to 5 times revenues, or higher. The significant difference between the multiple for the two industries is explained by many factors that are independent of the current revenue level. For example, expected growth in revenues, profitability, risk, and capital requirements will have an impact on the revenue multiple. The use of multiples is common among operating executives, investment bankers, and investors as an easily understood basis for valuation. It also facilitates comparing relative valuations across companies.

In applying multiples, it is important to use consistent measures of income and valuation. Specifically, we must determine if we are attempting to estimate the value of the firm (enterprise value) or the value of the equity. To illustrate these techniques, we will use the information provided in Tables 2.7 for LSA.

The effective use of multiples requires a thorough understanding of the key drivers of value that are essentially implicit assumptions in the valuation multiple. For example, in evaluating the purchase price of residential real estate, there are many factors that go into selecting "comps" and many drivers of value implicit in the value metrics. Figure 30.4 highlights the implicit assumptions in real estate and business valuation.

FIGURE 30.4 **Implicit assumptions in comparable valuations.**

Comparable Valuations

As with real estate, many implicit factors drive business valuation and valuation metrics such as Enterprise Value/Revenue or Enterprise Value/EBITDA

Implicit Assumptions:

Real Estate	Business
Location	Expected Growth
Size, Age and Condition	Margins, Expense Levels
School System	Intangible Assets
Neighborhood	Asset/Capital Requirements
Floor Plan/Decorating	Risk
Economy/Interest Rates	Economy/Interest Rates
Curb Appeal	Accounting Practices
Metrics: $ per square foot	Metrics: EV/Revenue, EV/EBITDA

For business valuations, great care must be exercised in selecting an appropriate set of comparable companies. I prefer the term *benchmark group* since it is unlikely that precise comparables may exist. Benchmark groups can be used to bound and understand valuation drivers as illustrated in Table 30.4.

The benchmark group includes direct competitors, participants in adjacent markets, and a few outliers for contrast and insight (e g., fast growing). In this way, we can compare the performance of LSA to each company across growth, profitability, and ROIC. The broad range of valuation metrics can be narrowed based on performance, industry, and other relevant factors. These most relevant multiple ranges can then be applied to LSA.

Enterprise Value to Revenue Ratio   The enterprise value to revenue (EV/ Revenue) ratio computes the value of the firm to the estimated or recent revenue levels.

TABLE 30.4 Valuation benchmark analysis.

Valuation Benchmark Analysis

Company	Business Description	Revenue $	Revenue CAGR (3 Yr.)	EBITDA %	Returns ROIC	Valuation Enterprise Value	Valuation EV/Revenue	Valuation EV/EBITDA
BM1	Mature Network/Storage System Manufacturer	1,100,000,000	5.0%	19%	45%	1,600,000,000	1.5	7.7
BM2	Direct competitor	75,000,000	4.0%	9%	18%	82,500,000	1.1	12.2
BM3	Adjacent Market	33,000,000	22.0%	7%	9%	82,500,000	2.5	35.7
BM4	Direct competitor	150,000,000	7.0%	17%	12%	210,000,000	1.4	8.2
BM5	Adjacent Market	200,000,000	5.0%	14%	20%	300,000,000	1.5	10.7
BM6	Direct competitor	90,000,000	10.0%	13%	8%	162,000,000	1.8	13.8
BM7	Adjacent competitor	275,000,000	6.0%	19%	15%	550,000,000	2.0	10.5
BM8	Direct competitor	20,000,000	75.0%	−20%	NA	200,000,000	10.0	−50.0
LSA Technology	Components and Systems for Networks	100,000,000	8.0%	18.8%	15%	190,030,000	1.9	10.1

18,750

Analysis	EV/Revenue	EV/EBITDA
All		
High	10	35.7
Low	0.9	7.7
Most Relevant		
High	2.2	13.8
Low	1.1	7.7

Indicated Valuation Range		
220,000,000	258,750.00	
110,000,000	144,375.00	

611

For example, LSA Technology Company has revenues of $100 million in 2023 and an estimated (enterprise) value of $190 million (debt of $10.0 and equity of $180.0 million).

$$\frac{\text{Enterprise Value}}{\text{Revenue}} = \frac{\$190m}{\$100m} = 1.9\times$$

Other companies in this industry have EV/Revenue ratios of 1.0 to 2.0. This would indicate a comparable valuation range of $100 million to $200 million for LSA Technology Company. The value to revenue ratio is within the range of similar or comparable companies, although at the high end of that range.

Advantages: The EV/Revenue ratio is a simple, high-level measure.

Disadvantages/Limitations: The measure requires many implicit assumptions about key elements of financial performance, including growth rates, margins, capital requirements, and capital structure.

Price/Earnings (P/E) Ratio The price/earnings (P/E) ratio compares the price of the stock to the firm's earnings. Using per-share information, the P/E ratio is calculated as follows:

$$\text{PE Ratio} = \frac{\text{Stock Price}}{\text{Earnings per Share}}$$

For LSA Technology Company:

$$\frac{\$10.59}{\$0.56} = 18.95$$

The valuation of companies comparable to LSA Technology Company indicates a P/E ratio range of 12 to 20 times earnings. The company's stock price of $10.59 is near the top of the range indicated by the market research ($6.72 to $11.18) using the comparable P/E range.

This measure can also be computed at the firm level:

$$\frac{\text{Market Value of Equity}}{\text{Net Income}} = \frac{\$180.0m}{\$9.5m} = 18.95\times$$

Advantages: This method is simple to employ and commonly used in practice.

Disadvantages and Limitations: Several problems exist with this technique. First, earnings are accounting measures and not directly related to economic performance or cash flows. This has become an increasing problem in recent years as accounting profit continues to diverge from the underlying economic performance. Second, this measure also requires many implicit assumptions about key elements of financial performance, including growth rates, capital requirements, and capital structure.

Enterprise Value/EBITDA   This method compares the total value of the firm to the earnings before interest, taxes, depreciation, and amortization. Since it is a measure of income before deducting interest expense, it represents income available to all investors, both equity (shareholders) and debt (bondholders). Therefore, we will compare this measure to the total value of the firm (EV). EBITDA is recognized as a proxy of operating cash flow since it adds back the noncash charges, including depreciation and amortization (D&A). It is one of the most frequent measures used by investment bankers and private equity firms.

For LSA Technology Company

$$\frac{EV}{EBITDA} = \frac{\$190.0}{\$15.0 + \$3.75} = 10.13$$

Other similar companies are valued at 8 to 10 times EBITDA. Based on ratios for comparable companies, LSA Technology Company is valued just outside the high end of this range.

Advantages: This method is simple to apply and is based on an approximation of cash flow, an important driver of value.

Disadvantages and Limitations: The primary limitation with this method is that it does not explicitly account for growth assumptions or future capital requirements.

Price/Earnings Growth Ratio or "PEG"

The price/earnings growth (PEG) ratio is a derivative of the price/earnings ratio that attempts to factor in the impact of growth in price/earnings multiples. The logic here is that there is a strong correlation between growth rates and P/E multiples. Companies with higher projected growth rates of earnings, for example, technology companies, should have higher P/E ratios than firms with lower expected growth rates.

The PEG ratio is computed as follows:

$$\frac{P/E \text{ Ratio}}{\text{Estimated EPS Growth Rate}}$$

For LSA Technology Company:

$$\frac{P/E}{\text{Growth }\%} = \frac{18.95}{8.0} = PEG \text{ of } 2.37$$

LSA Technology Company has a very high PEG ratio relative to the peer group. This may reflect a number of factors: perhaps strong cash flows or consistent operating performance relative to the benchmark group.

Advantages: This method reflects a key driver of valuation: expected growth.

Disadvantages and Limitations: Again, this measure does not directly reflect other key elements of financial performance.

Building Shareholder Value in a Multiples Framework Many investors, analysts, and managers use multiples of earnings in investment and valuation decisions. Using multiples, there are two ways to build value. First, the firm can improve the base performance measure, for example, earnings. The second way is to command a higher multiple. For illustration, let's assume that LSA Technology Company's valuation is being driven by capitalizing earnings (P/E ratio). The stock is valued at $10.59 because the firm earned $0.56 per share in earnings and the market has capitalized those earnings at approximately 19 times. The price of LSA Technology Company stock will rise when the earnings increase and/or if the market applies a higher multiple, for example, increasing to 22 times earnings. In the latter case, the stock would trade at $12.32 (22 × $0.56).

Factors that Affect Multiples

What factors would cause the multiple to expand or contract? A variety of factors can contribute, including some specific to the firm and others that relate to the industry or even the general economy. Examples include expected growth rates, the quality of earnings, cash generation, perceived risk, and interest rates. A firm's P/E multiple should expand if it demonstrates a higher expected growth rate, improved working capital management, and/or more consistent operating performance. It will likely contract if it consistently misses financial targets, utilizes capital less effectively, or increases the perceived risk by entering a new market. In addition, economic factors such as changes in interest rates or expected economic conditions will cause multiples to expand or contract.

Use of Multiples in Setting Acquisition Values Most of the multiples used in the previous discussion are typically derived from the valuation of other similar companies, industry averages, or broad market indexes. This is commonly referred to as the trading multiple, that is, the value set by trades in the equity markets. If a company is being considered as a potential acquisition target, the multiples will typically be adjusted to reflect a likely control or acquisition premium. These *acquisition values* are referred to as *transaction values,* versus trading values, and the multiples would be derived by looking at *transactions* involving similar companies. Control premiums are typical for two reasons. First, boards and management teams are unlikely to surrender control of a company unless there is an immediate reward to the selling shareholders. In addition, the acquirer should be able to pay more than a passive investor since it will be able to control the company and should be able to realize a higher growth in earnings and cash flow due to synergies with the acquiring company. Valuation for acquisition purposes is covered in Chapter 31, "Analysis of Mergers and Acquisitions."

Trailing and Forward Multiples   When applying multiples of earnings, sales and other measures, the analyst must select a base period. The value of the multiple will vary depending on whether the multiple is applied to actual past results (e.g., "trailing 12 months earnings") or a future period's estimated performance (e.g., "forward 12 months earnings"). The multiple applied to trailing earnings will be higher than the multiple applied to future earnings for two reasons: risk and the time value of money. There is risk associated with future earnings projections; they may not be achieved. The time value of money suggests that a dollar to be received next year is not worth a dollar today. These two factors result in a discount of the multiples used for future periods.

Adjusting or Normalizing the Base

Using multiples requires us to use a measure for a single period, typically a year. Many of the measures, such as sales or earnings, for the selected period may have been or are anticipated to be significantly impacted by a number of anomalous, or one-time, factors. For example, the current year earnings may include income that is not expected to continue into the future. Or perhaps the income includes a so-called "nonrecurring adjustment" to record a legal settlement or the closing of a plant. In these situations, companies and analysts may adjust the base to normalize the earnings, often referred to as pro forma or "non-GAAP" earnings.

This practice has become very prevalent beginning in the 1990s and led to a number of abuses. Certain companies were accused of being selective in choosing items to exclude, leading to a perceived overstatement of the earnings on a pro forma basis. The Securities and Exchange Commission subsequently placed significant constraints on reporting adjusted earnings. Several reasons gave rise to the use of pro forma measures:

- **Deficiencies in Generally Accepted Accounting Principles (GAAP).** There has been a continuing divergence between GAAP accounting measures and economic results. Specific issues relate to accounting for acquisitions, income taxes, stock options, and pension plans.
- **Significant Restructuring, Divestitures, and Acquisitions.** One-time or nonrecurring charges are reflected in earnings in a specific period based on very precise rules established by the accounting rule makers. However, a significant restructuring may be viewed as an investment for economic and valuation purposes. Acquisitions and divestitures may result in a disconnect between historical performance trends and future projections.

Some advocate using other measures, such as cash flow or economic profit, which adjust the accounting earnings to a measure with greater relevance in evaluating the economic value and performance of the firm.

Problems with Using Multiples   The use of multiples has several inherent limitations, especially for our purposes in linking shareholder value to operating performance.

Circular reference. The basic logic with multiples is that one company's value is determined by looking at the valuation of other companies. This is very useful in comparing relative valuations and in testing the fairness of a company's valuation. Management teams and boards rely heavily on the use of multiples to review the fairness of trading values and acquisition prices. However, if the industry or peer group is overvalued, then this method will result in overvaluing the subject enterprise. This was a contributing factor to the technology/internet (and other) market bubbles. The logic was that since dot.com1 was valued at 50 times sales, so should dot.com2, notwithstanding the fact that neither valuation was supported by basic economic fundamentals.

Implicit performance assumptions. Another problem with this methodology is that it is not directly related to key value drivers or elements of financial performance. It is very difficult to understand the assumptions underlying values computed using multiples. If a firm is valued at 18 times earnings, what are the underlying assumptions for revenue growth, working capital requirements, and other similar factors?

The market often attempts to cope with this limitation by increasing or decreasing the multiple over benchmarks to reflect factors such as consistency of performance, quality of earnings, lower or higher risk, and so forth. Such stocks would be described as "trading at a premium to the market based on. . ." certain identified factors.

Selecting appropriate comparables. Using multiples requires the analyst to select a set of comparable companies or a peer group. This can be a significant challenge. Few companies are so-called pure-plays that are serving a single industry or match up closely with other companies. Further, choosing an appropriate benchmark or peer group can lead to great debates since the process is both subjective and often emotionally charged.

INTEGRATED VALUATION SUMMARY FOR LSA TECHNOLOGY COMPANY

The individual valuation techniques described in this chapter should be combined to form a summary analysis of estimated valuation for LSA Technology Company. Each measure contributed a view of valuation that contributes to an overall picture. The numerical summary shown in Table 30.5 can be converted into a more user-friendly visual summary in Figure 30.5.

LSA Technology Company's current value is at the high end of the 12-month trading range and near or exceeding the top of the range for comparable companies. In this case, it would be important to understand the underlying performance characteristics of the benchmark group compared to LSA Technology Company. Is the company's valuation supported by better performance or higher future expectations of growth? The current market

TABLE 30.5 **LSA Technology Company valuation summary table.**

LSA Technology Company
Valuation Analysis: Multiples

	Value Basis		LSA	Benchmark Range Low	High
Revenue		2023 Result	$100,000		
		Multiple	1.9	1.1	2.2
	Enterprise	Value/Indicated Range	$190,030	$110,000	$220,000
	Equity	Value/Indicated Range	$180,030	$100,000	$210,000
Earnings		2023 Result	$9,501		
		Multiple	18.95	12	20
	Equity	Value/Indicated Range	$180,030	$114,008	$190,014
		Per Share	10.59	6.71	11.18
EBITDA		2023 Result	$18,750		
		Multiple	10.13	7.70	13.80
	Enterprise	Value/Indicated Range	$190,030	$144,375	$258,750
	Equity	Value/Indicated Range	$180,030	$134,375	$248,750
DCF	Equity	Value	$160,876	NA	NA

FIGURE 30.5 **LSA Technology Company valuation summary graph.**

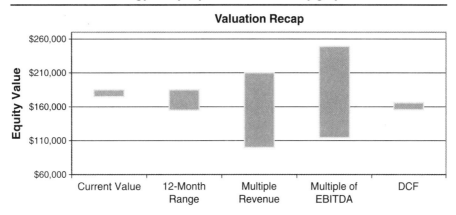

value approximates our estimate of the DCF value. This indicates that the market is probably expecting future performance in line with our projections used in the DCF.

Comprehensive Valuation Summary

For fans of dashboards or one-page recaps (including the author), the comprehensive valuation summary (Figure 30.6) may be of interest. It combines a number of the tools we have reviewed in this chapter to present a very comprehensive view into the dynamics of the valuation of this company.

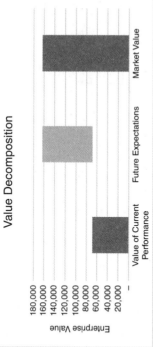
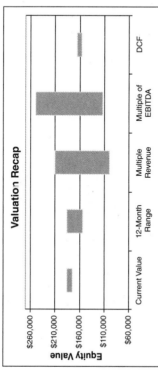
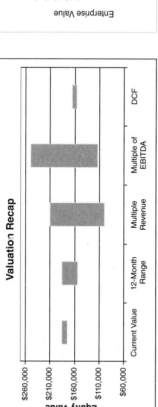
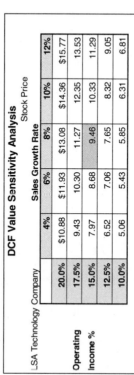
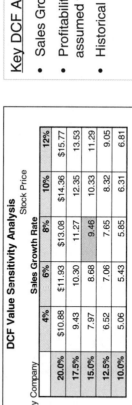
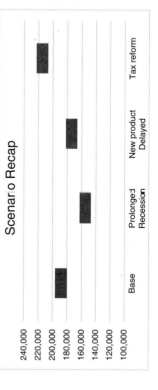

FIGURE 30.6 **Valuation summary.**

THE ELEPHANT IN THE ROOM: VALUATIONS OFTEN VARY SIGNIFICANTLY FROM FUNDAMENTAL METHODS

Over history, and especially over the past 25 years, market valuations have drifted far from the value established under fundamental economic methods, including discounted cash flow. The reasons for this, outlined in Figure 30.7, are varied and range across a number of factors such as irrational exuberance and extreme interest rate levels. The availability (or scarcity) of alternative investment vehicles, general economic conditions, tax and regulatory policy, and geopolitical forces all affect valuations. Managers and investors should be on guard when valuations diverge from DCF and other fundamental valuation methods. Market corrections often return values to approximate fundamental or fair-value levels.

FIGURE 30.7 **Factors impacting valuation.**

Valuation Dynamics: Factors Impacting Valuation

Factor	Reason	Examples
Company Specific		
Business Definition	How a business is defined and presented to investors has a significant impact on perceived value	Recurring Revenue Streams Automobile vs. Technology
Future Growth Potential	Demonstrated history of growth and future potential growth increase value	Revenue growth is the most significant driver of Long-term value creation
Profitability	Profitability (and expectation of future profitability) is a primary driver of value	
Cash Flow and Capital Requirements	Companies that require high levels of capital (Receivables, Inventories, Brick and Mortar, Equipment and Acquisitions) generally trade at lower valuations (multiples)	
Perceived Risk	Highly leveraged Capital Structure, Predictability and consistency of performance, recurring revenue streams, aggressive accounting policies. . .all increase perceived risk	
Controlling versus minority interest	Investments with a controlling interest are afforded a premium due to ability to "control" decisions and outcomes	
Liquidity, Float and Marketability	Valuations are discounted if the investment is not actively traded or marketable	
Macro and Market Forces		
Overall Market Sentiment	While valuation is in part quantitative, there is a significant subjective and emotional component	Bubbles: technology and internet, real estate Significant participation by hedge funds, retail investors FOMA: Fear of Missing Out
Market Rotations	Certain sectors are attractive to investors at different times based on economic cycles and other factors	Technology, Analytics, Healthcare vs. retail, energy, transportation
Economic Environment	A rising tide lifts all ships and a slowing economy or recession will impact revenues and earnings	
Interest Rates	Lower rates have a positive effect on equity values directly and indirectly	Lower interest rates encourage investment and economic activity. Low rates also make equity more attractive than investments in fixed income (bonds, Money funds).
Tax Policy	State and Federal Income Tax Policy affect earnings and cash flow; therefore valuation	The reduction in US Corp tax rates from 32% to 20% resulted in higher profits, investments and valuations
M&A Environment	A favorable M&A environment (e.g. low interest rates, strong valuations) will drive equity values higher	

VALUE DRIVERS

The fundamental objective for most companies is to create value for shareholders. For these enterprises, we have successfully utilized a framework that links value creation and value drivers to key business processes and activities.

In Chapter 15, we introduced the value performance framework (VPF) as one of several options to establish an overall framework for performance management. The VPF, presented in Figure 30.8, identifies six drivers of shareholder value:

- ❏ Sales growth.
- ❏ Relative pricing strength.
- ❏ Operating effectiveness.
- ❏ Capital effectiveness.
- ❏ Cost of capital.
- ❏ The intangibles.

Factors such as interest rates, market conditions, and irrational investor behavior will, of course, affect the price of a company's stock. However, the six value drivers identified are those that management teams and directors can drive to build long-term sustainable shareholder value.

FIGURE 30.8 **The value performance framework.**

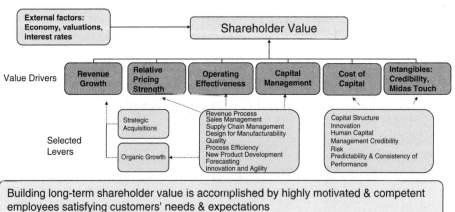

It is important to recognize that the significance of each driver will vary from firm to firm and will also vary over time for a particular firm. For example, a firm with increased competition in a low-growth market will likely place significant emphasis on operating and capital effectiveness. In contrast, a firm with a significant opportunity for revenue growth is likely to focus on that driver and place less emphasis on capital management or operating effectiveness. At some time in the future, however, this high-growth firm may have to deal with a slower growth rate and may have to shift emphasis to other drivers, such as operating efficiency and capital management.

In order to attain its full potential value, a firm must understand the potential contribution of each driver to shareholder value. It starts with the six value drivers that ultimately determine shareholder value. Underneath these value drivers are some of the key activities and processes that determine the level of performance in each value driver. In addition, the framework identifies some of the key performance indicators that can be used to measure the effectiveness of these activities and processes. For example, sales growth is a key driver of shareholder value. A subset of sales growth is the level of organic growth, excluding the impact on sales growth of any acquisitions. Organic sales growth will be driven by a number of factors, including customer satisfaction, which can be tracked by key metrics such as on-time deliveries (OTD) and the level of past due orders.

In order to create a linkage between the day-to-day activities of the employees and the company's share value, we must first create a discounted cash flow (DCF) model for the company. We can start with the model introduced in this chapter. We first input several years of historical performance as a baseline, and then project key elements of the expected future performance. The projections should be based on our best estimate of future performance. The projections should be realistic and should be reviewed against the recent historical performance trends experienced by the firm. This scenario, using our projections for the future performance, can be described as the "base forecast."

If the firm is publicly traded, the preliminary valuation can be tested against the current stock price. If the value indicated by the DCF model is significantly different from the recent trading range of the stock, one or more of your assumptions is likely to be inconsistent with the assumptions held by investors and potential investors. Identifying and testing the critical assumptions that investors are making in valuing the firm's stock can be very enlightening. The DCF model will allow you to easily change key assumptions and observe the potential impact on the value of the stock. It is very informative to iterate key assumptions until you can achieve a valuation consistent with recent market values for your company. For firms that are not publicly traded, this process can be performed for a comparable firm or firms that are in the same industry. Growth rates, other key drivers, and valuation metrics can then be transferred to the private firm to understand value drivers and expectations for the industry.

After developing a perspective on valuation and value drivers, the second step is to identify the critical activities and processes that impact each value driver. While many of these critical processes and activities are common from business to business, their relative importance will vary significantly among companies.

Further, every industry and firm has certain unique characteristics that must be identified and reflected in the framework. In Chapters 22 through 27, we examined each of the value drivers and linked those drivers to critical processes and activities.

This framework allows managers to evaluate potential improvement projects and identify high-leverage opportunities in the context of value creation. Too often, companies or functional managers embark on initiatives to improve certain aspects of the business without fully considering the impact on value creation. Will the initiatives be worth the investment of time and valuable resources? The VPF framework allows managers to rank various programs and address the following questions:

- How much value will be created if we accelerate sales growth from 5% to 10%?
- How much value will be created if we reduce manufacturing defects by 20%?
- How much value will be created if we reduce accounts receivable days sales outstanding (DSO) from 65 to 50 days? If we improve inventory turns from 4 to 6?
- Which of these programs will have the greatest impact on value?

Identifying High-Leverage Improvement Opportunities and Estimating Full Potential Value

Utilizing the tools of business process assessment, benchmarking, and discounted cash flow analysis, managers can estimate the potential improvements in the value drivers and quantify the effect on the value of the firm if the targeted performance is achieved. We start with the benchmarking framework, introduced in Chapter 18 (see Table 30.6).

In this case, LSA Technology has set preliminary performance targets to achieve top quartile performance in each key measure in Table 30.6. Using the DCF model, the value created by each change can be estimated and summarized in Table 30.7. The value of the firm could be increased from $162.9 million to $391 million if each of the performance improvements is realized. This may be a good place to start, but requires additional vetting. The targets should be refined by evaluating processes and operating effectiveness and testing the relative impact on value creation to develop a target business model. This exercise is not meaningful unless the team has a plan for *how* these improvements will be achieved.

A graphic presentation of this analysis is shown in Figure 30.9.

Projecting improved performance on spreadsheets is very easy. Achieving these improvements in actual results requires substantial planning, effort, and

TABLE 30.6 **Benchmarking summary.**

Benchmarking Summary and Target Worksheet

	LSA Tech	Median	Top Quartile	Best in Class	Best Practice	Performance Target
Revenue Growth	8.0%	8.0%	12.0%	15.0%	25.0%	12.0%
Gross Margin %	55.0%	52.0%	56.0%	60.0%		56.0%
Operating Expenses	40.0%	40.0%	38.0%	35.0%		38.0%
Operating Margins	15.0%	12.0%	18.0%	20.0%	25.0%	18.0%
Tax Rate	34.0%	30.0%	25.0%	15.0%	10.0%	25.0%
Operating Capital % Sales	30.0%	25.0%	15.0%	10.0%	15.0%	15.0%
WACC	11.99%	10.59%	10.13%	9.77%	9.07%	10%
Cost of Equity	12.4%	11.3%	11.0%	10.7%	9.8%	
Beta	1.24	1.05	1.00	0.95	0.80	
Debt to Total Capital						
Book	15.4%	30.0%	40.0%	50.0%	50.0%	
Market	5.3%	10.0%	13.3%	16.7%	16.7%	
(1) Assumes:						
Current RF 10 Treasury notes	5%					
MRP	6%					
Interest Rate	6%	6%	6%	6%	6%	
Tax rate	34%	30%	25%	15%	10%	

TABLE 30.7 **Summary of full potential value.**

Summary of Full Potential Value

	From	To	Enterprise Value	Increment	How?
Current Value			162.9		Current Performance Expectations
Increase Sales Growth Rate	8%	12%	194	31.1	Improve Quality and On-time Delivery
Improve Gross Margin %	55%	56%	209.3	15.3	Reduce Material Costs
Reduce Operating Expenses	40%	38%	239.7	30.4	Process Initiatives
Reduce Tax Rate	32%	25%	268	28.3	Tax Benefits from New Manufacturing Facility
Reduce Operating Capital %	30%	15%	289	21.0	Improve Supply Chain and Revenue Process
Reduce WACC	12%	10%	391	102.0	Improve Forecasting and Change Capital Structure

follow-through. Central to achieving these performance goals is the selection and development of effective performance measures.

SUMMARY

While each of the valuation techniques has limitations, they do provide insight from a variety of perspectives. It is best to use a combination of measures and techniques in reviewing the valuation of a firm. When an analyst summarizes

FIGURE 30.9 **Estimating full potential valuation.**

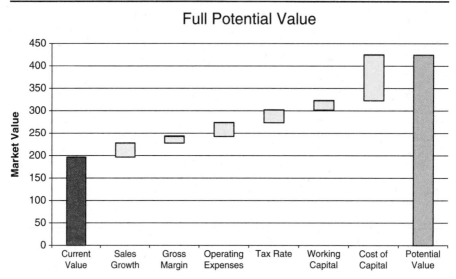

these measures for a firm and compares them to key benchmarks, significant insights can be gained. Conversely, inconsistencies across the valuation measures for a company are worth exploring and can usually be explained by identifying a specific element of financial performance that the measure doesn't reflect. For example, a company that consistently meets or exceeds operating plans and market expectations will typically be afforded a higher P/E multiple than its peers. This positive factor is reflected in a higher P/E multiple, and the company will trade at a premium to the industry norms.

Managers can use the DCF valuation model to estimate potential growth in value resulting from improving performance across key value drivers. Given this foundation in valuation, we will turn our attention to unique issues in analyzing and valuing mergers and acquisitions in Chapter 31.

31

Analysis of Mergers and Acquisitions

There probably is no other business decision that can create or destroy value more than mergers and acquisitions (M&A). Managers and boards pursue acquisitions for many reasons. Understanding the rationale for an acquisition is a key element of evaluating a potential deal, assessing the likelihood of success, and determining the reasonableness of the deal price. Successful acquirers have a clear acquisition strategy that flows out of a well-defined business strategy. In addition, they typically have competencies in evaluating and valuing potential acquisitions, discipline in pricing deals, and managers with experience in integrating acquisitions. We will focus on the analysis and economics of mergers and acquisitions in this chapter. Building a successful M&A program was covered in Chapter 9, "The Role of Finance in Supporting Growth."

THE ACQUISITION CHALLENGE

Many managers, academics, and advisers believe that it is difficult to create value through acquisitions. Research studies over the years consistently report a low percentage of acquisitions that are ultimately successful in creating value for the shareholders of the acquiring firm. The cards are stacked against acquirers since they typically have to pay a premium to close the transaction and assume all risk of integration and execution. In addition, many common mistakes lead to problems in valuing, negotiating, and integrating acquisitions, and are discussed later in this chapter. However, many companies do have successful acquisition programs that have resulted in building value for shareholders over a long period of time. The best practices that these companies employ are also discussed later in this chapter.

The stock market's reaction to proposed transactions can be informative. Following the announcement of a proposed transaction the price of the acquirer's stock will typically fall. At the same time, the price of a target's stock will generally rise to a price at or just under the announced acquisition price. Why does the market react this way? The market typically reacts negatively to the acquiring firm's announcement for several reasons. First, investors recognize that acquirers generally are forced to pay a significant premium and that most deals do not build value for the shareholders of the acquiring firm. Second, they may feel that this specific deal is overpriced. Finally, they recognize that all the risk of implementing the combined strategy and integrating the two organizations is transferred to the acquiring firm. It is interesting to note, though, that the market doesn't always react negatively to acquisition announcements. For companies with strong acquisition programs and track records, a clear strategic rationale and a reputation for disciplined pricing, the market price of the acquirer's stock may hold steady or even increase on news of a deal.

The price of the acquired company's stock will rise to approximate the proposed value of the deal. Since there is a good chance that the selling shareholders would receive the deal value at the time of closing, the price trades up toward that level. If, however, the market perceives significant risk that the deal will not be completed, for example, due to expected difficulty in obtaining regulatory approvals, then the stock will trade at a discount to the proposed deal price. As impediments to the deal are removed, the stock will trade closer to the deal price. If the market was speculating that another potential buyer might make an offer for the target, the stock price may even rise above the announced deal value in anticipation of an offer from another bidder.

KEY ELEMENTS IN VALUING AN ACQUISITION

In valuing acquisitions, it is useful to identify and value two components: the value of the company to be acquired (the target) as a standalone company and the value of any potential synergies arising from the acquisition.

Standalone Value   The standalone value is the worth of a company presuming that it continues to operate on a standalone or independent basis. Most publicly traded companies are valued on this basis, unless there are rumors or expectations that the company is a potential acquisition candidate. The standalone value is computed using the methodologies described in Chapter 30, "Business Valuation and Value Drivers." We will illustrate the merger and acquisitions (M&A) valuation concepts in this chapter building on the LSA Technology Company example, presented previously in Chapter 30.

Synergies   Synergies are a critical element in valuing acquisitions. Few, if any, companies will be sold on the basis of the value of that company on a standalone basis. Synergies are generally understood to result where the combined results exceed the sum of the independent parts. For purposes of this discussion, we will use *synergies* to mean the additional economic benefits that will be achieved by combining two companies. The term *economic benefit* is used here to emphasize that any synergy must be realizable in future cash flows to be relevant in valuation. Synergies can take many forms. Common types of synergies include higher sales growth, reduced costs and expenses, financial benefits, and improved management practices.

Revenue Growth. Revenue growth is always an important consideration in valuation. Drivers of sales growth resulting from M&A transactions include:

Leverage existing distribution channel(s). The growth rate of the target may be accelerated if the acquirer can sell the target's products through existing distribution channels (or vice versa). For example, the acquirer may have a strong international distribution organization in a region where the target's presence is weak or nonexistent.

Address a new market or develop new products with combined competencies. The combination of technical competencies from two organizations may result in a new product, channel, or technology that will accelerate sales growth.

Reduced Costs. Nearly all acquisitions contemplate some reduction in cost. Common examples include:

- *Eliminate redundant costs and expenses.* The acquirer may not need to maintain the target's procurement or administrative functions. For example, when two publicly traded companies are combined, many of the corporate functions at one of the companies can be eliminated, including the board of directors, investor relations, and financial reporting.
- *Leverage scale and purchasing power.* The combined purchasing power of the two organizations may result in reduced prices for materials or services.

Financial Synergies. Significant value can be created by leveraging the acquirer's lower cost of capital to the target. This is sometimes viewed as financial engineering by many operating managers. However, the cost of capital is a significant driver of value and even a modest reduction can result in a significant increase to value. By providing a previously independent firm with the acquirer's access to capital, borrowing power, and lower interest rates, a substantial increase in earnings power and valuation may be realized.

Transference of Best Practices. The acquiring company may have innovative business practices that can be transferred to the target (or vice versa).

For example, a highly effective product development process may reduce the product development cycle and time to market, thereby reducing product development costs and increasing sales. One of the companies may have a highly effective strategic planning framework or experience in improving operations that will lead to tangible improvements in financial performance for its merger partner.

Beware of Vague Synergies   Over time, the word *synergies* has taken on negative connotations because of the loose use of this term in describing dubious benefits from M&A transactions. Many deals have been justified over time by invoking the *synergy* word to describe vague or intangible benefits resulting from the transaction. Synergies must be specifically identified, supported by detailed implementation plans, and assigned to managers who will be held accountable for capturing the benefits that result in growth in value for shareholders.

Potential Acquisition Value

The potential economic value resulting from an acquisition is the sum of the standalone value and the value of expected synergies as shown in Figure 31.1.

FIGURE 31.1 **Standalone and synergies value.**

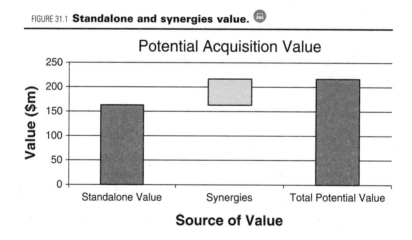

METHODS AND METRICS FOR VALUING AN ACQUISITION

A variety of valuation methods and metrics are utilized in practice, including:

- Accounting and comparable methods
  - Earnings per share accretive-dilutive test.
- Comparable or relative pricing methods: multiples of revenues, earnings, and cash flow.
  - Control premium analysis.

- Economic measures and tests
  - Discounted cash flow.
  - Economic profit/ROIC test.
  - Internal rate of return (IRR)/Net present value (NPV).

Each of these methods has strengths and limitations. Each can play a role in developing a comprehensive view of a potential deal. We will illustrate these methods using a proposed acquisition of LSA Technology Company (LSA) by Sheridan Acquisition Co. (SAC). SAC is offering to acquire all of the outstanding shares of LSA for $233.8 million in cash and will assume the $10 million in debt outstanding, resulting in a total acquisition cost of $243.8 million. Key assumptions are detailed in Table 31.1.

TABLE 31.1 **Sheridan Acquisition Company acquires LSA Technology Company.** 🖼

	Sheridan Acquisition Company Acquires LSA Technology Company
	Assumptions
$m	
SAC Forecast	**2024E**
Sales	1,000
PBT	100
TAX	−34
PAT	66
Shares	64
EPS	1.03
Price/Earning Ratio	20.0
Acquisition Financing:	
Debt, at interest rate of:	6%
Synergies	
Revenue	The merger would result in $20 million of additional sales beginning in 2024. The sales are estimated to result in a 55% gross margin and 30% operating expenses. Working capital requirements are estimated at 30% of sales; no additional capital expenditures will be required.
Cost savings	The merger would result in $6 million of annual savings beginning in 2024 and would cost $2 million in 2023 to implement.
	Cost Savings:
	G&A — 2.0
	R&D — 1.0
	Material cost savings — 1.0
	Plant closings — 2.0
	6.0

Accounting and Comparable Methods

Earnings per Share (EPS) Accretive-Dilutive Test. Since EPS is a critical measure of performance for a company, especially those trading in public capital markets, it is very important to understand the impact of an acquisition on EPS. The basic test is to determine if the acquirer's EPS will increase (accrete) or decrease (dilute) as a result of pursuing a specific acquisition. A "rule of thumb" used by many managers, bankers, and investors is that a deal should be accretive within a short period of time, often 12 months. The method involves identifying all of the various ways an acquisition will affect EPS. Examples include:

Favorable to EPS	Unfavorable to EPS
Profits contributed by the acquired firm	Expenses related to the acquisition
Profits from sales synergies	Amortization of goodwill (in certain cases)
Reduced costs	Amortization of other intangibles
	Capital required to finance the acquisition: • Additional shares issued to acquire company • Interest expense on debt issued to finance deal • Forgone interest on cash utilized

Goodwill arising from an acquisition is carried on the balance sheet and evaluated for recoverability on an annual basis. Historically, prior to 2001, goodwill was amortized and reported as an expense in the income statement. Under current rules, goodwill amortization expense is typically excluded from the Income Statement, thereby lowering the bar in the accretive-dilutive test. Since the EPS test does not fully reflect the true cost of capital for the acquisition, it will result in a positive impact on earnings long before earning an economic return. Table 31.2 illustrates the accretive-dilutive test for the SAC-LSA transaction.

This deal as presented would be accretive to earnings in the first full year after the acquisition since the earnings contributed by the target and expected synergies exceed the financing costs. EPS will increase from $1.03 prior to the acquisition to $1.17 reflecting the acquisition. If the investors are focusing on EPS and using a P/E multiple to value the company (and if the P/E multiple remains constant), the price of the acquiring company's stock will rise from $20.63 to $23.36 per share.

What about the economics of the transaction? What is the hurdle rate implied in this EPS analysis? That is, what is the required rate of return on the capital used to purchase this company to break even on EPS? The hurdle

TABLE 31.2 **Accretive-dilutive test illustration.**

$m	Sheridan Acq. Co.	LSA Tech	Synergies	Financing	Amortization	Total	Combined
Sales	1,000.0	116.6	20.0			136.6	1,136.6
PBT	100.0	16.9	11.0	−14.6		13.3	113.3
TAX	−34.0	−5.7	−3.7	5.0	0.0	−4.5	−38.5
PAT	66.0	11.2	7.3	−9.7	0.0	8.8	74.8
Shares	64.0	64.0	64.0	64.0	64.0	64.0	64.0
EPS	1.03	0.17	0.11	−0.15	0.00	0.14	1.17
Implied SAC Stock Price	$ 20.63						$ 23.36

(Header spanning: "Acquisition" spans LSA Tech, Synergies, Financing, Amortization, Total. "Steady State–first fiscal year (2024)" and "Accretive Dilutive Test" above.)

rate implied in this EPS accretion test is 4.0%. If profit after tax (PAT) exceeds the after-tax financing costs of $9.7 million, the deal will be accretive to (i.e., increase) earnings. Since the total purchase price of the acquisition, including assumed debt, is $243.8 million, the hurdle rate is 4.0%, as follows:

$$\frac{\text{After-Tax Financing Expense}}{\text{Purchase Price}} \quad \frac{\$9.7m}{\$243.8m} = 4.0\%$$

Is 4.0% an appropriate return for shareholders on this transaction? Hardly. Historically, investors could typically earn a higher rate by investing in essentially risk-free U.S. Treasury notes. In all investment decisions, the hurdle rate should be based on the specific risk associated with the investment. In acquisitions, the hurdle rate should be based on the target's risk profile adjusted for any perceived addition/reduction in risk due to the acquisition.

In spite of the reduced usefulness (under the rules eliminating goodwill amortization) of the accretive-dilutive metric, bankers, managers, and analysts continue to use it as a primary measure of the financial performance of an acquisition. If you listen to any conference call announcing an acquisition, EPS accretion-dilution will likely be prominently featured. It is certainly important to understand and communicate the EPS effect of a deal. However, it is not a comprehensive economic test.

COMPARABLE OR RELATIVE PRICING METHODS: MULTIPLES OF REVENUES, EARNINGS, AND CASH FLOW

Nearly all acquisition decisions will include an analysis of the pricing of similar companies in recent acquisitions. This is an important tool to determine how pricing of a proposed transaction compares with the pricing of other recent deals. This process is no different than evaluating the pricing of residential real estate. Prior to negotiating on the purchase price of a home, real estate brokers provide a comp listing, which summarizes transaction prices on recent home sales in the area. In a similar way, investment bankers and corporate development managers will identify recent transactions in the industry and compute key valuation metrics such as enterprise value/EBITDA and EV/revenue. These valuation metrics are then used to set or evaluate the pricing of the deal under review.

Generally, acquirers must pay a "full" or "strong" value (often euphemisms for overpaying) in order to convince the target's management, board, and shareholders that they should sell the company. Sometimes acquirers offer preemptive bids to discourage the target from considering other potential acquirers. Further, many companies are sold through auctions, where they are essentially marketed to a large number of potential buyers. The winner of this process is typically the highest bidder. All of these factors put upward pressure on the transaction prices. Therefore, managers who wish to build economic value through an acquisition program must recognize that the comparable transaction valuation methodology has a strong upward bias on transaction pricing.

Control Premium Analysis. A control or acquisition premium is the difference between the acquisition price and the market value of a public company prior to the acquisition announcement. Control premiums are often measured from the date preceding the announcement of a transaction ("undisturbed price"). If the market is anticipating an acquisition, it is likely that a substantial part of an expected premium is already reflected in the stock price. Therefore, it is important to examine the stock trading history for the target over the past 12 to18 months. It is possible that investors are expecting an acquisition and have partially or fully reflected an acquisition premium in the price of the stock. Table 31.3 shows the control premiums for the SAC- LSA transaction.

SAC's proposed purchase price of $13.75 per share represents a 38% premium over the price the day preceding the announcement of the deal. It represents a 25% premium over the 12-month high and a 50% premium over the 12-month low.

ECONOMICS-BASED MEASURES

Despite their shortcomings, both the accretive-dilutive test and comparable methods are useful tools in the decision process. The danger in placing

TABLE 31.3 **Control premium analysis.** ⊞

Equity Control Premium Analysis			
LSA Technology Company			
Shares Outstanding (m)	17.0		
		%	$m
Acquisition price (per share)	13.75		233.8
Price (1 day prior to announcement)	10.00		170.0
Acquisition premium	3.75	38%	63.8
12 month trading range –High	11.00	25%	
–Low	9.15	50%	

too much reliance on these methods results from two factors. First, neither method reflects the full economics of the deal since they do not utilize an appropriate measure of return on the capital invested. Second, the measures do not require explicit assumptions about the total performance of the combined businesses. Therefore, it is difficult to understand the performance expectations that are built into a comparables pricing analysis. How can operating managers understand what performance they are signing up for under these measures?

The use of the EPS accretive-dilutive test and multiples pricing methods should be complemented by economic tools, including discounted cash flow (DCF). The DCF analysis should include a "base case" valuation and sensitivity/scenario analyses to understand the impact of critical assumptions on valuation. Similarly, acquirers should estimate the expected economic return using return on invested capital (ROIC) or similar measures.

Discounted Cash Flow. Discounted cash flow (DCF) should be an integral element of any valuation and certainly in acquisition analysis. The advantage in using DCF is that it requires managers to make explicit assumptions about future performance. We would start with the discounted cash flow projection presented earlier in Table 30.1. This DCF for LSA would be for a standalone or independent valuation since we have not yet considered any changes that may result from an acquisition by another company. A simplified version of the standalone DCF for LSA is presented in Table 31.4.

We must now determine the potential value of LSA if acquired by SAC. There are two ways to estimate the economic value of proposed synergies. One method is simply to change the financial projections in the DCF for higher sales growth or reduced costs arising from the acquisition in the DCF analysis and record the revised value (see Table 31.5).

TABLE 31.4 **DCF Standalone.**

		DCF Stand alone		LSA Technology Company							
		2022	**2023**	**2024**	**2025**	**2026**	**2027**	**2028**	**2029**	**2030**	
Sales		100,000.0	108,000.0	116,640.0	125,971.2	136,048.9	146,932.8	158,687.4	171,382.4	178,237.7	
Gross Margin	55%		59,400.0	64,152.0	69,284.2	74,826.9	80,813.0	87,278.1	94,260.3	98,030.7	
%			55%	55%	55%	55%	55%	55%	55%	55%	
Cost Synergies											
SG&A			43,200.0	46,656.0	50,388.5	54,419.6	58,773.1	63,475.0	68,553.0	71,295.1	
Total Operating Expenses			43,200.0	46,656.0	50,388.5	54,419.6	58,773.1	63,475.0	68,553.0	71,295.1	
%			40%	40%	40%	40%	40%	40%	40%	40%	
Operating Income			16,200.0	17,496.0	18,895.7	20,407.3	22,039.9	23,803.1	25,707.4	26,735.7	
%			15%	15%	15%	15%	15%	15%	15%	15%	
Tax	32%		5,184.0	5,598.7	6,046.6	6,530.3	7,052.8	7,617.0	8,226.4	8,555.4	
EBIAT			11,016.0	11,897.3	12,849.1	13,877.0	14,987.1	16,186.1	17,481.0	18,180.2	
Depreciation			5,000.0	5,400.0	5,832.0	6,298.6	6,802.4	7,346.6	7,934.4	8,569.1	
Capital Expenditures	−30%		−5,400.0	−5,832.0	−6,298.6	−6,802.4	−7,346.6	−7,934.4	−8,569.1	−7,130.0	
WC Increase			−2,400.0	−2,592.0	−2,799.4	−3,023.3	−3,265.2	−3,526.4	−3,808.5	−2,056.6	
FCF			8,216.0	8,873.3	9,583.1	10,349.8	11,177.8	12,072.0	13,037.8	17,562.8	
Acquisition Costs			0.0	0.0	0.0	0.0	0.0	0.0	0.0	0.0	
TV									TV		228,316
Cash Flow (CF)			8,216.0	8,873.3	9,583.1	10,349.8	11,177.8	12,072.0	13,037.8	17,562.8	228,316
Present Value C^F (discount rate):	12%	162,927	8,216	7,923	7,640	7,367	7,104	6,850	6,605	7,945	103,279
Sum PVFCF		162,927						PHGR		4.0%	

Estimated Value of the Enterprise	162,927
Excess Cash	7,944
Value of Debt	(10,000)
Estimated Value of Equity	160,871

634

TABLE 31.5 **DCF synergy and standalone.** 🖩

SAC Acquires LSA Technology Company

DCF Synergy + Standalone

		2022	2023	2024	2025	2026	2027	2028	2029	2030
Sales	55%	100,000	108,000	136,640	145,971	156,049	166,933	178,687	191,382	198,238
GM			59,400	75,152	80,284	85,827	91,813	98,278	105,260	105,260
%			55%	55%	55%	55%	55%	55%	55%	55%
Cost Synergies			2,000.0	−6,000.0	−6,000.0	−6,000.0	−6,000.0	−6,000.0	−6,000.0	−6,000.0
SGA			43,200.0	52,656.0	56,388.5	60,419.6	64,773.1	69,475.0	74,553.0	77,295.1
OP Exp			45,200.0	46,656.0	50,388.5	54,419.6	58,773.1	63,475.0	68,553.0	71,295.1
%			42%	34%	35%	35%	35%	36%	36%	36%
Operating Income			14,200.0	28,496.0	29,895.7	31,407.3	33,039.9	34,803.1	36,707.4	37,735.7
%			13.1%	20.9%	20.5%	20.1%	19.8%	19.5%	19.2%	19.0%
Tax	32%		4,544.0	9,118.7	9,566.6	10,050.3	10,572.8	11,137.0	11,746.4	12,075.4
EBIAT			9,656.0	19,377.3	20,329.1	21,357.0	22,467.1	23,666.1	24,961.0	25,660.2
Depreciation			5,000.0	5,400.0	5,832.0	6,298.6	6,802.4	7,346.6	7,934.4	8,569.1
Capital Expenditures			−5,400.0	−5,832.0	−6,298.6	−6,802.4	−7,346.6	−7,934.4	−8,569.1	−7,130.0
WC Increase	−30%		−2,400.0	−8,592.0	−2,799.4	−3,023.3	−3,265.2	−3,526.4	−3,808.5	−2,056.6
FCF			6,856.0	10,353.3	17,063.1	17,829.8	18,657.8	19,552.0	20,517.8	25,042.8

TABLE 31.5 (*Continued*)

SAC Acquires LSA Technology Company

DCF Synergy + Standalone

	2022	2023	2024	2025	2026	2027	2028	2029	2030
Acquisition Costs		–	–	–	–	–	–	–	–
TV									290,649.5
Cash Flow		6,856.0	10,353.3	17,063.1	17,829.8	18,657.8	19,552.0	20,517.8	315,692.3
									87,376.1
Present Value (discount rate) 12%		6,856.0	10,353.3	17,063.1	17,829.8	18,657.8	19,552.0	20,517.8	87,376.1
Sum PVFCF	218,543	6,856	9,244	13,603	12,691	11,857	11,094	10,395	142,803
Estimated Value of the Enterprise	218,543								
Value of Debt	(10,000)				TV LSA Tech Co.: 4% growth				
Excess Cash	7,944								
Estimated Value of Equity	216,487				TV PHG Synergies: 0%				

Test

DCF Value Standalone	160,871
DCF Value Synergies	55,616
	216,487
	–

The second method is to compute the economic value of each synergy directly. The projected cash flow for each synergy is discounted to estimate the economic value today in Table 31.6. Note that the two methods result in the same value.

The value of equity from Table 31.5 is $216.5 million. This is consistent with the sum of:

LSA standalone (Table 31.4)	$160.9m
Value of Synergies (Table 31.6)	55.6
Total	$216.5m

TABLE 31.6 **Synergy valuation and control premium test.**

Synergy Valuation and Control Premium Test				
LSA Technology Company				
Cost of Capital	12%			
Tax Rate	32%			
Synergy Valuation:		EBIT	EBIAT/CF	PV
Revenue	20.0	5.0	3.4	28.3
Cost Savings				
G&A		2.0	1.4	11.3
R&D		1.0	0.7	5.7
Material Cost Savings		1.0	0.7	5.7
Plant Closings		2.0	1.4	11.3
Total		11.0	7.5	62.3
PV of Synergies			62.3	
Less Working Capital on Revenue Growth	30%		−5.4 (1)	
Implementation Costs (Synergies)	2.0		−1.4 (2)	
PV of Estimated Synergies			55.6	
Control Premium ($ millions)			63.8	

Excess/(GAP)

−8.1

Notes
(1) $6 million in year 2024, discounted for 1 period
(2) $2 million pre-tax in 2023

The advantage in using the detail synergy method in Table 31.6 is that managers understand the specific contribution to value of each projected synergy as well as the standalone value of LSA. This is useful in evaluating the probability and risks associated with each synergy. Not all synergies are created equal. For example, there may be substantially more risk associated with sales growth expected in three to four years. However, the probability of achieving expected administrative savings should be relatively high.

In addition to estimating the value of each synergy, this analysis indicates that the total value of estimated synergies approximates the control premium in this deal. Presuming that the market is valuing the LSA at a reasonable economic value (indicated by the standalone DCF analysis), the full value of potential synergies is being transferred to the shareholders of the selling firm. Comparing the value of potential synergies to the control premium is a useful test. The dynamics of this macro test are shown in Figure 31.2.

FIGURE 31.2 **Control premium-synergies macro test.**

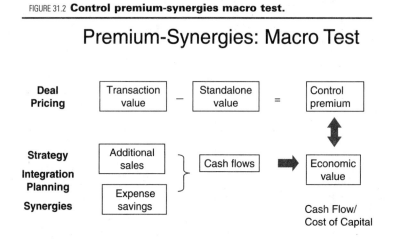

Combining the estimated standalone valuation with the estimates of each projected synergy results in the DCF valuation summary in Figure 31.3.

FIGURE 31.3 **Sources of acquisition value.**

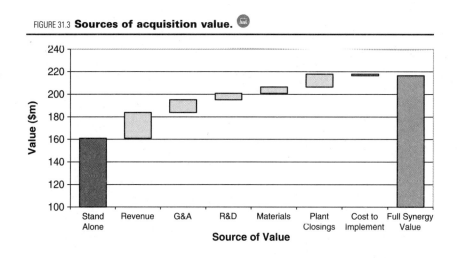

Economic Profit Test. Another sobering test in M&A analysis is to estimate the economic profit required to earn an acceptable return on the capital invested to acquire the business. Management must earn a return at least equal to the firm's cost of capital to create value for shareholders. Table 31.7 illustrates the economic profit/ROIC test for the LSA acquisition. The total economic purchase price of $243.8 million will include the market value of the target (standalone), the control premium, and assumed debt. Based on the estimated cost of capital of 12%, the required economic profit can be computed and compared to the projections of the target and estimated synergies. In this case, the projected earnings before interest and after taxes (EBIAT) doesn't reach the required level to achieve economic breakeven over the forecast horizon. Consistent with this result, the analysis also indicates that the ROIC will not achieve the cost of capital of 12% until some point beyond the forecast period.

TABLE 31.7 **Economic profit/ROIC test.**

$m	Economic Profit Test SAC acquires LSA Technology Company							
Market Value of Company (prior to announcement)	$170.0							
Control Premium	63.8							
Assumed Debt	10.0							
Total Transaction Value (invested capital)	243.8							
Cost of Capital	12%							
Required Annual EBIAT for economic "breakeven"	29.3							
		2023	2024	2025	2026	2027	2028	2029	2030
Projected EBIAT (Table 31.5)		9.7	19.4	20.3	21.4	22.5	23.7	25.0	25.7
Required EBIAT		29.3	29.3	29.3	29.3	29.3	29.3	29.3	29.3
Excess (deficit) EBIAT		−19.6	−9.9	−8.9	−7.9	−6.8	−5.6	−4.3	−3.6
ROIC (on transaction value)		4.0%	7.9%	8.3%	8.8%	9.2%	9.7%	10.2%	10.5%

The management team of the acquiring organization has several options in this situation:

1. Consider reducing the acquisition price.
2. Walk away.
3. Increase the projected performance to justify the price.
4. Proceed with the transaction (and overpay).

Unfortunately, too often managers select either option 3 or 4. Many proceed with the deal terms and argue that the economic analysis is not relevant or indicative of the value in the transaction. Often, they argue that the deal is strategic and that the financial analysis does not properly capture the strategic value. If the financials do not fully reflect the strategic case and expected synergies, then they should be revised. In other cases, the financial projections are increased to support the deal price. Presuming that the base projections were realistic estimates of future performance, this option may increase the risk of failing to achieve the financial results.

Internal Rate of Return and Net Present Value Analysis. An acquisition of a company is a specific and complex form of a capital investment. Therefore, it should be subject to the same tests as a new product proposal, plant expansion, or other capital expenditures, which were described in Chapters 28 and 29.

		Source
Present Value of Cash Flows—Standalone	$160.9	Table 31.4
Present Value of Cash Flows—Synergies	55.6	Table 31.6
Total Present Value of Cash Flows to Firm	216.5	
Purchase Price	(243.8)	
NPV	(27.3)	
IRR	8.4 %	

The NPV is a small negative result and the IRR falls short of the cost of capital of 12%. This test indicates that the economics of the transaction do not satisfy the economic tests. These results in NPV and IRR are consistent with the economic profit/ROIC test that indicated that breakeven returns would not be attained until at least sometime after 2030. Since the deal fails to satisfy the economic tests, management of SAC should consider whether the value created and returns earned are commensurate with the effort and risk in proceeding with the transaction.

Comparative Summary of Valuation Methods

We have reviewed a number of different valuation methodologies and metrics. It is helpful to summarize the indicated values from these differing methods, as illustrated in Figure 31.4. It is quite common for the methods to result in a wide range of potential transaction values. A useful exercise is to compare and contrast the estimated value ranges and understand the underlying factors, resulting in wide valuation ranges and sometimes even inconsistent results.

FIGURE 31.4 **Comparative value summary acquisition of LSA Technology Company.**

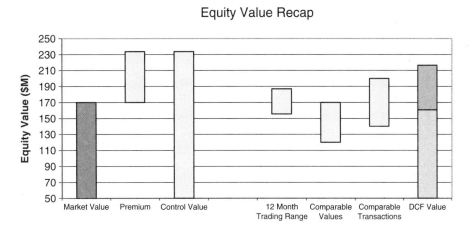

Day of Reckoning for Underperforming Acquisitions

The goodwill resulting from an acquisition (illustrated previously in Table 25.3) will be tested for recoverability at least annually under the accounting rules affecting most organizations. This test will require an annual review to determine if the acquisition is performing at levels sufficient to justify carrying the assets on the Balance Sheet. The test utilized is essentially a market-based valuation, often utilizing discounted cash flow analysis. This annual test has and will continue to result in a day of reckoning for many acquisitions. In fact, since the new standard was adopted, billions of dollars of goodwill have been written off, indicating that the acquisitions did not perform at a level that would earn an acceptable return on the original purchase price.

COMMON MISTAKES IN M&A

A number of common mistakes contribute to the difficulty in earning a return for shareholders of the acquiring firm. Many managers feel compelled to pursue acquisitions because their companies' organic growth rate has or is about to slow. Sales growth is a key value driver and the public capital markets place a huge premium on growth. Associates, executives, and directors want to serve growing organizations. In addition, mature organizations typically generate cash that exceeds operating requirements and are pressured to deploy this cash (or return to shareholders). As the business matures and organic growth begins to slow, they may embark on an acquisition program. This is fine if the program is well thought out and if the team acquires or develops resources necessary to execute an effective acquisition program. Many do not.

Poor Strategic Rationale and Fit

Some acquisitions are based on weak strategic cases. On the surface, the acquirer believes and articulates a strategy for the combined companies and points to synergistic benefits. Observers who are knowledgeable of the markets and the companies involved may recognize that the strategic case is weak and that some, or all, of the expected synergies may be difficult to attain. In these cases, a year or two after the deal is closed, the company will announce that the acquisition is not meeting expectations and will have difficulty in achieving the strategic and economic goals.

Poor Planning, Communication, Integration, and Execution

Well-planned and well-executed integration activities and strong communication plans are essential to achieve the objectives of an acquisition. Most successful acquirers also value speed in integrating acquisitions. Time is money, and getting the benefits of the acquisition earlier is better. More important, there is significant uncertainty and concern in the management and employee ranks about the potential impact of an acquisition. The sooner changes are made, the sooner employees will settle down to the tasks at hand. In the absence of well-planned, well-communicated, and timely changes, employees will lose significant productivity to speculation and fear. In addition, many will explore opportunities outside the firm.

Overpaying   Several factors cause managers to overpay for an acquisition. Paying too much for an acquisition may make it next to impossible to earn an acceptable rate of return on the investment, even if all other aspects are executed flawlessly. Many advisers and academics believe that it is difficult to purchase a public company at a price that will allow the acquiring shareholders to earn a return. Managers and boards have a fiduciary responsibility to maximize shareholder value. They have an obligation when selling the company to obtain the highest potential price for shareholders.

Managers often become emotionally charged when engaged in the acquisition process. After spending a great deal of time and emotional energy, it feels like losing to walk away from a deal. *Winning* is defined as "doing the deal," contrasted with doing the deal at a sensible valuation. Projections are often modified upward to support a higher offer. It is very easy to change expected savings or growth rates on a spreadsheet to yield a higher potential transaction value. Of course, achieving those lofty projections is another matter. The objective should be to buy a good company at a sensible price, not to buy a good company at any price. Ground the pricing discussions with DCF and other economic tests so that all parties understand the assumptions about future performance required to earn an economic return.

Managers should establish walk-away boundaries on price and other terms early in the process. The walk-away price should be supported by key assumptions. By putting a stake in the ground (or at least on paper), it will be easier for managers to recognize the inevitable upward pressure in transaction pricing. Only when significant changes in assumptions can be validated, should they consider migrating to another pricing level.

Unrealistic or Unspecified Synergies   Acquirers should be cautious about unrealistic or unspecified synergies. Red flags include unsupported statements such as:

- Sales growth rates will increase from 3% to 10% as a result of the acquisition.
- Selling, general, and administrative (SG&A) levels will decrease 3% points after the acquisition.
- Test these statements with questions such as these:
  - What new products will contribute to this growth? And how much?
  - What territories and customers will contribute to the growth? Have they been identified?
  - Has the sales organization signed up to these projections?
  - How many jobs will be eliminated to achieve the lower SG&A levels? Have these positions been identified? When will they be eliminated? Have related costs to implement these reductions been quantified?
  - Do we have commitment from the managers who will be responsible for the financial performance of the acquisition?

Failure to Anticipate and Address Soft Issues

People make acquisitions work. Too often, key managers are excluded from early stages of the M&A process. Unless everyone is in the boat and rowing hard, it will be difficult to make forward progress and achieve the challenging objectives of most acquisitions. Clear, timely, and well-communicated decisions about organizational structure are essential.

Inadequate Due Diligence   Due diligence must go far beyond traditional areas such as accounting, legal, and environmental. Strong acquisition programs will test the key areas contributing to future value, including: people, intellectual property, customer relationships, and other critical drivers of future performance.

BEST PRACTICES AND CRITICAL SUCCESS FACTORS

Companies that have a track record of success with acquisitions avoid these common mistakes and potential pitfalls with a strong acquisition process.

Successful programs tend to adopt best practices that improve the probability of creating value through acquisitions.

Sound Strategic Justification Acquirers always present a strategic case for a transaction. The key for managers, directors, and investors is to understand and test the strength of the strategic case. Most deals make sense, at least at a high level. Some questions to consider:

- Is this a move that is consistent with stated strategy and prior actions? Or did it come out of the blue?
- Does the acquisition address a competitive disadvantage?
- Does it leverage a key advantage?
- Does the acquisition accelerate progress on a key strategic initiative?
- What are the specific, tangible synergies that result from this transaction?

Discipline in Valuation

The objective of an M&A program is to acquire a strategic asset at a price that will create value for shareholders. It should not be to complete a transaction at any price. It is very useful to establish a walk-away price at the beginning of an acquisition review. Managers and boards must not view walking away from a potential deal that is overpriced as a failure. After passing on or being out-bid on a potential deal, managers do a lot of hand-wringing and questioning. What is wrong with our valuation methodology? Are we too conservative?

Different buyers will determine value very differently. Some buyers will perceive and are also capable of realizing higher synergies from a potential deal than others. It is also possible that another buyer may not have priced the deal on a rational basis. Remember that most acquisitions are not successful and many are overpriced. After one particularly emotional post-mortem session with a management team over a deal that got away, some members of the team predicted that the buyer would have substantial difficulty in earning an acceptable return at the final price. Within a short time, the management team of the buyer announced that the deal would not meet expectations, wrote off the goodwill, and announced that the company was exploring "strategic options" for the unit. That company was available again, for substantially less than the value that would have been required to win the deal from an irrational buyer the first time around.

Identify Specific Synergies

Synergies must be specific. They must be supported by detailed estimates and implementation plans. There must be buy-in from key managers and accountability must be established. Incentive and compensation plans must incorporate key value drivers in the deal, including achieving projections.

Strong Acquisition Process

Companies with solid track records in M&A have a strong acquisition process. Candidates are identified in the context of the firm's strategic assessment and plan. These companies devote considerable attention and resources to identifying, evaluating, and valuing potential targets. Thorough due diligence is conducted, well beyond the legal and financial basics to confirm key value drivers, including customer relationships and intellectual property. Synergies are confirmed and detailed execution plans are developed. Substantial effort is made to communicate the deal to key constituencies, including employees, customers, and investors. Integration is achieved as quickly as possible and monitored against the detailed implementation plans. Post-acquisition reviews are conducted to ensure follow-through and to identify lessons learned to improve the process for future transactions. The role of finance in supporting M&A was covered in more detail in Chapter 9.

Identify and Address Key Issues before Finalizing Deal

Successful acquirers identify and address key issues before announcing and proceeding with a deal. These issues often relate to post-transaction organization and people issues. How will the combined organizations be structured? Who will be the CEO and CFO of the combined organizations? What will happen to redundant organizations and positions? Will compensation and benefit plans be changed?

Communicate With, Retain, and Motivate Key Human Resources

It is extremely important to reduce uncertainty in the workforce as soon as possible. Details of integration plans and combined organizations should be communicated soon after the deal is announced. Key employees must be signed up and on-board on day one to ensure a smooth transition and integration. Employees whose positions will be eliminated should be informed and provided with details of termination dates and benefit programs.

Best Practices Summary

- Sound strategic justification.
- Discipline in valuation:
  - Success defined as acquiring a strategic asset at the right price.
- Identification of specific synergies.
  - Action plan and timely execution.

- Solid acquisition programs:
  - Objectives.
  - Acquisition criterion.
  - Process.
  - Pre-deal planning.
  - Due diligence teams and rigor.
  - Integration speed.
  - Establish line manager ownership early in process.
- Address key issues before finalizing deal.
- Retain and incentivize critical human resources.

UNDERSTANDING SELLER BEST PRACTICES

I have learned as much about acquisitions by participating in the *sale* of companies as I have learned by participating in the acquisitions of many businesses. In addition to watching buyer behavior and practices, it has been enlightening to understand the advice of investment bankers and consultants retained to assist in selling businesses. Here is what I took away as seller best practices.

"Dress Up the Performance"

Most sellers of businesses attempt to improve the performance of the business to increase the potential sales price. Obviously, it makes sense to paint the house and clean the carpets before listing the property. It also makes sense to address any areas that may detract from the value of a business that will be sold. However, no buyer would be happy if a major flaw was hidden by a fresh coat of surface paint. Similarly, potential buyers need to be thorough in their evaluation of businesses. For example, a business may be sold because of an emerging competitive or market risk. Other sellers may reduce investment in R&D or marketing to increase profitability in the short term; this may have a negative impact on the competitiveness of the company, and future sales and earnings.

Meet the Current Plan

Sellers are advised to meet or exceed their current operating plan. Falling short of the current plan provides a potential buyer with an opportunity to question future projections and the ability of the organization to execute to those plans. Beware of either modest plans or Herculean, unsustainable actions taken to meet the current plan.

Sell through an Auction Process, or Sell to Best Potential Parent or Partner

Sellers and their advisers recognize that they are likely to realize a higher selling price if they create a competitive bidding process. Many establish processes that encourage as many as 20 to 30 companies to consider preliminary bids for a business. Obviously, the relative bargaining position tilts to the seller in these situations. In addition, sellers should identify the best potential parents or strategic partners since those parties are likely to identify the highest level of potential synergies and therefore to offer a higher price.

Sell into a Strong Market

This is a variation of the investment advice buy low and sell high. Where possible, managers tend to offer businesses for sale at the top of valuation/market cycles. If the company is cyclical, the valuation will be substantially higher at the top of the cycle than at the bottom. There have been dramatic swings in the values of companies over the past 20 years and only a small part of the variation can be explained by the underlying performance or prospects of the companies.

KEY PERFORMANCE INDICATORS FOR M&A

Managers can use performance measures to evaluate the effectiveness of the M&A process and to track the progress in achieving the objectives for a specific acquisition.

Effectiveness of M&A Process

Companies that are serial acquirers should look at the performance of each of their acquisitions to evaluate the overall effectiveness of the entire process. Are we achieving the sales, profits, and returns anticipated in the acquisition proposal? What is the level of intangible assets arising from acquisitions? Have these acquisitions resulted in subsequent write-down of goodwill? This evaluation may identify potential improvement opportunities in the acquisition process.

Actual versus Planned Sales and Profits. Compare the actual sales to the level planned for in the acquisition proposal for the current year. Are the acquisitions achieving the sales estimates in the plan? If not, then the team should identify the underlying reasons for the shortfall and consider these in future acquisition proposals.

Actual versus Planned ROIC. Are the acquisitions achieving the return on invested capital (ROIC) projected in the acquisition proposal? ROIC is an important measure in M&A since it reflects the capital invested in the transaction. Again, what can we learn to improve our process for future acquisitions?

Goodwill and Intangibles Turnover. This measure provides a view into the relative significance of acquisitions to the firm. For highly acquisitive firms, this ratio will likely be low and will have a significant impact on return measures such as return on equity (ROE) and ROIC.

Asset Write-Offs and Impairment Charges. Goodwill impairment charges result from acquisitions failing to perform to expectations that supported the original purchase price. Significant charges to write off or write down assets may indicate an ineffective decision or implementation process for these capital investments. Companies that have frequent asset write-offs and impairment charges (and other nonrecurring charges) likely have an opportunity to improve capital investment, acquisition, and strategic processes.

Specific Acquisitions

The following measures are intended to provide real-time feedback on the performance of a specific acquisition. The objective is to select measures that provide a leading indication of progress toward achieving the financial and strategic objectives of the transaction.

Progress on Key Acquisition Activities. During a sound acquisition process, a number of actions are identified that are vital to achieving the objectives of the acquisition. These may include retention of critical human resources, benefits integration, and consolidation of the sales force and manufacturing plants. Progress on these action plans is a leading indicator of being able to achieve the financial goals of the acquisition.

Acquired Sales and Synergies. Most acquisition plans anticipate growing the acquired sales base from the time of the acquisition and realizing revenue synergies from the combined companies. Both components of sales growth should be closely monitored on a frequent basis.

Annualized Cost Synergies Achieved. Cost savings from combining organizations are an important contributor to the economic success of the merger or acquisition. Progress toward achieving the annual synergies included in the acquisition proposal should be tracked early and often (e.g., monthly or quarterly).

Key Human Resources Retention. The success of most acquisitions is predicated on retaining and motivating key human resources. Key human resources may include some or all of the executive team, functional managers, and technical, manufacturing, and customer relationship personnel. During the acquisition planning process, these individuals should be identified and a program put in place to encourage continuation of employment. Success in retaining the key people should be closely monitored.

DASHBOARDS FOR M&A

Based on the specific facts and circumstances, several performance measures may be combined to measure the overall effectiveness of the M&A activity and the progress in achieving the objectives for a specific acquisition. These dashboards are illustrated in Figures 31.5 and 31.6, respectively.

FIGURE 31.5 **M&A dashboard.** 🖼

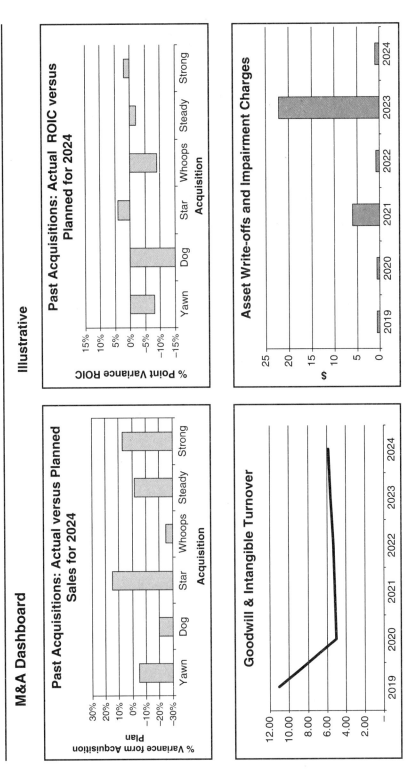

FIGURE 31.6 **Dashboard for a specific acquisition.** 📊

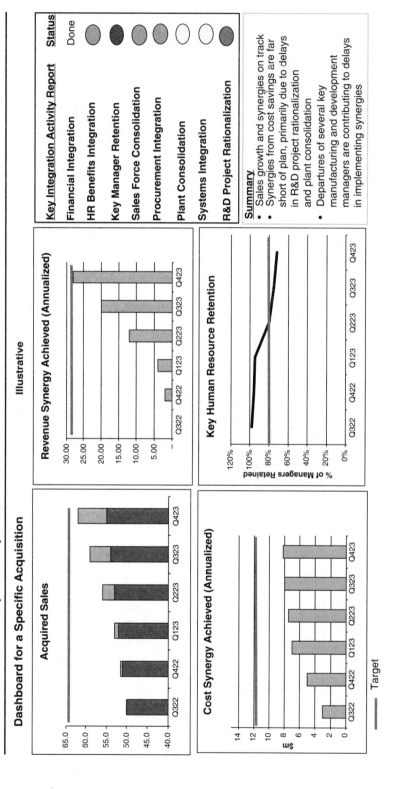

Dashboard for a Specific Acquisition   Illustrative

SUMMARY

Do acquisitions create value for shareholders? The answer is that value is nearly always created for the selling shareholders, but not as consistently for the shareholders of acquiring firms. Firms that have strong acquisition programs have developed competencies to execute well on all steps in the acquisition process. A key element of a successful acquisition program is to be disciplined in setting pricing and other terms, ensuring that the acquisition pricing is supported by economic analysis based on realistic projections of future performance. *Synergies* is not a bad word if the synergies are specifically identified and supported by a detailed implementation plan with clear accountability. The objective should be to do a good strategic deal at a reasonable price. Successful acquirers focus considerable attention on due diligence, synergy identification, execution planning, and post-merger integration.

Part Seven

Summary

32

Summary and Where To from Here?

This chapter will recap key takeaways from this book and provide suggestions for accelerating improvements in partnering to drive performance and value.

KEY TAKEAWAYS

Whether you have read this book from cover to cover or focused on selected topics of current interest to you and your organization, I offer the following summary of key points on elevating the contribution of finance as a partner in driving performance and value.

The current business and economic climates, as well as the pace of change, have significantly increased the need for effective FP&A, performance management, and overall financial partnership. *Most managers and executives desire better analysis, advice, and service.* Finance teams must rise to the occasion and improve the effectiveness of financial business partners. FP&A and performance management generally represent the areas of greatest potential impact for the finance organization.

Organizations should *assess the current effectiveness of financial business partners (FBPs)* and develop a plan to implement best practices and other improvements. In Chapters 3 and 7, we introduced several frameworks and specific tools, including a best practice assessment and client survey, to assess performance and identify improvement opportunities. Finance teams must develop or acquire skills and competencies to meet high expectations and needs of our clients.

Analytical works are incomplete and ineffective until they are presented and communicated to our clients. Spreadsheets are seldom the best communication tool. The ability to develop and present the findings of our analysis is a critical skill for analysts and financial managers. Improving our ability to deliver the message will improve the effectiveness of the analysis and the standing of the analyst. Chapter 5 detailed actions that can be taken to improve our ability to communicate and also provides specific examples of graphics, dashboards, and reports.

The *human capital* of an enterprise is generally a significant component of total cost and is also its most valuable asset. Finance must promote effective human capital management best practices across the company and specifically within the finance team, which were presented in Chapter 7.

Finance must contribute to and participate in the development of *strategic plans*. FBPs can earn a seat at the table by developing strategic analysis and sharpening our business acumen. Strategic analysis and planning were addressed in Chapter 8.

Finance must *contribute to revenue growth,* a critical value driver, by participating in the analysis and review of new programs, product development, and other growth activities. The role of finance in supporting growth was covered in Chapter 9.

Most significant threats and opportunities arise outside the organization. To be effective, financial management and FP&A must *maintain a view of external forces,* including economic, market and competition, and geopolitical. The external view was covered in Chapter 10.

At some point during an organization's life cycle, it will need to respond to inevitable challenges and changes in the marketplace to ensure the viability of the enterprise. *Business restructurings and transformations* were discussed in Chapter 11.

We live and operate in a world full of uncertainty and rapid change. Finance must adapt by utilizing and *promoting scenario management and organizational agility.* These topics were addressed in Chapters 13 and 14.

Technology continues to affect the way we live and work. Finance must monitor these developments and promote and use of new tools to improve productivity and analytics. Chapter 12 presented an overview of the rapidly changing technology, including artificial intelligence.

Finance professionals must be committed to *continual learning and development (L&D).* Business practices, best practices in financial management, technology, and society are all evolving at a rapid pace. The need to stay abreast of changes and create a personal L&D plan is vital to remaining employable and contribute to the success of our business.

Performance management, including the use of key performance indicators (KPIs) and dashboards, must be integrated with FP&A efforts in order to maximize effectiveness. A key to successful performance management is to develop a context that allows us to focus on key business and value drivers, strategic issues and objectives, and other critical issues. The selection of KPIs and the development of dashboards is very important since it implicitly defines priorities and key areas of emphasis. There is a tendency to measure areas and activities that are easy to track. Care should be exercised to include areas of great importance, including innovation, agility, human capital, and external forces. Finally, performance management must be fully integrated into other management processes, especially those dealing with acquiring evaluating and compensating team members. These topics on performance management were covered in Part III, "Enterprise Performance Management."

The ability to develop robust *financial projections* is a core competency for finance teams. Because the future is increasingly difficult to predict, new techniques and practices must be employed. Detailed financial budgets must be replaced with operating plans and business outlooks that focus on key drivers, operating processes and activities, upsides and downsides, and an ability to monitor key assumptions and indicators of future performance. Part IV, "Business Projections and Plans," presented best practices in developing projections, including business outlooks on demand and long-term projections.

FP&A teams must be able to plan, measure, review, and identify improvements in *critical business and value drivers*, including revenue growth, margins, and operating and capital effectiveness. Each of these drivers was reviewed in detail in Part V, "Planning and Analysis of Critical Business and Value Drivers." These business and value drivers typically are the core of most analytical efforts.

Capital investments decisions (CIDs) play a critical role in the overall success of any organization and have a direct impact on value creation. These decisions include purchases of equipment, product development projects, and acquisitions. Since CIDs require estimates of future performance, often over an extended time horizon, analysts must identify risks and upsides, a range of potential outcomes, and management options to optimize the project results under different scenarios. Capital investment decisions were covered in Chapters 28 and 29.

Valuation and shareholder value are important factors in assessing business decisions, setting goals, and purchasing businesses. Value creation is the primary objective of companies and should be a focus of FP&A and FBPs. Identifying value drivers and understanding the relationship among operating processes and activities, financial results, and value creation are essential. Valuation and value drivers were covered in Chapter 30.

Discipline in evaluating, valuing, and integrating acquisitions is essential, and finance must play an active role in this process. The M&A process was addressed in Chapter 9, and the analysis and evaluation and valuation subjects were addressed in Chapter 31.

Finally, it is important to direct our efforts in FP&A and performance management to *important business drivers and issues.* Specific suggestions to assist in this challenge were provided in Chapter 15, "Enterprise Performance Management and Execution."

WHERE TO FROM HERE?

Many finance teams struggle with the overwhelming number and magnitude of possible improvements to the current state of finance and our ability to contribute to improving performance and create value. This problem is exacerbated by other demands on finance and limited resources to deal with these demands. In addition, many teams encounter resistance to implementing improvements in performance management, typically because of fear and misinformation that arise about how performance management will be utilized, in some cases, to limit discretion or intuition or to more objectively evaluate employees' performance.

These initiatives to improve the enterprise performance management represent changes for the finance team as well as the entire organization. Those in leadership roles must consider these soft issues and utilize change management principles. In addition to the suggestions in Chapters 3 and 7, the following suggestions may be useful in driving for significant improvements in FP&A and performance management, and other value-added areas of finance.

Develop a Case. Document the current state of FP&A, performance management, and other services provided by finance. This can be accomplished in two areas. First, an assessment of finance effectiveness can be made. This can include a benchmark and identification of best practices as well as client feedback. The second area of assessment is a view of the overall performance of the company or organization. This can include benchmark comparisons on everything from value creation to capital management, and from revenue growth to costs and expense levels. These assessments will identify different needs for each organization and help to identify the specific areas warranting attention.

Build Consensus and an Execution Team. I cannot recall any successful endeavor of this magnitude that did not include building consensus and developing an execution team. The development of a case for change will provide a starting point for building consensus. Many executives are surprised at the amount of effort required to effectively communicate the case. In addition, catalysts for change also find that they must repeatedly drive home the critical need for change.

The execution team should include representatives from finance, information technology (IT), and key business processes and business units across the organization. This will help ensure that the changes and solutions are accepted, rather than viewed as a finance or IT project.

Plan for Success. The creation of a project plan with clear deliverables, milestones, and responsibilities is critical. The absence of a plan almost ensures falling short of objectives.

Provide Tools and Resources. Most efforts to significantly improve the contributions of the finance team will require investments in technology, training, and development, and outside resources. In addition, a significant level of human resources in finance must be devoted to improving, and then subsequently delivering high-quality service.

Build Momentum. An important aspect of leading change is to identify and execute on some early successes. The overall project should be planned to address some low-hanging fruit, in other words, relatively easy improvements that have high visibility. In organizations that resist adopting performance management, it is useful to direct initial efforts toward problem areas. For example, if the organization has difficulty in developing and meeting projections or in managing receivables, initial efforts can be directed to those areas. Skeptical managers can be won over after witnessing the useful role that performance management can play.

Monitor and Adjust. Progress on the plan should be reviewed frequently. In addition, the project results must be reviewed to ensure that intended objectives of the plan are achieved. For example, if one of the efforts is directed at improving the planning and forecasting process, has the project resulted in intended and measurable improvements? Circumstances and priorities change frequently, and the ideal of an effective business partner is a moving target. Efforts to improve financial services must be continually reviewed to ensure that they are directed at important areas and drivers of performance.

Finance Transformation Is a Journey, Not a Destination. Efforts to improve the contributions of finance will be an ongoing challenge. Changes in business conditions, technology, and competition will ensure that finance will continue to evolve and rotate focus across various aspects of the enterprise.

Good luck and enjoy the journey!

Glossary

Accrual Accounting   A basic principle of accounting that requires revenues to be recorded when earned and expenses recorded when incurred, regardless of the timing of cash payments.

Agile Employees   Those employees who demonstrate agility, enabled by key characteristics such as fast learners, flexibility, ability to plan and execute, and so on.

Agility   The ability to observe, recognize, and respond to required changes in the business environment.

Amortization   A periodic charge to earnings to reduce the book value of intangible assets, including goodwill.

Analytics   The discovery, collection, interpretation, and communication of meaningful patterns and trends in data.

Artificial Intelligence   The ability of a digital technology to perform tasks commonly associated with human (intelligent) beings.

Artificial Intelligence, Generative   Any type of artificial intelligence that can be used to create (generate) new text, audio images, video, or code.

Asset   Any tangible or intangible item or claim owned by a firm.

Asset Turnover   A measure of how efficiently assets are utilized to generate revenue, computed by dividing revenue by total assets.

Backlog   The level of open (i.e., not shipped) customer orders at a point in time.

Balance Sheet   One of the three primary financial statements, providing a schedule of assets, liabilities, and owner equity.

Base Case   In projecting performance or identifying potential scenarios, the most likely or most probable outcome.

Benchmarking   A process of comparing processes, performance, and valuation of one company to a group of other companies.

Beta   The risk associated with a specific investment or security estimated by the correlation of price movements in an individual stock to a broad market index.

Bias   An inclination or predetermined view about a person, subject, or decision that may be entirely controlled by the subconscious, including recency bias and confirmation bias.

Black Swan Event   A low probability, and often unpredictable event that will have a significant impact (e.g., Covid-19, geopolitical events).

Book Value   The value of an asset on the balance sheet, reflecting original cost less any accumulated depreciation.

Breakeven   The level of a particular assumption (e.g., revenue) that results in a measure, such as net present value (NPV), income, or cash flow equaling zero.

Business Model   A financial representation of a firm's strategy and operating practices, usually expressed as a percentage of each income statement line item (e.g., selling, general and administrative expenses) to sales.

Business Outlook   A preferred term to describe a forecast, generally inferring a broader business perspective than simply a financial projection.

Business Partner, Financial   Members of the finance organization who support and assist the organization in achieving goals for performance and value creation.

Capital Asset   A tangible asset of a firm, such as real estate and machinery.

Capital Effectiveness   A key driver of value, representing the firm's ability to manage and control capital levels in the business, computed as revenue/ net fixed assets.

Capital Intensity   A measure of the level of capital requirements for a business, which varies significantly across industries.

Capital Structure   The mix of capital sources for a company, including debt and equity.

Common Stock Equivalent   An instrument, such as stock options and convertible bonds that can be converted into common stock under certain conditions.

Comparables   A method used to value a company that involves selecting similar companies to compare valuation measures such as the price/earnings (P/E) ratio.

Compound Annual Growth Rate (CAGR)   A multi-year measure of growth that reflects compounding.

Confirmation Bias   A bias toward searching out or valuing information that supports or confirms our existing view.

Control Premium   The premium over market value required to purchase a company.

Cost of Capital   The weighted average return expected by all investors in a firm, based on the opportunity cost incurred in making an investment in that firm.

Cost of Equity   The return expected by shareholders in a firm, based on the opportunity cost incurred in making an investment in that stock.

Cost of Goods Sold (COGS)   The total cost of products sold, including material, labor overhead, and other manufacturing costs and variances.

Customer Acquisition Cost (CAC)   The cost of acquiring a new customer, including sales, marketing, promotion, and discounts divided by the number of new customers acquired during the period.

Customer Lifetime Value (CLV)   The total revenue or profit expected from a customer over the life of the relationship, less the cost of acquiring new customers (CAC).

Dashboard   A one-page, visual summary or screen presenting graphs and charts of key performance measures.

Data Lake   A central repository that facilitates storage of data. The centralized data can then be processed to create or enable analytics, performance dashboards, statistical analysis, and artificial intelligence.

Data Science   A broad term that includes developing insights from large amounts of data using statistical methods, algorithms, and processes. Data science integrates skills and techniques from computer science, mathematics, statistics, data visualization, and business analytics.

Data Scientist   A professional trained or experienced in the acquisition, cleansing, storage, retrieval, analysis, and interpretation of digital data.

Data Visualization   The visual representation of data, using graphics and other visuals to identify and communicate patterns and trends that might not otherwise be evident.

Days Sales in Inventory (DSI)   A measure of the level of inventories on hand relative to sales.

Days Sales Outstanding (DSO)   A measure of the average time to collect accounts receivable from customers.

Debt   A formal borrowing obligation of the firm, including bonds, notes, loans, and short-term financing.

Depreciation   A periodic charge to earnings to reduce the book value of long-term assets, including equipment.

Depreciation and Amortization (D&A)   Periodic charges to earnings to reduce the value of long-term and intangible assets. D&A is a noncash charge and is often an adjustment to income to estimate cash flows for valuation purposes.

Discounted Cash Flow (DCF)   A valuation and decision tool that considers the cash flows of an asset or project and the time value of money.

Distribution Channel   Refers to the method of selling and distributing the firm's products, including internal sales force, third-party distributors, and value-added resellers.

Earnings per Share (EPS) The accounting net income per each share of common stock and equivalents outstanding.

Earnings per Share (EPS) Accretive-Dilutive Test A decision test to determine if a project, acquisition, or financing alternative will increase or decrease earnings per share.

EBIAT Earnings before Interest after Taxes, aka "NOPAT" (Net Operating Profit after Taxes). This measure estimates operating earnings after tax. It excludes financing costs, but does reflect income tax expense. It is useful in comparing the operational performance of firms, excluding the impact of financing costs.

EBIT Earnings before Interest and Taxes. This measure reflects the income generated by operating activities before subtracting financing costs (interest) and income tax expense.

EBITDA Earnings before Interest, Taxes, Depreciation, and Amortization. EBITDA adjusts EBIT (operating income) by adding back noncash charges, depreciation, and amortization. This measure is used in valuation and financing decisions since it approximates cash generated by the operation. It does not include capital requirements such as working capital and expenditures for property and equipment.

Economic Profit A financial measure of performance that subtracts a capital charge from earnings to arrive at an economic profit, consistent with other economic techniques including NPV and DCF.

Engineering Change Notice/Order (ECN/O) A transaction used to initiate changes in a product's bill of materials or manufacturing process.

Enterprise Performance Management A comprehensive set of measures, analysis, reviews, and responses to an organization's overall operating and financial performance.

Enterprise Value The sum of a firm's market value of equity and debt.

Equity The book value of shareholders' equity or investment in the firm, including common stock and earnings retained in the business.

Expected Value A probability weighted average of possible outcomes.

Financial Accounting Standards Board (FASB) The accounting standards-setter in the United States.

Financial Leverage The use of debt and other liabilities to leverage the investment of equity investors. Computed as total assets divided by equity.

Fixed Assets Another term used to describe property, plant, and equipment.

Fixed Cost A cost that cannot be eliminated in the short term (e.g., six months) and that does not vary with changes in sales levels.

Forecast A financial projection, generally referring to a short-term horizon, less than 12–18 months.

Free Cash Flow to Equity (FCFE) The cash flow available to equity investors after providing for working capital requirements; investments in property, plant, and equipment; and payments to service debt (interest and principal).

Free Cash Flow (to the Firm) (FCF/FCFF) The cash flow available to all investors after providing for working capital requirements and investments in property, plant, and equipment.

Generally Accepted Accounting Principles (GAAP) The cumulative body of accounting rules issued by the FASB, SEC, and other rule-making organizations.

Gross Margin The residual of revenue minus cost of goods sold (COGS).

High Potential Employees Those employees with significant growth potential, perhaps as a senior manager or executive.

Income Statement One of the three primary financial statements, providing a summary of the firm's sales, costs, and expenses for a period.

Innovation The introduction of something new or the process of radically changing, transforming, or achieving breakthrough results.

Intangible Assets The assets of a firm that are not tangible, physical assets, such as reputation, brands, trademarks, patents, and goodwill.

Internal Rate of Return (IRR) The economic return of a project based on its cash inflows and outflows over time.

Invested Capital The total capital invested in a business, including equity and interest- bearing debt. Invested capital also equals the total net assets invested in the business.

Key Performance Measure/Indicator (KPM/I) A measure of a business process, activity, or result that is significant to the overall performance of the firm.

Lagging Performance Measure Measures that are computed after an event, transaction, or the close of an accounting period such as DSO or ROE.

Liability An amount or service due another party.

Machine Learning (ML) Refers to the ability of digital technology to learn autonomously from human control, intervention, or guidance.

Market Capitalization (Value) The market value of common stock outstanding, computed as the price per share times the number of common shares outstanding.

Multiples A ratio of value to one of several financial measures, including price earnings and price to revenue ratios. These ratios are used to compare values of similar companies.

Net Income Represents the "bottom line" of the Income Statement, the excess of revenues over all costs and expenses for a period.

Net Present Value (NPV) The present value of cash inflows less the present value of cash outflows.

Operating Capital The level of net working capital required to support the business, reflecting the excess of current operating assets over current operating liabilities. The measure excludes financing components of working capital, including cash and debt.

Operating Effectiveness An important value driver that reflects the effectiveness and efficiency of the firm's business processes and activities.

Operating Income/Profit   A pre-tax measure of operating performance, reflecting all operating income and expenses for a period.

Operating Leverage   A measure of the proportion of fixed costs to total costs that causes wider variations in profits, resulting from changes in sales levels.

Operating Profit after Tax (OPAT)   This measure estimates the "after tax" operating earnings. It excludes financing costs, but does reflect income tax expense. It is useful in comparing the operational performance of firms, excluding the impact of financing costs.

Pareto Analysis   Based on Pareto's (also known as the 80/20) rule, this analysis focuses on the 20% of a population that generally accounts for 80% of the total value of that population.

Payback   The period of time it takes to recover the original investment in a project.

Performance Management Framework (PMF)   A comprehensive system of management practices to measure, report, and improve business performance.

Perpetuity   A measure of time, typically used in valuing an asset or cash flow, meaning forever.

PESTEL Framework   A tool utilized to assess an organization's strategic environment, covering political, economic, social, technology, environmental, and legal forces.

Predictive Analytics   Use of analytical techniques to predict or forecast the future, based on trends and relationships in historical data.

Predictive (Leading) Performance Measure   Measures that cover key business drivers, processes, and activities on a current basis, providing an early indication of future business and financial results.

Present Value   The value today of a future payment or cash flow, reflecting a discount for the time value of money.

Price/Earnings (P/E) Multiple   A key valuation measure representing the ratio of the firm's share price to earnings per share.

Pricing Strength   The ability of a firm to command a premium price for its products and services based on a competitive advantage that will result in acceptable or above-average economic performance for the firm.

Proxy Statement   A filing with the SEC required for publicly traded companies that presents matters to be voted on by shareholders. The Proxy Statement also contains disclosures on the company's stock performance (total return to shareholders) and management compensation levels and policies.

Recency Bias   The tendency to assume that future trends or events will be a continuation of recent experience.

Residual Cash Flow   The cash flow available to equity investors after providing for working capital requirements; investments in property, plant, and equipment; and payments to service debt (interest and principal). Also known as free cash flow to equity (FCFE) investors.

Return on Assets   A measure of overall effectiveness, computed as net income divided by total assets.

Return on Equity   A measure of overall effectiveness, computed as net income divided by total shareholder equity.

Return on Invested Capital (ROIC)   A measure of overall effectiveness, computed as after-tax operating profit divided by the total of shareholder equity and interest bearing debt. Since it considers all capital invested in a firm, this measure is independent of the mix of capital.

Revenue Linearity   The pattern of revenue within a period (e.g., quarter). A linear pattern would result from a constant level of shipments over the entire period.

Revenue Process   The entire process that supports delivering a product or service to a customer, commencing with pre-sales activities and concluding with the collection of cash from customers.

Rolling Forecast   A technique for extending the horizon of financial projections by adding an additional month or quarter into the future.

Scenario Analysis   A projection or forecast version based on a specific set of conditions that varies from the "base" case, for example, a recession.

Scenario Planning   Scenario planning is a tool used to assist in making decisions under uncertainty, by considering alternative outcomes to a base plan.

Securities and Exchange Commission (SEC)   The U.S. federal agency tasked with monitoring securities markets and financial reporting of publicly traded companies.

Selling, General, and Administrative Expenses (SG&A)   An Income Statement line item that captures all costs and expenses associated with sales, marketing, and administrative activities of the firm.

Sensitivity Analysis   A summary of the changes in a decision outcome (e.g., net income or net present value) based on changes in one or more input variables.

Statement of Cash Flow   One of the three primary financial statements, providing a summary of cash inflows and outflows during the period.

Storytelling   A method of communicating that avoids a recitation of facts and figures in favor of developing a well-thought-out story to engage listeners.

Strategic Alternatives   Potential alternative strategies to the primary or base strategic plan, for example, selling a business unit rather than continue to operate it as contemplated in the base plan.

Strategic Planning   The process of assessing an organization's performance, opportunities, market, and competitive environment to develop a set of long-term goals and an execution plan to attain those goals.

Supply Chain Management   A key business process incorporating all aspects of planning, procuring, manufacturing, and distributing a firm's product.

Synergies   The incremental savings or income that results from a business combination beyond the sum of the two independent companies.

SWOT Analysis   A tool utilized in strategic planning to identify and address an organization's strengths, weaknesses (or limitations), opportunities, and threats.

Terminal Value   The estimated value of a company at the end of the forecast period in discounted cash flow valuations. Also known as post-horizon value.

Times Interest Earned   A measure of the ability to service debt, computed by dividing profit before tax by interest expense.

Total Return to Shareholders (TRS)   An overall measure of returns earned by shareholders that reflects both capital appreciation and dividends paid over a period of time.

Valuation   The process of estimating the value of an asset or company using one or more commonly accepted techniques, including multiples and discounted cash flow analysis.

Value Driver   A factor that has a significant impact on the value of the firm, for example, revenue growth.

Value Performance Framework (VPF)   A comprehensive performance management framework that emphasizes building and sustaining long-term shareholder value.

Variable Cost   A cost that varies with changes in revenue levels.

Vertical Integration   The extent to which a firm directly owns its supply chain and distribution channels.

Weighted Average Cost of Capital (WACC)   The blend of returns expected by all suppliers of capital to the firm (weighted by market value).

Working Capital   The excess of current assets (cash, accounts receivable, inventories, and prepaid expenses) over current liabilities (accounts payable, debt, and accrued expenses).

Yield to Maturity   The current rate an investor will earn on a bond, adjusting the bond's stated (coupon) rate for current market conditions.

Zero-Based Budgeting (Cost Analysis)   A fresh look, challenging every position, cost, function, project, investment, and program in the organization.

Acknowledgments

I have been blessed in many ways both in my career and in my personal life. In my professional career, I have been blessed to have exposure to a number of businesses and industries, work with and for great people, and observe and participate in business from several different perspectives. The experience gained as an auditor, division finance and general manager, controller, CFO, educator, small business owner, and consultant has all contributed to the development of the tools and insights incorporated in this book.

Prior to embarking on my teaching and consulting track, most of my professional career was with a terrific company, EG&G, Inc. The company had a large and diverse portfolio of businesses that provided ample opportunity for learning, as did the period of radical transformation during the 1990s. EG&G had very strong financial management and strategic planning practices that continue to influence me to this day. I had the pleasure of working with and learning from a number of talented people at the division, group, and corporate level, including Bob Nicol, Gary Hammond, Dave Botten, Luciano Rossi, Mike Gallucio, Paul D'Adamo, Jim Mellencamp, Sam Rubinovitz, Dick Delio, Murray Gross, Fred Parks, Dan Heaney, Mark Allen, Peter Broadbent, Dan Valente, Ted Theodores, Debbie Lorenz, Jim Dobbins, Peter Walsh, Don Peters, Bill Ribaudo, Will Weddleton, and many more. Special thanks to John Kucharski for both his leadership and as a model of managing with integrity.

The time spent teaching at Babson College was both rewarding and enlightening. I learned a great deal by teaching, especially how people learn and process information. I also learned a great deal from my time at Coopers & Lybrand (now PriceWaterhouseCoopers) in Philadelphia. The exposure to a wide range of client companies, process orientation, accounting and reporting, and great people provided a solid foundation for future growth.

I have also benefited greatly by knowing and working with a number of external business partners over the years, including investment bankers, consultants, and public accountants. Working with many directors, analysts, and investors over the years also contributed to my understanding of business, finance, and value.

A number of friends and colleagues were very helpful in providing encouragement and feedback on this project, including Nate Osborne, Warren Davis, Caroline Exley, and Gary Olin. The perspective on technology was greatly enhanced by suggestions from Martin Winkler and the Apliqo team. Finally, thanks to Bill Falloon, Executive Editor, and the team at Wiley for guidance and assistance on this project.

Thanks to my parents for everything, including passing on values of faith, integrity, hard work, and perseverance. And special thanks to my wife Suzanne for her unending support and love.

"I can do all things through Him who strengthens me."

—Philippians 4:13

About the Author

Jack Alexander is an experienced financial and operating executive turned consultant, author, and lecturer. He provides advisory services to businesses across a wide range of financial and operating areas, including strategic planning, value creation, M&A, improving profitability, and cash flow, financial planning and analysis (FP&A) and business performance management (BPM). His firm, Jack Alexander & Associates, LLC, also offers customized training and workshops on FP&A and financial management. Jack is a frequent speaker on FP&A and financial management.

Prior to founding the consulting practice, Jack served as Chief Financial Officer (CFO) of EG&G Inc. (renamed PerkinElmer), a global $2.5 billion technology and services company with over 40 operating units and also as CFO with Mercury Computer Systems. He was previously employed by General Refractories and Coopers & Lybrand.

Jack was a Senior Lecturer in Babson College's MBA program and School of Executive Education, and serves on the advisory board to the finance and economics department at Coastal Carolina University. He is a CPA and earned an MBA from Rider University and a BS from Indiana University of Pennsylvania.

He is the author of *Performance Dashboards and Analysis for Value Creation* (Wiley, 2006), *Financial Planning and Analysis and Business Performance Management* (Wiley, 2018), and *Financial Management: Partner in Driving Performance and Value* (Wiley, 2024).

About the Accompanying Website

This book is supplemented with a companion website:

www.wiley.com\go\alexander\financialmanagement

A password is required to access the website files: Alexander123

The password is case sensitive.

Should you encounter any difficulty accessing the website, please visit https://support.wiley.com for assistance.

WHAT'S ON THE WEBSITE

The following sections provide a summary of the software and other materials you'll find on the website.

Content

A number of illustrative performance dashboards, analysis, tools, and Excel models used in the book are included in the accompanying website. These items are identified in the book with a website logo 🌐. These tools are intended as working examples and starting points for the reader's use. An important theme of this book is to underscore the importance of selecting the appropriate measures and dashboards. It is very important to carefully select the measures and analytical tools that are most appropriate for each circumstance. Accordingly, most of the dashboards and models will have to be tailored to fit the specific needs of each situation. Please note that in order to facilitate changes to the analyses, none of the formulas in the worksheets are "protected." A copy of the original files should be retained in the event that formulas are inadvertently changed or deleted.

The tools contain the data used in the examples provided in the book. In order to fully understand the worksheets, including the objective, context, and logic of the analysis, the user should refer to the appropriate example in the text. For each worksheet, the data input fields are generally highlighted in color. All other fields contain formulas. The reader should save these files under a different name and use them to begin developing dashboards and analysis for the reader's specific needs. Using the models on the website requires Microsoft Excel software and an intermediate skill level in the use of that software. Many of the worksheets are standalone analyses that are not linked to the other spreadsheets. However, some of the workbook files contain models that require data input on the first worksheet to drive the models on subsequent worksheets in that file.

The website also includes a Quick Reference Guide (Table 2.8) that can be printed, laminated, and retained as a reference for financial terms and ratios and key aspects of valuation and performance measurement.

Chapter 2   The Fundamentals of Finance and Financial Statement Analysis

Chapter 3   Skills, Knowledge, and Attributes for Finance Business Partners

Chapter 4   Developing Predictive and Analytical Models

Chapter 31   Analysis of Mergers and Acquisitions

Modifying the Charts and Graphs   The user should modify the charts and graphs on the website in order to substitute specific performance measures for those contained in the sample dashboards and analyses. In order to modify chart titles, alter axis labels, and make other changes to charts, click on the chart, then select "Chart" in the menu commands and next select "Options." A menu of available chart options will be presented, including titles, labels, and scale selections.

The user may also want to change the scale of the charts to better present the data for each situation. This can be accomplished by double-clicking on the "Value Axis" label on the graph, and selecting "Scale" to change axis minimum and maximum values.

Index

Page numbers followed by *f* and *t* refer to figures and tables, respectively.